Kaiso!

STUDIES IN DANCE HISTORY

A Publication of the Society of Dance History Scholars
Constance Valis Hill, Hampshire College, Volume Editor
Claude Conyers, Holmes, New York, Volume Editor

TITLES IN PRINT

The Origins of the Bolero School, edited by Javier Suárez-Pajares and Xoán M. Carreira

Carlo Blasis in Russia by Elizabeth Souritz, with preface by Selma Jeanne Cohen

Of, By, and For the People: Dancing on the Left in the 1930s, edited by Lynn Garafola

Dancing in Montreal: Seeds of a Choreographic History by Iro Tembeck

The Making of a Choreographer: Ninette de Valois and "Bar aux Folies-Bergère" by
Beth Genné

Ned Wayburn and the Dance Routine: From Vaudeville to the "Ziegfeld Follies" by
Barbara Stratyner

Rethinking the Sylph: New Perspectives on the Romantic Ballet, edited by Lynn
Garafola (available from the University Press of New England)

Dance for Export: Cultural Diplomacy and the Cold War by Naima Prevots, with
introduction by Eric Foner (available from the University Press of New England)

José Limón: An Unfinished Memoir, edited by Lynn Garafola, with introduction by
Deborah Jowitt, foreword by Carla Maxwell, and afterword by Norton Owen
(available from the University Press of New England)

Dancing Desires: Choreographing Sexualities on and off the Stage, edited by
Jane C. Desmond

Dancing Many Drums: Excavations in African American Dance, edited by
Thomas F. DeFrantz

Writings on Ballet and Music, by Fedor Lopukhov, edited and with an introduction
by Stephanie Jordan, translations by Dorinda Offord

Liebe Hanya: Mary Wigman's Letters to Hanya Holm, compiled and edited by
Claudia Gitelman, Introduction by Hedwig Müller

*The Grotesque Dancer on the Eighteenth-Century Stage: Gennaro Magri and His
World,* edited by Rebecca Harris-Warrick and Bruce Alan Brown

Kaiso!: Writings by and about Katherine Dunham, edited by VèVè A. Clark and
Sara E. Johnson

Kaiso!

WRITINGS

by and about

Katherine Dunham

EDITED BY

VèVè A. Clark and Sara E. Johnson

THE UNIVERSITY OF WISCONSIN PRESS

The University of Wisconsin Press
1930 Monroe Street
Madison, Wisconsin 53711

www.wisc.edu/wisconsinpress/

3 Henrietta Street
London WC2E 8LU, England

This book was published with the support of the Katherine Dunham Legacy Project
in the Library of Congress and by the Doris Duke Charitable Foundation.

5   4   3   2

Printed in the United States of America

Library of Congress Cataloging-in-Publication Data
Kaiso! Writings by and about Katherine Dunham / edited by
VèVè A. Clark and Sara E. Johnson.
p. cm. —(Studies in dance history)
Includes bibliographical references and index.
ISBN 0-299-21270-X (hardcover: alk. paper)—
ISBN 0-299-21274-2 (pbk.: alk. paper)
1. Dunham, Katherine. 2. Dancers—United States—Biography.
I. Dunham, Katherine. II. Clark, VèVè A. III. Johnson, Sara Elizabeth.
IV. Series.
GV1785.D82K35 2006
792.8´028´092—dc22
2005008258

Contents

PART 2 *Dunham the Woman:*
SCHOLAR, ARTIST, ACTIVIST

Acknowledgments

The editors wish to thank many people who have made the publication of *Kaiso!* possible. First and foremost, we thank Katherine Dunham.

Over forty contributors participated in this volume, and we are deeply appreciative that they have allowed us to include their scholarship.

The original mimeographed version of *Kaiso!* appeared in 1978 with a limited printing of one hundred and thirty copies. Margaret Wilkerson, Jahleezah Eskew, Phyllis Bischof, and Roy Thomas were instrumental collaborators on the monograph and the accompanying Katherine Dunham exhibit at the University of California, Berkeley. Over the course of the many years that it has taken to prepare this new, expanded edition, numerous individuals have shared their expertise. Special thanks are due to Jeanelle Stovall, Robert Lee, Glory Van Scott, and all of the former Dunham Company dancers who generously contributed photographs, verified information and made themselves available as resources.

It has been a pleasure working with the Society of Dance History Scholars, which has long been committed to making *Kaiso!* available to a wider audience. A grant from the Katherine Dunham Legacy Project at the Library of Congress, funded in part by the Doris Duke Charitable Foundation, provided critical support. We are sincerely appreciative of Claude Conyers's painstaking editorial assistance, and we thank Constance Valis Hill and Susan Manning for their encouragement. In addition, we are deeply grateful for Lynn Garafola's unflagging support, especially throughout the extensive process of securing permissions.

Phil Karg of the Jerome Robbins Dance Collection at the New York Public Library and Duane Sneddeker from the Missouri Historical Society were of great assistance in locating photographs. We also wish to thank our editors at the University of Wisconsin Press, Sheila Moermond and Erin Holman, for their patience and commitment to realizing a shared vision.

Note on Orthography

The spelling of the French Creole languages spoken in the Caribbean islands of Haiti and Martinique is varied. Grounded in complex historical circumstances surrounding the legacy of colonialism in the region, the choice of orthography has been the subject of sustained debate and is often indicative of political and class divisions in each nation. The controversy largely revolves around which spellings are most appropriate, phonetic ones or those based on some degree of etymological approximation to French. In the case of Haiti, this question of etymological approximation is complicated by the fact that orthographic systems propagated by North American missionaries during the middle of the twentieth century utilized English as their point of reference.

In our editorial notes, we have followed the trend in current scholarship to employ a Creole orthography that is essentially phonetic and based on the two-volume *Haitian Creole-English-French Dictionary* by Albert Valdman et al. (Bloomington: Creole Institute, Indiana University, 1981). In an effort to preserve the integrity of the contributions, we maintained the original variant spellings throughout the volume, although some updating has been done for the sake of ensuring consistency when several variations were used within the same selection. Miss Dunham most frequently employed a Gallicized rendition of Creole words in her own writing, and the glossary provides a sampling of the most common variant spellings as well as their corresponding definitions.

In *Kaiso!* the question of Creole orthography is most frequently an issue with the Haitian religion *Vodun/Vodou.* Frequently spelled *Vaudou, Vodoun, Vaudun, Vaudoun,* or *Voodoo,* especially in older scholarship, we have opted for *Vodun,* although *Vodou* is also in current usage. Likewise, the term *l'ag'ya,* the Martinican martial arts dance, has many variant spellings, including *ag'ya* and *ladja.*

Chronology

1909	Katherine Mary Dunham is born on June 22 in Chicago, Illinois, to Albert M. Dunham and Fanny June Dunham.
1928	Begins to study ballet with Ludmilla Speranzeva, Vera Mirova, Mark Turbyfill, and Ruth Page
1929	Enters the University of Chicago.
1930–31	Forms the Ballet Nègre, one of the first African American ballet companies in the United States; the company makes its debut in 1931 at the Chicago Beaux Arts Ball.
	Marries her first husband, Jordis McCoo, who she divorces in 1938.
1933–34	Appears in Ruth Page's production of *La Guiablesse* at the Chicago Opera.
1935–36	Awarded a fellowship from the Julius Rosenwald Fund that allows her to conduct fieldwork in Haiti, Jamaica, Martinique, and Trinidad.
1936	Awarded a Ph.B. in social anthropology (bachelor of philosophy degree) from the University of Chicago.
1937	Performs at the Young Men's Hebrew Association in New York City as part of *A Negro Dance Evening*. Other performers include Edna Guy, Asadata Dafora, and Clarence Yates.
1938	*L'Ag'ya*, Dunham's first full-length ballet, performed at the Federal Theater in Chicago.
	Appointed director of the Negro Unit of the Chicago branch of the Federal Theatre Project.

Tropics performed at the Goodman Theater in Chicago.

Submits a thesis entitled "Dances of Haiti: Their Social Organization, Classification, Form, and Function" to the Department of Anthropology at the University of Chicago in partial fulfillment of the requirements for a Master of Arts degree.

1939   Appears in her first film, *Carnival of Rhythm.*

1939–1940   Collaborates on the International Ladies' Garment Workers' Union (IGLWU) Broadway production *Pins and Needles;* also performs with the Dunham Company in *Tropics* and *Le Jazz Hot* at the Windsor Theatre in New York.

1940–41   Appears in the Broadway and touring productions of *Cabin in the Sky.*

1941   Marries John Pratt.

1943   Impresario Sol Hurok presents Katherine Dunham and her company in *Tropical Revue,* which opens at New York's Martin Beck Theater and then tours nationally until 1945.

Appears with the company in the film *Stormy Weather.*

1944   Dunham School of Dance and Theater, later known as the Katherine Dunham School of Arts and Research, opens in Caravan Hall in New York City; in 1945, the school moves to West 43rd Street, where it operates until 1957.

1946   *Journey to Accompong* published.

Bal Nègre tours nationally.

1947   "Dances of Haiti," Dunham's thesis translated into Spanish and published as *Las danzas de Haití,* subsequently published in French as *Les danses d'Haïti* (1950) and in English as *Dances of Haiti* (1983).

1947–49   First tours of Mexico and Europe.

Albert Dunham Jr. dies.

1950–55   Dunham Company tours South America, Europe and North Africa; premieres her ballet *Southland* at the Teatro Municipal in Santiago, Chile, in 1951.

1951   Dunham and Pratt adopt Marie-Christine, a four-year-old girl.

1956–58	Tours Australia, New Zealand, and Japan.
1959	*A Touch of Innocence: Memoirs of Childhood* published.
1959–60	Third European tour; Dunham Company disbands, although it will occasionally regroup for special performances.
1962	Performs in *Bamboche,* her last Broadway appearance.
1963	Choreographs *Aïda* for the Metropolitan Opera House.
1964	Becomes an artist-in-residence at Southern Illinois University at Carbondale; retires in 1982.
1965	Attends the First World Festival of Negro Arts in Dakar, Senegal as the official U.S. representative.
	Last performance with the Dunham Company at Harlem's Apollo Theater.
1967	Performing Arts Training Center founded in East Saint Louis, Missouri.
1969	*Island Possessed* published.
1979	Katherine Dunham Museum and Children's Workshop opens in East Saint Louis, Missouri.
	Katherine Dunham Gala at Carnegie Hall, where she receives the Albert Schweitzer Music Award
1983	Receives Kennedy Center Honors Award.
1984	Dunham Technique Seminars inaugurated in East Saint Louis, Illinois.
1986	John Pratt, Dunham's husband and artistic collaborator of forty-five years, dies.
	Receives several awards, including the Samuel H. Scripps American Dance Festival Award; the Medal of Artistic Merit in Dance, given by the International Council on Dance, UNESCO; the Distinguished Service Award from the American Anthropological Association; the Southern Cross, Award of Honor and Merit from the Government of Brazil; and the Oral Self-Portrait from the National Portrait Gallery of the Smithsonian Institute, Washington, D.C.
1987–88	Alvin Ailey Dance Theater reconstructs Dunham's choreographies in "The Magic of Katherine Dunham" performances.

1992   Fasts for Haitian refugees.

2000   Named one of "America's Irreplaceable Dance Treasures" by
            the Dance Heritage Coalition.

2002   Honored on the occasion of her ninety-third birthday at the
            Jacob's Pillow Dance Festival.

Kaiso!

Introduction

Diamonds on the Toes of Her Feet

SARA E. JOHNSON

Katherine Dunham. For many, the name calls to mind a trailblazing icon—artistic director of one of the first African American dance companies to tour internationally, intrepid anthropologist, committed social activist. Legends abound of the woman who allegedly had her legs insured for a million dollars, seamlessly negotiated Vodun ceremonies in rural *ounfò* while rubbing shoulders with the intellectual and artistic elite of several continents, and doggedly refused to abide by Jim Crow laws wherever she traveled. This legendary stature is complicated by the fact that Dunham is not a household name as she should be. Given a career that has spanned close to seventy years and influenced countless people, her low profile is cause for critical conjecture; her myriad accomplishments merit renewed attention if we are to minimize the incongruous coexistence of her pioneering, yet undervalued, legacy in the public eye.

The breadth of Dunham's accomplishments is perhaps one explanation for the underappreciation of her work. Creating paths where there were none, she resists easy categorization. Dunham has catalogued, interpreted and transformed New World, African-derived sensibilities from the vantage point of multiple disciplines, consistently putting them into dialogue with other epistemological frameworks.[1] She is rightfully lauded as a dance celebrity that redefined the concert stage. One of the first black performers to garner sustained critical acclaim, Dunham forged new kinetic models that challenged traditional paradigms of "high" cultural expression. Likewise, she pioneered the study of comparative religions of the African diaspora, as can be seen in her study of Haitian Vodun, Cuban Santería, Jamaican Obeah, and Brazilian Candomblé. Although she has yet to receive her due credit, the value of this work alone earns Dunham a place alongside renowned scholars of Caribbean and Latin American studies, including Jean Price-Mars, Fernando Ortiz, and Gilberto Freyre. She is, in fact, one of the few women belonging to a pantheon of scholars that spearheaded movements analyzing the legacy of slavery in the region and championed the worth of African-influenced traditions in various national milieus. Her pursuits embody a lived dimension of a theoretical construct of diaspora. As a social activist, Dunham's activities also have international dimensions. Whether participating in relief efforts for the Republican movement during the Spanish Civil War (1936–1939), building a public medical clinic at her residence in Haiti, or facilitating pan-African exchanges that promoted ideological shifts in how Africans and Africans in the Americas viewed their interdependence, Dunham exemplifies the ideal of an informed, engaged global citizen. These are but a few examples of Dunham's interdisciplinary trajectories; ignoring the diversity of the sociohistoric contexts in which she operated and the various frameworks that she used to understand them minimizes the significance of her unique vision.

Borrowing its title from a calypsonian term of admiration, *Kaiso!* unites dozens of voices in appreciation of the profound contributions Dunham has made to our understanding of how intercultural communication enriches human experience. A collective praise song, the anthology hopes to make a new generation aware of Dunham's continued conviction that artistic expression has transformative, even emancipatory potential.[2] The nearly one hundred selections that follow offer a broad overview of her career while also providing detailed documentation of Dunham's varied interests. While never completely out of the public eye, "Miss D.," as she is affectionately called by those close to her, has been the focus of much new critical material examining her achievements as a performer, pedagogue, and anthropologist. Written over a sixty-year period by more than forty contributors, the pieces are multi-generic and come from a wide variety of sources—magazines, academic journals, monographs, public lectures, original programs, interviews with Dunham and former Dunham Company dancers, personal papers, and photographic archives. As she nears her hundredth birthday, it is especially fitting to offer this tribute with the hopes of stimulating further explorations into the immense richness of Dunham's legacy.

Dunham is best known as a performer; her life's work has been guided by her belief in the communicative power of dance, its ability to record social phenomena and effectively mine the conscious and subconscious worlds. In the essay "Notes on the Dance," she posits that dance is a constitutive principle in all societies. She writes:

> The emotional life of any community is clearly legible in its art forms, and because the dance seeks continuously to capture moments of life in a fusion of time, space, and motion, the dance is at a given moment the most accurate chronicler of culture pattern. The constant interplay of [the] conscious and unconscious finds a perfect instrument in the physical form, the human body which embraces all at once. Alone or in concert man dances his various selves and his emotions and his dance become a communication as clear as though it were written or spoken in a universal language (519, this volume).

Dunham's oeuvre is a philosophical meditation on how individuals can achieve some degree of equilibrium within larger community formations, a sentiment she describes as a "unity that directs itself toward an idea of the divine, toward nature, toward the unifying of the various personalities making up each individual self, toward a search for a concept of good . . . [and] some degree of relief from malaise" (515–16). Repeatedly reminding us that "the inner life must be fed," she has generated her own methodology for fostering these connections, locating dance as a primary means of stimulating self- and communal discovery. The selections included in *Kaiso!* explore Dunham's development of a corporeal, spiritual, politically engaged aesthetic, one that revels in the sheer physicality of expressive movement even as it coaxes one to explore what that same movement says about the world around us.

An archivist at heart, Dunham's legacy is indelibly linked to building bridges through the creation of institutions. Mechanisms for producing, preserving and disseminating knowledge, these institutions include her touring company and the various Dunham schools and performing centers. Likewise, her choreographic repertoire, the Dunham Technique, and her vast corpus of written and film work function as archives that institutionalized decades of research. Dunham has always been immensely aware, even during her early fieldwork, of the need to document the traditions she studied and to arrive at some understanding of their importance. Crediting this interest in the interrelatedness of form and function to her training in social anthropology, she transferred that conceptual framework from the field to the theater. "What would be the connection between the carnival dances, whose function is sexual stimulus and release, and almost any similar situation in a Broadway musical, for example, the temptation scene on the River Nile in *Cabin in the Sky*?" she wrote in the early 1940s.[3] Her attention to the psychic dimensions of accumulative tension and catharsis, both as an investigator and performer, is just one example of Dunham's intellectual imperative to simultaneously understand the particularities of local traditions and their universalist applications. Dunham's "research-to-performance" methodology provided a critically innovative paradigm, one that demonstrates that the most profound humanism emerges out of a deep knowledge of cultural specificity.[4] Not only did Dunham's work succeed in documenting the traditions of communities neglected by elite historiographies and "re-stylizing" them on stage, it also challenged—and continues to challenge—audiences worldwide to acquire a new literacy regarding the meaning of such material both in its "original" context and in relation to the contemporary moment. Our hope is that readers will continue this dialectic, using the wide range of primary and secondary sources included herein as a resource to cycle from performance to research and back.

When trying to categorize any creative process, Dunham reminds us that one always risks "over-complexity" or "over-simplicity" and that defining can in fact be an inherently limiting process ("Notes on the Dance," 515). Editing the new edition of *Kaiso!* posed a similar challenge, as the more we organized and reorganized the text, the more arbitrary it seemed to separate categories Dunham has always managed to fuse. The arrangement presented herein is thus one thematic road map among many. Part 1, "Autobiographical Reflections," contains excerpts from Dunham's published and unpublished autobiographical writings. Documenting her early childhood, fieldwork in the Caribbean as a Rosenwald fellow, and her first performance experiences, the section provides a point of departure for understanding Dunham's personal and professional journeys. As she makes her way from Glen Ellyn, Illinois, through Jamaica, Martinique, and Haiti, to eventually settle in the great urban centers of Chicago and New York, one is struck by her adaptability, intellectual curiosity, and deep respect for family and community ties. At the same time, one senses the vulnerability of a young woman constantly seeking both her family's approval and an always elusive sense of belonging as she struggles against race, gender, and class barriers in predominantly white- and/or male-dominated public spaces such as the University of Chicago and the professional theater. This vulnerability is easy to forget, given the determination and self-confidence that characterize most accounts of her life. Dunham's own words open a window into a more fragile, private side of a public persona.

Excerpts from *A Touch of Innocence* recount Dunham's childhood in Illinois. Focusing on the family dynamics of the Dunham household, particularly following the premature death of her mother, they explore her relationships with her father and idolized older brother, Albert Dunham Jr. *Journey to Accompong,* originally published in 1946, contains selections from the thirty-day field diary Dunham compiled while she was conducting research in Accompong, Jamaica, in 1935. Reputedly the first outsider to spend more than a day in the maroon community, Dunham describes "going native" in a delightful series of anecdotes that document the uncertainties and first triumphs of the blooming anthropologist. *Island Possessed* provides further insight into Dunham's field methodology, specifically her study of the sacred dances associated with Haitian Vodun. The excerpt focuses on the Congolese-derived *Petwo* branch of the religion in Haiti and her flirtation with future president Dumarsais Estimé, who, like many other members of the Haitian bourgeoisie of the time, heartily disapproved of her excursions into what was denigrated as "superstitious" peasant culture. Incidentally, it should not come as a surprise that her memoirs on Haiti were written while in residence in Senegal, and that *A Touch of Innocence* was composed while on tour in Tokyo. Dunham's geographic peregrinations played a fundamental role in developing her understanding of the world.

Part 1 concludes with excerpts from "Minefields," a previously unpublished memoir documenting Dunham's return from her fieldwork in the Caribbean and reinsertion into the performance scenes in Chicago and New York. The three selections focus on her work for the Federal Writers' and Theatre Projects; her early courtship with her future husband and co-artistic director, John Pratt; and her collaboration on the Broadway production of *Cabin in the Sky.* Looking back on the 1930s and 1940s from the vantage point of the early twenty-first century, Dunham reflects on her legacy and the inevitable "explosive devices" that marked obstacles along the road to stardom. A virtual who's who of what she terms the "New Negro" scene in both cities, this memoir is an archaeological treasure of African American dance scholarship that reveals the cross-pollination of music, theatre and dance in collaborations that revolutionized the performing arts.[5] The narrative records how the Dunham Company came into being—from the recruitment of dancers, many of whom went on to enjoy critically acclaimed careers, to the logistics of rehearsing, costuming, and touring. The piece offers an especially haunting tribute to her brother, who died in a psychiatric hospital after severing his connections with the outside world.

Part 2, "Dunham the Woman: Scholar, Artist, Activist," provides a holistic perspective on Dunham's intermingled academic, artistic, and political activities. Presented in rough chronological order, the section oscillates between Dunham's voice and those of both her contemporaries and more recent scholars. Beginning with the reminiscences of Mark Turbyfill and Ruth Page concerning their tutelage of Dunham during the early years of her dance career in Chicago, the selections also explore the formative influence of her first mentors in anthropology. Articles inspired by her research in the Caribbean, some published under the pseudonym Kaye Dunn, follow. Given her glamorous reputation as a performer, Dunham's scholarship occasioned great interest as well as curiosity. For example, we have included a review by another young anthropologist of the era, Dunham's unspoken rival Zora Neale Hurston, who was asked to review *Journey to Accompong* for the *New York Herald Tribune*. Although she slyly commented that "thirty days in a locality is not much in research and hardly affords time enough for the fieldworker to scratch the surface," Hurston praised Dunham's engaging style and acute observation skills. These talents are evident in all of Dunham's work as a dance historian, as her scholarship is remarkable for its comparative nature and combined insider/outsider perspective. As she delves into the socio-historic and aesthetic elements of African-influenced dance traditions in both the Caribbean and the United States, Dunham grounds her eyewitness observations in careful research into the specific legacies left by French, British, Spanish, and North American colonialism. Elaborating on what she terms the different "stages of acculturation" evident in the continuum from nonindustrial to industrialized societies, she effortlessly melds examples from Congo Square in nineteenth-century New Orleans to contemporary Jamaican, Haitian, Martinican, and North American dances that she observed both in the field and in locales such as New York's Savoy Ballroom.

Reviews by influential dance critics and lifestyle columnists provide another perspective as Dunham became the "hottest thing on Broadway," the scholarly "siren" who seduced the theater world. These reviews suggest what both the mainstream dance community and Dunham herself thought about what was then known as Negro dance. Dunham emerged at a time when John Martin, the most influential dance critic in the United States, could say in the *New York Times* that "there is nothing pretentious about it [Negro dance]; it is not designed to delve into philosophy or psychology but to externalize the impulses of a high-spirited, rhythmic, and gracious race."[6] Dunham's artistic agenda belies these comments. The selections documenting the late 1930s and first half of the 1940s trace the company's early appearances in Chicago, their initial New York performances in *Tropics* and *Le Jazz Hot—From Haiti to Harlem,* then the Broadway and touring productions of *Cabin in the Sky.* Recent scholarship by Constance Valis Hill draws critical attention to Dunham's choreographic contribution to *Cabin* and her long overlooked partnership with George Balanchine. New scholarship by Susan Manning analyzes how African American, leftist, and queer audiences understood the Dunham Company's productions. Manning's analysis builds upon the scholarship of VèVè Clark, whose theorization of the "memory of difference" as a way of reading Dunham's oeuvre has had a wide-ranging impact on performance studies. Clark's essay is reproduced in its entirety. Finally, praise songs from two anthropological legends, Alfred Métraux and Claude Levi-Strauss, indicate how the anthropological community evaluated Dunham's contributions twenty years after she had decided to pursue a professional career in dance.

Given that Dunham spent almost a third of her life on tour, this section also includes material documenting life on the road. A program from *Bal Nègre,* dating from the late 1940s, provides an example of the repertory that the company took on extended tours throughout the United States, Europe, Latin America, Africa, Asia, and the Pacific Rim. An interview with John Pratt, who designed the company's costumes and scenery for over thirty years, as well as interviews with and reminiscences by former company members, including Vanoye Aikens, Eartha Kitt, and Julie Robinson Belafonte, detail the challenges and rewards of worldwide recognition. These pieces also chronicle the Dunham Company's ongoing encounters with racial discrimination. In venues from Louisville, Kentucky, to São Paulo, Brazil, the predominantly black company often had trouble finding lodgings and restaurants that would serve them, and it frequently confronted racially segregated audiences and artistic trade unions. In addition to revolutionizing the concert arena, Dunham waged a constant battle for equality off-stage. The powerful critique of American race relations depicted in her 1951 ballet *Southland,* which documented a Southern lynching, is an example of Dunham's ability to infuse her art with political overtones. Constance Valis Hill documents official response to the ballet, suggesting that the U.S. State Department effectively blacklisted the company, with-holding financial support that indirectly led to its demise.[7]

After the Dunham Company permanently disbanded in 1965, Dunham took up residence in East Saint Louis. This was a period marked by her renewed commitment to educational training in the arts, both in the local community and abroad. She continued to write about her travels, pub-lishing several articles aimed at introducing North American audiences to life in the Caribbean. Dunham's friendship with the newly-elected pres-ident of Senegal, Léopold Sédar Senghor, also led to collaborations with the Senegalese cultural ministry. Ruth Beckford and Dunham herself doc-ument the heady days of early independence, an era marked by Dunham's consulting work for the first World Festival of Negro Arts and plans for an arts academy on the island of Gorée.[8] Dunham was thus an integral figure of the Black Arts Movement of the 1960s and 1970s, using cultural production as a way of linking local struggles to international ones. Her fight for arts programming for the youth of East Saint Louis, one of the most economically depressed cities in the United States, is indicative of her hands-on approach to demolishing racial and class barriers wherever she encountered them. Part 2 concludes with selections that further doc-ument the whirlwind of Dunham's activities in the United States, rang-ing from choreographing *Aïda* for the Metropolitan Opera House to her forty-seven day fast in 1992 to protest the federal government's repatria-tion policy towards Haitian refugees seeking asylum in the United States.

Another example of how Dunham integrated her cultural and political vision can be found in her creative writing. Part 3 of the anthology in-cludes short stories, poems, and a selection of song lyrics that she incor-porated into the Dunham Company's choreographies. Some of these short stories were originally published in anthologies edited by the likes of W. E. B. Du Bois and Langston Hughes. For instance, "Come Back to Arizona," which Dunham wrote when she was only twelve years old, was included in Du Bois's influential volume of children's literature in 1921. She also wrote *Kasamance,* the fantasy novel from which "The Census Takers" is excerpted, with young readers in mind. The cosmopolitanism of the fictional worlds evident in these selections is noteworthy; the action unfolds in places as disparate as the North American southwest, a Mexican bull-fighting ring, a Haitian marketplace, and rural West African villages. Her in-corporation of linguistic elements of these imaginative settings—Spanish, French, and French Creole—serves as a reminder that Dunham's diasporic literacy was inextricably tied to her commitment to multilingualism.

Part 4 engages another dimension of Dunham's work, exploring Dunham Technique. While the technique has been the subject of some study, in Dunham's own words, "the analysis of my own technique or even the description of it has been one of the most difficult problems of a long and rewarding career" ("Dunham Technique: Prospectus," 524). Acknowledging the formative influence that innovative Russian ballet artists such as Ludmilla Speranzeva and Vera Mirova had on her early training, Dunham has stated that the development of her own movement vocabulary corresponded to the need to create an idiom that validated African American body types. Leaving an indelible mark on American modern dance traditions through innovations including isolation of the knee and pelvic areas as a source of energy and power, the technique also places an emphasis on cultural contextualization and attention to spiritual well being.

Disseminating the principles of this technique was one of the prime objectives of the Katherine Dunham School in New York City. Though the school was founded at the close of World War II, its faculty roster and its curriculum in the brochure reproduced here could serve as a model for today's African diaspora and performance studies programs. Offering an extensive curriculum in the humanities that combined dance, drama, language, philosophy, and anthropology components, the school anticipated by decades the interdisciplinary, historically-grounded discipline of cultural studies that emerged in institutions such as the Birmingham School in the 1970s. This pedagogy is also evident in later Dunham institutions. Joyce Aschenbrenner describes the curriculum and participants associated with the annual Dunham Technique seminars held in East Saint Louis, Illinois, since 1984, the principal forum established after the closing of the Dunham School for training in Dunham's philosophy. No account of the technique would be complete without a sampling of movement exercises; Albirda Rose provides a sequence of barre work and across-the-floor progressions.

Millicent Hodson's insightful article on Dunham's dance literacy serves as an introduction to the second half of part 4. Documenting Dunham's theorization of the relationship between form/technique and the corresponding social impact of the dances under study, "The Anthropological Approach to the Dance" and "Notes on the Dance" offer especially rich investigations into the sociological and material aspects of rhythmic activity in societies at various stages of economic development. Concerned that many dances from "tribal" and "folk" communities were in danger of extinction, Dunham proposed using film to document these traditions as well as to preserve her own technique. As early as the mid 1930s, she lugged a Kodak 16mm motion picture camera through the rugged back roads of the Caribbean in an innovative approach to fieldwork. Roy Thomas analyzes Dunham's own pioneering endeavors as a filmmaker and posits her appearance in several Hollywood films as a watershed moment for black performance's entry into mainstream media.

Part 5, "Preserving the Legacy," concludes the anthology by detailing efforts made to sustain Dunham's legacy. In East Saint Louis, Illinois, she established the Performing Arts Training Center (PATC), a program affiliated with Southern Illinois University that offers academic, performing, and community service initiatives to the local community. Both Dunham and Eugene Redmond examine the importance of the center as a mecca of artistic life in the 1970s. As one of only two groups authorized to perform Dunham's choreographies, the Performing Arts Training Company plays an especially important role in preserving the Dunham oeuvre for future generations. Jeanelle Stovall, a longtime collaborator of Dunham's, describes other institutions that became bulwarks of the East Saint Louis community, outlining Dunham's sustained involvement with the Dunham Dynamic Museum and the Institute for Intercultural Communication.

Given her international stature as a pioneer in the performing arts, it is fitting that Dunham's contributions have been recognized by a series of awards, honorary degrees, and public events. *Kaiso!* documents many of these moments, beginning with a speech made by St. Clair Drake at the opening of the 1976 Katherine Dunham exhibit at the University of California, Berkeley. The juxtaposition of Drake's personal anecdotes about Dunham's influence on a generation of anthropologists with his commentary on her importance as a global ambassador of cultural knowledge encapsulates the tone and message of many accounts concerning her legacy. Glory Van Scott, a former Dunham dancer, provides a memorable analogy in the interview herein, comparing Dunham to a comet whose trailblazing activities always drew people along in her wake. In addition, Van Scott discusses the staging of an intergenerational performance of Dunham choreographies at the 1979 Katherine Dunham Gala at Carnegie Hall. A recipient of the 1983 Kennedy Center Honors alongside Frank Sinatra, Jimmy Stewart, and Elia Kazan, Dunham also had the pleasure of seeing her choreographies staged by the prestigious Alvin Ailey Dance Theatre in 1988. *Kaiso!* includes press clippings detailing both the Kennedy Center award and the rehearsal period and production merits of the Ailey reconstruction.

More recently, a group of scholars gathered by Marta Moreno Vega and New York's Franklin H. Williams Caribbean Cultural Center convened in 1999 under the rubric of the Conceptualizing the Legacy of Katherine Dunham committee. The group helped broker arrangements with the Library of Congress to develop the Katherine Dunham Collection; met with filmmakers and former Dunham Company dancers and staff; and explored the most efficient means of preserving material housed in collections throughout the United States, Europe, Latin America, and the Caribbean. Rex Nettleford's contribution to this volume characterizes the objectives of the meeting, as it highlights how scholars worldwide were influenced by Dunham's work and calls for sustained, serious inquiry into the significance of her endeavors. We include Moreno Vega's article as another illustration of the circles of influence generated by Dunham's activities, as she emphasizes the critical role Dunham played in collaborating with master drummers who were instrumental in introducing Santería and Vodun religious practices to North America.

Anticipating cultural movements, and in many cases initiating them to some degree, has been a hallmark of Dunham's career. Halifu Osumare argues that this was the case regarding Dunham's anthropological work as well. Questioning theoretical deficiencies long current in the study of other cultures, Dunham was ahead of her time in developing an integrative, participant–oriented approach to fieldwork that Osumare posits as a decidedly postmodern methodology long before the term was ever coined. The section concludes with recent articles in *Dance Magazine* that discuss Dunham's legacy and the effort to keep it alive through initiatives such as the Dunham Institute, a project sponsored by the New York Department of Education to introduce Dunham's work to educators throughout the city.

In closing, I invoke two images that highlight Dunham's remarkable talents and ingenuity. The first is documented in "Minefields" and demonstrates the many hats that Dunham wore professionally. Lest one forget the obvious, yet understudied importance of music to the success of the Dunham Company, Dunham reminds us how she often led performances "from the platform, the several drummers squatted on Cuban, Haitian, African and Pacific instruments on stage, as well as the orchestra in the pit, with trap and timpani in the percussion section." As she led, she "had to work closely with the conductor to hold the rhythms together" (120).[9] Picturing her onstage directing a host of instrumentalists and dancers allows us to see a mastermind at work. Like Anansi, she is a spider weaving a web that connects disparate traditions from around the world, directing the action in such a way that new traditions are constantly in the making. This process of creation, the rhythmic melding of visual and sonic stimuli, stresses the value of interaction—among musicians, between musicians and dancers, among the dancers themselves, and between these elements and the audience. Many accounts of Dunham's career speak of her formative influence on a variety of traditions, and it seems appropriate to value her legacy not only as a researcher and performer, but also as an enabler; she is a conduit who continues to inspire dialogues between a host of related yet frequently estranged fields.

In my own work on pre-revolutionary Saint-Domingue (present-day Haiti), I came across another image that provides a fitting point of comparison. In a memoir chronicling the antagonistic relations between free women of color and their elite white counterparts, a French woman laments the futility of colonial legislation designed to destroy her darker rivals' reputations for unparalleled beauty and exquisite taste. She bitterly recounts how the authorities "issued an order that forbade this degraded class from wearing shoes. They then appeared in sandals, with diamonds on the toes of their feet."[10] More than 150 years later, Dunham relates an episode when an agitated theatre manager refused to allow the company to appear onstage without shoes as it would be unseemly to perform barefoot. In a response that echoed the ingenuity of her historical predecessors, Dunham and her husband John Pratt "tied blue-gold straps around the big toe and across the arch to give the illusion of slippers."[11] The show went on to much acclaim and this costume improvisation was subsequently used for years in Dunham's choreographies (see Figure 8 in the photo gallery, *Rara Tonga*). I cite these two anecdotes as a means of placing Dunham into a diasporic continuum characterized by bravado, the capacity to improvise and the wherewithal to defy the status quo in environments that had very fixed notions about the appropriate behavior of young black women. Savvy enough to challenge restrictive and often blatantly racist and sexist traditions, Dunham has used humor, grace, and strength of character to modify her surroundings to suit her own vision. A humanist in the most exalted sense of the word, Dunham still has a lot to teach us.

By way of conclusion I mention her recent response when asked about what she'd like to see included in her epitaph. Jokingly she replied, "She tried." We cannot do much more than that, so we hope that readers will enjoy the show. *Kaiso!*

Notes

1. For example, much research remains to be done on Dunham's incorporation of Polynesian and East Indian traditions into her work.

2. Similar to a secular "bravo" or a sacred "amen," *kaiso* is a term used during a calypso performance to acknowledge an exceptionally virtuoso display of talent. For more details concerning the use of the word, see Keith Warner, *Kaiso! The Trinidad Calypso: A Study of the Calypso as Oral Literature* (Washington, D.C.: Three Continents Press, 1985): 8.

3. Dunham frequently used this example when explaining how the discipline of anthropology could provide provocative insights into theater production. See, for example, Katherine Dunham, "Thesis Turned Broadway," *California Arts and Architecture* (August 1941) and "A Lecture-Demonstration of the Anthropological Approach to the Dance and the Practical Application of this Approach to the Theater, " a lecture delivered at the University of California, Los Angeles, October 1942. Both essays are reproduced in this volume, pp. 214–16 and 508–13.

4. This conceptual term was coined by VèVè Clark to engage Dunham's methodological approach to theater production. See "Performing the Memory of Difference in Afro-Caribbean Dance: Katherine Dunham's Choreography, 1938–1987," reproduced in this volume, pp. 320–340.

5. The excavation metaphor is borrowed from Thomas DeFrantz, *Dancing Many Drums: Excavations in African American Dance* (Madison: University of Wisconsin Press, 2002).

6. John Martin, "The Dance—A Negro Art; Katherine Dunham's Notable Contribution," *New York Times*, 25 February 1940.

7. For more information about the Cold War, its implications for cultural production, and racial politics, see Frances Stonor Saunder, *Who Paid the Piper? The CIA and the Cultural Cold War* (New York: New Press, 1999); Penny Von Eschen, *Satchmo Blows Up the World: Jazz Ambassadors Play the Cold War* (Cambridge: Harvard University Press, 2004); and Mary Dudziak, "Josephine Baker, Racial Protest, and the Cold War," *Journal of American History* 81 (September 1994): 543–70.

8. Gorée, an island located off of the coast of Sénégal, was one of the major points of embarkation for slaves destined for the Americas during the course of the Atlantic slave trade. See note #3 on page 411 for further information.

9. In 2004, Caney produced a long-overdue compilation of Dunham's recordings called *Katherine Dunham, The Singing Gods: Drum Rhythms of Haiti, Cuba, Brazil.* Featured musicians include Francisco Aguabella, Julito Collazo, Chocolate Díaz Mena, Albert Laguerre and Antonio Rodrigues.

10. Madame Laurette Aimée Mozard Nicodami Ravient, *Mémoires d'une créole du Port-Au-Prince.* [1844]. Cited in Joan Dayan, "Codes of Law and Bodies of Color," *New Literary History* 26.2 (Spring 1995): 297.

11. Katherine Dunham, "Minefields," book 2, 79, Katherine Mary Dunham Papers, Special Collections, Morris Library, Southern Illinois University, Carbondale.

PART I

Autobiographical
Reflections

The Rabbit Hunt

KATHERINE DUNHAM

She stood first on one foot then the other, leaning on the BB gun and gazing across the dreary field of winter corn which seemed, overcome by the leaden sky, to be trying to curl back into the snow that lay ankle deep as far as the eye could reach. Its sweep was interrupted by the black jagged ribbon of a stream winding along one edge of the field and by a tired storm fence leaning at a crazy angle as it trailed along the other edge and finally lost itself in a drift.

Somewhere beyond distant sparse trees there must be a farmhouse, and the child thought for a while how it would feel to be inside it. She drew deeply on the mucus escaping from her chapped nose and swallowed hard, trying to shut out the bitterness of the cold and the intensity of her loneliness by conjuring up that unseen interior.

On a Sunday in the country the "big" meal would be at noon and so would be just about over. It would be better if the dishes were washed, too, and the family (mother, father, brother, and sister, like her own) all seated

SOURCE: Katherine Dunham, *A Touch of Innocence: Memoirs of Childhood* (New York: Harcourt, Brace & World, 1959; reprint, University of Chicago Press, 1993), chap. 1. Copyright 1959 by Katherine Dunham, Reprinted by permission.

A Touch of Innocence was Dunham's first book. The following note to the reader appears in the front matter: "This book is not an autobiography. It is the story of a world that has vanished, as it was for one child who grew up in it—the Middle West through the boom years after the First World War, and in the early years of the Depression. And it is the story of a family that I knew very well, and especially of a girl and a young woman whom I rediscovered while writing about the members of this family. Perhaps from their confused lives may come something that will serve as guidance to someone else, or something that will at least hold attention for a while as a story."

in the spacious linoleum-floored kitchen. No, it would be better in the living room, opened once a week, with a fire in the huge pot-bellied base-burner covered all over with isinglass windows like merry eyes.

Her thoughts took flight beyond what she knew from country Sunday visits now and then, into a world of fancy, often evoked when times were hard to bear. The First Mother (spoken of only on rare occasions and secretly, with the child's brother, who, being older, held memories not patched and faded) would be seated at the harp. She would of course be pale, sad-eyed, a little aloof; because to the child all fine ladies should be just a little aloof and never never let out sounds or show things that would attract the neighbors' or anyone's attention, unless in such a way as to make them think that everything was pleasant and charming in the happiest and most well-to-do of families. The father would be as he had used to be—younger-acting and playful and companionable—before bitterness and a foreboding of defeat set in, perhaps before he began to question himself, to realize that for the second time he was married to a woman who could have been in years his mother. On this Sunday, in this house, safe and warm and filled with the orange glow of the base-burner and the rosy glow of love, he would be reading something amusing in the *Sunday Tribune* and chuckling to himself about it, stopping now and then to read an item aloud.

What more could she construct in her fantasy for the brother and sister than that they be allowed to pause, unmolested and out in the open instead of hidden in a closet with a flashlight or candle, lying on the tan carpeting in front of the burner, close to where the ashes dropped glowing through the grate and into a small pit below, reading the pulp of the day: dreaded Dr. Fu Manchu, the thought of whom made one go around the block rather than cross in front of the Chinese laundry; *Science and Invention,* obviously published to delude the gullible into imagining conquests beyond what already seemed unreal, even ungodly, such as wireless and airplanes for everyday use; books of comic strips; and some others that her brother reserved for himself alone. . . .

Two streams had emanated from her nostrils during these reveries, and by now her eyes had overflowed with tears of cold and of an insupportable longing. She wished that the hunters would come back. The bitter cold and the desolation of the cornfield had congealed blood, bone, and cartilage into a condition that she felt sure was like death or might even be a state of near death. She lifted one foot, was surprised that it moved, and took a few steps toward the delivery wagon, black (though in fact it was dark green) against the slate sky, its dull gold hand-painted letters saying WEST SIDE CLEANERS AND DYERS, and underneath, 237 NORTH BLUFF STREET and in one corner TEL. 4513, and in the other corner, A. DUNHAM. She walked wide-legged to keep from chafing her already raw thighs, where the hated gray-flannel long underwear hung sodden with urine, released twice as she had stood there in the cold, so she wouldn't have to go behind a tree and expose bare flesh to the bitter still air and squat like a *girl*—so letting them know, if they came upon her, that she was weaker and different and therefore should have been left at home.

She eyed the stream, drawn by a perversity stronger than herself, knowing that if she moved near enough to hear its murmured complaint the suggestion would overrule her reflexes; and this time, from the already sodden gray flannel, the wetness would move down calves and into wool socks and galoshes. Her brother would shake his head the moment he saw her and smile wryly with a twinkle in his eye for her only, and she would hang her head in shame, already suffering in anticipation the episode from which there would be no escape that night: the long-delayed bedtime, after the dinner of fried rabbit or rabbit stew if the hunters were successful, or of leg of lamb if they returned empty-handed.

The kerosene stove, the kerosene lamp on the piano in the living room, would help at least a little to diminish cold and shadow; and when undressing time came—resolve though she might to face the glacial cubicle that was her room now that she was too old to sleep with her brother— she would end by crawling miserably behind the stove and reluctantly start peeling off middle garments, to arrive all too soon at the telltale, still damp underwear. And though she herself would hold her breath or breathe lightly and only on the top surface, invariably her brother would look up from his book—a serious one, thought-provoking for the brilliant philosopher to come—and glance slyly at her, then concernedly at their father to see if he was really asleep behind the newspaper or if he would look over it and say, "Young lady, it's about time you learned not to wet your underclothes," and then say, "Get the strap," if it had been a black-mood day or just grunt disgustedly if it had been an average day. Her mother would stop her reading or mending to say, "Oh, Katherine, that is disgraceful, a girl of your age who doesn't even know when to go to the toilet certainly shouldn't be allowed out." But worst of all was the quizzical look her brother would give her, because it seemed to destroy once and for all her half-formulated idea of herself as the girl of his choice, the ideal sister.

Standing between the delivery wagon and the stream, she became more dismal at the thought that, seeing the wretchedness of her condition, her brother would ask her why she hadn't gone to bundle down among the carpet ends in the back of the wagon. She knew but she would not be able to tell him. She would never be able to put into words the primordial need to be near where he was, so that even when she couldn't follow because she was a handicap to their tracking—slipping and falling and hurting her ankles in treacherous hoar-covered wagon ruts frozen glacier-hard and sharp as knife points—and had to turn back and follow the tracks to the wagon, still she felt less alone if she stayed out in the open, where there was a chance to hear the occasional "ping" from the twenty-two or louder reverberations from her father's shotgun, or maybe even see her father's pulled-down gray felt hat or her brother's blue knitted earmuff hood.

Again marveling that she could move at all, she walked over toward a giant elm tree, to which a few brown leaves still clung. Halfway there she heard the twin reports of the twenty-two and the shotgun. She wondered if there would be two rabbits or if one would bear the clean hole of the twenty-two and at the same time the perforations of the buckshot, which sometimes buried deep and was recovered only when bitten down on, hidden under meat and gravy. Her teeth grated at the unpleasant recollection, and this physical sensation seemed to bring to life the numbed nerve ends and aroused an urge to recover from utter mortification before the hunters returned.

She moved to the tree and hit first one foot and then the other against its rough bark. The aching sting that traveled as far up as her knees was reassuring. A leaf or two fell on her gray knitted hood, and when she started to remove these she discovered that, while shoulder and elbow still responded, her four fingers separated from her thumb in fur-lined mittens refused to unbend from the barrel of the BB gun. Frightened now, she began to swallow hard and fast to hold down the gasping sobs that were trying to push out of her throat. To keep from a breakdown into complete "girl" or "baby" helplessness, she stuck her tongue out and took into her lips the edge of the blue steel BB gun barrel. But the comfort she sought was rudely displaced by the sharp pain of contact between the warm moist tip of her tongue and the icy steel. She jerked her head back; the shock diverted her attention from her other grievances, and the sudden indrawing, away from the instrument of pain, caused a flow of life into her rigid fingers. Gently she let the BB gun slide between her legs into the snow; then she gingerly eased fingers and thumbs from the mittens and made a fist inside the shelter of her palms. Circulation seemed still to be there, and gradually the blood flowed again, and she could feel a slight sting of warmth in her fingers. The raw tip of her tongue burned, and she dared not touch the end of her nose, raw, too, from the constant flow of mucus. She fell again into waiting, comforted a little by the nearness of the tree.

A fine snow began to sift from the ominous blanket of sky, and a wind starting low on the cornfield rattled the numb stalks as it swirled the powder-dry drift, which stayed close to the ground for a while and then climbed up to lose itself in the falling flakes. She saw the hunters approaching in the distance, obliquely stumbling now and then in sleet-covered furrows, each with gun in one hand and furry spoil dangling head down from the other.

Her own interest merely token, she had on other occasions followed the chase through woods and across fields, her heart thumping madly, as startled as the flushed quarry, dragging the BB gun, and once or twice taking fraudulent aim and firing just to seem really a part of things. But though she dared not admit it, the idea of killing was distasteful to her; and the sight of the victim stopped in panic flight by rifle or shotgun—splattering the white snow with red dots, perhaps not giving up immediately or still trying to hop or contort out of pain to safety—brought revolt and repugnance; and some vague element of the abomination became transferred to the doers of the deed. Not to her brother so much: there was no violence in his nature, and no fear was conjured up at the sight of blood that he had let, because he seemed to have killed impersonally, as an expected duty. Her father's smile of satisfaction and the bloody burden he carried, however, gave her a squeamish sensation, which she felt should be associated with him but could not understand.

As they neared her, crunching across the road in front of the delivery wagon, she reached down into the snow for the gun at her feet and started toward them, hoping that what had happened to her during their absence didn't show and that she looked brave and unconcerned and useful, in what way she didn't try to define. She glanced anxiously at her brother and wiped her aching nose with her blue wool coat sleeve so that she would look less un-neat. He was staring into the tree above her head.

"Hey, look!" he said, gesturing with the rabbit. "Look, Kitty!" ("Kitty" was reserved for times when he himself felt playful or when he knew that she felt alone and needed love and warmth.)

Well out from under the almost bare branches, dusted now with the white snow powder, she turned to look up. She blinked water out of her eyes to see better and a second later wished that she hadn't looked at all. One of the forks in the tree seemed swollen: a tumorous, bark-colored growth bulged at the point where limb joined trunk. With her eyes cleared of moisture she could see the slightest movement in the bulge—a settling into position, a shifting into deeper closeness. A revulsion quite different from that caused by the sight of the dead rabbits came over her. Her spine and a band around the center of her stomach seemed to be in the grip of some creeping thing. She was looking at a knot of hibernating snakes, perhaps water moccasins, perhaps only harmless field or water snakes, but nevertheless congenitally loathsome, intrinsically repulsive—to her, the quintessence of everything abhorrent.

"Shoot, Katherine," her father said, pointing upward, too, with his rabbit. "Go ahead. See if you can hit one."

Unconscious of her movement, she stepped back from the tree, at the same time raising her loaded gun. Still mittened, she forced her fore-finger into the trigger and pulled, discharging all of her loathing at the noxious bundle under which she had stood unaware a moment before. The bullet must have hit, because some extremity, head or tail, uncoiled itself sluggishly, reached blindly into the cold air, then recoiled again. Her father laughed at her, while she stood and forced down the thin saliva that oozed from the depressions under her tongue and made her want to be sick.

The hood of the delivery wagon was covered with blankets, but in spite of this and other precautions, there was always the tense, shivering wait while the starter was tested, hopefully and persistently to the last, slow, grumbling protest of the unwilling motor and weakened battery. Then always the hand crank was resorted to.

Her brother could climb out first and sometimes, though he strained to the point of sweating, he was frustrated by the groaning motor. Then he and her father would switch positions; her brother would sit next to her and manipulate the mysterious lifeline, while her father puffed and panted and said "Damn!"—until, with a vicious kick that sometimes ejected the crank into the snow—in its flight striking vindictively at the hand that gripped it—the motor would turn over, and her father would catapult around the side into the driver's post. He would take just enough time to throw the crank under the seat as her brother stood up to transfer the controls and then slid past her to sit on the outside, so that she would be somewhat protected from the cold.

And then would begin the long journey home, with familiar landmarks seemingly deliberately retarded by her urgency. A storm-windowed farmhouse sending out one curl of smoke, as differentiated from another sending out two; a steepled church at a crossroads, with its biparietal outhouse; the truck garden of Nick, the Greek, shut down for winter now; the long stretch of Plainfield Road, its closer-together, occasionally lighted cottages indicating the nearness to town; finally the careful descent down the slope of Buell Avenue with much use of brakes and shifting of gears; then the top of Western Avenue and the even more hazardous descent down a steeper slope, where one had to be expert on roller skates and cautious on a bicycle and where sometimes in the night the accustomed stillness had been ruptured by futilely grinding brakes and screeching tires, prelude to a collision and the split second of stopped-time stillness that followed.

From the top of the hill she could see, immediately after the crossing of Bluff Street, the beginning of Cass Street and the Cass Street Bridge. Over this bridge on one memorable occasion, on a starry winter night not so cold as this one promised to be, she had risked punishment by strap to do the unmentionable, the thrilling-to-the-utmost, the longed-for-in-secret by every child in the town. Going out with their sled, she and her brother had promised to stay on Bluff Street; but on this occasion, overcome by some sense of daring, some perversity, some madness brought on by a full moon, they had decided—taking turns at policing the four corners for danger—to start at the top of Western Avenue and belly-flop down the vertiginous descent at meteor speed, across the Bluff Street intersection.

There had been the trudge up, the last-minute look down, the signal for the take-off, the impact on belly of sled. Speed gathered on speed, and, helpless under momentum, she had screwed her face into a knot against the needle sting of upflung snow, and, not having known before that snow smelled, had smelled its whiteness along with the smell of steel and sulfur from the sparks flying up from the runners. The approach to the bottom of the hill marked the greatest danger, and passing over it the greatest triumph. Pressed flat, shooting past the very spot where the hideous accidents occurred, she could imagine wheels crushing her body, bursting skin, cracking bones, smashing her skull so that her brains spattered out and froze to the ground.

The intersection was passed so quickly that fright and rapture mingled in a suffusing triumph, and before she knew what sensations had passed through her she was skimming lightly and safely over the stretch of bridge and coasting slower and slower to a gentle halt against the wooden elevation that divided pedestrian from vehicle. Trembling, eyes streaming, cheeks stinging, walking as though for the first time and as though descending from a great flight into space, she had dragged the sled back across the bridge to her waiting brother and taken her guardian's post.

This was in many ways more tormenting than the jeopardies of her own descent. Suppose some car was approaching without lights. Suppose she misjudged, and a vehicle presumably crawling on the ice-covered pavement was in fact moving at top speed, to mete out the extreme of punishment and make her her brother's murderer. Suppose he would be the one lying there mangled, brains frozen to pavement, sled smashed into splinters, runners twisted beyond recognition, gray overcoat soaked with blood and intestines? She stood with her hand raised in an agony of incertitude until, impatient, he called out from the top; and the voice drifting down from the waiting figure posed under the flickering streetlamp at the top of the hill activated the waiting figure motionless under the flickering streetlamp at the bottom of the hill. With a last anguished look in all directions, she dropped her arm. Then she stood in wait for him to catapult past the corner of Bluff Street, past the danger spot, and felt—as she stood planted square in the middle of the street, vulnerable herself to vengeful parents or oncoming vehicles—that with her own small body she would hold off any danger to him blind seeker after an unattainable planet, Iphigenia already begun.

She held her breath now as they descended the hill in the delivery wagon, but tried not to show that she recognized, inexperienced as she was, her father's lack of driving skill, never to be overcome.

The Closed Room

KATHERINE DUNHAM

People were always amused when Katherine Dunham told them that she remembered the circumstances of her birth. At five and a half she told her new mother all about the other mother who had died, and about riding home from the hospital in her mother's arms, and how the horse had shied at the shadow of a butterfly as the pale lady with black hair piled in a pompadour stepped from the surrey.

It was a warm day just nine days after the twenty-second of June. As the horse shied, her father took her in his arms, then gave her back to her mother, who walked up the driveway trailing her white linen dress and looking down at her seventh child—her second by the child's father, the young tailor.

Katherine Dunham tried once or twice to go back even farther than that and tell about the nine babies in a row at the hospital, all in baskets and all screaming for attention at the top of their newly discovered lungs, and how she howled louder than all the others when her father picked her up and put her into her mother's arms. But at that point the attention of listeners, willing to indulge her fantasies thus far, began to wander, discouraging her from further retrospect.

What she knew nothing of was Albert Dunham's trip to the village of Glen Ellyn shortly after his wife, twenty years his senior, had been delivered of their first child, Albert Millard Dunham Jr.

SOURCE: Katherine Dunham, *A Touch of Innocence: Memoirs of Childhood* (New York: Harcourt, Brace & World, 1959; reprint, University of Chicago Press, 1993), chap. 2. Copyright 1959 by Katherine Dunham. Reprinted by permission.

Albert Millard Dunham, the father, was fully aware that his marriage was unusual, and not just because of the discrepancy in age between him and his wife. There was her fair skin, her French-Canadian background; in addition, she was a divorcée, with five children and four grandchildren. All these factors provided material for social discrimination and malicious comment and gave rise to a variety of disagreeable situations which could be avoided, as he saw things, by a removal from the city's congested South Side, already stirring uneasily at hints of invasion by raucous Southern cousins. Her charm, beauty, intellect, and musical accomplishment had placed Albert Dunham on his knees before Fanny June Taylor; her property holdings on Prairie and Indiana Avenues and her assistant principalship at one of the big city schools made it easier, once the marriage had become a fact, to leave the city and make a home in the suburbs.

Just beyond the train stop of Maywood was the village of Glen Ellyn, untouched at the time by the economic pressures or racial discriminations or restrictive codes of the city. It was composed essentially of the middle-class—upper white-collar workers, lesser business executives, commuters to the city at seven o'clock and back again at seven, with, in addition, a few retired gentleman farmers and building contractors and modestly well-to-do bankers and businessmen, who represented noncommuting elite. There had been no occasion for concern over invasion by persons of unorthodox colors, creeds, or religions. The rare chauffeurs and numerous maidservants and cooks and gardeners were almost all Negroes; like the office workers, they commuted, but in the reverse direction. Years before Albert Dunham's arrival on the scene, a distant relative of his, Marie Clark, had worked her way through kitchen after kitchen of the village, while her husband, Earley Clark, clipped and mowed his way through as many gardens and lawns; until, like blemishes grown so familiar that they are at last unnoticed, they had settled in the lowlands of the village, bought property, become voters and taxpayers. By then it was too late for decent action, so they were indulgently overlooked or referred to with the affectionate condescension reserved for retired family retainers or illiterate relations.

It was through the intervention of Marie and Earley Clark that Albert Dunham, chafing more than ever at the inconvenience of the city because of his newborn son, came upon a choice property in an outlying area still in the stage of subdivision. When he first looked at it, a dirt road had just been cut through a wheat field and cement sidewalks were still fresh in their wooden frames. A few brick bungalows were under construction, a few were finished, and new grass was sprouting in front yards behind sparse green hedges. After much bargaining, many trips, and with the last-minute intervention of his wife, the young man finally took title to a plot of wheat field; in a short time the foundations were laid and the framework was started for a two-story wooden house.

A neighborhood committee was waiting for one false move on the part of the interloper. The people of Glen Ellyn had discovered, soon after the purchase, that the dark young man was married to, not just acting for or employed by, the tall, fair-skinned woman who often accompanied him to offices of realtors, contractors, and builders, and this caused no end of chagrin and unconcealed resentment. The neighboring landowners felt duped and misled but lacked a definite incident to seize upon; they sulked, held meetings, and foresaw the irreparable decline of property values. It happened that most of the scattered dwellings completed or under construction were of brick; a hastily set up zoning commission, drawing boundaries as irregular as the markings of a rabbit warren, concluded that Albert Dunham's lot fell into a division reserved for brick houses. The owner of the wheat field, a farmer in the process of retiring on the profits of these subdivisions, saw in this strategy a double-edged knife with one side of the blade turned toward himself. He opposed the coalition and won. But he could not change the spirit of men, and the next night an ineffective, home-manufactured explosive shattered the downstairs windows, which had just been installed. Albert Dunham's reaction was swift and to the point. Told what had happened by Earley Clark, he descended from the six o'clock interurban armed with a double-barreled shotgun, determination in his stride, murder in his eyes. The neighbors had counted on no such reaction and withdrew behind their piles of red brick and cement bags to confer, or peeped between starched bungalow curtains, watching the angry young man inspect the damage, look about defiantly, and then install himself in the tool shed on the front of the lot. Here he settled down for a vigil that extended through that night and every night, until the last coat of paint had been applied to the house and the carriage barn behind it.

The house was roomy, planned to accommodate, in addition to the immediate family of Fanny June Dunham, several members of her extended clan, who, until her death, took advantage of her generosity. The rotation of these guests was so regular as to make them seem fixtures. The eldest daughter, Louise, and her children hardly said goodbye before they were again on the doorstep, with suitcases and parcels and tales of abuse by a drunken husband and father. This youngest daughter by the previous marriage visited at regular intervals, and her visits were protracted, beginning as they did at the earliest stage of her successive pregnancies and lasting through parturition. The middle daughter—also named Fanny June—had married before her mother's second marriage, and it was George Weir, her husband, who had been responsible for the meeting that resulted in Albert Dunham's marriage to the much-courted divorcée.

George Weir was of the colorful classification known as "octoroon" and freely circulated between the two opposing color groups of the city. He also was a tailor's apprentice, and when the ambitious Albert Dunham decided to leave the firm of German tailors where both young men were employed, George Weir joined him in the daring adventure of an independent business in the Fair Building, a structure in the very center of the city which in those days was considered a skyscraper. Here they attracted much of the clientele from their former employers, and only they knew of the scanty meals they shared sitting cross-legged on the cutting table or of the coffeepot that simmered in the washroom from early morning until late at night, giving them stimulus when food had been too scanty.

George Weir introduced his friend to his bride, and Albert Dunham met and fell in love with the bride's mother. By the time he felt that he could ask her to marry him, George Weir was the father of a girl, Helen. By the time the Weir family paid its visits to the house in Glen Ellyn, a boy, Everett, was out of diapers. George Weir was happy with the life of the city and with his children, so fair of skin that they like him would have free access to all of the accompanying benefits. He had no aspirations beyond the immediate enterprise, which daily was proving more lucrative.

His partner, on the other hand, was set on suburban or even country life and could wish for nothing more desirable than the transformed wheat field and the two-story frame house with a carriage barn behind— even though he had not bargained for the heterogeneous household that he had inherited with his handsome wife. But he was aware that, despite her devotion to her new life and the responsibility she felt toward first the son and then the daughter, Fanny June was inevitably torn in her affections by the demands of her grown children. She was, in fact, unable to refuse the hospitality or even the financial help needed from time to time by one or more of them. But the least worrisome of her many responsibilities was the family of George Weir.

Katherine Dunham liked her unnaturally placed niece and nephew well enough, but even before she could talk intelligibly she took a strong dislike to the children of her half sister Louise and to their father also. One of her reasons for disliking the girl child in particular was that she always ended up wearing her clothes. And she mistrusted her half sister Louise's husband because she had once seen him in the ugly condition of drunkenness that resulted in violence. He was careful to call at the house only in the afternoon, when he was certain that the parents had left for the day, and he always went back to the city before they returned.

Henry, the youngest of Fanny June's children by her former marriage, was one of the permanent residents of the gray house. When left alone, he seemed quite tractable. When aroused, he fell into a fury, striking out at anything near and uttering cries only partly human. Katherine Dunham was fond of him because sometimes when she lay all alone and bored in her crib, he would creep into the room and lean over and look deep down into her eyes as though searching for understanding. They would communicate in their secret language, and what he said pleased the child, who always laughed. Sometimes he would sit for a long while catching stray flies that wandered into the room in summertime and show them to her before throwing them out of the window. Their frantic efforts to escape distressed him, and she felt that he caught them and threw them out not only to please her but to save them from the fly swatter. When Louise and her husband and children and callers teased Henry just to see him tormented into a speechless rage, she would feel very sad and want to stroke him or murmur something in their own language. But he was too far gone by then to be reached and would be led, frothing at the mouth and with eyes rolling far back in his head, to Grandmother Buckner's room, because she was the only one who could calm him, being a little different in behavior from the others herself. Once the child heard her mother, as she sat stroking the unhappy boy's head, offer an explanation about Henry's erratic behavior and frequent communications with inhabitants of a world that only he could see. He had fallen from a highchair as a baby and fractured his skull, and he had never been in possession of all his senses since then. Henry was fortunate enough to die early.

Grandmother Buckner tried again and again to tell the polygenetic members of the Glen Ellyn household what she knew from her Indian forebears and what she had learned from the family of dolls that lined the shelves of her bedroom. The only listeners were her daughter Fanny June and two small children apparently attached in some way to her daughter, but just how and in what relationship the old lady couldn't quite figure out.

Her daughter had always been a good child, as far back as when she was a little girl, dark-eyed and long-haired, in Winnipeg. Visits to Fanny June's old Indian grandmother, Grandmother Buckner's mother, had not frightened her, as many second-generation children of such unions had been frightened. Mother and child would drive deep into the country, sometimes in winter when the snow was piled higher than the rooftop of the log cabin where the old Indian woman lived alone. Then they would have to go by sleigh, and the little girl would never complain of the cold or cry at the sounds of animals when the horses turned into the woods near the log cabin. They would stay overnight, and the old Indian woman would prepare infusions of herbs and dried berries to make the little girl strong, because she was always frail and pale and too tall for her age. They would drive back the next day, and Grandmother Buckner would feel pleased with herself because she had taken the child, against the wishes of her school-teaching, French-Canadian husband, to the people he called "heathen."

When he died, Grandmother Buckner—whose people were English farmers and had little use for the descendants of the French settlers—changed her name from Guillaume to Williams and married the man whose name she carried thenceforth. The daughter, Fanny June, proved to be exceptionally apt in school, and soon after the family moved to Windsor, the mother decided to send the girl, then fifteen years of age, across Lake Michigan into Detroit for further schooling. Immediately after graduation from a school for elementary schoolteachers, the daughter fell in love with and married a man named Taylor, about whom little was known by the family except that he had sired five children and that his own father had been a Russian Jew. He was swarthy of skin, so everyone supposed that he had on his mother's side some mixture of Indian or Negro or Asiatic blood or perhaps all three.

Grandmother Buckner stayed in Windsor until her second husband died. As she was packing her belongings to make the trip to the Middle West to live with her daughter, she fell from a stepladder and broke her leg. Incompetent medical care led to its amputation, and it was during this confinement that the old woman, feeling herself alone and not being at all sure of welcome by her daughter's new husband in an already multiplied household, began collecting dolls. She had always wanted a large family, and the dolls were a kind of substitute for all the sons and daughters she had never had; they also became the friends and counselors of her declining years.

Some of the dolls had belonged to her when she was a child. These were dressed in worn and faded gingham, some in fringed suede or buckskin jerkins and skirts. They were very old, and if they had originally been painted, time and the affectionate handling of a lonely child had removed all traces, leaving only the crude torso and features fashioned long ago by some north-woods craftsman. There were dolls that had belonged to her daughter Fanny June and to Fanny June's daughters also. These had china features, with bodies of cloth stuffed with cotton or sawdust. One or two of the most elegant had bodies of fine kid leather, and delicate hands and feet of china, and heads and shoulders and elaborate coiffures of china or porcelain. Some were babies in long, time-yellowed baptismal dresses. Their faces were round and for the most part blank. One or two tried to smile, but because they were paintless, with an eye missing or the end of a nose chipped off, the effect was grotesque. Some of the dolls were more recent, gifts from the indulgent daughter who recognized the withdrawal of the old woman from a world she neither understood nor wanted to be a part of, but from which at the same time she would have liked to have some regard.

Her grandchildren laughed at her when she brought the dolls to the table to share her meals, and, if she left the room for a moment, brought their friends to look at the array. She would run them from the room, stumping after them as fast as she could on her wooden leg, sometimes forgetting that she was waving one of her precious family in the air as a weapon. Henry was often with her, and he, too, would join in the routing of the enemy, which only occasioned more taunts and jeers and laughter, until the old woman, exasperated and worn out by her efforts, would retreat to her room and bar the door with chairs and tables.

Of all this Fanny June remained unaware, seeing only the steady unhappiness and decline of both the misfits, the solemn introspection of her young son, and the concern of her young daughter. Sensing the affection that the children felt for the old woman and their defective half brother, she took them from time to time to her mother's room and explained the doll family and told them not to be afraid of Grandmother Buckner as the other children were. They examined the wooden leg as the old lady held her skirt for them to see, and looked with great interest at the doll in the old-fashioned babies' highchair, and the one always sleeping in the little wooden crib, and at the others on shelves all around the room. The old lady talked to the dolls and listened to their answers. She fed them bits from her own meals, which were brought to her on a tray after she refused to leave her room. Those with cavities for stomachs were neatest; the others were forced all the same to partake of the repasts, which included cooked cereal, soft-boiled eggs, mashed potatoes, and different kinds of fruit. Like overstuffed Roman senators or uncooperative children, they sat with bits of food smeared around their mouths and over the front of their clothing, taffeta as well as gingham. Since Grandmother Buckner had done with washing them when she took to her room to stay, the food remained stuck to their vacant smiles and overflowing from their partly open lips.

The youngest half sister seemed to have installed herself and her children permanently in the Glen Ellyn house, and although her husband continued to live in the city, he paid frequent and fruitful enough visits to ensure the enlargement of his family. A hardship was worked on the two children of Fanny June and Albert Dunham, who had to relinquish their room to the half sister and her children. The brother slept on the parlor couch, and the girl's iron-barred crib was moved into her parents' bedroom. The air was heavy with trouble, both present and to come, and in the midst of it all the child reacted by standing for long stretches of time looking out of the front window at the houses that had sprung up on all sides, trying to identify the few neighbor children that she knew, trying to recall her waking and sleeping fears of the night before.

At night when she was undressed and placed inside the crib and the protective iron fence was hooked into place, she always looked around the room, stealthily so that the others would not know of her secret fears, to see if there were any indications of "Them." A light would be left burning on her mother's bedside cupboard if it were dark, or the shade only partly drawn if it were light outside. Then she would be left alone to listen to the sounds of a still, closed room and to wait for Them. She always went to sleep and didn't even awaken when her mother and father went to bed. Later in the night, however, something would happen that would start her wide-awake, and she would sit up in bed damp with perspiration and cold with fear. There would be no identifiable sound, and she could see no strange form. But she knew that the creatures were there, and that They were in some way interested in her, and that They would do her harm if they could. She knew just what They looked like, and there was nothing especially outstanding about their appearance; it was an evilness which exuded from Them that began a fortification inside her, once she realized that this was something she had to face alone.

On one occasion she had cried out in the night, and her mother had taken her into her own bed. But this hadn't pleased her father, and she was afraid to be ejected altogether from the room, where she felt at least some protection in the black of night, at least some comfort from the regular breathing of her father and the fitful breathing of her mother. If she were moved into the open space of the parlor, her brother would be there, but he was, to her, not much more equipped than she to deal with such malevolence; and, besides, there was no door between the parlor and the hallway where (it had somehow become imbedded in her consciousness) these creatures had their abode. In the daytime she looked upon the hall tree in the hallway with mistrust and avoided it altogether when she was alone or at night.

But They were somehow also connected with the upstairs part of the house, where there had been other mysterious happenings, and where later the greatest mystery of all was to take place, the closed door behind which her mother lay to await her death. In the room in the middle of the night They lay in wait for her, and once she knew that there was no outside aid, she lay waiting for Them. They were called "Crandalls"—why, she didn't question; They just were. And They wore gray striped baseball suits and caps, which she must have seen once when her father took her to a baseball game. The faces were formless and evil, with no defining color or features and more of the dead than of the living. They wanted her badly, but though she might be afraid of them, she was not afraid enough to give in to them. They were familiar to her and were a family, and more than this she could not figure out. Her brother, in whom she confided, could help her only by accompanying her to the hall tree and taking off all the coats and umbrellas and showing her that no people lived there. He also took her to any upstairs room that happened to be unoccupied and made her look under the bed and in the closets, and she let him believe that she had dreamed it all. But within herself she knew that They were there waiting and she thought of these things when she stood in front of the plate-glass window of the parlor looking out at the children playing in the front yard across the street.

As she learned to walk more freely by herself, her world took on new sizes, shapes, and colors. The changing season helped, too, and as spring warmed into summer, she took a great interest in the barn and in the end of the lot where it merged into fields no longer planted in wheat, but green with long grass and dotted white with daisies and yellow with buttercups and blue with gentian and pale wild violets. She noticed her brother more, because his was the task of following her, of finding her when she wandered into hiding places, of trying to keep her out of trouble, of trying to answer her never-ending *whys* about things and people and events. With others she was silent and withdrawn. With him she always sought communication, half the time not waiting for answers, which he gave only after deliberate and full certainty, feeling the responsibility of his position as guide and mentor.

Somewhere, either at the end of the lot on which the house stood or farther out in the middle of the daisy field, was a hoary old apple tree. It stood alone, the next trees being on the property of a neighbor on the other side of the path that loosely marked a future road. The subdivision could still be considered in a pastoral stage, particularly on the side of the road where Albert Dunham's house stood. By accident or intention the fields behind the house and on each side were still vacant, and for this the father was grateful. The carriage horse was put to pasture in these fields and the skittish mare was led around an improvised exercise track on Sunday mornings.

During the lazy summer afternoons the children, who by now had settled into the foursome of Helen and Everett Weir and Albert and Katherine Dunham—on rare occasions joined by children from one of the more friendly families of the area—would gather under the apple tree to play at housekeeping, exchange confidences, make necklaces of the daisies and wood violets they collected in the field and under the apple tree, and climb into the upper branches of the tree itself.

A new world opened for the child with communication on the level of the others. The excitement was not so much in talking, because her niece and nephew were so voluble and clever that they automatically took over the conversation wherever they were, even with elders, who never tired of the witticisms and repartee that they had developed as a kind of defense mechanism in the competitive world they had known in the city, and in the often conflicting inner circle of their own family. Her brother did not say much, but what he said was always wise, and she found herself listening more and more to his counsel and trying more and more to please him and make up for not being a boy.

The excitement of articulation in a comprehensible language came in mastering numerous jingles and songs, some of which were re-edited from the original by her niece and nephew into cleverer or more amusing versions, as for example, in the case of a song called "Under the Old Apple Tree":

In the shade of the old apple tree
A hobo sat down on a bee.

She sang this version lustily, with, when she sang it in front of grownups, consequences remarkably close to those of the hobo's experience. But they were proud of her recitation of

I had a little pony whose name was Dapple Gray
I lent him to a lady, to ride a mile away.

Saddened by the thought of the unhappy pony, ridden under whip and lash and through mud by the ungrateful lady, she would say the verse over and over in a monotonous chant, until she had worked herself into a kind of abstracted melancholy in which she and the pony and the mud and the switch were all one in a dreary, thankless world.

The melancholia of this period was rooted in actual events. One of these was the disappearance of the white mare Nellie from the stable, on a late spring night during one of the electrical storms that hit the Middle Western states without warning—sometimes with accompanying winds that turned into tornadoes, sometimes simply splitting trees and setting fires to barns and causing lightning rods to discharge into the overcharged atmosphere like Fourth-of-July sparklers.

On one such storm-charged, rainless night the mare panicked in her stall and attempted to escape under the stout oak beam that barred the exit; she broke her back in the attempt. The storm and the noises and the shouts woke the child, and she was glad of an excitement stronger than the presence of the leering "Crandalls." She could see the lightning all around and, in its flashes, the grass of the fields bowing low under the sweep of the wind and the old apple tree yielding up twigs and leaves and blossoms and finally whole branches. She could not see the barn, but she could see that her father was not in his bed; and soon she heard, above the noise of the storm and sound of voices calling and shouting, an explosion like the banging of a large door. As she looked at the empty bed in the flashes of lightning, she began to try piecing together something else that had been worrying her for some time. But as the questions were taking form in her mind, the storm subsided, and she dozed off; and by morning she had forgotten all but a dim uneasiness.

The excitement about the mare took her mind off this worry. She was told to stay in the front part of the house until well into the afternoon, even though the day had become calm and beautiful after the storm, and she would have liked to visit the apple tree and gather the fallen branches of blossoms. When no one thought that she was listening, they talked of the pity of the white mare. Her father had stayed home from his work to survey the damage of the storm and was in an unusually disagreeable mood, not wanting to talk about the horse and finding the children too much underfoot. When she asked why it was a pity about the white mare, and what was a pity, and where was Nellie going now, the adults looked at each other in surprise and said that Nellie had run away in the night. But, standing at the front window, she had seen a wagon, pulled by two horses and with several men and lots of rope and iron bars on it, turn into the driveway. She couldn't follow its progress because the back part of the house was forbidden to her until afternoon, but she waited patiently, and after a while the wagon went out of the driveway again, and Nellie lay on it while two men kept trying to adjust a tarpaulin to cover her from sight.

She passed this off as another of the strange whimsies of adults and wished that she could move on to something else now and not worry about what had been gnawing at the back of her mind during the storm last night. There was something mysterious about it, and the reason came to her as Nellie's limp body, legs thrust awkwardly into the air—she who had been so proud and graceful—jolted around in the wagon as it turned out of the driveway and off down the road away from the house. The mystery was connected with the empty bed during the storm.

She woke less often in the night than during the cold dark winter months, but she was aware of the fact that there was now only her father's steady breathing from the large bed and that the fitful breathing of her mother, which sometimes of late had been interspersed with groans and once or twice with weeping, no longer accompanied his. Once she had experimented with sliding from her crib, which was now uncomfortably small for her and therefore left with the fence down, and tiptoeing to the side of the bed where her mother had always slept to see if she had simply not been hearing correctly. She was frightened to discover that in fact her mother was not there, and she crept back to bed to think about it; but then she fell asleep and in the morning didn't remember.

A few days later she did remember and asked where her mother was and why she never came from the city in time for supper any more and why she was always gone in the morning. Her brother didn't answer, and the others repeated what they had said on other occasions, that her mother was very busy and returned always after the child was asleep and left before she awoke. She tried staying awake when she was put to bed but always fell asleep before either her mother or father came into the room, and was cross with herself the next day when she thought about it. After the storm this thought was continually with her, especially because on Sundays also her father was in evidence but her mother was not. Once she complained so much and followed everyone about making such a racket, trying to solve her loneliness and fill in her loss, that a conference of the grownups was held and some decision reached in her favor.

That night, just at her bedtime, her mother came into the room as she had done so often, dressed in the clothes that she had worn to the city to teach school in, wearing a straw sailor hat with a black bow, on top of hair piled high into a shining black pompadour. The child could not know the effort that this deception cost Fanny June, nor was she more than vaguely aware of the whiteness of her mother's skin or of the deep shadows of suffering under her sunken black eyes. She could not tell that her mother could scarcely walk, much less carry the nightshirted, ecstatic child to the darkened kitchen, where by lamplight, as on so many occasions before, she went to the screened-in cooling shelf of the pantry and came back with a pitcher of milk and poured a single glass and, with the child on her knee, took a sip and then held the glass to the child's lips. The child paid no attention to the fact that all the others were suddenly out of sight or that the shades were drawn even though it was summer and the nights darkened later. She did not know that this would be the last time that she would see her mother alive.

Fanny June Dunham must have known for a long time that her illness was a malignant one. She must have hated to have her husband know it and to realize that the blow of her death would be a bitter one to him, and the responsibility of the children's upbringing a cruel one. And she didn't see anyone prepared at the moment to take over the task of her departure. Her daughter Fanny had her hands quite full and, moreover, was absorbed in her own interests. A sister of Albert Dunham, Lulu, was fond of the children and they of her, but she lived in the city in what was virtually a tenement, and all sorts of odd people circulated around her just because she was goodhearted and unsuspecting and generous. In the opinion of the mother, that was not a proper environment for her children, especially for the oversusceptible daughter. The son seemed to have a mind of his own and was wise enough to choose and discard and select from life around him those things that would serve him best, and to look at people from a great distance and with far more discrimination than his years warranted.

Tears ran down the mother's face and over her lips and into the glass as she sipped the milk to please the child, then held it to the child's mouth. The child reached to her and patted her cheek, feeling safe and eternally secure and so full of contentment that she thought only of the goodness of things; though the exact picture as it was, tears and all, remained with her as her last remembrance of her mother.

Death came slowly and painfully to the woman in the closed room, and as she wasted into death she wanted to be alone. The daughters and their families had moved into the house to wait with her, and a nurse came from the city and sat through the long nights. The young father stayed more at home through the winter and made every effort to know his children better, even at the sacrifice of his business, which needed more of his attention at this time than at any other. The child hung around the fringes of these vicissitudes, picking up what information she could and storing it for late assimilation. She was thwarted in her efforts to gain access to the upstairs room: the mother did not wish to be remembered by her children as she knew herself to be during her dissolution.

On Sunday afternoons the father would take his daughter on one knee and, with an arm around his son, would try to recapture his own Memphis childhood long enough to relay to them stories that his father and *his* father had told among themselves, with the children listening in front of a fire where hoecake browned in the ashes. He hit with great success upon the saga of Br'er Rabbit and how he outwitted Br'er Fox and all the rest of the Tennessee woods animals, until the Tar-Baby outwitted *him*.[1] Br'er Rabbit dressed up and leaving church on Sunday and bowing low to Br'er Fox, who waited outside licking his chops and planning how to work out an ambush for Br'er Rabbit, who had selected Br'er Lion as walking companion through the woods that morning and therefore felt very smug and took off his hat and bowed low to Br'er Fox, grinning all the time. Br'er Rabbit courting the same girl as Br'er Fox and always arriving by a short cut, so that by the time Br'er Fox arrived hot and tired, Br'er Rabbit was sitting cross-legged in the porch swing, fanning himself and drinking lemonade and making pretty speeches to the lady. And then sometimes Br'er Rabbit singing another tune, finding himself all alone in the woods, with Br'er Fox burrowing into his doorway or staring greedily at him through a clump of bushes where he had injudiciously taken a nap; and Br'er Rabbit having to do some fast talking and many times just barely escaping Br'er Fox's cooking pot. . . .

The child would demand over and over again the description of the Tar-Baby that the farmer made and put in his corn patch, knowing Br'er Rabbit's inclination toward courting fair ladies, and how the Tar-Baby melted in the hot Tennessee sun and wouldn't answer when Br'er Rabbit addressed her in the courtliest of manners—so that he became angry and hit her and stuck to the soft tar and would have been apprehended by the farmer and severely chastised and maybe even eaten if his enemy hadn't come along and, after taunting him, let himself be talked into releasing him, only to be made fun of later for his gullibility as Br'er Rabbit gaily skipped off to safety.

So the mortal feud unwound itself through episode after episode, and when Br'er Monkey and Br'er Lion entered the scene, the flavor of ancestral Africa delighted the child, and her pleasure was unmarred by any attempt to rationalize the seepage of this distant continent into not-so-far-off Tennessee.

The boy listened but preferred the tales of Great-grandfather Dunham, who, of his own free will and dodging, as it were, between projectiles from the muskets of the Union troops, had hitched two steeds to the Big House family carriage and maneuvered the young and the womenfolk of the family—with silverware, heirlooms, and all—to safety across the line. The father explained that the father of John Dunham, his own father, had been a Malagasy, which meant that he had been one of the few of the slaves recruited on the east coast of Africa, and that they came from an island named Madagascar. In their blood flowed the blood of Malay people as well as a type of African different from the Guinea or West Coast African people, one of whom the father of John Dunham took as a wife.

On winter Sunday evenings the child missed the sound of music as she lay in her bed waiting for sleep. Before, when her mother had been with them, there had been music from the small organ in the parlor and sometimes the delicate tinkling tones from the instrument in the corner under a cover that they were never to touch. It was called a harp, and once she had stood in the doorway of the parlor and watched her mother seated behind it, face against the wooden frame, arms extended to embrace it as it tilted into her lap between her knees. Her mother was moving her fingers over the instrument and changing little pegs and listening to the result as she plucked the strings, and her father sat nearby doing the same thing to the guitar that he loved to play on Sunday evenings. After the child was in bed again they seemed to reach some sort of tonal rapport, and she fell asleep to music that they were practicing together.

With her father alone, there was seldom music. Once she saw him come down from the room upstairs and go straight into the parlor, where the fire had gone out in the grate, and sit with his face buried in his hands, while his shoulders shook and sounds like crying came from between his fingers; but then he stood up and went to the guitar and took it from its case and sat and began to make the plucking sounds while he turned screws at the top and his face was in the light, and while it looked wretchedly unhappy, it was not wet from tears, so he could not have been crying.

Katherine Dunham loved new clothes, especially because, long before her old ones were outgrown or outworn, they were swiftly appropriated by the rapacious Louise for her own daughters who were the child's approximate age. During the last winter in Glen Ellyn she wore rompers and overalls almost always, inheriting her brother's outgrown ones when no one seemed to have time to replenish her depleted wardrobe. She remembered with nostalgia the times when her mother had dressed her on Sunday afternoons in woolen dresses with flounces or cotton dresses with softly starched pleats before a Sunday buggy ride. Her lower lip thrust forward as she saw the same dresses on the two disagreeable half nieces who, with their mother, were again among the multitude feasting on the hospitality of the dying mother. The fact that she might not now fit into the dresses made no difference whatsoever.

Her deprivation was given emphasis by these constant reminders, and as her own condition became sorrier, her dislike for her relatives increased. Her father no longer troubled to cut her hair on alternate Sundays, and the difference in quality between her own and that of her relatives was brought home to her by the fact that the longer it grew the more unmanageable it became; no one was able to untangle the snarls and knots, so that after a while it resembled more the brier patch in which Br'er Rabbit outwitted Br'er Fox than hair on the head of a three-and-a-half-year-old girl. She would stand in front of a mirror long enough for her to see into, and she would comb at and pull at and scrape over the nappy surface without ever being able to approach the roots, and tear away at the matted ringlets until her scalp was too sore to touch. Applications of Vaseline did not help, and she felt trapped by her unbecoming attire, her unkempt coiffure, and the gathering gloom of the household, underneath which ran currents of cross-purpose reaching beyond the life and death of the woman upstairs.

By now Albert Dunham had learned that the greater part of his wife's worldly goods had been cozened from her by her children, that a house on

Prairie Avenue and a flat building on Indiana Avenue in the city had gone for the reparation of some folly of one of the daughters or for the hospitalization and burial of Grandmother Buckner, who had gone with her dolls to the cemetery in Glen Ellyn the spring before, or to committing Henry, who had become dangerously unruly under vicious baiting, to an institution. Her insurance had been borrowed against in full for this last illness, and, foreseeing disaster, she had denied herself the comforts of hospital care and even tried with her last feeble energy to persuade her daughters to dismiss the nurse who ministered to her at night and increased the dosage of sedatives as ordered by the attending physician. As he stayed at home to take stock of things and to try and prevent his household from falling into total chaos, the distracted father saw for the first time the true pattern of his brief conjugal life, instead of the idyllic moments of his courtship and the first bloom of fatherly conceit and the pride of possession. He had been immersed in love of the wife who had, in accepting his youth, gratified in full measure all his innermost and strongest yearnings. Now grief over her loss was already turning him toward bitterness; the thoughtless dependency of her grown children, at the expense of a good deal of his own effort and of the future security of her two youngest children, instilled in him a resentment that stayed with him for most of his life, so that mere mention of one of "that" side of the family had the same effect as mention of a Hatfield to a McCoy. The household seethed with resentments; with the arrival of the child's Aunt Lulu and the more frequent visits of Marie and Earley Clark, the schism became one of color— the "near whites" against the "all blacks."

Aunt Lulu was welcome to Katherine Dunham, because she brought a present of clothing and because her first deed even before visiting the upstairs bedroom, was, on seeing the disorder of the child's hair, to set about dividing it into microscopic partitions and, with a gentle, professional touch, brushing, oiling, persuading the crinkles from their tangled state into some sort of order. Then she undid her parcel, and there was—instead of a dress with flounces and ruffles and pleats which stood out starched below the waist—a skirt of dull gray wool, and a gray sweater which buttoned down the front, and a gray knitted hood with knitted roses on each side and two long knitted bands with which to tie it under the chin. Her Aunt Lulu, thinking way ahead, had bought them all far too big for her. The skirt reached her shoe tops, the sweater her knees, and the hood hung over her face almost hiding it, even when the ties were pulled so that they crossed each other. The roses, instead of adjusting over the ears, hung down below her chin like fat woolen whiskers. She was not happy about all of this, but the hairdo made up for much: the fact that it was new and obviously not soon to be outgrown compensated to some degree for the outfit's dowdiness, of which she was conscious even without the side glance from the "other" side of the family or the expressionless stare with which her brother made his inspection.

One cold day late in January the upstairs bedroom released its guest. The girl was not present for the act itself, the children having been ushered into the attic for the occasion. When later she saw her mother, it was in the chill, darkened parlor, where the two factions of the family had arranged themselves on opposing sides of the room, with the glass-covered casket between. A man in a black suit read from a small book. People on both sides of the coffin wept; at some words from the man who was reading, the ones on the other side looked in the direction of her brother and herself and wept harder. Her father sat beside her, and she pulled back the gray hood and tilted her head down and to one side so that she could look up into his face, because his head was bent.

His hands were folded tight together in his lap between his knees, and he was looking down at nothing. His face looked terrible and miserable at the same time, and she wondered if she should cry as the others were doing, even the children, nervous from the long wait for something that they couldn't understand and infected by the unaccustomed behavior of the adults. She looked at the quiet face of her brother and decided not to cry, but to keep her sadness inside until its reason was made clear to her. When the man finished reading, everyone bowed his head and the room was very quiet, with only little sounds from her Aunt Lulu and her half sister Fanny. She saw her brother glancing at her and stopped squirming and looking around until people lifted their heads again. Then they all stood up, and there seemed to be a question of who would move first to walk over to the glass-covered box and look in. Her father lifted her, and she was the first. She looked at someone she scarcely knew, then looked away quickly, as though prompted by a gentle hand that turned her head aside so that this memory would not outshadow all of the others. The flowers were pretty, and her new sweater matched the gray of the velvet-covered coffin.

NOTE

1. The Uncle Remus stories of Joel Chandler Harris first appeared in the *Atlanta Constitution* in the late 1870s and were later published in a series of books. "The Wonderful Tar-Baby Story" appeared in the first book of Uncle Remus tales (1881) and is perhaps the best-known of all the stories of Br'er Rabbit and Br'er Fox *[Eds.]*.

Excerpt from
Journey to Accompong

KATHERINE DUNHAM

FIRST DAY. The "cockpit," this country is called. The levels of rustling bananas and wide mango trees stretch off into the distant hills. Occasionally, there had been a tunnel through the foothills, but now we are actually in the mountains. The little train climbs a precipice, winding and winding, and finally, behind us there is only a thread of a road beside the mountain, hanging over tangled green forests in the sharp, sudden valleys. It is cooler than the lowland of the island; almost the coolness of another land and another people. I looked around at the few who occupied the swaying coach; a bandannaed old lady with a crateful of travel-sick chickens; two silent East Indian men; a father in mourning with three little children also in mourning; that was all. I wondered if they guessed my secret or felt my excitement. I kept trying to cover it. After all, other lone women had taken field trips; other people by the hundreds had earned fellowships from foundations and probably with less ambiguous titles than "Anthropology and the Dance," but somehow this was me. And as I looked back at that thin little thread trailing down into the lowlands, I couldn't help but feel a strange ecstasy as though all of the steel-mill drabness of Joliet, Illinois, and the dark winter pinch of Chicago, and the confusion and bewilderment of New York City were sliding rapidly downhill and right off Kingston Bay into the ocean.

Then a rickety automobile from Maggotty, where the Colonel and the native boy Shirly met me, and now we are at Whitehall. I am anxious to

SOURCE: Katherine Dunham, *Journey to Accompong,* with an introduction by Ralph Linton (New York: Henry Holt, 1946), 1–27, 51–52. Copyright 1946 by Henry Holt and Company. Reprinted by permission of Holt, Rinehart and Winston.

see the "beasts" to which the Colonel has referred so often. Whatever they are, they have something to do with the rest of the journey. The beasts are mules, and I must go into a little shack that houses the Colonel's daughter-in-law and "grannies," or grandchildren, to change my clothes. I am not a rider and I could only pray that the beast would not become aware of my apprehension.

As we rode, I was only dimly aware of the wild splendor of the place. The narrow rocky road, the tangles of banana, breadfruit, and pimiento trees, and a dull rush of water as a foamy stream rushed on beside us. There were the sudden deep pits that give the country its name. I could only cling onto the beast, in despair of the slipping saddle, and watch the bearers who trotted rapidly ahead, barefooted, shirtless, dripping with sweat, my trunks and luggage balanced on their heads, as we climbed and descended at incredible angles.

Finally we reached the last precipice and were at the Colonel's "yard" at the foot of the Maroon village proper. Here I will stay for the night. His eldest daughter, Iris (pronounced Ee-ris), has prepared a savory stew of fowl, pimiento, coconut oil, peppers, and a bowl of rice. The food, I soon find, is very African both in its preparation and in kind. Later I grew accustomed to the excessive seasoning, but this first night the spice odor and sweet coconut oil found no favor with my jaded appetite.

My hosts discovered and coolly took possession of my phonograph. Here I am dying to hear wild exotic native music and watch weird ceremonies and I must sit up and listen to Duke Ellington, Cab Calloway, Benny Goodman, and Billie Holiday (with all respect to these worthy artists whom I admire very much, but who I felt were standing in the way of fieldwork). Later I learned to use these American idiom records to evoke native parallels.

During the evening the chief men of the village called to share a bottle of rum and inspect the newcomer. It was quite late when I crawled into the hard bed with its banana trash mattress thrown over a *marosh*, or mat of river reeds. I felt rather guilty, for I had the bedroom, and I knew that some complications must have arisen in the distribution of the Colonel, his wife, two daughters, son, son-in-law, and four or five grandchildren between one other bed and two rooms.

SECOND DAY. Last night I slept little. The excitement, the strangeness of the country and the people, and above all, my noisy mattress of banana "trash" kept me awake long after the others had retired. Nor were these waking hours too happy. The country which had seemed so splendid in the setting sunglow suddenly became terrifying. There were no windows in my room, but through the open door the dampness of night rose from the deep cockpits. A blackness entirely new to me had settled over the valley and the mountains, and there was no moon, scarcely a star to relieve its monotony. I turned my back on the open door and wondered why I was here instead of staying in Haiti where I had stopped off for a week en route to Jamaica. The language was almost unintelligible, despite the fact that it is only the Creole dialect of the English language. I was hungry, and the people, while hospitable enough, left me feeling very much alone. But worse than all of this, I just could not imagine them dancing.

The silence made me afraid to move for fear of disturbing it with the noise of my mattress. While I was sleepless I thought I might as well arrange some plan of field method and compilation of reports. The uncertainty of everything and the real lack of preparatory material (Dr. Melville Herskovits had told me a little, but he himself had stayed with the Maroons only for a few hours at a time, and no reporter to my knowledge had lived with them longer than a night) made me decide that I would simply examine what I could of their total life and recount each day as it happened. I would wait patiently for the music and dances and not get in the way. Though reports had it that the Maroon people were reluctant to reveal themselves to outsiders, and evasive about arriving at fact, I was sure that my childhood in Joliet, Illinois, had equipped me with enough patience to outwait them. I doubled into a knot and slept that way until late morning.

While I was asleep this morning the Colonel made plans for my living quarters. When I finally woke up it was all settled. Captain Holiday, the Colonel's assistant (this military terminology had misled me at first, and even though I had a general idea of what to expect, still the picture of this wrinkled little man in a worn sun helmet as "colonel," with his assortment of "captains," continued to strike me as being very incongruous), has still kept possession of a house which once belonged to his father, a prominent figure in the village in his day. This is the only spare house in the town because ordinarily it seems that a Maroon possesses only that which he actively uses. However, the Colonel assures me that I am indeed fortunate to have such a fine house. It is a mile or so up a winding rock and mud road which climbs a sheer mountainside. At the top of this road is the rickety gate to Accompong proper. The Colonel lives just outside the village, on his own personal property. This, I believe, gives him a slight feeling of superiority. He is a Rowe, and the Rowes had held chieftainship more than once and have always been a little more acquainted with the outside world than the rest of the Maroons.

We dickered over the price for a moment. There was no point in hurrying to see it, because after all there is no other choice. And I will spend another night here while things are being put in order at my own establishment. We agreed on five shillings (a dollar and a quarter) for the month as rent, another five shillings for Mai. Mai somehow goes with the house, and I hope we will get along. I hope she will be a little warmer of nature and more demonstrative than Iris and the Colonel's wife, and the house less cheerless. Though, let me repeat, they have been very hospitable.

Today, after the Colonel had made all final arrangements for my living quarters, we went to sit for a moment on his narrow back porch, which hangs dizzily over a steep cliff. We sipped white rum, of which I am not really fond, and talked. He had been expecting me for many days, thanks to my professor at home who had written him well in advance. He would be very happy to have me stay in Accompong for a while. The professor and his wife had been there only for a few hours, but in that time he had learned to feel very warmly toward them.

Thinking of the expression of surprise and disdain on the face of the suave manager of the South Camp Road Hotel when I had announced my intention to leave Kingston for the Maroon country, I asked the Colonel if visitors were in the habit of spending any time here. Oh, there had been many, many visitors. And he called to Iris to bring the Book. The Book was an ancient ledger dating back a number of years with the signatures of those who had visited Accompong. They were surprisingly few, many of them of the clergy. I repeated my question, and the Colonel finally admitted that I would be the first to stay among the Maroons longer than a day. I looked around at the majesty of the country, and wondered why. Then I remembered the night spent tossing on the close-smelling, crackling *marosh,* and the food which was not to my appetite, and the weird tales of the Maroon peoples that circulate around Kingston, and wondered no longer.

We talked of the dances I had come to study and to take part in, the Koromantee war dances most of all. This led us on to talk of the early Maroons, of their deeds and valor, and I was glad of the hasty afternoon spent in the Jamaica Institute over wormy volumes by Long and Higginson and Renny and Phillips and Sloane and others as worthy. The Colonel was surprised that I could match him date for date, tale for tale. And so while the sun sank into the tangled bottoms beneath us, and the white rum grew less fiery, we sat and reconstructed.

When the Spanish left Jamaica under pressure from the English, they left behind them about fifteen hundred Negroes and Mulattoes. These slaves were difficult to retain in a servile state, and had already begun to show some of the resistance which later made the complete settling of Jamaica such a problem to the British. The Negroes had come from the most warlike tribes of West Africa: Mandingoes, Gold Coast Koromantees, Eboes, Whydahs, or Papawa, Nagoes, Samboes, Congoes and Angolas. They, with some Mulattoes, a result of Spanish crossing, fled to the wildest mountains and constructed huts, hunted wild hogs, cultivated some vegetables, and wandered through the woods in a "state of nature." The females, according to Robert Renny (*An History of Jamaica* [J. Cawthorn, London, 1807]), from whom I quote at great length, were "remarkably prolific." From time to time these roving bands were joined by runaway slaves from British plantations, and often they descended to plunder a small village or a lonely plantation. During this period they were given the name "Maroons," said by some to be an adaptation of the Spanish *marrano,* meaning "hog hunters," by others to be from *cimarrón,* meaning "wild." They settled in the northeast of the island in a section called the Blue Mountains; there they built a town fortified by nature called Nanny-town. In 1690 a rebellion of the slaves of Jamaica added considerably to the numbers of the Maroons. The mountain retreat continued to flourish on the spoils of hunting and plundering, and the British government, spurred on by pressure from harassed landowners, sent out one scouting party after another, only to have them return, or at least part of them, with tales of black magic, forests that moved, and fierce black warriors who descended from nowhere, worked their destruction, and were as quickly lost in the bush and tangle of the cockpits. And into the secrets of these cockpits they dared not venture too far. Whole detachments had been wiped out in the treacherous mountain passes, and innocent-looking ravines had suddenly become furies of armed demons.

There were some who had scouted the Maroon camps after a victory or of a Sunday afternoon when the enemy was far away. Then there was feasting. All day the wild boar roasted over pits of hot stones, and the women and children were busy carrying water and preparing food, while the men lolled in the shade polishing their weapons, telling jokes, and talking of warfare. Then later there would be some wild dancing.

At their midnight festivities they often engage in dances the most licentious and wanton . . . they also engage in a warlike dance in which they display great ability by running, leaping, and jumping accompanied with many violent and frantic gestures and contortions . . .

There, too, they must have practiced that bush-fighting technique which so baffled the British and led them to tell of the walking forests and black magic.

During the early part of the eighteenth century a separate body of Maroons formed in Clarendon County under an able little black chief named Cudjoe. Cudjoe was ill formed, ragged, evil of face and figure, but an apt leader and a warrior who would do honor to the history of any people. He appointed his brothers Accompong, and Johnny as leaders under him, and for many years Cudjoe held the south and the old body of Maroons held the east, and British subjects were prevented from settling in these parts.

Cudjoe's force was also increased, though at what period it is not certain, by another tribe of Negroes distinct from the rest in many respects; their figure, character, language and country being different from those of their sable companions. Their skin was of a deeper jet than that of any other Negroes; their features more clearly resembled those of Europeans; their hair was of a loose and soft texture like that of a Mulatto or Quadroon; their form was more delicate and their stature rather lower than those of the people they joined . . . although they had probably lived with Cudjoe's people seventy or eighty years, their original character could still be observed. They were called Madagascars . . .

After several skirmishes with British troops, Cudjoe was obliged to retreat.

He retired to a spot in the parish of Trelawney, near the entrance of the great cockpits, or glens, to the North-west, the first of which, called Petty-River-Bottom, has since become well-known. This cockpit is accessible only by a very narrow defile, and is considered a large one, containing nearly seven acres of land, and an excellent spring of water . . . He now augmented the body placed under the command of his brother Accompong, and established them on the northern border of the parish of Saint Elizabeth above the mountains of Nassau, *where there still is a town called Accompong.*

Thus did these people maintain themselves for several years in a state of savage freedom, living in indolence while their provisions lasted, and ravaging the country when excited by their wants. In their inroads they exercised the most horrid barbarities . . . [it must be remembered that the writer of this report is a loyal British subject] and though some were no doubt more humane than others, yet when commanded to embrue their hands in the blood of the whites, they all paid implicit obedience to their leader, and the work of death once commenced, no hand could arrest, no power could control, their fury, till all within reach of their vengeance were destroyed . . .

At length, to the great satisfaction and mutual advantage of both parties, the articles of the treaty were drawn up and ratified under a large cotton tree, growing in the middle of the town . . . the principal terms of the agreement were, that Captain Cudjoe and his followers should all be allowed to remain free; that they should be suffered to possess fifteen hundred acres of land; that they should reside in Trelawney-Town; and that two white men should constantly reside among them; and that they should deliver up all runaway slaves who might in future take shelter with them . . .

The colonists were relieved from the most alarming apprehensions and from a rude, dangerous and implacable enemy, whose very wretchedness rendered him formidable. The Maroons were blessed with liberty, property, and security; blessings of the value of which they were fully sensible, but which they had never before enjoyed. As to the other Maroons of Accompong and Nanny-town, a party was sent against them; this party was waylaid by the Maroons, lost several in killed and wounded, fled with precipitation, and retreated to Saint George's parrish, harassed, fatigued and disgraced; and all this without having seen their enemies, although hey had heard their voices. Some time after the ratification of the treaty with Cudjoe, a similar treaty was arranged with the other Maroons.

During the rebellion of the slaves in 1760 under Tacky, a Koromantee chief, the Maroons aided the English. In 1795, however, the Maroons of Trelawney Town rebelled, for unstated reasons. Owing to the conditions in the other islands of the West Indies, particularly the formation of the Black Republic of Haiti on the island of Santo Domingo, the government felt that it must spare nothing in an effort to crush these insurrections. Through all of this the Maroons of Accompong remained faithful to the British government and to the treaty; but in other parts of the island a general insurrection broke out. The British, unsuccessful in combating the Maroon methods of warfare, resorted to Spanish *chasseurs,* or bloodhounds. In this way they subdued the rebellions, and in a new treaty of 1796 the

Maroons were required to beg pardon of his Majesty on their knees, go any place and settle on any ground which the government might allot them, and give up all runaway slaves.

By this time Captain Cudjoe and Accompong had passed away. The leader was now "Ol' Montague" in laced red coat and hat with gold lace and plumes. Six hundred of the rebellious Maroons were sent to Halifax, others were sent with Old Montague to Sierra Leone.

In 1835 there were sixty families in Accompong, eight in Moore Town, ten in Charleston, twenty in Scott Hall.

Today there are only the Maroons of Accompong.

In the process of acculturation their chiefs came to be known as colonels. After Chief Accompong, the Colonel named for me in succession Austin, Cross, McLeod, Write, White, Rowe, Wright, and the present H. A. Rowe as leaders.

In one place I read: "The Koromantyns are represented as possessing all the worst passions of which imbruted humanity is susceptible, the tribe that had generally been of the head of all the insurrections, and original and part stock of the Maroons." But I prefer to end on a pleasanter note: "Their record still retains its interest as one of the heroic races of the world."

THIRD DAY. We went for a walk this morning, after I had moved into my house. Maroon town is proud of this house. It has a living room and a bedroom and various little alcoves. It also has a glass window, an almost unknown luxury in Accompong. In the backyard is the hut which is the kitchen. That pleased me most. Black, mellowed posts with a high patina support the thatched roof, thick black gum coats the roof beams and clings to the walls in sooty streaks. The dirt floor is packed smooth from the bare feet of many a housewife. Everything is lightly dusted with the red ashes that settle from the hard redwood fuel, which gives the food a smoky taste. We cook on the ground, and the iron pots are black and comfortable looking. Mai is comfortable too. She is not a Maroon. She was brought in from the outside, I learn, by the sister of the owner of my house, to care for an invalid mother while she herself went to Kingston to marry. The invalid died and Mai stayed on. Though her position in the community is uncertain, she always finds a hut to sleep in and breadfruit to roast.

One end of the cookhouse is partitioned off, and in it is a huge, flat wooden bowl which serves as both bath- and wash-tub. There is no way to describe accurately the sensation of lying doubled in half in a bath in this wooden bowl after a hard day's trudging through the damp cock-pits. The wood is polished by the natural process of many, many years of constant usage. It is satin smooth and sweet-smelling and the warm water which Mai keeps adding at a leisurely pace is softer than is possible to imagine.

In the yard is a long cook-table called the "barbecue" where Mai prepares the food and washes dishes. There are also coffee vines with tiny white flow-ers and, most blessed of luxuries to an outsider, an entire bush burdened with dead-white waxy gardenias. Unaccustomed to sounds and smells that aren't of the city, I awaken in a room flooded with their heavy scent and can pick a trayful in the early morning while they are still cool and damp.

FOURTH DAY. Our walk carried us up to the highest hilltop, the "parade." There the town dances and festivities, feasts, weddings and council meet-ings take place. As we left the tiny open pavilion, I saw that we were being followed. It was old Maria. The Colonel brushed her aside because she was begging a tuppence. But I would see more of her, perhaps because she greets my smile with "pretty Missus!" and a pert curtsy. She leaned on a stick, one hand on her lame hip. When I told her that I had no tuppence with me, she promised to come and get it one day.

The coconut palms are scattered, sometimes there is only a solitary palm in a grove of bananas and breadfruit. I learned something about owner-ship when I accepted an offer of coconut milk. A boy started to climb a tree at the far end of the parade.

"Here, you! What you tink! Dat no me tree, you dat me brudder tree!" At the Colonel's angry reprimand the boy obediently slid down and fol-lowed us, machete in hand, from the parade and by a winding path into another breadfruit grove. The Colonel owned the land of the parade but the coconut tree was his brother's. In like manner, true to an old Ashanti custom, lone palm trees were pointed out to me as owned by one man but in another man's field. The owner may be far away, but the proceeds of his tree go to him or his family. Ownership of this single tree passes from father to son, and a Maroon would sooner touch a man's wife than the green fruit that grows on his palm tree, though he may own and tend the land on which it grows.

I learned something, too, of custom, as we sat by the roadside and watched the boy ascend the proper tree. He brought back two large green nuts, and with his long machete knife hacked away the tough outer fiber, and at the tip scooped a small hole in the soft white meat. We were on the path in front of a little hut. The Colonel called for chairs. We sat drinking from the shell, and the Colonel pointed out a girl in the doorway of the hut as his "datter."

But I thought you had only three!"

"Oh, yes, dem's me yard chillun. Me datter here got grannies too. Me got sixteen grannies!" From the twinkle in his old eyes I could well believe him. The mother of the datter stood at a respectful distance, regarding the stranger. A faded remnant of what she might have been in the Colonel's more active years. She bounced a tiny baby and finally she brought it over to us. It wriggled in the bright sunlight, and poked a pointed pink tongue in and out.

"Me grannie," the Colonel said proudly.

"And didn't your wife mind?" I ventured later as we slowly descended the path to my house.

"Oh, no! She no mind. Why for she mind?"

The "datter" too, it seemed had not yet been joined in holy wedlock. The Colonel explained that this was the hardest custom to do away with. For my part, I see no reason to change an age-old custom which fits beautifully into the picture of palm thickets, a clear moon, a million stars, the braying of a lone donkey, and that heavy gardenia scent which keeps me always a little intoxicated at night.

FIFTH DAY. Mai came puffing up the hill with great excitement. Tonight there will be a dance. This seemed too good to be true at such an early date, especially as I had only heard about the dances and had not come right out and asked for one. The fiddler has come from Whitehall, there is rum, and tonight we dance "set" dances at the parade. It was hard to wait for night to fall. There is an undercurrent of excitement, for the Maroons love to dance, and it is only very special occasions that boast both fiddler and rum. There is a steady procession from cockpit and hillside up the steep precipice to the council house. Lanterns and smoky kerosene candles lighted the way, for the moon was young and the road inky black. Mai labored beside me, a tin of water balanced on her head, and a jug of rum under her arm. I had no idea what the set dances were like and was all anticipation, in spite of my disappointment that this dance had nothing to do with Koromantee war dances.

The little open pavilion was rapidly filling, and as we entered, a sea of faces, old and young, familiar and strange, parted so we might pass, then closed again and pressed in on us until I had to hold my moving-picture machine on high and the water on Mai's head splashed over the side of the kerosene can and down her neck. Some were friendly, some openly curious and some reserved almost to the point of being hostile. I was relieved when the Colonel pushed through the crowd and took charge of me, and then I saw Iris and the Colonel's wife and the boy from Whitehall.

At the first passing of white rum everyone suddenly became animated except the fiddler. He was a middle-aged "yella" man with one crippled leg, and he kept shifting the leg about impatiently, making sham efforts at tuning his ancient fiddle, and banging his tin cup on the floor for more rum. When I spoke to him he only grumbled about his fee and glared at me so ferociously that I quickly took refuge in my circle of friends.

"'Im only ackin' up," whispered Captain Holiday, whom his closest friends affectionately called, interchangeably, "Ba' Teddy" and "Big John." "Don pay eem no min'. Ee soon cum 'roun."

So we patiently sat and waited, and I had time to observe the gathering. Old women, young women and girl babies all wore clean white kerchiefs on their heads. My yellow one and Mai's shapeless red cap were the only exceptions. The regulation costume for women consisted of a loose sacklike gingham dress tied around the waist and falling well below the knee. The men wore blue denim or faded khaki trousers, and occasionally a white pair, straw hats, and perhaps a sack coat of some vintage past and forgotten. All were barefoot except the most prominent and the affluent, such as council members and their immediate families, the shopkeeper, and young dandies of "cotin'" age who wished to make an impression.

Suddenly the hush into which we were rapidly falling was ruptured by a series of disharmonic chords and squeaks and loud thumps of the game leg and the bow on the floor. There was a moment of tension, a sigh, a violent expectoration over the pavilion railing, and the fiddler had "cum 'roun." First he warmed up on a bit of this and that: improvisations, snatches of old English airs and Creole melodies. Meanwhile two lines formed, one of men, one of women. The men vied for partners, the women modestly looked down and fingered their dresses, and then as if by silent agreement, fiddler and dancers were under way. There was a great flourish of curtsies, and gradually it dawned on me that this was the Maroon version of the quadrille.

The dancers interested me more than the dance. As they swung into the second figure, the polka, I noticed that of the six women dancing, four were quite elderly, and all of the men except Shirly were well onto three-quarters of a century, if one could judge age by physical appearance. In my country these old women would be the dignified chaperons; here they were the belles of the evening. Before the night was over, I began to realize that, at the dances at least, the attitude of the Maroons toward their elders is that of many another primitive community—what the years heap upon one in infirmities, that much also do they add in knowledge and wisdom and perfection of artistry—"The Colonel would rudder dance with Mis' Ma'y den all dem young 'uns put togedder," Mai told me.

And truly I marveled as I watched the wrinkled little bent figure suddenly straighten up as she tied her kerchief more tightly over her straggly gray knots, and step forth to take the Colonel's arm with all of the aplomb of a seasoned ballerina.

There were brief pauses for rum and to "kotch a bref." The music grew wilder, and even those of us who were observers were sweating with the excitement. The gentlemen no longer saluted the ladies with sweeping bows, but with a leap to the center of the square, a clicking of the heels high in the air, entre-sixes, backbends, and elaborate turns. The women's skirts began to climb, their eyes shone, their step was high and light, and the flashing of bare black calves brought about many a change of partner. The fiddler was inspired and became a veritable orchestra as he swung from the stately "valse" into the sixth figure of the quadrille with much thumping of foot and bow, and frequent vocal accompaniment. Someone beat out the tempo with two sticks, the mouth harp joined in, and before I knew it the Colonel had passed Mis' Ma'y on and I was thick and fast in the throes of the "shay-shay." This last figure of the set dance must undoubtedly be a Creole improvisation. Indeed it seems to have no place with the other conventional figures, variegated as they are. For the first time I began to feel that the Maroons belonged to the sultry side of the Caribbean and that their Spanish and Indian and African ancestors must have known passions other than warfare.

But perhaps it is the rum and the smoking lanterns. The unveiled hip movements of the shay-shay (sometimes called "mento") may have done things to me which I project into the innocent Maroons. For hours later, through a fog of smoke, I see that the old women are still the favorites. Then suddenly, very tired and spent, I decide that the Maroons do not dance for the sex thrill even as we Americans do, or as do their cousins in Kingston.

Many a hot night in Kingston, friends and I had slipped through the low stone passageway, paid tuppence, and joined the throng of lithe black bodies that rhumbaed, shay-shayed, and paso-dobled to the saxophone and drum that predominated in "Cooks Red Devils" native orchestra. There in Kingston, between brief variations which express every sort of individuality, the steaming couples clung to each other in a close embrace which was only little short of copulation itself. But the Maroons seem to dance purely egotistically, for the thrill of the perfection of art—for exhibitionism, if you wish. The dance has not yet reached urban degeneration here, or the old women wouldn't be the belles.

Or at least so I felt as I stumbled and slid down the precipice from the parade, Mai and I offering little support to each other, Shirly behind with the water tin, camera, and empty rum jug, the tattoo of the two little sticks following us even to my deserted cottage.

So that is the set dance!

TWELFTH DAY: FOOTNOTE ON GOING NATIVE. At first I made a wide circle around the path where the mules had been, boiled my own water religiously before drinking it as I did not trust Mai, constantly wore a hat against the sun, scorned all food unless I saw it prepared, and at that, ate for the most part from tins brought from Maggotty, and spread a net at night for imaginary mosquitoes. I also saw that my dishes were properly scalded, saw to my makeup immediately upon rising, slept late and retired long past the community hour, after reading by the unsatisfactory flame of a kerosene lamp, a luxury here.

Now I follow the path like the rest, brush aside the tiny fish when I dip fresh spring water to drink, wind a bright band around my head in lieu of a kerchief, eat heartily whatever Mai brings me, and sleep with only a rough sheet between my sunburned skin and the hard mat of river rushes. I have also learned to appreciate the cleansing qualities of red ashes and cold water on pots and dishes, or even just a good rain as they lie spread over the barbecue, face up.

I have learned to rub coconut oil into my skin to counteract the burn and to take the place of cosmetics, to go to bed not long after the sudden dusk except on special occasions, and then to be prepared to stay up until dawn without a murmur and to rise when the warm sun reaches my open shutters. I even contemplate taking off my shoes, I have long since done away with stockings, and exchanging my linen sport dresses for loose, knee-length gowns tied at the middle with a rope. I am the first to take position for the square dances at the council house, and among the last to leave, and have learned to listen well, talk little, and enjoy a humorous situation even if the joke is on me. I drink white rum in preference to red, and have practiced, though disastrously, mounting the ravine from the spring with a small tin of water on my head. This was one occasion when the joke was decidedly on me.

I have also made numerous other little adjustments in personal habits to conform with the accommodations at hand and with custom. Perhaps I shall even sit sidesaddle on a mule, or wrap my legs around the neck of one of the cavorting donkeys to get to Maggotty.

I wonder if this is what anthropologists call "going native."

Excerpt from *Island Possessed*

KATHERINE DUNHAM

Dumarsais Estimé's similitude to Toussaint Louverture is marked. Toussaint never forgave betrayal; and Estimé never forgave Borno, feeling that his support of the Americans and his refusal to make an effort to reestablish the constitutional government was the supreme betrayal of his country.[1] It can be believed that color distinctions within the country were tolerated if not condoned by Borno, which attitude would have aroused the same bitter resentment in Toussaint as it did in Estimé. Both men were slight, not totally black in color, not robust in health, not conventionally handsome. Both were self-educated in higher learning, both were philosophers and humanists. Toussaint, though with doubts as to the sincerity of Roman Catholicism, hated the Vaudun.[2] He saw in it a threat to his own personal authority. Estimé also hated the Vaudun, or I should say held it in ridicule, feeling that the worship of African gods tied the people to ignorance, diverting them from recognition of their immediate and real problems. Soon I was to find my own way without the deputy's car to the street corners of my friends, and to the Cul-de-Sac for visits to Cécile and Téoline. But I did not give in easily, and it was only after an experience which even I admitted was more than I would have accepted in like circumstances. . . .

The day I told Estimé's chauffeur that the deputy would not need him for the night and had given permission for me to be driven to Thomazeau, I had been to visit Camille Lhérisson, who had just returned from a trip to

SOURCE: Katherine Dunham, Excerpt from *Island Possessed* (New York: Doubleday, 1969; reprint, University of Chicago Press, 1994), book 1, chapter 2. Copyright 1969 by Katherine Dunham. Reprinted by permission.

the army medical post at Terre Rouge in the vicinity of Thomazeau . . . .
There he had learned of the death of one of the last really high-category
bocors in Haiti. The *bocor* was a very old man, wise in the knowledge of
feuilles, or herbs, poisons, *gris-gris,* had taken the *prix-de-cloche* in the
Congo and was clairvoyant without having taken the *prix-des-yeux.* He
was the most important *bocor* in the plains and valley region, perhaps in
all of Haiti, and he had been dead for three days, lying in state in his own
special sanctuary in one of the huts of his compound, surrounded by
mourning and party-making acolytes and relatives. I have never known
whether or not the people serving *bocors* are known as *hounci*—as they
would be in the vaudun. Generally a *bocor* works alone, that is, he is not
dependent upon a hierarchy of *serviteurs* for the execution of his offices.
He may, however, have about him a corps of trainees and apprentices of
high and low status, and these I have called *hounci.* The greatest obligation of one of these bush priest-custodians of the medicines and magic of
Africa is to transmit this knowledge, this ancestral wisdom to the highest
in order of his disciples, the most likely in his brotherhood to have those
qualities that have distinguished his own career.

My avidity for information and firsthand experience led me to the lie
that was almost the end of a friendship turned romance. Estimé's chauffeur, given by me only the general whereabouts of our destination, held
out bravely over rough roads with no signposts but plenty of potholes, fis-
sures, and animals half-asleep rising from ditches on one side and plunging into our headlights, almost driving us into the ditch on the other side.
Nearing Thomazeau we began to inquire for the compound of the *bocor.*
We were directed wrongly, followed the skeletons of aqueducts nearly to
the Dominican border, turned back, and finally at the end of a road of
rocks and pebbles heard drumming and singing, which indicated a fête
of some sort. I was accustomed to festivities for the dead from experience
at like occasions among the Maroon people of Jamaica, but I recognized
none of the familiar songs or rhythms of the Vaudun and was hesitant to
present myself with no introduction at such an occasion. The compound
could not be seen from our dead-end road. When the car lights were
turned off, as the chauffeur invariably did when the motor was stopped,
considering this as an economy for the deputy, there was absolutely no
light, not from stars, moon, sky, or the unseen source of festivity. I sat in
the car trying to find courage to descend and make my way up the stony
hill in front of us to see what was on the other side of it. The chauffeur
had begun to sulk, suspecting my falsehood. I bit my fingernails, fumbled

in my travel kit for matches, thought up a few unkind things to say to Camille Lhérisson when I next saw him for not having offered to accompany me, then took the plunge. I got out of the car and asked the driver in what I considered a scathing manner if he would be good enough to turn the headlights on until I had climbed the hill, and to wait for me until I had verified the locale and returned to him with further instructions. The ceiling light went on when I opened the rear door and I saw the driver's face. I knew then that I would have light only as long as it would take him to reverse the car and find the road leading eventually to Port-au-Prince. He was gray with fright, and some of this fear he transmitted to me. I turned in desperation toward the sound of the drums, then back to the car, just about decided to give up this particular expedition and return to Cécile's *caille* in Pont Beudette where there were always clean sheets and kerosene lamps. It would take some miraculous event to keep me in this godforsaken outpost, and a miracle is what happened. At the top of the hill a light appeared. The driver started the motor of the car and would have taken off then and there had I not had one foot on the running board and my hand on his open window frame. The light drew closer and was raised, not to look at us but to show us the face of its carrier.

The man approaching us was perhaps forty years of age, of medium height but strongly built. The face lighted by the lantern was mahogany brown, the color of many Haitians who have lived for generations near the Dominican border. He was dressed in the usual workman's denim trousers but was bare to the waist, though the night was cool and I wore a sweater over my shirt and corduroy skirt. A red handkerchief was tied around his neck, and another around each forearm. He wore sandals and a straw hat. These latter details we saw as he approached the car. He smiled, and I had the impression that it was in amusement at us, that my efforts at insouciance had ended up in the same fright even more apparent now in the chauffeur. I was certain that the driver's apprehension was due to stories of zombies and reincarnated buried-alive slaves especially fond of haunting former plantations. Mine was the nervousness of the unexpected. I was relieved when our apparition laughed and greeted me by name. Then I was astonished. Camille Lhérisson would not have had time to tell anyone of my intention to visit this area. I had not been sure of it myself when I had spoken to him that afternoon.

The man spoke in French. He regretted that I could not go directly to the *bocor*'s house because of special preparations being made there, but offered me the hospitality of his *caille* for the night if I wished to be near when the spirit of the *bocor* transferred into the head of the *bocor*'s nephew. This is what I had come for. I looked at the chauffeur, hoping for a sign of encouragement, but he had actually shrunk into his clothing and I knew that no amount of bribery would keep him in this place longer than the time necessary to shift gears and back down the road. I nodded agreement and followed my guide, determined not to ask questions until we had arrived at wherever we were going. At the time it did not seem strange to me or even daring. I had never known physical fear in Haiti and had no occasion to feel distrust. One of the remarkable things about Haiti even today is its low crime rate in a world moving with speed in the opposite direction. Perhaps it is because the gods are always there to punish misdoings; perhaps it is a gentleness of spirit come out of a great deal of suffering with satisfaction in the end, as when the gods of the brought defeat to the French and freedom from slavery, or when the prayers on the Champs-de-Mars softened the spirit of the American Occupation Commission; or perhaps it is just a respect for others which is one of the qualities of the true Haitian. I am not referring to that new group of hybrid terrorists surrounding the present president. Until the advent of the *Ton-ton Macoute* I had never been aware of fear in Haiti, that is, fear of other men. There was anger against men during the Marine Occupation, as there must have been in various revolutions. Otherwise, one is afraid of the gods and their doings and creatures of magic and the havoc played by nature and the ancestors if they are not appeased. That is more like being afraid of demons in the dark created by oneself. It leaves room for friendly relations with one's fellow men. . . .

The hut which I entered with my guide was clean, with straw matting on the floor, a Congo altar covered with a red cloth, and on the altar a row of Congo figurines, stylized dolls of blue and red spangled satin. They had fat round bodies, arms like pitcher handles, and tiny feathered heads. On the altar were also hand-decorated *canaris*—clay water jugs—a pack of worn playing cards, and strings of red and blue beads. A boy of twelve or thirteen sat at a table, reading by lantern light. This confirmed my impression that the owner of the *caille* was among the rich of the peasantry, that is, with enough money to send a child to school, which all Haitians passionately want to do but can seldom afford. The child rose to greet me and I was about to settle comfortably on the floor mat indicated by my host when I noticed an odor which never fails to set the hairs on the back of my head on end. It was the dry, insidious, insinuating, penetrating odor of Damballa in person, the odor of all serpents, hard to describe but always repugnant to me.[3] This would be from a *couleuvre,* a Haitian variety of python, nonvenomous, harmless—there are no poisonous snakes in Haiti—but something which I preferred at a distance, not close enough to smell. I froze halfway seated. My host pointed to the rafters, where I had not looked in my inspection of the hut. A *couleuvre* of approximately eight feet was curled through the thatch and crossbeams above us. A stranger had entered and its head was raised, tongue darting, beady eyes fixed in inspection. The whirring "ric-tic" which set its throat quivering may have been a warning or a greeting. My knees refused to support me and I sank to the mat, wanting to turn to my host in supplication but not daring to look away from the creature above my head. With all the respect I have for Damballa, the gratitude for life guidance even though with constant reprimand, the reverence when in one of his sanctuaries, I have never overcome a fastidiousness since childhood when near serpents. Many Haitians welcome *couleuvres* in their homes because of their appetite for rodents. It seems to them better to allow a serpent to curl up in the corner of the house or wayside store, or take up residence in the rafters, than have produce and food destroyed by rats. Sometimes saucers of milk are left out, or an egg or dish of flour as a sign of welcome. The eggs and flour are Damballa's diet, so there may be some confusion in the mind of the casual observer when seeing these offerings on a doorstep. *Houngfors* frequented by Damballa and Aïda Ouedo encourage the visits of *couleuvres* and at 'Nan Campêche near Cap-Haïtien they come in answer to the rhythm of Damballa and are a permanent part of ceremonies. At least it was so when I visited 'Nan Campêche.

The snake has no place in the Congo cult as I know it, and the dead *bocor*'s cult was Congo; so I supposed the one lodged above me must have been a simple house pet. Because of it my night was sleepless, and because of it I left early the next morning in a downpour of rain, though I would have liked to stay through the full ceremonies of spirit or soul transfer.

I must have passed the test of inspection. The serpent above me undulated its way back to a resting position, head and tail lost in the folds of its plump, indolent body. This variety is sometimes called *couleuvre dormante* in Haiti because, when not eating, its preferred state seems to be sleeping.

My host introduced himself as Antoine, the boy as his son, Calvaire. His wife was at the ceremony, but he had prepared a charcoal fire outside and on it heated a tin pot of sweet burned Haitian coffee. Calvaire served us in thin coffee cups, chipped but elegant, probably from some pre-Revolution plantation cupboard. I tried to forget the serpent and asked about the ceremony. At the bottom of the hill, standing outside the *caille,* we could see the compound, a spread of huts inside a barrier of *chandelle,* poisonous cactus plants frequently used for enclosures, called "candle" because of branches resembling candelabra. Outside in the courtyard, light came from a charcoal fire in which an iron rod stuck upright glowed red. This is the sign of the god Pétro, whether Pétro Simbi or Pétro Kita, but it also has some magic significance.

Around the fire were squatted a few people, all with heads turned toward the central hut of the compound—the only one lighted—as though awaiting some sign. A rocky slope of hill and knotted trees kept me from seeing more, but as we drank our coffee, seated on stools beside our fire, Antoine promised to take me close, to one of the windows if not into the room. He was waiting for word as to when and how far I could go, but in the meantime would like to deliver a message the Congo gods had brought to him for me some time ago. He had been waiting for me to come, and the death of the *bocor* had provided the occasion.

We went back inside the hut and Antoine went to the altar, removed the deck of cards, and waved his son away from the table. Antoine and I sat facing each other. From here I could look across the room at the *couleuvre* asleep in the rafters over the altar and could hardly smell its obnoxious odor. In Chicago and New York I had indulged in divinations by chiromancy, cartomancy, trance, and spirit recall. I was aware of the practice of divination in Haiti but had spent most of my time until now in research into religious and magic and herb cults. The reading of cards in this remote plains setting came as a surprise, as did the further proof of clairvoyance when Antoine turned the cards to read my life, past, present, and future. Until now I had told no one in Haiti of the supreme tragedy of my life, my brother's illness. Our closeness as children during our early years, my dependence on him during the trying years of my adolescence, the abrupt interruption of his intellectual brilliance as a shining emblem of security for me at a crucial period of my university life, these things were closely guarded by me in my effort to establish a new career of dependency on myself alone, bereft of my brother's criticism and guidance. Antoine told me all about my family, delivered messages from my brother and the dead mother who bore me, predicting my marriage to Damballa and cautioned me about the jealousies that would result from this union, and the jealousies that would pursue my adult life, personally and professionally. At the time I was prepared to continue and take my doctorate in anthropology, and all anthropologists that I had known so far had been surprisingly free from professional jealousies, rather inclined to share findings and theories. So I was somewhat skeptical of this prediction.

As far as my personal life was concerned, I realized that Fred [Fred Alsop] was jealous of Roger Anselm, and Dumarsais Estimé of Fred, and the fiancé I had left behind of a number of people, but I did not see this in its full symbolism. It just seemed to me that people were unreasonable and nonrealistic and over-possessive, and that sooner or later all of this would adjust itself in my life. There I was wrong. The pattern was set and there was no adjustment. As for the advance knowledge that Antoine had of my arrival and my name, this was all explained in revelations from the Congo gods. I am afraid that I felt a little sorry for myself as we delved into past and future, and my eyes were wet when a voice spoke to Antoine from the doorway and he rose to confer with the messenger from the compound of the *bocor*.

Antoine returned to tell me that the trial had been a hard one, that the old *bocor* was tired and did not want to return to his body from the shades where he had been hovering near the head of the corpse since his release. Reluctantly, after much pleading, celebrating in his honor, dancing, reciting of magic formulae, and weeping, he had entered his former abode, weakly at first, but at that very moment with enough strength to rise to a sitting position and point a withered finger at his successor. By the time Antoine and I had scrambled down the hill trying to make as little sound as possible, the messenger had disappeared. I would not be able to enter the sanctuary for fear of upsetting the already tenuous, hesitant spirit of the *bocor*. We pushed through bushes, avoiding the vicious *chandelle* cactus, and leaned against a window through which only a crack of light showed. I saw the stiff corpse of the *bocor* sitting upright in the brass bed, one arm rigidly pointing at a younger man kneeling beside the bed. The other windows and door must have been closed because clouds of incense in the room scarcely moved. I could see a few people who came within range of the crack in the window, and by the positions of their bodies judged the room full.

No one seemed to be breathing, and I imagined that at any minute someone would come to the window drawn by the sound of my heart, which was beating rapidly and, it seemed to me, loudly. There was no singing and no drumming, just silence. Then from the mouth of the handkerchief-bound head of the grizzled old man there was an unmistakable sigh. The younger man rose, crawled onto the bed without raising his eyes from the hand of the corpse, and placed his forehead against the wrinkled brow.

There was a long period without sound or movement. Another sigh, and the body seemed to crumble, sinking onto the pillow behind it as lightly as a feather would fall. The hand fell with the body, and the new *bocor* seized the hand and pressed it to his lips. People were beginning to crowd around the bed, weeping and moaning, and the whole sound became an anguished chant. I felt guilty at being an eavesdropper to such emotion and was quite ready to respond to Antoine, who touched my shoulder and guided me away from the window and up the hill. Behind us the chant became singing and looking back I could see the light from the open door and shadows of people streaming into the courtyard. They were dancing, singing, rejoicing. The transfer had only begun, Antoine told me when we were back at the *caille*. Now the spirit would have to be fed, food brought before the bed, and feasts eaten by the acolytes and family. There would be a long recitation of the vitae of the *bocor* and his most outstanding achievements, then ancestral prayers, and the group would return to the silence of the room to untie the kerchief which bound the jaws of the old man, thus freeing the spirit to speak and give further instructions to the new priest. All of this might take another day and night, but the body must be interred under water before the fifth morning. I felt sorry for the old man, who must have been quite ready for requiescence, now being obliged to work after death. The responsibilities of leadership are indeed heavy. I wondered, too, what balms and ointments would conserve the flesh for more than four days.

Not wishing to offend either my host or Damballa, I accepted a sleeping mat where I had been sitting earlier that night, right under the heavy reptilian knot. The odor stung my nose, and even burying my face in a handkerchief soaked in *eau de cologne* did not help. Antoine had returned to the ceremony and the boy was sound asleep leaning on the table, his head on his arms. A lantern had been left burning, but whether it was the presence of the serpent, or the scene that I had just glimpsed fragments of, or due to the black Haitian coffee, I could not remain still and twisted from one side to another, moving as far as I could from under the serpent while still remaining on the mat. Finally I sat up. My restlessness alerted the *cou-leuvre dormante* and it began a slow series of convolutions that separated head from tail and undid the folds of its shiny gray length. Now I was really in distress. If I moved it might become aware of my fear and decide to fold around me. If I sat still it might descend by the rafter closest to me and slither over me. Either I felt would be fatal. It took awhile for the serpent to undo itself, and while it did I tried concentrating on Antoine. If his

Congo gods could tell him so many intimate details of my life they should be able to transmit my predicament to him across the few yards that separated us from the *bocor*'s compound. I had kept my head still but rolled my eyes from altar to doorway and tried to recall the words to one of the two Congo songs that I knew. The song was profane, but that didn't matter in my urgency. I sang, softly. Antoine came to the doorway and I tried to smile but couldn't quite manage it. I went outside and was sick over the side of the hill behind the *caille,* then I pleaded emotional upset and an early morning appointment in Port-au-Prince and asked how far away the nearest Army post was so that I could telephone a friend to come for me.

The friend was Fred, so many times my rescuer. In those days few phones worked, but one could always count on those of the Army posts, and Fred was on night duty at the all-night garage where he worked so I was likely to find him even if he might be asleep. It was four in the morning and had my host been an ordinary person he would have thought me deranged. I counted on his being extraordinary, which he was. He called a man from the compound below and gave him a lantern. There are times when thanks are inadequate. I pressed Antoine's hand and turned my back on the serpent, which had gone back to its curled-up-asleep position. As far as I was concerned its sleep was only feigned. As I started down the hill with my guide, thunder flashed and rain started. It was the beginning of the rainy season, and was early for such a torrent. But as though Damballa were punishing me, the rain poured in torrents and the road turned to mud and stones. My guide was ahead with the lantern, and I kept my eyes on the ground beneath my feet though it was impossible to see. I held to his shirttail and followed as best I could, thankful that I had worn boots. Then the path was smooth as pavement and I tried conversation with my guide, shouting into the wind and rain. I wanted to know where we were and how much farther we would have to go and if he thought the rain would stop soon. It must have been anything to make conversation, but though my Creole was not all bad at that time, there was no answer.

Then the man stopped suddenly and I bumped into him. He caught me in his arms and I flushed, thinking that after all of my kind thoughts about absolute safety when in the Haitian countryside I would have to defend myself at the other end of nowhere and going God knew where. The man looked past me and down, holding the lantern so that I could see our path. I gasped and practically threw myself at him. We had been walking on the edge between two irrigation canals, which could not have been very deep but which seemed bottomless. The path was tricky, because bricks were loose on each side and the rain made the pavement slippery. From now on I would have to walk on the heels of my guide, some of the time with my arms around his waist. I was ashamed of my earlier fears and saw now that nothing was further from his mind than physical violence or violation on this precarious path in a tropical downpour with only a flickering lantern and an occasional flash of lightning to keep us from catapulting into a washed-out colonial canal. In the lightning I could see barren fields and ahead the aqueduct we had passed on the way to the *bocor*'s compound. The canals and aqueduct were short cuts to the Army post. For me the way was long and I was weary, my cotton stockings were in ribbons, scratches on arms and legs and face were beginning to burn, and I was hungry.

Halfway across the aqueduct I sat down. My guide squatted and managed to turn his back to the wind and light a pipe. He sat over the lantern, looking into space, until I had strength to continue. He was about twenty years old, black, friendly-looking and by that time, I decided, extremely patient. He had been taken away from an occasion which might not happen again in many years, if at all. *Bocors* of really high category were dying out and there were few candidates for replacement. The old man who lay dead might have been a relative of his. There was feasting and dancing besides praying and magic séances, and here he sat in the downpour of rain waiting for a foreign young woman to collect herself and find strength to continue the road. Then he would have to return immediately the long way and it would be full morning. To me it didn't make sense. I resolved to find ways of field research that did not demand such services of others as I had exacted that night.

At the army post a disgruntled corporal listened to my story that the driver of my taxi who had taken me to Thomazeau to look for a fellow student had misunderstood my directions and returned without me. I had seen my friend but could not find a car to take me back to Port-au-Prince in time for my classes, which I was teaching at a *lycée* the name of which I made up on the spur of the moment. Fred was asleep, cursed so loudly that I had to hold the phone away from my ear when I told him where I was, then promised to come right away. The guide left me and again I didn't try to find words of thanks for his help. The rain stopped and pale gray streaks were in the sky when I heard the rattle of Fred's faithful old Chevrolet. The corporal eyed Fred as though he were a returned Marine, and did not acknowledge my efforts to thank him. Fred scolded all the way back to Port-au-Prince. I was thoughtless, obstinate, unkind, inconsiderate, and finally stupid in his estimation to follow continually this obsession to get to the bottom of things. He as well has said that I might as well have fallen into the canal and saved him the trouble of the trip. I of course had no answer, so much of what he said being true. I wondered if my fellow researchers had such troubles, or if they could manage things alone and never involve others or blunder or have food taboos or panic at snakes. I refused to believe that all these invectives were because I was a woman or that my failings were incorrigible. I did not feel quite up to Doc [Reeser] and the questions of the Pont Beudette community, so I crawled to my rooftop at the Excelsior, treated my scratches, took a potassium permanganate bath, and went to bed as Titine brought early morning coffee. Now I had lost two friends and a great deal of self-confidence. I did not relish seeing Dumarsais Estimé again soon.

It was a week before Estimé came by the Hotel Excelsior. Most of the week I had spent at Pont Beudette recording songs on my old Edison cylindrical recorder. This gave me a feeling of being useful. I also tried to write up in coherent form the experience of the *bocor*'s spirit transference, but until now it has remained elusive, something which comes back to me over and over but which isn't clear in detail. I have intended many times trying to find Antoine and the compound of the *bocor*. Perhaps that was the only meeting intended for us.

Estimé took off his jacket and stretched out on my bed as he always did when staying the afternoon. Usually he removed his pistol and holster and put them over the back of the chair with his coat, but this time he left them on and I supposed that meant I was not to stretch out beside him on the bed. I sat at the window and talked of everything I could think of excepting the subject that troubled me. But Estimé was not angry; he was offended and hurt that I had lied and that I had involved an innocent person, the driver, and that I spent so much of my time pursuing the unimportant rather than seeing the important things evolving in the country, and that I made no distinction in my affectional life, as by now there was hardly an interested person in Port-au-Prince who did not know that Fred Alsop and I had arrived at the Hotel Excelsior at seven in the morning, I in a shocking state of disarray, due of course to my night's experience. As he talked I was ashamed and for the first time realized how little I knew about this man who must care for me or wouldn't put up with the way I was, and who had so impressed me when I heard him speak at the opening of the Chamber of Deputies shortly after [Senator] Zépherin introduced us.

Even in moments of what I would have called tenderness in anyone else, Dumarsais Estimé had seemed hard and aloof. The day he told me about the wickedness of what I had done at Thomazeau I felt closer to him than ever, and after I had tried to explain and apologized as I could, knowing that he had spared me the most damning accusation, which was disregard for his public office and career, he agreed to remove his pistol and holster, which he never allowed me to touch, and have me lie beside him on the bed and try and make up for the wrong that I had done by being quiet and letting him speak and letting his problems and tension drain into the afternoon sun that flooded the little room. This is the way I remember Estimé, and these were the occasions when he taught me in his oblique way, instructing me in the tools of humanism, awakening a conscience which had been selfish, not social.

I had seen women coming to town from the hills and plains with small children who might not return to the hills and plains with them. There were child servants at the hotel, usually kept in the back quarters, but doing their share of sweeping and cleaning and scrubbing. There were these *'ti moune* in all urban Haitian homes, a regular part of Haitian social structure. But I had not realized or my conscience was not stirred enough to admit that these child servants should be in some institution of learning, have shoes, clothes rather than the rags one usually saw them wear, and their labor have some recompense.

The *'ti moune* system was one of the preoccupations of the Estimé whom I knew—and education for the masses, and shoes for everyone, and sanitation in market places, which were the disseminating points of disease, and recognition of Haiti on an equal level in the rest of the world. In broad, less defined terms, Erich Fromm had prepared the way for my receptivity to the thinking of Estimé; I had failed his teaching in my total absorption of self as a means to knowledge. It was now up to me to turn this thirst for knowledge to a way of service, as Estimé's ambition was not for self, but for service. At first I interpreted the rarity of personal approach, the afternoons without handclasp or overture as rejection, and my vanity was hurt, though at the same time I was aware that Estimé was aware that I was not starved for personal attention.

Gradually I began to see the things around me with his eyes, with his evaluations, though never losing the intense preoccupation with what I had come to Haiti for, the Vaudun and the complex surrounding it.

NOTES

1. Dumarsais Estimé (1900–1953) came to power during the "Revolution of 1946" and was the president of Haiti from 1946 to 1950. Toussaint Louverture was an ex-slave who became leader of the Haitian revolutionary forces and governor general of Saint-Domingue. A brilliant strategist, he led his armies to victories against French, British, and Spanish imperial forces. He was captured by General Leclerc, the French commander-in-chief, in 1802 and deported to France, where he died in exile *[Eds.]*.

2. The Vodun is the hierarchy of gods, or spirits, in the religion of Haiti, also known as Vodou. For definitions of other special terms, as well as orthographic variations, see the glossary at the back of this book *[Eds.]*.

3. In Vodun, Damballa (Danbala) is the supreme Rada serpent deity associated with water, wisdom, fecundity and the rainbow. He is often evoked with his wife Ayida Wèdo *[Eds.]*.

Prologue

KATHERINE DUNHAM

The following note describes Dunham's philosophy when writing "Minefields":

It would have been of no help to the reader, to the biographer, or to me, the writer, for me to follow a pattern of strict chronology, to chart each person and event and geographical location at a given time, in perfect juxtaposition. The research would be self-defeating for my way of thinking, because then, my recall, hampered by detail, would not give me the pleasure in documenting my life, which I hope the reader will also find. What is important is what I experienced, or felt I experienced; and this last is important in the sense, I am told, that Alfred Adler was just as interested in the fiction in what one thought one remembered from the act or dream, as what may have been fact. Of course I could phone a company member here and there or ask a manager or producer for exact dates and places of this and that—sometimes I do so—but our many tours of the United States and Canada and Mexico, the period which covers the years before we went to Europe and the rest of the world, are so hurried and criss-crossed with surprises, changes, developments, confrontations (remarkably few), and responsibilities that I would rather, in total freedom, extract what was meaningful to me and, I hope, of value to others. My major preoccupation, aside from theater presentation with its attendant choreographing for and grooming of my nucleus company, was fighting the relentless practice of apartheid, especially

SOURCE: Katherine Dunham, excerpts from the prologue of "Minefields," an unpublished work in progress. Copyright 2005 by Katherine Dunham. Used by permission. The majority of the manuscript was written between 1980–1989. Minor corrections and changes of editorial style have been made.

in lodgings and eating places. . . . My efforts to break down, to the extent
that I was able, the prejudices of hotels and eating places took more time
and energy than I felt that I could spend in this fashion. But as I review
these trials, probably fewer for the Dunham Company than for other less
fortunate traveling minstrels, I find that each time an advance was made
or a battle victorious or a minefield circuited, I gained myself, in wisdom,
levity, forbearance. And the more severe the testing, the greater the anger,
until I became aware of subtle changes within myself which, without my
knowing it, were forming the entity I am today.

In this book I must recreate the anxieties of Chicago and New York, a cross-
country tour with *Cabin in the Sky,* Hollywood, San Francisco, Mexico,
some films, the Hurok tour, and again New York to appear in *Carib Song*
and open a school on Forty-third Street, across from the Times building.[1]
All of this period was heavily set with explosive devices of one kind or
another. I learned to feel out, at first meeting, the theater managers who
would be condescending, in spite of our prestigious impresario, the audiences that would at first be resistant to any extravaganza of overtures, the
hotels where I might manage to stay because of a white husband or secretary, or an entire white stage crew, this latter union dictated. Those were
difficult times. I became more and more aware of arthritis in both knees,
especially if under stress, which was most of the time, but more and more
alert and, strange to say, creative.

At first, true to character as portrayed in *Touch of Innocence,* I acted,
even created, intuitively, and leaned heavily on my affective self. My
life was made up of a mother lion's protectiveness toward the Dunham
Company members, my turbulent romance with John Pratt, and a guilty
feeling toward my university professors and the Rosenwald and Guggenheim Foundations for what I thought to be their lost investment in my
academic self. I didn't realize until later that foundation boards and university professors often know more about us than we do about ourselves.
They watched my career with curiosity and a kind of benevolent tolerance, even approval. They saw much in me that I didn't see in myself.

I would also like this book to lead the company and myself on our
travels until our departure for Europe. This should be a work of value for
others who might be contemplating a career such as mine. My first advice would be to be, or become, impervious to every known chemical sol-
vent or element of nature. Excepting time, of course, and then in the final

analysis, when it no more enhances us spiritually and physically, ignore that, since time is a round thing and all experiences are repeated in one form or another. We really go on as long as we want to; but one must know where lies the limit and then recognize the ever expanding horizon as we delve into our many partitions and find in ourselves undreamed of riches, even including, if we are lucky, discerning, and work hard at it, some form of superior being. And if we are more lucky and more discerning, we realize that the only God is our discovered selves . . .

Surely I have overlooked many people and experiences in trying to reconstruct these years [1937–1948]. But my gratitude I hereby express, enough to cover everyone and everything during those wonderful, turbulent, tortured years of triumph through anguish. Each day brought a new challenge, and there is nothing like this feeling of being an arrow in a taut bow that sharpens one for life. Of course there were days, even weeks, when all went smoothly. But all too soon would come warnings of dangers ahead, obstacles to be overcome, some hint of the vast minefield that would be my life. For my survival, I owe most to my brother.

My brother Albert and our relationship as children, motherless in childhood until our father remarried, has been clearly set forth in the account of my first eighteen years, *A Touch of Innocence.* Older and more prescient than I, a good deal of our relationship consisted in his fending off my childish amorous overtures, growing, no doubt, from the deprivation of bonding in childhood and a normal family life. This he did so efficiently that at times I would retreat into blind misery, feeling him to be needlessly cruel for something understood by me only instinctually, and then obscurely.

Before my Caribbean excursion my brother Albert had received a fellowship from Harvard University for work on his master's degree in philosophy. This would necessitate his moving to Boston. He had finished from Chicago a very young Phi Beta Kappa and had intended devoting his life to propagating the theories of those with whom he had studied: Alfred North Whitehead, Charles Morris, and T. V. Smith among others, as well as Santayana, whom he had never met but whom he admired greatly. (Albert was one of Whitehead's last students. I remember seeing the old fellow parking his bicycle outside one of the buildings where I would be going to a morning session in one of my aborted philosophy classes. He seemed then to be well into his eighties.) I was crushed that

Albert would be leaving Chicago. No matter how active my life, it in effect revolved around him and his guidance and approval. To make matters worse, before leaving Chicago and with scarcely any warning, he announced his plans to marry Frances Taylor, my closest friend. This seemed to me a betrayal by both. In the all too few days before the marriage I cried almost constantly, which greatly irritated my brother when he found out. I presumed that Frances had alerted him and for this reason resented her doubly. She could not know and he surely had forgotten that one night returning from one of the rare occasions when he had accompanied me to one of those Chicago "elite" promenades, he lightly touched my shoulder (aged eighteen and a half, I allowed myself the luxury of a home-remodeled taffeta dress demurely off the shoulder) and vowed not to marry until he found a girl with shoulders like mine. There was in his voice more tenderness and affection than I had ever known from him or anyone else. (The Dunhams are by nature reserved.) This intimacy, added to two or three dances with my brother during the otherwise dull promenade, created a heaven for me filled with almost more bliss than I could bear.

After his announcement of his plans for marriage to my now roommate Frances, I found myself looking at her shoulders, and at my own as something detached from my body or being. Having no indication of what measure he had used, I was obliged to believe that he had found what he wanted or that he had chosen his bride on other criteria.

With no ado there was a small and intimate wedding in a chapel on campus, remarkable for the fact that at that time black students didn't attend service at this particular chapel, much less get married there!

Months later my brother returned to Chicago with his very pregnant wife, to complete his Ph.D. at the university while I was still in the Grand Boulevard apartment. To Frances's pregnancy I seemed to have adjusted or resigned myself to realizing that here was a field of competition into which I could not enter. But I did notice that my brother seemed far more high-strung and sensitive than I had ever known him to be. He was fulfilling a teaching assignment as well as terminating his doctoral thesis, "The Concept of Tension in Philosophy." On the first day of his teaching, half the class walked out, not all of them Southerners. I knew that he was the first black person to have a teaching position at the university, and that this exception was due to the admiration and daring of his mentor in the department, T. V. Smith. It was not until later that I was aware of the trauma of that summer, the damage that was not repaired even after his classes, which on their own merit and due to some prodding from the deans of his department, reached an abundance of attendance for which he would not have hoped.

It was while he was under these pressures as well as feeling a reluctance, I suspected, to add to the populace of a world with which he felt no affinity, that on one occasion, to dispel, I hoped, some of the growing tension in our small household, I playfully ridiculed a hat that he wore almost continually, and which was very dear to him. It was a flat felt dark grey thing that, to all appearances, had been exposed to every kind of climate and usage. Was its generic appellation "Pork Pie"? I do not know. But when I pointed it out as being unbecoming to a University of Chicago Professor, my brother went into a rage of cold fury. Among other things, he counseled me to never again enter into or comment on his person, his dress, or his personal affairs. He then stormed out, slamming the door, leaving Frances and me stunned, her perhaps less than I because the tirade had been directed at me.

One early morning well before dawn, shortly after that episode, I opened the door to imperious knocking. My brother brushed past me holding one hand in the other. A friend with whom he frequently walked in the area of the university followed. He was white and had been a close friend to my brother in high school in Joliet. They had played in the high school string quartet, and the friendship, though sporadic, had lasted through the years. My brother ran cold water on a quite deep cut in the fleshy part of the palm of his right hand. Ralph, the friend, in spite of my brother's protests, phoned a taxi to take them to an emergency hospital for stitches, which seemed to be indicated. Frances, by now seemingly doubly swollen in front, stumbled half asleep from her room to find out what had happened. Days later the story was pieced together. The two men had wandered from an all-white campus neighborhood into the all-black one of Chicago's Southside Grand Boulevard. There, while arguing a point of stars and philosophers, they had been attacked by a black brigand challenging their right to meander through the streets of this neighborhood at three o'clock in the morning. He stripped them of their purses, and as my brother protested, flashed a knife and left the deep gash on my brother's hand.

My brother was deeply shocked, but the only comment made by him that night was one dragged from his innermost being, declaimed in abysmal despair. "There isn't a man alive who wouldn't kill his brother for money." Between them they had given up wallets, identification, and five dollars in cash.

In my opinion, this was the turning point in my brother's total retreat. He was lauded for his doctorate, and his thesis was published in Harry Stack Sullivan's *Journal of Psychiatry*. He returned to Washington to take up a post in Alain Locke's department of philosophy. His child, Kaye Lawrence, was born. Then my brother entered the Howard University Hospital for a tonsillectomy. He must have found what he was searching for most of his life while under ether. He never recovered; that is, he spent practically all of the next twenty years incarcerated in St. Elizabeth's Hospital in Washington. During this period he coedited a collection of Whitehead's works with Charles Moore and published in the *Journal of Psychiatry*. He was also called on two occasions before release boards but talked his way out of leaving the hospital. By the time I had returned from the Caribbean, many world-renowned psychiatrists and analysts, at the expense of the Rosenwald and other foundations or because of professional or personal interest or admiration, had tried to reason Albert out of his fixed sense of doom, out of his sincere belief that this world we live in was too tormented for human living and was soon to be destroyed anyway so why return to this chaos rather than seeking to escape in death. When it came to logic, point by point he argued the psychiatrists into a corner from where they could not with logic exit. And so he remained closed up in St. Elizabeth's Hospital in Washington. He had decided to leave this planet, and there was just nothing to do about it. But he had left me in good hands. I had met Erich Fromm,[2] and those beliefs in social justice and individual freedom, beliefs that made Chicago such a great school in those days, were firmly founded in me.

Before departing for Boston and Harvard University, on his last visit to Chicago my brother had insisted that I see the University analyst, a Dr. Sniffen. He himself had started analysis at Chicago under Douglas Campbell, an Alderian. I knew nothing about psychoanalysis; I only knew that it was a new field and still an experimental addition to the many new approaches to student problems introduced by the very young president Robert Maynard Hutchins. I took my brother's word that it would decentralize my growing inner pain and loneliness. Dr. Sniffen helped by telling me about Paul Robeson, with whom he had gone to school, and whom I should meet. He compared Robeson's college life to mine. He had had just as much to overcome, and had done so brilliantly. Just as I was becoming fascinated by this realm of self-study, of putting myself and life in a wider perspective, my analyst committed suicide. Then I truly felt lost. He had accomplished much in a brief time. I no longer felt that my brother had abandoned me by his marriage. I thought a great deal of my childhood and of the mother who had died when I was three.

Dr. Sniffen was particularly interested in my dreams. Some of my most impressive and persistent dreams had been of drifting on stagnant water towards ruins that might have been Greek or Etruscan, Byzantine or Egyptian. I was afraid, but not totally so, because before me and beside me a woman, pale and clothed all in diaphanous white, seemed to be guiding the boat or raft on which I drifted toward the ruined marble staircase of a crumbling temple which descended into quiet water. I seldom reached the bottom of the immense stairway, but could feel towering above me great pillars and statues and buildings. Sometimes there were the bodies of people lying on the edge of the water or on the stairway as though trying to escape something which had ruined the city. I stopped at the insistence of my guide before reaching the steps; the dream would just repeat itself. I would dream also of swimming very hard in clear ocean water trying to reach a drowning baby. I would reach it with the help of this translucent phantom in white that, during my unraveling of fears and confusion with Dr. Sniffen, I realized was my first mother. I no longer felt guilty of even thinking of her as I had when Annette Dunham would find me rummaging in forbidden drawers of the bookcase on Bluff Street in Joliet, looking for the one or two pictures there were of her.

In that short period of time before Dr. Sniffen took his life I found that I did not hate my father—to the contrary, I felt pity for him and what he must have suffered at the death of my mother. I even felt a sort of diffused family love which heretofore I had showered on my brother, who at an early age saw the dangers of this. I was in love with my brother as my father was with me; but instead of resentment toward my father and sister-in-law, and in spite of what was undoubtedly an incestuous love for my brother, I was able to see both as clearly as I had seen that drowning baby. Myself, saved by me, guided by the woman in white. The message wasn't as clear at the time as it was to be later, but at least I had been shown a way to help myself to survive and grow. Always with the gentle guidance of my dead mother.

Generally the fears of being alone, of living at night with one or more sentient beings walking behind me as I left the library or rehearsal or waiting in the dark hallway where I lived on Grand Boulevard at Thirty-fifth Street in Chicago weakened in their impact but were there nevertheless. The bed didn't rock or jump as before my Caribbean experience, but something remained in the room, even when other people were there. My life's work was then set out: to depend on my strong, intuitive self and let all things of a nether world gradually die of diminished energy. The Crandalls, those molesters of my babyhood, gradually disappeared.

My Haitian initiation must have helped, giving the feeling of the *loa,* or saints, as protection. As they entered my life, even in Chicago I remembered Toline and Desgrasse assuring me that if I would respect Damballa, the serpent god to whom I had been ritually married, no harm could come to me. Immediately on my return from Haiti, I had set up a provisory altar in the closet at the head of my bed. There, in a corner, rested the saucer of flour, a raw egg, together with a bottle of syrup of orgeat and Florida water, basic paraphernalia of Damballa, and my initiation beads. I began to pit the strength of Damballa against the malevolent beings that so far had been able to terrify me from babyhood through adolescence and into adult life. If I gravitate towards places where these forces may have originated or which they still occupy, as the burial grounds of Mitla and the pyramids at Giza, or even cemeteries at night in Haiti as I have had to do during the course of years as I moved from the degree of *hounci* to *mambo asegue,* the highest degree now accorded in the Vodun hierarchy of adepts in Haiti, then I am aware of these presences. But they are now far in the background and unable to gain my attention or pass through the many layers of magnetic circles that I have accumulated these many years in many countries from many sources. Bush priests in Senegal still send me by traveling countrymen small packets of protective charms folded neatly and meticulously sewn into square or rectangles of animal hide.

Following Dr. Sniffen's advice I went backstage after one of Paul Robeson's concerts at Orchestra Hall in Chicago to present myself to that extraordinary man. A warm friendship was established, though our meetings during the years were infrequent.

My sister-in-law brought Kaye to Chicago when he was only a few months old. They did not stay long, and I have wondered if I had not begun to build barriers between us to keep from being tempted to try and emulate my brother as homemaker and provider for the small family. One time after they left to return to Washington I was so torn that I asked Erich Fromm for help. Erich would never analyze me, but we did talk often when he happened to be in Chicago. Later we saw more of each other when I was more or less established in New York, and years after that in Mexico. On this occasion he did as he usually did—asked me questions that would help me solve problems myself. He wondered if I wasn't trying to follow my brother as I had always done, or wished to do. He congratulated me for not choosing the path of mental collapse; but with a twinkle in his wonderfully perceptive blue eyes and the suspicion of a smile, wondered if I might not be a little rash in even considering the assumption of a family in my own distressed financial condition and hopes of a career.

He was, of course, very right. I would have resented for a lifetime anything that would deflect me from the path becoming clearer every day; a life in dance, if possible, combined with academic research. I visited Albert once alone when on my way to the Caribbean. He had just recently been incarcerated, and all who had ever known him, or even of him, hoped that this was just a temporary shock, perhaps due to the anesthesia of his tonsillectomy; a hiatus in a brilliant career. At my insistence both Harry Stack Sullivan and Erich Fromm had already visited Albert on more than one occasion. Erich was rather amused at Albert's manipulation of academic logic and saw little possibility of a return from that limbo in which he had taken refuge. I was actually on my way to the diminutive Royal Netherlands ship that would carry me to Port-au-Prince, my first stop on my Caribbean research trek. But like so many others, I was hopeful of breaking through that bland barrier that had baffled so many well-wishers.

The superintendent led me up a flight of stairs at the top of which was a grillwork barrier surrounding a large dormitory; in the enclosure were, as I remember it, a number of sleeping and pacing and glaring and peering male inmates in various stages of catatonia. In the middle of the second row of camp cots my brother stood, stark naked, peering through the steel barricades as though expecting someone. I was stunned by the odor of mental sickness, by his emaciated body, and by the unmentionable, semi-alert, semi-pendulant in full view. It could have only been seconds before the voice of the superintendent boomed out cheerfully, "Albert, your sister is here to visit you!" At the same time a male orderly wrapped a blanket around my bother's nakedness. Which stunned me most I don't remember—the sight of my brother in his dreadful surroundings, tragically vulnerable, or the use of his first name, which in our family was reserved for family and close friends, peers or at least a generation removed. Strangers, I felt, especially under the circumstances, should address him as Dr. Dunham. (Though a recipient of a number of honorary doctorates, I still refuse to address myself as "doctor." But that was some time ago, and his appellation was arduously won.)

I sat in a small waiting room while my brother was made ready for the meeting. During my sports days I had begun chewing gum to ensure a flow of saliva. My mother and father detested this habit, and my brother loathed it. I was desperately chewing gum when he was led into the small room. We were left alone and I looked out the door to see if the attendant was near, which he was not. My brother looked at me so strangely that I could think of nothing to say—not even trivia. I went to a balance scale in the corner of the room, and must have been deeply involved in shifting the gum from molar to molar, which if expertly done produced a loud pop, later a trademark of mine on stage in a number called *Barrelhouse— A Florida Swamp Shimmy*. I played with balancing the scales and did not hear my brother approach behind me. I turned and he would have seen my panic had he not been studying a profound question which, judging from the expression on his face, deeply puzzled him.

"Hey Kitty," he said—I was "Kitty" only to him—"did you ever try chewing gum with your asshole?" I doubt if I had ever heard the word, but I certainly knew what it meant. I could feel a deep red flush spreading from my cheeks to my hair and then downward. "No," I said, "I haven't." Then I removed the gum, wrapped it in paper and dropped it in the wastebasket. My brother smiled for the first time, maliciously it seemed to me. The attendant was there as though on cue. I kissed my brother on the cheek and left down the stairs and out of the building. I turned once. He stood at the top of the stairs, again looking puzzled, and fingering the web between the third and little fingers, which he often did. At that moment I wondered, all things considered, if perhaps he weren't from another planet, and I too, constantly just missing something that should have been evident.

The next time I visited my brother I had returned from the Caribbean. Kaye was a toddler, and I remember remonstrating with Frances that she should not leave him behind, nor dissemble about our visit to the hospital. I have always felt that small children should not be left in adumbration. Their little minds are wise with the wisdom of innocence, and the drawing of curtains of protection may do more injury than good. Kaye stood in the window as our taxi drove off. He was not very pleased and has since confided in me that he knew that something was wrong with his father and that we were going to see him. We were both sad, and he remembers his own sadness.

This time Albert was in a different section of St. Elizabeth's or in some different facility, I do not know which. But he was well dressed, had gained weight, and was referred to as "doctor," this change of attitude probably due to the flux of illustrious psychiatrists, professors, and well-wishing (or curious) friends who had not yet given up hope for his recovery. There had even been talk of sending him to Europe for therapy, and in the eyes of the administration this had no doubt set him aside from the run-of-the-mill population of St. Elizabeth's. We went for a walk, and sitting on a well-kept lawn, I tried to interest my brother in rhythm. His disinterest didn't discourage me from pursuing in our New York school the use of primitive rhythms related to their therapeutic functions in society—catharsis, hypnosis, stimulation and diminution of aggression, and so forth— in the attempted therapy of the mentally ill. We were allowed a session or two at Bellevue, and I remember some encouraging correspondence with the Mellon Institute.

That was the last time I saw Albert, but I did write frequently. Years later, after a lobotomy, he wrote me. His frame of reference was our childhood. I was about to go on stage at La Martinique Club in New York when I received a telegram that Albert, after having been thwarted in several attempts at suicide, had removed his left eye with his own hand. This is the way it was so often in my life; my brother's sudden death while resting after a day in the hospital library where he had worked since the lobotomy, a surgery that I, the responsible, had approved in desperation. A phone call from my mother just before an "on stage" in Amsterdam a few years after the eye incident. The phone call from Joliet to the Palais du Chaillot in Paris, where I was literally about to step on stage, announcing my father's death after a prolonged illness. Then my mother Anette's death announced in a cable to me from John, between acts at the Sankei Theatre in Tokyo. In a way, it is a relief not to be waiting in the wings of a dressing room of some theater nervous, at times terrified with apprehension, for the dreaded phone call or telegram from Joliet, Illinois.

NOTES

1. *Cabin in the Sky* (1940) was a musical play staged by George Balanchine, with music by Vernon Duke (Vladimir Dukelsky), sets and designs by Boris Aronson, and lyrics by John La Touche. Katherine Dunham played the role of the temptress Georgia Brown, and the Broadway production co-starred Ethel Waters, Dooley Wilson, and the Dunham Company. The choreography for Dunham and her dancers was a joint collaboration between Dunham and Balanchine.

Sol Hurok was a Russian-born impresario who immigrated to the United States in 1906. He was one of the most popular and powerful agents in the performing arts and represented the Dunham Company on their 1943 tour of *Tropical Revue [Eds.]*.

2. Erich Fromm (1900–1980) was a German psychoanalyst, philosopher and social activist. His most well-known works include *Escape from Freedom* (1941), *Man for Himself: An Inquiry into the Psychology of Ethics* (1947), *The Art of Loving* (1965), and *The Sane Society* (1955). He immigrated to the United States in 1934 and eventually resettled in Mexico City, where he maintained a clinical practice and taught at UNAM, the National Autonomous University of Mexico *[Eds.]*.

Survival

Chicago after the Caribbean

KATHERINE DUNHAM

To be perfectly honest, I believe I married (my first marriage to Jordis McCoo) out of loneliness. I longed for companionship during my brief hours at home or on holidays, but forgot to take into consideration the fact that Jordis McCoo was a postal clerk and seemed to be locked into a night shift. When I returned to Chicago from the Caribbean, nothing had changed, so he gallantly agreed to a divorce or an annulment, whichever was easier. It was more logical for him to be the plaintiff since I had spent practically all of my time out of the country for the previous year and a half. Desertion: it was easily and swiftly done.

The apartment on Thirty-fifth and Grand Boulevard was, in some ways, all I could want, in other ways very lacking. The building was one of those baronial brownstone townhouses, which descended from medium-rich brewery and stockyard executives and landlords to the "colored" people of the city. It included what was known as an "English basement" a few steps below street level with living quarters in the front for a superintendent, in the affluent days, and laundry and storage behind. Now the English basement at 3560 Grand Boulevard was only used for storage and the front room was dusty, shuttered and to me, sinister. The first floor was a flight of stairs above the basement and it was there that I tried to make a three-room apartment into a suitable nest. There was a salon and a large dining room converted into a bedroom. Between, there was a mirrored marble

SOURCE: Katherine Dunham, excerpts from Book I of "Minefields," an unpublished work in progress, in the Katherine Mary Dunham Papers, Special Collections, Morris Library, Southern Illinois University, Carbondale. Copyright 2005 by Katherine Dunham. Used by permission. The majority of the manuscript was written between 1980–1989. Minor corrections and changes of editorial style have been made.

washbasin in which I frequently relieved myself of urine if pressed or afraid of the dark in the hallway. There was a kitchen where a bathroom had perhaps been and a toilet, bathtub and washbasin farther down the hall. Paint, folding shutters, a few odds and ends of furnishing from the Salvation Army, and this became home to me for half of the three years before New York and *Cabin in the Sky* . . .

My first serious problem upon returning to Chicago was how to live, mere survival. I had a part-time position with the Chicago Public Library, which had been my first job upon arriving in Chicago from Joliet. In Joliet I had filled in an application that my niece had sent me and with great astonishment learned that I had passed the civil service examination and at a very high level. Whoever made the placement decisions decided to place me at a Hamilton Park Branch, an upper-middle-class white community, decidedly racist, where there had been no black people living and only a very few working, these as domestics and delivery persons. There I stayed until I had to resign in order to keep up with Melville Herskovits's classes at Northwestern and Robert Redfield's, Radcliffe-Brown's and Malinowski's at Chicago. My Rosenwald fellowship sustained me for the period directly before the West Indies as well as the field trip. Leaving the country for Haiti had also cost me my seniority in the library and my position as junior clerk, so after the Caribbean field trip, how to live became my number one, top-priority problem.

Charles Johnson of Fisk University and Erich Fromm, writer and psychoanalyst, were both largely responsible for my fellowship. Erich had visited me frequently during his short stay in Chicago in 1935 and briefed me on fellowships from the Rosenwald Fund. He also had offered to write a recommendation suggesting that the Fund interview me for a fellowship to the Caribbean, which I had decided during our few meetings was the place for me to begin serious study in dance *and* anthropology, I stressed, not wanting to be negligent of one or the other.

On my return from the highly profitable first field trip, the Guggenheim Foundation paid my tuition for a master's degree, with a little left over for a stipend. I asked Erich, who was again in Chicago, if he could possibly help with perhaps the monthly twenty dollars for my parents. I knew that I could count on some small sum from teaching, but that involved the expenses of a studio and accompanist, and income from that was sporadic. With Erich's help I was able to resume a more or less stabilized pattern of living. He did not stay long in Chicago, but continued his quest for repatriating Jewish humanists and intellectuals.

During this period of my life, I met Bill and Ruth Attaway. Both were interested in theater, and both were in classes at the midtown University of Illinois. They were fortunate in having a small allowance from their mother, a schoolteacher. Because of our mutual interests, and because I would soon not be able to pay for my apartment on Grand Boulevard, we scoured the South Side and found a stable with minimal living quarters above. We looked at it on a warm fall afternoon and didn't notice that there was no heat anywhere in the building. There were gas, water, and electricity, separate in the main house, which we found had become a lower-class boarding house. What had been stables for horses years before had been converted by removing the stalls and cementing the floor into a garage. This was our studio, the floor above our living quarters. Hot water pipes serving the big house in front of us had been installed in the garage, and the first chilly days we thought these would be sufficient. By winter we had hooked up two small heating stoves to gas outlets in the alley behind us, and with a little manipulating of the gas meter, Bill found a way, by devious rubber-tube attachments, for us to have at least the chill off the air at no cost to us. When the real Chicago winter took over, however, we were more often than not freezing cold.

In this, my first real studio, I taught two classes a week to children bundled up in long woolen underwear under their tights, and two or three sweaters and scarves. They wore shoes and rubber boots to keep from freezing their toes on the cement floor in ballet shoes. Ruth Attaway taught acting techniques, and Bill listened to music or wrote, which later became his profession. I have never been very good at remembering names, but we had some very staunch supporters in those days—mothers who would bring their children through rain and snow to take their lessons in ballet and "primitive," the material gathered from the Caribbean, chiefly Haiti, which would eventually develop into the Dunham Technique.

Once Erich was in Chicago from Davos, Switzerland, where he was institutionalized much of the time now for care of his lungs. Again he was meeting with moneyed American Jews hoping for assistance in the diaspora of persecuted Jews being planned by several intellectual Jewish groups of Europe. He was a founding member, I believe, of the Institute for Sociological Research, which later became attached to Columbia University in New York. The group had moved from Berlin to Switzerland, partly prescient of what was to take place in Germany, and partly because Fromm, one of their key members, needed to live in Davos. It must have been a great hardship for Erich to send me the monthly help that he did for my parents. He spent one night at our studio (we had cots around the central gas heater), then begged off because of a cold. We were in no position to extend hospitality.

The freezing winds blowing across from Lake Michigan finally overcame our staunch determination to stay in the stable. My own recourse was to ask my former husband if he would move to his mother's apartment and let me return alone to the haunted apartment on Grand Boulevard. Ruth and Bill returned to their family house, but having signed a lease for the studio, we were still obliged to pay and therefore used it on days and evenings that were mild enough for lessons and rehearsals.

Some of my professors knew that I had written not only "Dances of Haiti," which was accepted as a master's monograph (other examinations were interrupted by multiple other activities), but a book of my experiences with the Maroon people in the cockpits of Jamaica, where according to Melville Herskovits, I was the first outsider to spend time with these liberated slaves. He had been there overnight a few years before. I had kept a diary of my twenty-eight days living in the village Accompong which was, and still may be, pretty well cut off from the surrounding tax-paying counties of Jamaica. The Colonel, the chief of Accompong, related to me tales of the warriors Johnny, Cudjoe, and Accompong who, with their ragged armies, fought off British Red Coats and founded three villages, each in his own name. Accompong was the only one that I could research at the time. In these mountainous cockpits, twenty miles from the nearest village, most of my time was spent playing Duke Ellington records on my old portable record player to a group of fascinated listeners, writing, listening to folk tales and learning a few steps of dance. After these many years *Journey to Accompong* has become a textbook for explorers into folk culture, especially as methodology for a lone woman investigator.

I asked Dr. Redfield, our department head at Chicago, to read *Journey.* He, aware of my financial stress, suggested that I take it to the Works Progress Administration (WPA) Federal Writers' Project to see if this, with his recommendation, would qualify me as a superintendent of a special project. This I did, and went prepared with an outline of a project that would make use of some of my background in sociology and anthropology. This was to be a study of the cults burgeoning in Chicago and their relationship to deprivation. The title changed a few times but I was allowed to select the people who would research the project as I would outline it, and there were some others who would write their own material as gleaned from research. I took responsibility for the finished document. Mary Fujii, one of the few other women in my department at the University of Chicago, was in most of my anthropology classes, so I chose her and Frank Yerby to work on the project. Frank was a cousin of one of my few financially non-deprived friends, Barefield Gordon.

Excepting for Frank Yerby and Nelson Algren, other names on the writing project escape me, but the overall director was a wonderful person, a Mr. Fredericks, who submitted *Journey* to Henry Holt and sent me flowers when I learned of its acceptance for publication. I settled on "The Occurrence of Cults among Deprived Peoples" as a title for our WPA monograph, and built a quite good questionnaire for the researchers. I went to most of the projects under study, but some, as the Temple of Islam Number Two, directed by the prophet Elijah Muhammad, were not too keen on visitors. I did attend a few meetings and managed to meet the prophet. I was impressed by his sincerity about his role in the Temple. Also, we had to do a bit of maneuvering to get what we wanted from some of the "storefront churches," but between these and the Muslims, Pentecosts (which were then not in the main stream of church respectability), Adventists, Holy Rollers, Father Divine and even Amy Semple McPherson (as much as we could document from a distance since she was stationed in California), we were all kept pretty busy. I especially appreciated the Father Divine storefront restaurants, where for twenty-five cents one could have home-cooked chicken and dumplings and peach cobbler at any time. For some reason I was always seated to the right of the empty chair on which one of the Father's cloaks was spread. A complete dinner service was placed in front of the chair, and behind it on the wall was a larger-than-life tinted picture of an old gentleman. They could have seated me in the kitchen and I would have been content, as long as the Father Divine kitchen did its good work at its more than reasonable price.

My arrangement with the Works Progress Administration's Writers' Project lasted for perhaps six or eight months. Twice during that time our files were rifled and all of our Temple of Islam notes disappeared. Fortunately I kept a set of notes at home for reference for the paper I was writing, but the occurrences were upsetting, and we began to look at each other circumspectly. During this time I wrote the ballet *L'Ag'ya* set in Martinique and in some ways influenced by Ruth Page's *La Guiablesse* in which I had danced a featured role at the Chicago Opera before going to the West Indies. Our writing project was about finished and I would soon be out of work. I took this ballet script, *L'Ag'ya* (the name of a Martinique fighting dance) to the heads of the Theatre Project of the WPA, George

Kondolf and Harry Mintern. Just before the Writers' project closed, I was engaged to absorb about fifty nondancers into the ballet and prepare it for a gala presentation—one of three ballets. The others were by Berta Ochsner and Kurt and Grace Graff. Rehearsing *L'Ag'ya* took weeks—how many I don't remember, but it was a colossal undertaking. I had always wanted to work with people—that is, proletariat or lumpen, and this was a golden opportunity. There were hordes of out-of-work cooks, chauffeurs, maids, typists, everything and everybody, aside from elements of small acting groups, because the Depression was still in full swing.

I must have auditioned for two weeks before I had my full complement of fifty. It has always been difficult for me to audition people. I suffer more than they do at these ghastly eliminating examinations. Finally, years later, the New York Dunham School of Arts, Sciences, Humanities, and Applied Skills and the Dunham Company had reached such a prestigious level that people from the Dunham Company or School were excused from auditioning for other companies or Broadway shows. This is not true today, but having been in the company still furnishes keys for many doors, both in this country and many others in the world. (In Sweden alone, for example, there were at one time seven teachers of Dunham Technique privately and in universities; this pleases me.)

Having a little more money, or should I say, having a guarantee of money from the WPA, I was able to relinquish the stable and rent a small room part-time in the Auditorium building on Wabash Street for rehearsals and a class twice a week. Most of the featured roles of *L'Ag'ya* were rehearsed in this studio or when a full complement, in WPA work space. My biggest problem was male dancers. I finally recruited my former husband Jordis McCoo and Charles Sebree, already known as a painter and an intimate of our small group, which met now at the Cube Theatre on Harper Avenue, near the university. Henry Pitts, a true Black Adonis, was my first partner for *L'Ag'ya*. When the project closed, he continued his studies and became an outstanding doctor of psychology at a university in Phoenix, Arizona. How on earth I managed to keep up with all of these activities, I don't know. I regretted having to forego poker with the Attaways, but by Sunday I was too tired to do anything but sleep. There were now and then university classes which I succeeded in attending. I tried classes at seven in the morning for a while, then gave up half way through my Master's exams and threw myself into the production of the Martinique ballet *L'Ag'ya*.

Mary Hunter—niece of the writer, mystic, seer of American Indian folklore and mythology Mary Austin—was directing the acting groups

at the Cube.[1] There I would appear as often as possible to see Alain Locke
(author of *The New Negro*); Rose McClendon, costarring with Frank
Wilson in *Porgy and Bess;* or James T. Farrell, timid, more often hungry
than not, beginning then his great writing career; Studs Terkel, writer,
then a television host in Chicago; Canada Lee, that great actor; or W. C.
Handy, incomparable trumpet player and composer of the "St. Louis
Blues," and whomever else we could entice to make an appearance,
thereby enhancing our little theater movement and testifying to the fact
that black and white could certainly meet on the level of the arts. (And
science, I insisted, since my haven from racial discrimination at the university had been anthropology.) Little by little, thanks to Charles Johnson;
Erich Fromm; my brother, Albert, and his philosopher friends, among
them Nick Matsoukas; Mary Hunter; Ludmilla Speranzeva, my teacher
of the Kamerny Theatre in Moscow (in America by way of the Chauve
Souris); Ruth Page and Mark Turbyfill, my patrons who opened the doors
of professional dance for me; John Alden Carpenter; Alain Locke; Isamu
Noguchi; and others whose forgiveness I ask for not remembering their
names, I began to cultivate an international as well as local circle of friends
and acquaintances. And then of course my horizon was broadened by
John Pratt.

When I returned to Grand Boulevard, a superintendent for the WPA, I felt
myself to be in a position to do a small amount of entertaining. There I
met Darius Milhaud, brought to my apartment by Quill Monroe, designer
friend of Mark Turbyfill. There were also Radcliffe-Brown and Malinowski, Oxfordian anthropologists, and Alan Lomax, musicologist, who would
drop in on our anthropology meetings at my place. I felt affluent enough
to buy two Sebree paintings from his then-current Blue Period and an
Abercrombie, at friendship prices of course.

   I had met John Pratt when he was introduced to me as the costume
designer for *L'Ag'ya.* He began to come regularly to rehearsals, but it wasn't
until some weeks later when it was time for all involved in the ballet productions to meet and agree or disagree on final touches that I suggested he
come directly to the spider's web, first floor, Grand Boulevard. We argued
about the ending of *L'Ag'ya* because I wanted a third scene set behind
scrims in a sort of Giselle return-from-the-dead atmosphere. John argued
for ending the ballet when the hero Alcide is killed by the treacherous
Julot. This proved to be a valuable suggestion, and the ballet has ended
this way over the many intervening years. It was rare for anyone to correct

or criticize me in any of my creative work, and unheard of that I would listen and consent to change.

One evening John came over to my haunted apartment to discuss the ballet. In those days I drank very little, but I had fallen into the habit of offering visitors a small rum punch as done in Martinique—rum with heavy cane sugar syrup and lime. I had a small quantity of Martinique rum left from the five-gallon jug I had brought into the country on my return from the Caribbean a year before. It had been reduced to quart bottles for convenience, but these bottles were on a closet shelf in the front room and I needed a chair to reach them. Barefoot, I climbed on a chair and had just grasped a bottle of the precious liquid when I was given a terrible fright. John Pratt had followed me and had seen for most of the evening whenever I stood up and turned my back to him, a split in the seam of my blue corduroy pajamas. Now, both hands inside the aperture and clasped in front, he lifted me from the chair and spread me on the sofa before I knew what was happening. He placed the rum bottle on the floor, undid what was left to undo of the one-piece blue corduroy pajamas, and began kissing me in a way I had never been kissed before.

I couldn't act surprised, because feeling as I did, that would have been just too hypocritical. Although I did not know of the rip in the seam of my pajamas, from the moment I noticed John Pratt watching our rehearsals and sketching, I knew that here was someone special, someone with whom I could take wings and fly. And we did, because he seemed to feel the same way. It wasn't easy. After the episode of the lounging pajamas, John was at Thirty-fifth and Grand Boulevard as much as he was at his mother's apartment on North Clark Street. He was very tall and slender, not thin, and grey-eyed and blonde, with wavy hair that still stays with him all these years later. His nose was perfect and his lips were perfect and I stepped willingly where there was danger because I couldn't do otherwise. I suppose I might have known that there were others before me, just as there were afterwards, though not enough to be troublesome. But none of that counted, and what has happened in all of these between and late years is of no consequence beside the glowing fusion that has remained. It was love then, on both parts, as it is love today. Age, sickness, exhaustion, world travel, accolades, separations, quarrels—professional and personal— it was at times difficult to know just how much this love could bear. Looking back, I can say enough. Many times, however, at a given moment I have sworn to liberate him and myself from this deadly charm. But it never happened, no matter what temptations or near replacements. I believe that I have always loved John and always will, which is brought closer to me by his three serious bouts with cancer, all kinds of dehydration and malnutrition crises brought on, I suppose, by a daily liter of brandy, rum, or in later years, vodka. But he pulls through, riding on the tide of his own will to live, prayers on my part to various saints—Cuban, Haitian, Brazilian, Christian, and now Buddhist—many physicians and hospitals and a kind of thread that holds him where I am. There are some who believe our lives charmed, and they may be.

Where the record with *"Campanitas de Cristal"* on one side and *"Son"* on the other came from, I cannot remember, but these Dominican boleros permeated our lovemaking, our before and after dancing together, alone, on Grand Boulevard, enveloped in a substance of physical and spiritual need and want that bound us into a core from which not one or the other could, or really wanted to, escape.

I have heard over the years other such enticing entrapment music in Egypt and Argentina, Cuba and Paris, and Singapore and New York: tangos, blues, boleros, rumbas, danzones, sambas. My happiest after-theater rendezvous I danced with John. When he wasn't there I went dancing with Serge Tolstoi, or Porfirio Rubiros when Doris would invite me with the two of them, once with Aly Khan or other friends or admirers, in night spots of Europe or South America or Beirut while it was still the Paris of the Middle East. Or, I stayed in my hotel room and read, wrote, planned new stage material, listened to music, or went to sleep.

John Pratt, christened John Thomas Jones Pratt, and his brother, Davis, had agreed to share an apartment with their mother, Gertrude, who had been divorced after a twenty-five-year marriage that she felt to be secure. The ten large, high-ceilinged rooms on North State Street were filled with an amazing collection of Victorian furniture, including an almost complete set of John Belter sitting room sofas, armchairs, side chairs and ottomans all carved in grapes and roses and gilded and burnished, dozens of gilt and polychrome Venetian blackamoors holding up tables, candelabra, shelves, walls covered by white framed heavy rococo mirrors and wide matted Braque pouchoirs. (It took some time for me to distinguish these objects by name or kind!) There was a large grand piano bearing candlesticks of bronze gilt-formed calla lilies and usually a very large Waterford bowl of living ones. Mrs. Pratt had been an honors graduate of the Cincinnati Conservatory of Music and would periodically play a few exercises or sonatas or rhapsodies on their imposing super large grand piano as though not to lose contact with a world long gone. An only child, daughter of a college president, she had married the son of a prosperous wheat farmer in Saskatchewan, north of Montana. The ranch was given to them as a wedding present while the father moved further west into Alberta to take advantage of new territories being opened up for wheat ranching in this period of Canada's expansion. Gertrude had little chance to pursue her musical career in that sparsely settled prairie country and did much of the unfamiliar, necessary work: canning, gardening, baking twice weekly, feeding a battery of hired men spring and fall. Their first child, John, was alone much of the time, wandering the tall-grass prairies with a dog, picking crocuses and lilies and saskatoon berries for his mother and once bringing her a gaudy prairie snake, longer than he was tall, because it was "pretty." He was sometimes the object of search parties, since he would hide in buffalo wallows where the grass grew extra long in order to avoid occasional passing Assiniboine Indians dressed in black, with shapeless black felt hats pulled very low over their braided hair. These silent figures were John's "Crandalls," he told me, and haunted his dreams until they were replaced by more vivid images of terror from his years spent as a soldier.

John's brother, Davis, was born six years after John, in Indiana, matrix of his parents, grandparents, and most of his great grandparents. The family later moved to Winnipeg, where their father was editor and publisher of the *Grain Growers Guide,* the largest farm paper in Canada. In 1922 the family moved to Chicago, where the father worked for various newspapers, the *Daily News* as a representative of the North American Newspaper Alliance and later for the Hearst papers as an advertising manager. After being embroiled in Chicago politics for several years, the Pratt father accepted a position as editor and publisher of the *Louisville Herald Post,* later worked for the Frank Gannett syndicate in New York and returned to Chicago to head the National Physician's Committee, a sub rosa auxiliary of the American Medical Association. All of the movement of this very active life was bewildering to Mrs. Pratt, and she grew so apart from it that divorce became inevitable. She never really accepted the divorce but devoted herself to her sons. I never knew Gertrude Pratt to be surprised by passing events, not even by me. I feel sure that she had never associated with black people but with complete sang-froid would prepare a platter of scrambled eggs and bacon and toast for my dancers, some of whom were billeted from time to time in her Indiana limestone house on North Dearborn Parkway, one of the few in the area which had survived the great Chicago fire. Mrs. Pratt acted as though neither of her sons could do wrong, but I always felt John to be her favorite. The boys' father married again, and his old age was brightened by a daughter forty years younger than John.

The first few days after Federal Theatre checks we circulated from place to place in taxis to eat at small Italian, Chinese, or German restaurants (the only ones where I felt comfortable) or in a South Side chicken shack or "society" restaurant where, again, I felt uncomfortable, these times because of John, since there the clientele was never fairer than octoroon. We rode streetcars rarely, because with time to just sit and stare or be stared at on the South Side by black riders, on the North Side by the white ones, our impervious shield of love and respect for the privacy of others would show signs of disintegration. There would be times when I would accuse John of racism if he happened to be morose for some reason of his own and went for some time without speaking or would walk ahead of me long enough for me to catch up and shout "I'm not your Indian squaw!" People would stop to turn and stare. This always exasperated John to no end. Score one for me, until we arrived at my house or wherever we were going. Then for punishment I would be up against an icy wall of frigid silence, cold politeness, and chain-smoking, which I became accustomed to over the years. Fortunately these dramas were short-lived. But it did not help that both of us were hypersensitive Cancerians.

John had a great number of Chicago North Side society and "literati" friends and, being gregarious, was constantly invited to cocktail parties and soirees in the company of the rich and the famous. Sometimes he would tell of these occasions beforehand, sometimes afterwards, and other times I would learn quite by accident. On rare occasions I was invited too, and if the invitation did not come by way of his own largesse but directly to me by way of others, John would be furious. It took me some time to realize that he was jealous, both of me and because of me. After all, he was already, at two years younger than I, an established designer and painter. Two of his paintings still hang in Special Collections in the Art Institute of Chicago. I had to be firmly and irrevocably established in stardom before I could recall objectively this period in our lives.

Dodo Badger was a good friend of John's. He was frequently at her small penthouse apartment and finally, since he spoke of her so often, I inveigled him into stopping with me by her place, conveniently on the North Shore not far from our WPA rehearsal hall. If this was such a good friend, why had we never met? By now our relationship was fairly well established in most of Chicago, sanctioned or not. Dodo Badger's apartment was quiet, elegant, and quite in contrast to the somewhat "rococo" (as I remember it) Pratt residence. The salon was dominated by a Travertine marble fireplace. Things went extremely well until I, for some reason, decided to smoke. To emphasize some point in conversation I was standing by the fireplace, leaning on the mantle. At that time I smoked now and then, perhaps a cigarette a week. A box of matches was on the mantle, and hardly being aware of what I was doing, I struck one of them on one of the curved designs of the fireplace. John froze, but Dodo continued our conversation without the blink of an eyelash. My lack of astuteness vis-à-vis this priceless work of art and antiquity trailed our confrontations for years, being a prime example of my ineptitude. Had I not learned to shed, as some fowl do water, this sort of judgment from John, whether it be about art, people, my own theater performances, or household furnishings, then I would never have been able to disregard his need to try and make me believe myself callow, naive, and untutored as he became more and more tied to me, or we to each other, unable to tear ourselves apart. Finally he accepted my ascendancy to stardom as a thing apart from his own, as no threat or challenge, certainly not intentional, and things became less turbulent.

Inez Cunningham Stark was altogether different from Dodo Badger.[2] To begin with, she was not only John's patron in the arts but his mistress when I first met him. But of course I didn't know this.

Chicago has always been a city to take to its vast smoky bosom dignitaries and famous painters and musicians and composers. I refer to its "smoky bosom" because that was much of my experience when I was confined to the Loop (Midtown). One part of my induction into the sanctum of North Side townhouses, apartments and mansions bordering Lake Michigan was engineered by Mark Turbyfill, Ruth Page and Quill Monroe; another and probably more important (for a while) introduction into Chicago North Side society and unpolluted air came via John Pratt. He became more confident as he found that he was not shunned by patrons and friends because of his association with me (color). Some chose to think of this association as professional; others truly enjoyed hearing me tell about my West Indies voyage; some wanted to feel worldly, and beyond the barrier of race, emulating Nancy Cunard and going out of the way to "adopt" Negroes famous in the arts or entertainment fields, or those giving promise of future notoriety. There were some who, friends and sycophants of Inez Cunningham Stark, resented deeply my violation of her established relation with John, of which I repeat, I knew nothing. This was the age of the New Negro . . .

Everyone wanted to know about the ballet *L'Ag'ya,* which John as stage and costume designer helped to publicize. It was a simple story, very reminiscent of *Giselle,* which Arnold Haskell, the English critic, immediately perceived. He wrote of *L'Ag'ya* as the "Tropical Giselle." The fact that I had lived in the tiny fishing village of Vauclin in Martinique gave me a certain confidence in spite of the piece's vague resemblance to Ruth Page's *La Guiablesse,* the story of a Martiniquan devil creature in which I appeared on the Civic Opera stage as the lover of a young Martiniquais beguiled by the devil woman, played by Ruth Page. This was before my research in Martinique, and I felt on very safe ground in spite of young lovers and witchcraft and a tragic ending analogous to both ballets. The program note from *L'Ag'ya* gives a sketchy storyline, but one would have had to see the luxuriant stage decors, from fishing village to zombie jungle, and the vibrant costumes of John Pratt to understand the comment evoked by Arnold Haskell.

The scene is Vauclin, a tiny eighteenth-century fishing village in Martinique. Loulouse loves Alcide and is desired by Julot. Julot, the villain, repulsed by Loulouse and filled with hatred and desire for revenge, decides to seek the aid of the King of the Zombies. Deep in the jungle, Julot fearfully enters the lair of the zombies and witnesses their strange rites which bring the dead back to life. They give Julot the charm needed to secure the love of Loulouse. Frightened, but remembering his purpose, Julot pursues Roi Zombi and obtains from him the *cambois,* a powerful love charm.

The following evening; it is a time of gaiety, opening with the stately creole mazurka or *mazouk,* and moving into the uninhibited excitement of the beguine. Into this scene enters Julot, horrifying the villagers when he exposes the coveted *cambois.* Even Alcide is under its spell. Now begins the *majumba,* love dance of ancient Africa. As Loulouse falls more and more under the charm, Alcide suddenly defies its powers, breaks loose from the villagers who protect him, and challenges Julot to the *l'ag'ya,* the fighting dance of Martinique. In *L'Ag'ya* and its ending is the consummation of the forces released in superstition and violence.

The first casting was Jordis McCoo, replaced later by Henry Pitts, who was actually not bad in the role of my lover; Woody Wilson, as the wicked Julot; and in the featured roles of full ballet numbers Roberta McLauren, the Brooks sisters, Carmencita Romero, and others. There were the former cooks and maids and chauffeurs and waiters of all sizes and shapes, at first protesting the idea of stage dancing, then in full swing as the realistic presentation of village folk unraveled in rehearsals and on stage. The music was composed by Robert Sanders of the University of Chicago music department. It was inspired by old Edison cylindrical recordings I made in Martinique, as well as popular recordings of Creole mazurkas and waltzes and beguines, songs and music that I had learned, thinking perhaps of a future theater repertoire for myself, because, encouraged by Quill and Mark, I periodically thought of a solo number here and there. Robert Sanders was at every rehearsal, and though a piano was not his instrument, he often accompanied on the old upright piano that had been installed in the basement of the Elks Temple on North Dearborn; measure by measure, practically step by step, phrase by phrase, composing for the Federal Theatre Orchestra what would later be played by symphony orchestras from San Francisco to Buenos Aires to Santiago, Chile, and beyond. His presence spurred me on to greater heights of creativity.

Some of the cast of this first ballet venture I have never forgotten: Roberta McLauren, epitome of acerbity, not terribly good looking but a marvelous dancer. Patti Bee Yancey who, when John asked for scissors at a fitting, obliged with a six-inch bone-handled folding knife. It was true that the streets between the Dearborn Street elevated and Thirty-fifth and State elevated were dark and dangerous after our late rehearsals. I always went home on the Grand Boulevard bus and, if John were not with me, had only a short walk by myself to the middle of the block. The apartment had been greatly exorcised of its malevolent occupants by John's presence and my sporadic entertaining and a few libations of toilet water and orgeat to my Haitian Vodun husband, Damballa, the serpent god. Nevertheless, I was always relieved to pass from the menacing hallway into the familiar feel and smell of my own living quarters.

Lily May Butler, soon to be known as Carmencita Romero, was one of the dancers. (She claimed relationship with Cesar Romero, and wrote him as such. He called on her backstage when we were playing at the Philharmonic in Los Angeles; I don't know if the contact was continued after his face to face encounter or not.) Carmencita, after many years and much world travel, is one of the exponents of Dunham Technique now teaching in New York. John has often recalled the confusion among the wardrobe seamstresses when they might do a fitting on Lily Butler and find that there was no Lily Butler, but a Carmencita or a Joan Amour. Carmencita Romero took precedence over the other names and has been her professional and legal name ever since. She was a great asset to our later performing company, and I believe spread the gospel of Dunham Technique on her far and wide travels.

The Brooks Sisters were also very good dancers, and of course there was Tally Beatty who, though young, was showing promise of the stardom that he reached after branching out from our company in New York. But my real delight and sense of achievement was derived from the "proletariat": the chauffeurs and maids and cooks and so forth. Many of them were devoted churchgoers, conventional or storefront, and not only had never danced publicly before, but were nervous about retaining church membership in view of the hip-swaying, shoulder-shaking, lusty enjoyment of such indigenous Martiniquan dances as the *majumba* and beguine. The creole waltz and mazurka they performed like true veterans, bowing, curtsying, shuffling, fluttering their beribboned fans and embroidered lace kerchiefs, swaying to Robert Sanders's suave rhythms as I had imagined the slave population of those islands would have done in the mimicry of the masters in the big house. Their presence on stage was solid and reassuring. They enjoyed every moment of it, and though they started out as background, these non-professionals soon gave the stage the dimension of reality that made the folk myth believable. They were moderately paid, but they were saved from the inconvenience and ignominy of bread lines and were mature and experienced enough to appreciate it. Many were not so fortunate during those frightening days of the Great Depression.

One night, John's father came to see *L'Ag'ya*. I didn't know until some days after the fact, but I was annoyed that John had not insisted that he come backstage. Until he died, ten or more years later, I still had not met him. By that time I had categorized him as a racist and let things go at that.

L'Ag'ya, performed on the same bill as Grace and Kurt Graff's *Alt Wien* and a ballet by Berta Ochsner, was immediately a great success. We rehearsed daily, a habit I maintained until dissolution of the company, nearly thirty years later. Daily rehearsals and on-stage corrections between acts became a trademark of mine, causing problems with new stage managers watching time clocks for the union-controlled intermissions. Before long, they too saw the wisdom of keeping the company keyed to the determination for perfection.

During this period, I would go at times with Vera Mirova, who was as insolvent as I, to sit in the farthest gallery seats at Orchestra Hall or the Auditorium for performances of soloists or ballets or orchestras. At other times I went alone, in the least expensive, highest-up seats in the gallery. If it happened to be a pianist (Rachmaninoff, Rubenstin, Paderewski, especially the great romanticist, Horowitz), I would listen enraptured, choreographing madly, transported to far countries and magic scenes. Since Ludmilla Speranzeva and Vera Mirova could often buy tickets at reduced rates for ballet and concert dance performances and at times were given seats by the touring managers and conductors and impresarios, I might sit in a balcony or orchestra or box seat to see the Ballet Russe or La Argentina or Harald Kreutzberg or Massine with his refreshing new choreography. These were my most impressionable years, and whole new vistas were opening at such a great rate that anthropology receded much of the time into the background, diminished by the stirrings of a desire to create something new and wonderful, to include myself in it, and to make of it something permanent.

L'Ag'ya ran for six weeks at the Great Northern Theatre. Again out of a job, I worked as often as possible with a small group of members selected from the Federal Theatre. In 1934 I had done, with Ludmilla, a Negro spiritual, *Sinner Please Don't Let This Harvest Pass.* It was sung by a tenor who now and then appeared at the Cube, and played by Margaret Bond, who helped us immeasurably by working out music and rehearsing with the nucleus post *L'Ag'ya* group. Quite desperate, I turned to the Chicago Public Library again. It so happened that they welcomed my application for my old position of Junior Clerk. (I had never taken the examinations for Senior Clerk.) This time my assignment was near the university. While I was not entirely welcome (Hyde Park color prejudice), I was not as ostracized by the staff as I had been on my first library assignment, Hamilton Park. Nevertheless, I resolved never to be put in this disagreeable position again. I returned to classes at the university as soon as possible, took and taught lessons and choreographed for this small group to which I could now offer carfare, so attendance was quite regular.

During this period, a sorority in Indiana and the Young Men's Hebrew Association in New York both requested performances. The fee was small, but expenses were paid. Dancers and costumes were in the trailer of the old Cadillac that I drove to Indianapolis. I was proud of our success, and my personal success, and the spirit of the trip was only dampened by the fact that I really did not know how to manipulate a trailer, but didn't want to admit it. I drove into a dead end, leaving the after-show party at the sorority house, and tried to back out, but the trailer kept going in the direction opposite to where I thought I was guiding it. I tried not to panic because I had been warned by several well-wishers of the illegality of carrying passengers in a windowless, cramped commercial trailer. All of us disembarked, and by lifting and pushing we edged the trailer into the right direction and were off to Chicago. Of the trip to New York and the performance at the YMHA I shall write later.

During the depression years my father's dry-cleaning business went farther and farther downhill. My mother stayed more and more at her sewing machine and did more mending and remodeling; this probably saved the West Side Cleaners and Dyers from total bankruptcy. By now my mother and father lived in the house, which, with much foresight, my father had moved several blocks to a larger plot of ground. To the astonishment of inhabitants of the streets, the eight-room brick house passed through on massive wooden rollers en route to the vacant lot on Joliet Street. My father left much of his equipment on Bluff Street, where we had lived before, because it was not only worn but was embedded in cement for stability. He salvaged what he could of the whirlpools and tumblers and set up what he dreamed would be an interim miniature dry-cleaning establishment in the garage of the new old house. His work suffered, he could not afford help, and of this situation I was the only one to benefit.

My father's discouragement at this business failure and his inability to buy the best gasoline and chemicals for cleaning and removing spots from delicate fabrics caused him to lose more than one of his best customers. Replacing expensive evening dresses cost him far more than proper cleaning essence would have. And so I inherited from the rich and well-dressed Joliet elite two dresses which I particularly appreciated. One was ivory satin, an irregular hemline of the period, skirt dipping slightly in back, a plunging back line and straight line from shoulder to shoulder in front. A white fox stole crossed the front and was attached at the bottom of the plunging back. The fur was slightly off-color, and this may have been the cause for the owner's dissatisfaction and the devastating indemnity that worked to my advantage. The other dress was pearl grey crepe de Chine trimmed in silver. It was long, with a skirt that fell from a low waist in fine gathers. The boat neck was outlined with an inch wide band of Egyptian-like design in silver, as were the wrists of long slightly gathered sleeves. The bodice was form-fitting to a low waistline that was emphasized by a band of the same geometric design. My father had been unable to remove spots, probably red wine, from the dress. I returned one Sunday from a visit to my parents in Joliet, thrilled at the prospect of two elegant evening gowns, just a little sorry for my father, who must have struggled and scrounged for some time in one way or another to make good his failure on the merchandise.

The grey dress I had dyed a royal purple at the best shop in the neighborhood. The spots disappeared, the dress was a perfect fit, and I was complimented for it at Cube parties and receptions, even by John Pratt. I guarded the secret of the provenance of the dress, letting it be believed that my mother, who was indeed a fine seamstress, but engulfed now in the drudgery of repairs and remodeling, had made it. The white satin dress was another matter. John had long known that my deep respect for his taste in all things, design especially, would make me conform, more and more willingly, to his judgment. The ivory satin dress he loathed at first sight. And first sight happened to be at Inez Cunningham Stark's soiree for the Maestro Stravinsky. Paul Schofield had been assigned to delivering my invitation and to seeing that my former husband was invited. There, John reminds me, was our first meeting (his and mine); a brief introduction a few days before our joint assignments for the Federal Theatre Project. I do not remember how other women were dressed, or who they were. I believe that John's analyst, Edith Menser, whom he rarely saw and whom I was to meet later, was there, as was India Moffett, society writer for the *Chicago Tribune*. Inez Stark, I learned later, was in the throes of extreme jealousy toward our good friend Gertrude Abercrombie, who was truly her rival in John's love life before John and I met. Mrs. Stark never invited Gertrude, who couldn't have cared less, to these soirees though she was one of the best known of Chicago's young painters. Inez's famous turquoise eyes, colder than ice, were not turned on me that night. But she made up for this later. The anthropologist Laura Bolton was there, as was Tyrone Power, then playing in *Romeo and Juliet* opposite Catherine Cornell. The apartment was as elegant as its hostess, whom I instinctively and with reason disliked and started to scrutinize critically. I decided that her flaming red hair was dyed, reluctantly that her black crepe dress, long, with long tight-fitted sleeves was ultra chic, that her jewelry was to be envied, that she was over forty, which seemed to be terribly old to me then, and that she was being polite to me because as hostess, she had to be. She was obviously attracted to a tall, handsome young man with grey blue eyes and blond hair. I should not have been sleeveless. In fact, I should not have worn the fox-trimmed dress at all, and Jordis looked uncomfortable in his rented black-tie ensemble. Stravinsky charmed me as he did everyone else, and it was great fun when he insisted that I talk about the "Colonies," and that we speak in French. Realizing that my textbook French lacked correct grammar, I interspersed Creole into our conversation, which relieved me of the embarrassment of competing with the other guests, most of whom had lived in France as part of their finishing school experience.

For years after that night, my first real introduction into Chicago "society," John made scathing remarks about the fox-trimmed satin dress. He also set out on a campaign to change my choice of perfumes; to turn me, by gifts of his choice, from l'Heure Bleue, first given me by Dumarsais Estimé, president of the Chamber of Deputies of Haiti and later president of Haiti, and Black Narcissus, both of which were very expensive but available in miniscule quantities at Woolworth's for less than a dollar. John liked flower scents—Bellodgia (Carnation), delicate violet and rose, Fleurs de Rocaille. Because I had no winter coat, having worn to shreds the panne velvet one trimmed in mink remade from Annette Dunham's wardrobe of affluent days as a teacher in Alton, Illinois, before she married Albert Dunham Sr., I had applied for and miraculously received a charge account at what was just about the most expensive and fashionable store on Michigan Boulevard—Blum's Vogue. I had looked longingly into its display windows as I sat on top of the Michigan Boulevard bus going to Thirty-fifth and Grand in summer, or inside on the lower level in winter. I always sat on the right side of the bus and would twist and crane my neck for the last glimpse of the enticingly designed windows. Blum's Vogue was almost my undoing. My first indiscretion was a charcoal-colored nubby woolen coat with a fox collar (black this time) that John took several years to reveal his dislike for. Then, as though to compensate for my adolescent shoe deprivations, I would pounce avariciously on Italian and French handmade slippers at frequent sales, imperiously waiving aside price tags as though a charge account would be inexhaustible. As a result of these extravagances I was soon reduced again to the survival level, and was terrified at threats of salary attachments. Somehow I managed to liquidate these foolish expenses before leaving Chicago.

My economy was helped by occasional engagements of our Negro Ballet Company. I would always try to clear something, however small, after expenses were paid. Ludmilla and I co-choreographed a program at the Punch and Judy, a small theater where foreign and avant-garde motion pictures were shown. When the screen was moved up or back, I don't remember which, it allowed space for a lecturer, varied concert artists, and for the first time, a dance company. The most notable aspect of the program was the accidental sliding down of precariously tied bandana brassieres while six young women hurled themselves into the footlights in the climatic finale of Debussy's *Golliwog's Cakewalk*. Standing in the wings of the little theater, I prayed that this would go unnoticed by the audience. My prayers were in vain; one morning-critic reported in full detail the mishap of the *Golliwog's Cakewalk,* even speculating as to whether or not the virginal bosom exposure of the finale had been intentional. This irked me to no end, even though the requests for a repeat performance were more than welcome for reasons of box office. Erich was in town and gave us—at what must have been a great sacrifice for him—the twenty-five dollars necessary to secure the theater for a further performance. I was pleased that he need no longer send help to my parents.

We began to develop, aside from the Cube and my own personal following, an enthusiastic audience from what might be called the "far left." Communism was making inroads into the university, two of its strongholds being the Cube Theatre and the North Side Dill Pickle Club. The personnel being on government salaries, little inroads were made into the WPA Theatre and Writers' Projects. But gradually I had become aware of requests for appearances not altogether to my liking. Incendiary parades and speeches were more and more frequent. I found one excuse or another to avoid close affiliation with something about which I knew so little and which seemed a camouflage for deception and hypocrisy. Where I would attend (rarely) parties in dismal ballrooms or candle-lit artists' studios I noticed that attempts to mix the components racially were undeniably heavy-handed. Rumor had it that the young white women dancing with and accompanying black young men, students or working class, were very often recruited from among prostitutes and girlfriends of so-called labor leaders. Refreshment was invariably sandwiches or unevenly cut black bread and bologna or salami sausages with pickled cucumbers and hard-boiled eggs, along with soft and hard cheese. My snobbism did not keep me from eating heartily, because all of us seemed to be constantly hungry. The drinks were, of course, bathroom-confected gin, cheap red wine, or homemade beer. Something at these noisy gatherings was not quite right for me, but not being politically aware I did not grasp what it was. I just stayed away most of the time, as did John. Periodically we would dance at a fundraising party, and the remuneration was most welcome.

One cause I embraced with open arms. That was the Spanish Civil War. I was proud of the Lincoln Brigade without knowing exactly what it was and fervently practiced heel-stamping and castanets as often as I found studio space to rehearse and Vera Mirova to coach. The *Spanish Earth* was my first ballet of protest against social injustice, otherwise known then as fascism. The John Pratt costumes were in earth tones, brown, black, and

grey, and in felt. The movement was fluid yet ponderous. Much of the
music was recordings of *"La Niña de los Peines."* The *"Bulerias"* starred
Carmela el Khoury, an Arab Palestinian girl as passionate as I for dance,
and even more economically deprived. (We wheedled a slice of bread with
gravy on it from the Greek cafeteria next to the auditorium which cost ten
cents until the proprietor, seeing no dividends from his largesse, intervened.) Carmela was with our company off and on until we went on our
tour after Hollywood, and I learned much of Bedouin and Arab dance
from her. The *"Saetas"* was a lament for the war dead. Talley Beatty was
magnificent as a leader of the Resistance. I represented the roots of peasant Spain with heels and castanets in a fiery protest to the fascist armies
of Franco. For years I refused to appear in Spain as my own private protest,
until impresarios and well-wishing citizens convinced me that nothing
would be gained for the cause by my depriving the Spanish people, those
who needed the nourishment of the outside world, of our art form. Indeed,
Spain was one of the rich experiences of my touring career.

Vera Mirova was not my only coach in Spanish dancing. Quill Monroe,
Paul Schofield, and Paul Dupont, another designer, worked assiduously
with me on heels and castanets. As I remember it, Chicago's North Side,
the streets two and three blocks in from the lakefront, was becoming
known as a colony of painters and designers. American "haute couture"
was replacing Coco Chanel and Schiaparelli and Mainbocher. The war
may have had something to do with it. Of all these young men, Quill, to
me, was the epitome of the aesthete. He first designed for me a beautiful, simple Spanish peasant dress of cotton printed in tiny muted beige
and white flowers. It inspired me to all sorts of whirling turns, *jotas,* and
the wide, closely-fitted waist band and bloused sleeves also inspired me
to stand for whole evenings in front of Quill's fitting mirrors experimenting with castanets and arm positions. Quill had been himself a partner
of La Argentina, the first one, before his couturier days. He was exceedingly tall and thin and while acting as mentor would tell hilariously funny
tales of the rigors of touring in provincial Europe and the capitals of
the world. Quill had a great collection of Spanish records, including the
saetas and every kind of guitar music from classic to flamenco. He also
played frequently, at my request, a German song, *"Ich kusse deine Hande,
Madame."* In Spanish it was *"Yo beso sus manos, Señora,"* and I fanta-
sized singing it one day in concert performances as Lucienne Boyer had
sung *"Parlez-moi d'Amour"* in concert at the Blackstone Theatre in Continental Varieties. The electric blue of her fitted velvet dress became my

trademark in *Barrelhouse—A Florida Swamp Shimmy,* but the song did not materialize. One of the few times John and I attended a theater performance together was when we saw Lucienne Boyer. Quill and Mark also helped me confect two of my very rare solos, *The Wine Door* (Debussy) and an Indian nautch dance, with the help of Mirova. These Quill designed the clothes for, and they were never danced after the Chicago period. . . .

We had become very popular doing benefits for the Lincoln Brigade. *Spanish Earth* was performed almost weekly until we branched out into less politically specific performances, such as the one at Lincoln Center on Thirty-ninth Street between Grand Boulevard and Cottage Grove. I was attending the university from time to time then and beginning to worry about a growing fissure between my life as an aspiring anthropologist and as a fledgling performer. I took my problem to Robert Redfield, dean of the department, and he answered in approximately the same words he had used when I asked the same question before going to the Caribbean. I felt an urgency to decide whether to turn my back on one and pursue the other. His answer was "Why not pursue both?" He did, though, question me about my feelings of success as a dancer. Certainly my grades in anthropology were not outstanding. I suddenly had the bright idea of asking him if he would come see a performance if I could arrange it. It was not too hard to persuade the director of the Lincoln Center that we could fill their small auditorium for one, perhaps two nights on a weekend, and we ended up with a matinee and night performance on Sunday. Our following from the Punch and Judy Theatre, friends and friends of friends from the Cube and the university filled the theater. One big disappointment was that John could not be there—he was in the midst of moving the huge Clark Street apartment into the relatively small two-story house on Dearborn Street. But in front row center, Robert Redfield, my moral sponsor, smiled when I was onstage, and applauded spontaneously for me as well as for the rest of the program. Backstage after my Moroccan dance I suffered feelings of guilt for having been so critical of the women who lost their brassieres in the *Golliwog's Cakewalk* at the Punch and Judy Theatre. To my great embarrassment I had put on the hat, veil, embroidered bodice, jewelry, and transparent voile skirt. But I had forgotten my underpants. A cool breeze and feeling of freedom while dancing I had attributed to the whirlwind speed of my nautch turns! In spite of this, Dr. Redfield came backstage to compliment me—to reassure me on a dance

career. Anthropology I could pursue as convenient, which is what I have
done . . .

By now everyone in my acquaintance knew that I was suffering from
arthritis, my lifelong nemesis. As a child, going up and down stairs was
frequently painful, and that may have been the reason why I invariably
fell out of a tree as soon as I climbed it. In high school I was forced to give
up high jumping, though I did hold a record (approximately four feet,
eight inches) for some time. At first, it was only pain in my knees at any
extra effort, which I learned to support (our family doctor, Dr. Williams,
would now and then prescribe a mildly ineffective white powder, much
in appearance like his antidotes for my summer malaria or my mother's
headaches). Finally, one morning in high school gym class, an excruciat-
ing pain shot up the shinbone of my right leg when I landed on a mat
under the bar. Reluctantly, I stopped high jumping, then, gradually, all the
sports in which I had some indication I might excel. But I would not give
up dancing. Many times in Mark's or Ludmilla's classes I would be roundly
scolded for my dilatory pliés. I offered no explanation, thinking my silence
would will away the pain, and feeling embarrassed by its handicap.

I don't remember how I met Max Obermayer, a Viennese dermatolo-
gist who arrived with that influx of gifted scientists just before and during
World War II. It may have been by way of Julian Lewis, a young research
professor at the university. Julian Lewis I would have met at one of Bertha
Moseley Lewis's (no relation) receptions as, with his green eyes, fair skin,
crinkly light hair and two years' post graduate study in Paris, he was surely
of the typical Chicago "colored" elite class. He loved to practice his French
on me and was a great help in physical anthropology when he approved
a paper of mine: something having to do with the high incidence of
protruding calcaneous in people of African provenance. That protruding
heel, I wanted to prove, helped black athletes' elevation and track abilities.
I measured over a hundred black school children, and, whether my conclusions were a priori or not, my enthusiasm and Julian's approval helped
in procuring a passing grade.

Another reminder of my affliction was an unbearable knee pain on
striking a Spanish pose, my weight supported on one bent knee. This was
when I attempted to augment my always diminished income by modeling
for a South Shore portrait painter. Two life-size canvases later, I resigned
but gladly took a job washing dishes at eight o'clock in the morning, after
the breakfast of two young teachers at the university. I had two hours in

which to scrape hardened eggs off the plates and bacon grease from the skillet, make the bed, dust here and there, and look in on a sleeping six-month-old baby, changing his diapers if he woke during my two hours. Fifteen minutes had to be allowed after the two hours for one of the parents to return home and, of course, waiting was part of my job. I always needed whatever they were paying me, perhaps a very generous dollar an hour, and my knees were not abused.

Julian Lewis had heard of a new osteopath, also from Vienna. He did not know him but was certain Max Obermayer would. Max and I became good friends; once or twice a month I would join him for dinner at his small apartment near the university. He attended only one of my soirees; the Negro South Side was a little difficult for him to assimilate, I suppose. But he immediately made an appointment for me to see the doctor, whose name I have forgotten. He was very Germanic, very brusque, and only reasonably sympathetic. He must have realized that there would be no cure, but he was then experimenting with bee venom injected directly into the knee joint. I dreaded those bi-weekly sessions more than I have anything since, even a gold and fever treatment in Buenos Aires. It was a kind of unique pain, like slowly freezing on the corner of Michigan and Randolph in dead of winter waiting for a South Side bus with sidewalk and streets like glass and a hundred kilometer wind doing its best to push you out of whatever doorway you might be huddled in. It ended in a sharp, feverish throbbing.

It seems that at the time of my treatments someone had decided that bee farmers suffered hardly at all of osteoarthritis. Bee venom was extracted from a number of these insects and injected into the cartilage between patella, tibia, and fibula. It was unadulterated agony, the concentrated stinging of a hive of furious bees. My knees would swell, and they were hardly back to normal before the routine would be repeated. While it may have done some good, I would not swear by it. This doctor ominously predicted that if I didn't stop dancing I would not be ambulant after two years.

This spurred me on to greater effort, to more choreography for others, to more stretches and off-the-knee exercises to build support for my ailing connectives. I have always stressed an emphasis on the inner rather than the outer muscle. It was not at all unusual to see old-school ballerinas with protruding shoulder blades, muscular arms and lower legs, and thrown-forward chests and backward buttocks. These things have fortunately changed due to the revision in ballet teaching inspired to a great extent by George Balanchine. For me they are serious defects, which detract

from the economy and purity of line so necessary to meaningful choreography. Having inherited generous buttocks and more than a hint of a
lumbar curve, most of my adult and performing years were spent in creating from "primitive" societies a technique and language of dance that
would satisfy the demands of Western, then world theater. A holistic
approach, taking into account physical structure, personality, culture, the
variables within an individual or society that would make a dynamic,
complete, ecstatic experience for performer as well as observer. . . .

Some of the friends so important to me were unknown to John Pratt
because I knew them before we met. Others were outreach from the university, woven into the fabric of Thirty-fifth and Grand Boulevard evenings when I didn't have to teach or rehearse or work at the library. When
my small barrel of Martinique rum ran out I would concoct some kind
of punch or fruit juice and brandy. Whatever else, I don't remember, but
in retrospect the evenings were small gatherings of people who might not
know each other but whom I felt should. This has been a manner of entertaining still practiced by me; that part of my contribution to life as
a catalyst, a pioneer, I suppose. University professors, composers, musicians, painters, designers, writers, anthropologists, psychologists—more
of these than dancers. My ambivalent nature has always been apparent in
the social gatherings rooted in these budding Chicago days. I cannot say
who was responsible for my meeting whom. Count Korzybski through
my brother; Darius Milhaud through Mark Turbyfill; Langston Hughes,
Canada Lee, and Rose McClendon by way of the Cube Theatre, as were
Studs Terkel and Ben Hecht; Arna Bontemps, the writer; and Richmond
Barthe, the sculptor who created several of the statues of Haitian heroes in
the Champ de Mars in Port-au-Prince. I conferred several times with Alan
Lomax, foremost musicologist and researcher into almost lost and forgotten Southern and Western folk melodies. I saw Ben Davis, whose father
was the first Black American general and who himself eventually became
an Air Force general after persisting through four years of West Point, suffering with courage the silent treatment of never having a word addressed
to him directly until his third year.

One evening Mary Hunter phoned and asked to come by with a surprise. The surprise turned out to be a slender, very alive young woman
about our age, obviously a ballerina by every move and gesture of graceful
hands and small, high-arched feet. She was Agnes DeMille, daughter of
the playwright, William DeMille and niece of the movie producer, Cecil

B. DeMille.[3] Her reddish blonde hair was gathered into a chignon, a style she wears today, more than fifty years later. We knew nothing of each other, but Mary Hunter brought us together and Agnes was from the first meeting a good friend. She has written and spoken such glowing words of me and all that I have attempted to do in life that it is at times hard for me to realize that this is the great Agnes DeMille, blending her solo works with her company choreography, with uniquely innovative Broadway musicals and many books, until she seems to have achieved all her aspirations. I don't know what we talked about at that first meeting, excepting that she was eager to see what I was doing with a company of black dancers and wanted, some day, to work with such a group in which she imagined untold and unexpected riches. She did present more than one ballet using black dancers on Broadway, but I have never seen these. So much of the period after our company became professional was spent in Europe or somewhere in the rest of the world.

At parties after performances at the Cube, I would burst forth in my dyed purple silver-trimmed dress. Folding chairs would be removed from the small theater and lined against walls or put away by our stage manager, Jack Sullivan. Mary Hunter, our director, knew everyone: Max Bodenheim; Charles White, the painter; Horace Caton and St. Clair Drake, sociologists in some of my classes but more in my brother's age group. Zora Neale Hurston and I would eye each other warily, she being a kind of senior authority on the Sea Islands. When she published on Jamaica and Haiti I felt offended. It was some time before I allowed myself to appreciate her writing, which, after all, derived from serious fieldwork.

We talked and danced, and we drank more than we ate. We listened to all kinds of music, and if W. C. Handy were there, his trumpet was for good measure. We took so much for granted but we worked hard for our freedom. . . . We were the prime motivators of the "New Negro" rage. It was more than a vogue. In Chicago we were inundated by media waves—films and lectures and photographs from Paris and New York. Picasso and the cubists, Gershwin and Handy, Nancy Cubard and Noble Sissle—even without realizing it we were touched by them. More than that, we felt *ourselves* to be the New Negro. . . .

I surely stepped on a high explosive when I decided to take steps to sever John Pratt from Inez Cunningham Stark. She did not take to this well at all. Of course it would have been beyond imagination that she would invite me to her house again after establishing the facts of John's and my relationship. That I didn't mind at all. But there was a constant tug of war as to where John would spend nights, especially on weekends. Since his mother had been relatively newly divorced, he felt obliged, and rightly, to spend some token amount of time with her, at least so he said. The very hot summer weekends when John was always invited to one Lake Shore beach fiesta or another were miseries for me. I could read only so much and avoided friends, who soon became accustomed to my lapses into widow's weeds when John was not available. Once I went to visit Gertrude Pratt and poured out my feelings to her. She was a good listener, and a kind person, but of course could do nothing about my situation. Secretly, I felt that she disliked Inez Stark as much as I did. The woman had a propensity for taking over things or persons touched by her or patronized by her "lock, stock, and barrel," as my father would sometimes say.

John was a very talented painter and designer before he met her, but once she had sponsored one or two sold-out exhibits in New York and Chicago, and other hostesses clamored for his presence at their own affairs, with or without her, she became passionately obsessed with the determination to give no ground. I am certain that because of me she had engaged the services of the Pinkerton Agency, because no sooner would John and I arrive together at my place than the phone would ring. There would be no acknowledgement at the other end. Then she would leave messages with John's mother to ask him to call her, which he might or might not do. This must have been infuriating. Then things reached such a state that if I were home alone I could count on four or five phone calls with, in the beginning, only silence. Later there would be heavy breathing, and now and then whistling. The Pinkerton man was earning his fee. But finally, in exasperation, I picked up the phone one night and said in a loud voice as menacing as I could manage, because I will admit that I was nervous, "Mrs. Stark! Stop phoning me or I will have the police do something about it!" or some such. The phone slammed in my ear and I was not bothered again by its ringing.

Then Mrs. Stark fell critically ill—a heart condition. Charles Sebree and I discussed the situation and came to the sensible conclusion that there would be no way to prevent John from going to the bedside of a sick dear friend. I tried to ignore his absences and lived through them as resignedly as I could in order not to create disorder in the times that we were together. I took from my bedroom closet the white plate with the mound of flour and egg on it (the egg for Damballa's dinner was changed weekly) and the small bottles of orgeat and of Florida water and put them under the head of my bed. I don't know whether Damballa intervened or not, but I doubt it, as he is a very jealous god and has no reason to aid and abet his competitors. What did happen, though, was that I grew more philosophic, not losing my feeling of inner security that John and I had solidified during the past months. I used these evenings without him to see some of the people I have mentioned and to rehearse more.

By then I had resigned from the library and lived on what I earned teaching and on payment from Ruth Page for a repeat of the ballet *La Giablesse.* There were also advances from our two major appearances due that year. We had gained recognition because of our Spanish War series of vignettes, because of the Cube Theatre, and because of a growing number of followers who were either attracted by their own need for this new diversion or were caught up in the still popular vogue of "New Negroism." I had not been thinking much about my writing career as an alleviation to my monetary situation, but my affiliation with the Writers' Project of the WPA brought, out of nowhere, with no known direct association, a number of encouraging encounters with publishers. Though the articles published did not bring high fees, each came at a time when the exposure solidified my position in the literary world and the remuneration was welcome and put to good use.

Journey to Accompong was accepted by Henry Holt during this period. Various articles on the Caribbean and on dance, particularly on Negro Dance, were published in the *Chicago Post* and in feature sections of other daily newspapers. During this period and the years to May 1948, before leaving for Europe, I surprised myself by publishing in periodicals, anthologies, and journals. At times, exhausted by the battle for survival with the responsibility of two to four dozen aspiring, at times aggressive young artists, I have thought of trying to become a professional writer and leaving the stage behind. At that time, just back from the Caribbean, however tempted I may have been by the response to my efforts at authorship, in the end the stage became not only a calling but a physical and spiritual necessity.

My most gratifying literary recognition at the time came from two articles published in *Esquire,* September and November 1939.[4] One day, I have no idea by whose instigation, the secretary of Al Smart, who with his brother, David, published *Esquire,* asked if I would be able to see Mr. Smart at his outer drive apartment to discuss an article for their magazine. With pleasure I accepted the invitation and met there Arnold Gingrich, close associate of the publishers and editor-in-chief of *Esquire.* I had heard of Gingrich from John who had been hired to design suggestions of minimal, seasonal costumes for a calendar featuring the Varga girls, usually undraped and bare bottomed. Arnold Gingrich was afraid that Varga, a gentle South American, was too unworldly to turn out the sophisticated nothings that *Esquire* readers could expect. Too, there was E. Simms Campbell's erotic Little Sultan and his buxom harem with impudently suggestive bylines. These features and its reputation for being "For Men Only" added to a certain circumspection on my part about being able to write for *Esquire*. But they had seen some of my feature articles in newspapers and felt that I could write for them; the catch was that no woman had, as yet, written for their magazine and I would have to use a pseudonym. But I would be well paid, and there might even be a third article. E. Simms Campbell would illustrate. I quickly accepted the offer, choosing the name "Kaye Dunn." My brother's son name was "Kaye," and "Dunn" was about as close as I could get to Dunham.

I had to send in my two articles as soon as possible. In the pleasant atmosphere of the luxurious apartment, I presented my subjects then and there. I already had outlines and copious notes for "La Boule Blanche" and "L'ag'ya," sketches of dances in Martinique, replete with folklore, photographs, social comment, and colorful atmosphere. They were pleased with both ideas. As soon as the articles were written, I was to go to New York to see E. Simms Campbell, who was living at that time somewhere in Westchester, I believe. I was sorry that Charles Sebree or John Pratt couldn't do the illustrations but awestruck at the proposal that such a prominent artist, admired by our group of friends as the first black artist to occupy a position of prominence with such a prestigious publication, would be illustrating the articles and that I would meet him in person to offer personal suggestions. . . .

While waiting for John to choose camps (Inez and I were both women who refused to give ground), Ruth and Bill and Sebree and I had discovered a beer garden on Lake Street, a real haven for the financially deprived. I had to, more than ever, curb some of my tendencies to extravagance. I think I was the only one with an assured income for the next couple of months. But my advances on two performances at the Goodman Theatre, which adjoined the Art Institute, and my windfall from *Esquire* had to cover a lot of ground because there was still carfare to pay for the rehearsing company, costumes and scenery to be made, my own living expenses, and fare from New York for Archie Savage and Papa Augustin, who had appeared at the YMHA in New York. I had sent for Archie because Talley Beatty was too young and immature to serve as my partner in such a number as *Barrelhouse Shimmy*. Archie was tall, sophisticated, and with a body like some of the better known Greek statues, a Praxiteles, perhaps. He had worked with Orson Welles in the Federal Theatre Harlem project and was famous in the New York theater world for his fall from a fifteen-foot tower to the stage floor in Welles's production of *Macbeth*. Papa Augustin was from Haiti and aside from being a Vodun priest, he was a master of Rada drums, some of which had been baptized with me at my *lavé tête*. He sang in a typical bush voice, an accompaniment to rhythms, singing himself the responses that I should have sung. He was determined to be my acolyte and granted me *mambo* status long before I had earned it.

The Lake Street beer garden was especially attractive to us because with every mug of ice-cold, foaming beer drawn from barrels behind an improvised bar, there would be, free of charge, a frankfurter, the like of which I have only found sold from wagons on the streets of Munich, late at night. They were long and thin (they must have been stuffed into the small intestines of the pig), highly charged with garlic, and dripping, now and then, with paprika-seasoned oil. There was no distracting music, but a good-natured hum filled the sawdust-floored arena, which could, and often did, accommodate two hundred people at long tables. Consuming free hot dogs and beer at ten cents a mug, an evening would pass quickly. John, when he was again in our camp, went with us, and sometimes our group would include boisterous Ike Clark and our more affluent friend, Barefield Gordon, son of a doctor who had migrated with his family to Chicago and lived down from the street from me on Grand Boulevard. Sometimes we would all go to one of the all-black or black-and-tan clubs proliferating on the South Side. Some of these had entrance fees, but most of them had no entrance or cover charge, and by careful planning, one could nurse two glasses of beer at twenty-five cents apiece or two gin or bourbon drinks at fifty cents each.

I especially remember those clubs which were territorial—that is, when Noble Sissle or Duke Ellington or Count Basie or Lionel Hampton came to town they played at the Terrace Garden on Grand Boulevard. (Most graduation, fraternity and sorority, "coming out," and seasonal dances for New Year, Christmas, Valentines Day, et cetera were at the Terrace Garden, but I had left these sorts of parties behind when I came to Chicago to live.) When the Terrace was not sold out for these formal affairs, there was still a cover charge so we didn't often go. The De Lisa Club was home to the drummer Red Nichols and his Five Pennies Band and where Ziggy Johnson, master dancer, who, with his elegantly shod, very small, lightning-fast feet, looking smaller because of his rotund body, trained and led the De Lisa Dancers. There I first saw Mae Barnes and Paul and Thelma Meers, tanned, more athletic replicas of Irene Castle and her husband Vernon. Ethel Waters was at home at the Pioneer Lounge, and Meade Lux Lewis, Pete Johnson, and Albert Ammons played classic boogie-woogie at the Clairemont club. They were with us later at the Martin Beck Theatre, where we made our first full company, Hurok Broadway opening and introduced the show at their two grand pianos, boogie-woogie concert style. They introduced a complete American third section to our *Tropical Revue* show. The classical virtuoso violinist Eddie South was, I believe, most often at the Pioneer Lounge. Sammy Dyer trained the Regal Chorus where Snake Hips Tucker frequently appeared, shiny hair and shiny black pants and cummerbund accentuating his double jointed "camel walk," undulating "Snake Hips," and collision-style bumps after a series of grinds. There was the Sunset Lounge on Thirty-ninth Street, which I vaguely remember as having excellent fried chicken and barbecue.

John and I were in the black-and-tan (mixed black and white audience) Dave's on Garfield Boulevard, second floor, when we spotted Lucille Ellis. There she was, a slender, agile Josephine Baker. Without Lucille, and later on Lenwood [Morris] and Van [Vanoye Aikens], I don't think there would have been a Dunham Company. Certainly not of the stature it was. Each contributed in his own way, but Lucille, who couldn't have been over sixteen then, became company mother, first assistant to John in wardrobe, rehearsal deputy for Lenwood, and prima ballerina, ranging in technique from ballet to primitive to Dunham. Just now she is in Chicago battling her way into establishing a bona fide school of Dunham Technique. Lucille's dependability became almost as important to our institution as her dance, which was frequently nothing short of sensational. She interpreted *Los Indios, Tango,* and *Flaming Youth* as no one else could. And in between she picked up clothes backstage after novices, ironed ruffles on *Shango* dresses, or scolded some of the newcomers about faulty on-stage delivery.

One of several barbecue stands frequented by John and me was the small, nameless shack on State Street between Thirty-seventh and Thirty-eighth. It was on the east side of the street facing the stockyards, and any breeze from the west brought an odor of death, animal excrement, singed hair, and freshly dried blood. The outdoor smells were replaced by the mouth-watering smells of the pits inside. As we entered, the left side of the shack was ten feet of glowing charcoal and hickory logs on which sides of pork spareribs and pigs' feet, tails, and snouts sizzled on first contact with the fire, then were moved to the back of the grill to luxuriate in the pungent spicy smoke of the pit. We could see at the far end behind the counter a glass case with piles of raw parts of pork, beef, lamb, and chicken stacked awaiting the fire ritual. A cook wearing a bloodstained apron decided when the fire should be fed. He was the owner and butcher, we learned, but the various wives or women who served the counter, a different one every few weeks, handled the orders of those of us who ate in the small front area and the orders to take out, which were many. The light of a single bulb scarcely illuminated the whole, but the barbecue pit threw a dim glow onto the plasterboard ceiling and hospital-green walls. John was the only white person to frequent the place the many nights we were there, but now and then someone who was Mexican or Chinese would stand at the carry-out counter, tourists in the exotic climate. We would stand patiently in line, picking out cuts of ribs to take to one of the three tables in the room. We were disappointed if some itinerant pianist were not there to play the battered old piano and sing the blues or some of those lonely, defeatism work songs, or maybe a gospel hymn set to blues harmony and rhythm. The hot sauce for the ribs reminded me of Haitian *ti malis* sauce—more liquid than one uses now for synthetic barbecue sauces, with no sugar, many jalapeño peppers, onions, garlic, just enough vinegar to counteract the richness of the ribs, and swirls of lemon rind.

The tips of those who sat at the tables compensated whatever musician happened to pass by. Occasionally someone standing in line at the counter would do two or three dance steps over to the piano and drop ten cents into the cigar box on top. We never saw the pianist eat, but the glass beside the collection box was never empty; a nod without breaking the rhythm of his rendition would bring the proprietor from behind the bar counter to fill the glass from a bottle carried under his apron. As we became known at the place we would now and then order a drink of what must have been "moonshine," though Prohibition was over at the time, as I recall. Otherwise we drank a dark pink soda-pop labeled "strawberry" on the bottle top. That was before the craze of assorted colas and diet drinks. Strawberry soda goes exceptionally well with barbecue. From time to time, whatever entertainer would go into his own reveries, carried far back into some hazy vision of the past. I wonder if cocaine was as popular here as it was, I was aware, among most black performing artists of the day. But though appearing to be what is known as "stoned," I decided that in places like this (I knew no other quite like it in Chicago, but in Detroit and even here in East Saint Louis I have seen near facsimiles) the energy generated by the heady smells from the pit, the down-to-earth expressions of appreciation from the audience, and some form of alcohol supplanted any need for other stimuli. When appearing in Chicago in later years, I tried several times to locate this place, but it had been long forgotten, probably returned to the warmer climate of the black ghettos of the South. Or just put aside till some later day.

It was here at this barbecue shack that I first met Kokomo, guitar player from Kokomo, Indiana, that state of Garveyites, bitter steel mill strikes, and deep-seated racial prejudice. Kokomo played the guitar and sang the blues as I never heard the blues played or sung. The pain in him came from a deeper source than the violence of Indiana. I danced one of my rare solo offerings to a blues of Kokomo's, winding around him on the floor of the Lincoln Theatre stage clothed in a white shirt and the worn navy blue corduroy skirt that had done me such faithful service when I followed the drums and rituals in the Caribbean. Onstage, Kokomo sat in a center spotlight on a battered wooden chair like those at our barbecue shack.

It was at the barbecue shack that I heard the "Barrelhouse Shimmy," anonymously composed and played. I believe the first concepts of the movement of the shimmy came from these after hours spots; even way back when, as a child, I would see Ethel Waters at the Monogram Variety House with a feather duster tied around her waist, bouncing it back and forth as she described in what manner she would welcome her absconded man when he returned, with the robust side to side twist of the shimmy. *Barrelhouse Shimmy* with *Batucada* and *Floyd's Guitar Blues* became trademarks for me over the thirty and more years of the company touring. My first *Barrelhouse* partner was Archie Savage, whose mother made us so welcome on our first engagement in New York. Archie, with his New York street savvy, helped in the creation of the number. After Archie had left us to follow Ethel Waters when *Cabin in the Sky* closed in Los Angeles, Joe Stevenson came as *Barrelhouse* partner (Los Angeles); then Roger Ohardieno, a New York Haitian; then Vanoye Aikens, who was my last partner and one of the three lead dancers for more than twenty years. . . .

The Goodman Theatre was a small, perfectly equipped theater. Those dancers who preferred its intimacy to the theaters of the Loop, or who couldn't afford the demands of these tightly union-controlled houses, waited in line for opening dates at the Goodman. Vera Mirova, Jack Cole,

Grace and Kurt Graff, Agna Enters, and Agnes DeMille were among those to whom the Goodman became home. After our two performances, our only returns to Chicago would be in the largest of the downtown theaters. I never felt comfortable appearing in Chicago after the Goodman. Our audiences were large but unresponsive compared to other cities, as though expecting some miracle from their native daughter. Evidently I could not or would not produce what was expected of me. But I doubt if I would have altered the show anyway. The critics seemed to be waiting to inflict some lethal blow, but some were kind, even enthusiastic. Somehow, until many years later, the local girl made good was never to be a prophet in her own land. Then, the unfreezing came after the rest of the world had proclaimed her, after she had written books, after she had trail blazed with a company of fifty, never subsidized by the U.S. government, and pioneered a new system of performing arts education in America and other countries. It was disappointing but not entirely unexpected.

At the Goodman Theatre, as part of the Americana I introduced *Br'er Rabbit an' de Tah Baby,* a folk tale told me by my father, which portrayed one of Br'er Rabbit's many escapades. This time he falls in love with a tar baby set as a scarecrow in the middle of the cabbage patch, the patch surrounded by a low white picket fence. Talley was Br'er Rabbit. Uncle Remus passed down the road at the opening, and the tar baby began to melt little by little in the hot sun. Br'er Rabbit ignores him until after his solo, relating chiefly to the cabbage patch, when he leaps lightly over the picket fence. His courtship is brief, and then he entices the tar baby to dance. Now well on the way to melting entirely, the tar baby manages a few steps with Br'er Rabbit before he becomes hopelessly entangled. I was the tar baby. John designed my costume, which was black-glazed chintz, a long-sleeved bodice, a black tutu, black tights, black ballet slippers, long black shiny gloves, and a perky boater hat with small braids sewn in the back over my own hair. Charles Sebree did the rest of the costumes and the decor, with the exception of outlandishly large cabbages placed around the tar baby behind the picket fence, all made by John's brother Davis.

A curtain after the pas de deux allowed the removal of the fence and cabbages, and Uncle Remus is discovered seated down stage right in an overhead spotlight. Dancers enter from the stage left and right with the left-right shuffle rhythm of "traveling" plantation dances, arms swinging loosely, greeting each other with the festivity of a Saturday-night get-together. Noble Sissle had shown me a few of these all-but-forgotten plantation square-dance steps, but it wasn't until I had done some coaching with Tom Fletcher, in his eighties I should imagine by the time we met in New York in the early forties, that I was able to complete these authentic plantation dances and their lively calls.

"Good evenin', Sister, good evenin'!" "Good evenin', Brother! Right fine thank-y!'" The dancers immediately formed a square without breaking rhythm. Then they took orders from the "leader," which I was at the Goodman concerts. I have stood in the wings of whatever theater we were playing, transfixed by the flow of choreographic orders from the leader— Gordon Simpson's rich basso profundo, or Ural Wilson's baritone. Seated on a stool carried from stage right to left, downstage of the dancers, the calls would direct and the dancers in the square would respond.

"Salute your corners,
Now your partners.
Now all grab hands and sashay to the center!"
Bottoms swaying, they would all bend over into the center gossiping.
"Now pas mala back."

After that came a series of directions. Many of them humorous, many double entendre—like walking up the steps and knocking at your neighbor's door, going on in and grabbing her tight before swinging her. It was bright, gay, and exuded an air of exuberance and authenticity that I felt surpassed the western and southern white country square dancers. Perhaps I was just prejudiced, as surely Agnes DeMille's square dances in Oklahoma left nothing to be desired, and surely the Western square-dance revival in America was due to her. We ended with a call for the "juba," and after high leaps in the air, the dancers formed a circle on the floor, rocking side to side to begin the circle dances. As some stood up whirling and keeping rhythm on their thighs, slapping an open palm and back of the hand in the "hambone," others in the center of the circle one at a time demonstrated "fallin' off a log," "Palmer House," and other mimetic steps known only to black folk and finally revived after a hiatus of more than fifty years. My reasoning in presenting these robust but graceful dances was that if I could research and present the equivalent from other countries, I could not consider myself a conscientious field anthropologist if I neglected the rich heritage of the American Negro. I have had to defend on more than one occasion the Americana section of the program, always in the United States. At one time it was to a group of "comrades" who in the early days in New York somehow felt this exposé of black culture to be undignified; at another time in San Francisco years later, when a group of militant brothers failed to see the historic value of their own roots.

But all were highly amused by the Caribbean counterparts, beguine and *majumba* of *L'Ag'ya*.

Another number that made its debut at the Goodman was *Rara Tonga*. There was a program-cover drawing of me with Tommy Gomez and Roger Ohardieno by Sebree with costumes by John Pratt [see figure 8 in the photo gallery]. I had borrowed an African telegraph drum from one of my library friends and sat at this on a platform in a circle of light upstage. The drum was a magnificent example of Congo craftsmanship, a solid instrument carved from a tree trunk. The wood was paper thin at the two horizontal slats, which were separated from each other by about three inches. The interior wood thickened to the bottom, about fourteen inches from the slit at the top. The drum was about four feet long; both ends were about four inches in thickness. It had a remarkable range of tones, and since its original use was to send messages for miles over field, mountain, valley, and jungle, the tones penetrated the largest of theaters. In the end, on tour I was leading from the platform, the several drummers squatted on Cuban, Haitian, African, and Pacific instruments on stage, as well as the orchestra in the pit, with trap and timpani in the percussion section. I had to work closely with the conductor to hold the rhythms together.

Archie and Papa Augustin arrived in Chicago early to rehearse the show with us. Although I knew what I wanted in *Barrelhouse,* Archie, laconic and experienced in the way the man in *Barrelhouse* had to be, added dimensions to the choreography I had dreamed of since the barbecue shack and Kokomo. Papa Augustin was a legitimate priest of the Rada-Dahomey cult in Haiti and of course had carefully followed all of my initiations through the chain of Vodun priests extending through the Caribbean, South America, North America, and Africa. As I began to know Papa better I trusted him with just about all of my problems and aspirations. He carried with him a small altar in front of which he practiced his alchemy—sometimes to the Rada-Dahomey gods, sometimes to the Congo warlike Petro gods. Of course we petitioned Damballa before the Goodman opening. The right invocations; the powders that Papa brought with him, perfumes, and a white rooster sacrificed on Mrs. Hall's back porch with my own necklaces and rattles and bells, orgeat and Florida water ensured the success of the two day performances. The theater was sold out, and the critics were more favorable than ever, with the exception of the *Chicago Tribune,* which at that time went out of its way to ignore or diminish most black achievement.

These performances, along with Papa Augustin's sorcery, promoted a number of changes in my escalating career. The publicity manager of the Goodman Theatre, Louise Dale Spoor, decided to take on Katherine Dunham and Company. But before she could arrange a tour, Mary Hunter, whom I had not seen since the E. Simms Campbell New York experience, brought Louis Schaeffer of the International Ladies Garment Workers' Union to see us in rehearsal, having in mind the transport of a large part of the company (fifteen members) to New York, where I would place them in the musical *Pins and Needles,* the first of the Broadway topical musicals, written by Harold Rome.[5] But the only way of supporting the company, which by now had begun an inveterate, and, I found out, irreversible habit of depending on me for increased financing, was to look for other work while waiting for these dreams to materialize. There was the matter of daily carfare for rehearsal and classes and a number of other expenses associated with rehearsal and performance.

The Sherman Hotel on the corner of Randolph and Clark streets advertised a special dining and dancing room called the Panther Room. . . . Things went well at the Panther Room. . . . I sang with more daring than voice, and *Cumbancha* and *Bruja Manigua* became part of our future nightclub engagements. There was no limit to our dreams after the stunning success of the Sherman Hotel, and in the years that followed Hollywood, we were habitués of Las Vegas, Palm Springs, Reno, Ciro's, and other much fought-over nightspots in this country.

An immediate pleasant surprise came when George Balanchine appeared one night after our first show. (We did two nightly.) Of all things, he had been spurred on by Mary Hunter, who, now married to Jack Sullivan, had long since moved to New York to become a featured performer in Dan Golenpaul's show *Easy Aces* with Goodman Ace. Mary, it seems never stopped thinking about us or planning for my personal growth. Though Louise Schaeffer had in hand our acceptance of the contract for the Labor Stage he had hastily sent me after seeing us at the Goodman, the prospect of playing Sweet Georgia Brown in Ethel Waters's *Cabin in the Sky,* assisting George Balanchine in choreography, and staging all of this at the same time left me dumbfounded.[6] I insisted that our entire company appearing in the new version of *Pins and Needles* be requisitioned for *Cabin.* Mary also arranged with Louis Schaeffer to cosponsor a Sunday afternoon and night performance at the Windsor Theatre on Forty-fifth Street, where *Pins and Needles* was playing. I had to make a few changes in the company; not all had their parents' permission to travel such a distance with me and for an indeterminate period of time. Just about now I began that costly enterprise of taking into the company potential members as apprentices. Louise Dale Spoor realized that she would have no position in my escalating career. We parted good friends and she continued with her recent marriage and her work at the Goodman.

The cost of putting on the Sherman show had been terrific, as I was unaccustomed to producing on such a scale. John and I both had dedicated whatever money was on hand or available to clothes and properties and rehearsals with Paquita Anderson for the nightclub show. Now began frantic efforts to borrow for rehearsal and transportation costs. Further costumes, scenery, and props for our descent on New York were needed. We would have to count on Mary and Jack Sullivan for assistance and counsel. For the first time I began to have stage fright.

I was unquiet about my position with Ethel Waters, and rightly. There would be summer rehearsal with a fall opening of *Cabin in the Sky*, after the Windsor Theatre. I had recent memories of her in a Chicago nightclub and recalled her as a majestically tall woman with a scowl on her face as frequent as that famous smile exposing the separation between her two front teeth as she often erupted into her incomparable banter with Butterbeans and Susie, or into poignant or raucous song. And I remembered the feather duster tied around her waist and jerking a foot in front of her as she executed perfectly timed bumps and grinds intended for her missing or future man, I don't remember which. This latter memory stemmed from early childhood when Irene or Aunt Lulu would take my brother and me from our kerosene-heated cold-water flat to the Monogram Variety House to keep warm for a few hours.

We frequently stayed through two or three shows, often sleeping through a whole show burrowing into each other for further warmth in the moist malodorous atmosphere given off by unwashed bodies and undigested cheap wine and gin. It is not only the warmth from the freezing Chicago winters that I remember, but here were imprinted on me the nostalgias and humor and pathos of the black race. Harry Stack Sullivan (psychiatrist) calls it "diffused optimism," this sustaining quality of the black race expressed in song and rhythm. Frantz Fanon calls it "tragic optimism." I have recognized both in myself but have added a third after so many years, "incurable. . . ."

So I left the apartment—lock, stock, and barrel—and packed my personal belongings to prepare for the trek to New York. John opted to accompany the company and baggage on the train. I would fly alone. I welcomed this because I had begun to enter a zombie state in breaking, I knew, forever, the ties of Chicago, which had after all given us so much. I concentrated with an organic confidence on the overriding task before me of conquering Broadway, because without this I could foresee, in a paranoid fashion this new thing, the company to which I had devoted entirely my cognitive and affective capacities, drifting from one anxiety to another, probably nightclubs and the Goodman Theatre. But, I was so buttressed by "diffused optimism" that fear of failure was quickly routed. The full meaning of "tragic" optimism affected me much later.

NOTES

1. Mary Hunter Wolf was a producer and theater director who founded the American Actors Company in New York and collaborated with artists including Katherine Dunham, Jerome Robbins, Horton Foote, and Agnes DeMille during a long career that spanned work in theatre, television, and radio. She was the founder and executive director of the Stratford, Connecticut, American Shakespeare Festival Theater [Eds.].

2. Inez Cunningham Stark was a wealthy Chicago patron of the arts who is best known for her association with the Pulitzer prize–winning poet Gwendolyn Brooks, who attended a modern poetry workshop of Stark's at the South Side Community Art Center in 1941 [Eds.].

3. Both articles from *Esquire* are reproduced in this volume, "La Boule Blanche," pp. 195–200, and "L'ag'ya of Martinique," pp. 201–207 [Eds.].

4. Agnes DeMille (1905–1993) was an American dancer and choreographer credited with incorporating popular dance idioms into ballet and reconceptualizing the Broadway musical scene. She choreographed *Black Ritual* (1940) for the American Ballet Theatre, thought to be the first to use African American dancers, including Lavinia Williams, a future principal dancer with the Dunham Company. Some of her best-known ballets include *Rodeo* (1942), *Three Virgins and a Devil* (1942), and *Fall River Legend* (1948). She choreographed some of the biggest Broadway hits of the 1940s and 1950s, including *Oklahoma* (1943), *Carousel* (1945), *Gentlemen Prefer Blondes* (1949), and *Paint Your Wagon* (1951) [Eds.].

5. *Pins and Needles* was a long-running musical revue, with sketches by several writers and music and lyrics mostly by Harold J. Rome. Produced by the International Ladies Garment Workers' Union Players, it was first performed at the Labor Stage Studios, New York, in June 1936, with dances directed by Adele Jerome. It opened on Broadway at the Labor Stage Theatre on 27 November 1937, with dances directed by Gluck Sandor and choreography by Benjamin Zemach. Katherine Dunham was dance director during the run of the second edition, entitled successively *Pins and Needles 1939* and *Pins and Needles 1940,* after the show had moved to the Windsor Theatre on 26 June 1939 [Eds.].

6. Ethel Waters (1896–1977) was a blues vocalist and actress. She was reportedly the first woman to sing W. C. Handy's "St. Louis Blues" on stage, and went on to record

classics, including "Down Home Blues," "Oh Daddy," and "Stormy Weather." After performing on the vaudeville circuit, she began a successful career in many Broadway productions, including *Rhapsody in Black* (1931), *As Thousands Cheer* (1933), *Cabin in the Sky* (1940–41) and *The Member of the Wedding* (1950). The latter performance earned her the New York Drama Critics' Circle Award. During her career she performed with musicians such as Duke Ellington, Fletcher Henderson, and Benny Goodman, and she and is recognized as one of the first African American artists to receive equal billing as her white colleagues. Waters also appeared in many television productions and was nominated for an Academy Award for Best Supporting Actress in 1949 for the film *Pinky.* She wrote two autobiographies, *His Eye Is on the Sparrow* (1951) and *To Me It's Wonderful* (1972) *[Eds.].*

Early New York Collaborations

KATHERINE DUNHAM

My first weeks in New York, while we were rehearsing with the Labor
Stage production *Pins and Needles,* there were no problems of where to
live. Mary Hunter and Jack Sullivan had taken an apartment on East
Twenty-third Street in a new building facing Gramercy Park and invited
me to stay with them, at least temporarily. It had a doorman, which made
late-night return more comfortable, and was easily accessible to the Windsor Theatre, Forty-fourth and Seventh Avenues. Even after the show was
under way and I had designed for our company the biblical scene *Mene
Mene Tekel Upharsin* ("You have been tried in the scales and found wanting"), an opening, a finale and some staging of crowd scenes, I continued
to stay with Jack and Mary. Harold Rome's music was exceptionally
effervescent, and for the first time, a musical of social commentary took
Broadway by storm. With the exception of two or three professionals
whose names I have forgotten and, of course, our company, the show was
cast entirely from the International Ladies' Garment Workers Union
(ILGWU), and it was produced by Louis Schaeffer and Labor Stage. My
days were filled with hard work and anxieties while we prepared for our
Windsor Theatre Sunday afternoon and night performances.

Mary Hunter and Louis Schaeffer were our producers at the Windsor.
There were considerable changes from the Goodman Theatre program.
Woman with the Cigar became a full production number, which closed

SOURCE: Katherine Dunham, excerpts from Book 2 of "Minefields," an unpublished
work in progress, in the Katherine Mary Dunham Papers, Special Collections, Morris
Library, Southern Illinois University, Carbondale. Copyright 2005 by Katherine
Dunham. Used by permission. The majority of the manuscript was written between
1980–1989. Minor corrections and changes of editorial style have been made.

the first act. Harl McDonald's *Mexican Rhumba,* with its setting of two immense pylons, one broken and its fragments resting on the steps to the platform, brought applause when the curtains opened and again when, from stage left, six ladies entered. They came in with a sweeping, hip-emphasized movement, wearing huge, heavy white butcher's linen dresses trimmed with what John called "blind lace" over-embroidered with cotton ropes, long black braids hanging down their backs, white baskets filled with flowers and long blue pheasant feathers on their heads. I had fallen in love with a Brazilian song, "*Batucada,*" written by Don Alfonso. When I had first heard it, I do not know, but once in the program it stayed for the duration; its haunting melody trailed us through all of the countries of the world where we appeared for almost thirty years. Originally the five men in dark blue poplin and black felt hats were rope makers. As years went by, the nets draped downstage and in the second portal transported the scene, as reported by critics, to a fishing village. I was astonished to learn that the rope that was thrown to me off stage and that I wove into and out of, playfully flirting with the men, was presumed to be a fishing line! It made no difference in the enthusiastic reception of the number I sang and danced with a languorous abandon that delighted me as much as it did the audience. With time it seemed to become more seductive, and the audiences even more seduced!

All of this time I also taught at Labor Stage. It was a rewarding experience and allowed me to audition many dancers for the larger company needed for *Cabin in the Sky,* the contract for which by now was signed and sealed. *Tropics* and *Le Jazz Hot,* for so the Sunday shows were called, used many of the Goodman Theatre and Sherman Hotel dancers: Archie Savage; Carmencita Romero; Rita Christiani, beautiful Rita who was, I believe, from Trinidad and is now a nurse in Chicago; Talley Beatty and his cousin Laverne French; and Lavinia Williams; among others. Windsor Theatre additions were Lauwanne Ingram, Claude Marchant Brown (later Claude Marchant), Bobby Gray, Gino Moxier, Alexander McDonald, Richardena Jackson, Delores Harper; and some from the short-lived *Tropical Pinafore,* including Lucille Ellis, Carmela el Khoury, Tommy Gomez, and Frank Neal, who later became a painter of note. Joining the augmented corps de ballet for *Cabin in the Sky* were Enid Mosier, Royce Wallace, and others. Agnes DeMille was very helpful in steering some of her black company, gotten together for a special performance of Ballet Theatre, to the Dunham Company, which she assured them would run longer. After thirteen triumphant Sundays, we closed in order to concentrate on *Cabin.*

Louis Schaeffer's dream was to have some enormous spectacle showcase for, if not all, at least hundreds of ILGWU members. My special contribution to *I Hear America Singing,* the pageant he planned, was to be choreography and the staging of such numbers as Vachel Lindsay's *Rivers.* The show was to be presented in the vast old Madison Square Garden on midtown Eighth Avenue. When he told me that thousands would perform, I told Louis about John's expertise in costuming huge numbers of people for very limited funds for the Federal Theatre. Louis Schaeffer was convinced by my enthusiasm and by what he had already seen. John was sent for and rather reluctantly (he had come to New York when the *Swing Mikado* had been taken over by private producers and found himself a sort of greenhorn, out-of-town boy in the Big City) established himself in a low-ceilinged dirt-floor basement cave of the ILGWU headquarters building with a solitary black lady with severely twisted, crippled hands, stitching up hundreds of outfits which he was cutting out of hundreds of yards of garment wholesale-area cheap material. The most important ones were surplice-inspired robes for the lady mandolin players, more than five hundred of them, who were the pride of the ILGWU Recreation-for-Everyone program. There were hundreds of American Indian braves' outfits, fringed buckskins actually made of Japanese cotton duveteen. John found some time to work on our concert at the Windsor Theatre, especially costumes for *Honky Tonk Train,* incredible patchworks of every tartan, every plaid, in every material to be found. Their kaleidoscope effect was heightened by dangling patches of large multicolored paillettes. Having finished *I Hear America Singing,* John was contracted to costume a Labor Stage serious drama, *Altged of Illinois,* in early stages of rehearsal, but it died and John returned to Chicago to work on *Tropical Pinafore,* in which we were both very much interested.

Mary Hunter had arranged for a one-hour, color television broadcast for CBS, its first full-length dance program. I had never seen television but was thrilled at the idea of being another "first." Our show turned into a travelogue of many places, with Mary narrating; the Pacific Islands (*Rara Tonga*), Haiti (by now I had developed a suite of Haitian songs and dances), Cuba (a suite of dances: *Son, Rhumba*), the deep south of North America (square dances, *Barrelhouse Shimmy*) and, of course, the Brazilian *Batucada.* I do not remember what else, but I do know that the light required for television in those days blistered the lino on which we danced as well as our bare feet. By the time the program reached *Honky Tonk Train,* our only shod number in the entire repertoire, we could hardly squeeze into our Capezio shoes. For some time afterward I was shy of television, but I made up for any hiatus once we reached Europe. . . .

So many people entered my life at this time. I think especially of Alfred Fisher, who for a brief period was our manager. How I met him I do not remember. He was an extremely neat, almost self-effacing European, probably from Vienna. It was unfortunate that he fell in love with me, or so acted, because, although John Pratt had not come to New York [to live] during all of this period, there was no question as to where my emotional interest lay. My phone calls to Chicago were frequent, then frantic. John would promise to arrive in two days, or wonder why I had not received his last letter. It took me awhile to realize that he was either fence-mending his finances or making an effort to straighten out the tangled and confused web of his personal life. I knew that most of the confusion came from Inez Stark, and on more than one occasion Papa Augustin stayed late in my dressing room at our improvised altar to petition, invoke, demand, and insist on aid for my troubled heart from my Haitian protectors. . . .

Before the opening of *Cabin,* Alfred Fisher began trying to dress me and there trod on dangerous ground. John had made me several outfits he considered high fashion and suitable for my New York debut, but Alfred Fisher envisioned me in casual European modes. I could not appreciate the Swiss and Austrian sports clothes; I would see all sorts of French imports far more to my liking, but also beyond my financial means, on Lexington and Madison and Fifth Avenues. After one exhausting afternoon rejecting one Viennese creation after another, I gave in and borrowed enough from Alfred Fisher to purchase a green gabardine raincoat and skirt with dark green leather trimming. There was a matching Australian soldier–type hat, turned up on one side, that completed the outfit I had just barely tolerated, discarding it the minute I saw Karinska's fabulous designs.

Karinska, the Russian designer who had been engaged for *Cabin in the Sky,* was the most important designer in my life, after John Pratt, but somehow I could not feel comfortable in her designs for *Cabin.*[1] She was sought after, practically fought over, by theater and concert producers. I felt at home with my Russian cohorts; Balanchine, staging and choreography (I was deep into both of these with him); Vernon Duke (Dukelsky), music composer; Boris Aronson, scenic designer; Karinska, costume designer except for my own costumes. In addition to the coterie of Russians, there was John La Touche, who wrote the lyrics and became my good friend over the years.

Alfred Fisher represented me as much as I would let him. In desperation, after my refusal to wear Karinska's wardrobe, he sent for John Pratt. Karinska seemed to be happy to execute John's designs and to be relieved of the pressure of trying to satisfy me. Wardrobe mistresses were cajoled into making last-minute adaptations and remodelings for the company dancers. I had anticipated a certain coolness from the rest of the staff, but things went smoothly, especially after costume rehearsals that satisfied everyone. They all admired John's clothes and were fond of him personally.

Alfred had engaged a Viennese singing coach for me. So far, I had sung in whatever key Paquita Anderson and Jose Manzanares decided for me. Truthfully, I was more frightened of the singing demands than the acting ones. The voice professor Alfred found had coached the famous of the Metropolitan Opera and the celebrated of the European scene. He was especially fond of telling me the various "Aidas" who owed their success to him. At first he seemed too operatically inclined for my limited experience, but he was patient and before or after my lessons, whether to put me at ease or to acquaint me with others who were not necessarily known as vocalists, he would introduce me to such pupils (Viennese all) as Dolly Haas and Elizabeth Bergner. Thanks to Alfred Fisher I entered my opening night with more assurance vocally, and at the Martin Beck and on return engagements to New York, the Viennese became solid supporters of our shows.

There were also those terrible days when I would wake up voiceless with inflamed tonsils. They had been removed earlier but were growing in again! I would rush to my professor's South Park West apartment for therapeutic vocalization or, with Alfred, to another Viennese, a throat specialist with a huge stomach. I remember this stomach because to be examined I had to spread my legs dancer-wide to allow him to direct his headlamp into my throat and probe with his life-saving instruments. Nothing was ever terribly wrong, but without this care I am sure I would have been relieved of my *Cabin* contract during the early days of the Broadway run. I knew that much of my problem was psychosomatic. Ethel Waters was not an easy person to confront. My role as Sweet Georgia Brown dictated that I be in the company of Miss Waters for two hours every night, to say nothing of rehearsals and matinees. Many a day I docilely wore a neck brace and refrained from speaking at all until performance time. Periodically I would be fortunate enough to have an appointment with Max Jacobson, my medical guru, and always felt more secure and fortified after one of his "cocktails," chiefly a mixture of vitamins, enzymes, minerals, and perhaps even a trace of amphetamine. Max saved my life over and over again during my many years of stressful travels.

Ethel Waters and ailing tonsils were minor afflictions compared to the overwhelming problem of where to live in mid-town New York. My widened horizons, beginning with my Caribbean research days, made me sensitive to being confined to Harlem. I had been there to late-night bars and the equivalent of soul-food restaurants but, by chance or design, saw no evidence of the environment in which I would like to live, especially alone. Also, I seemed driven to trail-blaze again, and whether John was in town or not, I thought of him and realized that, outside our protective coterie of Chicago, or circumscribed New York professional friends or acquaintances, we not only had no true milieu in which to circulate, but no roots, which all Cancerians must have to survive. Because of coinciding birth signs, we have understood each other over the years. Sometimes I have wondered if it is best to be mated to the same sign of the Zodiac, if there isn't such a thing as knowing more about each other than one should. I have taken great consolation from examining the differences between male and female character analyses of "Moon children!" With a certain acerbity I have pointed out to John the almost irremediable failings of Cancer men in juxtaposition to Cancer women. I gave that up long ago as an unrewarding, nonproductive sport. Life became easier.

Ruth Attaway had opened on Broadway in *You Can't Take It with You* some months before my debut in *Cabin*. We saw each other rarely but with the same friendship as always. She had found a small apartment on West Sixty-sixth Street, off of Central Park West. The location was ideal, but she had no place for me in what amounted to one room, kitchen, and bath; and also, her building was full. It was one of those small places that one came upon in New York by word of mouth or accident. It was the only apartment of its kind that I knew of for years. Most property owners avoided, and still do, black or a growing group of Hispanic apartment seekers like the plague. The Sixty-sixth Street building was next door to a fashionable riding academy stable. When I visited Ruth there, the building seemed to be a fixture growing out of the stable; the sounds and smells of horses dominated the narrow little apartment building but it seemed the most desirable location in all of New York to me. Once in a while someone would move because of the sound and smell of the stable or whatever, and this gave me hope for the future, but the in-between period was one of the strangest in my life before and after *Cabin*. . . .

[One day Ruth] brought me the exhilarating news that the sixth-floor apartment in her building would be free in two weeks! "Tragic," "diffused," or "incurable," my optimism had carried me through one of the most difficult, utterly isolated periods of my life. How carefully I walked those days. I didn't need a minesweeper to avoid confrontations with Ethel Waters. I simply reacted to her antagonism by immersing myself in the company until the show opened, and then in the audience and what I must do to conquer and retain at least some portion for Dunham and Company. The apartment house on West Sixty-sixth Street was in the middle of the block and, as I have said, just about as close as it could get to the stable next door. It was one of those unlikely situations in which a white landowner had, for reasons unknown to the occupants of the building, gradually introduced black tenants unsuccessfully scouring for midtown housing. Many of these were in theater or students or aspirants. The superintendent was also white, and I paid him monthly with alacrity. To my knowledge, I never saw the owner. At any rate, for me it was a lifesaver.

The apartments were tiny—one in front and one in back on my floor, the sixth, which was the top. Being so far up presented a problem from the first day. I learned to stop and rest my ever-ailing knees at the second and fourth floors. I also put a small chair on the fourth-floor landing because it was there that I felt completely depleted by what I learned from my University of Chicago physician was degenerative arthritis. My arthritis was undoubtedly helped by the fact that I did not take his advice and stop dancing. My faith in Papa Augustin as a conduit to my Haitian protectors was also comforting. The element of hope is extremely important to those who suffer from any chronic illness; somehow I feel this is even more so in the case of arthritics, being now firmly established as one myself. Once in the apartment, I did not have to engage in circumspect Vodun ceremonies behind a locked dressing-room door. (I wonder what was gossiped about concerning these meetings with my Papa Augustin? My reputation as an initiated follower of the Haitian Vodun had not yet flowered outside the country of its origin.)

My miniscule apartment—a front room, a miniature bath, the smallest kitchen I had ever seen, known by some as a "Pullman" kitchen—was a luxury to me. The living room was also my studio bedroom and had a small altar in the corner where Vodun and later Santero paraphernalia were stored behind a Second Avenue folding screen. Santería, or Cuban Vodun, was just entering my life by way of two Cuban drummers, La Rosa Estrada and Julio Mendez, as well as one Dutch Antilles drummer, Gaucho Vanderhans. All three had been with us at the Windsor Theater and now livened the "Hell" scene in *Cabin*. Little by little I was being introduced into a Cuban–Yoruba–West-Coast African belief, close to, but different from the Haitian Rada-Dahomey-Congo-Pétro experiences of mine in Haiti.

Ruth lived on the fourth floor but soon moved into a larger place in Harlem. The apartment just behind mine became vacant, so, to diminish noise, since I would be sleeping late once *Cabin* opened, I kept the front apartment for an office and room for a secretary-bodyguard, of whom I shall write later, and for the overflow of our not-too-frequent parties. John and I shared the back studio when he was in town, and the room became quite attractive once we had paid a few visits to the second-hand furniture and antique shops on Second Avenue. I remember especially a pair of tufted General Grant–period armchairs covered with canary-yellow brocade, their black walnut bases lightly traced with gold. (I wonder if Talley Beatty remembered these antique chairs? He lived in my apartment for a while while I toured with *Cabin,* and he managed to mistreat them beyond repair!) A studio couch was covered with a red and yellow Indian-print spread. The windows of the back apartment overlooked the roof of a brick building that must have been added to the stable, leaving room for a fire escape between the two buildings. Whenever I felt inclined to be annoyed by the restless stomping of the horses tethered in the stalls on the other side of my wall, or the odor of stable accented by quantities of Glover's Mange Cure, with which they sprayed the animals at the least sign of skin irritation I thought of the house on East Sixty-sixth Street and accepted with pleasure the vicissitudes of the two small cupboards which were my apartments on West Sixty-sixth Street. (I recognized Glover's mange cure because my mother used it on my hair for dandruff. I carried its tarry odor in my hair and on my pillows for days. It was supposed to make the hair grow and, wanting long braids, I supported it for this reason.) The windows were curtained with billowing white cotton, which blocked the view of the roofs below but allowed just enough sun to seep in on bright afternoons.

John had brought from Chicago a pair of his Blackamoors, Venetian guilt and polychrome figures, and a huge clam shell from the Great Barrier Reef of Australia. The very heavy shall was placed on the black-lacquered commode and finally ended up, years later, at the bottom of my private swimming pool on our Leclerc property in Haiti. On a low coffee table with supporting columns pickled in antique gold (by me) sat a small tray with my most prized possession, a set of *millefleurs* demitasse cups, lined and banded in gold. For some reason the landlord had recently replaced linoleum floors with natural oak, lightly varnished. Somehow I found space for my Thirty-fifth Street, Chicago record player. My salary was often spent before the week was out, but advances to stars, which I felt myself to be before long, were easily come by on Broadway. John and I did a lot of Second Avenue shopping and went to nightclubs and to Sardi's and to expensive Chinese restaurants in midtown. These restaurants were a striking contrast, especially in price, to the smaller family restaurants in Chinatown, Chicago, where we had eaten in student days. We went to the Museum of Natural History, to some Madison Avenue art galleries, as well as the Metropolitan. We made plans for the future of the Dunham Company and solidified our love far beyond earliest expectations.

Most of the time during the nine-month run of *Cabin* at the Martin Beck I slept late, prepared a combined breakfast and lunch, and rehearsed, as by now I had taken advantage of the Martin Beck being dark five days a week in the afternoon. Mr. Beck himself had given me permission to use the spacious lobby of the mezzanine for rehearsals, with the provision that I'd be especially careful to see that no damage came to his treasure, a grand piano lavishly trimmed with ormolu and exquisite painted miniatures. We began rehearsals for a proposed concert sometime after the closing of *Cabin*. With tragic optimism we all, that is, *our* contingent and our friends on the side of the divided camps of the Waters-Dunham veiled feud, foresaw no end to the Broadway run of the show that, according to critics, should set a record and then, surely there would be long years of touring in the United States and Canada, maybe even Europe. Vinton Freely, our producer, was more realistic. We had full houses, but many of us on stage were too Broadway-inexperienced to recognize what are called two-fers (two tickets for the price of one) or houses sold out at reduced rates to clubs or fraternities. Nor were we aware of the Music Publishers strike, which crippled any new show then opening on Broadway since a good part of financing came from the sale of sheet music and records.

I suppose I could look back on those days as being ones of "wine and roses." It was during this period that Eleanora Deren (later known as Maya Deren) came backstage after a matinee. She was full of enthusiasm and praise and intelligent comments. After several visits from Eleanora, I was convinced that she was needed in our growing consortium. She was the daughter of a college professor, Dr. Deren, a practicing psychiatrist, and must have started very young to plan an exotic career. She plunged into our classes, began a bookkeeping system, took care of ever-growing fan mail and of meeting people at my dressing-room door, whom I had heretofore turned away for the most part. Before long she was proofreading my writings (I had copious notes from the West Indies, which were later the basis for several books and articles) and preparing the proposal for her own fellowship from the Guggenheim Foundation to go farther than I had in analyzing Haitian folklore and religion. Her book, published eight years after she left us in Hollywood, is one of the classics of Haitian folk and religious customs.[2] Eleanora was bright-eyed, bushily red-haired and generously freckle-faced, quite a contrast to my masseuse-bodyguard Evelyn, who more resembled, until she began to talk, a somber, angular Mexican. Evelyn smoked constantly, a habit I tried hard to break her of long before smoking was billed as a health hazard. Not allowed to smoke in my dressing room or apartment, she chewed on a carved ebony cigarette holder. Her speech was Louisiana mixed with Harlem argot. Two front teeth were outlined in gold. Her hair was black and wavy. I knew that Evelyn was from New Orleans but little else.

Evelyn came about in this way; with a heavy schedule of dance and exercise and at least once a day up and down the six flights of stairs at West Sixty-Sixth Street, I felt obliged to alleviate the growing discomfort in my knees. More and more I thought of the University of Chicago's Viennese doctor's advice to give up dancing if I intended to continue to walk. He had given me three years at the pace I was keeping at the university. Three years had just about gone by when certain exercises presented serious risk and pain. With a featured, practically starring role in a successful show on Broadway, my own company, more solidified each day, infinite vistas opening in choreography, I simply could not afford knee problems in the future I had begun to hope for. As therapy I had began to concentrate on building what was established by now as the Dunham Technique as a support and protection to my troubled connectives. I started advanced stages of stretching, of muscle building from inside to outside. This inside muscle emphasis was to diminish almost certain formation of bulges in calf and upper arm and thigh muscles, of correcting skeletal deficiencies in some of us and developing undreamed of possibilities in others, always building a protective muscle support around the knees. In Paris, Stockholm, or Beirut a member of the Dunham Company could be recognized from far off by carriage and stance by those who may have seen the show only once.

Massage seemed logical, but I had little experience with its therapeutic character. I did not feel financially able to afford the major salons that

advertised in *Vogue* or *Harper's Bazaar.* Also, I did not feel up to challenging their established ways or making an issue of the composition of their
clientele. I looked in the yellow pages of Manhattan and found a massage
parlor in the safe confines of Harlem. The man who ran the place called
himself "doctor" and the masseurs and masseuses were labeled nurses.
After a steam bath (when shut up in the coffin-like contraption for steaming I thought of the steam bath parlor not far from Grand Boulevard in
Chicago where an elderly women expired while steaming, neglected by a
poker-playing attendant), my attentive nurse led me to a small cubicle.
After I had cooled off by being wrapped in a sheet and blanket, a nurse
attacked expertly those areas where I was having muscular pain and those
areas where I had always been, to a degree, over-fleshed, my hips and bottom. As she worked, my constant companion, arthritic pain, decreased and
I decided that one of these massages daily would allow me to welcome the
difficult exercises I was then creating for new choreography, rather than
dread them as I had. To teach or create without participation was foreign
to me; every day the dancers were developing to where singly and in concert they moved ahead, becoming the company I wanted and at the same
time challenging me in demonstration of my own creations.

Before the first massage was over, Evelyn Vaughn, my masseuse from
the beginning, had agreed to come to the theater with a portable table and
set up shop on her nights off. Little by little Evelyn became a real necessity until, when I felt financially able, she began to work for me exclusively. She had her own Studebaker coupe, which was a great convenience
when, after the theater, I would want to go to the jazz hangouts on Fifty-
fourth Street, or to the newly developing Greenwich Village spots. On
Fifty-fourth Street we heard Sid Catlett, Big Bill Broonzy, the drummers
Mead "Lux" Lewis and Albert Ammons playing twin boogie-woogie pianos
(here without Pete Johnson, who added a third piano at the Clairemont
Club in Chicago), Louis Armstrong, Roy Eldridge and Wingy Manone
with their trumpets, and such singers as Sarah Vaughn, Billie Holiday and
Maxine Sullivan. John and I would often go to the Blue Angel and to
Mabel Mercer's Penthouse Club where the international "jet set" of those
pre-jet days would convene to hear nostalgic songs more spoken than sung.
I wondered then if I would ever see and capture the far places they spoke
of—a community of wealth, French designer clothes, the Cote d'Azur,
the most recent vernissages, and the finest restaurants. Mabel Mercer was
beautiful and charismatic and stayed that way for the forty years or so after
I first saw her until her death. She was wise and much loved, even more

so after her voice became gravelly and she needed a microphone even in the smallest of rooms. In Harlem I learned the fine points of jitterbugging, which always reminded me of the Jamaican mento or shay-shay. We danced Cuban rumbas and boleros at the Campo Amor on Lennox Avenue and Lindy Hop at Small's Paradise, one of Harlem's brightest spots.

After the show I would remove my makeup, which was complicated because in the "My Old Virginia Home on the River Nile" scene I used a light coating of Max Factor's pancake (Egyptian) #9 over most of my body. I would shower carefully, remembering that fresh laundry was at a premium at Sixty-sixth Street, not so much for the cost as for the inconvenience of changing sheets and towels and carrying them to the Chinese laundry on Columbus Circle. In order to have one-day service I had to have them in the laundry before ten in the morning, and because of late nights this was not easy. On the other hand, especially while John was there, I disliked sleeping in makeup-stained sheets. So I was just about the last person leaving the theater, and during all my years performing I would be in the theater two hours before curtain time to warm up, exercise, review mail, and carefully apply makeup. For many years the theater was more home to me than our rudimentary nest-making in many, many countries of the world.

If John were in town, which was only some of the time during *Cabin,* we would go to my favorite after-theater fried chicken dinner club, Jimmy Daniels's on 125th Street. Jimmy was still the handsome young man who had so charmed me at Harry Stack Sullivan's party. Now he was sure of himself and his audience, more professional. The club was small and very intimate: two grand pianos, three or four tables in front of cushioned banquettes, a table squeezed into each side of the entrance, bird's-eye spotlights on the pianists and center floor for some other entertainer and for Jimmy. The other entertainer might be May Barnes, who sang in suggestive tones about the "Li'l Old Lady from Baltimore, truckin' on down and Susie-cueing," demonstrating on the six-by-six dance floor what the little old lady from Baltimore might do. Or perhaps two pianists (white) playing Broadway hits, or Jimmy's accompanist, Garland Wilson. A full-page photograph of Garland at a grand piano with its top up, wearing a striped T-shirt while I lounged inside the piano, dressed in a *Cabin* costume designed to expose legs covered with net stockings, had appeared in *Theater Arts Monthly* and occasioned unpleasant remarks from the Waters Camp [see figure 5 in the photo gallery].

At Jimmy's I felt as though I should drink champagne, sometimes in a cocktail; if we had guests I would have a bottle. John drank scotch almost exclusively, as did my masseuse-bodyguard-chauffeur, Evelyn. She always mixed hers with milk, a habit as firm as her invariable dousing of anything edible put in front of her with Pick-a-Peppa hot sauce, a bottle of which she always carried in her purse.

After John returned to Chicago and his unfinished projects, Evelyn and I would often end the evening at Jimmy's, eating his famous fried chicken or a T-bone steak, enjoying the floor show and always Jimmy, spotlighted in the curve of a piano silhouetted against a huge bouquet of fresh flowers. We always had our usual drinks. I was never attempted to try Evelyn's mixture. I think I spent two or three days in widow's weeds after John left. Then Evelyn and I started on our rounds of Harlem, Fifty-fourth Street, Chinatown, and the Village. Sometimes Ruth would be with us, but her show had just closed and she was preparing for a new one, studying and taking classes, and hence late nights were not on her agenda. Evelyn surprised me, shocked would be a better word, when I started back to the car for something after arriving in Jimmy Daniels's one time, and saw her remove a small revolver from the glove compartment and put it in her oversized bag. She explained it was only wise since she carried the payroll for the next day and had a permit that she had gotten by some means or other to live up to her self-appointed cognomen of "bodyguard."

Though Evelyn gave me at least four massages a week, she came to be known as my bodyguard, both in my presence and behind my back. The company took this upgrading of Evelyn's position in stride. After all, the more important I became, the more important they became. Not realizing the practicality of a bodyguard in my impulsive life, they considered it one of my devices to maintain my position in the face of Ethel Waters' constant upstaging. She had what we derogatorily called "her girls" to sustain her against the vicissitudes of my growing popularity. These were seven young ladies from some southern Bible school who surrounded her off stage and on if they could. They were her hand-picked choir and, when not in one of the five choral pieces directed by Rosamund Johnson, were seated on the floor around Miss Waters in her dressing room practicing church hymns and listening raptly while she read from the Bible. I would love to know what her selections were. I know that she thought of all of us (my contingent) as totally corrupt and unsalvageable.

Once in the dead of winter I accepted an invitation from the theater and anthropology departments at Yale University to speak on what I termed "An Anthropological Approach to the Theater." It was terribly cold, the highway was slippery, and I was anxious all the way to New Haven about the innovative approach in this lecture, and all the way back for fear of arriving late for the Martin Beck curtain. After a long preamble, I spoke of *Rites de Passage* and the company demonstrated. Paquita and our drummers were our orchestra. It was a great success, and we arrived at the Martin Beck well in time. I had no sooner started makeup when Evelyn brought me a copy of the *Daily News*. On the front page was my picture, one made by Dorian Basabe in Chicago, captioned "Anthropologist turned Dancer," or something like that. The article went on to elaborate on my featured role in *Cabin* and to marvel at my lecture-demonstration at Yale. As I started to dress for my first entrance, I heard a commotion stage right, which was just below my dressing room. Ethel Waters was in a real state, to put it mildly. She was complaining bitterly to Al Lewis, one of the associate producers. She had grabbed him by the coat lapels to emphasize her statement. "Ah don' know nothin' 'bout no anthropology," she stormed disdainfully, deliberately distorting her language, "but Ah sho' know a lot of naked asses wigglin' when Ah see 'em!"

Of course, Alfred Fisher had cleared the Yale engagement with the management, but no one had seen fit to advise or ask Ethel Waters. The company was in stitches laughing, which didn't help matters. I had to cross in front of Miss Waters as she sat on a stool on the side of the stage. She covered her nose with a handkerchief. Archie, who was by then three-fourths of the way into the Waters Camp, said that it was because the dry ice smoke in the "Hell" scene bothered her breathing. We all thought it was a comment on our perspiration-streaked bodies as we left the stage, running over each other for a quick costume change. Be that as it may, I would say "Good evening, Miss Waters," when I first saw her, "Excuse me, Miss Waters," if I passed in front of her and "Goodnight, Miss Waters," if I passed her on leaving, which wasn't often, because I purposely took longer to leave my dressing room and shower than she did. After the publicity about our appearance at Yale, through the run of the show, she refused to answer or acknowledge me in anyway. I was so deeply immersed in the singing lessons, massage, music research with Paquita Anderson and the daily two-hour class rehearsal with the company that I cared little about my relationship with Miss Waters. What I did mind, however, was the blatant (or so I thought at the time) defection of Archie Savage. Miss Waters seduced him away from us early after the Yale lecture, and at one time I thought would succeed in prohibiting him from appearing in any of our stage numbers. In this she did not prevail, because the producers would not have agreed, even if Archie had, and Archie had no intention of restricting his visibility in a successful Broadway show. Archie was, however, absent from our extracurricular rehearsals, so our new show developed without him. Shortly after, when *Cabin* closed in Los Angeles, Archie was displaced by a handsome "high yaller" young man who flashed around from West Hollywood to Central Avenue in Miss Waters's new Lincoln Continental. Archie's fall from grace was some sort of poetic justice. Although I could sense this predictable turn of events, I wondered if Papa Augustin, my spiritual protector, had anything to do with it.

My social life, with or without John, who was often in Chicago, slowly, almost imperceptibly, expanded into more nights out, and more lunches in restaurants where I was not regarded with curiosity because of my color. Ann and Dan Golenpaul, producers of both Goodman Ace's *Easy Aces,* a radio show that featured Mary Hunter, as well as the very popular *Information Please,* took me out at times with Mary and Jack Sullivan. This would be the Second-Avenue seafood places or French and Italian restaurants on the East Side. Their Park Avenue duplex was on a scale heretofore unknown to me, stretching out into terraces on all sides with potted palms in unusual corners. Now and then Alfred Fisher would take me to the Russian Tea Room to see and sometimes meet European artists who, little by little, were recognizing my name. Louis Schaeffer phoned occasionally to ask me to lunch at the Lobster on Forty-fifth Street, or the Blue Ribbon, a German restaurant in the same neighborhood.

I knew little of Evelyn's background but that she was from New Orleans. One day she invited John and me to dinner at her mother's apartment on Sugar Hill, the most fashionable section of Harlem. I remember it as dimly lighted, with fringed lampshades, an upright piano, overstuffed sofa and chairs, and a dining room decorated with a huge Boston fern in a shiny ceramic pot. There were artificial flowers and plants in the bedroom where we left our coats on a bed covered with bright pink damask. We met Mrs. Vaughn, a sweet-faced large woman with a small head made even smaller by a very close shingled haircut of a style ten years past. Her son, Earle, who looked as if he had never left the apartment in daylight, retired to his room. John suspected that he was the source of the stream of silver fox furs and French perfumes which Evelyn was always offering me at extremely low prices, although I was not in the market for such. The only other guests were several light-skinned, highly made-up young women who spoke not a word during a delicious New Orleans meal, and all of whom wore hats, some with the turned-up nose veils that were fashionable at the time. These ladies were introduced as cousins and old family friends from Louisiana. I vaguely noticed but didn't pay much attention to a continuous interruption from phone calls. Evelyn had set the table while a cook's helper stayed in the kitchen. Sometimes Evelyn would answer the phone, sometimes her mother. Then a girl would be called from the table for a whispered conversation. The girl might or might not go out immediately, but when this occurred all through the meal, we had ran out of not only conversation, but also of guests. As each young lady left, she would curtsy to John and me, kiss Suzie Vaughn on the cheek, and excuse herself from the remainder of the meal. It did seem strange to me, these sudden departures. Mrs. Vaughn asked us into the very dim parlor, where she invited us to make ourselves comfortable, even stretch out if we felt drowsy, then seemed to lose herself in her music as she played a meandering stream of ragtime songs from the turn-of-the-century. Once alone at home with John, he enlightened me. I had not associated the apartment with what was apparently the case—a stable of well-mannered call girls. I was amused at my own naïveté and found ways to be excused from later invitations to dinner. John referred to Mrs. Vaughn as Harlem's Polly Adler and wouldn't have been surprised if Susie had once worked for that august Madame.

At times I would invite company members to my Sixty-sixth Street apartment for music, food, and drinks, much as I had in Chicago on Grand Boulevard. Sometimes Papa and his lady friend, Joan Smith, who later helped us with the founding of the New York Dunham School, would prepare Haitian food—rice and beans *collé,* or stuck together, with red bean sauce and *grillot,* bits of marinated fried pork. I didn't know who lived beneath me but, even though our hours were late and more than likely there would be resounding Cuban and Haitian drumming and singing and barefoot dancing, there were no complaints from below. Once or twice Balanchine with Vernon Duke, and on one occasion Stravinsky, came over after the show. I remember Vernon and Balanchine planning for a Cuban vacation and my shock that they would be looking for fun with little girls. I, of course, thought sixteen or more, but it was hysterically funny to them that I hadn't realized an age of eight or ten was what they meant when speaking of "little girls." Now I feel they were teasing; somehow I had managed to conserve the naïveté of my school years. When Stravinsky was there we discussed what of his music I might choreograph and ended up with an unpublished tango. I especially enjoyed Balanchine's sense of humor as a little acerbic. While staging *Cabin,* we often saw the same things as amusing. I have learned no better way to build a friendship.

The version of *Cabin in the Sky* that opened at the Martin Beck Theater was not the original version planned by the Russian quartet and their American lyric writer, John La Touche, and the producers. The original book was a combination of satire and fantasy, but in a Russian context. The opening chorus, for instance, was rehearsed with Ethel Waters only once because it seemed sheer sacrilege to her that black folk mourning the death of Little Joe would sing Russian dirges rather than deep south gospel. I must say that I, too, found the Russian-flavored version confusing. The script was rewritten to accommodate Ethel Waters and her cohort choir director. Todd Duncan, concert singer who played the part of the Angel Gabriel, and the singers and actors who had been in *Green Pastures* must also have been influential in the revision. Rex Ingram, the Devil, and Dooley Wilson, the wayward Little Joe, couldn't have cared less, as their acting parts would have changed little and as veteran actors they counted on a certain leeway in interpreting their roles. As for wicked Georgia Brown, inexperienced in the acting, singing and dancing demands of Broadway, I was willing to go along with the majority. Gradually I molded the role to my own specifications and capacities. Balanchine was easy to work with, and though he didn't agree to staging or choreography credits in print, on stage we worked well together. It would have been difficult for the company to have accepted total direction from someone else as long as I was in the picture.

The "Hell" scene, which portrayed vividly the delight of sinning, billowed with smoke from dry ice, reverberated with banshee cries and Cuban-style howls from Dunham dancers, and exploded with unrestrained frenzied rhythms from our drummers, who in my opinion dominated the scene, even after my entrance. I seldom entered this scene without thinking of an old Bert Williams song, a record played on an old hand-wound machine in my childhood. A preacher had been exhorting his flock for indulging in Saturday-night sin. He described a scene just about like the one we presented nightly. In the mist of graphic pictures of biblical sin, hellfires burning and orgiastic revelry, a sinner in the congregation (Bert Williams) jumps up, crying in a loud and ecstatic voice, "If hell is what you say it is, oh Death, where is thy sting?"

What Balanchine had in mind choreographically for the "Hell" scene I don't know, but Karinska had clothed us as feline creatures, our pelts of thick, furry wool mounted on, I believe, hand-knitted leotards. The one time we tried them on we were all gasping and suffocating from the heat engendered, and not even Archie could manipulate his heavy, six-foot-long tail. We were paralyzed. Without my prompting, Alfred Fischer again called John Pratt to the rescue. Leotards, tails, and masks with ears and whiskers were abandoned; strides and brassieres of leopard print edged with black wool fringe were salvaged. Men were bare torsoed and ladies had midriffs and thighs exposed. I had a black-and-white rumba dress with a train, the alternating taffeta ruffles vertical rather than the conventional horizontal. This is the only time in my memory that I was not ecstatic about John's design. I did, however, admire the mass of black horsehair curls that sprouted from the top of my turban and bobbed and shook as I danced. Neither was I pleased with my choreography. I have often regretted that I did not at least try the scene as planned by George. It might have been pure Kamerny Theater avant-garde or, better still, Balanchine.

Dooley and I had a duet in which he pleaded with me, while on the lookout for his vigilant wife, to love him tomorrow, but to leave him alone today. I insisted that "this life is short, never wait until tomorrow" and only today is what counts. I wore a tight wrap-around black poplin skirt, tight satin underpants with monogrammed initials embroidered in rhinestones, the inscription reading G.B. It never occurred to me that some might interpret this as a tribute to George Balanchine.[3] At certain moments a slight movement of the skimpy skirt revealed a great deal of thigh and the inscription that, of course, stood for Georgia Brown. An orange velvet, heart-shaped hat, a vivid teal blue poplin bolero jacket, orange gloves and slippers, and black elastic meshed stockings completed the outfit. Not being a singer of that particular sort of ballad, I flirted outrageously with Little Joe to compensate. The number was successful; Dooley was a real charmer. Since Dooley didn't sing conventionally either, we muddled our way through with mime and a great deal of fun.

The biggest dance number took place in Little Joe's backyard while his wife, Petunia (Ethel Waters), was away at the store. A clothesline hung with washing served as the curtain, which parted to reveal the dancers dressed in brief costumes made of red bandanna over-dyed with yellow. Between the open bed-sheet curtains I entered in my soon-to-be-famous Egyptian costume. Before exiting for her trip to the store, Petunia had sung with Little Joe of their "Old Virginia Home on the River Nile" and Little Joe's subsequent dream fantasy gave me ample occasion to be glamorous. Little Joe was dreaming, and Georgia Brown took advantage of Petunia's absence to entice him as I imagined an Egyptian queen would. I had rejected Balanchine's and Karinska's idea that I should enter rolled up in an Oriental carpet carried by Nubian slaves; after which the rug was to be unrolled to reveal a mummy wound up in white linen. I was then to be unbound, unraveled to reveal a skimpy costume of multicolored knit flowers, knitting being one of Karinska's passions at that moment. John, who has an invincible memory, pointed out that Ida Rubenstein had once made such an entrance, and I remembered something similar in one of Ruth Page's ballets, perhaps *Aïda*.

Eventually I was dressed in a costume made of fine tie-died East Indian silk scarves pinched up all over into tiny multicolored knots—red, lavender, and orange on a pale yellow background, the whole blended under lights into a diaphanous suggestion of a fitted bodice flowing into a translucent skirt split up the front to just under my bust. The tall headdress, covered with the same material, was copied from that worn on the celebrated head of Nefertiti in the Berlin Museum. The illusion of rich jewelry was created by diamond-shaped yellow brilliants that covered anklets, wide-cuff bracelets and a dog collar. I wore a yellow floss-fringed loincloth, the front of which fell to the floor. Pictures of me tempting Little Joe in this flimsy, scant costume appeared in *Time* and *Collier's,* and I knew it would be difficult for Ethel Waters to digest it. But she could hardly act more ungraciously then she had already done, although she resorted again to throwing wrong lines for cues as she had on opening night. Now I was more stage-wise and answered in kind until the producers had to interrupt such nonsense and we returned again to following the script more or less.

I would say that Balanchine and I contributed equally to the staging of my big number in the second act, "Honey in the Honeycomb." I quickly learned from Ethel Waters (an adept of double-entendre), and even I believe, from Bessie Smith, who was frequently at the Monogram Theater, where as children my brother and I would take refuge from the bitter Chicago cold, how to use lyrics. This was done by playing against a background of the most agile and good-looking Dunham Company young men and teasing just enough for the audience to wonder if they were reading too much into the lyrics. "Honey" became a staple in our nightclub and variety shows until our big, full company closing at the Apollo Theater in 1963. The first "Honey" costume from *Cabin in the Sky* was rose satin with a short, knife-pleated skirt, a magenta net overdress with a circular skirt, bordered Irene Castle–style with bronze coo feathers, which also trimmed a bolero jacket. Silver-fox heads set with ruby eyes trimmed to the décolletage and hat, which also sported silver fox tails wired to stand jauntily erect. It is now one of my favorite costumes in our museum display in East Saint Louis, Illinois, though the one there is a second or third replica of the original.

Ethel Waters was not the only contretemps in my determination to move forward toward a more secure ground in *Cabin* and an immutable Dunham Company capable of sustaining itself after the closing of the show. When Balanchine and the producers first talked to me about the composition of the dance contingent, they had already seen our company at the Sherman Hotel and the Windsor Theater. Following the fashion of the day, they expected that those added to the show, so as to approximate the number of dancers in current Broadway shows, would be made up of what were known as "mulatto" or "high yellow" Cotton Club girls, whom I knew would never integrate into our well-trained unit. I argued and fumed against it, but Balanchine stepped aside and let the others finally wear me down into accepting eight Cotton club girls, whose main contribution to the show was to sit at or drape against the bar in the "Honey" scene. Soon we were all accustomed to them, even missing them when we parted in Los Angeles. They were pretty, as the Sherman Hotel Panther Room New Orleans mannequins were pretty, but had no aspirations to dance as we knew dance, and I suppose they were worth the effort and expense if only to demonstrate the panorama of color and culture found in Black America. Agnes DeMille's dancers, added to our company, were indeed a great help.

I began to tire of nights outs, after-theater parties, the occasional dinner at the Russian Tea Room or Sardi's, or the one or two French or Viennese late-night restaurants introduced to me by Alfred Fisher. A few times I had lunch with Erich, who, due to his increasingly heavy schedule of patients, seldom went out at night. Erich's health had never been what one might wish for since hospitalization in Davos, and he preferred to lunch in his office-apartment on Central Park West. He was rather frail, so I would therefore not dream of inviting him to my-sixth floor home. More and more frustrated by John's unfulfilled promises to return to New York, I spent much of Erich's and my time together talking of him—or my talking and Erich's listening. Erich refused to take me on as a patient. He was opposed to analysts taking on close friends as clients, but probably aided and molded me more by his friendship than he would have been able to in a strictly professional relationship. He always gave me a feeling of self-worth, particularly when I felt torn to shreds by John's deliberate attempts to leave me so. When Erich and I met, Erich made it a point to see that I felt renewed confidence (what I had gained in the Caribbean would diminish under attack); that I mattered in a *world* sense of things, not just on stage, where he had seen me on several occasions, but in the broadest sense

of life acquisitions. Once, leaving his apartment, I dropped something—
a handkerchief or flower or something of little significance. I bent to recover it and Erich said, "Liebchen, I wonder if you know with how much
grace you make every move. Just that one, for instance." I was, of course,
pleased. Maybe his beholding me as beautiful in the "human" sense, as
full of grace, were reflections that I needed. Since knowing Erich Fromm,
reading his timely and profound analysis of the state of man and society,
listening to him, a part of my life has always been measured in my own
mind by how Erich would think of this or that. In the case of John Pratt,
he could help little. But through Erich's guidance I became strong enough
not to be shattered by the fiercest of assaults that we launched (I, too,
though not as effectively) on each other through the years. For instance, I
felt lying to John would be a sign of weakness, whereas I discovered he dis-
simulated so much that it is only lately, in the past ten or twelve years [out
of forty-nine, the year of his death] that he has made an effort to separate
fact from fiction.

Perhaps I should have been more discreet or prevaricative about my own
peregrinations, which might have shocked or injured him. At any rate,
from the very beginning, because after all I knew Erich a few years before
I met John Pratt, Erich tried to steer me away from the abyss of blind,
exclusive love over which I was clinging for life or death. Erich met John
very few times over the years and felt we were not for each other, that
sooner or later I would be terribly hurt by John's sadomasochism, which
he didn't need to analyze professionally to recognize. Somehow, in round-
about gentle ways, by treating me not as a patient but as a friend, Erich
molded me from what I was when we first met into the substance of what
I am now, more than fifty years later. I felt adrift for a short while after the
immediate shock of his death, but what I do not remember of his words,
I find in the priceless wisdom of his books. After a few years practicing in
New York, he moved to Mexico. Stricken, not knowing that I would soon
be there myself, I asked him why. His answer revealed a great disappointment in the value systems of America, where in New York he had lived and
practiced long enough to experience them. Furthermore, he had decided
that his greatest contribution to human improvement would be to analyze
only analysts, thus indirectly, and without the certain failures and disillusionment of individual practice, he would establish a following among
professionals, and only the worthy ones. That would ensure a wider influence on world thinking, as those chosen adopted his method of analysis.
Once understanding what he meant by the words "love" and "humanism"

and "humanity," I willingly let myself be guided by his words. More directly, Mexico, having high altitudes, would be better for his lungs.

Finally, *Cabin in the Sky* closed on Broadway. We went first to Toronto, which I didn't appreciate because of its blue laws and early curfews on bars and restaurants. To circumvent the blue laws, Evelyn carried a flask to the Chinese restaurant where we met with the Dunham Company, at least most of them, every night. Some went to the few and far between black restaurants that I do not recall frequenting; I suppose it would have to be Jimmy Daniels's or nothing. I enjoyed a few parties—one of my classmates in anthropology had taken his doctorate, married, had two children, and was teaching at McGill. But happy as I was to talk of the old days and to have a change from our nightly Chinese meals, I thought nostalgically of the parties of the anthropology department at the University of Chicago. Perhaps I was missing John, because it was seldom that I had a direct word from him.

The exact itinerary of the tour I do not remember, although some stops stand out. In Boston, Bill Gaston sent flowers on opening night and came backstage with an invitation to dinner. I had first met him in New York under similar circumstances and had lunch with him at the Harvard Club. He had come to New York to see *Cabin* after seeing my picture in *Time* and had written more than once, which inspired me to write and ask him before the opening in Boston if he would arrange for hotel accommodations. I described what became my standard requirements: an older but first-class hotel and a double room (there was always the possibility that John would appear) on the quiet side of the hotel or high enough that I would not be awakened by street or hotel kitchen noises. I must have been thinking of the Sherman in Chicago when stipulating this last. Additionally, I would also need two single rooms, one in my hotel for Evelyn and one where the company would be staying for Eleanora. This would be in the black neighborhood in those days, and it now occurs to me that I may have been testing Eleanora's durability under conditions where she might not be accepted in a black hotel. If she were refused, then she would arrange for accommodations wherever our technical crew would be staying, all white, there being no black union members in those days. When I challenged the union, they offered to show statistics that no black person had applied for these positions, indicating that they were technically untrained anyway. These positions were as wardrobe mistresses, dressers, stagehands, electricians, propmen, stage managers, company managers, spotlight operators, and so forth. I know that John pioneered in changing this, his friend Vernon Enoch being the first black person in the electricians' union. Eleanora always chose to stay with the company when possible, and, knowing her as I did later, I would not be surprised had she analyzed each and every one of these instances to put her findings aside for some scientific book or article. Her later fieldtrip to Haiti for research writing and recording and photography (after she met her husband-to-be, Sascha Hakenschmitt) allowed her little time for fulfilling all of her talents, especially in view of her early and untimely death.

The Boston hotel was all that I could have wished for; always fresh flowers in the lobby, women having afternoon tea in the dining room, and men, all about Bill's age, holding forth at the comfortable old-fashioned bar. We were a success from the start to finish of two weeks in Boston, except for a certain publicity which I could have done without but which the producers welcomed.

Boston has always been a city of great contrast in moral behavior. It had a wide-open red-light district, rough waterfront bars, and small restaurants frequented by sailors and ships' mechanics. On the other hand, suspected vice in the theater was controlled by a civil servant who took his position very seriously.

In the Egyptian scene my navel was uncovered and seemed to this man the only thing to look at in spite of a chorus of daringly dressed ladies and torso-bare young men. After the show he stormed into the lobby looking for our road manager, a kind little man with thick glasses and a worried expression. Within earshot of the newspaper critics (including the celebrated Elliot Norton) and lingering audience, he denounced my exposed umbilicus and promised to close the show if it were not covered by the next performance. When the manager and producer—the latter traveling to any important opening, which Boston certainly was—came to my dressing room after the final curtain, they were accompanied by the head wardrobe mistress, Mother Duncan. This could only mean one thing: some conciliatory modification of my costume. I postulated that my midriff was not, in fact, bare. The costume required a yellow diamond in my navel and I had always put it there where it sometimes got lost in the little folds of flesh and was only seen when some errant spotlight hit it and returned a flashing glitter. I had what turned out to be a brilliant idea. The jewel was really a button of many-faceted glass with small holes around it. Why not sew it to a piece of flesh-colored gauze, which could be pasted with liquid adhesive to the offending area? Thus the diamond was thrust forward with no possibility of its presence being hidden in the design of my umbilicus. The newspapers the next day elaborated on the censorship, and of course, the next performance everyone wanted to see how the mishap had been handled. . . .

We played major cities between New York and Chicago without serious confrontation. Alfred Fisher gave me very good advice before bidding us farewell in New York. He felt he had done as well by me as possible, given the fact that I was an understandably difficult person, wary of restraint and council, and, much of the time, doing too many things at once. We parted in friendship, but he advised me to go no further along the path of growing success without having an agent or manager, preferably both in one person or one office. I soon engaged Ethel Waters's managers. They were the lawyers Goldie and Gumm, spinster-like characters from Dickens in appearance and manner. They must have been capable, I decided, to have handled Miss Waters for the many years they had. They did not tour with us but appear occasionally to control bookkeeping with the company manager, give advice on bookings and settle trivial and not-so-trivial problems between Miss Waters and the press agent or advance man. Goldie and Gumm had been called upon to placate Miss Waters when she was claiming that the stage manager (responsible for distributing the dressing rooms) had deliberately and maliciously assigned her a dressing room adjacent to the backstage toilets. We could hear all over backstage as she declared she would not appear for the performance one more time if she had to be assigned a dressing room next to one of those "shit houses." Useless for the crew backstage and the staff at the front of the house to argue that, since in those theaters where there were not toilets in the Star dressing room, it seemed accommodating that she be placed close to conveniences even though they were to be used by the rest of the cast. Things were shifted about somehow without my losing my privileged dressing room—the choicest of the second-floor ones.

I once sat with Goldie and Gumm as we traveled to our next performance, and I gathered a lot from the two exasperated lawyers. One little tidbit told in the deepest confidence was the true gauge of the star's moods. If content in her love life, she was amiable, compliant, and—most important of all—became and stayed slender. Between love affairs the wardrobe women made continuous progressive alterations, or even complete costume replacements. Between New York and Los Angeles, a period of some weeks, Miss Waters remained dramatically thin. What had begun as a spiteful compulsion on her part to try and disrupt our close-knit company, by enticing Archie Savage from our camp to hers, became a passionate attachment of such proportions that the more conservative of the cast—of which at that time I was one—felt uncomfortable if, by chance, they happened to be at the same bars or eating places or black neighborhood "lounges" frequented by the two of them.

NOTES

1. Barbara Karinska was a costume designer who enjoyed a long career in the New York theater world, collaborating with artists such as George Balanchine, Agnes DeMille, Mike Todd, Louis Jouvet, and Jerome Robbins *[Eds.]*.

2. Deren's book is *Divine Horsemen: The Living Gods of Haiti* (New York: Thames and Hudson, 1953). She also made a film of the same name that was released posthumously in 1977 *[Eds.]*.

3. Apropos of misunderstood monograms, I dedicated my first autobiographical book, *A Touch of Innocence,* to B.B., a tribute to my revered friend Bernard Berenson. I was startled to find later that many supposed that B.B. stood for Brigitte Bardot, a French cinema star.

FIGURE 1. Portrait of Katherine Dunham and her brother Albert Dunham Jr.,
July 1930. Photographer unknown. Courtesy of the Katherine Dunham
Collection. Missouri Historical Society, St. Louis.

FIGURE 2. Katherine Dunham as a child. Photographer unknown. Courtesy of the Katherine Dunham Collection. Missouri Historical Society, St. Louis.

FIGURE 3. Katherine Dunham (far right) doing fieldwork in Haiti alongside her friends Cécile, Doc Reeser, and Fred Alsop, 1936. Photographer unknown. Courtesy of the Katherine Dunham Collection. Missouri Historical Society, St. Louis.

FIGURE 4. Katherine Dunham and company in the dream sequence of "My Old Mississippi Home on the River Nile" from *Cabin in the Sky* circa 1940. Photograph by Bob Golby. Courtesy of the Katherine Dunham Collection. Missouri Historical Society, St. Louis. (This image is discussed in "Early New York Collaborations," page 143.)

FIGURE 5. Katherine Dunham and Garland Wilson in a New York nightclub, 1940. Photographer unknown. Courtesy of the Katherine Dunham Collection. Missouri Historical Society, St. Louis. (This image is discussed in "Early New York Collaborations," page 136.)

FIGURE 6. Katherine Dunham and company in the film *Stormy Weather,* 1940. Twentieth Century Fox Pictures. Courtesy of the Katherine Dunham Collection. Missouri Historical Society, St. Louis.

FIGURE 7. Katherine Dunham with Roger Ohardieno in *Florida Swamp Shimmy*. Date and photographer unknown. Courtesy of the Jerome Robbins Dance Division, The New York Public Library for the Performing Arts, Astor, Lenox and Tilden Foundations.

FIGURE 8. Roger Ohardieno, Katherine Dunham, and Tommy Gomez in *Rara Tonga,* 1943–44. Photographer unknown. Courtesy of the Jerome Robbins Dance Division, The New York Public Library for the Performing Arts, Astor, Lenox and Tilden Foundations.

FIGURE 9. Katherine Dunham and Vanoye Aikens rehearsing. Date and photographer unknown. Courtesy of the Jerome Robbins Dance Division, The New York Public Library for the Performing Arts, Astor, Lenox and Tilden Foundations.

FIGURE 10. Katherine Dunham as "Woman with the Cigar" with Ricardo Avalos, Vanoye Aikens, and Ural Wilson in *Tropics*. Date and photographer unknown. Courtesy of the Jerome Robbins Dance Division, The New York Public Library for the Performing Arts, Astor, Lenox and Tilden Foundations.

FIGURE 11. Promotional program advertisement for *Tropical Revue*, circa 1944.
Courtesy of Katherine Dunham.

FIGURE 12. Katherine Dunham with Cuban drummers during a visit to Cuba. Photograph by Carmine Schiavone, 1947. Courtesy of Carmine Schiavone.

FIGURE 13. Katherine Dunham (as Loulouse), Vanoye Aikens (Alcide), Lenwood Morris (the Zombie King), and Tommy Gomez (Julot) in *L'Ag'ya*. Date and photographer unknown. Courtesy of the Jerome Robbins Dance Division, The New York Public Library for the Performing Arts, Astor, Lenox and Tilden Foundations.

7

FIGURE 14. Katherine Dunham in *L'Ag'ya,* 1948. Photograph by Roger Wood. Courtesy of the Jerome Robbins Dance Division, The New York Public Library for the Performing Arts, Astor, Lenox and Tilden Foundations.

FIGURE 15. Katherine Dunham and company drummers, 1946. Photograph by the Vandamm Studio. Courtesy of the Jerome Robbins Dance Division, The New York Public Library for the Performing Arts, Astor, Lenox and Tilden Foundations.

FIGURE 16. Students (including Eartha Kitt, left center) at the Dunham School in New York, New York. Photograph by Jean Polacheck, circa late 1940s. Courtesy of the Jerome Robbins Dance Division, The New York Public Library for the Performing Arts, Astor, Lenox and Tilden Foundations.

FIGURE 17. Katherine Dunham Company rehearsing *La Valse.* The dancers include Tommy Gomez, Lucille Ellis, Wilbert Bradley, Richardena Jackson, Julie Robinson, Lenwood Morris, and Dolores Harper. Photograph by Roger Wood, 1948. Courtesy of the Jerome Robbins Dance Division, The New York Public Library for the Performing Arts, Astor, Lenox and Tilden Foundations.

FIGURE 18. Katherine Dunham in *Bal Nègre,* circa 1946. Photograph by the Vandamm Studio. Courtesy of the Jerome Robbins Dance Division, The New York Public Library for the Performing Arts, Astor, Lenox and Tilden Foundations.

FIGURE 19. Portrait of Katherine Dunham and John Pratt, Paris 1952. Photographer unknown. Courtesy of the Jerome Robbins Dance Division, The New York Public Library for the Performing Arts, Astor, Lenox and Tilden Foundations.

FIGURE 20. Katherine Dunham relaxing backstage, seated on trunk, 1955. Photograph by Arnold Taylor. Courtesy of the Jerome Robbins Dance Division, The New York Public Library for the Performing Arts, Astor, Lenox and Tilden Foundations.

FIGURE 21. Katherine Dunham Company on tour in Greece, 1961. Back row: Ricardo Avalos, Laura Anderson, Clifford Fears, Lucille Ellis, Ural Wilson; Center row: Virginia (last name unknown), Barbara Wright-Craig, Jorge LeFebre, Camille Yarbrough, Dorothy Speights, Katherine Dunham, Leslie Harnley, Lenwood Morris; Front row: Walter Mayfield, Pearl Reynolds, Vanoye Aikens, Glory Van Scott. Photographer unknown. Courtesy of Glory Van Scott.

FIGURE 22. Katherine Dunham with Léopold Sédar Senghor, President of Senegal, 1962. Photographer unknown. Courtesy of the Katherine Dunham Collection. Missouri Historical Society, St. Louis.

FIGURE 23. From left, Delores Harper Autuore, Julie Robinson Belafonte, Katherine Dunham, Glory Van Scott, Anna Grayson, and Gloria Mitchell Thornburg at the reception for the Katherine Dunham Gala, 1979. Photograph by Ayoka Chenzira. Courtesy of Glory Van Scott.

FIGURE 24. Katherine Dunham speaking at the ceremony "Divine Drumbeats" at her residence, Habitation Leclerc, Haiti, circa 1980. Photograph by Johnny Sandaire. Courtesy of the Katherine Dunham Collection. Missouri Historical Society, St. Louis.

FIGURE 25. Katherine Dunham and Glory Van Scott in rehearsal for the television broadcast *Divine Drumbeats: Katherine Dunham and Her People*, 1980. Photographer unknown. Courtesy of the Jerome Robbins Dance Division, The New York Public Library for the Performing Arts, Astor, Lenox and Tilden Foundations.

FIGURE 26. A portrait of Katherine Dunham at ninety-three, taken during the seventieth anniversary season of Jacob's Pillow, 2002. Photograph by Mike van Sleen, Jacob's Pillow Dance Festival. Courtesy of Mike van Sleen.

PART II

Dunham the Woman

SCHOLAR, ARTIST, ACTIVIST

The Lost Ten Years

The Untold Story of the
Dunham-Turbyfill Alliance

PART I

Dunham's Contribution

ANN BARZEL

Katherine Dunham celebrated her seventy-fourth birthday on June 22 [1983]. An unexpected gift was a letter from Roger Stevens, chairman of the John F. Kennedy Center for the Performing Arts in Washington, D.C. Stevens may not have been aware that it was the great dancer's birthday, but the timing was appropriate because his letter informed Dunham that she was to be a recipient of the Kennedy Center Honors, presented annually "to individuals who, through a lifetime of accomplishment, have enriched American life by their achievement in the performing arts. The primary criterion is excellence." Other honorees this year are Frank Sinatra, Virgil Thomson, and Elia Kazan. The Honors will be presented formally the weekend of December 3 and 4 in Washington. The schedule includes a dinner hosted by Secretary of State and Mrs. George P. Schultz followed by a reception in the White House hosted by President and Mrs. Reagan. The Honors Gala that follows will be held in the Kennedy Center Opera House. Katherine Dunham's achievements are well known to dance world veterans. For the past five decades Dunham has contributed to dance and society in many ways—as a glamorous dancer, as an innovative choreographer, as an anthropologist who has researched the roots of ritual

SOURCE: Ann Barzel, Mark Turbyfill, and Ruth Page, "The Lost Ten Years: The Untold Story of the Dunham-Turbyfill Alliance," *Dance Magazine* (December 1983), 91–98. Copyright 1983 by *Dance Magazine,* Inc. Reprinted by permission.

dance, as a teacher of the exciting dance form she created, as a catalyst who stimulated scores of dancers and choreographers, and recently as an artist committed to inspiring a depressed community to a richer life.

Dunham burst upon the New York scene in 1939, a beautiful young woman with a company and a repertoire of picturesque dances based on Afro-American experiences. She herself had choreographed all the dances for her fifteen black dancers. Presented first at the 92nd Street YM-YWHA, the show was moved to the Windsor Theatre for thirteen weekends.

From this start, Dunham next devised a revue format of short numbers and longer ritual-based ballets which she presented in the various shows she produced in her long career in Broadway theaters, concert halls, and opera houses throughout the United States and on world tours. For several years the Dunham Company toured under the aegis of Sol Hurok, then Dunham went on her own. For two decades she toured the capitals of Europe, South America, the Far East—Paris, London, Rome, Mexico City, Buenos Aires, Lima, Tokyo.

The pieces, all choreographed by Dunham, were based on the Americana of her own life experiences and on the authentic folk and ritual dances she had researched as an anthropology student in Haiti, Martinique, Cuba, and other neighboring countries. As an anthropology major at the University of Chicago in 1935 she had been awarded a Rosenwald fellowship that took her to the West Indies on the first of several research trips. Stunning features of Dunham's presentations were the lavish and colorful costumes and scenery designed by John Pratt, brilliantly theatricalized from authentic sources.

Her other activities included Broadway shows, most notably *Cabin in the Sky,* starring Ethel Waters, with her own and Balanchine's choreography. There was a season in San Francisco that included a performance with the San Francisco symphony conducted by Pierre Monteux. And there were a number of films, the first being a twenty-minute short, *Carnival of Rhythm,* produced by Warner Brothers and directed by Jean Negulesco. Of the several full-length films, the most memorable was *Stormy Weather* (1943), in which Dunham and her company appeared in her choreography. Unsubsidized, the Dunham Company, although intrinsically an art-dance group, was able to exist because it could find work in many milieus. In part it was because of the beauty and glamour of its star. Added to that was the attractiveness of the company, which included Janet Collins, Eartha Kitt, Talley Beatty, and Tommy Gomez. And always there were John Pratt's gorgeous costumes. Dunham dancers appeared in opera houses, concert halls, legitimate theaters, vaudeville theaters, and often in cabarets—such as Ciro's in Hollywood, El Rancho in Las Vegas, and College Inn in Chicago. One of the company's last engagements was in 1965 at the Apollo Theater, the famous vaudeville house in Harlem.

During her world tours, Dunham was a close friend of the great and celebrated, among them art connoisseur Bernard Berenson, poet Langston Hughes, music-hall idol Josephine Baker, heiress Doris Duke, and President Senghor of Senegal.

Sandwiched in with all this activity was Dunham's New York school on 43rd Street. It had a profound effect on Broadway performances, as well as the world of show and concert dance. The Dunham Technique included anatomical bases of ballet and modern dance that emphasized the torso movements of the primitive ritual of Caribbean-African dance and jazz rhythms. Among the students were Marlon Brando, Peter Gennaro, Syvilla Fort, Eartha Kitt, and Arthur Mitchell.

This brief description of Dunham's career has appeared in greater detail in the world press and in her books. However, there is a lost decade, the 1930s, spent in Chicago. Sometime back Dunham wrote to me, "I surely do wish someone from the old background would do the Chicago period, which after all was the real formation ground." I know bits about this period, some by hearsay, some through personal experiences.

Dunham's first important professional appearance was in 1933 in a supporting role in Ruth Page's *La Guiablesse,* described in notes concluding this article. I saw Dunham later when she danced the lead in this ballet on a ballet evening with the Chicago Civic Opera. Page gave *La Guiablesse* and its costumes to Dunham for her first group. I remember Dunham as leader of a group taking classes and rehearsing with Ludmilla Speranzeva in the Berenice Holmes studio in Chicago. Speranzeva, a dynamic Russian with some modern dance background, was interested in Dunham and influenced her to concentrate on modern dance instead of the ballet she had been studying. She presented a program starring Dunham in what was then the Punch and Judy Theater. The show included a ritual dance about an African sun goddess, a synthetic but effective piece. What many who saw it remember most was that four attractive young black women carried in the portly sun goddess on a litter, and while undulating to the African rhythms their strapless upper garments slipped and they finished the dance topless—and looking great.

At this time Dunham became interested in the roots of her African heritage and was studying anthropology. As mentioned above, as a result of her interest in dance origins she received a fellowship and did research in the West Indies. On her return, she expanded her choreography, which became more authentic as well as more picturesque. With the authentic music, she added singing.

Dunham was popular with local dancers and was very much involved with the Chicago dance scene, taking lessons in oriental dance with Vera Mirova, appearing in a lecture for the Chicago Dance Council, cooperating with modern dancers. In 1938 she worked on the W.P.A. Writers' Project, then, when there was an opening, transferred to the W.P.A. Theatre Project, for which she created (not without administrative difficulties) her ritual ballet *L'Ag'ya*. And it was at this time she met fellow W.P.A. artist John Pratt, who became her collaborator and husband.

In 1938 Dunham produced her first major group performance, a concert in the Goodman Theater that included the premieres of some of the dances—such as *Barrelhouse* and *Béguine-Béguine*—that remained in her permanent repertoire.

These were some of the Chicago beginnings to which she referred, but before all these activities there was the real seed, the forming of the dream, the efforts with Mark Turbyfill in 1929–1930 to found a "Negro Ballet." Recently, on the occasion of the re-publication of one of Turbyfill's volumes of poetry, Dunham sent a letter of congratulations assuring him of her personal affection and recognition of his part in her career. She wrote, "How wonderful that in my youth I knew, was taken over by, and launched on this strange career of mine by people like you . . . my post-adolescence anguish and deprivation were so much alleviated by you."

Octogenarian Mark Turbyfill, now a recognized painter, still lives in Chicago. In the 1920s and 1930s he was a very handsome young dancer, the *jeune premier* of the Adolph Bolm Ballet. He danced with Ruth Page and participated in experimental and avant-garde projects. He was also a noted poet who received several awards. He was the only writer in those lively years of Harriet Monroe's *Poetry* magazine to have an entire issue devoted to one of his epic poems, *A Marriage with Space*. Turbyfill was very much a part of the artistic and social life of Chicago's "golden age," with its exciting Chicago School of Literature, lavish opera company, flourishing symphony orchestra, and repertoire ballet company directed by Bolm. Turbyfill had a studio in the row of storefronts at the edge of Jackson Park near the University of Chicago. Relics of the 1893 World's Fair, the buildings were a low-rent haven and artistic beehive for writers and artists of every form. The poet-dancer met the very young Dunham around 1930, and with her he became interested in founding a "Negro Ballet." Their early efforts are recorded in his unpublished autobiography. Most fascinating is the monthly diary Turbyfill kept, which told of the progress and the setbacks, creating the ambience of what was almost an impossible dream.

Excerpts from this diary, a hitherto untold tale of Katherine Dunham's beginnings, are published here for the first time.

PART 2

Excerpts from the Diary

MARK TURBYFILL

In *The Borzoi Book of Modern Dance* Margaret Lloyd wrote, "Katherine Dunham came dashing on to Broadway in a one-night Sunday stand that lasted for thirteen consecutive Sundays. . . . Who was this brilliant new dancer from Chicago? . . . In Chicago she studied with Mark Turbyfill, a gifted, eccentric poet and dancer, who sometimes appeared in Ruth Page's ballets."

Katherine Dunham was dashingly beautiful on the night I was called to meet her at the apartment of my friend, Mary Hunter, in the old "Coudich Castle" near the corner of Harper Avenue and 57th Street. My young friend Mary subsequently gained fame as a New York theatrical producer. It was in 1929 or 1930 when Mary introduced me to Katherine, but I recall feeling that there was perhaps something a little eccentric in my nature (as Margaret Lloyd would have said) that caused me to accept Mary Hunter's urgent request, namely that I undertake the training of an ambitious Negro girl, who had never had a lesson in her life in the art, but who wanted to become a ballet dancer. At the outset of my rash undertaking, I had no studio of my own in which to begin giving instruction to Katherine and a few others who would, supposedly, form a nucleus for the black ballet. The first efforts were made during rented time in studios maintained by other dancers and teachers. With the moral support of book reviewer Marion Neville Drury, I decided to open a studio on 57th Street in one of the storefront shacks of Columbian Exposition vintage, overlooking Jackson Park. The novelty of a Negro ballet appealed to Marion, and she offered her services as secretary and general factotum.

I was soon interviewed by the *Chicago Herald-Examiner,* and in the issue of July 20, 1930, a picturesque story appeared: "Not since writer Margaret

Anderson moved into the 57th Street art colony has so bizarre a figure as Mark Turbyfill appeared there. He arrived, so he says, for the same reason that brings many artists to the district, 'because the rent is low.' He is one of the few, so his neighbors say, who can afford to live elsewhere. Dubbed an experimenter in the field of the arts, Mark Turbyfill is widely known as a poet and dancer. . . . In his studio he is working on his theory of poem-dance, a philological ballet to be called *Play of Words,* in which the beauty of words is shown with three-dimensional entities. He is also working on an experimental ballet on Negro themes, for which Eric DeLamarter, assistant conductor of the Chicago Symphony Orchestra, is composing the music. Mark Tobey, well-known artist of New York, will probably design the settings and costumes for the ballet."

Plans were being made for the Negro Ballet. The persons listed in the letterhead of our stationery included a theatrical producer, a newspaper publisher, a sculptor, a couple of composers, and an attorney. All this was in hopes that we would "catch on." As it turned out, our "catching on" was a long time away. Though deferred, when it did catch on the Negro Ballet was astonishing in character. It was years later that Mary Hunter and I and a few sympathetic friends had the satisfaction of seeing our potential ballerina come out on top.

But that is a later story. Meanwhile, I enjoyed both grave and merry discussions with the advisory board. There was puzzling talk about publicity and cultural interests with publisher Robert S. Abbott in his office at the *Chicago Defender,* the popular Negro daily newspaper. I waited an inordinately long time in the anteroom before being ushered into his private sanctum. . . . There were leisurely and entertaining drives through Jackson Park in attorney (now prominent judge) Edith Sampson's car, as she returned me to the 57th Street studio after we had solicited yet another prospective guarantor for our impalpable Negro Ballet. "We can't give up yet," said Edith.

A month by month record, which I kept of our black ballet project—from its birth to its death—in the early 1930s, stirs my memories. As I reread it nearly forty years later, in a world of violence, I realize our incredible innocence and unworldliness.

January: Mary Hunter telephones and invites me to come to her apartment in "Coudich Castle" to meet Katherine Dunham. I am charmed by Katherine and her desire to pattern a career, holding Isadora Duncan as her ideal. The idea of a Negro Ballet is born. We discuss plans for the future.

February: Katherine rounds up a few Negro pupils. I explain our plan to Adolph Bolm and persuade him to rent me some evening time in his studio on Michigan Avenue. We start with three or four in class. Mrs. E., Negro society leader, expands on her enthusiasm for our exciting undertaking. She promises to see to it that her small daughter is always in class. Interest and acceptance of our work is slow. Few come to class.

March: Katherine's interest wanes. She has some hidden fear. I continue to hold classes. Katherine introduces sculptor Barthe. We become doubtful of our success, but keep at it. Mrs. N. appears and offers to bring in pupils on a commission basis. A large class comes once or twice. We are inspired. We plan to give a studio demonstration. I begin arranging and rehearsing "string ballet" (reminiscent of the Massine-Tchelitchew *Ode*). Mrs. Mildred Blair invites me to a dinner party in her North Shore Dive apartment where I meet Baron ———. (He said he was a nephew of Anna Pavlova.) During the dinner I discuss the Negro Ballet project with the Baron and Mrs. Ellen Waller-Borden. Mrs. Borden recalled with pleasure my dancing with Ruth Page in her drawing-room at 1020 North Lake Shore Drive, the Borden baronial castle. I am hopeful that she will take a substantial interest in the black ballet. The Baron asks me for an invitation to see our studio demonstration. I am happy to tell Katherine the news, and we begin to feel we are getting somewhere.

April: Bolm moves his studio to another floor of the Blum Building on Michigan Avenue. He confides that the manager of the building is not pleased to see Negroes coming to my class. I have to give up Bolm's place. I look for another studio, but everywhere I go I am indignantly refused. Finally, I go to the small dingy R—— studio and succeed in renting time. Pupils lose interest and drop off. We talk of taking a place of our own. Katherine and I are forced to stand on street corners and on El platforms while making plans for the Negro Ballet.

May: Eric DeLamarter sends me a donation to help get started. I decided to rent one of the historical 57th Street studios. Byron Hemphill and Lillian Hall advise taking studio 1547. It has the best floor. Byron calls attention to his scribble on the wall, "Scavenged April 10 by B.H." He jeers at my efforts to scour and renovate the place and watches and laughs as I crawl on the floor, painting old furniture. He carelessly splashes water on the freshly painted canary yellow walls. Mrs. S. hints she might round up more pupils if her commission were substantially increased. Classes become discouragingly small. I am mortified to discover it was the novelty of their access to a Michigan Avenue studio that the Negroes valued most. Settled with great effort in more attractive headquarters of our own, their interest in our project falls to a demoralizing low. Lillian drops alarming hints that Negroes are unwelcome on 57th Street.

June: We decide to give a big opening tea party. Katherine and I work on lists of socially prominent Negroes. Barthe takes me to a church concert where I meet cordial and enthusiastic Negroes. Barthe produces a list of "really elite" Negroes to be invited to our tea. Agnes DeMille (in Chicago on a visit to see Mary Hunter) asks to spend a morning in the studio rehearsing for her next concert. She counsels me that the idea of a ballet for Negroes is all wrong. She reminds me that it has never been done, that it isn't physiologically in the picture. I tell her that I'm not thinking of a physiological picture, but rather an abstract one.

I send Mrs. Waller-Borden an invitation to our tea and ask her to pour. Blanche Mattias accepts invitation and promises to pour. We begin preparing the studio. Designer Quill Monroe helps to hang my paintings, "Ballet Crucifixion," "Ballet with Strings," and others. I make arrangements with Joseph B. Biggs, caterers, to supply food and accessories. I receive regrets from Blanche Mattias, Cara Verson, Ruth Page, and Thomas Fisher. June 19 arrives. Joseph Biggs Co. sends slender, gold chairs, resplendent silver tea service, flowing lace tablecloth, crates of exquisite food and ice and maids. My longtime friend, the poet Eunice Tietjens, makes a prompt appearance and pours tea. The studio is jammed with some two hundred guests. Among the few white faces are those of poets Gladys Campbell, George Dillon; John Drury, and dancers Bentley Stone, Walter Camryn, and Diana Huebert. I am cheered to see Rudolph Weisenborn, acclaimed abstractionist painter. He chats with everyone nibbling aquamarine and pale pink *petits fours*. Eunice Tietjens, exhausted after two hours of service at the urn, asks to be relieved. Mary Hunter comes to the rescue. All during the party Katherine clings to the walls, pretty, aloof, and silent as a flower. . . . At last the studio is empty and we are filled with wonder about the future. Two days later Mrs. Waller-Borden's note arrives explaining that the day of the party was also that of her daughter Ellen's birthday, and that she spent it with Ellen in the country. She said that she was extremely sorry not to be at the party. Katherine and I were sorry, too. [Note: Years later young Ellen married Adlai Stevenson, a twice unsuccessful Democratic presidential candidate, who became governor of Illinois and, as a distinguished statesman, was the U.S. representative in the United Nations.]

July: Our search for talent for the future Negro Ballet appears to be

less rewarding day by day. In the hope of carrying the message to more
"understanding members of the race," Barthe invites me to several parties
given by the Negro elite. Pupils are now as scarce as hen's teeth. I decide
to advertise a special summer course in a leading Negro magazine. Miss
Marshall of Washington, D.C. is attracted by the ad and arrives to take the
course. Miss Fishback comes from Louisville to join the class.

August: S., young daughter of Mrs. E., attends class infrequently. On
the days that she appears she is brought safely to the door in a shining,
chauffeured limousine. After class the chauffeur calls for her. Though we
feel something of a letdown, Marion Neville Drury and I determine to put
on a drive for white pupils, so as to be able to pay the rent, hold on to the
studio, and possibly save the Negro Ballet. I persuade Byron, who is fresh
out of cigarettes, to accompany the class for an hour at the piano, at a fee
of twenty-five cents for the hour. Eric DeLamarter sends me another
donation, and says that he is working earnestly on his score for our ballet,
The Dance of Life.

September: Utility bills are mounting. To help meet expenses I get a
tenant for a cot in the back room, social worker J.H. I get the electric paid
just in time to keep the service going. Katherine comes to class irregularly.
She develops a habit of arriving late, just in time to miss her lesson. She
sits and watches the last five minutes of the class. . . . I am asked to write
an article on the Negro Ballet for the first issue of the forthcoming *Abbot's
Monthly.* On further missionary work for the Negro Ballet, attorney Edith
Sampson and I drive hither and yon in her car. On Sunday afternoon
Katherine brings her brother Albert, the philosopher, on his first visit to
the studio. We discuss our perplexing problems. Albert sums up the situation, "Mark, I think you and Katherine are sitting on top of a gold mine
and you don't realize it." We discover that someone is opposing the publication of my article in the first issue of *Abbott's Monthly.* I manage to get
an interview with editor Robert S. Abbott. I leave his office at the *Chicago
Defender* with a feeling that all is not well.

October: The first issue of *Abbott's Monthly* is delayed. We are all holding our breaths. Quill Monroe and I are admitted backstage at the Eighth
Street Theatre to watch a Negro dance concert. Suddenly we are asked
to leave. "No white people allowed back here," we are told. The first issue
of *Abbott's Monthly* appears. My article on behalf of the Negro Ballet is
missing.

November: My article appears in the second issue of *Abbott's Monthly.* . . .
The weather is getting cold. There is no stove in the studio. The two

remaining Negro pupils shiver in their thin practice dresses. I give more strenuous lessons, not only for art's sake, but to keep the youngsters warm. I borrow electric toasters and grills from the neighbors. They don't heat up much under the high, cold, blue ceiling. But the canary yellow walls are cheerful. I go shopping on Cottage Grove Avenue and buy a "monkey" range. Marion Neville and I hustle to a coal yard and purchase a bushel of coal. We take it to the studio in a taxi. We warm the studio a little, but now we have no pupils at all.

December: The Chicago Symphony Orchestra plays Eric DeLamarter's *The Dance of Life,* his score for our Negro Ballet. Eric conducted the orchestra. There were no dancers on stage, but there were the words of the scenario quoted in the symphony program, suggesting the choreography that might have been. I had written:

> That fantastic jungle in which the Black Flowers of the ballet first stir is a region not to be found on an ordinary map. Amidst that strange and fleshy architecture of leaves and monstrous flowers with bellies and mouths, torturous and choking vines, the Black Flowers stir and feel the vehement urge of the thrusting jungle; to rise out of the darkness, free in the light to blossom, to scatter pollen and seed, seeking to conquer the earth. . . . Men and Women look into this prodigious struggle, and see mirrored therein their own struggle. In the development of the them, all blend in the swift-turning girdle of Mother Earth, entwined in a gigantic, human garland, the destiny is synthesis.

As I listened to Eric DeLamarter's stirring score, I thought how lovely Katherine might have been in the adagio. And I visualized Miss Marshall of Washington and Miss Fishback of Louisville doing their bits. Their journeys to Chicago would not have been in vain. . . . In the studio it is very cold. I borrow a scuttle for coal from the artist next door. We think long thoughts in the studio on Christmas Day. Shall we go on?

January: *Can* we go on? We take "Ballet Crucifixion" and the other paintings down from the walls. We send the borrowed piano back to the Bissell-Weisert Co. I sell the stove, the folding screens, the pineapple-patterned curtains. Social worker J.H. helps me pile a few odds and ends into a taxi bound for the North Side. The Negro Ballet gives up the ghost. I was haunted for a long time by a recurring nightmare, an impossible dream. . . . I heard a ghostly voice wailing, "impossible . . . impossible . . . it's all utterly impossible."

PART 3

In Appreciation

RUTH PAGE

Mark Turbyfill may have thought the Negro Ballet an impossible dream, but he invited his friend Ruth Page to see Katherine and give an opinion. Ruth Page remembers the occasion.

Mark was giving Katherine a private lesson in some dingy studio, I don't recall where. After the lesson I told Mark she would never be a classical dancer. She had started too late.

However, I remembered the attractive, sincere young girl, and some time later, when I was preparing *La Guiablesse*,[1] a ballet based on a West Indian legend, I asked Katherine to take part. William Grant Still, the distinguished black composer, had been commissioned to write the score. I scoured Chicago's South Side for black dancers, male and female, and among the lively horde of amateurs, willing and surprisingly able, were Talley Beatty and Archie Savage. The dancers were more reliable than the props, several dozen cane poles required for the action and the atmosphere. The poles disappeared regularly to reappear as fishing-rods on the lakefront.

The ballet was an item on a gala program during the summer of 1933, an activity connected with the fair, the Century of Progress. I danced the lead, and Katherine had a small role; most of the large cast was black. The ballet was a success and the administrators of the Chicago Opera, on which I served as ballet director, asked me to repeat it in the Opera House during the regular season. I was involved in choreographing a new piece, *Hear Ye! Hear Ye!* to a commissioned score by Aaron Copland, and did not have time to work on *La Guiablesse*. I told the opera people that there was this very intelligent and attractive dancer named Katherine Dunham. If they wanted the ballet she could rehearse it and dance the lead. They agreed, and Katherine was put in charge. She remembered every step. *La Guiablesse* with Katherine in the lead was presented in the Civic Opera [i.e., the Chicago Opera] in an all-ballet program with *Hear Ye! Hear Ye!* Again it was a success, and Katherine had an experience of directing a large group, some of whom, like Talley and Archie, became part of her permanent group that later toured the world.

In the years that followed I was happy to see Katherine's career advance. It was interesting that after *La Guiablesse* she turned more of her attention to the dances and culture of the displaced Africans in the West Indies.

I saw Katherine many times on the stage in her glamorous heyday. As I had predicted, she did not become a classical ballerina, but she had found herself in the colorful culture of her people,[2] a culture that she had researched and brought to wider attention. She was an exciting artist. And she was fortunate to have the collaboration of designer John Pratt, who added theatrical flair to the excitement of the Dunham presentations.

I was also right about Katherine's intelligence, for she was more than an attractive dancer. She has been a force in bringing wide recognition to the dance and culture of black America.

NOTES

1. *La Guiablesse,* based on a story by Lafcadio Hearn, is a Martinique legend of a she-devil who lures a young man away from his true love. Adolph Bolm and Ruth Page read the book when on a return voyage from performances in South America. They were excited about the possibilities of this story and its milieu for a ballet, and Bolm asked Miss Page to write a libretto and create the choreography for such a piece. It was announced in a 1926 program for the Allied Arts but was not presented until 1933 as described above by Miss Page. Participating in this was Katherine Dunham's first experience with ritual dance and certainly stimulated her to become involved in the African-based culture of the West Indies.

2. Katherine Dunham has two homes. One was acquired during her years of research and touring. It is Habitation Leclerc, a lovely estate in Haiti, once the mansion of Pauline Bonaparte, sister of Napoleon. Dunham spends more time in her home in East Saint Louis, Illinois, one of the most dismal towns in the United States. It is there that Dunham has established her Performing Arts Training Center and also maintains the archives of her distinguished career. Through the recommendations of Davis Pratt, Dunham's brother-in-law who is a professor at Southern Illinois University in Carbondale, the dancer-anthropologist was invited as an artist in residence at the university. She expanded her work to the SIU branch in Edwardsville. There the needs of that desperate community captured her attention. During the difficult years of the late 1960s, Dunham worked with the angry militant youths of the street gangs. She made them, as well as the more sedate members of the community (which is over 90 percent black), aware of their culture. The Performing Arts Center functions with a nucleus of teachers from Dunham's original company and has been training a group that performs throughout Illinois.

Miss Dunham Is Sensation in Haitian Dances

Edward Barry

Few dance recitals are punctuated with applause as loud and enthusiastic as that which rang through the Goodman Theater again and again on Wednesday. Frances Allis, Katherine Dunham, Diana Huebert, and Marian Van Tuyl had pooled their resources for an elaborate program sponsored by the medical bureau of the American Friends of Spanish Democracy and designed to raise badly needed funds for child victims of the civil war.

The chance to see in one evening such an unusual collection of dancers and to part with a little money for the cause drew to the theater a large audience which never missed an opportunity to give audible testimony of its approval.

The success of Katherine Dunham and her group approached the sensational. She is the young colored woman who went to Haiti on a Rosenwald travel fellowship to study and collect the native dances of the island. These dances are of such a singularly exotic character and were so superlatively well executed Wednesday that they constituted for the majority of the audience nothing less than a revelation.

In the Haitian ceremonial dances Miss Dunham demonstrates the emotional potency of sheer monotony in a most remarkable manner. There is an uncanny impression, when the curtain closes, that the dance and the

SOURCE: Edward Barry, "Miss Dunham Is Sensation in Haitian Dances," *Chicago Daily Tribune*, 4 June 1937. Copyright 1937 by *Chicago Tribune*. Reprinted by permission.

steady rhythm of drums are still continuing and that they will continue forever and ever.

Getting more metaphysical still, it seemed that the impassive faces and motions of the dancers provided a more vivid description than words ever could of the very essence of mysterious primitive humanity. In this impassivity and this monotony lay something volcanic, a suggestion of immense power and darkly realized forces.

The Negro in the Dance,
as Katherine Dunham Sees Him

FREDERICK L. ORME

And who is Katherine Dunham?

Let's call her a crusader, for the want of a better word. An intelligent girl with a sense of values, interested chiefly in the progress of her own people. Sympathetic by right of birth, though never unnecessarily prejudiced. An artist with an objective.

In 1929, after an elementary study of the dance, she met Mark Turbyfill of the Chicago Opera Company. Together, they caught a glorious vision of a Ballet Nègre, to resemble in effect the Ballet Russe. But the idea was too startling and the response indifferent. Failure was inevitable. Turbyfill gave up. They disbanded. And it wasn't until the next year that the idea could be revived. This time, with a different premise.

"I carried on alone," Katherine Dunham will tell you, "once again hoping for the best. I had been studying with Ludmilla Speranzeva (Ludmilla of the Wigman School and later of the Kamerny Theater), and she had agreed to help me with the training of the group. I brought together girls who were older and more interested, and we composed several numbers and gave two recitals. These were admittedly modern, but far from successful—the time was not ripe."

They called themselves the Negro Dance Group, but—that was a surprising mistake.

"Can you believe it," she laughs. "The Negro mothers immediately disapproved. They refused to send their children to me, for fear they might be taught Negro dancing!"

SOURCE: Frederick L. Orme, "The Negro in the Dance, as Katherine Dunham Sees Him," *American Dancer* (March 1938). Copyright 1938 by *American Dancer*. Reprinted by permission of *Dance Magazine,* Inc.

When Ruth Page produced her ballet *La Guiablesse* with the Chicago Symphony Orchestra, Katherine Dunham danced one of the three leads.

"This aroused a small amount of interest and I was able to put my school on an almost paying basis. But the group itself improved slowly. Girls were constantly dropping out, and in each succeeding class there were new faces. It was disturbing, to say the least, for I had to re-teach them a dozen times a year! And the reason for it was simply that the Negro believes in a certain fallacy the white person has bequeathed him—namely, that the Negro is a natural-born performer and needs no training. I am sure that any Negro will agree with me, if, of course, he has reached any status in the artistic field, that the one thing we face most often is a double standard of judgment, and the result is an appraisal of good for the Negro that is far below the expected good of any other artist. We are too quickly complimented and unless we are exceedingly strong and discerning our work is apt to be aborted in its very beginning. This ready acclamation retarded our progress."

And as though to further depress them, Ludmilla and Miss Dunham were told by any number of white dancers that their standard of training was much too rigid. That rather than being constructive, it was detrimental, and they were canted that hackneyed phrase: "inhibiting natural talents."

But Katherine Dunham refused to listen.

"Frankly," she explained to me, "I had to look at things more scientifically. The African Negro is habituated to a certain kind of musical technique in which rhythm is basic. In America and the Islands we harbor an appreciation of this rhythm over and above melody. Of melody we have only a minimum, even in our blues and spirituals. But this appreciation is not based on any physical difference, nor is it psychological; we are sociologically conditioned by our constant contact with it, and it continues from babyhood up. In the West Indies, women dance to the drums almost until the hour the child is born—and they nurse it, still dancing. But that does not mean there is no technique. There is. And it is every bit as essential that we train as rigorously as any other group, even in presenting ordinary folk material."

Early in her career, her aim had been to present only this "ordinary folk material," but her horizon widened and she decided differently—preferring to develop a system of primitive pattern that could be as substantially articulate as anything either modern or classical. She sought to do this, not because she believed herself better adapted, but rather "because our struggle for a permanent and dignified recognition must come through an outstanding contribution. We must always do twice as well and be twice as original to be accepted as genuine artists—and not on any basis of condescension, ever!"

Then too, she wanted to be freed of that psychological chaos through which she feels the modern dance is being forced to wade. She knows from experience that there is much valuable material, still unexploited, among the primitive peoples. And that it can't help but enrich the concert stage, if time be taken to provide it a specific technique. Therefore, she is studying impartially both the modern and the ballet media, hoping to incorporate from these schools that which will be most useful.

"I am about to get my master's in anthropology," she asserted diffidently, "majoring, as is to be expected, in primitive dance. But I feel that the value of transplanting the dance as such is mostly educational. My West Indian examples, so far, have been authentic, but my ultimate achievement must be to modify this, that it may be applicable to whichever theme I choose."

Then . . . will you state more simply just what you mean by your anthropological approach to the dance?

"Certainly. It is to view it functionally—its meaning and significance in the personal and social lives of the people who participate in it; to grasp its ritual, its ceremonial, and its recreational values. Also, in a comparative analysis, a careful study of the dance form itself is necessary. Necessary for purposes of weighing its contact with other peoples and the results of such contact—best illustrated in Haiti, where West Africa meets eighteenth-century France, and does it so often in so many dances."

She insists that all primitive peoples dance—the Negro no more than any other—but since our peasant Negro is our only approach to a folk or peasant group here in America, he presumably dances more than the white man. It isn't really true.

"It is merely that all primitives solve their psychological difficulties most easily in motor activity—often in a form of exhibitionism. Thus, because of the minority position of the Negro here, we unfortunately are apt to become exhibitionists. And, since a carry-over of our native rhythm has become a part of our tradition, obviously expected of us, we dance a lot. It's a healthy release-mechanism, but I can't agree that it is a more natural medium of racial expression."

And what of the white dancer dancing the Negro spiritual?

"I think she should if it is within her background and emotional understanding. For instance, I am a Negro, but I was reared in the North, and in white schools with white associates. Naturally, I heard spirituals, but until I was fully grown, I probably heard them much less than a white girl in the South. Why, then, should I dance them and she not? Some dancers, however, attempt them for the exotic, for publicity, or to satisfy some longing to champion the oppressed. Motives such as these speak for themselves."

And in conclusion?

"The one big worry is still a stereotyped idea of what the Negro should do. This, plus a seeming distaste of my people for discipline. Perhaps they can see no future. At least, I like to think that when I'm about to give up— it trebles my determination to help make that future for them!"

And your plans?

"To establish a well-trained ballet group. To develop a technique that will be as important to the white man as to the Negro. To attain a status in the dance world that will give the Negro dance-student the courage really to study, and a reason to do so. And to take our dance out of the burlesque to make it a more dignified art. We lack a tradition in the dance as we present it now, and the young Negro has no esthetically creative background."

I give you these comments of Katherine Dunham as she gave them to me, and that you may know her sincerity, I repeat myself: an intelligent girl with a sense of values, an artist with an objective.

La Boule Blanche

KATHERINE DUNHAM
writing as KAYE DUNN

Only occasional white visitors to the island misunderstand
the pure love for dancing behind the *béguine*.

Upturned faces form the arched bridge of the canal. Even the boatmen stop
as though hypnotized. One franc fifty centimes and the Palais Schoelcher
is yours. Without that you stand outside, on the bridge, if possible,
because the bridge is arched and the arch carries you that much nearer the
coveted goal. If not to dance, just to see. To hear the insinuating clarinet
and to feel the pulse of the bass viol. A slight twitching in the muscles
of your neighbor's abdomen. He takes up the tune, and unconsciously
rotates his haunches in the double rhythm of the *béguine*. His hands are
low on the hips of the girl before him. We are crowded on the bridge . . .

> Ancinel levée,
> Ancinel tombée—
> Di laisse les hommes
> Moin ka vini di mettez lumié!
> Ancinel levée
> Ancinel tombée

Ancinel is the chief of police. Cigar in his mouth, a shrewdness in his keen
blue eyes—get your bluff in first. He was a policeman in the States and is
indelibly marked. He hates the Negroes, and they hate him. Not only do
they hate him, they hold him in ridicule. He carries a gun and is always
accompanied by a vicious, green-eyed dog who has been trained to kill at

SOURCE: Katherine Dunham, writing as Kaye Dunn, *Esquire* 12.3 (September 1939):
92–93, 158. The original article contained painted illustrations by E. Simms Campbell.
Copyright 1939 by *Esquire*, Inc. Reprinted by permission.

any encouragement. The Negroes retaliate by writing a song about him. The tune was brought over by a Trinidad orchestra, by curious chance an ancient Calypso song written about a tyrant jailer. Someone in the streets of Martinique thought it a very fine vehicle for the ridicule of the chief of police.

> Ancinel rose
> Ancinel fell—
> Say let the men alone
> I've come to say put the lights on!

Verse after verse, sometimes senseless, sometimes double-entendre and ever more ribald. An excellent *béguine,* the tune on every creole lip and always exciting a burst of laughter.

> Ancinel tombée—Ai ya!

I slip away and the crowd melts into the spot where I stood. There are too many lights in the Palais Schoelcher, and I have been there many times. Tonight the Boule Blanche—

The Boule Blanche boasts a balcony. On the balcony two rows of chairs for those who wish to look the field over well before they choose a partner; for those who come as onlookers, not to dance; for the petite *femme taxi* who wishes to advertise that she is here for definite business purposes; for those who wish to remove their shoes and rest their aching feet. In the corner a rough bar and a nonchalant waitress, her striped *madras* tied in two points, indication that she is looking for a lover. Beneath the balcony, the orchestra. Clarinet, indispensable for the *béguine,* bass viol to simulate the vibrant throb of the hand drum, sha-sha made of seeds in a tin cylinder, banjo on special occasions, and a piano with every other note missing. There are two rows of chairs downstairs too. Colonial French prudery, the cavaliers and their ladies are never together in the interim between dances. They sit facing each other across the long dance floor. They eye each other speculatively. They form in little cliques of the same sex and discuss little cliques of the opposite sex.

There are *blancs* there—French, Martiniquans, Europeans of all descriptions. Sailors, and now and then ships' officers. Young *hommes de couleur* of the upper class. There is Monsieur Victoire, and with him a young doctor and two engineers. Monsieur Victoire is a professor at the *lycée.* Thursdays, Saturdays, and Sunday nights he alternates between the Boule Blanche and the Palais Schoelcher. We can exchange salutations unreservedly, though I am very friendly with his soft-voiced wife and six large-eyed boys. There is an unwritten law—the women of Martinique must know nothing about the Boule Blanche and the Palais Schoelcher. Others know of them only at Carnival season, that glorious fête of unrestricted purging of the inhibitions. Masked, they go places and do things that would be decidedly antisocial and immoral at any other time, and the *esprit du carnival* receives credit or blame. Madame Victoire is at home now, sleeping soundly . . .

The men are impatient from Sunday to Thursday, from Thursday to Saturday. There is nothing to do in Fort-de-France. No other amusement at all in Martinique, one might say, but the dance. At first I thought that these men of better families came for rendezvous with the many little attractive *femmes taxi.* But I know now that it is fundamentally a love of the dance that brings them. Only in Europeans, the *blancs,* do I see the actual degeneration of the dance to a medium of sexual stimulus. My creole friend André, for instance, always chooses a loose-mouthed, unattractive woman, old enough to be his mother, as dancing partner. She dances the *béguine* admirably. Every muscle in her worn, flabby body is conditioned to anticipate each gesture of her partner. André dances with her because she dances well.

There is not much variation. The *béguine* can be danced in two manners. One, a two-step with a very tricky little movement from side to side of head and shoulders, while the lower body swings to each side on slightly bent knees. This is the *béguine* taken from the sixth figure of the *contredanse* or *haute-taille,* Martinique versions of the European *contredanse* and quadrille. It is still the beguine of the salon, and now and then at the Boule Blanche a couple will separate, and with mincing steps advance toward and recede from each other before closing in the conventional *béguine.* But that is rare. The real *béguine* of the Boule Blanche, the *béguine-béguine,* is a work of muscular art, with no particular floor pattern. The sailor who watches drools at the mouth and calls for more rum. For him this is a paradise of debauchery which justifies deck swabbing and empty nights with only a star and the rolling of the inky sea, and wharves smelling of rotten fish and tar and spoiling fruits and sweating bodies. The young creole *blanc* who comes frequently to the Boule Blanche is either looking for a mistress, is under a *cambois* (some little Martiniquaise has put a charm on him), or, like the young man of color, he is merely seeking entertainment in the dance. Finding pleasure in this sole form of amusement.

Sometimes, too, the *béguine* is more fundamental. As with the Negro Delusuc. Delusuc is black. He comes from Saint-Pierre. He has not long been in Fort-de-France, and the bright lights are a little intoxicating. But he dances the *béguine* as his grandfather danced the *ma'jhumbwe*—intensely, fervently, passionately. He has a good partner, for though he is black (and this is no little consideration to the proud Martiniquaise), he is handsome. His black felt hat is on the back of his head. His wrinkled grey canvas suit is wet with perspiration. He holds his partner away from him, and his eyes gleam. She has a wide straw hat tied under the chin and tipped rakishly over one ear. Her bosom is high and well formed. Two dark circles stand on either side where the perspiration has made transparent the pink satin dress. She is brown. Someone gave her the dress and it is too tight. Her full buttocks are almost bursting out of it, but artistically, that is all the more perfect. They dance the *béguine* as a ritual of fecundity. The consummation is in the dance itself. The conventional two-step has reduced itself to a slight elevation of first one hip then the other—a shifting of the weight. Now her hips are moving and they describe a double circle at opposite ends of a loop . . . a figure eight . . . "*La Peau Fromage*" . . . *Béguine* of the old Saint-Pierre before the catastrophe. But Delusuc and his partner are dancing only to the tambour, and the movement is no longer side to side, but under and up, hips looping on rigid torso, knees bent, heads lowered as they look into each other's eyes, moving a half inch to the right with each under-and-up movement, each revolution of the abdomen. Strong feet and arches keep the rhythm smooth. They find a pleasure in the artistry of the dance.

The sailor thinks that they will leave the floor together to meet in a moment on one of the dark porches off the balcony. He watches them greedily as the music finishes and the floor clears. Without a word they turn apart, seek chairs on the opposite sides of the room, and await the next dance, eyes roving the opposite wall for another partner. The dance ends there for them. They have enjoyed it. They are satisfied in the accomplishment of an artistic feat—in matching techniques. Now it is a new conquest of another dance, another partner. The sailor is disappointed, but he is new here.

My first reaction to the *béguine* was basically the same as his. Extreme discomfort after an hour or so of watching the gyrating, undulating buttocks and abdomens. And then Henri suddenly left me to seek a little brown girl in a green *madras* and a yellow *foulard* tight around her hips. They danced together as one must dance at the Boule Blanche. When he returned to our table I asked him a question about her. "With one of those girls? *Mais non! Zut!*"

And he told me a thing or two about the wise little wench in the *foulard*. One of his friends had made the mistake and was just recovering. Then later—"But she's an extremely good dancer; I like to dance with her."

Another time I asked him, "But there are no other women here. Doesn't your sister or your fiancée or any of the girls of your own set ever come with you?"

"*Mon Dieu, non!* A girl's reputation would be ruined if she ever came here excepting at Carnival, and masked then."

I made the observation that only prostitutes and men are free in La Martinique. This, of course, started heated discussion which was drowned by the next *béguine*.

For Henri, then, it was simply a love of the dance that brought him here every Thursday, Saturday, and Sunday night. As with André and Monsieur Victoire.

Now I dance the *béguine,* and I find that it is not simply a matter of individual expression: the dance has certain standardized movements, and those who carry it to extreme or take advantage of these movements for an open sex thrill are in disfavor, even at the Boule Blanche. The sailor, for instance. The intricate basic rhythm has entirely escaped his Nordic mentality. He sees only breasts and hips and buttocks. He is dancing with a well-known "taxi-mama." She is thin, and her features are fine and Madonna-like. Excepting that her mouth sags and her eyes are a little bloodshot. Her brown hair is long and silky. She is a Dominican who came here for business, and she dances the *béguine* as a part of her advertisement. Mechanically she rolls her hips. Her movements are hard and deliberate; she has none of the smooth suppleness which melts the dance into the pulsations of the tambour-like bass viol. She is pressed tightly against the sailor, and she kneads his awkward body with her hard thighs and stomach. At the end of the dance she leads him onto the balcony at the far end of the hall and up the stairs . . . this is not really the *béguine* . . .

My attention is drawn to the wrinkled little woman in *grande robe* and three-pointed *madras*. She sells peanuts at the Boule Blanche, and she is a good dancer. She is much in demand. Every other dance she deposits her tray of "pistaches" under a chair in the corner. The full *grande robe,* trailing skirt tucked high on one hip, is a graceful accompaniment to her

stately yet supple movements. Her head balances from side to side coquet-
tishly, and her partner stands far enough away so that each is practically a
solo dancer. The *béguine* as the Empress Josephine would have known it.
When the dance finishes, the peanut vendor in *grande robe* returns to the
corner, retrieves her basket, and recommences her half-indifferent rounds
of the room.

There are other dances—the *valse créole* and the haunting *mazouk,* the
creole mazurka. Then suddenly in the midst of heat and perspiration and
the giddy high pitch of the sight and feel and smell of so much joy it is
black . . . *"La nuit"*—signal for all lights to be put out, and the night is
consummated in inky blackness while the clarinet whines the melody and
banjo and sha-sha and bass viol keep up the insistent throbbing that follows us as we slip away. Beneath, the silent canal, malodorous haunt of
myriad mosquitoes. And the black boatmen with upturned faces . . . La
Boule Blanche . . .

L'ag'ya of Martinique

KATHERINE DUNHAM
writing as KAYE DUNN

Two bodies rock, leap, fall and whirl into feigned attacks while the drum beats out the commands.

In Martinique a road to the south leads up and through cool green bamboo-shaded mountain passes, then down again and into open, flat plains of rolling sugar cane. In the south is Vauclin, idyllic village of fishermen. Here, as in all villages of Martinique, on all feast days or at any slightest provocation whatsoever, the *l'ag'ya* is danced.

When I first sought dances in Martinique, I was told that there was only the *béguine,* the national dance. Then, of course, the fox trot and the tango, the mazurka and the *valse créole.* The *l'ag'ya* was mentioned to me more than once, but no one seemed to see the qualities of the dance in the backbone of Martinique country entertainment. The *l'ag'ya* is known the entire island over. There is no hamlet or village where it is not danced at some time during the year. And a dance it is, in the fundamental sense of the word.

There are several explanations of the derivation and significance of *l'ag'ya.* It may have its origin in the Nigerian wrestling match, which is celebrated in the spring festival to the Earth Mother. Skill, prowess, strength: the Earth Mother must be proud of her sons. The Martiniquans themselves feel it for the most part only a competitive exhibition of strength on the part of the country fellows. They gather around the *l'ag'ya* with the same bloodthirsty anticipation that they attend the makeshift prize fights at Théâtre Gaumont, which calls to mind, even in the reaction of the audience, the combats of the gladiators of the court of Nero.

SOURCE: Katherine Dunham, writing as Kaye Dunn, "L'ag'ya of Martinique," *Esquire* 12.5 (November 1939): 84–85, 126. The original article contained painted illustrations by E. Simms Campbell. Copyright 1939 by *Esquire,* Inc. Reprinted by permission.

On the outskirts of the circle around the *l'ag'ya* they place bets on the burliest or the wiliest. They even offer ten francs to the man who will stain the torso of his opponent with the most blood, who will break the leg of his opponent in one of those amazing quick throws, or even his head or neck. "Just wait," they tell me as I am intent on following the movement of the dance. "They'll get all of that over with in a minute. That's just getting ready. Wait till they begin to fight. That big fellow there from Trinity killed a man in the *l'ag'ya* two years ago. Accident, of course, but nearly made it hard for the real honest-to-goodness *l'ag'ya* after that." And their eyes glisten as they offer another ten francs to get the preliminaries over with and really "show me something."

The *l'ag'ya* is also called *damier*. Delusuc at Saint-Pierre explains that if I watch closely, I can see the movements of the players follow the squares of a chess board. They move in the set pattern of the checkerboard game their slave ancestors must have often watched under the shade of stately palms in some quiet garden of the old days. Delusuc tells me also that the dance was one of pantomime, at times following the words of the songs. I watched that night at Saint-Pierre and felt that I could discern the patterns of the chess board; there is that principle in the *l'ag'ya* of a move, then a wait to watch your opponent, then a move again. I also observed the elaborate prancing, the falling on two hands and kicking the feet in the air of the two dancers during a particular song. The song was:

Gardez ça mule là,
Comme il cavoye pie.
(Look at that mule,
How he kicks his feet.)

But the pantomiming of the words of a song is more or less accidental. It depends on what the words are, and how the actor feels at the time. It is the player of the *'ti bwa* (*petit bois,* or little wooden sticks) who sets the basic rhythm, the drummer, who indicates the movements of the dance, the advance and the retreat, the feints, the sudden whirls and lightning-like leaps in the air to sharp drops flat on the ground. He indicates the marking time as the two opponents eye each other, each anticipating every gesture on the part of the other. He keeps them there, hypnotized marionettes on a string. Then he hurls them into an embrace and as suddenly tears them apart. He draws them to a crisis as their excitement and that of the crowd mounts, and again to a finale as they become exhausted. With the true finesse of a stage manager he arranges and re-arranges them to best advantage. With the quick perception of a director he senses the reactions of the audience. As the hidden prompter in the little box beneath the footlights carries each breath of the opera singer, so he lives the performance with the two contestants. A real *l'ag'ya* is a pantomime cockfight. But I have seen the dance of the cockfight in the cockpits of Jamaica; the cockfight itself in Haiti, and I find no parallel between the droll, staccato strutting, mincing movements of this mimicry and the deep roll of the *l'ag'ya*.

Monsieur Martino at Vauclin would have it this way. The *belair* is a *danse caraïbe*. His people learned it from their people, and so forth back to the early slaves who learned it from the now extinct Caribs. That Carib blood flows in his veins he has no doubt. And, indeed, the deep brown of his skin is redder and the curl of his hair smoother than that of his fellow fisherman, without evidence of Caucasian intermixture. The *belair*, says Monsieur Martino, was danced by men and women, and there were usually more men than women dancers. Then a man and woman alone took the center and danced the *ma'jhumbwe*, a dance more intimate and sexual in its import. There was jealousy on the part of the woman's mate, or another man who may have hoped for encouragement from her if he could have the opportunity to prove his prowess. So the jealous rival stepped in and became an adversary with the twofold purpose of overcoming his opponent and of exhibiting his own superior physical and personal attributes. He must show himself clever. He constantly invented new play. He must show himself witty. His must exhibit his physical charms; there are definite periods of the dance when the two circle before the crowd with the sole purpose of exhibiting themselves for appraisal. He must be strong; at times the feats of these *l'ag'yas* are nothing short of miraculous. They surpass the tales even of the gladiators in pure brute strength, and the lightning trickery of ju-jitsu finesse. And always to the steady staccato of the *'ti bwa* and the throb, and pulse, and swing of the goat skin or bull hide stretched over the barrel-like drum and tormented by palms and heel of the man astride.

Monsieur Martino's explanation is very likely, well thought out, and deserving of further consideration. But I think of the Nigerian Earth Mother, and I am again at Vauclin, on the shifting white sand under two rows of coco trees leading to the sea. We are between the little chapel of Nôtre-Dame-de-Pecheurs and the row of blue "Canots" in their palm-leaf shelters. We face the sea, and the cobbled streets of Vauclin wind in gentle ascent to the top of the hill, ending in the market, another the cathedral, still another winding in and out and then circulating the *hôtel de ville* to arrive with a flourish at the public square. But these are only mock destinations. They all really terminate at the market, which is the center of the town from which radiate all commercial and social activities; and from the market all activities lead to the sea.

And it is to the sea, then, this bright morning, to see the *l'ag'ya*. The housewives have finished with the fish vendors, and the fish vendors have stripped the fisherman of the last silver *p'tit balawoo*. It is all over now, and the *porteuses* can spare an hour or two to rest their trays on the sand. Cupped straw hats of the fishermen, wide straw hats of housewives, *madras* and *foulard* in the white sunlight. The *l'ag'ya* itself is on a surprising patch of green touching the edge of the sand. It is not Julot this time, but the dry little Cisseaux, perhaps nicknamed that because of his biting wit. Constance has finished the *ma'jhumbwe,* second movement of the *belair.* She is magnificent in gold jewelry, embroidered white chemise, and striped *jup-la* of the old days. Her fine black face shines with perspiration. She has danced from eight o'clock this morning, and it is now one-thirty. She is seven months pregnant. Now Constance has given way for the *l'ag'ya,* which as Monsieur Martino says, should be the order of things.

I continue to think of the sons of Nigeria. This is the *l'ag'ya* as I know it. As I love it. No lurid spectacle under flickering kerosene torches, while callow-faced men place a piece for the breaking of a companion's skull. No exhibition for the tourist to come and see and feel a little ill and go away and write about the savage beat of the tom-tom, the bloody attacks of the two naked combatants, and the mad, primitive frenzy of the onlookers. No stench from bodies that have soured all day in the heat and excitement of the fête. No odor of white rum grown fetid in feverish mouths. No reeling and crowding and cursing to enter the ring and place bets and offer insults to a lagging hero.

Such was the *l'ag'ya* at the fête at François, in the early morning hours. Now it is to the sun, and the small patch of green is the abundance of the Earth Mother, while the coco palms overhead are heavy with green fruit. Alcide and Tel'mach are jesting with each other and the crowd. They are both in the tight-fitting semi-nude striped tricot of the sailor, and Tel'mach boasts a ragged beret. They make fun of each other in good natured rivalry, and each tries to outdo the other in his demonstrations of wit and personal charm. This preliminary is all a part of the dance. The bright air is brittle with laughing and joking and anticipating. Even the sea seems to scintillate in reflection of our mood. And then the staccato of the *'ti bwa* and the deep rolling response of the tambour as the drummers take their places. They play together like this for a moment, deciding on a song, falling into the rhythm of each other, preparing us for the rite. Under the magic fingers of Cisseaux, the tambour becomes alive, not nervous and erratic as with Julot, nor, again, the mistress responding to the caress of her lover as with the man from Trois Îlets; deeply, subtly, mysteriously, it is a thing of flesh and blood. The abode of the *mystère;* the Earth Mother giving a message to her sons.

Alcide has made the circle of challenge, and Tel'mach has followed him with eyes only, seemingly rooted to the spot. Then they face each other, ten feet or so apart, and, arms in gesture of boxing, begin a slow rocking motion on half-bent knees, legs wide apart. This is the basic movement of the *l'ag'ya*. All else is variation and gesture and pantomime, with much improvisation. The balance is broken by shifting forward and back, across and back again, shoulders more than arms keeping the rhythm. The balance, too, is in the hips. A jerking, almost twisting, of the haunches that becomes more agitated with the tension of the drum beats leading to the attack. Then suddenly there is a snap. The drum booms out a command, and Alcide falls flat on his face, turns over, and bounces up again without seeming to touch the ground. Tel'mach has spun on one leg, the other half-bent and at right angles to his body. Both were remarkable feats of muscular coordination, and the crowd cheers them equally. They are balancing again now, this time more nervously. They look into each other's eyes, but not the slightest movement, no muscle in the body of one escapes the other. In these few seconds the perspiration has begun to stream down their faces and polish their naked shoulders. And now they are together, this time to lock in an embrace until one or the other weakens, or until the drum commands them to separate. The fascination of the real *l'ag'ya* lies not in the lust of the combat, but in the finesse of approach and retreat, the tension which becomes almost a hypnosis, then the flash of the two bodies as they leap into the air, fall in a crouch, and whirl at each other in simulated attacks, only to walk nonchalantly away, backs to each other, showing utter indifference before falling again into the rocking motion which rests them physically but excites them emotionally.

In one of these sudden attacks Tel'mach has ripped open Alcides' striped sweater and proudly exhibits it to the crowd. They take position again, Alcide bare to the waist, gleaming bronze in the white sun. And now they begin the *l'ag'ya* in earnest. But without losing for an instant the rhythm of the dance. Sometimes they are wrestlers, bodies entwined and pressed to the earth; they are boxers, dodging and swinging and thrusting to the staccato of *'ti bwa,* puppets on an invisible string controlled by a nervous god—turning somersaults over each other, spinning on one foot, and seeming to dangle in mid-air before falling to the ground. And gradually it is less pantomime, less play, and more a serious struggle—not so much a struggle to overcome the opponent as to fill some demand in the deep agitation of the drum. Now the tops of their heads are pressed together, and their arms are locked. Tel'mach seeks in vain to hold the oily, polished body of Alcide, but slowly he is being forced to the earth. With each beat of the drum Alcide rises and Tel'mach sinks.

Cisseaux is becoming hoarse, and the words of the song are unintelligible. Water runs from his chin and throat, the cords of his neck stand out like thin steel cables, and the face of the drum is moist from the perspiration which runs down his arms and into the palms of his hands. He rises slightly from the drum and sinks again and grasps it with his thighs as though to bring into it even more life by the passionate contact of his body. His eyes are bloodshot, and he is breathing heavily. He is bringing the *l'ag'ya* to a close. We of the crowd have stopped cheering and jesting and passing advice to the contestants. We are tense; even the coco trees have ceased to murmur. Life seems to be suspended for a moment halfway between earth and sky, with the voice of the drum a muffled warning of an impending disaster. Slowly as the dropping of minutes in the blinding sun, Tel'mach touches the green earth. Knees first, then thighs, then back. And over him Alcide, pressing him down and down until his whole body is flat, and in the final burst from the drum, Alcide has lifted his own face to the sun, triumphantly, ecstatically. There is a slow gasp from the crowd. It is almost as though an unseen being has arisen, satisfied, to take its departure, and has made its presence known only by its leaving. Then Tel'mach is released and springs to his feet, and we are laughing at the torn sweater which Alcide waves in the air, and cheering him as the winner. Cisseaux leans far back under a dem' john of white rum, and the wind stirs again.

The *porteuses* adjust burden and *foulard* and soon are swinging in a ragged procession up the hill and away from the sea, little gossips and comments on the *l'ag'ya* and free laughter floating behind them. Fishermen seek the dark recesses of their little huts for the much-needed siesta, and housewives pass a word or two of gossip, then scatter to prepare the late noonday meal. Children linger around Cisseaux and Tel'mach and

Alcide and the drum. The drum is voiceless now, and they caress it with grimy fingers and beat their first lessons on its submissive face. The *l'ag'ya* is over. The Earth Mother is appeased. Her sons have forgotten the significance of this dance, but the blood of their ancestors is strong. They have not forgotten the dance.

Designing Dunham

John Pratt's Method in Costume and Décor:
An Interview with John Pratt

VÈVÈ A. CLARK

John Pratt, painter, sculptor, and designer, was the Technical Advisor of the Dunham Company and the Consulting Director of the Katherine Dunham School of Arts and Research. The following is an abridgement of an interview conducted on 23 May 1981 in East Saint Louis, Missouri.

JOHN PRATT [hereafter JP]: Like many other things in the Dunham Company, costumes and scenery were redone and remade. The scenery was adapted for other numbers and we did use unit scenery so that various décors we had served for many different numbers; they would be transformed by either lighting or with scrims and that sort of thing because we traveled a completely soft show. It was made to hang. There wasn't anything stretch because it sometimes had to go into airplanes and so forth and so on. And we didn't travel very lightly as you know. *L'Ag'ya* was done for the first time for the Federal Theater and then those costumes were not available when Miss Dunham wanted to redo it. The Federal Theater was required by their regulations to keep all of their old costumes, but by that time they'd probably been torn up and made into a number of other productions. My job in the Federal Theater was to make the budget stretch and last by taking old clothes and tearing them up to make new clothes and I always kept track of them. I had a sentimental interest in the *L'Ag'ya* costumes and other productions at Federal Theater. But that set of costumes was not available to Miss Dunham and the scenery had been done by Clyde Rickenbar. I personally never liked

SOURCE: VèVè A. Clark, interview with John Pratt, 23 May 1981. Copyright 1981 by VèVè A. Clark. Used by permission.

the scenery very much because I always do prefer my own scenery. But the first version of *L'Ag'ya* was done with scenery by Clyde Rickenbar and he had done the scenery as sketches. It was done in black and white just as if it had been with chalk. It seemed to me to need a richer, and to some degree, a more realistic setting, and also something with a little more dimension rather than having these black and white sketches I had seen.

VÈVÈ A. CLARK [hereafter VC]: Was it the budget that would have made him use only black and white?

JP: No, I think it was his taste and that's what he wanted the scenery to be so that was apparently what was approved. I was so busy trying to help every other [show]. The workshops were turning out many, many different things and we were turning out the other ballets that were appearing on the same program as well as various other productions. We would turn out as many as five shows a week because we served Illinois and the six states around and we would send out touring companies. It was just a madhouse, really unbelievable. It was a wonderful thing. We will never see its likes again, but I'm only explaining how the first set of costumes just disappeared. They couldn't be kept together. I mean, they couldn't have been bought, say, by Miss Dunham for her own use because of the various red tape in the Federal Theater and then they were torn up and the material used for other things.

The next version of *L'Ag'ya* was put together in Chicago, and a large number of costumes, particularly the men's clothes, were made of Japanese materials which I liked very much, and which I had been able to buy at a considerable discount because the Japanese merchants in Los Angeles were trying to liquefy their entire stock because they were being moved out. We had just gone through Pearl Harbor, and I feel that I was doing them some good. They were stuck with all of their stuff, and I did buy an enormous amount of Japanese material, particularly that used for summer kimonos. I must say it stood us in very good stead for many years. Many of the Dunham Company costumes were made of Japanese material, Japanese summer kimono material. It was very color-fast, washed beautifully. It didn't fade, and it was very tough stuff. It was very nice.

Anyway, the second version was put together in Chicago, and my mother was very helpful in reconstructing many of the rather elaborately embroidered women's jackets that were used in the *Mazouk* and the *Béguine*. And she also made the headdresses, which were very tall, sort of an imitation of eighteenth-century colonial wigs. Then after that they were made of white material and draped with various hanging handkerchiefs. I always tried to control the color in *L'Ag'ya* very carefully. So, in the first act most of the women were dressed in white and men were dressed in Japanese material with mostly blue and white print. And it was very fresh and crisp looking. Miss Dunham wore a pale blue dress trimmed with embroidery, which I think she must have liked very much because while I was away at the war she also wore it in *Carib Song.* Anyway it served a double purpose. The scenery by this time was three-dimensional. We had started to use a two-foot high platform across the back of the stage and it had boxes piled on that permanent platform and then the whole thing was draped with a ground cover, happily, to look like hills; that was a permanent setting for all of the ballet. At that time we added a jungle drop. It served for every jungle number. So when the zombie scene came on, that was what we did. Otherwise it was done in cyclorama. Then the third time it was done over it was for the British Broadcasting Company, and the costumes by that time had gotten quite worn, even though they'd had a great deal of loving care, having ribbons and strings sewn on them to give them dimension. Many of them were duplicated at that time. So they've had a long history. The scenery also has been redone. The jungle eventually wore out so there was a new jungle. So it's been a very moving thing. A very living sort of theater at all times.

vc: Has anything survived from that second period of costume?

jp: Not to my knowledge. I think they finally went the way. And not having the company active for a number of years has made a great difference because the costumes, some of them just disappeared and some of them actually were worn out. I've always loved working in the theater because it is an illusion. When you saw these costumes up close they weren't very gorgeous, but the overall effect was quite satisfactory. So when they weren't in use they weren't particularly desirable or lovable or cherished. They just turned raggedly looking.

vc: So as far as costumes are concerned for *L'Ag'ya,* do you have any idea what's left?

jp: There aren't any.

vc: Nothing?

jp: I don't think there is one to be found, and none of Miss Dunham's even. There are a number of her [other] costumes that are in very nice shape. They've been very carefully kept and they're over next door [at the Dunham Museum].

Katherine Dunham's Notable Contribution

JOHN MARTIN

With the arrival of Katherine Dunham on the scene, the prospects for the development of a substantial Negro dance art begin to look decidedly bright. Her performance with her group last Sunday at the Windsor Theatre may very well become a historic occasion, for certainly never before in all the efforts of recent years to establish the Negro dance as a serious medium has there been so convincing and authoritative an approach.

Miss Dunham has apparently based her theory on the obvious fact so often overlooked that if the Negro is to develop an art of his own he can begin only with the seeds of that art that lie within him. These seeds are abundant and unique. Indeed, it would be difficult to think of any people with a richer heritage of dance begging to be made use of. Yet in the past (and even in Miss Dunham's present company in certain instances) there have been those who have started out by denying this heritage and smoothing it over with the gloss of an alien racial culture that deceives no one. The potential greatness of the Negro dance lies in its discovery of its own roots and the careful nursing of them into growth and flower.

Certainly this seems to be exactly what Miss Dunham has done. Several years ago she went to Haiti and the neighboring islands on a Rosenwald fellowship to study the native dances and rituals, and since then she has carried on the study of her subject under a grant from the Rockefeller Foundation. All of which has given her a basis for her work that is entirely solid and true. But manifestly if she were not possessed of creative gifts,

SOURCE: John Martin, "The Dance—A Negro Art: Katherine Dunham's Notable Contribution," *New York Times,* 25 February 1940. Copyright 1940 by the *New York Times* Company. Reprinted by permission.

no amount of research could possibly turn itself automatically into art. It is because she has showed herself to have both the objective quality of the student and the natural instinct of the artist that she has done such a truly important job.

Perhaps one of the most notable aspects of her program is the absence of all sense of self-importance. Here is simply a performance about which no explanations or announcements need be made to any normal human being who likes theatrical entertainment. It is, in short, a good show. That it is basically something far more significant does not in any way interfere with its sprightly and vivacious surface values.

This is quite in character with the essence of the Negro dance itself. There is nothing pretentious about it; it is not designed to delve into philosophy or psychology but to externalize the impulses of a high-spirited, rhythmic, and gracious race. That Miss Dunham's dances accomplish this end so beautifully can mean only that she has actually isolated the element of a folk art upon which a more consciously creative and sophisticated form can be built as time goes on. This is cultural pioneering of a unique sort.

To sit before a program such as this is to be impressed both with the existence of a constant element in it that is different from all other types of dance and with the great range and variety with which that constant element manifests itself. Miss Dunham has composed a primitive ritual in a somewhat mythological vein and has graduated her material from this point through rituals that are for the release of personal tensions in primitive and semi-primitive societies down to the jazz and swing variants of those same impulses that are current in sophisticated communities. This sounds tremendously anthropological and "important," and it is; but it is also debonair and delightful, not to say daring and erotic.

Because Miss Dunham's researches have been made in countries which have come under Latin and Gallic influences, she gives us rumbas and dances of coquetry that are almost Parisian in their chic. But in so doing she manages somehow to show them as fundamentally Negro underneath and links them up indefinably with the universal quality of the art she is working in. Her rumbas from Santiago de Cuba and Mexico, her *Island Songs* from Haiti and Martinique, her delicious little scene called

Tropics—Shore Excursion, are all as finely racial as her truly wonderful little genre piece called *Florida Swamp Shimmy.*

At present, if her version of *Br'er Rabbit an' de Tah Baby* can be taken as typical, she has not got to the point where she can make a ballet (or dance drama or what you will) out of independent material, but at least she has sensed the form upon which such a type of work can be built and the ingredients that belong in it. This present work is a failure, to be sure, but it is the kind of failure on which a future success can be based, for it clears the ground to a considerable extent.

In her supporting company Miss Dunham has in Archie Savage a dancer eminently worthy of her efforts. He can not only dance like a house afire but he is a good actor and a genuine stage personality. The group as a whole is handsome and competent, though there is among certain of the male dancers, including Talley Beatty, a distressing tendency to introduce the technique of the academic ballet. What is there in the human mind that is so eager to reduce the rare and genuine to the standard and foreign!

Musically the program is excellent, from the drumming of Gaucho (and of Miss Dunham herself) to the piano arrangements of Paquita Anderson. John Pratt's costumes are beautifully effective and ingenious, and the whole show is well staged and colorful. Happily, a whole series of further performances is to be given.

P.S.—Better not take grandma.

Thesis Turned Broadway

KATHERINE DUNHAM

In the great raft of publicity which, in the past few months, has appeared in connection with my role in the Broadway show *Cabin in the Sky*, I find myself referred to, and on the very same day, both as "the hottest thing on Broadway" and "an intelligent, sensitive young woman . . . an anthropologist of note." Personally, I do not think of myself as either one of these extreme phenomena. But eager reporters, confronted by the simultaneous presence of two such diverse elements, have often failed to grasp the synthesis between them; they have chosen, instead, to account for effectiveness by an exaggerated emphasis upon either one or the other. Then there is always the fact that the attempt to relate the dignified and somewhat awesome science of anthropology with the popular art of Broadway dancing and theater works the interviewer back to the question of which came first. Actually, that consideration is as unimportant as the chicken-egg controversy. Now that I look back over the long period of sometimes alternating, sometimes simultaneous interest in both subjects, it seems inevitable that they should have eventually fused completely.

Every person who has a germ of artistry seeks to recreate and present an impression of universal human experience—to fulfill either human needs or wants. The instrument is the specific art form which may have been chosen; the effectiveness depends upon skill in handling the form and upon the originality of the individual imagination. But the experience which is given expression cannot be either too individual or too specific; it must be universal. In the Greek theater, for example, the importance of

SOURCE: Katherine Dunham, "Thesis Turned Broadway," *California Arts and Architecture* (August 1941). Copyright 1941 by Katherine Dunham. Reprinted by permission.

the universals was so great that an entire system of formal absolutes was worked out of their expression. Consequently, any effective artistic communication is impossible if the artist's understanding of human experience is limited by inadequate knowledge. Anthropology is the study of man. It is a study not of a prescribed portion of man's activity or history, but a study (through some one of the five fields of anthropological specialization—ethnology, archaeology, social anthropology, linguistics, physical anthropology) of his entire state of being throughout his entire history. In such a survey, the student of anthropology gradually comes to recognize universal emotional experiences, common alike to both the primitive Bushman and the sophisticated cosmopolitan; he notes patterns of expression which have been repeatedly effective throughout the ages and which, though modified by many material circumstances, persist in their essential form; and finally, he acquires an historical perspective which enables him, in the confusion of changing maps and two world wars within a single generation, to discern the developing motifs and consistent trends.

As nearly as I can remember, I have been dancing since I was eight years old and it has been my growing interest to know not only how people dance but, even more importantly, why they dance as they do. By the time I was studying at the University of Chicago, I had come to feel that if I could discover this, not only as it applied to one group of people but to diverse groups, with their diverse cultural, psychological, and racial backgrounds, I would have arrived at some of the fundamentals, not only of choreographic technique, but of theater artistry and function. I applied myself to acquiring this knowledge and eventually, as a "Julius Rosenwald fellow, student of anthropology and the dance," spent a year and a half traveling through the West Indies in pursuit of this understanding.

In the beginning, I had great hopes of turning out a thesis for the University of Chicago which would take care of the entire field of primitive dance. It was to be entitled "A Comparative Analysis of Primitive Dance." I ended up by limiting my thesis to "A Comparative Analysis of the Dances of Haiti: Their Form, Function, Social Organization, and the Interrelation of Form and Function." (Still too much for one sitting!) In the West Indies the peasant natives (primarily Negroes of Koromantee, Ibo, Congo, Dahomey, Mandingo, and other west coast derivation, mixed perhaps with a little Carib Indian and varying degrees of European stock) think very much and behave basically very much as did their African forebears. Consequently they dance very much in the same fashion. Differences there are, of course, due to the shift from tribal to folk culture, to miscegenation, cultural contact, and other items making for social change. But the elements of the dance are still what, in my analysis, would be termed "primitive." Almost all social activity is dancing or some type of rhythmic motion (it may be the unified movement of the *combite* or work society of Haiti in cutting sugar cane, or a similar activity in the work societies of the Jamaican Maroons, or the cross-country trek of a Carnival band). Out of a maze of material from the concentrated fields of study—Jamaica, Haiti, Martinique, and Trinidad—one important fact stood out: in these societies the theater of the people ("theater" being practically synonymous with dance activity) served a well-integrated, well-defined function in the community; in the case of the Carnival dances of social integration and sexual stimulus and release; in the funeral dance the externalization of grief; the social dances, exhibitionism and sexual selection along with social cohesion; in the ceremonial dances, group "ethos" solidarity in an established mechanism of worship, whether through hypnosis, hysteria, or ecstasy. And so on through the several categories of dances arrived at.

It was one thing to write a thesis and have it approved for a master's degree. It was another thing to begin earning a living on Broadway. In making use of field training to choreograph for my group, I found persistently recurring in the back of my mind in some form or another "function." It never seemed important to portray, as such, the behavior of other peoples as exotics. But the cultural and psychological framework, the "why" became increasingly important. It became a matter of course to attack a stage or production situation in the same way in which I would approach a new primitive community or work to analyze a dance category. As in the primitive community certain movement patterns, which I cannot go into here, were always related to certain functions, so in the modern theater there would be a correlation between a dance movement and the function of that dance within the theater framework. And certainly a broad and general knowledge of cultures and cultural patterns can be advantageously brought to bear upon the problems of relating form and function in the modern theater. Or so has been my theory and so my practice in my own theater experience.

What would be the connection between the Carnival dance, whose function is sexual stimulus and release, and almost any similar situation in a Broadway musical—for example, the temptation scene on the River Nile in *Cabin in the Sky?* It would be the similarity in function, and through this similarity in function the transference of certain elements of form would be legitimate.

The Negro Dance

KATHERINE DUNHAM

The pressure of European culture upon the Negroes transplanted to the West Indies was of a different kind. . . . The political, economic, and social organization of the West Indies was no longer tribal, and the entire structure of social and art traditions which had been based upon the tribal form lost its functional validity. Accordingly, this structure began to disintegrate; and the process of disintegration was accelerated tremendously by the impact of European culture upon the now vulnerable African traditions.

My personal observation has been that the French, on the whole, were less concerned with dominating culturally their colonial peoples than the

SOURCE: Katherine Dunham, excerpt from "The Negro Dance," in *The Negro Caravan: Writings by American Negroes,* edited by Sterling A. Brown, Arthur P. Davis, and Ulysses Lee (New York: Dryden Press, 1941), 990–1000. Copyright 1941 by Holt, Rinehart & Winston. Reprinted by permission. The original editors' note included the following information:

This essay, too long to appear in its entirety, gave first a definition of the dance as "rhythmic motion, singly or in a group for any one of several purposes": for (1) play, (2) the stimulation or release of emotional or physical tension, (3) the expression of social relationships, and (4) the exhibition of individual or group skill. Since the dance is essentially emotional, forms of the dance have a tenacity greater than other cultural forms. The dances of the Polynesians, the Aztecs, and the American Indian show how dance patterns, though altered in function, remain fairly stable in form. The primitive African dance was largely "bound up functionally with the whole study of religious beliefs and practices," though of course there were war and social dances. In explaining her use of the word *primitive,* Dunham denies the connotations of "loose" or "inferior" or "simple," pointing out the integration and formalization of the tribal cultures of the West African empires, whence came most of the slaves for the New World.

English, and consequently the integrity of African culture and the sanctity of African religious tradition persists to a greater extent in, for example, Haiti and Martinique than in Jamaica or Trinidad. Even so, in the interior of most of the islands of the Caribbean, one can still find African forms which have survived vigorously in the almost-tribal organization of isolated communities; and these forms are replaced more and more by European influences as one nears the relatively urban communities of the port towns.

Although the survival of African dances in their intact form is most typical of inland communities in the West Indies, North America also furnishes material for observation.

Early in the 19th century, soon after the Louisiana Purchase, slaves were allowed for the first time to assemble for social and recreational diversion. The most popular meeting place was a large open field at Orleans and Rampart, known as Congo Square. In earlier times the space had been a ceremonial ground of the Oumas Indians. Today, landscaped with palm trees, it forms a part of the municipal grounds called Beauregard Square. The Negroes, however, still speak of the place as Congo Square, in memory of the days when it was an open, dusty field, its grass worn bare by the stomping and shuffling of hundreds of restless bare feet. A century ago, slaves met there every Saturday night to perform the tribal and sexual dances which they had brought with them from the Congo.

Before the Civil War the Congo Dances were one of the unusual sights of New Orleans to which tourists were always taken. At times almost as many white spectators as dancers gathered for the festive occasion. That the Negroes had not forgotten their dances, even after years of repression and exile from their native Africa, is attested by descriptive accounts of the times. . . .

Though discontinued during the war, the Congo Dances were again performed after the emancipation and were not entirely abandoned even two decades later, when a correspondent of the *New York World* reported: "A dry-goods box and an old pork barrel formed the orchestra. These were beaten with sticks or bones, used like drumsticks so as to keep up a continuous rattle, while some old men and women chanted a song that appeared to me to be purely African in its many-vowelled syllabification. . . . In the dance the women did not move their feet from the ground. They only writhed their bodies and swayed in undulatory motions from ankles to waist. . . . The men leaped and performed feats of gymnastic dancing. . . . Small bells were attached to their ankles. . . . I asked several old women to recite them (the words of the song) to me, but they only laughed and shook their heads. In their patois they told me—'No use, you would never understand it. *C'est le Congo!*'"

According to Herbert Asbury,[1] from whom the above description is taken, the favorite dances of the Negroes at the Congo Square were the *calinda* and the *bamboula,* both of which are still performed in Haiti. Both of these were, to be sure, embellished with copious borrowings from the French *contredanse,* but in their fundamental pattern and movement were clearly African.

Still another instance emerges when we compare the following description by Père Labat, a Jesuit missionary writing in 1742, of a dance performed in Santo Domingo, with dances performed on some of the islands off South Carolina.

> The dancers are placed in two lines, facing each other: men on one side, women on the other. Those who are tired of dancing and the spectators form a circle about the dancers and drum players. The most skillful sings a song that he composes on the spur of the moment on whatever subject he deems fitting, the refrain of which is sung by all the spectators and is accompanied by clapping of the hands. As for the dancers, they hold their hands a little like those who dance while playing castanets . . . they jump, execute turns, approach within two or three feet of each other, retreat in cadence until the sound of the drum commands them to come together, beating their thighs together, that is, the men against the women.

Persons who have visited the islands off South Carolina have described dances in a manner as to call Père Labat's description strikingly to mind.

However, such a direct retention of African forms in North America is certainly the exception rather than the rule, and the West Indies are still a more fertile field for the analysis of the survival of the dance in its shift from tribal to folk culture. Apart from the two extremes—the close-to-tribal organization of isolated interior communities and the cosmopolitanism of port rum-shops—the characteristic and predominant culture of the West Indies may be termed the folk stage of acculturation. Here the conflict between the disintegrating African traditions and the powerful European influences is still very active and has resulted in many and varied attempts at compromise and resolution.

For one thing, it was inevitable that as Negroes became more and more

inducted into the religious practices of various European cultures, the
dance and ceremonial forms which were an integral part of African religious practices would gradually become absorbed to some degree into the
new religious life, and to a greater degree into the new secular life. Haiti,
for example, offers an interesting instance of neatly combining Catholic
and traditional African ideologies. Every ceremony begins with a Catholic
litany which, once performed, is promptly forgotten for the remainder
of the ceremony, which is almost purely African. Another example is that
of associating the portrait of Saint Patrick driving the snakes out of Ireland with Damballa, the traditional African snake-god. And this inverted
interpretation is accomplished with apparently the greatest of ease!

In North America, however, there is less compromise and more real
assimilation of African religious forms into European religious ideology.
In 1938–1939 I had occasion to direct a group in the Federal Writers' Project in an investigation of religious and magic cults in the city. Here, while
the ideology was clearly and definitely Christian (with added flourishes),
the entire pattern of religious behavior associated with it was almost as
purely African. The rhythmic percussion-type hand-clapping and foot-
stamping, the jumping and leaping, the "conversion" or "confession" in
unknown tongues which is a form of possession or ecstasy (induced, in
some cases, by a circle of "saints" or "angels" closing in upon the person
in rhythmic motion of a dance), the frequent self-hypnosis by motor-
activity of the shoulders—all these African forms were present. This last
type of movement, for example, is called *zépaules* in Haiti and is formally
recognized there as a basic dance movement of great ritualistic importance
in practice. In general form, even in function, the motor activity connected
with the religious expression of "store-front" churches in this country is
strikingly similar to that of the Haitian peasant.

More often, however, the disintegration of African religious ideology
under the impact of European influences led to the incorporation of the
forms of its dance into secular dance. The West Indies, representing that
stage of folk culture in which such transitions are apparent, provides, once
more, some excellent examples.

In the more formalized of secular dances, in the dance-halls at carnival time, the young people of Haiti perform what they refer to as *do-ba*
dances, whose characteristic feature is a wavelike motion of the spine
performed in a squatting position, back forward, body bent double. The
do-ba begins in an erect position, but gradually, by a simultaneous forward movement of shoulders and back, is lowered until the dancer is in an

almost squatting position. Anyone who has seen the dance to Damballa, snake-god of the Rada-Dahomey cult, will certainly recognize the secular *do-ba* as a derivative of the ritual in imitation of the undulations of the snake-god. In the ritual, the low squatting position is the climax of the dance and usually indicates a state of supreme religious ecstasy, bordering on or participating in a state of possession by the snake-god to whom the dance is sacred. In the secular dance, the climax of intensity is also reached at the same point, although, of course, the ecstasy is not, in these cases, of the religious impetus.

Another instance of the secularization of a religious ritual is the *bonga* or *banda* of Trinidad. My experience with this dance was when it was presented to me as a part of a funeral ritual. It has a definitely sexual character, in keeping with African philosophy which closely associates procreation with death, perhaps as a compensatory effort. I have been told, however, that the same general movements and patterns are freely incorporated into Carnival dances also.

So far we have spoken first of the incorporation of African religious dance patterns into Christian ideology; and we have considered, as well, examples of the degeneration of African religious dance patterns into secular dance. It remains to consider the interaction of African secular dance with European secular dance. The *béguine,* which is practically the national dance of Martinique, is a striking example of just this type of combination. . . .

In interior Jamaica, as well, the "set" dances proceed step by step through seventeenth-century French court forms of minuet only to culminate in a finale the like of which no French court ever witnessed but which, to the Jamaicans, is part and parcel of the "set" dances. In Haiti, the *caribinea,* or *contredanse,* is a native adaptation of the European social dance. Innumerable such examples, especially from the French colonies, could be cited. . . .

Thus we see that in the history of the Negro, the transition from tribal to folk culture expressed itself in three ways as far as the dance is concerned: (1) the use of African ritual patterns for the expression of Christian ideology; (2) the degeneration of religious ritual patterns, by virtue of the disintegration of the ideology which sustained them, into secular use; and (3) the combination of secular African patterns with the secular patterns of whatever European nation happened to dominate the territory.

By the time we come to analyze the transition from folk to urban culture, as the next stage in the acculturation of the Negro, the problem becomes more difficult; for by now the patterns are so intermixed, and so dissipated and broken, that tracing them from one complex to another is at times almost impossible. Sometimes the transition is implicit in the difference in the organization, the social procedures which are involved, in the dance as we proceed from country community to urban center.

In Haiti, for example, the common dance of the rum shops and public houses in town is the *méringue*. This might be described under the general term of ballroom dance, but, as is true of the closely related national dances of the other islands, the *méringue* has definitely undergone radical changes in character on being introduced into an urban setting. These dances in town call for no unusual knowledge or skill, and no leader. Men pay to enter an establishment and dance with the women, or buy rum for the privilege of dancing, and leave at will. Here are all young or middle-aged people—people still very active sexually, who seek stimulus and outlet for a definite localized urge.

In the country, the dances which are performed at a *bamboche*—any get-together not connected with any religious rite and not falling into the category of a seasonal dance—are organized differently. The *bamboche* may have, as its primary feature, a wedding celebration, the departure of a notable in the community, part of a feast-day entertainment, or any other excuse. Here, in contrast with the organization of dances in the city, there is a *mait' la danse,* usually one of the best dancers in the neighborhood. He must have a female partner, and she too must be an outstanding dancer. Everyone usually knows each other well. Not only are both young and old equally active, but the older ones usually lead since here the premium is not upon physical attractiveness, but upon skill; and the repertoire of dances is so long and complex that only the older ones are competent to lead. In general, while there is no hierarchy of officials, there is a definite air of something more or less planned, definitely communal. Behavior and sanctions are understood. The dances are not just accidental or the outgrowth of an urge for personal excitement or expression. They are group dances according to a set pattern, and necessitate a certain amount of skill in execution, the exhibition of which is another factor in bringing these people together.

It is not at all necessary to remain afield for examples of the movement from dance patterns of folk cultures to those of our urban centers. It just so happened that, at the very time that the Lindy Hop was first becoming popular in New York, I myself was in Jamaica, studying the dances there. When I returned to New York and saw the Lindy Hop for the first time, it was apparent to me that almost the entire pattern and certainly many of the specific movements were very similar to those urban Jamaican popular dances known as the *shay-shay,* or *mento,* which I had just been recording. This similarity was due, in part, no doubt, to the influence of the Jamaicans who had emigrated to America in increasing numbers. But it was due, also, I feel, to the fact that the patterns and the movements were fundamentally familiar, as part of a deep tradition of folk-dancing, to American Negroes.

Another of our currently popular dance forms, the Big Apple, seems to me to have its derivation in the category of "circle" dances represented by the plantation Juba dance. In its original African form, the *juba* or *jumba* or *majumba,* as it is called in the West Indies, is primarily a competitive dance of skill. One person steps forward in the circle of dancers and begins exhibiting his skill, whereupon he is joined by a member of the opposite sex who joins him in this exhibition. The people in the circle may rotate for a certain number of measures in one direction, then in another for an equal number of measures, or may remain stationary, all the while clapping rhythmically and encouraging the competitors with song and verse. While this pattern is not exclusively African, it is typical. The Juba, as this dance in a modified form came to be known in America, was a very popular plantation folk dance and a whole tradition of Juba music was evolved in connection with it. No doubt it was influenced, to some extent, by the square dance. Certainly, however, the recently popular Big Apple belongs in this tradition and when danced with the particular rhythm and abandon characteristic of such Negro gathering places as the Savoy Ballroom in Harlem, assumes an aspect very similar to that of the original *jumba.*

This detailed consideration of the dances of tribal and folk cultures has been motivated by recognition of the fact that American Negro dance is a product of this particular line of development. The various European influences, the tribal origins, the disintegration of the dance of religious ritual into that of social and finally of individual expression are part of American Negro dance history. But here the dance has developed into the final urban stage under sociological pressures which do not exist to as marked a degree in the West Indies. The entire process has here been accelerated and condensed, not only by the uniquely rapid industrialization of America but also by the position of Negro culture within American society.

We have already discussed in some details those expressions of the transition from dance patterns of tribal to those of folk culture such as the *calinda* and *bamboula* in New Orleans, and the dances of the islands off

South Carolina. The plantation dances, most of them in the tradition of the circle-and-hand-clapping dances of Africa and influenced, at the same time, by the English square dance and the French quadrille, represent that period of American Negro folk dancing which can be compared to that of the contemporary West Indies. Out of this period emerged the minstrel tradition, which was in essence a forerunner of the urbanization of Negro folk-dance patterns.

The minstrel period of Negro dance is particularly important in that, for the first time, the influence of Negro culture upon the American white culture becomes apparent. Previously it had been the Negro culture which had experienced the effects of foreign influence. The Negro had borrowed from the quadrille just as he had borrowed the finery of American white culture, although, to be sure, he had interpreted them both in his own unique manner. Now the entertainment value of Negro dance and musical expressions became recognized and whereas these forms had previously been repressed[2] or looked upon with completely alien eyes, black-face minstrel bands now began to exploit those very forms.

The rise of the black-face minstrel bands achieved the induction of Negro culture into American culture not in terms of an appreciation of Negro cultural expressions as art forms but on the basis of their entertainment value. This instrument of fusion between the two cultures resulted not only in jazz bands, a fact of American musical history which is well known, but provided the meeting ground for sand-dancing, bucking, and winging on the one hand with the Irish clog on the other. The result was the current, highly-stylized form of tap dancing. The minstrel bands also served to make the Negro newly conscious of the value of his own expression and when he saw it adapted by the whites, he drew on his own inventiveness in addition to his store of culture material. It is not merely the inventiveness of the Negro, but this rich background which enters into white American culture and tempers its art forms much as that of the Moors tempered those of Spain.

The cakewalk tradition may properly be considered the urbanization of the plantation folk-dances, incorporating in the whole such separate figures as the Black Annie, the Pas Mala, the Strut, the Palmer House, and, later, Walkin' the Dog, Ballin' the Jack, and other individual expressions.

In moving pictures brought back from a West African sojourn, Dr. Melville J. Herskovits recorded ceremonial dances, some of the steps of which bore a remarkable resemblance to that popular dance of the post–World War I era, the Charleston. Again, in Haiti, I found the Charleston in the dance La Martinique; and in terms of the retention of choreographic forms through transition periods, I would say that such a dance must have been known during the North American folk period. I have certainly seen possessed devotees in "store-front" churches propelling themselves up and down the aisles with a practically pure Charleston step. It is not so surprising, then, that at one point the Charleston should have become such a popular and general expression of American culture.

Frequently, when watching the variations of the Lindy Hop in the Savoy Ballroom, I have seen individualizations which might have come directly from folk, even tribal, eras; and certainly the great sweep of Latin American dances brings with it choreographic patterns rich in African and Creole African lore.

In America, the inevitable assimilation of the Negro and his cultural traditions into American culture as such has given African tradition a place in a large cultural body which it enjoys nowhere else. While, during the cultural segregation, the African traditions were more modified here than elsewhere, those which persisted now have a sound functional relationship towards a culture which is contemporary, rather than towards one which is on the decline; and, therefore, such traditions as have been retained are assured of survival as long as the large, strong cultural body of which they are a part survives. With the re-establishment of a functional relationship towards society as a whole (rather than to a cult) the traditions are strengthened and re-emerge with new vigor. The current vogue of West Indian dances, bringing with it a refreshment of African traditions, adds enormously to this resurgence. The curious fact is that it will be the American Negro, in his relatively strong position as part of American culture, who, in the final analysis, will most probably guarantee the persistence of African dance traditions.

NOTES

1. Herbert Asbury, "The French Quarter," chapter 8 in *The Negro Caravan: Writings by American Negroes,* edited by Sterling A. Brown, Arthur P. Davis, and Ulysses Lee (New York: Dryden Press, 1941).

2. The legal measures taken in New Orleans (Asbury, "The French Quarter,") to prohibit the assembly of Negroes for any reason, including dancing, are typical. In 1751 "any assembly of Negroes or Negresses, either under pretext of dancing, or for any other cause" was forbidden entirely. Later, however, "recognizing the value of recreation and a measure of social intercourse in keeping the Negro contented with his lot," the American authorities, following the Louisiana Purchase, permitted assemblies which continued far into the night. This permission was later qualified, in 1817,

by an ordinance directing that "the assemblies of slaves for the purpose of dancing or other merriment, shall take place only on Sundays, and solely in such open or public places as shall be appointed by the Mayor." Congo Square was the place appointed for this purpose and such gatherings, held under strict police supervision, were rigidly terminated at sunset. Discontinued after twenty years, this custom was resumed in 1845 on the same basis.

An Amazing Aura

Interview with Katherine Dunham

VèVè A. Clark

The following is an excerpt from interviews conducted with Katherine Dunham in East Saint Louis, Illinois, on 24 and 25 May 1977.

VèVè A. CLARK [hereafter identified as VC]: If we look back from today to 1938–1941 . . . it seems to us that there must have been an amazing aura happening around you then. You were coming out of certain individual discoveries, followed by your research in the Caribbean, the magic of having Talley [Talley Beatty] and all the youngsters in your dance company. There was *Pins and Needles,* then *Tropics,* moving up to *Cabin in the Sky* on Broadway. Essentially we are interested in the artist you are and the definition you have given to the profession through your life and your activities.

KATHERINE DUNHAM [hereafter identified as KD]: I had the advantage of being a pioneer. I would say that its drawbacks were less at that period in America than were its advantages. I didn't realize that I was a pioneer. I just knew that with everything I wanted to do I had to start from the beginning, but this method didn't seem too unnatural to me. Here, I think anthropology helped me a great deal. The attitude of an anthropologist is, if one group can do it, another can, so that belief carried over into everything I did. There was no feeling of possible failure, which I think came from a social anthropological background.

SOURCE: *Film Culture Magazine* (1978); reprinted in VèVè A. Clark, Millicent Hodson, Catrina Neiman, and Francine Bailey Price, *The Legend of Maya Deren: A Documentary Biography and Collected Works,* edited by Hollis Melton (New York: Anthology Film Archives, 1984). Copyright 1978 by *Film Culture Magazine.* Reprinted by permission.

vc: Looking back on your career, what were some of the doors that opened for you during the Thirties?

kd: I had a professor whom I really adored, Robert Redfield.[1] His field was acculturation. Acculturation seemed such a natural phenomenon to me, and I believe that this was why Redfield wanted me to go to the Caribbean instead of just Africa. I think that his influence was great. I had come from a very conservative family which encouraged me academically but was not thrilled about my theater work. I thought, "What will my family and the Rosenwald Foundation think of what I'm doing? Being in *Cabin in the Sky*, being out here doing this, that, and the other." I really did suffer.

By then, I had taken most of my exams for my master's. I went to Redfield and said, "I don't know what to do. I have an offer to go into a Broadway show, *Cabin in the Sky*, and I don't know what to do." And he said, "Why can't you just do both? Why are you so worried about which is which? If you're sincere in both, you'll never stop being one or the other anyway, so go right ahead." He came to see a program of mine, a little program given at Abraham Lincoln Center in Chicago, and after seeing it he said, "I would advise you not to hesitate about going into this Broadway show. You can always do anthropology whenever you want to." So that helped me a great deal.

vc: Can you characterize what it was like to be around the Redfields and Herskovitses[2] in the Chicago of that period?

kd: There was something great about Hutchins[3] coming in. He swept in there so young, so handsome, and so wise. He captivated all of us. It was a transitional period when Whitehead[4] was going out. My brother was a Whitehead pupil, a humanist, one of his last students. It seemed as though anything could be done if you could get a degree without having to be at every class, every morning, exactly on time. The freedom that comes from substituting knowledge for formal education is what Hutchins contributed. The feeling against social injustice was so great there that I can practically recognize somebody from the University of Chicago during those years.

It was great for me to have been there then. I just wouldn't be the same person without it. One of the obstacles that Hutchins worked to eliminate was the segregated eating halls on campus. The University of Chicago was a very snobbish school—intellectually snobbish. The Board of Trustees and the people who gave them money were, I think, cardinals, Baptists, I'm not sure. I think that's why Hutchins eventually quit. My brother, too, was a great forerunner in breaking down racial prejudice. He and a friend of his in philosophy, Nick Matsoukas, formed a little theater group. I think my brother actually formed it for me because I had come from Joliet where certain racial prejudice existed, but I didn't understand it. I didn't meet nearly as much of it as he knew I would encounter later in Chicago.

My brother started this little theater, and somehow he must have sensed, not only through knowing me from the family but, I think, because he was intensely a philosopher, he must have known that I would have a much harder time surviving if I didn't express myself in some of the performing arts. Paul Robeson[5] once told me that I needed to continue in theater, and I think Redfield knew it too.

So Matsoukas and my brother formed this little theater group which was simply called The Little Theater Group of Harper Avenue. Harper Avenue was where we all met. [*Laughter*] They were little bitty things; may have been stables, I don't know, but they were rows of artists' studios where all fellow travelers met and all the avant-garde. You might find Louis Armstrong there. Armstrong would bring his trumpet and play on his way through town. Or you might find Canada Lee[6]; it was simply fantastic. Charles White, the painter; Frank Yerby; Jimmy Farrell [James T. Farrell]; and many other names that I probably don't remember.

Alain Locke used to come to our theater. We just had so many people who came. The place was always crowded, and we'd do these one-act plays. Then we began having parties, and there was a certain infiltration. The Communist infiltration after two or three years created an uneasiness, not because Hutchins or the campus would have been against it in any way, but I think the Board of Trustees was getting ready to move on Hutchins's liberalism, even though he didn't leave for some time after that.

Those were the associations that finally moved me into finding a dance berth. My very first dance school experiences in Chicago were with Ruth Page, Mark Turbyfill, and the Chicago Opera. They were in that same little art colony. There was another rival colony on the North Side called The Cube Theater. It was more famous for radical speakers, whereas ours was known for a cultural arts thrust with no color bars at all. So, gradually, without making the effort, seemingly, we broke down the social bias of segregated tables in the dining rooms, and gradually there were admissions to the residence halls.

I had been in and out of the University of Chicago for a number of years, because I went to work six months at the library to get the money to come back, and then borrowed from my brother. [*Laughter*] I was a long time there. Then I went to the West Indies and so forth. I think the big disappointment to people like me who came along in the Forties was that we thought we had won it all, especially when civil rights began to be discussed. We thought that we had really conquered everything that had to do with racial division. Going away to Europe in 1947 and coming back to stay in 1967, in effect, was quite a shock to me. I couldn't believe that everything we had done had not progressed but retrogressed.

I think that what we went through in the Thirties, and thought we had conquered in the Forties gave me enough stamina and, many times, strategy to live through the Fifties and Sixties. I think that's the only thing it could have done. I was inculcated with the idea of eliminating social injustice. Senator Paul Douglas told me that one day when he came here. He had been in the University with my brother—they were two or three years ahead of me. He came with a committee during one of the roughest periods here in East Saint Louis, about 1969. It was very bad here. He came, spoke of the University of Chicago, and said, "I see here an alumna of ours, of mine. I'm not surprised to find Katherine Dunham here because wherever there is social injustice, somewhere you will find somebody from the University of Chicago fighting it." I thought that was a great thing for him to say.

NOTES

1. Robert Redfield (1897–1958), professor of social anthropology at the University of Chicago, pioneered the anthropological study of social change, especially in peasant societies *[Eds.]*.

2. Melville Herskovits (1895–1963), professor of anthropology at Northwestern University, organized the first program of African Studies in the United States. He was the author of many books and articles, including studies on communities in Surinam, Dahomey (Benin), Haiti, and Trinidad, as well as the influential *The Myth of the Negro Past* (1941) *[Eds.]*.

3. Robert M. Hutchins (1899–1977) became president of the University of Chicago at age thirty in 1929, a position he held until 1945. From 1945 to 1951, he served as chancellor of the university *[Eds.]*.

4. Alfred North Whitehead (1861–1947), British philosopher and mathematician, joined the faculty of Harvard University in 1924 and remained there until his retirement in 1937 *[Eds.]*.

5. Paul Robeson (1898–1976), son of a former slave, became an acclaimed actor and singer on Broadway stages and in Hollywood films. He appeared in concert halls in the United States, Europe, and Russia *[Eds.]*.

6. Canada Lee (1907–1951), actor best known for his portrayal of Richard Wright's "Bigger Thomas" (*Native Son*), was born Leonard Canegata in Manhattan *[Eds.]*.

Modern Dance Owes a Lot to Lovely Katherine Dunham

SUE BARRY

Back in Chicago a score of years ago a rangy Negro high school girl spent all of her spare hours dancing. The joy of rhythmic motion was more important to her than anything else in her life. Her future, she thought, was decided. She'd be a dancer.

It was a wise decision, as the intervening years have proven. Recently, when *Cabin in the Sky,* the all-Negro revue,[1] played in San Francisco, the chief attraction of the show was the dancing of Katherine Dunham. This was her first appearance in San Francisco, and critics and audiences alike raved about her performance.

UNUSUAL BEAUTY. There was ample reason for the raving. Miss Dunham is not only one of the most accomplished dancers San Francisco has ever seen, but she's a rarely beautiful woman. Very tall, with a slender shapeliness, she has the kind of a face you remember for a long time. And it isn't only the beauty of her eyes, the charm of her features, and the rich brownness of her skin that impress you—there's something else that is more difficult to put into words. It has to do with a gentleness and modesty of manner—a genuine, simple kind of friendliness that has as much to do with beauty as do the standard requirements of coloring and regularity of feature. And, strangely, you feel that friendliness when you're sitting in the theater watching her. It comes out over the footlights while you're watching her strut around as the glamorous Georgia Brown. It's a very unusual feeling, because most actresses and dancers and singers are just up there

SOURCE: Sue Barry, "Woman of the Week: Modern Dance Owes a Lot to Lovely Katherine Dunham," *People's World* (San Francisco), 2 July 1941. Copyright 1941 by World Publishing Company. Reprinted by permission.

performing, and there's an unbridgeable gap between them and the audience. Only rarely does an artist possess it, and when he or she does, it goes a long way toward creating lasting popularity.

That was one reason why an interview with Miss Dunham seemed in order. You want to know friendly people, and learn as much as you can about them. And it was over a luncheon table that the opportunity came to get acquainted with this young lady who's lectured at Yale, who recently got more than a column of comment in a national news magazine, and whose lovely face is as familiar to savants as it is to concert- and theatergoers.

STUDIED BACKGROUND OF DANCE. For Katherine Dunham has been doing a lot more than perfecting her dancing technique since those high school days. For one thing, she's contributed more, in her particular field, to the knowledge of the dance than has any other American scholar or dancer. There's a world of background to Negro culture. Much has been done on the subject of music, less on the dance. That's a lack that Miss Dunham has done a lot to remedy.

Her interest in the background to Negro dance forms developed when she was a student at the University of Chicago. It led her to a study of anthropology. She found out that while there was much to learn from books on this subject, she'd have to go farther afield if she really wanted to get the necessary knowledge. So, on a Julius Rosenwald fellowship, she set off to the West Indies to prepare a thesis for her master's degree on "A Comparative Study of Primitive Dance."

SPECIALIZED IN PRIMITIVE FORMS. It was a large task she'd set herself, she found, when she reached the island of Haiti. So to do a thorough and complete job, she concentrated on Haitian primitive dances.

Since her return, concert audiences throughout the East have seen Miss Dunham and the troupe of dancers she has trained perform those strange and exciting Haitian dances. She's gained nationwide fame as the dancer who became an anthropologist in order to perfect her understanding of the dance.

You can see, in some of the dances she created for *Cabin in the Sky,* the influence of the primitive dances she has studied so closely.[2] And you find it a very stimulating experience—far different from the usual pretty or simply "jazzy" dances that you're used to seeing in musical shows.

BITTER STORIES. It is hard to get Miss Dunham to talk about herself. She'd rather talk about the theater, or, if there's an anthropologist around, about scientific matters. And she has a lot to say about her people, too.

She was particularly interested in hearing about the suit of several San

Franciscans and the great singer Paul Robeson against café-owner Vanessi for discrimination. She had a story to tell of a bitter experience girls of her own dancing group had in an Eastern city while *Cabin in the Sky* was on tour. They'd gone to a movie to while away the time between shows. But, because they were Negro girls, they'd been refused admission.

There were stories, too, about the things she'd seen in the West Indies. About the color caste system British imperialism has imposed in an attempt to split and weaken the ranks of dark-skinned people with the old and familiar "divide and rule" policy.

DANCED FOR SPAIN. Pretty soon the conversation was steered back to the subject of Miss Dunham, though unlike most people of the theater, she didn't do the steering. Chicago has been the scene of most of her activity. She'd "just about danced her heels off for Spain," she said, during those years when all right-minded people were aiding in every way they could the cause of democracy in that Fascist-beleaguered land. For a couple of years she did the choreography for *Pins and Needles,* the yearly musical revue of the ILGWU garment workers.[3] Just lately she had made a technicolor short in Hollywood of native Brazilian dances.[4] Some of the South American dignitaries there had caused a bit of a stir about a Negro dancer appearing in a film of their country, proving that in some ways it's the same old South, even below the Panama Canal. It had apparently slipped their minds, said Miss Dunham, that 80 percent of their countrymen possess dark skins.

She likes working in the movies. She loves dancing and the theater. Maybe that's one reason why, after wearying months on the road with *Cabin in the Sky,* she looks so fresh and alive and lovely. She's found life full of interesting things to do and learn. And you can tell, by talking with her, and watching her talk with other people, that her interest will never flag.

NOTES

1. *Cabin in the Sky* (1940) was not a revue. It was a musical play with a book by Lynn Root, music by Vernon Duke, and lyrics by John La Touche [*Eds.*].

2. *Cabin in the Sky* was staged by George Balanchine. The choreography for dances by Katherine Dunham and her company was jointly devised by Balanchine and Dunham [*Eds.*].

3. For Miss Dunham's personal reminiscences of this collaboration, see "Early New York Collaborations," book 2 of "Minefields," on pp. 125–149, this volume [*Eds.*]

4. *Carnival of Rhythm,* a short film written by Stanley Martin, directed by Jean Negulesco, and produced by Warner Bros., was shot in 1939 and released in 1941. Devoted entirely to Katherine Dunham and her company, it features four dance numbers set to Brazilian music [*Eds.*].

Collaborating with Balanchine on
Cabin in the Sky

Interviews with Katherine Dunham

CONSTANCE VALIS HILL

The following conversation is an abridgement of two lengthy interviews with Katherine Dunham that I conducted in November 1999 and January 2000 on behalf of Popular Balanchine, a project of the George Balanchine Foundation investigating Balanchine's work for the popular stage and screen. The interviews focused on Dunham's collaboration with Balanchine on *Cabin in the Sky,* the 1940 Broadway "musical fantasy" about a kindhearted but morally ambivalent Everyman who dies from being cut up in a craps game and is bound for Hell but is saved by his wife's prayers and given extra time on earth to qualify for Heaven. The production, which starred Dooley Wilson as Little Joe, Ethel Waters as his faithful wife Petunia, and Katherine Dunham as the sexy temptress Georgia Brown, along with an all-black cast that included the J. Rosamond Johnson Choir and Katherine Dunham's company of dancers and drummers, was staged by Balanchine, with music composed by Vernon Duke (Vladimir Dukelsky) and sets and costumes designed by Boris Aronson. Dunham was not credited in the program of the 1940 Broadway production of *Cabin in the Sky* as choreographer, but she has a legitimate claim to be credited as co-choreographer with Balanchine.

SOURCE: Constance Valis Hill, interviews with Katherine Dunham conducted on 18 November 1999 and 15 January 2000. Copyright 2002 by the George Balanchine Foundation. Used by permission. Opinions, speculations, and conclusions expressed herein are those of the speakers and do not necessarily reflect the position of the George Balanchine Foundation. Transcripts and audiotapes of the full interviews are in the Popular Balanchine Collection in the New York Public Library for the Performing Arts.

The following abridgement contains her reflections on various aspects of her career as well as her recollections of working on *Cabin in the Sky*. It does, I trust, reveal the extent of her artistic and choreographic contribution to the production and the unique relationship she enjoyed with George Balanchine as co-choreographer.

CONSTANCE VALIS HILL (hereafter CVH): Miss Dunham, when you first read the script for *Cabin in the Sky*, or read Lynn Root's story that it was based on, what attracted you to the musical?

KATHERINE DUNHAM (hereafter KD): I thought that it could be what was becoming a very popular form of theater presentation, fantasy. Like Balanchine, I had expected it, from the scene of Little Joe's death on, to be considered a fantasy, and I think certain liberties were given. "In My Old Virginia Home on the River Nile" and those things allowed us to keep that fantasy element in there.

CVH: Did it take place in a specific place in the American South?

KD: I don't think so. It was just a Southern cotton plantation, and it could have been anywhere that you would find that setting.

CVH: I have wondered about the plot—the fight between the devil's son, Lucifer, Jr. and the Lawd's General for the body and soul of Little Joe— and the sacred and secular aspects of the Southern black experience that are rendered with humor and sympathy in the play. These are aspects that are clearly not fantasy. Was there anything in that material in *Cabin in the Sky* that attracted you?

KD: Probably my sense of folklore, from an anthropological point of view, was attracted to the fact that we had so many folk settings and people, so much folk material that we had not really used. And I think that *Cabin in the Sky* gave an opportunity [to draw on that folk material]. Ethel Waters had her way. She had certain things that were just down-to-earth black action, black thought. At the same time, Balanchine got his touch of Russian fantasy, and I had my exotic material, so that I think the final presentation satisfied most of us.

CVH: When you say that Balanchine got his touch of fantasy, what do you mean? He was the [person] most foreign to the material.

KD: Well, he had a terrible time in the beginning. He was rather young and had his own Russian background to give him energy and life, and to bring something new to theater, certainly new to Broadway. He wanted the show to open with a Russian dirge, to open it and have a complete fantasy, and have these black people singing old Russian dirges instead of spirituals. And I thought that was a very clever idea, but Ethel Waters did not. She had a *fit!* And finally, we ended up letting Hal Johnson [J. Rosamond Johnson] use his choir.

CVH: *Cabin in the Sky* opened instead with the chorus singing "Wading in the Water." Do you think with Balanchine, in wanting to use a Russian dirge at the beginning of *Cabin,* when Little Joe lays dying from a stabbing and people are praying for him, that there was a sense of identity with the spiritual practices of Southern blacks?

KD: Well, you know, I think there probably, certainly, could have been and was.

I didn't know what Balanchine wanted. I really didn't. [Perhaps] he really wanted to see what this offshoot of American cultural society could do. I think that there was a lot in him of—I don't know if it would have come from the ideas of revolution in Russia or what, but a lot of him was "Let us see what other people can do." And then being a Georgian in Russia, I think that his feeling for the—I can't say "the underdog," and, still, that's what it actually was—his feeling for neglected groups. We'll say "the deprived," minor groups as the Georgians had been in Russia.

I would never have thought of Balanchine as a communist in the traditional sense of the word. In other words, you couldn't think of him in terms of a "Red"; you thought of him in terms of humanity, the color of which was like his own color, a sort of a sun-touched, cold-warm, reaching-out color, and that is what he was, and he came from people who were. When I think of Balanchine and the Georgians, I think of warmth and love.

CVH: I remember your saying in an interview that Balanchine came to see you and your company in Chicago.

KD: Yes. At the Sherman Hotel. That would have been in 1939.

CVH: What do you think it was that made Balanchine want you and your entire company of dancers and drummers to come to New York to perform in *Cabin in the Sky?* What was the attraction?

KD: I would say what we were doing then would have been heavily influenced by my training with Ludmilla Speranzeva. She had a school with Vera Mirova in downtown Chicago. I could not have rented a studio there at that time because of my color, and I couldn't afford it anyway. But I did [train with them]. I don't know how I met them, maybe through Ruth Page, but I went to take lessons from Speranzeva.

Speranzeva came to America with the Chauve-Souris.[1] I probably first heard of Balanchine from her. She was great on these things with explosive movements, and I guess she had the Russian spirit in them too, the real Russian spirit. I would say that the Chauve-Souris had more to do with this thing of bringing in the Russian spirit into night-clubs and Broadway than anything else. It was a little French in its approach. It was a little more—you might say—more daring than our musical things were. It sort of, in a healthy way, took a grab at you. I think it was in that period that Martha Graham called me the High Priestess of the Pelvic Girdle.

In the study I did with her [Speranzeva], for two or three years, there was the feeling of abandon, especially in Chauve-Souris. I don't know what it would have been in the Russian ballet. Chauve-Souris was more popular. I remember her as designed abandon—and that was very Russian in those days. I think I must have gotten a lot of that explosive feeling, and also a freedom of sexual presentation, that I didn't think much about, being in anthropology at the University of Chicago at that time. I went ahead and did what I thought was correct with the atmosphere. But I can see how I would have been influenced by her, which would have been a strong Russian feeling in the Chauve-Souris, which was more like a nightclub concert.

[*Dunham is looking at a scrapbook of clippings from* Cabin in the Sky *that Hill has collected and assembled.*]

CVH: Do you see this picture of Balanchine holding you up by the leg and stretching it? He looks like he is doing it with great glee. And look, in this picture, at the way the girls are perched high up on the shoulders of the men. That kind of lifting—does that look like something you would do on your company at the time?

KD: I think so. I don't want to take anything away from Balanchine, but I would imagine that that was part of our training.

CVH: That perching looks like a cross between ballet lifts and the aerial lifts of the Lindy Hop.

KD: It was Speranzeva, on the Chauve-Souris side, the music hall. They had a lot of European music halls at that time. You know, I'll tell you truthfully, it's the sort of thing we do all the time, and what I got exactly from Speranzeva or Balanchine I can't tell you. Because we were sort of intermixed.

CVH: When you first listened to Vernon Duke's music, did it resonate with the scenario of *Cabin in the Sky?*

KD: Yes.

CVH: How did he accomplish that? He was a Russian.

KD: He was Russian, but he was also sort of a vagabond, almost like a traveling troubadour. He picked up things as he went along. I think that Dukelsky will never be considered a great composer, but he was adequate. He was witty, he had love in him, and he was manipulative—all the things that would make him succeed.

CVH: You added music to *Cabin in the Sky*, didn't you, with your musicians? Two drummers [J. Emanuel Vanderhans and Cándido Vicenty] from your company were also working on *Cabin in the Sky*. Did they influence Dukelsky's musical score?

KD: I think so. Not to take anything at all away from him, but I think that our musicians were all root-core musicians. They knew what they were talking about, they knew the fundamentals of what they were doing, and they realized also that the achiever was the person who could create upon these fundamental beliefs, and they respected Vernon for that reason. They saw that he was creating on fundamental beliefs.

CVH: Did you enjoy choreographing to Duke's music?

KD: I did, but now that I think about it, I think I enjoyed, from my part, mostly what was touched by our influence. Take the "Hell" scene. I wonder if Dukelsky would have done the "Hell" scene as it was, without us. We had that mellowing, that—

CVH: I have a picture of it here. We can take a look at it. You said "the mellowing." [*Indicating a picture*] There were drummers in that scene.

KD: That [drumming] influenced Dukelsky, no question about it.

CVH: And [set and costume designer] Boris Aronson. Do you remember working with him?

KD: Yes. I worked with him. I liked him. I thought he was talented.

CVH: That was quite a modernist design concept for *Cabin*, and he designed costumes as well.

KD: I would say that my husband [John Pratt] did the costumes. I don't think Aronson had anything to do with our costumes, except to enjoy them or admire them.

CVH: Really? Did Mr. Pratt do the costumes for the dancing chorus and the entire cast?

KD: Oh, not the entire cast, [just the Dunham dancers]. Everything that we did, he costumed.

CVH: Miss Dunham, I want to ask you about act 2, scene 1, "In My Old Virginia Home on the River Nile." [*Laughs*] That's a great fantasy, with the scene going from Virginia to Egypt.

KD: Oh, honestly, it is.

CVH: How did it come about?

KD: Well, you see, Ethel Waters [in the role of Petunia Jackson] was sitting there in the yard. She had hung her washing out, was sitting there in the yard, singing about, reminiscing about, her old Virginia home. And she was smart enough to realize, after a while, the innovation and amusement and fun of having the exotic locale like the River Nile. And so "In My Old Virginia Home on the River Nile." And of course, among other things, I did not want to lose the exotic impact that we had made on American culture. Therefore, I thought of myself as being, in some way or another, depicted as an Egyptian or something from the River Nile that really amused itself with the Virginia concept.

Look at something like this. [*Indicating a picture*] That's Virginia, you see. And Talley Beatty, because of his structure, his beautiful, fine looks, practically Egyptian, fell into the River Nile feeling. And there I was, trying to act the way I thought Egyptians would act.

I think that, in trying to escape some of the racism that we were bound to feel in appearing in material that was audacious and new, I was looking for ways that would take us out of the stereotype of "My Old Virginia Home." [In all my] performances on Broadway, [in] everything [I did], I would draw shamelessly from my anthropological background.

If we were doing some archaeological study somewhere, you'd find me trying to think, "How can I use this? How can I put it on the stage for us?" Because that's part of us, too. And that finally took. It was a long time before the audiences, New York or otherwise, were able to see that I was not kidding and bluffing. It was a part of our culture that was coming through more and more and more.

CVH: Are you saying, in the fantasy part of "In My Old Virginia Home on the River Nile," that there was an escape from Virginia back to Africa, back to Egypt?

KD: Yes. It was, in a way, escape, but I think it was a little more subtle than that. It was a merging in, a recognition of, a kind of making a cake batter very smooth, you know, and not picking out little bits of it here and there.

CVH: I love that image. Making a cake batter smooth. [*Laughs*]

KD: Yes. I'm sure that's the way I felt about the whole thing.

CVH: And it so struck the theme of Afro-Americana, in terms of the way that you segue from Virginia to Egypt.

KD: Yes. I think that it preceded our Afro-American attitudes of today. You see people going around in robes and fezzes, with their hair bushed out or braided, and so forth and so on. It's always been there, but I think that it was a little timid about bringing itself out until we did it.

CVH: Miss Dunham, you had been doing Americana dances, or at least your Americana material was just emerging in this period. Right before *Cabin in the Sky*, when you performed in New York, in February of 1940 at the Windsor Theatre, you did *Tropics* and *Le Jazz "Hot."*

KD: The Windsor.[2] Yes.

CVH: You did some things at the Windsor that struck me perhaps as the beginning of your Americana repertoire. You did plantation dances. *Field Hands* was another number. I think *Br'er Rabbit an' de Tah Baby* may have been on that program. I know you also had *Florida Swamp Shimmy*. How did those Americana dances come into *Cabin in the Sky*?

KD: I think that my sense of injustice with my sense of correctness made me realize that even though I might be archaeologically or historically correct in bringing these exotic things into our performances, and as a part of our technique, I shouldn't forget that we were black. We were not African, but black Americans, and black Americans have never been clearly defined. It's why "Afro-American" is such a letdown. It's not quite true.

As I began to see what I was doing—in terms of reviews, photographs, and this, that, and the other—I began to see myself as looking for escape from the pulchritude, for conventional beauty outside of this country. It took me a little time to realize—and I think anthropology certainly had a lot to do with it—that it's in this country, too. [Just] because a [face] has a protruding jaw and thick lips, you don't have to think of it in terms of non-aesthetic. And that took me not too long, because I did have a pretty good University of Chicago point of view. You can't turn down anything, really. You've got to look at it and study it and put it in its place.

So I coasted along for some time, I think, realizing if I were perfectly honest about it that much of my success came from beautiful kids on stage and beautiful bodies and wonderful costumes and good presentation. People in the audiences felt a part of the beauty. They stopped resenting the fact that we were black doing it and sort of drifted along in escapism, but escapism which was based on scientific fact. And that's where I think I began to see that I must always keep that working along with me. And that's when I must have begun to see art and science as belonging together, each one supporting the other. I think that's what gave me the courage and the imagination and the strength to present what I thought went together. And they did turn out to go together.

CVH: Miss Dunham, how then did you begin conceiving of Americana?

KD: You know, in one way, it would have been as a counterbalance to the exotic things. My feeling was "Gee, I've got to do something about this." So the show automatically became divided into three parts instead of the average show then of two acts, because I had to get in there one impor-tant big expression of our combined creative and technical capacity.

CVH: Are you saying that in *Cabin in the Sky* you were doing those three elements?

KD: Well, I usually, with opening numbers in the first part like *Rara Tonga* [1937] and *Shango* [1945], acquainted the audience with sounds and sights and colors that would be found later in the show.

So, I'd say the "Hell" scene [in *Cabin in the Sky*] was pretty primitive. It wasn't dress primitive, but in motions, movements, sounds, and so forth. And then, I would say that there was an effort, like in "River Nile" ["In My Old Virginia Home on the River Nile"] to present a big ballet.

CVH: And then the scene with "Boogy Woogy" and "Lazy Steps"?

KD: Yes, yes.

CVH: Where did that go?

KD: There was your Americana. I had to be correct.

CVH: Miss Dunham, it has been claimed that with *Oklahoma!* [1943], the so-called ballet Americana gained prominence on the Broadway stage. But when I look at *Cabin in the Sky* [1940], I see there was this fusion of American vernacular dance, ballet, and Broadway show dancing. I don't want to put any labels on anything, but I would like to know what you think about the claim that *Oklahoma!* was one of the first to fuse these forms.

KD: I wasn't happy about that. Agnes [Agnes DeMille, choreographer of *Oklahoma!*] and I knew each other. It has happened to me several times: people taking some of the songs I have researched—you know, popular songs—and translating them. I guess it's bound to happen. I was really annoyed with her [DeMille] because I think her idea came from some-thing called the plantation dances, not in *Cabin in the Sky,* but in our concerts. I had prided myself on using my work and my discoveries for establishing certain things about black dance.

So we had a number called *Plantation Dances.* When I saw what she had done, I was annoyed, because it was true, there were these dances in *Oklahoma!,* and I thought, "Well, it would have been nice if she had mentioned [me] as a counterpart." . . . I don't know how she could have, because, after all, it was her show and her choreography. I remember feeling annoyed at her because I feel we were the first to do that. And that was really because of my concentrating on that in my work.

CVH: There is a general awareness that you were translating indigenous Afro-Caribbean dance forms at the time, but much less awareness that you were motivated to do the same with American vernacular dance forms.

KD: My feeling was how on earth could I go, as I had always done, to the West Indies and spend practically a year going off to the islands, looking for their root material in the performing arts, and not realize that there was this richness right there in our country. So when I got back— I don't think it was before my trip. My trip was maybe 1934, maybe 1935 or 1936, about a year and a half—I said, "We have that in our own country. I might as well put it on stage." That's when I began the plantation dances. The square dances, plantation square dances, cakewalk, all of that set of Americana, as I called it, was our third act in the show [i.e., performances of the Dunham Company] from then on. Always, all over the world.[3]

I know that the Americana idea came to me in the regret that it hadn't been otherwise used. It came to me from really starting to analyze the work of the Caribbean. [But] they were the same people, and they did evidently the same things, practically. We had a whole section of Americana. I don't have a program now. Plantation dances, and a blues sequence, and my *Barrelhouse* blues.

CVH: It's known you collected material from the Caribbean, but how was ballet incorporated in your work? What was it about ballet style and technique that fit with what you were doing in 1940?

KD: We might as well say my respect for and close relationship with Ludmilla Speranzeva, because again I say that when Chauve-Souris was here in the States, Russian concert material [was] made into musical comedy specials and things. And I say that I appreciated ballet because there was no technique for any other kind of dancing that we did.

You take a ballet like *L'Ag'ya,* and no one knew anything about it. Well, I was criticized by [name omitted], and she said that I pointed my foot, and that I was very eager to show that I knew classical ballet. Ridiculous. It was a love scene for me, and for the part that I was doing I could get out, wiggle around, take off my clothes, of course. But when it came to this particular love scene, I used the movements of ballet.

I think there are times when it just simply fit, if you know it well. I hate to see it when it's just thrown in there because somebody has seen a ballet or something. But I think it was well used by me. I don't think anyone else used classical ballet [as I did] in *L'Ag'ya*.

CVH: On the list of the classes offered at your school, when it first opened in New York, there are a number of ballet classes.

KD: Oh, yes, there was ballet. I always have it. I think it's a wonderful thing to get you acquainted with the strict kinds of things your body can do. With music, much of it is so much better expressed in the classical ballet than might be in others.

I wouldn't have a school that didn't have some form of classical ballet, because of what it does for your body.[4] There's a real difference.

CVH: Balanchine must have seen that your dancers had been classically trained, and he must have seen the expressive potential of ballet in your company.

KD: He did. But even so, ballet is not a thing you can just do, or that you can do with a few lessons, like some of the things we do in primitive Dunham Technique. It requires, I think, an exact image that's been there for a couple of hundred years or more—three hundred—and therefore there is a precedent that you just must not derange. You must not upset it. This is the way an arabesque is, you know, and you can't let your own personality enter into it or any of it. You just do it.

I will tell you that I liked the discipline in it, and at the same time the music and the things that went with classical ballet sometimes gave me relief from the drums.

[*Miss Dunham is looking in the scrapbook at pictures from the scene "Honey in the Honeycomb."*]

CVH: So that's your solo number, "Honey in the Honeycomb"?

KD: I'm sure of it. And the boys came in later. They were rolling me downstage, and they were on all fours, and in my last motion in the song I lay on their backs. And they scuffled right down to the footlights.

CVH: I have the music to "Honey in the Honeycomb." Let me play it for you. This is not the original, but I did get it from the 1963 theater production. I can play it for you.

[The recording of the 1963 Broadway revival, issued on EMI-Angel CD #64892 in 1993, begins to play. A woman is singing "Honey in the Honeycomb."]

KD: [*Singing along*] "What have I got that the others ain't?" [*Listening to recording, KD laughs.*] You know, if you'll notice, in most of my songs I seldom go into the second verse. If I can conquer that first one, I would leave it.

CVH: But then you dance in the second verse, don't you, Miss Dunham?

KD: Yes, I didn't have to learn those lyrics.

That's the way it began, and that gave it kind of a little-girl attitude. [*Singing*] "What have I got that the others ain't? That always seems to please." And then I'd say, "It ain't my perfume," and they'd say, "Fancy paint," and I'd say "Revlon paint." I just had to get something in, my own poetry. "Just like they was bees." That was my hardest thing, that "When I charmed, the men all swarmed. It was like they was bees, they is. And they got to wondering what there was. Honey." I learned how to drip those words out there. [*Laughs*]

CVH: [*Laughs*] Miss Dunham! Oh, I would have done anything to see that.

KD: Oh, it wasn't easy. It was not easy, but I had to get those engagements.

CVH: What was the dancing part like?

KD: The dancing part was like a chorus from any typical Broadway show, the boys coming behind me and me getting in the middle of them, you know, these things you see in the photograph. I don't know who danced with a chorus of boys like that, excepting Baker [Josephine Baker], and not having ever seen her.

CVH: And did Balanchine collaborate with you on the choreography for that number?

KD: With Balanchine, we had an understanding. I was a little bit outdone when I wasn't the sole person. But he did have a thing to say now and then about staging. After I worked with him—he was such a wonderful person—I enjoyed every minute of it.

He was staging the entire show, and it kept him pretty busy. I think he did pretty much trust me for the choreography, especially since the company was mine. I just couldn't tell you [if he helped choreograph the number]. When people are able to work together—He may have. I know one suggestion he made was in the last act. We were all up on the bar. It may have been the end of "Honey in the Honeycomb." And the company ended up standing on the bar, and they had to fall off of the bar—something sort of acrobatic. I remember that he came in and saved me on that one. I didn't know what to do about it.

CVH: And the idea of the Egyptian ballet in the Nile ["Fugue" and "In My Old Virginia Home (on the River Nile)"], was that Mr. Balanchine's?

KD: Let us say that the idea of an Egyptian ballet would have been Balanchine's. He told me what he thought, and then I tried to put it together. I don't think I would have thought of an Egyptian ballet, even though at the time I was deep in anthropology at the university. I'm pretty sure that was his idea. I don't think there was anything that had to do with staging and choreography that we didn't talk over together. I can't imagine that there would have been.

CVH: How would you do it? Would he say, "Katherine, I see it this way?"

KD: Well, he would say what had to be done next, and when he had an idea, like the Egyptian scene, maybe I'd add a few things. In the Egyptian scene, I can't tell which one of us did my entrance. There were clothes hanging on a clothesline drying, and Little Joe—I think Ethel [i.e., Petunia] may have gone to church at the time—and I came through the line of clothes. I would imagine that would have been Balanchine's [idea], because it was really a very clever idea, and sort of European. And that's the way we did things. You know, he said, "I think you should come through these clothes that have been hung up to dry."

CVH: But no steps.

KD: In some of them he would have the idea. I think in most of them he would go through the whole scenario and say where the dance was. That was the first musical I had ever done. And I was quite willing to have him give as much as he could. He never bothered me about the exact step of the choreography. And unless it interfered with the story, he wouldn't stop me in any theme in the way that I would want to do it.

As I think about it, and what I would want to say about it, I'd say that he deserves a great deal of credit for what I did. [He] put me in a position that I wasn't in before, I guess, that I was able to engage the company, to pay them by union [scale]. That's when, I think I remember, they were all contracted to me, and that's when, I remember, I broke off into just the company.

CVH: Miss Dunham, just one last question. What do you think Balanchine got or learned or brought with him after his experience of working with you and observing, intimately, you and your company?

KD: I think that there was a meeting of the Georgian freedom of expression and the Georgian heat, you know, that he found a response to in the whole black element. Freedom of the pelvis and all those things. While the Georgians weren't necessarily using them, they were implicated. The whole externalization of all these physical emotions complemented things that were in the Georgian temperament, but didn't come out in the same way.

In other words, I would see him dance or choreograph, and I would not see the blatant use of the pelvic girdle or the blatant whatever it was I was doing at the time, but I would feel behind it an affiliation with it. So I got to really appreciate him, that point of view. So I'd say that some of our things put him at ease, let him do things he might not have done otherwise. I do think the freeing of the pelvic girdle, I think he sort of was relieved to see it finally on the stage.

NOTES

1. Le Théâtre de la Chauve-Souris à Moscou (The Bat Theater of Moscow) played many performances on Broadway in different editions in 1922, 1923, 1925, 1927, 1929, 1931, and 1943. Billed as Balieff's Chauve-Souris of Moscow, all but the last edition were conceived and directed by Nikita Balieff, who also starred. The cast was composed of Russian émigrés who had moved to Paris. Ludmila Speranzeva appeared in the fourth U.S. edition, in 1925. When it closed, she remained in America and settled in Chicago, where she opened a ballet school.

2. Under the aegis of impresario Louis Schaefer, Katherine Dunham and Dance Group performed at New York's Windsor Theatre for thirteen weekends in a row during the spring of 1940, when the resident show, *New Pins and Needles,* was not playing. In the program for Sunday evening, 28 April 1940, a special benefit performance for the New York Urban League, *Tropics* and *Le Jazz "Hot"* are featured, followed by "plantation and minstrel dances from the ballet *Br'er Rabbit":* Square Dance, Juba, Jennie Cooler, Palmerhouse, Pas Mala, Ballin' de Jack, Strut, and Cake Walk. In programs for performances in May 1940, *Plantation Dances,* performed by the *corps de ballet,* is billed as a separate suite. In *Le Jazz "Hot,"* the *Barrelhouse* dance, performed by Dunham and Lucille Ellis, is identified as the *Florida Swamp Shimmy.*

3. The repertory of the Dunham Company (1938–1965) consisted mainly of dances based on Caribbean, Latin American, and African origins, but her programs also usually included dances of African American origin (blues, ragtime, honky-tonk, boogie-woogie, and jitterbug). In 1940 she began to include plantation and minstrel dances on her programs as well. The term *Americana* was not used in printed programs until about 1950.

4. The Katherine Dunham School of Dance and Theater, established in 1945 in New York City, first occupied premises in Caravan Hall but later relocated to 220 West 43rd Street. That location was closed in 1957.

A Talk with Katherine Dunham

DORATHI BOCK PIERRE

Katherine Dunham was born in Chicago and raised in Joliet, Illinois, where her father was in the cleaning and dyeing business. She attended public school there and was fortunate in being a student in a very progressive high school. In her second year she became a member of the extracurricular Terpsichorean Club, where her natural love of dancing was fired to ambition.

She was particularly interested in dance and rhythms as they applied to her own people, and, having theories of her own, she decided to teach and try them out when she entered the University of Chicago, and also as a means of paying her tuition. She tells with some amusement now of how when she taught straight ballet she had crowded classes, but when she taught basic rhythms as they related to the Negro her classes dwindled, for her students wanted something more showy and sophisticated.

She entered the university with no definite major in mind, but fate led her to a class in ethnology under Dr. Robert Redfield, and his remarkable insight and presentation of the subject so thrilled her that she made that her major, and later returned to the university for graduate work toward a master's degree in anthropology.

While a student at the university she studied educational dance techniques with a pupil of Margaret H'Doubler, modern dance from Ludmilla Speranzeva, ballet from Bentley Stone, and special courses from a number of dancers, including Harald Kreutzberg.

SOURCE: Dorathi Bock Pierre, "A Talk with Katherine Dunham," *Educational Dance* (August–September 1941): 7–8. Copyright 1941 by *Educational Dance* Company, Hollywood, California. Reprinted by permission of Katherine Dunham.

"My great interest in dance had been a subconscious feeling that it was more than a physical exercise; that it was somehow closely related to the people who danced, and naturally I was tremendously excited over the confirmation of this theory which I found in ethnology."

"My university work was very interesting, for I was off and on the campus for ten years before I completed work for my master's degree. I would attend classes until I had an offer of work and then I would stop sometimes as long as six months or more; the longest lapse was the eighteen months during 1936–1938 which I spent on a Rosenwald fellowship in the West Indies."[1]

I asked of her objectives, and what she accomplished during her stay in the Caribbean. "My desire was to see first-hand the primitive dance in its everyday relationship to the people; and anthropology, which leads one to origins and the simple basic fundamentals of art which is made complex and esoteric by civilization," was the answer.

"I spent six weeks in a tiny village waiting to get just one dance; and I spent much time on the many small islands as well as Jamaica, Martinique, and Trinidad. I made innumerable records of the songs and music of the people, wrote my thesis from these findings, and a book on my experiences, written in narrative form. But more than this, I learned about the people, how they dance and, especially, why."

"I had a very amusing experience when I first went to the Islands, for the urban society leaders questioned my desire for native research, and needing the moral backing of these leaders, I gave a concert for them and included only numbers which were traditional ballet or aesthetic interpretations. They loved it, and I was given a free hand thereafter to search out my 'primitives.'"

When Miss Dunham returned to Chicago she reassembled her group of dancers and started putting her findings into practical use. Having an offer from Labor Stage in New York she took six of her dancers with her. With her entire salary from this engagement she put on a concert at the Windsor Theatre in February 1940. It created such a sensation that she did thirteen Sunday night concerts, was acclaimed by critics and the public, and became firmly established as one of the outstanding concert dancers of the United States. She and her group appeared for a year with Ethel Waters in *Cabin in the Sky,* and this summer she made a motion picture short for Warner Bros. Studios of some of her primitive dances, called *Carnival of Rhythm.*

I asked her what her future plans and ambitions were.

"I want a school in New York where I can train dancers in the knowledge and use of primitive rhythms. I want to lecture on the subjects of anthropology and ethnology and dance; and of course I want to dance. I am not interested in dance routines. I am only interested in dance as an education, a means of knowing peoples, and I want students who want to learn and have a desire to develop people and tastes."

I was sure she had interesting opinions in regard to dance in education, and questioned her, especially as it affected the Negro student.

"I am opposed to any group, either Negro or white, slavishly imitating any leader or technique. The many Negro schools and colleges in the United States should use great care in their academic approach to dance."

"First they should know what people are, and what dance is. They should study religion in its relation to dance, and have a course in religious dance to overcome prejudice against dance in communities where it exists."

"The subject should be approached on the basis of the relationship of all things to the American Negro; the tribal and cultural strains which make up the people; and an examination of the music and arts which make up the cultural strains. I believe that a person who dances should know why they dance, and to do so they must have an historical background."

"To me physical education is more than simply body development, and I have always felt that classes should be arranged on the basis of intellectual viewpoint."

"Indirect connotation through rhythm offers endless opportunity. Men can be interested through an introduction of primitive war movements in rhythm; and working rhythm into the gymnastic is the genuine approach to what dance is. Manipulation and technique can find a parallel in history; basically we must move for a reason."

"Negro schools should study the intercultural results of dance. Such simple subjects as the Kentucky Mountain Squares in relation to Plantation Squares, which are different; and the changing rhythms between the Juba and minstrel and plantation dances. The same dance through different people becomes entirely different."

"I believe this general approach could be used to advantage in all educational dance programs, but I feel Negroes have an unusual opportunity to make a contribution to our total culture through this medium."

Notes

1. Dunham departed for Jamaica early in 1935 and returned to Chicago from Haiti in late spring of 1936. The dates provided, 1936–1938, are inaccurate [Eds.].

Better Race Relationships
Hoped by Seattle Dancer

That the work of the Katherine Dunham Dancers and other artistic and cultural groups operating throughout the country may some day bring a better understanding between races and wider opportunities for members of so-called minority races is the hope of Syvilla Fort, talented young Seattle dancer with the Dunham troupe now playing at the Moore Theatre.

"A fight that a lot of young people have, especially if they are of a minority race, is to get the training they want," Miss Fort said today as she rested between performances at the home of her mother, Mrs. R. E. Dill, 2320 N. 53rd Street.

SCHOOL FOR ALL ASKED. "Through the Katherine Dunham group of dancers and other groups, things are happening. Maybe it will finally bring about a school or a place of training which would be open to all for artistic or cultural training."

"If one day there could be a center for training it would be wonderful," she said enthusiastically. "It would give so many people an opportunity to do what they want to do." Although dancing is her first love, Miss Fort is almost as interested in music and regards it as her second choice for a vocation.

"I studied music for about eight years, and then I finally decided I wanted to study dancing," she recalled. She got her start on the stage in musical and dramatic productions in which she participated as a child at the Green Lake Fieldhouse.

SOURCE: "Better Race Relationships Hoped by Seattle Dancer," *Seattle Times,* 16 April 1943. Copyright 1943 by the *Seattle Times* Company. Reprinted by permission.

TWO YEARS AT UNIVERSITY. Miss Fort studied four years at the Cornish School, majoring in dancing, and studied two years at the University of Washington. She has taught dancing groups both in Seattle and in California. She joined the Katherine Dunham dance company a year and one-half ago.

The dancer is eagerly awaiting the release of a new motion picture, entitled *Stormy Weather,* in which the Dunham dancers appear in a number of scenes.

"It is much more difficult to sustain the mood when dancing before cameras than before an audience," she said. "When dancing before an audience they sort of 'warm up' to you and you to them at least before you're halfway through the program."

This is the first visit Miss Fort has been able to make to her home here since the troupe appeared here last year.

Dunham Weary of
Hotel Trek

"For the first time I am getting a little angry," Katherine Dunham, dancer, said when she arrived here the other day and found her management had been unable to reserve a hotel room for her because she is a Negro.

"It is gradually beginning to wear me down. Some of the kids in the company say they'd almost rather stop dancing than go through all this over and over."

After a short rest in Connecticut, she will return to make the usual trek from hotel to hotel in person asking for rooms so that she can conveniently start rehearsals at the Martin Beck Theater September 9.

San Francisco stands out like a shining light, she said. They gave her a three-room suite there at the Mark Hopkins, and she rented a charming apartment on Telegraph Hill, and she ate wherever she pleased. The company had pleasant accommodations.

CINCINNATI EXPERIENCE. She stayed at the Netherlands Plaza in Cincinnati, but this is what she said happened there:

Her stage manager had reserved the room. Not long after she moved in, Max Schulman, the manager, came and asked her whether she thought she'd better move because of what had happened. What had happened was that members of the AFL union of culinary workers had threatened to pull its members out of the Covington Club in the hotel unless she moved.

"I have to think about my business. I have to think about after the war," said Schulman.

SOURCE: "Katherine Dunham Is Weary of Hotel Trek," *PM*, 5 September 1943. Reprinted by permission of Katherine Dunham.

"If we don't win the war, your people and mine will be in the same fix," she answered.

He said he'd rented her room. She said she wouldn't move. And didn't. She stayed two weeks. Everyone was nice to her. She and Schulman had a long talk on discrimination against minorities.

"You think it will be better the farther north you go," she said. "Or that an art colony, for instance, will be more liberal. But it is not true."

"WHITE ONLY." In Portland, Oregon, signs have sprung up—"We Do Not Serve Colored," or "White Only." And in Carmel, California, the tour before this last one, the Dunham Company arrived to find their hotel reservations canceled, and not even an auto camp would take them in. (This time the hotels took them.) What she has learned as an anthropologist—she has lectured at Yale, and UCLA—Miss Dunham said, has made her more tolerant of the foibles of the white race. It has worked the other way, too, making her more resentful of the ignorance of race that makes discrimination against Negroes possible.

"I am getting good and mad about it now because of the war," she said. "It would seem ridiculous if it were not so tragic."

When Miss Dunham entertains at camps, she always has to make a strong stand against segregated audiences. At Fort Louis, where the commander himself backed her up in her insistence on mixed audiences, the Negro chaplain supported segregation.

Comment to a Louisville Audience

KATHERINE DUNHAM

It makes me very happy to know that you have liked us, that you have felt some of the beauty and happiness that we feel when we perform. But tonight our hearts are very sad because this is a farewell to Louisville. There comes a time when every human being must protest in order to retain human dignity. I must protest because I have discovered that your management will not allow people like you to sit next to people like us. I hope that time and the unhappiness of this war for tolerance and democracy, which I am sure we will win, will change some of these things. Perhaps then we can return.

Until then, God bless you—for you may need it.

SOURCE: Katherine Dunham made this comment to the audience after a performance of her company at Memorial Auditorium, Louisville, Kentucky, on 19 October 1944. Used by permission of Katherine Dunham.

Watching Dunham's Dances, 1937–1945

SUSAN MANNING

In a seminal essay published in 1994, "Performing the Memory of Difference in Afro-Caribbean Dance," VèVè Clark wrote that Katherine Dunham's "transformations of indigenous Caribbean, African American, and South American dances challenged her dancers, audiences, and critics to develop their dance literacy as they appreciated the changing same."[1] Here I would like to historicize Dunham's challenge to her viewers and ask how and when spectators learned to read Dunham's performance of diaspora. Or, more precisely, how and when spectators from different social locations learned to read Dunham's "memory of difference."

In so doing I adopt a cultural materialist approach that attends to conditions of production and reception and that interrelates social and artistic change. From this perspective, the years surrounding the Second World War constitute a paradigm shift in representations of race in American concert dance. Although leftist dance in the 1930s had patronized black artists to a greater extent than the emergent modern dance associated with Martha Graham, both leftist dance and modern dance relied on assumptions about the generalizing power of white bodies that created a critical conundrum for black dancing bodies. After 1940 mobilization for war distanced civil rights activism from leftist culture, and this realignment enabled black dancing bodies to acquire new meanings as signs of diaspora. Dunham's dances played a powerful role in this process of social and artistic change.

SOURCE: Susan Manning, "Modern Dance, Negro Dance, and Katherine Dunham," *Textual Practice* 15.3 (2001): 1–19. Copyright 2001 by Susan Manning. Thanks are due to the editor, Alan Sinfield, for granting permission to republish this case study of Dunham's reception.

Like other black concert dancers during the 1930s, Dunham had to improvise patronage at the interstices of leftist culture, elite black culture, commercial and noncommercial theater, and an emergent American ballet and modern dance. In fact, Dunham's affiliation with leftist culture took her from Chicago to New York in September 1939. Two and a half years earlier she and her company had made a one-time appearance at the Young Men's Hebrew Association on Ninety-second Street, where they joined with other black dancers to present a "Negro Dance Evening." A producer for the Labor Stage had seen the concert, and he remembered Dunham when he was looking for a choreographer for the 1940 edition of *Pins and Needles.* The Labor Stage performed at the Windsor Theatre, a small Broadway house. Taking advantage of her new position, Dunham booked her own company at the theater for a Sunday performance, which was such a hit that the company repeated the Sunday performances for another ten weeks.[2] In theatrical lore these concerts, titled *Tropics* and *Le Jazz "Hot,"* constitute the turning point of Dunham's career. For the next twenty years Dunham managed to keep her company afloat—and for a shorter period, her school—from income generated in the commercial theater.

What I want to probe is how and why the spectatorship of Dunham's dances so radically changed from the 1937 "Negro Dance Evening" to her 1940 production of *Tropics* and *Le Jazz "Hot"* and subsequent runs in New York during the war years. When Dunham first presented dances based on her ethnographic research as part of the "Negro Dance Evening," only one black critic and one leftist critic recognized what the concert organizers so clearly intended: to narrate the Black Atlantic through dance. When Dunham returned to New York three years later and appeared at the Windsor Theatre, her performance of diaspora became legible to a broad spectrum of theatergoers. Strikingly, only a few leftist critics dissented from the general acclamation, disappointed by what they perceived as the dancer's retreat from social protest.

Through the war years Dunham's performances drew audiences that, according to her own estimate, were nine-tenths white and one-tenth black.[3] Watching Dunham's dances, critics and audiences engaged in the dynamics of cross-viewing, the possibility for spectators to catch glimpses of perspectives conditioned by subjectivities and social identities that differed from their own. It is my contention that spectators learned to read the performance of diaspora in part through the experience of cross-viewing.

For the 1937 "Negro Dance Evening," Dunham collaborated with Edna

Guy, Alison Burroughs, Clarence Yates, and Asadata Dafora. An advance flyer clearly announced the artists' intent to narrate the Black Atlantic. However familiar this genealogy for African American dance became after the late 1960s, this was the first iteration in print that I know. The flyer stated:

> The program commences in Africa. This is to make immediately apparent to the audience the roots of the dancing in the Americas today. Then the scene goes across the ocean in slave ships to South and North America, and we see what becomes of the African in feast dances, war, religious and love dances. As generation succeeds generation of black folks, the memory of a free life based on hunting and farming becomes more and more vague. But the black builders of the New World must sing and dance in order to forget the awful misery of their new life which seems to hold no future. The third part of the program brings us to the present day. There is no more chattel slavery, but life is still difficult. . . . And then comes the contribution of the contemporary Negro artist.[4]

Although the advance publicity clearly articulated the frame of the Black Atlantic, it was less forthcoming about a second frame for the concert, the "contribution of the contemporary Negro artist" in terms of social protest. The first half of the evening opened with African dances choreographed by Asadata Dafora, moved to West Indian dances choreographed by Dunham, and closed with dances based on the Ring-Shout and Cakewalk choreographed by Clarence Yates. The second half of the evening, titled "Modern Trends," opened with solos by Guy, Burroughs, and Dunham and then presented a female duet and trio choreographed by Guy to the accompaniment of spirituals. The evening culminated in two dances of social protest: Dunham's *Tropic Death,* which cast Talley Beatty as the fugitive from a lynch mob, and a collectively choreographed work titled *Negro Songs of Protest.* Set to lyrics collected by Lawrence Gellert, the final work moved from a collective lament against injustice ("How Long, Brethren?") to a daring threat of violent resistance ("'Cause I'm a Nigger") to a specific protest against the fate of the Scottsboro Boys.[5] A photograph from the *Daily Worker* shows three male dancers in the final "Scottsboro." Displaying the separation of torso and pelvis characteristic of West African dance, the dancers performed social protest with an Africanist accent.

Only one critic from the dance press bothered to review the concert. Ignoring the advance publicity, the reviewer for *Dance* reiterated the limiting conceptions of Negro dance widely in evidence during the 1930s. Overall, the reviewer found "the combinations of primitive and French or American cultures" in the dances by Dunham, Guy, Burroughs, and Yates less effective than Dafora's African dances, described as "short—almost single phrases—and authentic." In other words, although the reviewer recognized the intercultural fusion in Dunham's dances, the reviewer favored Dafora's dances, because "primitive as they were, they contained a natural design which [sprang] truly from the people's imaginations."[6] Thus the white critic credited the value of Dafora's dances to an essential naturalness in black dancing bodies.

This was one half of the critical conundrum encountered by black concert dancers in the 1930s. On the one hand, if black concert dancers staged themes perceived as Africanist, then white critics considered them "natural performers" rather than "creative artists." On the other hand, if black concert dancers staged themes perceived as Eurocentric, then white critics considered them "derivative" rather than "original artists." In 1931 John Martin wrote in the *New York Times* that "it is not in these dances which echo and imitate the manner of the dancers of another race that the Negro dancers are at their best, but in those in which their forthrightness and simplicity have full play."[7] Yet Martin never chided modern dancers or leftist dancers for making references to "another race," which was an accepted convention in works from the 1930s that I have termed metaphorical minstrelsy. The most spectacular example was Helen Tamiris's *How Long, Brethren?*, set to the same collection of *Negro Songs of Protest* as the closing dance of the "Negro Dance Evening." Commissioned by the Federal Theater Project, Tamiris's work premiered three months *after* the "Negro Dance Evening" and received rave reviews. Accompanied by a black choir, the white dance ensemble protested the conditions of African American life, and only a few commentators found the configuration odd. Hallie Flanagan, director of the Federal Theater Project, spoke for many when she noted "One cannot tell where music becomes movement, where black voices become white bodies. *How Long, Brethren?* . . . is a powerful social document on freedom from racial prejudice."[8] Given the widespread acceptance of metaphorical minstrelsy among modern dancers, leftist dancers, and their audiences, it is no wonder that most white dance critics overlooked the "Negro Dance Evening."

Not so the black critic who reported on the concert in both the *New York Amsterdam News* and the *New York Age*. Attuned to the frame of the Black Atlantic, the critic described the evening as "an illustrative survey of the Negro dance from its origins in Africa to its present-day trends in America." Downplaying the dances of social protest, the critic singled out solos by the female dancers—Guy's *After Gauguin* and her rendition of *How Long, Brethren?,* Burroughs's *Composition,* Dunham's *Biguine-Biguine* and *Moorish Dance.* Thus the Harlem critic implicitly linked artistry not only to the performance of diaspora but also to female bodies in motion.[9]

The critic for the *Daily Worker,* Louis Mitchell, also recognized the concert's performance of diaspora. Yet, not surprisingly, the leftist critic reversed the valuation of the Harlem critic. Whereas the Harlem critic had praised *After Gauguin, Composition,* and *Moorish Dance,* Mitchell considered these works limited by their "studio influence." In contrast, he considered Dunham's anti-lynching dance, *Tropic Death,* "most successful for dramatic projection" and *Negro Songs of Protest* "moving" and "a new source of dance material." Not insensitive to the frame of the Black Atlantic, Mitchell lamented the omission of jazz dancing from the program. Yet he clearly valued most the concert's culmination in social protest.[10]

When Dunham returned to New York three years later with *Tropics* and *Le Jazz "Hot,"* she adapted the frame of the Black Atlantic from the "Negro Dance Evening." Significantly, she dropped overt dances of social protest and added jazz dancing. Her 1940 program began with dances based on Latin American and Caribbean sources and then moved to dances based on African American sources from nineteenth-century "plantation and minstrel dances" to twentieth-century jazz dances.[11] Although she did not script an extended program note, most white dance critics perceived her performance of diaspora. Not that they changed their preconceptions overnight, but it is clear that watching Dunham's dances in 1940 altered white critics' perceptions of black dancing bodies.

One example will have to stand for many. In the *New York Times* John Martin applauded Dunham's reliance on the "[rich] heritage" of Negro dance. Although he disparaged the integration of ballet into her intercultural movement vocabulary, he perceived an artistic authority in black concert dance that he had not seen before. Martin wrote, "To sit before a program such as this is to be impressed both with the existence of a constant element in it that is different from all other types of dance and with the great range and variety with which that constant element manifests itself."[12] Although Martin never used the term *diaspora,* he perceived a "constant element" in Dunham's dances that later commentators would term "Africanist."

Amplifying the response of the reporter for the *Amsterdam News* and the *New York Age* three years earlier, critics from the national black press reveled in Dunham's success. In *Opportunity* Blanche Matthias narrated her response in the first-person plural:

> From the beginning we were electrified, joyfully so. . . . Each time we returned to see Katherine Dunham and her group we were filled with wonder. The spirit which made gesture an art of glittering possibility, or of spontaneous reaction to just life with its magic yeas and nays, when that life meant love and story, plantations, hot jazz, rumbas, boleros, and was suddenly turned into a reason for being.[13]

Like John Martin's "constant element," Matthias's "reason for being" articulates the performance of diaspora. For many white critics, Dunham's 1940 concerts resolved the critical conundrum they earlier had scripted for Negro dance. For many black critics, Dunham's 1940 concerts realized the potential of Negro dance that they had barely glimpsed before.

Strikingly, the leftist press in New York registered less admiration for Dunham's extended run at the Windsor than did the black press and white dance press. The dance critic for *TAC,* a journal published by the left-wing Theater Arts Committee, wrote: "When Miss Dunham has her eye cocked on musical comedy, her numbers fall into the all too obvious patterns of white man conceptions of Negro dancing."[14] Where many black and white critics had seen the performance of diaspora, this leftist critic saw the performance of minstrelsy. Yet not all leftist critics agreed. Writing in *People's World,* a Communist paper published on the West Coast, John Pittman believed that Dunham's "social significance" was self-evident, because "the themes of her dances stem from the folk life of Negroes and of the peasant colonial peoples of Latin America and the Pacific."[15]

Of course, the few critics quoted here do not represent the views of all critics who recorded their impressions of Dunham's company on its non-stop tours across the United States. Nor do all the critics represent the views of all the spectators who flocked to see Dunham's company during the war years. Although it is clear that many black and white critics learned to read Dunham's performance of diaspora, it is equally clear that many spectators were drawn to the eroticism of Dunham's performances. For some spectators, Dunham's dances reinforced stereotypical images of sexy black female bodies, what a reporter for *Time Magazine* described as "a great scalawaggery of shimmying, shagging, rowdy flashing of black eyes and brown legs, a lively wigwagging of rumps."[16]

For other spectators, Dunham's dances presented legibly queer images. Here the evidence for dissident spectatorship is less direct than the unabashed account of dominant spectatorship in *Time*. Consider the line drawings that accompanied Walter Terry's rave review of *Tropics* and *Le Jazz "Hot"* in the *New York Herald Tribune*. Did the caption describing the 'gay good spirits' of Dunham's company carry more than one meaning for queer spectators, Terry included? Did the male dancers' jutting hips signify as gay as much as Africanist? Other evidence supports the possibility of a queer reading. Archie Savage, Dunham's frequent partner onstage, belonged to Carl Van Vechten's interracial gay social circle.[17] Gordon Heath, a gay black actor, remembered Dunham's company as "the highest prancing camp in the business."[18] And George Chauncey's ongoing oral history confirms the reputation of the Dunham Company as one center for gay life in Harlem during the 1940s and 1950s.[19]

Here as elsewhere in my research, it is easier to recover gay male spectatorship of Negro dance than lesbian spectatorship, and the same holds true for modern dance. Were lesbians simply less drawn to Negro dance and modern dance than were gay men? Or is lesbian spectatorship less evident in the archive because it existed along a continuum with straight feminist spectatorship? Although I suspect the latter, I cannot say for sure. Consider the example of *Tropics—Shore Excursion,* one of Dunham's signature works. The dance dramatized an encounter between Dunham, the "Woman with the Cigar," and Savage, a dock-hand whom Dunham "meets . . . [and] flirts with" but who "has a date down the road"—in the words of one critic.[20] Yet countering this narrative frame (or perhaps extending the narrative for spectators who knew Savage's reputation) was the spectacle of Dunham as the "Woman with the Cigar." On the one hand, the cigar alludes to the religious practices of Santería, a fusion of Yoruban and Catholic practices that originated in Cuba.[21] On the other hand, Dunham based the dance on Caribbean market women known as Madame Saras, market women who often supported "wives."[22] Photographs of the dance show Dunham clenching a cigar between her smiling lips. Clearly an allusion to fellatio and just as clearly an allusion to a butch femme, the image fused heteronormative with queer eroticism and both with the performance of diaspora. Like the male dancers' jutting hips in the line drawings published in the *Herald Tribune,* the image of Dunham as the "Woman with the Cigar" carried both Africanist and queer connotations.

To return to my earlier query: what accounts for the radically different reception of Dunham's choreography in 1937 and from 1940 to 1945? First, and most obviously, the decline of leftist culture. Leftist spectators had applauded not only the "Negro Dance Evening" but also Tamiris's *How Long, Brethren?* because in different ways both events realized the ideal of interracialism, the belief that only an alliance of black and white activists could dismantle the doubled legacy of capitalism and racism. But the rhetorical conjunction of socialist solidarity and ethnic self-representation came apart during the war years. Or, perhaps more accurately, ethnic self-representation came to stand for socialist solidarity, as exemplified by John Pittman's review of Dunham in *People's World.*

Second, and less obviously, wartime mobilization initiated a transition from the gay world that took shape earlier in the century to the era of the closet that descended after the war. As George Chauncey has demonstrated, the gay world used new spaces in the urbanscape—public parks, rooming houses, entertainment districts—to enable the expression of same-sex desire in ways that were boldly legible to insiders and not necessarily illegible to outsiders. In contrast, the era of the closet created discreet and discrete spaces for gay sociality.[23] During the war years the transition from the gay world to the closet was particularly clear within the military, which for the first time made homosexuality grounds for deferment or discharge but which also prompted legions of gay men and women to experience what Allan Bérubé has described as "coming out under fire."[24] The home front was equally contradictory, as massive geographic dislocation of civilians gave men and women, gay and straight, new opportunities for sexual expression. At the same time popular culture and government policy bombarded civilians with the rhetorical ideal of traditional domesticity—the return to normalcy promised and realized at war's end.[25] During these years civilians and soldiers on leave queued in long lines to see Dunham's company. Did they recognize in her dual performance of heteronormativity and queerness something of their own contradictory experiences during wartime?

Third, and most important, mobilization for war accelerated the momentum of the civil rights movement, as the NAACP launched its Double-Victory campaign, linking the fight against fascism abroad with the fight against racism at home. In a very real way, Dunham's appearances furthered the Double-V campaign. Touring across the country, her company often found itself booked into theaters with segregated seating, and the choreographer always mounted a protest, despite the risk this posed to her commercial success. In October 1944 Dunham addressed an audience in Louisville that a black journalist estimated as nearly a quarter black:[26]

Right now war is being fought. People the color such as we are . . . giving
our lives, and we come to a city like this and find that we cannot have
our people seated among you because of color. I will have to say that it is
impossible for us to return to you . . . as much as we would like, since
we see by your response you would like us to come back. But we cannot
appear where people such as ourselves cannot sit next to people such as
you.[27] Within the week the theater in Louisville had changed its policy on
ticket sales, and within the year the United States had won the war.

Desegregating theaters across the country through the war years, Dunham demanded that her audiences experience cross-viewing. Of course,
black spectators long had experienced one-way cross-viewing, sitting in
the balcony and watching white spectators watching black performers.
But integrated houses introduced two-way cross-viewing, where black and
white spectators watched each other watching. It is my contention that
spectators learned to read the performance of diaspora in part through this
two-way exchange.

Dunham's performances also encompassed another form of cross-
viewing, where queer spectators saw what straight spectators saw but also
saw another layer of meaning. Dunham did not necessarily reverse this
established pattern for spectatorship, a pattern introduced by the gay world
and continued by the era of the closet. Thus a work like *Tropics,* featuring
Dunham as the "Woman with the Cigar," participated in an established
dynamic for cross-viewing. In effect, Dunham's wartime performances
layered a new dynamic over a preexisting dynamic for spectatorship. What
resulted was a complex range of responses, many of which remain beyond
the reach of historical research. Yet the evidence makes clear that watching Dunham's dances changed many spectators' perceptions of black bodies in motion and that these new perceptions encompassed queer bodies
in motion. In other words, theatergoing changes the ways people interpret the social meanings of physical bodies. For those who were looking,
Dunham's dances made legible the performance of diaspora and of black
sexual dissidence during the war years.

Notes

1. VèVè Clark, "Performing the Memory of Difference in Afro-Caribbean Dance:
Katherine Dunham's Choreography, 1938–87," in *History and Memory in African-
American Culture,* edited by Geneviève Fabre and Robert O'Meally (New York: Oxford
University Press, 1994), 202.

2. There is some discrepancy concerning the length of the run of the 1940 production of *Tropics* and *Le Jazz Hot* at the Windsor Theatre. Some sources note that the show ran for thirteen weeks. Susan Manning has done extensive archival research and determined that the concert on 18 February 1940 was repeated on March 10, 17, 24, 31; April 7, 14, 21, 28; and May 5 and 12. She also determined that there was a three-week hiatus between the first and subsequent performances when Miss Dunham made changes to the program *[Eds.]*.

3. Ramona Lowe, "Being a Closeup on Miss Dunham," *New York Amsterdam News,* 18 September 1943, 8B.

4. Publicity Flyer, "Negro Dance Evening," 7 March 1937, Young Men's Hebrew Association, Jerome Robbins Dance Division, New York Public Library for the Performing Arts.

5. Program, "Negro Dance Evening," 7 March 1937, Young Men's Hebrew Association, Jerome Robbins Dance Division, New York Public Library for the Performing Arts.

6. "Negro Dance Evening," *Dance* 2.2 (May 1937): 32–33.

7. John Martin, "Dance Recital Given by Negro Artists," *New York Times,* 30 April 1931, 27.

8. Hallie Flanagan, "The Dance and the Modern Theatre," ms. in Federal Theater Collection, National Archives, p. 1. For an extended account, see Susan Manning, "Black Voices, White Bodies: The Performance of Race and Gender in *How Long Brethren," American Quarterly* 50.1 (March 1998): 24–46.

9. "An Interim of Dancing: Negro Dance Recital Enthralls Audience," *New York Amsterdam News,* 13 March 1937, 9; "Crowd at Negro Dance Recital: Folk Dances of Many Lands Featured in Dance Recital," *New York Age,* 13 March 1937, 9. Essentially the same review appeared in both newspapers, leading to the conclusion that one critic wrote both.

10. Louis Mitchell, "Panorama of Negro Dances," *Daily Worker,* 16 March 1937, 7.

11. Program, Katherine Dunham and Dance Group, 7 April 1940, Windsor Theatre, Jerome Robbins Dance Division, New York Public Library for the Performing Arts.

12. John Martin, "The Dance: A Negro Art," *New York Times,* 25 February 1940), 9:2.

13. Blanche Matthias, "Katherine Dunham," *Opportunity* 19.4 (April 1941): 112–13.

14. "Katherine Dunham," *TAC* 2.6 (1 March 1940): 9.

15. John Pittman, "Dunham Dance Group Returns for Another San Francisco Triumph," *People's World* (3 January 1942), Dunham scrapbook, Jerome Robbins Dance Division, New York Public Library for the Performing Arts. Dunham's program at the Windsor Theatre opened with *Rara Tonga,* based on a "Melanesian folk story." Since Dunham had not undertaken ethnographic fieldwork in the Pacific, her decision to place this dance first on the program underscored that artistic invention motivated her choreography as much as ethnographic research.

16. "Anthropology, Hot," *Time* 35.12 (18 March 1940): 32.

17. Bruce Kellner, ed., *Letters of Carl Van Vechten* (New Haven: Yale University Press, 1987), 205. In a letter to Hugh Laing dated 8 August 1944, Van Vechten wrote, "If you see Archie Savage, send me all the dirt. Is he free again? What did he do with the $10,000, etc?"

18. Gordon Heath, *Deep Are the Roots: Memoirs of a Black Expatriate* (Amherst: University of Massachusetts Press, 1992), 59.

19. George Chauncey, personal conversation, 28 December 1999.

20. Richard Buckle, ed., *Katherine Dunham: Her Dancers, Singers, Musicians* (London: Ballet Publications, 1949), 2–3.

21. Katherine J. Hagedorn, *Divine Utterances: The Performance of Afro-Cuban Santeria* (Washington, D.C.: Smithsonian Institution Press, 2001), 205, 216. My thanks to Deborah Thomas for drawing my attention to Santería as an obvious referent.

22. VèVè Clark, personal conversation, 13 October 2000.

23. George Chauncey, *Gay New York: Gender, Urban Culture, and the Making of the Gay Male World, 1890–1940* (New York: Basic Books, 1994).

24. Allan Bérubé, *Coming Out under Fire: The History of Gay Men and Women in World War Two* (New York: Free Press, 1990).

25. Elaine Tyler May, "Rosie the Riveter Gets Married," in *The War in American Culture: Society and Consciousness during World War II,* ed. Lewis Erenberg and Susan E. Hirsch (Chicago: University of Chicago Press, 1996), 128–43.

26. "Dunham Denounces Kentucky Jimcro," *People's Voice* (11 November 1944): 28.

27. Ruth Beckford, *Katherine Dunham: A Biography* (New York: Marcel Dekker, 1979), 69.

Goombay

KATHERINE DUNHAM

EDITORS NOTE: On a study tour of the West Indies, sponsored by the University of Chicago and Northwestern University, dancer and anthropologist Dunham made Jamaica her first stop. Her interest there was the Maroon people, an isolated, once warlike group who lived in the rugged cockpits in the north of the island. During her month's stay among them, she overcame their shyness and made friends. But up to almost her last day Miss Dunham was unable to discover if they still secretly performed their ancient war dances. The "Colonel," their chief, denied all knowledge of them, although Ba' Foster, one of Miss Dunham's Maroon friends, promised to make her a goombay, the drum that once accompanied these rituals. Then, two days before her departure, the Colonel went on a visit to another part of the island. . . .

It was growing dusk, and, glad for an excuse to leave the house, which seemed a little dreary in the half light, I decided to walk down the mountain to Ba' Foster's and find out why he had not brought me my goombay. Two weird little mouse bats whirled past my head as I stepped out into the yard, and settled under the rustling straw roof with a great flapping of wings and a contented squeaking. I had never liked them, and tonight they were especially repulsive with their flash of sharp white mouse teeth and webbed furry wings.

SOURCE: Katherine Dunham, "Goombay," *Mademoiselle* (November 1945). Copyright 1945 by Street & Smith Publications, Inc.; renewed 1973 by Condé Nast Publications, Inc. Reprinted by permission.

Nearing Ba' Foster's house, I began to feel an excitement in the air, and almost involuntarily my step quickened and I was breathing faster without knowing why. Then I became aware of a *drum*. Not the deep booming of the revivalist Salvation Army drum, but the sharp staccato of a goatskin drawn tightly over a small hollowed trunk and beaten expertly by gnarled black palms.

I skidded down the last rocky decline and directly into Ba' Foster's "yard." This was deserted. But farther down in the hollow, well hidden from the road behind a tangle of pimiento and breadfruit and coconut trees, I could see the smoky glow of kerosene torches. A circle of tense eager bodies, faces ecstatic in the flickering half-light, and in the middle of the circle, Mis' Ma'y and an old man whom I did not know, performing a strange ritual, more pantomime than dance. To one side Ba' Weeyums squatted over the goombay, *my* goombay, his face streaked with perspiration, his eyes brilliant, and his hard palms beating the goatskin, the tone changing from sharp to sullen, from a command to a coaxing by a deft sliding of the side of the palm along the face of the drum.

Ba' Teddy saw me first. Yes, even he was there.

"Evenin', evenin', Missus," said Ba' Teddy softly.

"Evenin'," I replied, winking back a tear. Ba' Foster stepped quickly forward with the goombay under one arm.

"Me *juh'* gwi' bring eem you, Missus!" he said, with too much emphasis. "Me on de way now w'en me meet up wid' Ba' Weeyums en eem ax er play eem jus' dis' once."

I looked at Ba' Weeyums. He was first on one foot and then on the other, twisting his little felt hat around his forefinger, and looking anxiously at me the while. Then suddenly I realized that this was the long-hoped-for opportunity—that here were the dances that I had waited so many weeks to see. It was my turn to look anxiously at Ba' Weeyums.

"But everyone's leaving!" I said. And to be sure, of the score of old and young who circled the dancers when I arrived, there were now less than half.

"De' goombay eem good 'nuf," said Ba' Weeyums slowly, "but eem need rum. Don' no goombay talk like eem *should* talk eef eem no had de rum."

The rum! The rum! Of course. I loudly asked Ral if he would go up to my cottage and bring down the jug of rum from under Mai's bunk in the kitchen. He was off with unusual alacrity, whether because of the rum or because of the chance that Mai might by this hour have retired to the bunk, I do not know.

While we waited, Ba' Weeyums explained that of course he could have beat the drum for me any day, but there had been no drum to beat. Ba' Teddy explained further that all of this was strictly forbidden by the Colonel, that he had cautioned them against doing these dances while I was there, that Ba' Foster's story was true that nothing had been planned but only by the accident of Ba' Weeyums's drum-beating had these passers-by gathered, and that were the Colonel not at Balaclava, even this would have been completely out of the question.

Ral returned, and Ba' Weeyums took drum and demijohn off to one side. There he poured rum on the goatskin head, rubbed it in, took a long drink himself, then spat a mouthful at the drum again. Between times he mumbled in a tongue which I recognized as Koromantyn. Then he poured a few drops of rum on the ground, and the baptism was over. This was for the spirit of the drum, he explained. Then he squatted over the drum again, and indeed it seemed to me that it was suddenly alive. Though the body of the drum was shallow, and it more resembled a square stool than any drum which I had previously seen, the tone was full and less staccato than before, and I was almost inclined to believe that it *was* alive, and that it *was* the spirit of some Gold Coast god come to life to grumble a protest against the long silence.

Gradually they returned, slipping from behind the coconut palms and up from the ravines and down from the mountains. I don't know how many, because I was in the midst, and there was now only one kerosene torch and the rum was going the rounds and it all became unreal, though it all happened because the dances are still very clear to me.

I might not have been present at all, for the difference that it has made. I am accepted. I am one of them.

The dance which I had interrupted was a *myal* dance. Ba' Teddy explained it as, fascinated, I watched Mis' Ma'y and the old man. They were facing one another. The old man took the part of the *myal* "doctor," and the dance was to entice into his power an evil spirit—the "duppy" of some dead worker of black magic. Ba' Weeyums led a chant in Koromantyn, and the women answered. The dance interested me too much for me to try and remember the sounds of the words. The evil spirit circles around the doctor, hesitant, advancing and retreating. Her eyes were fixed, mouth clamped shut tightly, body rigid. The doctor squats in front of her, arms wide as though to embrace her, fingers wide open and hands trembling violently. As he advances slowly toward her, his pelvis begins to move, and the duppy responds in like manner. They hesitate in front of each other, swaying. Then she eludes his embrace with a sharp convulsive bend and is on the other side of the circle, taunting, enticing, features still hard and set but body liquid and so full of desire that I can scarcely believe that it is old Mis' Ma'y, grandmother of goodness knows how many.

The doctor reaches out for her, gesticulating, grimacing, insinuating. Then she comes suddenly to life and the pursuit is reversed. The doctor is afraid of this thing which he has done, of this woman whom he has raised from the dead with these fleshly promises. They are face to face, bodies touching, both of them squatting now with arms pressed to sides, elbows bent, and widespread fingers quivering violently. The duppy leans over the man who cowers in fear from her, though their bodies are pressed tightly together. As I decide that I must close my eyes for a moment, Ba' Teddy mutters, trying to calm his voice and appear merely annoyed in spite of his quick breathing. I open my mouth to speak, but he anticipates my question and answers sharply. "Bes' don' ax no furder questions, Missus! Me don' see dat fer long time, en hit bad. Dat mix up wid bad biznuss. Better fer missus ef she fergit!"

I was almost relieved to be thus reprimanded. But the mood of the dance had already changed, and to a far livelier rhythm. Two men were hopping about in the circle, mimicking two cocks in the thick of a fight. They switched their middles, bobbed their heads, wrinkled their faces and stuck their necks far out, crowing a challenge. The audience, tense a moment before, is now in a hysteria of laughter. One picks his foot high and hops around in a circle, the other following at a gallop, hands thrust in coat pocket and flapping wildly for wings. Finally one is vanquished and with a feeble squawk rolls over sadly in the air. The other struts over to him, looks disdainfully around and flaps his wings in victory as he trots around in a circle.

I plead with Ba' Weeyums for a Koromantee war dance, and he finally consents. In this I join, along with Simon Rowe and others who have watched so far. The few young people who are here, however, do not join in these traditional dances. They are ashamed, and I am sure that I shock them greatly; on the other hand, I feel that they watch us rather wistfully, wishing that they had the courage to give themselves for a moment to their traditions and forget that there is a market at Maggotty and cricket games on the outside, and store-bought shoes.

The war dances are danced by both men and women. The introduction seemed to be a disjointed walking around in a loose circle, much like the warming up of an athlete. Then Henry Rowe and I are facing each other doing a step which could easily be compared to an Irish reel. Hands on hips, we hop from one foot to the other, feet turned out at right angles to the body, or well "turned out" in ballet vernacular. This hopping brings us nearer to each other, and I must closely watch the rest to keep up with Henry. We turn our backs and walk away, then turn suddenly again and hop together. The songs are in lusty Koromantyn, and from somewhere a woman has procured a rattle and shakes this in accompaniment to Ba' Weeyums. Some of the men wave sticks in the air, and the women tear off their handkerchiefs and wave them on high as they dance. Henry and I grab each other around the waist and run circles around each other, first one way and then the other. A few of these turns, and we are separated in a melee of leaping, shouting warriors; a moment later we are "bush fightin'," crouching down and advancing in line to attack an imaginary enemy with many feints, swerves, and much pantomime. At one stage of the dance Mis Ma'y and I are face to face, she no longer a duppy but a Maroon woman of the old days, working the men up to a pitch where they will descend into the cockpit and exterminate one of his majesty's red-coated platoons. She grabs me by the shoulders and shakes me violently, then we are again hopping around each other with knees high in the air, headkerchiefs and skirts flying.

When this is over we are all exhausted. The Maroons have not been accustomed to this sort of thing for a long time; nor am I, who until now have known only the conventional techniques and the far less strenuous "set" dances. We disperse and I am in possession of the goombay. Ba' Teddy and Ba' Weeyums and I labor up the mountainside, and behind us shutters close and candles are extinguished.

Thirty Days among Maroons

ZORA NEALE HURSTON

Katherine Dunham's *Journey to Accompong* is a lively and word-deft account of a thirty days' visit to Accompong, the Maroon settlement high in the mountains of Jamaica, British West Indies.

Dancer-anthropologist Miss Dunham has made the most of her material in the 162 pages of this book. In a more comprehensive work, the material in *Journey to Accompong* would have been compressed into a single chapter. But the keen observation of the author, professional and otherwise, plus her frequent humorous reflections, sustain the thin material to the end. After all, thirty days in a locality is not much in research and hardly affords time enough for the fieldworker to scratch the surface. Therefore, it is to the tremendous credit of the author that she has achieved such an entertaining book.

Katherine Dunham is a famous dancer and choreographer. Most of her dance compositions are founded on the folk dances of the Antilles. The material for them she gathered on two Rosenwald fellowships under Dr. Melville Herskovits, of Northwestern University.

Ted Cook's landscapes have an atavistic quality which is compelling. For that reason, this reader regrets that his human figures suffer from a kind of traditional triteness. The influence of Miguel Covarrubias, the

SOURCE: Zora Neale Hurston, "Thirty Days among Maroons," review of *Journey to Accompong* by Katherine Dunham, *New York Herald Tribune Weekly Book Report,* 12 January 1947. Copyright 1947 by International Herald Tribune (IHT) Corporation. Reprinted by permission.

NOTE: *Katherine Dunham's Journey to Accompong,* with drawings by Ted Cook. New York: Henry Holt & Company, 1946.

famous cartoonist of Negro life in Harlem, is left in Mr. Cook's work—the eternally overdeveloped buttocks, the over-long and skinny arms, the lack of human expression in the face.

In 1936, there were upwards of a thousand people in the Maroons' mountain settlement living in a sort of tribal fashion under their head, who wears the title of colonel. The settlement has been there for around three hundred years. Its origin is a product of phases of African slavery in the West Indies. First under the Spanish, then the British. The Maroons were ex-slaves who either ran away to the all-but-inaccessible retreat of the mountain or fought their way free and joined the others. Like the Indians in the United States, they live under a treaty arrangement with the government, have their own courts, and [keep] their own customs as far as they like. Miss Dunham's book is a day-to-day record of her observations: What has survived of the African cultures, and what has been absorbed from the outside world of Jamaicans, the traces of Obeah and African dances.

Miss Dunham's book is very readable; in addition to the lively style and the pert observations on the doings of the men, women, and children of Accompong, like Colonel Rowe with his official dignity, halting between the tribal and the customs of the outside world, Mrs. Mai and her fat self and loud snores, Ba' Weeyums and his Obeah, and Big John and his primitive cane-mill, the author includes several folk songs from Accompong and instances of Anansi folk tales. The Anansi folk tales, of which Br'er Spider is usually the hero, are the best known tales in Jamaica.

On Stage with the Dunham Company

An Interview with Vanoye Aikens

VÈVÈ A. CLARK

Vanoye Aikens joined the Dunham Company as a student in 1943 and remained a member until its final performance in 1965. After being promoted to principal dancer, he was Miss Dunham's partner in many of her ballets and dances. The following conversation is an abridgment of an interview conducted in Saint Louis, Missouri, on 14 August 1995, during the Dunham Technique Seminar.

VANOYE AIKENS [hereafter VA]: Miss Dunham has given me my life. I'm still paying my dues, to tell you the truth, I am. God, yes. I hope this is recorded because I mean every word of that. It was my life. It is still my life. And the funny thing is, it was not planned. My career came by sheer accident.

VÈVÈ A. CLARK [hereafter VC]: And how was that?

VA: You don't know?

VC: No, I don't know the story.

VA: You don't know anything? What do you know about me, please?

VC: I don't. And that's the point. The first question I have here was what kind of dance training you had. What I know of you I know from the pieces.

VA: All of my training came from Katherine Dunham. Now, we did have outside teachers [who were brought in to teach]. You were not allowed to study outside. First of all, you joined the Katherine Dunham Company as a student, not as a dancer. I don't care, you could have been dancing rings around the moon, you joined as a student. You didn't know that?

VC: I really hadn't heard anybody say that before.

VA: When you come into the Dunham Company, you have to forget what training you have and be retrained. That is not a simple thing. Because people who are already trained, they have certain habits and ta-ta, ta-ta, ta-ta. Miss Dunham, I can truthfully say, she can see a scrubby talent, that is, unscrubbed talent, and then she—I don't want to say "molded," because I don't like that "mold" business—anyway, what she saw in me I do not know.

VC: What were you doing before you joined the company?

VA: Well, I was in school. I had finished my sophomore year at Morehouse College. But finish? I didn't even get there, because we had no money. And I worked for the purser, or is it the bursar? On a ship it's what? A purser? And at school it's the bursar. And he was ill, so Dr. Hubert gave me a scholarship because I think my aunt and Mama got twenty-five dollars together. Mr. Gassett [the bursar] was becoming ill and he needed attending. To make a long story short, I worked all that time in Morehouse College, had no time to study, had to be up all night long.

That's where I learned to drive, because I had to drive him to school, collect him, bring him back, give him his lunch, back to school again, staying up all night, stoking the furnace. So I said, "Mama, I don't know how this is going to work. I want to be home and not spend the night out there, cutting grass and all that kind of crap. This has got to stop. I'm going back to Hartford, and I'm just going to find a job or whatever."

Then, I got into the Navy immediately, but they only kept me thirteen months. They knew perfectly well they had made a mistake, you understand. [*Laughter*.] I don't think that's funny at all. Well, I got out of the Navy in Boston, Massachusetts. I had thirty-four dollars in my pocket, and Mama had sent me my only suit, because I said, "Mama, I'm getting out of the Navy." And she said, "Thank God!" You know, one of those things. I said, "I don't know what I'm going to do." And she said, "I don't care what you're going do, but you get out of that place." I said, "Well, my one suit that you have in the closet, please ship it as soon as possible."

So when I got out of the Navy, I had thirty-four dollars and that one suit. And I got on the Greyhound bus and slept. It was practically empty, a midnight bus—I think the fare was about three dollars in those days—and I slept on the back seat. I had the whole thing to myself. I woke up—at that time the Greyhound bus stop in New York was around Fiftieth Street—and I went straight to—then you could get the subway for a nickel—the 134th Street YMCA, and they put me in the annex. That was all right.

I arrived on a Friday morning because it was a half a night trip. I was in the annex Saturday afternoon. I'm sitting on the steps of the YMCA, the main Harlem YMCA, because I said "Now I'm going to have to find a job as a dishwasher. And the first job I'm going to look for, I'm going to the Waldorf Astoria, so that if I have to wash dishes, it's going to be at the Waldorf Astoria." So I'm sitting there that Saturday afternoon contemplating, and who should come down the street but Lenwood Morris.

vc: [*Surprised*] No!

va: I don't tell lies. Lenwood. I'm sitting there, just, you know, looking and this, that and the other, and Lenwood came. It's Saturday afternoon and he looked at me and said, "Hi, Doll." I said, "Hello." And he said, "I have just joined Katherine Dunham." Lenwood auditioned for her in Louisville in a nightclub. That was one of their last appearances in Louisville. And Lenwood and Andre Drew went there and they were taken immediately because Miss Dunham was getting ready for *Tropical Revue* to be produced by Sol Hurok and she was going to extend the company. And I had seen Miss Dunham in Boston with Rochester in one of those war films,[1] and she said, "Man, you ain't only sassy, you is Haile Selassie" or something. And that's the first time I heard her name.

vc: You joined the company. Can you give me the year?

va: Do I have to?

vc: Yes.

va: Why? But the only thing is—I swear to God—I get it screwed up. Because I've told so many lies, like my age. I get it screwed up. No, I cannot tell you. I swear sitting here I can't tell you. I know when it was round about. Miss Dunham can tell you when *Tropical Revue* opened at the Martin Beck Theatre in New York. That was the debut.

vc: That has to be somewhere between—

va: 1940.

VC: I'm going to guess 1943.

VA: Somewhere in there. Because I swear, you're quite near the mark. *Tropical Revue* began at the Martin Beck Theatre, produced by Sol Hurok, and that was my debut.[2]

After that "Hi, Doll, I became a Dunham dancer," I said to [Lenwood], "You know, I've always wondered what it would be like to be a dancer." And he said, "You know, we're going to be down there, why don't you come and try out?" I said, "I wouldn't dare. I mean, I don't know." He said, "Tell you what, I'm on my way [to Philadelphia] and I'll be back tomorrow." Because Lenwood comes from Philadelphia, and he was coming from the West Coast [when] Archie Savage sent him to Miss Dunham to audition, and he was leaving that night to go to Philadelphia to see his daddy. The next day was Sunday. And I said, "Well, I'm in a room up there."

Well, up to Sunday night, no Lenwood Morris. So I went to Small's Paradise. In those days, it was—was it during the war or after the war?—anyway, Small's [was] a place for servicemen to get information. So I went. I met a man, his name was Gilbert, and I said, "Excuse me sir, but have you heard of Katherine Dunham?" And he said yes because he was helping the servicemen and all that. He said, "It's in the newspapers, and they're appearing at the Martin Beck Theatre." So I thanked him.

The next Monday morning I went to 125th Street, because I was on 135th, and bought myself a pair of beige boxer shorts and a beige shirt with blue and yellow and beige in it, you understand? And then I went to the Martin Beck Theatre and sat there. Early Monday morning, after I had gotten my little—No, that is not true. I didn't buy the beige outfit until after that. Wait a minute, wait a minute. Back up. I went the next morning, which was a Monday, to the Martin Beck Theatre. The entrance to go in the theater is on the same street as the stage door, and I just leaned against the wall. I mean, the entrance— the stage door and the front of the theater—is on Fortieth Street itself. It's not like backstage is in the alley. God, that was my first theater in New York, so I know very well.

VC: So you went into the theater.

VA: No, no. I stood out there. As a matter of fact, I think the doorman was there but he had no information for me. So I went outside and stood, leaned against the wall. And I saw this lady coming down the street in a sort of a brown two-piece suit, you know. And these heels, and I'm telling you, pretty legs—I don't look at ladies that often, but—and she walked right up to the stage door. Who was it? Lucille [Ellis]. And with the bangs she used to wear, and something up here [*gestures toward head*]. Now, Lucy was always in charge of wardrobe, you understand. So there she was coming and I said, "Excuse me, Miss, but could you tell me where the"—I don't know what I said—"where the cast is rehearsing?" or something. And Lucille has not changed to this day. "Yes, dear. Now listen to me. We will be at the F—— Studio in Greenwich Village on Twenty-something Street. Now, it's ten o'clock, but we won't be there until one."

Now I had three hours. So I went to the Paramount Theatre and saw vaudeville. I can't remember who was on stage. It doesn't matter. I kept looking at my ten-cent watch, and then I went up to Twenty-third Street—I think that's where the studio was—and found the number. Now, in those days, the studios were on the top, the very top, so you had to climb five sets of stairs. I got there and Lavinia [Williams] was teaching. Syvilla [Fort] was there. Everybody was there. And Lenwood said, "But, Doll! So glad you showed up." I said, "Well, what happened?" Whatever it was, it was not deliberate.

I didn't have any clothes to put on. Anyway, whatever happened, happened, and I was to return the next day. Because the good thing about the company is the dancers worked in front, and they put the new people behind them. And that saved me. To make a long story short, the second day, I had nothing to wear. And that's when I went to 125th Street and bought my outfit.

[In the studio] there was a skylight, and it was late summer because we opened in September, it would seem to me, and there was no air. And you've seen the way I perspire. I was always in the back, coming in the progression and on the floor. After the second day, I almost had to go to the hospital because Lavinia overstretched me. But I was still carrying on in my outfit. And when I got the outfit, it only lasted about a couple of hours, and I was dripping water. [*Laughter.*] I don't think that's very funny.

VC: [*Laughing*] But it *is* funny.

VA: Well, it's true. And we went in progression and there was a trail of water. It's true, I swear on my dead mother. I don't lie, and I'm not exaggerating. And Lenwood and I became buddies immediately. So when we were finished, with our little bit of money, we would go to Forty-second Street and get spaghetti and meatballs because you could get an awful lot for forty-five cents, you understand. So then about the third day, we couldn't go down the subway stairs, and we couldn't come up because that [the intensity of the rehearsals] went on all day. Syvilla was the ballet mistress, so when she would start the rehearsals, we weren't in a lot of, hardly any of that stuff, so we could leave. And that's the first time I saw Lawaune Ingram, this beautiful child. Oh, Lord, Lawaune was such a lovely creature. And so it went on for four days. And Miss Dunham was up there in the Klondikes someplace, and there weren't very many of us.

Have you heard of Josephine Premice?

VC: Sure.

VA: Josephine was fresh out of Haiti at Columbia. I think she was eighteen. But before [the final day] Miss Dunham had called in to find out if there were any possibilities. No one says anything to me. And what they said, I suppose, was "Well, there's one or two" or something. And I guess they said me and Josephine.

The last day we came in, Lenwood and I, and here was this lady, all stretched out like Cleopatra in blue. Blue top and the blue tights Miss Dunham always wore, but knitted, you know, blue and all these bangles. I shouldn't say bangles. Gold bracelets up to here. And the minute the progression started, and I'm behind, the first thing she said to me was "Would you go back and do that again?" And I looked around—it wasn't simple—and I said, "Me?" And she said, "Yes." And I went and I did it again. I still didn't know who she was.

Anyway, so Friday, that's enough. I'm sore, the money is down to nothing, and I said to Len, "You know, I'm not getting anywhere. I've got to find a job and pay the YMCA." We were sharing and spending our money together and didn't have any. I said, "I've had it." I didn't know what was going on. And so Saturday I didn't go [to rehearsal]. But I had forgotten my beige shorts and my top because Claude [had taken it] when I was dripping all that water, Claude Marchant, who was also a great part of the Dunham Company. Have you heard the name Claude Marchant? Claude is still in Gothenburg. Anyway, I wanted my shorts back because I thought, "When Monday rolls around I am going to the Waldorf Astoria to apply for a dishwashing job." I had no skills. I had no skills at all. So I went around eleven or twelve o'clock. I got to about the third landing and the drums were going and all hell was—I got to the top, entered that tiny little studio and Lavinia looked at me and said, "You're late." I said, "What do you mean? Late for what?" And she said, "Didn't you get the telegram?" I said, "What telegram?" "You were supposed to be here for photos and costumes at ten o'clock."

Well, the next thing I know I have nothing on. I was in *Rites,* standing up with a pole in front, and the next thing, they put me in the *Honky Tonk* costume. And I didn't know my butt from a hole in the ground. And that was the beginning of my dance career with Katherine Dunham. That is the God's truth. So all of my training comes from the company and Miss Dunham.

We did nothing but tour. But wherever we would settle for a week or ten days, she would go and find a ballet teacher. So our training—we were not allowed to train outside of the company. If we were in Chicago, as we were for weeks and weeks and weeks, she would find the teacher and the studio. And your day would begin with ballet. And then if it were not so, then *she* would teach a ballet class, which I hated. It was too difficult. But Miss Dunham would find our teachers for us. Otherwise, she taught. She would bring Ziggy Johnson from Detroit to give us chorus-line work, you know, and plain old gut-bucket Chicago chorus-girl jazz. We had to work between shows. I mean we had to have a class between shows. And we had flamenco. You name it. But that was our life. So my formal training came from the company and Katherine Dunham.

vc: And you stayed with the company until 1965? I understand that the last show was at the Apollo in New York?

va: That's true.

vc: But you stayed with them the whole time?

va: No.

vc: No?

va: But there was no whole time. We first parted company in Japan.

vc: Okay. I didn't know that.

va: What? The Dunham Company was first let go in Japan, and then we regrouped again. That's the first time that I went on my singing career, while I was in Japan, because I was the only one prepared with something to do.

vc: And what kind of singing did you do?

va: I did standards, and calypso was very heavy. I surprised Miss Dunham in Australia. I found a composer and had my songs orchestrated. I found a tailor and had my outfits made. I found a shoemaker and had my shoes made. And then, when I was completely ready—and she didn't know that our wardrobe mistress made my ruffled tuxedo shirt—when I was ready with full orchestration, rehearsals, and so on, I went to Miss

Dunham and said, "Please, may I show you something?" And on a Saturday afternoon between shows, I invited her and members of the company [to see me perform]. I had been to the director of the theater and gotten permission. The stage manager knew, so he asked a couple of the stage hands. I had lights, the whole theater, and a ten-piece orchestra on stage behind the curtain. And then they were all seated and I was in the wings, with a friend to hold my hand, because I was scared to death. And my theme was "Georgia." And so when the first chord of "Georgia" struck, the lights came on, and the curtain went up, and there was the full orchestra. As always, I let the first two go by. [*Sings*] And then offstage I would pick up, [*singing*] "I can't keep Georgia off my mind." And then I walked on stage in front of the microphone, and I did my whole act for Miss Dunham. That is the truth.

vc: So this was probably in the late 1950s?

va: Absolutely. You got that right. And so when we parted company in Tokyo, a nightclub thing was set up for me immediately. And I appeared there, and it was called the Benibashi, and it's where I started the night-club thing.

vc: Let me stop for a minute. [*VC then asks about VA's roles in the Dunham Company.*]

va: Now, do you mean as a principal or as a group? You know, because I was in everything. We had different programs, didn't we?

Let's use one program for example. All right? Whatever opening number, after the overture, we were always either doing *Tropiques* or *Woman with the Cigar.* After Roger Ohardieno, I suppose I did that longer than anybody. Or, if we were doing *Afrique,* then I was the head warrior in that and had the opening for the solo parts, and so on. And certainly, she didn't trust anybody, so I had to be with that platform. I mean, I was in charge. So, then one would have to change immediately to get ready for *Nañigo,* so it was La Rosa [Estrada] and myself and then the rest. And then one would probably have to immediately quick change and get it into *La Comparsa.* And after a while, I refused to perform in *Shango.* I just wouldn't. Then you would go into a whole second act of either the warrior in *Rites de Passage,* and there were times when I had to do the puberty ritual *and* fertility. Or, puberty and death, when we added the third part with Miss Dunham. And there were times when I would open the third act with *Field Hands.* A quick change into the blues, one blues or another, depending on the program. I was an original in *Flaming Youth.* As a matter of fact, when she choreographed that, it was all original, and so I was one of the first of the three crossing. And then, I was always in the finale, whatever it would be. Now, it would always depend on the program, but I would have practically as much to do in whatever program it was. It wasn't one thing in the first act, and one thing in the second act. No, I never stopped.

vc: You took a very different stance than other people. I also heard that from Tommy [Gomez] in part about how it was hard to even deal with a favorite when you were just changing from one to the next to the next, from a programmatic point of view. I thought it was really interesting that both of you, instead of dealing with the dances as isolated, you dealt with them in terms of the program. No matter what the program was. He said it was hard for him to think in terms of "favorite" or "least favorite," because what was more important was that you were changing constantly.

va: I looked at the question and I thought, "How am I going to [answer that]? But I did not like—I never felt comfortable doing the most famous number, the most famous piece, the one that Europe loved: *Batucada.*

vc: Why didn't you feel comfortable?

va: I don't know. First of all, throwing that rope completely across stage used to give me ulcers. Well, honey, now it's a trick. Here, you come out. The music starts. The thing is here. Well, then if I'm over here and the public is there—you be the public—[*demonstrating*] and you always had to be the first one to start, and you have a group.

  Have you ever seen *Batucada?*

vc: Yes, I saw a film.

va: And a group of fisherman or something, they come out, talking, and ta-ta, ta-ta, ta-ta. I have the rope. Now that damn rope must be in place. Now, that rope was *never* in place. Of course, the stage hands would have it wound, but then I had to rewind it and get it, you know, so I could feel it. Now, when that music starts [*sings song*], and here come these heavy men, you see, talking about—You forgot what you were going say, but you just sang all kinds of shit, you know, and it was supposed to sound like Spanish, or whatever. And cha-cha—Then you looked, that was always the thing. You look and you see something from afar. And then you have to lasso and get that rope completely across the stage. And it used to hang up sometimes in the wing, and I hated that shit. God! Is the rope going to get over? And Miss D, she always had someone there. Sometimes you were lucky and sometimes you were not. Now you done fucked up the whole thing if this rope did not get over there. Do you understand? [*Laughter.*]

VC: I got it. Now that's theater. I mean, people need to see behind the stage. That's what I always loved about theater. You know, the funny parts of it. Some of the things that you guys have said to me over this period, it's like, yes, you have your favorites, but you also have some things that really bothered you. Now, if we jump to the favorite—

VA: I mean the hardest, not the most difficult, but the most demanding would have been years of doing *L'Ag'ya*. *L'Ag'ya* is three acts, and I had a great response because of that fight at the end. It had to look realistic. I didn't look forward to the death scene because I'm there, getting my last breath. I perspired like a dog, and winter, summer, spring, or fall, I had pools of water—even in Columbia in freezing weather. That was burdensome and there was no one else to do that part except me. Do you understand? No one, ever. I had no understudy.

VC: Why do you think you were chosen for that part? Do you think it was your stature?

VA: I don't know what Miss Dunham saw. The first time I did it was at the Hollywood Bowl, the premiere, and I dropped the tambourine during the *pas de deux*. Oh, God. But I got it back in time. I enjoyed doing nightclubs. I don't know why but you had a certain sense of freedom. It was kind of campy. I mean, not campy, sort of, well, it was a different rhythm. And of course, it was not two and a half hours long. I really enjoyed the intimacy because you were right there with the public and it was a different thing. I did enjoy doing nightclubs. That I must say.

But as far as favorite numbers and non-favorite, it was the job. It was what you did. So I had quirks. I mean, like, that rope, not getting it across. I had quirks. In nightclubs our opening number was *Macumba* with Miss Dunham and three boys. And naturally, I had three lifts to do during the finale. After all that futzing around, and her taking off one skirt. And then the drums, ta-ta, ta-ta. And then I have one lift, and that was on the left shoulder. And then there she is carrying on, on my left shoulder. And she comes down, boom! And then some more foolishness and then, here we go, voom! And she's on my right shoulder. So then you turn around the other way, you know, and then ta-ta, ta-ta. And then, she would come down very slowly off that right shoulder, carrying on and carrying on. And you're still back there, and the cue was when she would go all the way downstage. Now she's down to her chemise, the one-piece thing, and she's going downstairs, and she would sort of do something. And then I knew that was it. Get set and come to me. Voop! Bam! And sit on my head.

VC: Now, this is the *majumba* in *L'Ag'ya?* In *La Comparsa?*

VA: No. It was just titled *Macumba.* And it was more Brazilian than anything else. [*Singing and clapping.*] It was a flash piece, and she was dressed beautifully. And when the drums started, then she would start peeling off [the costume]. First she would kick off the mules [lounging slippers]. You know, she was famous for the mules. Now that caused a little bit of anxiety, but, thank God, it was the first number. So somehow I missed sitting her on my head no more than three times because that was the cue for the orchestra to start and for us to go off the stage. You understand? So I think in all of my years, those were the only two anxieties I had, really.

VC: Back to my question about stature. I think it's a really important reason why you were in so many of these pieces. You were, and still are, a very strong man.

VA: Oh, Lord.

VC: And I don't mean to sound like typecasting

VA: No, no. I know perfectly well what you're saying. I think Miss Dunham saw—No, I can't say that. I don't know, but I guess I was pliable. Or, whatever she would put me in, I certainly didn't fail. Can we say that? That's the only way I can put it. And if you didn't fail, she'd put you in something else. Then off you go. And so that's the way it was. I was never technically strong, even with all the training, because at a certain age—You get your technique as you're coming up, you know. But anyway, I think I had the stature, the goal to fit into all of the scenery that she was producing. I look the type, I suppose. I had the rhythm. I was not a sissy on stage. I don't know. I guess I had the personality.

The boys—especially in the *Nañigo*—in the finale we had to do bup-bup-bup-bup-rup-bup-bup plié and do a double *tour en l'air* and fall flat to the floor. Now I'm in front, smack dab in front. The whole goddamn thing started with me, and of course it ended with La Rosa. I'm the first one on and the last dancer off. We all had variations. One would do one thing and then the other one overlapped that. It was so wonderful, really, very masculine. It was a very exhausting dance. Oh, the *Nañigo,* child, I'm already out of breath even talking about it.

Now, in the finale we're all out there doing the same thing, and the last thing is rup-bup-bup, voop, boom! [*Hums music and demonstrates movements.*] And then they would all go off and leave me there. I was there for days. Then, finally, La Rosa would get up and start around me. But now, they did a double *tour en l'air* and I did one. I was never good at it. Mr. P [John Pratt], because he was out in front, you know, he would come back and say at intermission "Katherine . . . ," you know, one of those things, because I looked as though I did three and the boys did two. Well, that has to do with stage presence. I wouldn't lie, I could never do a double *tour en l'air,* but the time they did two, I did such a gorgeous one, and in time, and down on the floor, you didn't see what they were doing at all. Thank you.

vc: I've got two more questions.

va: Ask away, dear.

vc: What kind of difference did you perceive in doing the Caribbean dances and performing the dances that were from African American lore? Say it's *Flaming Youth.* Did you see a difference, culturally and kinetically, within your body when you were performing, say, *Nañigo?*

va: When I performed *Nañigo,* I was a Cuban doing the *Nañigo.* And when I did *Barrelhouse,* I was a black from Catfish Row. No. Going from one role to another, you're trained. Now what was your question?

vc: What I'm getting at is maybe there's something in Dunham Technique that allowed you guys to switch codes, you know, as they say now?

va: But VèVè, we were trained. We were trained in everything. I was a Mexican in *Veracruzana* because we spent weeks working with these people, and roles were created. Don't you get into the atmosphere?

vc: To characterize the contributions—

va: What we did, what she did, that was new was to show the world various cultures in dance, I would say. It's the first time I've ever said that. And no one had ever done that. I would say that she *made* Caribbean culture, put it on the map. So much was copied after that. No one had collected Caribbean and Latin material and presented it in the theater the way that Katherine Dunham did. No one had ever thought of Voodooism without thinking of something kinky before Katherine Dunham. No one had ever seen a trained company in folkloric material re-choreographed without any of the ethnic qualities taken away and presented on stage with trained dancers. And that is what Katherine Dunham did. And I think that's the only way that I can explain that, because it wasn't done.

vc: It's powerful.

va: It couldn't be copied. It had never been done. People never thought of it. They saw Carmen Miranda in *La Cucaracha* [*Copacabana*]. They saw

Betty Grable in *Down Argentine Way* and *Moon over Miami,* doing a conga or something. But no one thought of ethnic dancing presented in a theatrical form. Because, face it, folk dancing is boring as such. But to keep the flavor, to keep the basic and add a little theater to that without disrupting it or making even the basic more interesting, that is what she did. And you needed trained dancers to do it, so she trained them in her own way. That is why she preferred people whom I suppose she could see with talent and could train. If you were turned out, then you had to learn to turn in. And don't bring anyone who's heavy in the classics, honey, because they know nothing about isolation at all. They dance with straight knees. So, that's the best way I can put it, I suppose. I don't know any other way of putting it.

VC: It's perfect. You know, as I said, I had this feeling that if I asked a question, you would go straight to the point on these issues. I don't know why I thought that.

VA: You better believe it. I don't beat around the bush, you know. I'm not a great intellect and all that sort of stuff. But, child, you tell it like it is. I don't like procrastination. I don't like to muck around. Get to the point. Do it, and do what you're supposed to do. Now, I guess I'm not going to have any more of that, because I can't even talk correctly. I'm too excited.

VC: I shouldn't have done this late at night.

VA: It's not late at night at all. We just had a lot to talk about. We haven't finished yet. Is there anything else?

VC: I just wanted to talk to you about the roles. That's the only thing I need.

VA: What do you call roles? *L'Ag'ya?* I wouldn't even call *Tropiques* a role because that was a fanfare. But when I think of roles, I would think, of course, you were right to name *L'Ag'ya,* because after all, Miss Dunham had done *L'Ag'ya* during her WPA days or something. And Woody [Lenwood Morris] was the Devil. I don't even know who Alcide was. She re-created the role on me. So that would have been a role in my mind.

A role for me would have been as the third lead taking over the warrior part of *Rites de Passage,* which was a very important piece in our repertoire. Still is. And it's a piece that could stand up forever. I just wish it could be done again and stored. I hate to talk about it. It was done on a television thing, "Dunham and Her People," but it wasn't done correctly. And it's too late, because I repeated the role, but I gained weight, and it was not to my liking at all. I suppose you have that film. Roger [Ohardieno] did it one way, but then I did it another, so that was a role for me.

Floyd's Guitar Blues was created on me. I stepped in as the third part in Barrelhouse, but it was originally done with Archie Savage. Being a member of the company, you may have been in a pinch of that, and a pinch of that, and so I can't say "roles." God! You were in every other number. Later on, everything that I appeared in I was the principal [dancer]. Whether it was Nañigo or Tropiques or La Comparsa or Batucada, we were all in a group, but then I was doing a principal part in it.

VC: I think the kind of distinctions you've made on every question I've asked you are very different, and I really liked your characterization of the contributions.

VA: Good. I hope so. I'm greatly relieved that I answered that one to your satisfaction.

VC: It was beautiful.

VA: Thank you. Then that's it. I can sleep.

NOTES

1. *Star Spangled Rhythm* (1942), a Paramount Pictures production, has a thin plot involving a soldier (Eddie Bracken), his girlfriend (Betty Hutton), and his father (Victor Moore), who works as a gate guard at a Hollywood studio. Intended as a wartime entertainment for troops fighting overseas, it featured a large supporting cast of Hollywood stars who appeared as themselves in cameo roles. Katherine Dunham and Eddie "Rochester" Anderson were among them. They perform a song-and-dance number to "Sharp as a Tack" *[Eds.]*.

2. *Tropical Revue,* a dance revue in three acts and eight scenes, was conceived, choreographed, and staged by Katherine Dunham. It opened on Broadway on 19 September 1943 at the Martin Beck Theatre, moved on 16 November 1943 to the Forrest Theatre, and closed on 4 December 1943 after eighty-seven performances *[Eds.]*.

The Dance in the National
Youth Administration

KATHERINE DUNHAM

The ballet as a theater production is extremely important because of the incorporation in it of the several arts of costume design, decor, music, at times voice, and choreography. Socially it is important because of the strong integrative influence of the dance in general, and because of its adaptability to the expression of the social and emotional trend of a society. To the individual it means expression through movement, the coordination of mental and physical activities, the concrete achievement of an act by means of the various disciplines, of the various techniques.

In primitive societies the dance has reached relative stages of development determined by the pattern of the society, its beliefs and needs. In our civilization the dance has become minimized in that it is confined in its more developed forms to the professional stage and to those who have

SOURCE: Katherine Dunham, "The Dance in the National Youth Administration," an unpublished paper, written c. 1941/42, in the Katherine Mary Dunham Papers, Special Collections, Morris Library, Southern Illinois University, Carbondale. Copyright 1941/42 by Katherine Dunham. Reprinted by permission.

NOTE: The National Youth Administration (NYA) was established on 26 June 1935 and operated for eight years, until 1943. It was first under the general auspices of the Work Projects Administration (WPA), although its administration was essentially independent. In 1939 the NYA was transferred to the Federal Security Agency, and in September 1942 it was placed under the direction of the War Manpower Commission. The purpose of the NYA was to provide education, jobs, recreation, and counseling for male and female youth between the ages of sixteen and twenty-five. Various programs operated at both the federal and state levels. Many states had separate programs for black youth. Although the NYA had a better record than other New Deal relief programs, the number of black participants never corresponded to the percentage of black youths on relief [Eds.].

mastered the techniques through years of serious training—in other words, a highly specialized group. This is, it seems to me, an unfortunate circumstance, and surely a great deal is lost individually and socially by this removal of natural and needed expression to the professional.

A compromise between the two uses of the dance falls to the serious dance leader of today who deals with the art in a humanitarian rather than purely professional manner. Until the establishment of government-financed theaters, this compromise seemed fairly hopeless. Now, however, a great contribution suddenly becomes possible in the willingness of federal agencies to develop the youth of America culturally, so that by this cultural development and appreciation, they may better adapt themselves to the society in which they live, and by so doing, better integrate that society.

It has been my experience in dealing with Negro youth in the dance for a period of years, that, being of a minority group, we, more than any other group, need a means of releasing the tensions caused by our minority position, and giving ourselves dignity in as many fields as possible. Unfortunately the dance, as important as it is, has been confined to the vaudeville and burlesque for the Negro. These recent years, and their accompanying cultural and artistic successes have, however, proven to me the value of establishing the dance in its larger, more useful and acceptable forms for the Negro youth. To the individual it brings a definite feeling of value and prestige, as well as artistic accomplishment: to the community a new evaluation of the tastes and abilities of the Negro, and a step forward toward removing him from the unfortunate burden of his minority position.

Attached to these comments are outlines of ballets which would be suitable for a group of youth. It is hoped that the establishment of such a dance activity would gradually develop into a larger cultural center—a collaboration of the arts in well-chosen, well-trained productions.

BALLET OUTLINES

L'Ag'ya. Produced for the Federal Theater, 1938. Martinique ballet. Traditional dances built around the story of witchcraft in a fishing village. Music by Robert Sanders. Originally for an 18-piece orchestra but being enlarged for 50 pieces. Ensemble of 32. 18 minutes.

Christophe. Dance drama of the first kingdom of Haiti. Text of spoken lines being done by Langston Hughes. Haiti before the revolution, the attempted betrayal of the black leaders at the salon of Pauline and

the court of Christophe at Sans Souci. Full orchestra. Ensemble of 35.
Approximately 30 minutes.

Br'er Rabbit an' de Tah Baby. Dance drama (without spoken words) built
around the tales of Uncle Remus. Action in the back yard of the 'big
house' and in the cabbage patch. Small or full orchestra. Ensemble of
22. Approximately 27 minutes.

Greek Incident. The episode of Odysseus and the Lotus Eaters. Two
pianos, small or full orchestra. Ensemble of 15. 14 minutes.

Rumba. To the music of the same name by Harl MacDonald. Dances of
folk Mexico in the region of Chihuahua and Sonora. Full orchestra or
two pianos. Ensemble of 20. Approximately 15 minutes.

Lil' Black Sambo. Dance drama (without spoken words) to the story of
Black Sambo, Black Mumbo, Black Jumbo, and the five tigers. Action
in the deep forest of Africa. Ensemble of 9. Two pianos or orchestra.
15 minutes.

Octoroon Ball. The famous masked Octoroon Ball of old New Orleans. A
short tone picture with action built around the symbolic auctioning of
the quadroon and octoroon daughters of darker mothers to wealthy
white aristocrats. Two pianos or orchestra. Ensemble of 15. 14 minutes.

Scenario for *Greek Incident*, A Ballet in Two Scenes

Orchestral Prelude to the Sea

SCENE 1: THE GREEKS. Wearied by the seven years' war with Troy, the
Greeks start for home, one band under the leadership of the warrior-chief
Odysseus. At the opening of the scene the warriors are standing and lying
in attitudes of war, more statues than men. The blast of a trumpet brings
them to life, and led by Odysseus they dance a farewell to the ruins of
Troy and an anticipation of Ithaca. The dance is brittle, stylized, gymnastic, with much use of design around shield and spear. Phrases may be built
up to a short climax then mechanically repeated to establish the mood of
routine activity. With a crescendo of music the men form a pyramid and
Odysseus points to the distant sea. *Curtain.*

Orchestral Prelude to the Lotus Eaters

SCENE 2: THE LOTUS EATERS. Turned from their course by the vengeful
Aeolus, many strange events befall the Greeks as they wander the seas. After
many weary months Odysseus and his men land at the island of the Lotus
Eaters. Here strange tropical people feed upon the flower of the lotus and

live under the spell of its drug. The scene opens with the Lotus Eaters in a dreamlike repose. They are suspended in strange, hypnotic poses, and in the foreground, among them is their queen. Very gradually a movement is felt, rather than seen, and they begin a rhythmic, almost static dance to woodwinds and percussion. The movement grows and recedes, directed somewhat to the huge lotuses among which they recline, and might almost be a seduction of the flowers. This dance reaches a climax, subsides, and again the Lotus Eaters sink into their torpor. As they again recline, the martial music of Odysseus and his men is heard, and the Greeks enter. In spite of the attempted intervention of Odysseus, they are lured among the Lotus Eaters, taste of the flower, and are almost immediately under its spell. Odysseus resists the offers of the queen of the Lotus Eaters at first; then he, as are his men, is relieved of shield and spear. A *pas de deux* of the two principals develops into a bacchanal of the Greeks and the Lotus Eaters. When the flower is offered Odysseus at the height of the bacchanal, he refuses it, and grasping his shield and spear bids farewell to his men. They no longer recognize him, and, as he leaves, they sink with the Lotus Eaters into the torpor of the opening of the scene. *Slow Curtain. FINIS*

Bal Nègre Program

Bal Nègre

A Katherine Dunham Production
Costumes by John Pratt
Orchestra under the direction of Gilberto Valdés
Presented by Nelson L. Gross and Daniel Melnick

ACT I

OVERTURE
    Ylenko-Ylembe . . . . Valdés
    Eartha Kitt, Jean-Léon Destiné, Mariam Burton, and
    Sans-Souci Singers.
    Congo Paillette—Haitian Corn-Sorting Ritual . . . . Native air
    Katherine Dunham with Lenwood Morris and Company.

1. MOTIVOS
    a. **Rhumba** . . . . Valdés
    Lucille Ellis, Eartha Kitt, Othella Strozier.

SOURCE: Program for performances of *Bal Nègre* at the Belasco Theatre, New York, in the week beginning Monday, 16 December 1946. Copyright 1946 by Katherine Dunham. Reprinted by permission.

NOTE: *Bal Nègre* opened at the Belasco Theatre on 7 November 1946 and closed on 22 December 1946 after fifty-four performances.

b. **Son** . . . . Cuban Slave Lament
Possessed dancer: Dolores Harper. *Singer:* Jesse Hawkins.

c. **Nañigo** . . . . Valdés
La Rosa Estrada, Vanoye Aikens, and Company.

d. **Choros**—A 19th-century Brazilian quadrille . . . . Gogliano
Gloria Mitchell, Richardena Jackson, Wilbert Bradley, Ronnie Aul

e. **La Comparsa** . . . . Lecuona
Alone in the deserted streets in the early morning hours after
Carnival, a woman encounters three men. She believes that one
may be her husband.
    Katherine Dunham with Vanoye Aikens, Byron Cuttler, and
    James Alexander.

2. HAITIAN ROADSIDE . . . . Anderson-Valdés
On the dusty roads of Haiti many things happen in the late afternoon.
Peddler with the guitar: Cándido Vicenty. *Other peddlers:*
La Rosa Estrada, Byron Cuttler, Julio Mendes, James Alexander.
Traveling priest: Jean-Léon Destiné. *Market girls:* Lawaune
Ingram, Gloria Mitchell. *Carnival kings:* Lenwood Morris,
Jean-Léon Destiné. *Chacoon:* Katherine Dunham.
Market people and wayside travelers.

3. SHANGO—Ritual and dance . . . . Bergerson
The Shango priest: La Rosa Estrada. *The boy possessed by a snake:*
Jean-Léon Destiné. *The leaders of the Shango dancers:* Lucille
Ellis, Eddy Clay.

INTERMISSION
(15 MINUTES)

ACT 2

L'AG'YA—From an original story by
    Katherine Dunham . . . . Robert Sanders
Loulouse: Katherine Dunham. *Alcide:* Vanoye Aikens. *Julot:*
Wilbert Bradley. *Roi Zombie:* Lenwood Morris. *Porteresses,
vendors, fishermen, townspeople of Vauclin.*
The scene is Vauclin, a tiny eighteenth-century fishing village in
Martinique. Loulouse loves and is desired by Alcide. Julot, the
villain, repulsed by Loulouse and filled with hatred and desire

for revenge, decides to seek the aid of the king of the zombies. Deep in the jungle, Julot fearfully seeks the lair of the zombies and witnesses their strange rites, which bring the dead back to life. Frightened, but remembering his purpose, Julot pursues Roi Zombie and obtains the *cambois,* a powerful love charm, from him.

The following evening: it is a time of gaiety, opening with the stately Creole mazurka, or *mazouk,* and moving into the uninhibited excitement of the *béguine.* Into this scene enters Julot, horrifying the villagers when he exposes the coveted *cambois.* Even Alcide is under its spell. Now begins the *majumba,* love dance of ancient Africa. As Loulouse falls more and more under the charm, Alcide suddenly defies its powers, breaks loose from the villagers, who protect him, and challenges Julot to the *l'ag'ya,* the fighting dance of Martinique. In the *l'ag'ya* and its ending is the climax of the forces loosed in magic and superstition.

INTERMISSION
(15 MINUTES)

ACT 3

1. Nostalgia
   a. **Ragtime**.................................... Medley
      Rosalie King with the Sans-Souci Singers. *Dancers:* Lucille Ellis, Lenwood Morris, and Company in the Waltz, Fox-trot, Ballin' the Jack, Tango, Maxixe, and Turkey Trot.
   b. **Blues** .... Floyd Smith
      Katherine Dunham and Vanoye Aikens.
   c. **Flaming Youth, 1927** .... "Brad" Gowans
      Blues singer: Rosalie King. *Kansas City Woman:* Lucille Ellis. *Dancers:* Lawaune Ingram, Wilbert Bradley, and Company in the Charleston, Black Bottom, Mooch, Fishtail, and Snake Hips.

2. Finale
   Havana, 1910 .... Navarro
   Para Que Tu Veas .... Bobby Capo
   Jean-Léon Destiné. *Entertainer:* Katherine Dunham. *Two Lady Tourists:* Richardena Jackson, Dolores Harper. Sans-Souci Singers and the Dunham Company.

MUSICAL ACKNOWLEDGMENTS

The Overture. Katherine Dunham has devised an overture to be seen as well as heard. "Ylenke-Ylembe," written by the brilliant young composer-conductor Gilberto Valdés, is a vocal and orchestral combination which emphasizes unrestrained Afro-Cuban themes. The second half of the overture, "Congo Paillette," is based on a native Haitian air.

Haitian Roadside. Native songs. "Soleil, O," an invocation sung by Jean-Léon Destiné and male quartet. "Apollon," a Carnival *meringué* sung by Jean-Léon Destiné. "Chocounne," sung by Katherine Dunham.

Ragtime Medley. "Chong." "Under the Bamboo Tree." "Ragtime Cowboy." "Oh! You Beautiful Doll." "Alexander's Ragtime Band."

MEMBERS OF THE DUNHAM COMPANY

Dancers. LUCILLE ELLIS, LENWOOD MORRIS, LAWAUNE INGRAM, VANOYE AIKENS. James Alexander, Ronnie Aul, Wilbert Bradley, Byron Cuttler, Eddy Clay, Roxie Foster, Dolores Harper, Jesse Hawkins, Richardena Jackson, Eartha Kitt, Floria Mitchell, Eugene Robinson, Othella Strozier. Syvilla Fort, *Guest Artist.*

San-Souci Singers. JEAN-LÉON DESTINÉ, EARTHA KITT, ROSALIE KING. Mary Lewis, Mariam Burton, Gordon Simpson, Ricardo Morrison.

Drummers. La Rosa Estrada. Cándido Vicenty, Julio Mendez.

ACKNOWLEDGMENTS

Advisor on ragtime material: Tom Fletcher. *Vocal arrangement on "Chocounne" and "Ragtime Medley":* Reginald Beane. *Musical arrangement and orchestration on "Ragtime":* Billy Butler. *Costumes executed by* Edith Lutyens. *Miss Dunham's gown for "Blues" by Leopold Kobrin.*

STAFF FOR KATHERINE DUNHAM

Technical advisor: John Pratt. *Assistant technical advisor:* Dorothy Gray. *Business assistant:* Dione Lewis. *Company assistant:* Lucille Ellis. *Assistant choral director:* Rosalie King. *Ballet master:* Lenwood Morris.

Schoolmarm Turned Siren
or Vice Versa

JOHN MARTIN

There are two schools of thought about Katherine Dunham. One group recognizes in her a woman of fine intellect, a sincere student of anthropology and its broader and more practical implications. The other group sees her as a beautiful, highly sexed theatrical entertainer, with surprisingly few inhibitions in the material she puts on the stage. Both groups are unquestionably right, for Miss Dunham is Siamese twins, in a sense, however little she may look it.

The Katherine Dunham School of Arts and Research is a phenomenal institution. It comprises the Dunham School of Dance and Theater, the Department of Cultural Studies, and the Institute for Caribbean Research. It has two-, three-, and five-year courses leading to professional, teaching, and research certificates; its faculty numbers thirty, its curriculum contains everything from dance notation through ballet, modern, and primitive techniques to psychology and philosophy, with acting, music, visual design, history, and languages by the way; its student body, unaffectedly interracial, numbers approximately four hundred; and—its deficits are enormous.

At this point the other Dunham steps in, whips together a tropical revue, wows them on Broadway and elsewhere, and sinks the profits in the school. It is a procedure that probably does not make sense, but no stubbornly idealistic project ever quite does.

SOURCE: John Martin, "The Dance: Dunham, Schoolmarm Turned Siren or Vice Versa; In 'Bal Nègre' at the Belasco," *New York Times*, 17 November 1946. Copyright 1946 by the *New York Times* Company. Reprinted by permission.

To imply, however, that this giving of money-making shows works a hardship on the total Dunham would be to deny the evidence. There is about her an obvious delight in being a successful theater figure—a choreographer, a director, a performer, and, by no means least, a glamour girl. Very few serious and competent pedagogues could hope to make the grade, and pride would seem here, if ever, to be altogether pardonable.

ANOTHER VIEW. But there is also, as it happens, a third school of thought about this whole matter. It is, perhaps, a small group, but it clings to the belief that the Dunham schizophrenia is more apparent than real, and will some day be conquered. In *Bal Nègre,* her newest production now ensconced in the Belasco Theatre for four weeks, this group finds great comfort, for here there seem to be indications of a developing rapprochement between the two hitherto apparently irreconcilable Dunhams. As in the simple performances of her early dance recital days, the breath of art is beginning to blow at least lightly down the neck of a retreating "show business." And in the healthy field of art both Dunhams should find themselves happy, unified, and fulfilled. If this be wishful thinking, make the most of it.

SOME OF THE EVIDENCE. In evidence one offers several specific items, as well as things more intangible. The novel overture, designed to be seen as well as heard, is one of them. It may well be too long, as the whole show is inclined to be, but it has imagination and a substantial charm.

The Shango scene, revived from *Carib Song,* manages to make a legitimately theatrical spectacle out of a primitive religious ritual. The final section seems to introduce extraneous matter simply to make for an effective curtain, but that is a secondary consideration.

L'Ag'ya, the atmospheric folk drama of old Martinique which was first produced for the Federal Theater, also has its faults. Its first scene is conventional and flat, but its scene in the jungle of the zombies is altogether admirable (though what has become of the old rocking chair that used to lend such a sense of reality to its mumbo-jumbo?), and the final scene of the béguine, the wrestling match, and Miss Dunham's hypnotic dance is rich and full.

Most engaging of all is *Haitian Roadside,* which is just a cumulative arrangement of folk items, not actually related to each other, but forming together a vivid and convincing picture of an exotic way of life.

Among the shorter numbers, a *Rhumba Trio* has, perhaps, the best choreography of the entire show, and the *Son* and the *Nañigo* are well done.

The *Choros* is spoiled by the introduction of *brisés volés* and the like, and *La Comparsa* does not come off. Also, the ragtime section is superficial and negligible. Miss Dunham has not studied these dances as an anthropologist or even as a historian. In general, some of the boys should be reminded that they are not Russian ballerinas and that it would be nice if they would comport themselves accordingly.

But over the show as a whole, including the many parts of it that are not new, is a new dignity, an absence of sensationalism, a new taste, that certainly interferes not at all with its values as theater entertainment.

Caribbean Backgrounds
Program

Caribbean Backgrounds

A program performed by
The Dunham Experimental Group of
The Dunham School of Dance and Theater

The Caribbean Islands offer wonderful source material for the investigator seeking authentic information concerning the dances and rituals of the peoples brought to the Western Hemisphere as slaves. Here in practically inaccessible and untouched interior places, rituals are preserved intact.

1. Progression and Improvisation in Primitive Rhythms.

2. Congo Paillette
   Semi-ritualistic dance of Haiti. Danced chiefly in the spring, it probably had its origin in fertility rites.

3. Chansons d'Ouvrage
   a. Haitian work song. Sung at a *combite,* a gathering of people brought together to complete a task such as cutting sugar cane, building a house, etc.
   b. Caribbean work rhythm. Danced by Talley Beatty and Tommy Gomez.

SOURCE: Program for a performance of *Caribbean Backgrounds* by the Dunham Experimental Group of the Dunham School of Dance and Theater at Howard University, Washington, D.C., on Thursday, 26 June 1947. Copyright 1947 by Katherine Dunham. Reprinted by permission.

4. Social Dances
   a. Traditional European mazurka. Danced by Syvilla Fort and
      Harold Gordon.
   b. The *mazouk,* West Indian form of the mazurka brought to the
      Islands by the French.

5. Chansons Haïtiennes
   Sung by Edward Rousseau.

6. Dance to Legba
   Legba is the household god of Haiti. Danced by Walter Nicks.

7. Ceremonial Dances
   a. **Yonvalou.** A rhythm dedicated to Damballa, god of dance and
      motion.
   b. **Zépaules.** A Vodun dance, a rhythm peculiar to the Arada tribe of
      Haiti. *Mambo:* Syvilla Fort. *Hounci:* Lillie Peace. *Knife Priests:*
      Harold Gordon and Melvin Jones.

8. Film
   Made by Katherine Dunham in Martinique showing *la savate* and
   l'ag'ya. La savate is a French form of fighting with the feet. *L'ag'ya* is
   the Martinique version.

9. L'ag'ya
   Demonstrating the skill, agility, and grace of combat.

10. Baile Afro-Cubano
    Nañigo rhythm, and Afro-Cuban folk dance. Danced by Talley
    Beatty and Tommy Gomez

11. Carnival Kings
    All of the Caribbean Islands hold carnivals during Lent. In Haiti the
    county people hold a Rara for forty days ending on Good Friday.
    Bands of people led by a "king" or "best dancer" travel from town to
    town visiting friends, seeing the countryside. Two such bands meet,
    the kings compete, and the crowd decides the winner.

Members of Dunham Experimental Group

Featured dancers: Syvilla Fort and Walter Nicks. *Girls:* Lillie Peace, Cleo
Walker, Madelaine White, Laura Lewis, Louise Fitzpatrick. *Boys:* Larl
Beechman, Harold Gordon, James Hunt, Peter Gennaro, Melvin Jones.

Leaders of chants: Louise Fitzpatrick and Ted Barnett. *Drums:* Henri
Augustin and Dean Sheldon.

Director of Dunham Experimental Group: Syvilla Fort. *Advisor on Haitian
rhythms and customs:* Henri Augustin. *Commentator:* Dorathi Bock
Pierre. *Accompanist:* Dorothy Jenkins. *Haitian singers:* Emarantes
Despradines and Edward Rousseau. *Guest artists:* Talley Beatty and
Tommy Gomez.

Katherine Dunham Raises Primitive Dance Art to New Heights of Sophistication

PETER WADDINGTON

Audience reaction to Katherine Dunham and her dancers is immediate and enthusiastic. It's the same everywhere they appear. There are two reasons for this: Miss Dunham is essentially a *personage du théâtre*. She understands the language of the theater, and this is evident in her dance technique, choreography, and in the choice of her assisting artists; too, a strong sociological purpose pervades her work, and this gives it a special flavor that sets it apart from all other dance and balletic groups now before the public.

An instance of the universal appeal of her art, and one that points up its individual character, became evident when Miss Dunham and her troupe arrived in a Mexican city twenty-four hours before their scenery and costumes. With only a backdrop, the company appeared in its entire program in street clothes and won the same enthusiastic reception that invariably greets it when performing in its full scenic regalia. This is not hard to understand because, if there is something fundamental in the Dunham dance technique, there is also something elemental and, therefore, universal in it. Miss Dunham says there are no cultist predilections about the dances in her repertoire although she is interested in the religious forms and legends of the Africans, West Indians, the American Negroes, and other peoples in so far as they are adapted to the theater.

Shango, Miss Dunham explained, is a case in point. It is a ballet based on the superstitions connected with an African god. The weird occult

SOURCE: Peter Waddington, "Katherine Dunham Raises Primitive Dance Art to New Heights of Sophistication," *Opera and Concert* (June 1948). Reprinted by permission of Katherine Dunham.

power of this deity lends itself admirably to theatrical treatment without profanation. Presentations of this kind, she said, not only help to explain the African people to us but they help to establish a bond of sympathy because the fears, aspirations, loves, and reverences of the Africans are also common to us. Anything that will help explain one group of human beings to another will tend to dissipate the misunderstandings, fears, and prejudices of one group of people for another. Miss Dunham has traveled to the West Indies and other Pacific islands and lands to study social and ritual customs of the people and their traditional rhythmical expressions, and the repertoire of her company is uniquely rich in balletic and dance numbers based on these studies.

"I am particularly interested in presenting to the public one segment of the American people—the Negro," Miss Dunham said. "To this end I have chosen the members of my company. None of them are professionals in the sense that they come from theatrical parents or have been in the theater previously to becoming a member of my company. They have been trained in my school, in the Dunham Technique, especially for the type of theater I am now presenting to the public. There is no doubt but what we are doing is creating a better understanding of, and sympathy for, the American Negro. From the beginning, I aimed at sociological as well as artistic targets. Now, however, I admit that a strong sociological purpose motivates my work and that there is a real drive in my purpose to present good looking, talented, clean, healthy-minded and healthy-bodied young American Negroes in a repertoire of dance mimes and sketches. How well I am succeeding is well illustrated by incidents both in this country and in Mexico, where, during our last tour, I was invited, with members of my company, to call on President Miguel Alemán, who was most gracious in his praise of our performance. He was particularly pleased that we spoke to him in Spanish, such as it was, an effrontery in view of his good English, but one that broke the contretemps and established a friendly feeling at once." People who underestimate this kind of propaganda are blind to its advantages. "In other words," Miss Dunham explained, "our appearances in Mexico, for example, did much to counteract Hollywood's clichés for the Negro. They discovered that the Negro can also be an artist and not always a shiftless, ignorant person. The famous Mexican artist Covarrubias brought his pupils to the theater to sketch the members of my company. They expressed surprise at the intelligence and the artistry of my dancers."

Those who have seen Miss Dunham and her company are often surprised at the great variety of numbers that go to make up her programs.

In addition to those based on religious forms and superstitions of the African and the West Indian, the dancer has found that numbers embodying the customs and foibles of the American Negro are extremely popular in view of the delightful humor, and frequently, the satire underlying these dance ideas. There is more poignancy in such humor and satire when they spring from the racial group in question, rather than from an outside source.

When asked how she creates her dance ideas, Miss Dunham said very often music inspires them, other times things said or historical facts repeated begin a train of thought which sometimes "jell." *"Comparsa,* by the Cuban composer Ernesto Lecuona, impressed me very strongly the first time I heard it and I began at once to devise a dance number from the music. This idea worked out very quickly because the music had great qualities for provoking images and ideas. On the other hand," Miss Dunham explained, "I was strongly impressed by an idea while in New Orleans. It was an historical fact that suggested a dance-play, but the more I thought of it the harder it was to resolve into theatrical terms. While in Mexico a few months ago, the whole idea worked itself out in my mind and I called on the noted Italian composer Mario Castelnuovo-Tedesco, and explained to him the idea of *Octoroon Ball,* and then danced it step by step as he improvised the music. Later the music was altered to fit the story and the steps and was written down."

Octoroon Ball, Miss Dunham explained, deals with an old custom of the New Orleans of the 1840s when the mothers of octoroons presented their daughters at specially contrived balls to meet eligible gentlemen. Marriage, of course, was not the objective, so men as far away as the courts of Europe came to see, be fascinated, and carry off a beautiful damsel.

Miss Dunham is satirizing an octoroon ball and it will readily be seen that it is a subject that will lend itself to colorful choreographic embellishments.

Miss Dunham is, in private life, Mrs. John Pratt. Her husband designs most of the costumes and sets used in his wife's productions. She was born in Chicago and attended school there. While in junior college, she switched from a heavy participation in athletics to dancing, "the most logical interest for a growing girl," and soon became absorbed in the sociological aspects of it. A journey to the West Indies was made possible after graduation and the next year and a half were spent in study and research. This work forms the backbone of many of the dance numbers Miss Dunham has created, as well as contributing to the "Dunham Technique," which the dancer insists, despite its strenuousness, actually permits the participant to *rest* in action.

So popular are her dances and so insistent have people been to learn her dance technique that Miss Dunham opened a school in New York where she employs some forty to fifty teachers for the following subjects: modern dance, ballet, Spanish dancing, Dunham Technique (primitive rhythms of West Indies), social dancing, percussion, drama, speech, voice production, stage management, acting, anthropology, esthetics, psychology, languages, and other cultural subjects. Pupils have come from all parts of the world to study at this unusual school.

In many of her dances, Miss Dunham employs the native drums which are different in size, pitch, and volume. The weird sounds of these drums supply all the music that is needed for some dances, and form the strongly rhythmical backgrounds for others of the native group.

But like most successful artists, Miss Dunham did not start at the top. She did concert work for a while before being invited by Ruth Page to join her company at the Chicago Opera Company in a production of William Grant Still's *La Guiablesse* (The Devil Woman),[1] and remained to train the members of the ballet at that opera. She inherited much of her artistic inclination from her father, who was musical, and her studious nature from her mother, a schoolteacher. She is the author of an autobiography and of *Journey to Accompong,* a work of fiction based on her trip to Jamaica.[2]

After leaving the Chicago Opera Company, Miss Dunham organized her own company and later joined the *Cabin in the Sky* company which played a successful engagement in New York before touring the country. The first time she appeared in a night club was in San Francisco at the Hotel Mark Hopkins, but this was during the time of organizing and augmenting her company to its present size and caliber.

Notes

1. *La Guiablesse* is a ballet by Ruth Page set to a commissioned score by William Grant Still. Created in 1933 and performed at the Chicago World's Fair, it was restaged in 1934 at the Chicago Opera with Katherine Dunham in the title role *[Eds.].*

2. *Journey to Accompong* is not a work of fiction. It is a day-by-day account of Katherine Dunham's experiences during her month-long stay among the Accompong Maroons of Jamaica in 1935 *[Eds.].*

Katherine Dunham,
Observed in London

If you cannot easily label a theatrical production, and cannot say at once: "This is a tragedy, or a comedy, a ballet, opera, or revue," you should be on your guard: it may, perhaps, be the work of a creative artist.

Certainly one cannot readily classify Katherine Dunham's *Caribbean Rhapsody*—the Negro show which has been filling the Prince of Wales Theatre and causing intense interest amongst professional dance producers. It is not a revue, or cabaret—although in various ways it is both. Chiefly it is ballet, but of a quite unusual kind.

Miss Dunham's success has been acclaimed on all sides, from the *Daily Express* to the highbrows of classical dance. The former calls her show "the fastest and most colourful that London has seen for many years," and has booked it for an Albert Hall festivity. While one of the latter remarked that her barefooted company made classical dancers seem like waxwork figures; and another compared the impact of her company's visit to the arrival in Paris of Diaghilev's ballet in the year 1908.[1]

The general character of her show is an interweaving of dance and song, mostly in the idiom of the West Indies and of Brazil—which means a mixture of African and Latin styles that is peculiarly exotic. There are short, highly stylized numbers, *Motivos,* such as a Cuban slave lament, a quadrille, and Miss Dunham's own Brazilian murmur-singing; these are followed by two longer and intensely dramatic compositions of great artistic wealth—one based on a Trinidad ritual, the other on the customs of eighteenth-century Martinique.

SOURCE: "Katherine Dunham," *London Observer,* 12 September 1948. Copyright 1948 by Guardian Newspapers, Ltd. Reprinted by permission.

The last act satirizes modern dancing, in a setting of Chicago in the Twenties; it is done with style and humour, but carries a meaning that is ironical and even tragic.

The extraordinary fact about this diverse and brilliant show is that it is entirely the production of one person. A "star," who is capable of more than executing her own part, is rare: one who can write, produce, and direct the work of a whole company, and do so with originality—without ever using clichés—must be something of a genius.

Katherine Dunham was born in an ordinary small town of the American Middle West (Joliet, Illinois) in 1910.[2] Her mother was a French Canadian—which may at once explain the strongly Latin quality in her work; her father, a Negro who ran a small business and was a strict Methodist.

This combination produced remarkable progeny. Katherine and her brother both went to the University of Chicago and became outstandingly successful students. The brother took a degree in philosophy, became a lecturer at Howard University in Washington, and a close friend of the philosopher Whitehead, whose recently published works he helped to edit.[3]

Katherine studied anthropology and gained her B.A. degree without difficulty.[4] But the special peculiarity of her mind—that it is at once artistic, scientific, and administrative—led her into other, more felicitous, fields.

While studying anthropology, she not only learned classical ballet but also formed her own little school of dancing. It was the first studio in which she could produce artistic creations. Her strong talent as a choreographer showed itself at once, and people began to talk of her.

Then that great American institution, the philanthropic trust—in this case, the Rosenwald Foundation—became interested in her unusual combination of abilities and gave her a grant that transformed her life. They asked her what she wished to study: she replied: "The dances of the West Indies, their primitive backgrounds, their choreographic and rhythmic patterns."

And so she set off for the islands of the Caribbean, equipped like an explorer, her mission solemnly entitled by the foundation "Anthropology and the Dance." And there she stayed for a year and a half.

It was not all easy. In Haiti, for instance, her excursions into the backwoods disturbed the respectable citizens of Port-au-Prince. So she hired its largest theater and audaciously announced a concert. Her audience came expecting to see shocking barbarities derived from the secret Voodoo rites that she was studying. Instead, she appeared in white tulle and gave a faultless display of classical ballet to music by Debussy, such as the little town had never seen: her conquest was complete.

When finally she returned to Chicago, she produced a thesis, which earned her a Rockefeller fellowship to continue work on her M.A. degree; and she wrote a book which Ted Cook of the *New Yorker* illustrated.[5]

And then she began her career as a choreographer and theatrical producer in earnest. She had collected a mass of Caribbean music and dance movements, and a whole world of ideas. She formed a company of dancers, singers, and musicians, and set them to work.

Now, had she been only scholastic in ability, she would simply have become an exponent of West Indian folklore. Or, had she only been after fame and money, she would have followed up the quick and exciting successes which she had on Broadway and in Hollywood with a career along their well-lit, well-worn paths.

But Katherine Dunham is a young woman of great independence, and she chose her own course. Together with her white husband, John Pratt, a gifted artist who designs all her costumes and stage sets, she added to her own company an ambitious school of dancing in New York.

It is unconventional in every possible way. First, its pupils have to learn not only the drill and routine of several schools of dancing, but also music, languages, philosophy, and much else. Next, her school is racially "mixed," and, therefore, controversial amongst the "whites" and not a medium of cultural propaganda for the Negroes.

While being strictly non-racialist, believing that art has no frontiers, she has unconsciously sought to show the deracinated coloured people of North America their cultural background; to link them to their less sophisticated and less corrupted cousins in the Antilles; and to build on their real talents for dance and music a valid, cultural style of their own.

She strives after great things—dances that mean more than entertainment and represent more than stereotyped cultures. Her ideas reach far back into history and sociology, go deep into human feelings, and yet move forward, creating something new.

Whether Miss Dunham—a charming, quiet, slightly wistful person—will continue to work within the social pressures of the U.S.A. is uncertain. She might settle in the artistically kinder surroundings of Mexico, Paris, or Rio: or she might explore the primitive cultures of Africa itself: she has no definite plans.

But she is never without consistency and drive. For example, she is *still* an anthropologist. The Royal Anthropological Society has invited her to address its members while in London. Although hesitant in accepting, she will probably speak on an intriguing subject—"The Occurrence of Cults among 'Deprived' (i.e., traditionless) Peoples."

Her most precious talent is the ability to utter, to interpret, to create through the medium of dance. Wherever she may be, that creative flame will burn, adding its light and warmth to the culture of a deprived world.

NOTES

1. In the spring of 1908, the impresario Sergei Pavlovich Diaghilev presented a season of Russian music and opera in Paris, as well as exhibitions of paintings by Russian artists. The following spring, he presented a company of dancers that was billed as the Ballets Russes de Serge Diaghileff. The first performance of this soon-to-be-famous company was on 19 April 1909 at the Théâtre du Châtelet *[Eds.]*.

2. Katherine Dunham was born in Chicago in 1909. She grew up in Glen Ellyn and Joliet, Illinois *[Eds.]*.

3. Katherine Dunham's brother, Albert Millard Dunham Jr., graduated from the University of Chicago and went on to do graduate work in philosophy at Harvard University with Alfred North Whitehead (1861–1947). The University of Chicago subsequently accepted his credits and his thesis from Harvard and awarded him a Ph.D. degree *[Eds.]*.

4. University of Chicago records show that Katherine Dunham was awarded a Ph.B. degree (bachelor of philosophy degree) in 1936. Her major field of study is shown as social anthropology *[Eds.]*.

5. Dunham's thesis, an analysis of forms and functions of native dances of Haiti, was submitted to the Department of Anthropology at the University of Chicago in 1937 or 1938. She never completed the requirements for her master's degree, choosing instead to give her time and energies to a performing career. Her book about her experiences among the Maroons of Jamaica, *Journey to Accompong,* with an introduction by Ralph Linton and drawings by Ted Cook, was published in 1946. Her thesis on the dances of Haiti was eventually published in Spanish (1947), French (1950), and English (1983) *[Eds.]*.

Touring Europe with the Dunham Company

EARTHA KITT

The idea of having royalty in our audiences now and then sort of stimulated our interest. The word would scale the walls, settling backstage, when a royal personality was anywhere nearby. Every theater in London, of course, contains a royal box, so it was natural for our eyes to glance there first on entering the stage. We were terribly disappointed when kings and queens did not look down on us.

The night that royalty did come in, there was a great discussion, involving Miss Dunham particularly, as to whether she should bow, curtsy, lower her head, or forget the whole thing. There was still a dispute as to what the American should do under the circumstances. Then, too, if Miss Dunham acknowledged the presence of royalty, what should the cast do?

We were in our places on stage, watching Miss Dunham's entrance with careful eyes, waiting for her to offer an American greeting to British royalty. On her cue, she came on the stage, almost facing the royal box. She nodded her head in rhythm with the drums, without disturbing the choreography. If one did not know, one would have thought it a part of the dance.

When time came for me to do my little number with Jessie Hawkins, I fixed my hair the way Miss Dunham always told me not to, because I wanted to be more attractive. Since I was singing a Spanish song, I could not understand why she made me wear a bandanna over my hair. She would watch from the wings when one least suspected, to see if her orders

SOURCE: Excerpts from Eartha Kitt, *Thursday's Child* (New York: Duell, Sloan & Pearce, 1956), 131–33, 141, 144–47, 148, 149–50, 154–55. Copyright 1956 by Eartha Kitt. Reprinted by permission.

were being carried out. They were not this night, for I fluffed my hair in bangs, with curls all over my head, and pinned the bandanna on a small portion of my hair with the hope that it would fall off at some interval. I was prepared to take the punishment afterward and went offstage prepared for the worst.

Since I had got away with that, I figured I could take another chance in the finale of the first act, a number called *Shango*. This involved the sacrificing of a white cock to the god Shango. We all got possessed, and one boy turned into a snake and slithered all over the stage. I stood on the shoulders of two boys, dove to the floor, and slid from one end of the stage to the other. It was murder on my breasts, for we were not allowed to wear bras. Anyway, in this jungle ritual, just as the boy was being prepared to become a snake, I, as a high priestess or something, grabbed a cowbell and, running across stage, started a chant.

The chorus answered. In a high shrill voice, I repeated the chant with variations, leaping to a table, where I stayed, doing various movements and shouting until the curtain descended. When the curtain did come down, I was near death. It is almost impossible to sing with any meaning and dance with any meaning at the same time. Also I was afraid to do too much movement on such a high level, for Miss Dunham always restricted us from expressing ourselves too freely in the dance. Then too she did not want her choreography distorted in the slightest manner. If she had seen what I saw from some of us, when she was not looking, she would have been shocked into her grave long ago. Dancing on a table was not easy either. Very often I had to jump off when it toppled over and, with this particular in mind, I could never concentrate on more than one thing, singing, dancing, playing the cowbell, or keeping the rhythm.

Another fetish of Miss Dunham's was our makeup. Very often we would want to emphasize certain features—mine were my eyes and my high cheekbones. But Miss Dunham would say, "Kitty, you have too much makeup around your eyes." Or, "Too much rouge . . . cover up your hair." From the front of the house we thought all the girls looked alike and all the boys looked alike.

For six months, the Prince of Wales Theatre was the center and the joy of the London theater district. Ours was the most exciting show that had hit London since the war. London still grieved from that horror—I could see and feel her wounds. I was glad that I was born in a part of the world that had been so well protected, but I was also ashamed of my protection. I carried guilt inside for being a privileged character when the rest of the world was being destroyed. My feelings made me realize how valuable my American passport was.

Paris was a fascination to me. The first night, in a cab on our way to the little hotel Julie's mother had told us about, Julie [Robinson] said, "Can you imagine, Kitty? Here we are in Paris. Isn't it exciting?"

We found the Théâtre de Paris about ten blocks from the hotel. This was convenient, for we could walk and save money. The blocks were short. After a few nights of walking, we found we had company once in a while. If there were four of us, we had little trouble, but with two of us—or one, it wasn't so good. Once in a while it took a long time to shake our followers. The first couple of times Julie and I were followed in the lobby of our hotel where we called the manager. When we were first seen at night, coming in from work or what not, the professional girls of the neighborhood were suspicious that we might be moving in on their territory. It seemed our hotel was in the middle of the streetwalkers' section. We were doggoned if we were going to move. We expected to be in Paris only a couple of months anyway. Why bother? The ladies swarmed around our little abode like flies to chicken gravy. We were a little embarrassed at times, going in and out, because our hours were pretty much the same as theirs, but we got used to it, until the morning we were awakened at eight by pounding on the door.

My room was nearest the elevator. "Who is it?" I screamed.

"Open the door."

"What have I done?" I thought. Maybe the hotel's on fire. The hell with it. They have the wrong door. I started back to bed. Bang! bang! bang! "What do your want? Go away."

There were voices in the hallway. Maybe something is wrong. I'd better open the door. When I did, everyone else's door was opened too. No one was around but men. One walked heavily into my room, his eyes glancing here and there.

"Your passport?"

"My passport? What for?" I tried to make him understand. If only I knew how to speak this language, I'd tell him a thing or two for waking me up at such a ridiculous hour. Other voices were getting louder. I searched my room, one handbag, then another, one bureau drawer, then another. Where was my passport? Could I have lost it?

I ran to Julie's room. She too was looking for hers. Then we remembered. The company manager had taken all the passports. We got on the phone to call him and he came over within the hour to rescue us from our fate. Of course we went back to bed.

But a French newspaper carried a small item: FOUR DUNHAM DANCERS SEIZED IN RAID.

During our first day at the Paris theater, our rehearsal had been witnessed by photographers, of course. Since publicity is publicity, we cooperated with the photographers, who posed us in various positions. Our rehearsal clothing being rather scanty, not revealing but scanty, it was just what the cameramen wanted. We were posed this way and that.

The following day Miss Dunham came into the rehearsal with a newspaper. Opening the paper to a picture of us girls, she proceeded to reprimand us for not knowing about photographers and how to protect ourselves from vulgarity.

She showed us the newspaper picture of the Dunham girls in rehearsal. When we saw it, we became hysterical. All that one saw was legs, legs, legs, no faces.

Opening night in Paris was fantastic. More silks, satins, sables, and lace than I had ever seen before. A stage was set up in the lobby. The decoration in the lobby was intended to create the atmosphere of a jungle. There was even a tiger peeking through the greenery. Animal skins and drums of all sizes and shapes, along with primitive artwork were displayed along the path to the theater.

As usual, just before the curtain was about to go up, something happened. I don't remember what it was this night, but word was sent to me to go into the lobby and sing a couple of songs to kill time until the proper show was ready. I was given a Haitian costume. That was bad enough, but to have to sing so close to people, as though at a party, was extremely difficult for me. With fear in my bones, I walked through the crowd to the temporary stage. I took the maracas and began my songs, not daring to look at anyone's face. Why one had to go through this kind of torture I could not understand, but I had my orders.

Finally the overture started and the ordeal was over. If we never danced before, we did that night for Paris. It was a wonder the Théâtre de Paris did not turn to charcoal when the curtain went down. Maybe it was because it was Paris—the beautiful woman with a controversial reputation. The one everyone wanted to make love to but few would accept for a bride.

For three months we went to bed at dawn. It was inevitable that I was awakened practically every morning by a bottle of perfume, champagne, flowers, or just a date for lunch. I got so tired I hated Paris and everything

she stood for. I was too worn out to care. Of course I could have refused
a lot of dates and hospitality, but I didn't want to miss anything.

The day we all took a chartered plane to Cannes was strenuous. We had
to be at the airport at seven, after going to bed at one. Six o'clock in the
morning in Paris is like six in the morning anywhere, except more so. I
was so sleepy I couldn't get my eyes open.

   It was my first time on a plane and I was sure I was dreaming the whole
thing. At first the new experience did not impress me. Then the engines
started up. As soon as my seatbelt was fastened, my forehead was pressed
against the windowpane. I sat in the first seat, just behind the propeller. I
wanted to see everything. When the propellers started one by one to twirl
the air, my fear became more acute. The vibrations shocked me out of my
wits. If I have to contend with this noise until we reach our destination,
I'll be out of nerves, I thought.

   I closed my eyes, feeling the airplane rise into the air with my imagination, though it had not left the ground. When I saw we were finally
gliding across the ground, I thought of all the horrible things I had done
in life. It would be just like me to get on a plane for the first time and
have it crash. When the machine left the ground, I calmed down. I had
never felt such serenity as I did when we glided though soft puff-puffy-
puffs of puff.

Brussels was an expensive venture for us. Since everything in the stores
was American, American prices prevailed. We were told that the city was
a little Paris and a miniature New York. This was no lie, because everything was American, including the taxis. We were grateful to be able to
walk into a grocery and see U.S. products staring at us from the shelves.
We bought up everything we could afford.

   After one experience in a restaurant, we all decided to stock up on milk
and milk products, bread, jam and butter, along with plenty of fruit. We
used to eat in a cheap place next to the theater, our one hot meal a day. The
hamburgers were great. That was our main dish, with a bowl of onion soup.

   We enjoyed this city, even so. No one bothered us, only stared from a
distance. Now and then a Watusi would walk by gracefully. Then it was
our turn to stop and stare.

When we went to Antwerp, I loved it, the old buildings and canals. The
most impressive thing was the monument in the main square. Then there

was the old castle on the water front. We were told there was a tunnel under it leading to Flanders Field on the other side of the lake.

Italy was next. Living in this country was cheap. There were so many lire to the dollar that large handbags came in handy. We could eat without remorse. Naturally, one's main meal consisted of spaghetti with various sauces, salad, and ice cream. I believe we ate nothing but ice cream the first two days because it was so different—tutti-frutti, spumoni, tortoni.

We were in Rome one month. This gave me a chance to walk at length through the streets. My soul reached up when I sat in the ruins of the Coliseum, and a visit to the city of the dead was a spine-tingling experience. The catacombs held my interest from the moment I descended beneath solid soil until I breathed fresh air again.

The people themselves were very friendly and curious. A group of people followed us for blocks the first few days trying to figure out what the devil we were. They soon found out from their newspapers and word of mouth. Our show was quite a shock for them.

Milano, Torino, Napoli. Poverty struck us in the face like a black cat leaping from a garbage can on a dreary night. Wherever we walked, children followed. Rags hung from their bony limbs as though God had forgotten them. Dirt sapped the color from their faces and hands. Their eyes glistened with expectations of a lira. Disappointed heads hung in fumbling hands when they did not capture a coin. Giving is a wonderful experience, but when it is endless?

When we left Italy, we went to Switzerland. Zurich was a city in a valley of high mountains. We were taken to a hotel pension. The beds were covered with a soft quilt of eiderdown that melts over the body in sleep. The stairs creaked from so much use.

We liked everything we saw in Switzerland. The quaint streets, the grand boulevards, the toy shops, the watch and clock shops, the lake running through the city, the high mountains, the snow peaks, the people— clean-shaven unless aged—no sign of poverty, the calmness, the serenity, the faces that continued to smile from one to another, the price of a heritage that made their eyes sparkle.

Our successful engagement came to an end, much to our regret. Just when we were finding new friends, we had to travel on.

Our next stop was Sweden, the city of Stockholm. We were put into a pension that was very nice. Miriam Burton and I had an apartment next to Othella [Strozier] and Jackie Walcott, sharing the same bath. We made ourselves very much at home in this part of the world, because the people were very friendly, very health conscious, and so clean it was frightening.

The city is built on little islands, which made it more interesting and unique. The shopping district was on one island, the sports and health centers were on another. The theater and amusement center was on one, the oldest parts of Stockholm were on another. All these were connected by little bridges.

The theater was a converted circus house. We were there for a month, not wanting to leave at the end of the engagement. The people seemed happier than anyone in the world. Every face and hand was immaculate. No torn clothing, no beggars, no drunkards. This was a perfect example of civilization. In amazement I went through the city without seeing one sign of a slum.

I could not get too close to these people, for friendly as they were, they kept very much to themselves in thought. The fact that there was never any drinking in a public place without eating kept drinking to a minimum. That is, until Saturday night. When you do catch a drunken Swede, he is really drunk.

I spent my days getting steam baths and massages and bicycling into the country with a boy I met who spent his weekends touring me around. The one thing that amazed me was the curiosity of the people. Not having the experience of seeing a Negro every day, they followed the darker members of the company around.

Katherine Dunham and Us

ABDIAS DO NASCIMENTO

In the July 9 issue of this city's literary supplement *Correio da Manhã,* in the section "Inquiries and Declarations," the journalist Yvonne Jean published "The Dignity of the Art of Katherine Dunham," a summary of an interview with the great African American dancer and choreographer Katherine Dunham, who is currently visiting us.

Among other things, Ms. Yvonne Jean credited the following statements to Katherine Dunham: "In Brazil, where the problem shouldn't exist, I was disagreeably impressed to see a newspaper called *Quilombo,* made by and for blacks. This is not a title which seems appropriate according to the books I have read by Gilberto Freyre; it seems that here, where the situation is not the same as in the United States, blacks should read the same press as everyone, not segregate themselves voluntarily, as this could lead to distressing results. When I discussed these problems with the 'leader' of the 'black' movement, I told him he reminded me of Marcus Garvey."

The report of the French journalist, who has resided for a long time in Brazil, occasioned surprise among Brazilians of color, given that Katherine Dunham has shown us in successive interviews that she is ready to understand our struggles, lamenting that in a country such as ours it was necessary to create a black press and a black theater. Meanwhile, the statement "I had a disagreeable impression" and the allusion to Marcus Garvey, both

SOURCE: Abdias do Nascimento, "Katherine Dunham e Nós," *Quilombo* 2.10 (June–July 1950). English translation copyright 2004 by Sara E. Johnson. Used by permission.

of which demonstrate a lack of understanding of our struggle and our problems, were due to a faulty interpretation of our brilliant comrade and collaborator of the *Correio da Manhã*.

When she became aware of Ms. Yvonne Jean's report, Katherine Dunham sent her the following letter from São Paulo, where she is currently appearing with her company at the Teatro Municipal:

> I sincerely thank you for your splendid article in the *Correio da Manhã*. I received many favorable comments and am very satisfied with the article, with one exception.
>
> As you know, I am a great friend of Abdias [do] Nascimento in Rio de Janeiro, and his associates who form part of the Black Folkloric Theater. I am well aware of their problems, as well as those faced by all black Brazilians, especially since I too have been a victim of racial discrimination here in São Paulo.
>
> If you recollect my conversation with Gilberto Freyre in the house of Mrs. Francisco Chamie, you probably recollect that however strongly I objected, on a purely scientific basis, that black Brazilians should segregate themselves from the rest of the community, be it in the form of a journal specially dedicated to representing and serving the black community or in the form of a theater specifically established to give opportunities to black authors, at the same time I also considered this a necessary and inevitable development given the present situation at the heart of Brazil. In other words, I believed that in normal circumstances, an organization dedicated to expressing the sentiments of the black population as distinct from those of the rest of Brazil would not be necessary.
>
> Speaking also from a purely scientific point of view, and I believe that this was clearly understood between Gilberto Freyre and myself, the publication of *Quilombo* is a recognition of the segregation of the black Brazilian, and Abdias [do] Nascimento, if one were to follow the thesis presented at my conference, the point of departure for all of this discussion, could justifiably serve as a "messiah" for a humiliated and oppressed people. I cannot confirm that this was the intention or even the desire of Mr. Nascimento because he never expressed as much to me. I only know him to be a person profoundly preoccupied by and knowledgeable about existing conditions, and he is ready and willing to attempt to ameliorate the current state of affairs. I believe, in fact, that your reference to my commentary with respect to this issue of self-segregation was misinterpreted or taken out of the general context of the

conversation, and I fear that this offended Mr. Nascimento, who certainly can count on my complete cooperation.

I would be deeply grateful if you could write a note with the following declaration to your readers, or at least to Mr. Nascimento, saying "I regret that the black population of Brazil finds it necessary to segregate itself in whatever form, as ideally and normally it should be an element completely integrated into Brazilian social and economic life such that this separation need not occur."

I thank you once again for an article that I otherwise found extremely accurate and admirable.

Sincerely,
Katherine Dunham

Performing the Memory of Difference in Afro-Caribbean Dance

Katherine Dunham's Choreography, 1938–1987

VèVè A. Clark

Ironically, the development of *lieux de mémoire* as a concept among scholars of French revolutionary history presupposes emotional and intellectual distance from memory and history. In African diaspora cultures where peasant communities continue to survive—and their memories with them—the evolution toward *lieux de mémoire* has been far more simultaneous. Distinctions among memory, history, and *lieux de mémoire* in Africa and the Caribbean result primarily from class distinctions rather than the erosion of trust in telling one's history which currently defines the deconstructionist agenda in France. Pierre Nora's rereading of the French Revolution and his notion of *lieux de mémoire* can be applied universally to traditions of historiography and history, and to significant events celebrated worldwide.[1]

Milieux de mémoire, alluded to briefly in Nora's essay, are especially relevant to an understanding of *lieux de mémoire* in African American dance, largely because certain obscured black environs or *milieux* retained the memory from which choreographers of the 1930s drew their artistic inspiration.[2] To name the more obvious cases, Asadata Dafora Horton,

SOURCE: VèVè A. Clark, "Performing the Memory of Difference in Afro-Caribbean Dance: Katherine Dunham's Choreography, 1938–1987," in *History and Memory in African-American Culture,* edited by Geneviève Fabre and Robert O'Meally (New York: Oxford University Press, 1994), 188–204. Copyright 1994 by Oxford University Press. Reprinted by permission.

A version of this essay was presented at the Dunham Symposium organized by Yvonne Daniel and Halifu Osumare of the Committee on Black Performing Arts, Stanford University, 12 May 1989.

Katherine Dunham, and Pearl Primus represented on the concert stage dance cultures they had studied in either Africa or the Caribbean. When Dunham and Primus transferred these dances of the diaspora to performance spaces in North America, their choreography challenged the norms of male-centered African American performance of the 1930s and 1940s confined significantly to nineteenth-century formulas, namely shuffling and tap—no matter the degree of improvisation (e.g., Baby Laurence or Bill Robinson) or attempts at sophisticated representation (e.g., Coles/ Atkinson or Astaire/Rogers). I shall focus here on the transition from research (*milieux*) to performance (*lieux*) as one significant tradition within African-American dance history. While many of these *milieux* exist to this day, it is clear that some of the dances had lost their cultural base of support even in the 1930s and could, with the passing of an older generation, depart from memory.[3]

Early in the twentieth century, ethnology replaced both colonial historiography and alleged scientific theories that prevailed in the colonies and in France during the nineteenth century. Ethnologists became present-day historiographers whose studies in West Africa, for example, reflected memories and a history forgotten deliberately by the keepers of Hexagonic records.[4] Certain Caribbean historians of the eighteenth century, like the Creole writer Moreau de Saint-Méry, early on had published chronicles attempting to blend memory and history.[5] In 1935–1936, when Katherine Dunham sought out *milieux de mémoire* in various Caribbean countries and succeeded in documenting aspects of dance culture, she uncovered cultural artifacts revealed to only a small cadre of scholars during that era. Between 1937 and 1945, Dunham established a research-to-performance method to which her first dance company was exposed. She would use this method of scholarly inquiry as a means to recreate the memory of regional dances among her dancers and a variety of audiences in North America and abroad. For this essay, I shall focus on the *memory of difference* to examine Dunham's research methods, dance technique, and performance principles, and to evaluate critical response by reviewers.

ETHNOLOGY, THE NEW HISTORY

An epistemological break with the narrative of European history and memory occurred during the Haitian Revolution (1791–1804). No longer would black history be remembered solely as an appendage; a former colony was producing a memory of its own. Later in the nineteenth century—during the period when Nora claims that certain French historians were becoming more scientific in their analysis—French writers, such as Gobineau, were defending the notion of European racial superiority in response to Darwin's theories of evolution. To European arguments for racial hierarchy, several Haitian writers responded vehemently in opposition.[6] Their views were dismissed and did nothing at the time to influence or overturn the prevailing white colonial versions of memory and history. Having inherited a tradition of exclusion from Western narrative history, a number of Caribbean and African intellectuals of the 1920s turned to ethnology for support. Ethnology, or the history of the Other, established in the 1820s and 1830s by the nation-states of Europe (notably England, France, and Germany), created a branch of memory and history whose purpose was to record tribal practices in the regions dominated by European powers. The French historian Delafosse and others, writing at the turn of the century, revealed the integrity of African sociopolitical structures as well as a hitherto ignored memory of family/clan rule—Africa's forgotten history, as it were.[7]

In *Ainsi parla l'oncle* (1928), Haitian scholar Jean Price-Mars attempted to prove the continuity of memory and history in the New World colonies, particularly Haiti, despite colonialist narratives arguing the contrary. Ethnology soon became the new history, the preferred methodology, which encouraged the inclusion of folk memory in historical narrative; more importantly, however, Price-Mars's study became an antidote to the warped historiographies that colonialists wrote based on their memory of exile in the colonies. Price-Mars was followed by Herskovits, Roumain, and Métraux.[8] In the 1930s, such ethnologists accumulated a *memory of difference* deriving from folk memory and ritual observance that ultimately challenged official histories written by European colonists.

Price-Mars and others uncovered what Nora would call *milieux de mémoire*—discrete, regional remembrances beyond the pale of official history—so insignificant as to be known only among practitioners, a living chronology revealed to members only. In the Caribbean, *milieux de mémoire* survived in Haitian Vodun, Shango cults of Trinidad, and the urban dance halls of Martinique and Jamaica. Dunham was attracted to all of these *milieux*. In 1935–1936, when she traveled to Jamaica, Haiti, Martinique, and Trinidad, she was following an ethnological tradition established a decade before by her mentors, Robert Redfield and Melville Herskovits. Ethnology in the 1930s did indeed privilege the study of peasant culture or the *milieux de mémoire* of rural, non-literate communities, and Dunham followed the precedent into the field. She was interested especially in observing and documenting dance cultures that had been overlooked by others. The privilege Dunham gave to peasant culture persevered throughout her career but was accompanied by an equal devotion to urban and rural black dance research in the United States. Consequently, the Dunham shows became a repository of black dance of both North America and the Caribbean. Moreover, Dunham's research became the basis for character dances and ballets, all of which demonstrated her extensive knowledge of dance forms recreated from African diaspora memory. When the dance steps, music, and other cultural forms were transformed for stage representations, they become *lieux de mémoire,* reworkings and restatements of historical danced events whose memory Dunham had also preserved in writing or on film.[9] Dunham's *lieux de mémoire* became at once a celebration of Caribbean memory and history preserved in dance form and a reminder of cultural artifacts one should not forget.

In four of Dunham's works, one witnesses a creative dialogue between *milieux* and *lieux de mémoire.* The dialogues appear in the choreography she created for the film *Stormy Weather* (1943), with the full ballet *L'Ag'ya,* set in Martinique (1938–1944), and two overtly political works, *Tango* (1954) and *Southland* (1951), first performed in South America. My interpretations here are meant to encourage innovative critical approaches to black dance, particularly to the work of choreographers who, like Dunham, participated in a research-to-performance method. I urge dance historians to provide readings that go beyond pure description, beyond the choreographer's biography, beyond the definitions of black dance as "ethnic" dance or as "concert" dance, the genre ghetto to which much of black dance history has been banished.[10] In Dunham's case, one must set her research and performance style in historical context. Her writing on the dances of Haiti applied a form/function, structuralist analysis to the dances she observed, while her choreography belongs to the narrative, modernist tradition.[11] When we view the Alvin Ailey dance company's recent reconstructions of several Dunham pieces, we as audience members, critics, and scholars perceive them in poststructuralist/postmodern intellectual and artistic environments, whether or not we acknowledge the existence of this fundamental change in artistic form and audience expeditions. Given the current taste for non-narrative, decentered, or abstract choreography, the postmodern perspective may, indeed, inhibit our abilities to appreciate the history and memory embedded in Dunham's Caribbean and African American dances.

The challenge, then, is to develop a critical literacy for dance analysis so that we may decipher and interpret choreography just as we read literary texts closely or "read" the language of cinema. Performance studies by such scholars as Richard Schechner, Victor Turner, Judith Lynne Hanna, and Robert Farris Thompson provide models for analysis of this kind.[12] When dance scholars participate more fully in current critical discourse, their work will, no doubt, encourage comparative studies across genres—with the novel, with theater, and with the fine arts.

Developing a critical discourse that is appropriate for the Dunham *oeuvre* is a complicated affair, because unlike most choreographers, she was trained both in dance and in anthropology. Consequently, her sources and allusions are extensive, and refer to dance styles she learned in Chicago as well as to the dance vocabularies she observed in the Caribbean and South America between 1935 and the mid-1950s. The South American dance idioms appeared in her shows as individual numbers (*Congo Paillette* or *Choros*), while the Caribbean dances were incorporated into ballets the likes of *L'Ag'ya* (i.e., *Béguine, Creole Mazurka*). Dunham applied a similar method of recovery when she studied urban black dances of the 1920s (Charleston, Black Bottom, Mooch), which reappeared in *Flaming Youth*. Long before Dunham sought out black dances of the diaspora, she was trained in modern and character dance by her Russian-born instructors Ludmilla Speranzeva and Vera Mirova; her exposure to black community theater and ballet came by way of Ruth Attaway, Mark Turbyfill, and Ruth Page. These eclectic influences would later define the dance training style known as the Dunham Technique, a specific set of exercises and movements that she developed in the early 1940s, whose vocabulary evolved through the late 1960s to include Asian performance styles as well.

Inevitably, critics not as learned as Dunham have applied their own standards to evaluations of the Dunham Company's performances. Many expected Dunham to represent Caribbean regional dances in documentary form. When she did not do so, she was chided for stylizing authentic dance forms.[13] Criticism of this kind is irrelevant, because it fails to understand that Caribbean dance has been stylized and transformed throughout its history. More important, stylization has been a tradition in American modern dance since its inception. Note, however, that other moderns were not criticized when they visualized *milieux de mémoire* that no longer existed (e.g., Martha Graham's *Primitive Mysteries)* or that never possessed a danced tradition (e.g., Helen Tamiris's *Negro Spirituals*).

RESEARCH TO PERFORMANCE INVERTED

My original method for studying Dunham's choreography was to trace her research and/or creation process to the ultimate performance of a particular piece. Useful as that approach was in the research stages begun in 1983, I decided to change direction when I overheard negative responses to the Dunham ballets during the 1987 Ailey reconstruction of her choreography in New York City. At that point, I realized that American audiences have not been trained to see black dance historically. Consequently, I reversed my process of analysis by following the performances backward to research and by setting my analysis in the postmodern climate that informs our contemporary perceptions of dance. That inversion has raised questions that my chronological approach had failed to notice. Before turning to the study of specific dances, however, I shall describe the dance research environment a half century ago into which Dunham was drawn as dancer and scholar.

In the 1930s dance ethnology offered American scholars a new field within cultural anthropology where the potential for rediscovery seemed limitless. The discipline attracted the attention of social scientists, dancers, folklorists, and writers alike. Franziska Boas, daughter of the eminent Franz Boas, was among the neophytes who brought credibility to the burgeoning field, as were Geoffrey Gorer, Harold Courlander, and two African American choreographers, Pearl Primus and Dunham—the former directed toward African dance, the latter focused primarily on Caribbean culture and dance.[14] With the support of a Rosenwald grant in June 1935, Dunham departed for the Caribbean with dance archaeology on her mind. The significance of her first eighteen-month stay in the Caribbean lies in the breadth of her exposure to sacred and popular culture and the example she later established as a black choreographer for herself and others who were, in the 1930s and 1940s, reinterpreting for staged presentations the secular and sacred dances indigenous to African diaspora communities in the Caribbean and North America.

Dunham was drawn to folk culture rather than elite society because of her interest in African art forms surviving (albeit transformed) in the Caribbean. Her orientation reflected the scholarly concerns of her mentors Redfield and Herskovits, who were respectively attempting to reveal the dimensions and integrity of Mexican and African diaspora culture. Dance had been neglected prior to 1935 primarily because anthropologists and sociologists had gravitated toward the "hard" specializations of their disciplines. Dance was not among them. Moreover, none of these scholars was a trained dancer who could understand the language of dance without the aid of an interpreter. Herskovits, whose field experiences in Dahomey and Haiti were well known, directed Dunham's work. He suggested approaches that influenced her way of seeing and her subsequent manner of documentation. Nonetheless, Dunham diverged radically from prevailing methodology by becoming a participant-observer in Haitian Vodun during an era when only a minority of social scientists practiced this form of information gathering. Herskovits cautioned against such engagement in a letter dated January 6, 1936:

> Once again, I am disturbed at the amount you are trying to do, this time principally because of your health. I hope you haven't contracted malaria, but whatever it is, you owe it to yourself not to try to do quite as much as you are. I am a little disturbed also at the prospect of your going through the *canzo* ceremony, and I am wondering if it would not be possible for you to attend merely as a witness. Of course, as you know, the trial by fire is an integral part of this initiation, but I wouldn't like to see you suffer burns as a result of going through it. However, you know best in such matters. I am not surprised that the natives are amazed at the way you pick up the dances, and that it induces them to believe that you probably have inherited *loa* [ancestral spirit] that makes this possible.[15]

Dunham did not follow her mentor's advice, nor had she done so previously in Jamaica, Martinique, and Trinidad, where she gained entry into *milieux de mémoire* whose practices were shrouded in secrecy and mystery as a means of protection against censure by adversarial religious orders—Catholic and Protestant—ultimately the keepers of the status quo in the Caribbean of the 1930s.

When the research-to-performance method is reversed, a viewer's attention is drawn first to Dunham's stagings—the *lieux de mémoire* that exist on film and in the recent Ailey reconstructions. Looking back from performance to research inspires a number of questions, and when one studies the archival footage Dunham shot in 1935—say, in Martinique—issues of reconstruction for the stage become apparent. In the case of the martial dance form *l'ag'ya*, an explicitly male *milieu*, one wonders how Dunham gained access. Given the potential for bodily harm during these bouts, I question whether the *l'ag'ya* was repressed by the constabulary or, as one sequence suggests, these bouts may have been sanctioned by local authorities and their constituencies as well. In her filming of the *l'ag'ya,* Dunham documented a *memory of difference* that has been forgotten by most Martinicans. The dance form does appear frequently in advertisements for tourism; however, representations of the *l'ag'ya* in contemporary Martinique are equally as stylized as were Dunham's presentations in the 1930s and 1940s. To my knowledge, no historical record exists in Martinique to remind us of the distinctions which must be made between the *l'ag'ya* as *milieux de mémoire* and the *lieu de mémoire* it has become in recent decades.

The relationship that exists between mimesis and figuration is a central issue in the research-to-performance method; the process is highly complex, particularly when the transfer of research is cross-cultural, as it was in Dunham's case. The notion of performing the *memory of difference* may suggest ways in which historians of black dance might assist contemporary audiences and those of the future in seeing and appreciating the dialogue, both cultural and performative, that Dunham's better-known choreography represents.

Performing the Memory of Difference

The *memory of difference* in dance provides a paradigm for examining the dialogues between research and performance; between research and the training of dancers; and between the established order of repertoire and the ways it changes over time as well as the portrayals of class and gender differences that have not always been acknowledged as significant elements in Dunham's choreography. As of this writing, I have isolated seven elements, all or some of which may affect our readings of dance when difference in diaspora culture is represented on stage. These elements come into play on several levels whether the problems refer to research, performance, criticism, or scholarship:

1. historiography of a researcher's individual memory of regional dances;
2. representations of African-American and Caribbean *milieux de mémoire* on stage;
3. style and mood conveyed to the audience through characteristic movements memorized, as it were, during the training and rehearsal process;
4. allusions in the text to which audiences respond differently as a company tours (e.g., *L'Ag'ya* in Japan);
5. subtle differences in performance over the period of a company's history as principal dancers are replaced;

6. responses to cultural difference on the part of mainstream critics whose literacy of black dance varies;

7. class and gender differences that challenge an audience to recognize variations in black culture.

In *L'Ag'ya,* for instance, we are confronted with the lives of peasants in a small fishing village in Martinique. Through mime, posture, and costume—all mimetic in character—the Dunham Company brought us closer to peasant environments that, in the 1930s and 1940s, were viewed principally from the outside. Gender differences appear in pieces Dunham choreographed for the men in her company who, as she says, needed a display of their own. Thus *Nañigo.* Dunham's ballet *Women's Mysteries* from the 1950s was another attempt at developing gender-specific dance language and settings. *Stormy Weather,* although designed for a mixed group of performers, privileges the lead woman dancer. This convention dominated American dance throughout the 1930s and 1940s, when dance dramas created by women choreographers replaced male fantasies and prowess as they appeared, for example, in Nijinsky's *L'Après-midi d'un Faune* (1912) and Asadata Dafora Horton's wonderful display of male athleticism, *Kykunkor* (1934). In illustrating the various modes of rereading the process of performance to research, a number of approaches seem relevant, including stylistic/aesthetic (à la Robert Farris Thompson), agitprop (as in Dunham's *Southland* and *Tango*), cultural, and semantic. The latter two are representations of memory I shall discuss in *Stormy Weather* and *L'Ag'ya.*

The Break in *Stormy Weather*: Envisioning Modernism in Black Dance

Stormy Weather (1943) is a *lieu de mémoire* that serves as a dictionary of black dance including nineteenth-century forms such as the cakewalk and shuffling as well as twentieth-century versions of cool tap performed by Bill Robinson. In addition, black performers parody the Astaire-Rogers elegant variety, and in one short sequence a young man performs modernized tap accompanied by interpretive moves that would later become the sign of Gene Kelly's cinema dance.

The section in which the Dunham Company appears occurs during the break as Lena Horne performs Harold Arlen's urban white version of the blues, "Stormy Weather." Her blues is uptown, sophisticated, and smooth, stylistically well removed from the Ma Rainey and Bessie Smith variety largely because technical advances like the microphone and boom had erased the need for singers to belt out their lines. Dunham's choreography literally replaces the section in a blues song during which musicians improvise on the theme; in this instance, black dance is improvising, and it is here that Dunham's visions of modernism in black dance are expressed forthrightly. The vision contrasts dramatically with the opening scene in which the performers (all but Dunham) lean forward on each other and in a casual but deliberate manner recapture the movements of 1920s black American get-down social dancing. Their style is meant to be mimetic, and John Pratt's wonderful costumes suggest a reality of the Chicago streets. The angular lines in the costumes reflect the reticulations of the elevated train tracks above, under which this disparate group has huddled. This same angularity will be restated in the following section. I would argue that both sections are *lieux de mémoire:* the first is mimetic, representing the tradition of black popular dance and its transmission from generation to generation; the second is figurative and visionary.

As the music becomes increasingly jazzy in the second section, the dancers' movements take on an off-center perspective. (I am speaking here of the leaning, falling, shoulder, and pelvic moves that Dunham chose to illustrate her vision of black modern dance to come.) Only recently had this modernist tradition been established publicly, in 1937, during a presentation by Edna Guy, Dunham, and others at the YMHA in New York.[16] Dunham's vision of a new dance is also ironic considering the background theme to which the dancers perform—namely, stormy weather. As many black choreographers and dancers of the era and afterward would testify, their art was indeed caught in the "stormy weather" of unpredictable obstacles that would confront a black company performing the *memory of difference* in the United States.[17]

Paradox in *L'Ag'ya*

This ballet was Dunham's first. It was performed for the WPA series of productions in 1938 and has always intrigued me. Even though I have written elsewhere on the structure of *L'Ag'ya,* I have felt that my analysis was insufficient, that there was far more to learn from the narrative and from Dunham's use of various Caribbean dance idioms.[18] When I began to focus on the sequences, I realized how deeply this *lieu de mémoire* expresses the paradoxical nature of black culture in the "New World." History in *L'Ag'ya* visualizes dramatic moments in the silenced working and

recreational lives of peasants and working-class individuals. The setting
is a village in rural, southern Martinique of the 1930s, known as Vauclin.
Mundane fishing and marketing activities in which the dancers participate daily are offset by feast days when they transform themselves into
"another." To dance the Creole mazurka, the *mazouk,* villagers dress in
former colonial apparel imitating ruling-class behavior of a century ago.
This type of transformation seems to be socially acceptable. When Julot,
one of the featured characters, engages in sorcery as a way of seducing
Loulouse (played by Dunham) away from her lover Alcide (Vanoye
Aikens), his attempts to transform reality are considered antisocial and a
transgression against the community. The ballet ends with a martial-arts
duel, the *l'ag'ya* between Julot and Alcide. The latter is killed in the process, and Julot is chased away from the scene and the community as a form
of reprimand.

Memory in the ballet is cross-culturally presented through a sequence
combining ballet, modern dance, and Caribbean dance. Of the Caribbean
dances, the sequence includes the *habanera* (Cuba), *majumba* (Brazil),
mazouk, béguine, and *l'ag'ya*—the latter three from Martinique. *L'Ag'ya is*
the quintessential ballet of memory because of its composite representation of dances from the wider Caribbean. Dunham's mélange of cultural
references in the piece leads to a more profound portrayal of Martinican
society of the 1930s. At the time, Caribbean culture was entering a second
phase of creolization through emigration on the one hand and cross-
cultural communication among intellectuals associated with the Harlem
Renaissance, indigenism, *indigenísmo,* and *négritude* movements. Some of
these intellectuals would share their coming to consciousness in the salons
of Paris or meeting halls of New York City.

The syntax of Dunham's choreography in *L'Ag'ya* reflects the profound
class and color antagonisms that existed in 1930s Martinique. *L'Ag'ya* is a
perfect example of oxymoron in dance; the narrative opposes work days/
feast days, seaside/jungle, love/fantasy, respectable, community-oriented
behavior/questionable, ego-centered desire. The subtext of the ballet re-
inforces such a reading: consider the constant use of dance movements
which by their style are opposed—modern/ballet; Old World/New World;
colonial/post-emancipation; ecstatic/martial. Dunham's choreography reflects social oppositions existing simultaneously and paradoxically in a
society governed at a distance from France, and further controlled economically and socially in those days by former plantation families known
as *bèkès* or their elite mulatto co-conspirators. In such an environment,

dance of the majority black population demonstrates the contradictions of New World acculturation.

Having settled on paradox and oxymoron as the principal semantic devices operating in *L'Ag'ya*, I looked back at one of Dunham's letters to Herskovits written in September 1935 when she reported on the barriers she was then facing:

> This is a very difficult country. It is small, and the people are much amalgamated. There is much more to be done here psychologically than artistically or anthropologically. The country is slowly decaying and the people with it. I have been not so well here physically, partly because my work has gone so poorly, I suppose. There is just nothing to see, but I hang on, hoping. I've seen several phases of the *béguine*, the *l'ag'ya*, an acrobatic dance that much resembles the Dahomean thunder dance, and Sunday I go to see an (East) Indian ceremony which is climaxed in cutting the throat of a sheep. But I can't seem to get any pictures.[19]

Seventeen years later, the Martinican theorist Frantz Fanon would analyze some of the same behavior, using as documentation two literary works written by Antilleans rather than the opposing traditions of their danced history that Dunham had observed.[20] While the sequence in *L'Ag'ya* in which *mazouk* is followed by *béguine* maintains an established custom during set dances in Martinique where the memory of Old and New World forms persisted side by side, Dunham's juxtaposition of other dance traditions was unconventional. *L'Ag'ya* was Dunham's "Ballet des Antilles," the title she gave to the work in an early summary.[21] It was her attempt to consolidate the various dance styles of her training and research efforts. In the company's repertoire, *L'Ag'ya* represented Dunham's vision of diaspora culture, a concept that in the 1990s seems more real than imagined.

AGITPROP TRANSFORMING *Lieux de Mémoire*

Agitprop is not a performance technique associated generally with dance. Normally, the practice has been confined to dramatic representations: workers' theater of the 1920s and 1930s in both Europe and America; subsidized versions during the Federal Theater Project; experiments in the 1960s among, for example, the San Francisco Mime Troupe and El Teatro Campesino.[22] Throughout the 1930s, however, several choreographers associated briefly with the Workers' Dance League, the likes of Anna Sokolow and Sophie Maslow or Helen Tamiris, participated in their versions of social protest in dance, and did so following the precepts of agitation—propaganda as a showcase for left-wing political objectives.[23] In the historiography of the Dunham Company, *agitprop* is a term which does not appear—perhaps because it may seem abrasive in its suggestion that control has been lost, the very reverse of the company's aesthetic. The Dunham style was elegant, intense, and at times raunchy in the ballets and single pieces based on the reformation of American, Caribbean, and South American dance idioms for world stages.

Yet two works, a dance piece and full ballet—*Tango* and *Southland*—both of which were first performed during the 1950s in South America, Dunham engaged in agitprop to respond to political situations as they were then unfolding. Unlike the choreography analyzed earlier which focuses on modernism and transcultural adaptations, the agitprop works in the Dunham corpus were deliberate recastings of regional dances designed to express anger and protest against certain sociopolitical practices. These two texts were part of the European tours seen first in South America and later in Paris but, in the case of *Southland,* never performed in the United States. As *lieux de mémoire,* the dances were evaluated as sites of comparison by critics who had enjoyed the Dunham Company's performances earlier, in the late 1940s and early 1950s. Although these works were newly created, they reworked familiar idioms, such as the tango, plantation dances, and the blues, in a performance climate playing clearly upon difference.

Reviews of *Southland* from Paris bristled with expectation not only because the ballet dealt with lynching but also because four years after the initial tour the program generally had become a *lieu de mémoire* critiqued by association with memories of earlier performances.[24] In part, the return of the Dunham Company to South America or Europe, and later to the United States, was a typical lesson for reviewers and audiences in *reading choreography* as Susan Foster has defined the phenomenon that I am calling the *memory of difference:* Only the viewer who retains visual, aural and kinesthetic impressions of the dance as it unfolds in time can compare succeeding moments of the dance, noticing similarities, variations, and contrasts and comprehending larger patterns-phrases of movement and sections of the dance-and finally the dance as a whole.[25]

Tango (1954), presented for the first time in Argentina for audiences accustomed to the forms of their national dance, allowed "readers" of Dunham's choreography to appreciate the ways in which the tango might be used to express defiance.

Buenos Aires theaters were not new to the Dunham Company in 1954. The dancers had performed there in the fall of 1950 a program including *America!, Son, Choros, Nañigo, Batucada, Shango, L'Ag'ya, Flaming Youth, Barrelhouse,* and *Jazz Finale.* But no *Tango.* During that first tour, the company participated in a benefit performance for Eva Perón's Fundación de Ayuda Social. Four years later, the political climate had changed so significantly for the worse that Dunham used the tango as an agitprop form of persuasion that would both distance her company from former support of the Perónist agenda and record the degree to which disappearance (*la desaparición de personas*) was becoming a mainstay of Argentinian political life.[26] In advance of her arrival, she informed the composer of *Tango,* Osvaldo Pugliese, and the pianist-conductor, Bernardo Noriega— both Argentineans—that she intended to make a political statement with this particular number in which she was to appear with the black Argentinean Ricardo Avalos, a member of her company, and three others, Vanoye Aikens, Lenwood Morris, and Lucille Ellis.[27]

There is no filmed record of the dance, although it stayed in the repertoire well into the 1950s. Only a few photographs remain, but these are striking because they show Dunham in the lead role and angry in performance. These pictures, housed in the Dunham Archives in East Saint Louis, prompted me to inquire about the tone of *Tango,* with what seemed a dramatic departure from Dunham's usual persona on stage. According to her recollections, *Tango* played upon the implied Argentinean audience's probable readings of sentimentality, sexuality, and brutality in her reconstructed work. Members of the audience knew that Dunham intended to use their national dance as a form of protest and were prepared that the usual confrontations between male and female would allude to a particularly disturbing occurrence within their midsts. Dunham's remembrances of *Tango* explain how she used the *memory of difference* as an agitprop technique among an audience that would implicitly comprehend her political statement about death and repression advancing under the Peróns:

> *Tango* is a street number. I used to go walking in a Buenos Aires district which is very much like Les Halles in Paris, and used to do so well past midnight after our shows had closed. There were a number of taverns and cafés nearby where tangos were played, and when the dance was not being performed socially, I thought of it as though it were occurring on a street in Afro-America. When the woman in *Tango* enters, she is going somewhere with great urgency, looks back over her shoulder as if she were being

pursued. She meets one partner, then two others, and has a brief tango step with the first partner. She is suffering from high, nervous tension. When she performs with her central partner [Vanoye Aikens], she demonstrates several authentic tango steps, but she also engages in confrontation with him. She executes a series of movements in which she very sharply opens her thigh due to his pressure; he hits her with his knee so that she opens hers, and there are two or three movements like that which imply sexual motivation but also refer to the clashing of two people ideologically even though they are politically on the same side. In the process, however, she seems to fling away everything around her in an intent to express another political position. The piece ends on a harsh, sharp note of defiance. The defiance is directed toward the Argentine people, the Peróns, and the situation. I was a different person then. That was my second trip back to Argentina, and I had no illusions about the political situation by then.[28]

The political references in this danced text were so clear that audiences previously drawn to the Dunham Company's performances in 1950 either gave a standing ovation after *Tango* was premiered or stayed away, possibly for fear of reprisals.

Why was Katherine Dunham so angry, in 1954, when she returned to Buenos Aires? The program notes, reworked as the company toured throughout the 1950s, suggest in understated form the political context surrounding her own emotions at the time: "In the Argentine, there have been many changes in recent years but the vast city of Buenos Aires still covers the underbeat of the tango. In the *cantinas* of the street people, Katherine Dunham felt the nostalgia of the tango and the restlessness of the times."[29] Other versions of these notes contain equally personalized references to Dunham's experiences in the city and to the memory of Pepita Cano, a personal friend and one of the first women to become a radio announcer, who died in the interim between the 1950 and 1954 tours. She died under mysterious circumstances and might have been murdered by the tango player whose career she had launched—as either a *crime passionnel* or a political assassination connected with "disappearance" methods of dispensing with activists, or both. Moreover, *Tango* was reacting to similar harassments of the composer and the conductor—the former jailed and the latter known for his anti-Perónist sentiments.[30] The *memory of difference* in *Tango* contains a quality of agitprop which some members of the audience feared to sanction and others applauded forthrightly. Such, indeed, is the contrastive climate within which this particular style of performance has been received since the 1920s in both theater and dance.

Southland became Dunham's Achilles' heel after its premiere in Santiago de Chile in January 1951. This full-length ballet depicting lynching was her undoing as a trusted representative of American culture abroad as far as the U.S. State Department was concerned.[31] By portraying overseas our country's dirtiest social laundry, Dunham betrayed a trust of silence. As in *Tango*, the work expresses anger, this time reporting about the trial of the Martinsville Seven and Willie McGee in a replay of the rape *topos* surrounding the Scottsboro trials of the 1930s. Having recently experienced institutional racism herself during her company's tour of Brazil in the summer of 1950, Dunham was reminded of similar acts of discrimination against which she had fought legally during the 1940s within her own country.[32] She believed in the 1950s that the practice was typically American, and moreover had been resolved. In Brazil, the pervasiveness of color prejudices surfaced once again when she was denied entry into one of the better hotels because she was black. From this personal experience and news about the recent lynchings back home, she created *Southland*.

The work is a dance drama in the Kamerny Theater tradition and closer in aesthetic to tragic ballets presented by Diaghilev's Ballets Russes. As such, it reflects Dunham's early training with ballet dancer Ludmilla Speranzeva, who had worked at the Kamerny in Moscow, and the choreographer's expressed desire in the 1930s to create her own Ballet Nègre. Before arriving in Chile for the premiere, Dunham composed dialogue for *Southland* in two acts that the dancers, to their dismay, had to memorize in preparation for actually performing these feelings in pantomime on stage. In production, however, dramatic action was sustained by a "Greek chorus" of singers who explicitly express and comment upon the dialogue, which the dancers enact but do not express in words.[33]

At intervals, the chorus engages in irony and allegory. In the opening scene they literally signify upon Southern plantation sentimental melodies, "Is It True What They Say about Dixie?" by responding ironically with the Other truths about the plantation South known among black Americans. When the lynching occurs, the tone of the chorus shifts to allegory as Claudia McNeil sings the Billie Holiday version of "Strange Fruit," thereby setting in broader perspective the endurance of this pernicious social phenomenon in American social history.

The curtain opens to reveal a huge magnolia tree and the whitened pillars of an old, Southern mansion—a wonderfully understated set by John

Pratt. Throughout *Southland* the time frame is condensed so as to associate the memory of plantation oppression with segregation and despair
among the urban black populace. Briefly, the problem of this dance drama
unfolds in the following manner. Two young country folk (Lucille Ellis
and John Lei or Ricardo Avalos) express affection for each other. The
joyful ease of their relationship is reflected in the carefree performance of
plantation square dances drawn from the company's Americana repertoire. Following this opening sequence, a young white woman (played by
Julie Robinson) is battered by her white companion (Lenwood Morris)
and left unconscious just below the magnolia tree. The field hands returning to the scene come upon the woman's body, and one of them shows
compassion while the others draw away, knowing instinctively that a black
man should not try to console a white woman in such a state of disarray.
The tragic consequences of such an effort were implied. When the woman
awakens to a black man hovering over her, she calls him "Nigger," and
through pantomime arouses an invisible mob to defend her pristine virtue and punish a "reckless black eyeballer" instead of the white companion who actually abused her. Although the young black man attempts to
escape mob violence through every possible exit on stage, he does not
succeed, and in the next sequence his body is seen hanging from the lofty
branches of the magnolia tree. In the final act the performers are on Basin
Street, dancing the blues. They are anesthetized equally by segregation and
alcohol, as a New Orleans-style funeral cortège passes through the café
bearing the lynched body. Most of the clients do not know how to react.
At ballet's end, only a blind beggar recognizes the depths of the tragedy
that has transpired.

In 1951 *Southland* was a daring dance drama indeed. Beyond the subject
matter itself, the use of *lieux de mémoire* exemplifies agitprop in dance. All
of the four dance idioms were familiar to Dunham Company members,
audiences, and critics alike, as the company toured Europe following the
South American engagements. Basically, Dunham transformed the setting
of these *lieux de mémoire* within the repertoire in order to make a political statement. The *apache* in the pseudo-rape scene had appeared in *Windy
City* (1947), the *habanera* performed to incite the mob was used in the
zombie scene of *L'Ag'ya* (1938); the plantation dances and blues had been
long-standing numbers within the company's repertoire since the 1930s
and 1940s. But here they were performed with a difference. The *apache*
and *habanera* signified anger and arousal on the part of a woman "victim";
the American dances provided comforting yet paradoxical brackets for the

violence developing at the center of the drama. For those viewers aware of how these dances appeared earlier in Dunham shows, they were witnessing the *memory of difference*. References to a culture's authentic dances suggested that communities surrounded by familiar traditions—whether square dances or blues—might be disrupted periodically and perhaps predictably by racial hysteria with its own set of "performance" tactics learned, practiced, and ultimately leading to the death of an individual hanging without trial by the neck.

As one would expect, the U.S. State Department responded negatively to *Southland* during a period of Congressional conflict prior to the McCarthy proceedings and the civil rights movement between 1952 and 1954. Criticism of the ballet was mixed, particularly in Paris, where the ballet was performed in 1952. As in the response to *Tango,* the reviews were partisan—from Communist Left to conservative, from enthusiastically supportive to bored.[34]

On a broader level, agitprop in these two works is not nearly so unconventional in the Dunham *oeuvre* as it might appear to be. In fact, *Tango* and *Southland* are examples of a persistent choreographic tendency, beginning with the early experiment *Tableaux of Spanish Earth* (1937), one of many pieces performed at the time in support of the Abraham Lincoln Brigade's efforts during the Spanish Civil War, through the Federal Theater Project in Chicago where *L'Ag'ya* premiered (1938), followed by a show sponsored by the ILGWU, *Pins and Needles 1940,* for which Dunham served in 1939 as dance director. These commitments to the representation of political issues prepared the way for *Tango* and *Southland,* as well as Dunham's work with poet Eugene Redmond on *Ode to Taylor Jones* (1968) in East Saint Louis, Illinois. *Ode* was a dance drama dedicated to the memory of a black activist killed in an automobile accident the year before.[35] When this type of dedication to representing social issues radically in dance is recognized as part of the Dunham legacy, the move to East Saint Louis and the work with gang members of the 1960s are not the startling and abrupt changes in life style that they appear to be among many observers of her company's successes in America and worldwide throughout the 1940s and 1950s. The *memory of difference* in Dunham's choreography is complex and still misunderstood. This brief survey of several works provides glimpses of the ways in which her transformations of indigenous Caribbean, African-American, and South American dances challenged her dancers, audiences, and critics to develop their dance literacy as they appreciated the changing scene.

NOTES

1. Pierre Nora, "Entre mémoire et histoire: La problématique des lieux," in *Les lieux de mémoire,* edited by Pierre Nora (Paris: Gallimard, 1984) , xvii–xlii.

2. Ibid., xvii.

3. Katherine Dunham, *Journey to Accompong* (New York: Henry Holt, 1946).

4. Fred W. Voget, *A History of Ethnology* (New York: Holt, Rinehart & Winston, 1975).

5. Médéric-Louis-Élie Moreau de Saint-Méry, *Déscription topographique, physique, civile, politique et historique de la partie française de l'Isle Saint-Domingue* (Philadelphia: Imprimeur Libraire, 1797–1798); and *Dance: An Article Drawn from the Work of M.L.E. Moreau de St.-Méry* (1796), translated and with an introduction by Lily and Baird Hastings (New York: Dance Horizons, 1975).

6. The major writings are by Arthur de Gobineau, *Essai sur l'inégalité des races humaines* (1853–1855; reprint, Paris: Belfond, 1967), and Clémence Royer, "Du groupement des peuples et de l'Hégémonie universelle," *Journal des économistes* 6.5 (1877). Gobineau has been translated into English by Michael D. Biddiss in *Gobineau's Selected Political Writings* (New York: Harper & Row, 1970), and his works studied by Biddiss in *Father of Racist Ideology: The Social and Political Thought of Count Gobineau* (New York: Weybright & Talley, 1970). The Haitian response appears in Louis Janvier's *L'égalité des races* (1884), Anténor Firmin's *De l'égalité des races humaines* (1885), and Hannibal Price's *De la réhabilitation de la race noire* (1900).

7. Maurice Delafosse, *Haut-Sénégal-Niger* (Paris: Payot, 1911), *Les noirs de l'Afrique* (Paris: Payot, 1922), and *Les civilisations négro-africaines* (Paris: Librairie Stock, 1925).

8. Jean Price-Mars, *So Spoke the Uncle,* translated by Magdaline Shannon (Washington, D.C.: Three Continents Press, 1983). Melville Herskovits, *Life in a Haitian Valley* (1937; reprint, New York: Doubleday, 1971). Alfred Métraux, *Voodoo in Haiti* (1959; reprint, New York: Schocken, 1972). Jacques Roumain's writings on Haitian culture are summarized in Carolyn Fowler's biography *A Knot in the Thread: The Life and Works of Jacques Roumain* (Washington, D.C.: Howard University Press, 1980), 213–23.

9. Katherine Dunham, writing as Kaye Dunn, "La Boule Blanche," *Esquire* 12.3 (September 1939): 92–93, 158, and "L'ag'ya of Martinique," *Esquire* 12.5 (November 1939): 84–85, 126. Katherine Dunham, *Las danzas de Haití* (1947), published in English as *Dances of Haiti* (Los Angeles: Center for Afro-American Studies, 1983). The film footage shot in 1935–1936 is in the archives of the Dunham Fund, East Saint Louis, Illinois.

10. Joyce Aschenbrenner has reviewed the early critical response to Dunham Company performances in *Katherine Dunham, Reflections on the Social and Political Contexts of Afro-American Dance* (New York: Congress on Research in Dance, Inc., 1981). For a comprehensive history of African American dance, see Lynne Fauley Emery, *Black Dance in the United States from 1619 to 1970* (Palo Alto, Calif.: National Press Books, 1972).

11. Katherine Dunham, "Form and Function in Primitive Dance," *Educational Dance* 4.10 (October 1941): 2–4.

12. Richard Schechner, *Ritual, Play, and Performance* (New York: Seabury, 1976). Victor Turner, *Dramas, Fields, and Metaphors* (Ithaca, N.Y.: Cornell University Press, 1974). Judith Lynne Hanna, *To Dance Is Human* (Chicago: University of Chicago Press, 1974), and *Dance, Sex, and Gender* (University of Chicago Press, 1988). Robert Farris Thompson, *Flash of the Spirit* (New York: Vintage, 1983).

13. See Aschenbrenner, *Katherine Dunham,* 41–59.

14. Franziska Boas, ed., *The Function of Dance in Human Society* (New York: Dance Horizons, 1972). Includes papers from 1942 by Gorer and Courlander delivered during a seminar organized by the editor.

15. The correspondence between Melville Herskovits and Dunham (1932–1939) is in the Herskovits archives at the Africana Library of Northwestern University.

16. The "Negro Dance Evening" occurred on March 7, 1937, and included Edna Guy's Dance Spirituals and Asadata Dafora Horton's and Dunham's choreography performed by members of their respective companies. See Emery, *Black Dance,* 251–52.

17. Racial discrimination in hotels and Southern concert halls presented the major barriers as the Dunham Company toured North America. See VèVè A. Clark and Margaret B. Wilkerson, eds., *Kaiso! Katherine Dunham: An Anthology of Writings* (Berkeley, Calif.: Institute for the Study of Social Change, 1978), 37–38, 85–88.

18. VèVè A. Clark, "Katherine Dunham's *Tropical Revue,*" *Black American Literature Forum* 16.4 (Winter 1982): 147–52.

19. Letter to Melville Herskovits, September 10, 1935.

20. Frantz Fanon, *Peau noire, masques blancs* (1952), translated by Charles Lam Markmann as *Black Skin, White Masks* (New York: Grove Press, 1967).

21. The document is in the Katherine Mary Dunham Papers, Morris Library, Special Collections, Southern Illinois University, Carbondale.

22. Douglas McDermott's article "The Workers' Laboratory Theatre: Archetype and Example" provides an excellent performance history of agitprop from its inceptions in both Europe and America. See Bruce McConachie and Daniel Friedman, eds., *Theatre for Working Class Audiences in the United States, 1830–1980* (Westport, Conn.: Greenwood Press, 1985), 212–42.

23. McDermott, "The Workers' Laboratory Theatre," 123–24.

24. The reviews of the opening in Paris at the Palais de Chaillot on January 9, 1952, and subsequent critiques are from the scrapbook of Julie Robinson Belafonte. Those to which I am referring are from *L'Humanité,* a French Communist party newspaper, and other periodicals, none of which is dated.

25. Susan Leigh Foster, *Reading Dancing: Bodies and Subjects in Contemporary American Dance* (Berkeley: University of California Press, 1986), 58.

26. On the disappearances of some eleven thousand Argentineans during the 1970s, see Argentina Comisión Nacional sobre la Desaparición de Personas, *Nunca Más: The Report of the Argentine Commission on the Disappeared* (New York: Farrar, Straus & Giroux, 1986). Robert Cos has argued in "The Second Death of Perón?" (*New York Review of Books,* December 8, 1983) that the police state of Juan Perón prepared the way in the 1950s for these horrors to occur and be repressed.

27. Interview with Katherine Dunham, July 22, 1983.

28. Ibid.

29. Program notes in the Dunham Papers at Southern Illinois University, Carbondale.

30. Interview with Katherine Dunham, July 22, 1983.

31. The Dunham Company's unofficial status as artistic-cultural representatives and issues of censorship during the 1950s is related in Ruth Beckford's biography, *Katherine Dunham* (New York: Marcel Dekker, 1979), 59–60. Proof of the latter assertion will not emerge until Dunham's FBI file, if it exists, is released through the Freedom of Information Act.

32. See the column by Mason Roberson in *Daily People's World,* March 23, 1951, 5.

33. The working notes for *Southland* are in the Dunham Papers at Southern Illinois University, Carbondale; the lengthy program notes were reproduced in Clark and Wilkerson, *Kaiso! Katherine Dunham.* The action summary here is drawn from these two sources and from interviews with Katherine Dunham, July 23, 1983.

34. See note 24.

35. See Eugene Redmond, "Cultural Fusion and Spiritual Unity: Katherine Dunham's Approach to Developing Educational Community Theater," in Clark and Wilkerson, *Kaiso!,* 265–69 [reprinted herein].

Southland Program

A Dramatic Ballet in Two Scenes

KATHERINE DUNHAM

Original Scenario and Choreography by Katherine Dunham

Music by Dino di Stefano

PROLOGUE. [English translation of the prologue narrated in Spanish by Katherine Dunham at the world premiere of *Southland* in Santiago de Chile, January 1951.]

The man who truly loves his country is the man who is able to see in it the bad as well as the good, and seeing the bad, declaim it at the cost of liberty or life.

For countries are no different than men, and all men are made of good and bad, and must see these things within themselves, and strive toward the good if there is to be any upward moving.

North America is a great and wonderful country. I know it and love it from the hills of San Francisco through the prairies of the Middle West to the rugged puritanism of the eastern sea coast.

The people of North America are great and wonderful too, in their newness and youth and energy. But there is a deep stain, a mark of blood and shame which spreads from under the magnolia trees of the Southland area and mingles with the perfume of the flowers.

And though I have not smelled the smell of burning flesh, and have never seen a black body swaying from a Southern tree, I have felt these things in spirit, and finally through the creative artist comes the need of

SOURCE: Program for the world premiere of Katherine Dunham's ballet *Southland*, Teatro Municipal, Santiago de Chile, January 1951. Copyright 1951 by Katherine Dunham. Reprinted by permission.

the person to show this thing to the world, hoping that by so exposing the ill the conscience of the many will protest and save further destruction and humiliation.

This is not all of America, it is not all of the South, but it is a living, present part.

EXTRACT FROM PROGRAM NOTES. Of *Southland,* Katherine Dunham says: *"El hombre que ama verdaderamente a su patria, es aquel capaz de ver lo bueno y lo malo que hay en ella; y al descubrir lo malo, debe denunciarlo a costa de su libertad y su vida."*

This is the story of no actual lynching in the Southern states of America, and still it is the story of every one of them because behind each one lies the violence of the mob against the defenseless, and behind most of them lies the violence of anger, fear, and lust, which generates a sickness of profound guilt.

Lynching is not acceptable to the statutes of the United States of America, but stronger than these statutes is the mass hatred aroused by the girl Julie, which culminates in the lynching of Jon Lei. Jon Lei's sweetheart is Lucille Ellis, and it is Lenwood Morris who is discovered with Julie in the roots of the magnolia tree. Claudia McNeil sings "Strange Fruit." Dolores Harper sings "Basin Street Blues." The other singers are Freddye Marshall, Gordon Simpson, Milton Grayson, and Ural Wilson.

The ballet *Southland* is a comment on violence and its attendant guilt, which often acts in the human individual as the most powerful agent of destruction. In 1952 for the first time in the seventy years that such incidents have seemed newsworthy, there was no recorded lynching in the United States. Mob violence, racial hatreds continue there, however, as in many other great nations of the world. The ballet is directed, insofar as its intentions surpass purely theatrical and artistic aspirations, toward the conscience not of one nation but of all human beings who are not yet aware of the destructive dangers of hatred.

SCENE 1. The first scene is perhaps even too obvious. The Greek chorus of singers who reflect the stage action in song and mime, represent the fundamental simplicity, the earth-dignity of the Negro. At the opening of the ballet, standing before the portals of an antebellum Southern mansion, they ask with a certain amount of ironic doubt "Is it true what they say about Dixie? Does the sun really shine all the time?" One of them sings a standard concept of a Negro's nostalgia for the Suwannee River, another with the same ironic touch sings "Carry Me Back to Old Virginie." Then one steps forward to sing "Steal Away" with the ecstatic force of the true Negro spiritual and another unifies the group in the revival hymn "Dry Bones."

The Southern mansion gives way to the magnolia tree and at its base the chorus continues its observation on scenes that follow. First a group of field hands on their way to work. Then plantation square dances and the more African "Juba." Lucille and Richard, lovers, linger behind and after dancing together separate reluctantly.

The pleasant flow of the lazy magnolia-scented afternoon is interrupted by the appearance of Lenwood and Julie, who have been in an embrace behind the magnolia tree. A moment of ridicule, a reaction of resentment and the warm Southern atmosphere becomes one of violence, which leaves Julie lying unconscious under the magnolia tree after the attack of her companion. The field hands enter again. Despite the mute warnings of the chorus and the flight of his comrades, Richard remains, torn between his natural instincts to help and an awareness of the taboo situation which exists between white and Negro people in this community. When he touches the girl, she regains consciousness and, more terrified than he, cries the hated word *Nigger*. Almost immediately, however, she becomes aware of the possibilities of drama and excitement and seizes the opportunity to escape from the sordidness of her own life by becoming the heroine of a self-created saga of lust and violation. She cries for help and against a background of the denials of the boy and the chorus, tells the lie which is the determining factor in his murder.

The boy is lynched. In her solo dance, the *habanera,* the girl epitomizes the fury of all acts born of hatred and fear and guilt. She is interrupted by the growing flames, the smell of burning flesh which announce the accomplishment of the crime. The chorus watch her. It is only at the moment when the body of the lynched boy swings toward her in full view, suspended from the magnolia tree that she feels the full impact of the crime that she has committed.

Left alone, the sense of power drains from her. But, fascinated by what she sees of herself in the disfigured figure of the man, she approaches the body, rips a piece of cloth from it as a souvenir of her moment of triumph and in a deeper sense as a reminder of her guilt. Leaving, she meets the girl Lucille and for one moment falters in her bravado. The moment passes and she moves on. Lucille dances in her grief as Rosalie sings of the "strange fruit," which hangs from the limbs of the sweet-scented magnolia trees in the south. The chorus becomes the cortège of mourners which leaves with the broken body of the lynched boy.

SCENE 2. The last scene is "Basin Street" or any other street where because of color, creed or forced economic inferiority a people are relegated to enjoy in a spirit of frenzied cynicism what substitutes they may find for the deprivations of their daily lives, what compensations for its tragedies. A singer stands in a café doorway. A blind beggar passes and the street activity merges into a smoky café. At the height of the tragi-comic diversions of this urban aspect of Negro life, the passage of the chorus bearing the body of the lynched boy through the café is purely symbolic. It is inconceivable that the essential tragedy of a people could escape them, even in the midst of pleasure. The passing of the funeral cortège is that profound moment of realization of one's own tragic situation which occurs at some time or another to all of us, intensified certainly in the lives of those people, in no matter what country, who are denied full freedom to enter into and partake of every aspect of the community in which they find themselves. The cards fall from the hands of one boy—a girl weeps—another boy opens his knife and takes out his chagrin in plunging it into the floor—a couple bury themselves in the sexual embrace of a slow dance movement—another couple dance disjointedly, heedlessly, bumping into the blind beggar.

The blind beggar is the only one who sees the true fact at the moment of the passing of the cortège. Herein for me lies the true human tragedy—the rest feel but cannot define; the blind beggar at that moment has eyes and sees the true fact. He leaves seeking the answer, which all of us who love humanity seek more than ever at this moment.

Katherine Dunham's
Southland

Protest in the Face of Repression

CONSTANCE VALIS HILL

The man who truly loves his country is the man who is able to see it in the
bad as well as the good and seeing the bad declaim it, at the cost of liberty
or life.

—KATHERINE DUNHAM, prologue to *Southland*

In 1951, at the dawning of a decade that would be known for its suffocating conformity and political intolerance, Katherine Dunham created
Southland, a dramatic ballet Americana about what was by then the century-
long practice of lynching. In the program notes to the ballet, which premiered at the Teatro Municipal in Santiago de Chile, Dunham wrote,
"This is the story of no actual lynching in the Southern states of America,
and still it is the story of every one of them."[1] She spoke the prologue on
stage, in Spanish, "Though I have not smelled the smell of burning flesh,
and have never seen a black body swaying from a Southern tree, I have felt
these things in spirit. . . . Through the creative artist comes the need to
show this thing to the world, hoping that by exposing the ill, the conscience of the many will protest."[2] *Southland,* a protest as much against
lynching as against the destructive powers of hatred, was created before
the Selma march of 1965, the Freedom rides, the student sit-ins; before the
Montgomery bus boycott and the lynching of Emmett Till in 1955. Unlike

SOURCE: Constance Valis Hill, "Katherine Dunham's *Southland:* Protest in the Face
of Repression," *Dance Research Journal* 23.2 (Fall 1994): 1–10; reprinted in *Dancing
Many Drums: Excavations in African American Dance,* edited by Thomas F. DeFrantz
(Madison: University of Wisconsin Press, 2002), 289–316. Copyright 1994 by Constance Valis Hill. Reprinted by permission.

the 1960s, artistic expression in the late 1940s and 1950s provoked suspicion and outright repression. It was a time when dissent itself seemed illegitimate, subversive, un-American. The story of *Southland* tells of the consequences of social protest in the 1950s, the decade once described as "the happiest, most stable, most rational period the Western world has known since 1914."[3] But it also reveals the temperament and perhaps the very soul of protest expression rooted in the African American political struggle, an expression that was for Dunham both a public act and private *rite de passage,* affirming how dancing is a healing process as well as a political act.

THE 1940S

In the postwar years, Dunham was at the height of a stage and film career that had been launched on Broadway with *Cabin in the Sky* in 1940. Fame seemed limitless for the woman most remembered as "decked out in singular hats and dresses, daring to wear feathers, bright colors, soft fabrics,"[4] though the woman who was making brilliant-textured transformations of indigenous Caribbean dances was still limited by racial discrimination. There was the ongoing critical debate as to whether she was a serious artist or a popularizer, whether comment and integrity in her work were "sacrificed to conform to what Broadway expected the Negro dance to be."[5] There was Dunham's perennial double-image, in which she was simultaneously viewed as "the hottest thing" on Broadway and "an intelligent anthropologist of note."[6] Perpetual intimations of a split personality appeared in such headlines as "Schoolmarm Turned Siren," "Torridity to Anthropology," "Cool Scientist or Sultry Performer?" and "High Priestess of Jive."[7] However, the clever phrases invented to cheapen her talent and tarnish her beauty diminished neither her popularity nor her creative output. The Katherine Dunham School of Dance and Theater opened in New York in 1944 and through the 1940s—from club work at Ciro's in Hollywood and the Martinique Club in New York to musicals in Chicago and performances in Mexico City, London, Paris, and Rome—Dunham and her company of singers, dancers, and musicians were on what seemed a perpetual tour across America and around the world.

Touring did not keep Dunham out of touch but instead only heightened her awareness of America where, simultaneous with the optimism of postwar prosperity, there was the ever-presence of Jim Crow in transportation, education, and public accommodation. Though lynching was rampant and went without condemnation in the South during the 1930s, it declined in the 1940s. However, violence continued against blacks, countless and perpetual acts of violence that were part of an overall pattern of retaliation against postwar egalitarianism.[8] From 1936 to 1946, forty-three lynchings of mostly Southern blacks were reported, though the lynchings went unprosecuted. The most notorious lynchings were the 1944 drowning of a fifteen-year-old black youth in the Suwannee River, an act that the boy's father was forced to witness, and the quadruple killing in 1946 of two black men and two black women in Monroe, Georgia.[9]

America's fight against Nazism and Fascism abroad highlighted the hypocrisy of racism at home and provided a catalyst for African Americans, whose long-suppressed anger and outrage sought new expressions of protest. In dance, for the most part, social protest was accepted. About her 1943 solo *Strange Fruit,* an interpretation of the Lewis Allan poem[10] that presented the residual emotions of a woman who witnessed a lynching, Pearl Primus recalls, "In the forties you could protest, in fact, I was most encouraged."[11] Primus openly stated at that time that the "'Negro problem,' so-called, in reality was a problem of democracy" and asserted that as people in other countries fought against Hitler's suppression of minorities, so they needed to fight against fascist ideas in the United States.[12] Talley Beatty, whose 1947 *Southern Landscape* dealt with the terrorization of black and white sharecroppers in the South during the Reconstruction, confirms, "I thought everybody back then was doing protest dances."[13] Nor was Dunham a stranger to political activism during the thirties and forties. Touring in a segregated society such as America's presented problems she faced head on, from curtain speeches to segregated audiences to a staunch insistence in finding decent housing for her company. "There comes a time when every human being must protest in order to retain human dignity," Dunham announced to a segregated audience in Louisville in 1944, explaining she would not return but that she hoped the war abroad for tolerance and democracy would change things in America.[14] Sometimes there were outrageous confrontations, such as the story company members tell about how Dunham, in a segregated theater in the South, turned around and showed her rear end to the audience, saying, "Until people like me can sit with people like you," the company could not and would not perform.[15]

However, by the late 1940s the times were changing, as overt expressions of dissent were suddenly construed as being politically incorrect. The political climate was chilling with the Cold War and a new Red Scare so powerful that many social causes identified with liberal principles could be tarred with the fatal brush of being called subversive. The politics of anti-Communism exerted such a cooling effect on all progressive causes that even blacks in government who actively opposed segregation were accused of disloyalty.[16] In 1949, the House Committee on Un-American Activities (HUAC) continued to investigate members of the movie industry and then escalated its assault against Paul Robeson, who in bold counterattack challenged HUAC's "ominous silence" in the face of the continued lynchings of black citizens.[17] Katherine Dunham was abroad with her company at the time, but she was neither safe from nor immune to the onslaught of news from America that both haunted and assaulted her.

She remembers hearing about the lynching of an American Southern black youth and, during an airplane ride over the Nile River, she wrote, "The mud that turns in the Mississippi, is it able to cover those black bodies, or would any river do?"[18] In a bar in Genoa, company members were threatened and insulted with racial slurs by American sailors in an incident that brought them late to a cocktail party given by Ambassador Pell. And in the summer of 1950 in Brazil, Dunham was denied entry into one of the better hotels because she was black, a bitter reminder of the pervasiveness of color prejudice.[19] It was the fall of 1950, the aftermath of the Eighty-first Congress which became the graveyard for the NAACP's thirty-two-year fight for federal anti-lynching legislation. In response to this travesty, Langston Hughes's character Simple, expressing the reactions of the black community, declared the federal government could find the means to pass espionage and security legislation, "yet cannot and will not and won't pass no bill to keep me from getting lynched if I ever look cross-eyed at a white man when I go down south."[20] It was amidst hearing news about the trials of the Martinsville Seven and Willie McGhee, in which black youths in Virginia and Mississippi convicted of raping a white woman were sentenced to death,[21] that Dunham's response to America from afar took shape in *Southland*.

THE MAKING OF A PROTEST DANCE

Commissioned by the Symphony of Chile, and with a premiere in Santiago set for January 1951, *Southland* was researched, composed, choreographed, designed, and rehearsed in the last months of 1950 in Buenos Aires.[22] The musical score by Dino di Stefano, a Jesuit priest based in Argentina, was an orchestral arrangement of African-American spirituals, blues music, and popular American songs. Designed by John Pratt, Dunham's husband and artistic collaborator, the set's centerpiece was a sprawling magnolia tree in full bloom that evoked the warm and sunny American South. However, while Dunham, speaking the prologue, praised America for its youthfulness, she probed its dark underside: "There is a deep stain, a mark of blood and shame which spreads from under the magnolia trees of the southland area and mingles with the perfume of the flowers. This is not all of America. It is not all of the South, but it is a living, present part."[23]

The curtain opens on a chorus standing before the portals of an antebellum Southern mansion.[24] "Is it true what they say about Dixie? Does the sun really shine all the time?" they sing, and the mock nostalgia of "Swanee River" and "Carry Me Back to Old Virginie" contrasts with the ecstatic force of the spirituals "Steal Away" and "Dry Bones."[25] The Southern mansion gives way to the magnolia tree where field hands on their way to work dance a suite of plantation dances, leaving behind a pair of lovers, Lucy and Richard. Their tender *pas de deux,* in which he reaches her up into the tree to pluck a magnolia blossom, combined dramatic gesture with dance movement. What Dunham described as "a mixture of mime and motion" in her dance drama was an ingenious mixing of fact and fiction. She meticulously researched the history of lynching in the United States by consulting the records on file at the Tuskegee Institute. She then wrote a detailed scenario and working script, complete with dialogue written in Southern dialect, as the following segment from the "Love Scene" for Lucy and Richard demonstrates:

HE: Lucy.
SHE: Huh?
HE: Come ova heah, Lucy.
SHE: (*small cry of joy as she dances to him*) Oh.
HE: Love ain't a big enough word for what I has for you, gal. (*When she is in his arms*) De Whol' worl' ain't big enough to hol' it. (*When she reaches for flowers*) Here, gal, let a big fella help wid dat. (*Carries her to flowers*)[26]

The script was used by dancers for rehearsal and discarded when the dialogue was replaced with motivated action. The names of the characters in the script were the actual names of the dancers playing them—the characters of Lucy and Richard, for example, played by company members

Lucille Ellis and Ricardo Avalos. The dance movement was created through a collaborative rehearsal process in which Dunham worked with dancers onstage while di Stefano composed at the piano. Newly choreographed scenes were supplemented with well-known dances from the company repertory. The square dances and patting jubas in the opening plantation scene, for example, were longstanding numbers from Dunham's Americana suite from the 1930s and 1940s. Dunham's dance drama, then, recontextualized historical "facts" and dancers' biographies, new dramatic choreography and old musical numbers, thereby enabling dancers to more truthfully internalize, or embody, the materials. To borrow dance scholar VèVè Clark's term, it was a kind of "method dancing" that motivated a complete transformation into the world of "the play," a play that was a thinly disguised exposé of truth.[27]

After the "Love Scene," Lucy and Richard separate and a white couple, Julie and Lenwood, tumble out from behind the magnolia tree. The role of Julie was played by the only white dancer in the company, Julie Robinson, with a bleach-blonde streak down her long brown hair to represent Southern white society; the role of her boyfriend Lenwood was played by Lenwood Morris, wearing a red wig and whitened makeup. Julie and Lenwood are drunk, and he takes her teasing as a sexual insult. Chasing her around the tree, he catches her by the hair and in the ensuing *apache*-styled duet, he beats her viciously, strutting away like a proud cock to leave her unconscious. Julie is discovered by the field hands who flee in fear, though Richard remains. He lifts her head, and she opens her eyes to see his face. In that moment, between feeling the humiliation of being discovered in that state and recognizing the opportunity to capitalize on it, Julie decides to makes him the perpetrator of her attack. Pointing an accusing finger, she cries out the word "Nigger!" and skillfully draws in an imaginary crowd, inciting them to believe she's been raped. Dancing a *habanera,* she strips her blouse, whips her hair and then twists it around her neck to advocate his lynching. Trapped by this imaginary crowd-turned-lynch-mob, Richard cowers on the ground in complete animal fear. He mimes being kicked offstage by the white mob, moving into an offstage pool of red light. Onstage, Julie dances herself into a fury born of hatred, fear, and guilt as, offstage, the pool of flaming red light intensifies as the mob hangs and burns the black man. It is only when Richard's body, swinging by his neck from a branch of the magnolia tree,[28] swoops toward her in full view that Julie feels the full impact of her lie. Fascinated by what she sees of herself in the disfigured body, she rips off a piece of Richard's charred shirt and on her exit, meets Lucy face-to-face: one woman clutches the burnt cloth, the other holds the magnolia blossom. The chorus, turning into a cortège of mourners, gathers up the remains of the body as Lucy dances a searing adagio solo that is filled with back-spiraling descents to the floor and recovers. Ellis recalls that Dunham, coaching her, said, "Lucille, feel you are that child again and you just lost something you had, come out completely limp and innocent."[29] Lucy dances and weeps; and in her final descent, she wraps herself around the legs of Claudia McNeil, who sings:

> Southern trees bear a strange fruit,
> Blood at the leaves and blood at the root,
> Black bodies swaying in the southern breeze,
> Strange fruit hanging from the poplar trees.
>
> Pastoral scene of the gallant south,
> The bulging eye and the twisted mouth,
> Scent of magnolia sweet and fresh,
> Then the sudden smell of burning flesh.
>
> Here is a fruit for the crows to pluck,
> For the rain to gather, for the wind to suck,
> For the sun to rot, for the trees to drop.
> Here is a strange and bitter crop.[30]

The second scene opens with the "Basin Street Blues" and takes place, writes Dunham in the scenario, on "any street where, because of color, creed or forced inferiority, people are relegated to the frenzied cynicism that substitutes for the deprivations of their daily lives."[31] In a smoky café inhabited by couples dancing, men gambling, and a blind man begging,[32] the funeral cortège passes bearing the body of the lynched man. Singing a funeral dirge, the chorus moves across the stage dragging Lucy, whose arms are wrapped around the legs of the bass singer. For a moment, every-one is motionless. Then cards fall from the hands of a gambler, a woman weeps silently, and couples tighten their embrace to grind slowly and dis-jointedly, like somnambulists; while a man opens his knife and continues to plunge it into the floor, retrieve it, and plunge it again.[33] The blind man suddenly stands straight up. "Seeing" what the others feel but cannot de-fine, he follows the funeral procession, "seeking the answer which all of us who love humanity seek more than ever at this moment."[34]

The Public Response

It was not only the graphic depiction of a black man swinging by his neck from the end of a rope that made *Southland* so shocking; as Dunham says, "It was the whole thing."[35] She remembers on opening night that some in the audience wept while others, members of the diplomatic corps, sat rigid. If the ballet ended on a note of mournful resignation, with the field hands carrying off the body, would Dunham have gotten the response she was delivered the next morning? A reporter from the Communist newspaper, who asked to secretly meet her in the hotel garden, told her that the review that he wrote of *Southland* was the only review she would receive in Santiago. Every newspaper in Chile depended on America for newsprint, he explained, and members of the press were "informed" that all newsprint would be withdrawn if anyone dared to write about *Southland*. It wasn't only the explicit violence of the first scene that was intimidating, but also the implicit threat of violence in the second scene. Dunham remarks about the last scene in *Southland:*

> If you were at all sensitive, you would pick up this thread of violence. The guy with the knife—a 1960s type—and the crap players, they were mean; they wouldn't take it very long. And we do get the feeling of something going to happen, not the feeling it's hopeless. I should think that any white person, whether they belonged in that setting or not, would feel particularly uneasy.[36]

It was January, 1951, ten months after Senator Joseph McCarthy claimed there were 205 known Communists in the State Department.[37] That an American artist, a black woman in a foreign country known for its strong Communist base and anti-American sentiment, had dared to expose America's darkest side, was a flagrant betrayal of her country. This action appeared totally out of character for Katherine Dunham so often perceived as the glamorous entertainer. She recalls, "People who thought I was having such a success as a figurehead goddess, whatever that was, couldn't understand how I could do a thing like that on stage."

The paranoia aroused at the American embassy in Chile—which was under the ambassadorship of Claude G. Bowers, whose 1929 book *The Tragic Era* justified the Ku Klux Klan as being organized "for the protection of women, property, civilization itself."[38]—can only be imagined. While reprisal on the part of the State Department was indeed insidious, it was at first invisible. *Southland* was immediately suppressed in Santiago:

the company was forced to leave within days. There were no more reviews, nothing more was written, and nothing was publicly said; what followed was a cold and sustained silence. Dunham had been warned, after all, by officials who attended rehearsals in Santiago to remove "the lynching scene." Since she insisted on presenting the ballet as conceived and rehearsed, there would be no more calls or invitations from the members of the embassy who had wined and dined her. The intention of the ensuing silence was to pretend that *Southland* never happened. Nevertheless, word about the ballet traveled quickly over the Andes. When the company returned to Argentina, there was also a cold silence from the embassy in Buenos Aires, and it was a silence Dunham clearly understood. In the company's second command performance in Buenos Aires for Eva Perón, *Southland* was not performed, nor was it performed the rest of 1951 during the company's tour through South America, nor in all of 1952. "Dunham's whim," as her impresarios deemed it, was a financial hazard that was to be avoided.

However, by the end of 1952, in preparation for the company's Paris season, rehearsals for *Southland* started again in Genoa, Italy. Anticipating criticism and possible repression, Dunham sent John Pratt ahead to inform the American embassy in Paris that she intended to perform the ballet. Arriving in Paris with the company, Dunham was besieged by members of the press who wanted to know more about her "lynching ballet." They knew she had been heavily criticized and ousted in Santiago, and they asked Dunham what she thought the Americans might do if she performed *Southland* in Paris. A few days before the opening, Dunham tried to see American ambassador James Clement Dunn, but he was supposedly out of town. She spoke instead with his cultural attaché, who reportedly told Dunham, "We trust you and your personal good taste, and we know that you wouldn't do anything to upset the American position in the rest of the world." Pressing for a definitive answer as to whether or not she should present *Southland*, Dunham says, "He wouldn't go any farther. So I did it."

Southland opened at the Palais de Chaillot on 9 January 1953 to a swarm of radically bipartisan reactions. There were praises by the French Communist newspaper *L'Humanité* for the ballet's remarkable powers of expression and its contribution to "the emancipation of the blacks by rising against the racist assassins," and complaints by the conservative *Le Monde* that "Katherine Dunham had changed since those wonderful evenings in Paris. . . . What has happened to the anthropologist we once admired?"[39] A *Paris Presse* review refused to even acknowledge Dunham's creation of *Southland*.

The critical responses, as she later wrote, sounded to Dunham like "the repeated rhythm of an out-of-gear piece of machinery" and ranged from pronouncements such as "cerebralism," "Sorbonnism," and "betraying racial origins in emphasizing the orchestra instead of the tam-tam" to "beauty," "unforgettable theatre," "courage," and "going beyond the folkloric and anecdotal into the realm of classicism."[40] While *Southland* marshaled criticism from radio commentators, who advised Dunham not to show blacks hanging on the stage, several of the Communist newspapers felt she hadn't gone far enough to show her anger and wanted to see the burning of the body on stage.

There were as many congratulations as criticisms for Dunham's breaking away from the limiting categories that had been placed on her by the French. However, she was deeply grieved by the criticism, especially from her friend the noted art historian and critic Bernard Berenson, who saw the production in Paris. Berenson's rejection of *Southland* symbolized the American response: "I know and respect all of your feeling towards the State, many of which I have," Dunham wrote in a response to Berenson after the Paris opening, "but I have not been approached by either Communists or the Communist press who I believe do not see anything, either in the ballet or in the material, for anti-American usage. . . . In my heart of hearts . . . I know this has done more good for the American government than perhaps even they know. It has proven to the world that the thing of which they are being accused every day, due to the acts of such people as Senator McCarthy, has not yet become a fact and that freedom of speech still remains one of our basic principles."[41]

Southland was never again performed after the Paris production. Dunham says, "I didn't do it after Paris. I was personally spent. I didn't have the spiritual strength, because it takes that." She was burned out, not only from battling critics but from fighting her own company who, she discovered, never wanted to perform *Southland:* "I was surprised at their reaction because they didn't want me to do it at all. Their idea in leaving America was to lose any feelings of racial difference, to try to forget what the whole thing was about. And when I first mentioned it, they asked why was I doing it. They had never really known me, I discovered." Dunham remembers talking to the company, for days that seemed like an eternity, about a situation they had shut their eyes to. She explains: "It's not easy to take a company who had defended themselves all their lives, and then been protected because of the constant touring, from the indignities of their color. They felt they were untouchable and were afraid of losing that.

And this took them down to the very bottom, to a reality they felt they had never known."[42]

However, members of the company had a different perspective. "Why bother getting into something so deep when everything was fine, the ballets we were doing were expressive enough," says Lucille Ellis, who joined Dunham's company in 1938. "We were not ready to go into anything that was racial because it was back to a history we wanted to rest. Paris had accepted us, we weren't going to change the world."[43] Ellis remembers that when Dunham explained to the company who the principals were, how the characters would react to each other and that Julie Robinson was going to play a white girl, "all of a sudden, some members of the company realized that Julie was white—they never thought about that before."[44]

Says Julie Robinson Belafonte about creating the role of the "white trash" girl, "The only way I could do it, because I almost didn't, was to analyze it as an acting problem and transpose my hatred of this person I'm playing into the character."[45] It was the word "nigger"—the only word spoken in the ballet and by Julie—that triggered hostility and confusion within the company. At a midnight rehearsal, which the entire company witnessed, Belafonte remembers how Dunham, directing the moment when Julie opens her eyes and sees Richard, said, "All right, open your eyes and you're in shock. All of a sudden, you could be somebody. And you start to think how you could use this situation. You've got it, you're going to accuse him of rape and tell everybody a lie. Yes. Now with all your everything, and in an accusing way, scream out 'Nigger.'"[46]

There was no way Robinson could say the word out loud; weeping, she begged Dunham to let her find a way to get the word across without speaking it. "When the word finally came out, I couldn't believe it was coming from my own body," says Belafonte. It was only when she overheard a dancer remark, "Do you hear the way she says 'Nigga'? Nobody would say it that way if they didn't really mean it,"[47] that she realized how *Southland* forced members of the company into an awareness of their own color prejudices and fears. "It meant that color came into play, shades of color," Lucille Ellis explains, "because some dancers were white and some were lighter than others: And then Julie and I had to stay apart in rehearsals to acclimate to our roles because we weren't those same people. And she was afraid to hurt my feelings and I was afraid to hurt hers. We were all walking on eggs."[48]

Most difficult was that right after performing *Southland,* the company on the same program had to turn around and perform a lighter piece from the repertory, like *Minuet* or *Cakewalk*. Ellis remembers, "Out of the depths of hell, we were coming back to 'Oh, fine,' and the transition of personal emotions was very difficult."[49] *Southland* put a strain on the entire company. They worried about whether they could do it, whether or not they were doing the right thing, whether it would ruin the company's reputation, whether it would ruin Dunham. Says Ellis: "*Southland* took our security blanket away. If we were run out of the country, where would we be? We were in limbo. Until finally, we said we can fight it—we can do what we want to do, because this is what it's all about. And that's how we all came together."[50]

The Aftermath

Though she was never called before the House Committee on Un-American Activities, Dunham was not spared the most devastating of reprisals from the State Department. In the 1950s, when the U.S. State Department began sending representative American artists abroad as cultural diplomats—a policy that was, ironically, a direct outgrowth of the Cold War—Dunham was continually denied both support and subsidy and never chosen to officially represent the United States.

In 1954, the José Limón Dance Company was chosen as the first State Department–sponsored dance touring company to perform in South America. In Montevideo, the Limón company's opening was booked on the same evening as Dunham's opening. It was a seeming surprise to the embassy, who hosted a cocktail party for Limón to which Dunham was not invited, and who insisted that Dunham's impresario attend the Limón premiere and forgo Dunham's. In Greece, with an engagement next in Lebanon, Dunham learned that the State Department had almost succeeded in getting the theater owner in Lebanon to say the theater was occupied, which would have made the company sit for days in Greece at their own expense until the day before the Lebanon performance.[51]

In San Francisco in 1955, from the high cost of keeping the company going and dancers decently housed to exorbitant fees that had to be paid to the theater and musicians' unions, Dunham faced her company's greatest financial crisis. "I have been closer these days than ever to complete annihilation," she wrote to Berenson. "When we arrive in New York, I shall put my case before the proper authorities and try to obtain some sort of government aid."[52] Still battling segregation, she began a lawsuit against the landlords who leased an apartment to Dunham and Pratt and then changed their minds after discovering they were an interracial couple "disgracing their respective races."[53] Dunham changed her mind on the lawsuit, thinking it petty compared to the recent lynching in Mississippi of Emmett Till, which, along with the other difficulties encountered in San Francisco, had led her to believe that very little had changed since *Southland:* "I am thoroughly discouraged by and about America and what is happening here,"[54] she wrote.

In Australia in 1956, a representative of the Chinese Opera invited Dunham to visit the People's Republic of China. The invitation was an honor as well as a breakthrough in cultural relations, while it also provided a convenient continuation in travel for the company with subsequent engagements in Manila and Tokyo. Dunham's request to go to China was obstinately refused by the U.S. embassy, which told her she could go if she was willing to give up her passport and pay $10,000 fine for each company member. Dunham reasons, "I think it was because they would not want anything as attractive as a black company, as we were, to go. It would give us too much prestige." It wasn't until the late sixties that American contact with China resumed. At that time, it was claimed that a United States table tennis team made the first breakthrough in communication with Red China.

In the sixties, the State Department continued to give Dunham the excuse that the company was too large and therefore too expensive to sponsor. Dunham, to no avail, offered to send as few as five dancers and two pianos abroad, despite the fact that Alvin Ailey's company of dancers, singers, and musicians toured the Far East and Australia for thirteen weeks in 1962. Duke Ellington's orchestra was treated to an extravagant State Department–sponsored tour through Europe and the Middle East in 1963.[55] For Dunham, these inconsistent policies, embarrassing oversights, and reports that she was under a secret investigation by the F.B.I., indicated an intentional blackballing. "I had fallen from grace. I never had aid from the State Department. I had all sorts of encouragement and cocktail parties wherever we went, but never financial aid."[56] Physically exhausted and financially bankrupt, the Katherine Dunham Dance Company gave its last performance at New York's Apollo Theatre in 1965.

PROTEST AS A SEARCH FOR IDENTITY

Artistic confrontation and struggle is a way of life; it is neither a badge pinned on and taken off nor a placard carried and put down. Dunham's commitment "to expose the ill so that the conscience of the many will protest," is a deep one, as she wrote to Berenson about *Southland:* "Somewhere in me are roots stronger than I am based more on intuition than reason, and which walk hand-in-hand with my own will and judgment so that I seldom falter in an act, and if I do I am almost always regretting and ashamed.[57] Not to confront, not to respond to the social injustices of her people, was to sin: it was a lesson Dunham learned early in childhood, when in a courtroom she unwittingly abetted in the loss of a custody suit between members of her family and bitterly learned that "there is no absolution in innocence and even unwilling collaboration was at least stupidity, which has no place in uprightness; and that betrayal of the trust of others and pride of self is more guilt-engendering than just plain, willful sinning."[58]

Propelled by a search for truth, *Southland* is rooted in the African American struggle for self-definition in a society that has often refused to acknowledge its humanity. From the innocent Lucy to the trusting field hand Richard; from the gospel-like chorus to the "seeing" blind man searching for answers; from the Basin Street Blues people, who absorb the tragic lynching through the sheer power of their dancing, and the knife thrower who fiercely refutes it, to the chorus who in the end is practically triumphant, the characters in *Southland* struggle to confront and transcend their historical restrictions in an attempt to affirm meaning in their lives. They refuse to allow the racist perception of black humanity to be reduced to the sum total of their brutalization.[59] They are what made *Southland* such a powerful protest expression.

Dunham wrote to Berenson, "I have turned every possible searchlight and inner eye on *Southland* and I must say I feel absolutely innocent. It was a thing to me of great beauty, an expression of the passion in me. I grieved the unkind remarks, but I would have more deeply grieved had I betrayed myself."[60] The act of creating *Southland* was absolutely crucial to Dunham's well-being, just as the act of performing it was to her dancers, however painful it was. Dunham believes that "a person who dances should know why they dance, and to do so, they must have an historical background.[61] Dancing is a way to knowing, hence it is an affirmation of self and of one's culture. The "fiction" of *Southland,* the artwork itself, becomes the healing agent for the more brutal "fact" of it. As Lucille Ellis confirms for the company, "*Southland* was the beginning of knowing the quality of life and the human element. It made us all respect life and people. It made you feel you must do something. And in the doing, you finally begin to find yourself."

Southland was silenced, though Dunham was not. Nor were those she touched. "She was my Toussaint l'Ouverture," Talley Beatty says about the woman who made him a dancer and gave him the courage to choreograph from the center of his own experience. Though *Southland* was suppressed, and never even performed in the United States, its fierce spirit and bold theatrical form prefigured such black protest expressions of the late 1950s and 1960s as Beatty's *Road of the Phoebe Snow,* Donald McKayle's *Rainbow 'round My Shoulder,* Eleo Pomare's *Blues for the Jungle,* and Alvin Ailey's *Masekela Language.* These protest expressions by African-American artists followed Dunham's conviction: "Your daring has to backed up with a willingness to lose that point. To make a bigger point, you might have to lose one. I like to avoid confrontations if I can. But if I cannot, I want to be totally prepared to solve them or eliminate them, one way or another."

Although *Southland* instigated the dissolution of Dunham's company, it laid the moral groundwork for subsequent expressions of affirmation and dissent and will forever embolden all those who dare to protest in the face of repression.

NOTES

1. Katherine Dunham, Program: *Southland* in Santiago de Chile, World Premiere, January 1951, in *Kaiso! Katherine Dunham: An Anthology of Writings,* edited by VèVè A. Clark and Margaret B. Wilkerson (Berkeley: Institute for the Study of Social Change, 1978), 118.

2. Ibid.

3. Quoted by Leon F. Litwack, "The Nifty Fifties" in *Advancing American Art: Painting, Politics and Cultural Confrontation at Mid-Century,* ed. Taylor D. Littleton and Maltby Sykes (Tuscaloosa: University of Alabama Press, 1989), 2. Litwack does not identify the writer except to say that his observation was published in *Commentary.*

4. Clark and Wilkerson, "Dunham the Woman: Perspectives," in *Kaiso!,* ed. Clark and Wilkerson, 5.

5. John Martin, "The Dance: *Tropical Review,*" *New York Times,* 26 September 1943, sec 2, p. 2.

6. Katherine Dunham, "Thesis Turned Broadway," in *Kaiso!,* ed. Clark and Wilkerson, 55.

7. John Martin, "The Dance: Schoolmarm Turned Siren or Vice Versa in *Bal Nègre* at the Belasco," *New York Times,* 17 November 1946, sec 2, p. 9; "Torridity to Anthropology," *Newsweek* (27 January 1941): 62; "Cool Scientist or Sultry Performer?" *Dance Magazine* (May 1947): 11; "High Priestess of Jive," in Katherine Dunham, Scrapbooks: Clippings, Programs and Photographs, vol. 5, 1937–1949, Jerome Robbins Dance Division, New York Public Library for the Performing Arts.

8. Howard Smead, *Blood Justice* (New York: Oxford University Press, 1986), xii. The Tuskegee Institute conservatively reports that between 1937 and 1946, two hundred blacks were rescued from threatened lynchings, twenty-one blacks alone in 1946; see *Crimes against Lynching: Hearings before a Subcommittee of the Committee on the Judiciary United States Senate* (Washington: U.S. Government Printing Office, 1948), 50.

9. The January 1944 lynching of an unnamed fifteen-year-old Negro youth in the Suwannee River, and the quadruple lynching of Roger Malcolm, Malcolm's wife, George Dorsey, and Dorsey's wife in Monroe, Georgia, on 20 July 1946 are cited in *Crimes against Lynching*, 50.

10. The poem "Strange Fruit" was written in 1938 by Abel Meeropol, a Jewish schoolteacher and union activist from the Bronx. When he set it to music in 1940, he used the pseudonym Lewis Allan.

11. Pearl Primus, telephone interview with the author, 23 March 1993.

12. Primus, in 1944, quoted by Bragiotti and cited in Beverly Hillman Barber, "Pearl Primus: Rebuilding America's Cultural Infrastructure," in *African American Genius in Modern Dance*, edited by Gerald E. Myers (Durham, N.C.: American Dance Festival, 1993), 10.

13. Talley Beatty, telephone interview with the author, 2 July 1992. Beatty was one of the nine original dancers in Dunham's dance company; *Southern Landscape* was created after Beatty left Dunham to form his own group.

14. "Miss Dunham's Comment to the Louisville Audience at Memorial Auditorium, October 19, 1944," in *Kaiso!*, ed. Clark and Wilkerson, 88.

15. Julie Robinson Belafonte, interview with the author, 14 April 1993. "People forget," writes Agnes DeMille about Dunham, "Now people can go anywhere, stay anywhere, but in the thirties and early forties, it was terrible for blacks, particularly on tour. . . . Every city she went to posed the same problem: how should she house and protect her company and keep them out of dreadful rooming houses and filthy hotels. . . . The dimensions of this persistent problem and the amount of trouble it caused her have never been discussed, but they were significant" (*Portrait Gallery* [New York: Houghton Mifflin, 1990], 45).

16. William H. Chafe writes that any program that deviated from a 100 percent conservative Americanism might have been attacked as reflecting a Moscow party line: "If you believed in civil rights, you were critical of America's racial customs and therefore an ally of those who, from abroad, also criticized American racism" (*The Unfinished Journey: America since World War II* [New York: Oxford University Press, 1991], 108).

17. Martin Duberman's *Paul Robeson* (New York: Knopf, 1988) provides a detailed account of Robeson and the 1949 Peekskill riots.

18. Katherine Dunham, interview with the author, 29 January 1993, East Saint Louis, Illinois.

19. VèVè A. Clark, "Katherine Dunham: Method Dancing or the Memory of Difference," in *African American Genius in Modern Dance*, ed. Myers, 8.

20. Langston Hughes, in Robert Zangrando, *The NAACP Crusade against Lynching, 1909–1950* (Philadelphia: Temple University Press, 1980), 204.

21. On 2 February 1951, the seven black defendants known as the Martinsville

Seven—Joe Henry Hampton, Howard Hairston, Booker Millner, Frank Hairston, John Taylor, James Hairston, and Francis Grayson—were executed at Richmond, Virginia, for allegedly having raped a white woman. On 8 May of the same year, Willie McGee was executed by the state of Mississippi, after having been convicted of raping a white woman, Mrs. Willamette Hawkins. Though evidence indicated Hawkins forced McGee into a relationship he later tried to sever, once the charge of rape had been raised, Mississippi was incapable of legitimizing the concept that a white woman sought a sexual relationship with a black male. The racist stereotype of the black rapist served to justify execution of black defendants who had been convicted in trials that mocked proper judicial procedures. Herbert Shapiro, *White Violence and Black Response* (Amherst: University of Massachusetts Press, 1988), documents the chilling details of McGee's trial and execution. Dunham remembers following the news of the trials, which lasted from 1949 to 1951. By March of 1950 the seven youths, who were convicted in Virginia on 8 January 1949, were in the midst of applying for a change of venue, the details of which are documented in *Hampton v. Commonwealth*, 58 South Eastern Reporter, 2d Series, 290.

22. Dunham dancer Lucille Ellis recalls that *Southland* was produced by special arrangement with the Symphony of Chile and performed on the company's day off. Dunham arranged to have the theater open, prepared a special concert of three premieres (*Southland* and two shorter dances) and the audience invited through special invitation. "It was regal—the embassy and all the dignitaries were there," said Ellis in a telephone interview with the author, 8 June 1993.

23. Program: *Southland* in Santiago de Chile, in *Kaiso!*, ed. Clark and Wilkerson, 117.

24. The singers in the chorus included Freddye Marshall, Gordon Simpson, Milton Grayson, Ural Wilson, Claudia McNeill, and Delores Harper and acted as what Dunham described as a "Greek chorus" reflecting the action in song and mime.

25. The program, prologue, and scenario for *Southland* are reprinted in *Kaiso!*, ed. Clark and Wilkerson, 117–20. Details of the ballet were recounted during the author's interview with Katherine Dunham, 29 January 1993 in East Saint Louis, during which time Ms. Dunham described the action of the ballet while playing a tape of di Stefano's musical score. Unless otherwise indicated, descriptions of the ballet come from the interview with Ms. Dunham.

26. Katherine Dunham, unpublished script for *Southland*.

27. "Method dancing" is aptly termed and elaborated on in VèVè Clark's article in *African American Genius in Modern Dance*, ed. Myers, 5–8.

28. Ricardo was literally swung by the neck onto the stage; Dunham remembers on opening night, "He was dying for air and choking," because the stage hand forgot to put on his harness.

29. Lucille Ellis, telephone interview with author, 8 June 1993.

30. Lewis Allan (pseudonym of Abel Meeropol), "Strange Fruit" (1938); music and lyrics copyright 1940 by Estate of Abel Meeropol. Reprinted by permission. The song "Strange Fruit" was made popular by Billie Holliday. Lillian Smith's best-selling novel *Strange Fruit* (1944) dealt with the topic of interracial sex and romance, not rape, and caused quite a sensation.

31. Katherine Dunham, Program: *Southland,* in *Kaiso!,* ed. Clark and Wilkerson, 120.

32. The character of the blind man in the Santiago production was played by a Haitian priest by the name of Sisemone, who also drummed for Dunham's dance company.

33. After the chorus's dirge, the music changes back to jazz, but it's in a minor tone. Dunham says, "It was never perfected, they should do what they're doing but with an understanding of the futility of their situation. It should have hatred in it, like the knife that showed it" (Interview with the author, 29 January 1993).

34. Ibid. Julie Robinson Belafonte adds that "the character of the blind man is one of searching for answers." Belafonte, interview with the author, 14 April 1993.

35. Katherine Dunham, interview with the author, 29 January 1993.

36. Unless otherwise indicated, all remarks by Katherine Dunham in this section are from her interview with the author, 29 January 1993.

37. Athan Theoharis, *Seeds of Repression* (Chicago: Quadrangle Books, 1971), 16.

38. Claude G. Bowers, *The Tragic Era: The Revolution after Lincoln* (Boston: Houghton, Mifflin, 1929), 309. Bowers (1878–1958) was the United States ambassador to Chile from 1939 to 1953.

39. Gilbert Bloch, *L'Humanité,* 10 January 1953; Dinah Maggie, *Le Monde,* 12 January 1953.

40. Katherine Dunham, unpublished letter to Bernard Berenson, 1 February 1953.

41. Ibid.

42. Dunham, interview with the author, 29 January 1993.

43. Ellis, telephone interview with author, 8 June 1993.

44. Ibid.

45. Belafonte, interview with the author, 14 April 1993.

46. Ibid.

47. Ibid.

48. Ellis, telephone interview with the author, 8 June 1993.

49. Ibid.

50. Ibid.

51. The State Department incidents related by Dunham during her interview with the author are substantiated by Ruth Beckford in *Katherine Dunham: A Biography* (New York: Marcel Dekker, 1979), 58–62.

52. Dunham, unpublished letter to Bernard Berenson, 12 October 1955.

53. Ibid.

54. Ibid.

55. See Duke Ellington's "Notes on the State Department Tour" in *Music Is My Mistress* (New York: Doubleday, 1973), 305.

56. Dunham, interview with author, 29 January 1993.

57. Dunham, unpublished letter to Bernard Berenson, 1 February 1953.

58. Katherine Dunham, *A Touch of Innocence* (New York: Harcourt, Brace & World, 1959), 66.

59. I am very much taken with James H. Cone's argument, in his discussion of the blues, that it is only through the "real" or "disclosed" in concrete human affairs that a

community can attain authentic existence, and that "insofar as the Blues affirm the somebodiness of black people, they are a transcendent reflection on black humanity" (*The Spirituals and the Blues* [New York: Orbis Books, 1972], 113).

60. Dunham, unpublished letter to Bernard Berenson, 1 February 1953.

61. Katherine Dunham, quoted in Joyce Aschenbrenner, "Katherine Dunham: Reflections on the Social and Political Contexts of Afro-American Dance," *Dance Research Annual* 12 (New York: Congress on Research in Dance, 1981), 7.

62. Katherine Dunham, quoted in Brian Lanker, *I Dream a World: Portraits of Black Women Who Changed America* (New York: Stewart, Tabori & Chang, 1989), 28.

An Anthropological
Band of Beings

An Interview with Julie Robinson Belafonte

VÈVÈ A. CLARK

Julie Robinson was a principal dancer with the Dunham Company in the late 1940s and early 1950s. She is remembered particularly for her remarkable performances in *Choros* and *Southland*. She married singer-actor Harry Belafonte in 1957 and, with him, has since taken an active part in many political and humanitarian causes. The following is an abridgment of an interview conducted on 23 November 1983 in New York City.

VÈVÈ A. CLARK [hereafter VC]: What do you think are the greatest carry-overs for you from your years with Dunham?

JULIE ROBINSON BELAFONTE [hereafter JRB]: There are so many, starting with the years at the Dunham School, which were very important middle adolescent years for me. I was in high school. And this was even before the school was on Forty-third Street, when she'd just opened up at Caravan Hall.

VC: 1944?

JRB: Yes. Syvilla [Fort] and Talley [Beatty] and Lavinia [Williams] were my first teachers. I was a high school art student, and I never dreamed of becoming a dancer. Though I had been dancing since I was about ten on Saturdays at the New Dance Group. I had a scholarship at the New Dance Group when I was very young. But I did it because I loved it. I loved dancing. My mother is a painter and I was sort of going into sculpting; on Saturdays I would try to take a dance class. I was always

SOURCE: VèVè A. Clark, interview with Julie Robinson Belafonte, 23 November 1983. Copyright 1983 by VèVè A. Clark. Used by permission.

very athletic, you know, being born on the streets of New York, as I was out playing handball. I loved sports. And I am also from a musical family, that's why I'd always loved dancing. Plus, wherever the latest social dances were I was always hanging out. So then when I went to the Dunham School, I had a scholarship. I never thought Dunham would take a white girl. I never thought of performing, actually, but I loved the technique, so I thought I would teach. I became very interested in teaching, and when I was seventeen, I lied about my age and took a job at a summer camp teaching children, for experience.

vc: You were in New York?

jrb: Well, it was not in the city. That was in Massachusetts. I taught a hundred children, and at the end I had to put on a little show, and I had to use every kid. So you know, when I came back I said "Well, I have tremendous experience, [even though] I know I'm very young." So I started to be like a student teacher at the Dunham School. I'd warm up Syvilla's classes; I'd give the barre and then Syvilla would come in and do the rest of the class. And I started teaching and then finally I had my own classes and I taught at the school till I joined the company—the Dunham Technique.

vc: Can you really describe to me the kind of training you were getting at the New Dance Group, before you went [to the Dunham School]?

jrb: Very definitely. Pearl Primus. As a matter of fact, it was her drummer Simba [who encouraged me]. When I was ten, he told me I should dance, that I had a feel. And I took Jane Dudley's class. Sophie Maslow. Hadassah.

vc: Oh, my God.

jrb: I took them all. I was just fascinated by all techniques. I even did Hawaiian dancing for the USO. I would say that my strength really was modern dance background and Pearl Primus.

vc: So you had a good background in modern and African dance. Did that training clash with the Dunham Technique?

jrb: No, because I also had street training in the dance halls. I can't explain it. It's like you can always tell someone that is overly ballet-trained. No matter how they move, no matter where they are, whether they're walking, no matter what they are doing. [*VC does an impression. Laughter.*] But with me, I always liked to feel like being a part of where I was. Like if it was . . . the Palladium. And, I just always felt I belonged where I was, whether it was in the streets, or in the dance hall, or in that dance class. And when I was taking modern, like Jane Dudley's class,

[my] personality changed. I've found that. It's hard to explain. It's like the kind of dancing [I was] doing always affected my whole personality. Or, I don't know if it's that I have the capability of adapting to it. I really can't answer that. It's like in *Buck and the Preacher.* I had a good ear for languages—that language taught me where to put it in my body, in my throat.

VC: So, coming in with the Dunham Technique, the ballet part of it sounds like it was fairly new to you.

JRB: That's right. I hated it.

VC: Tell me why.

JRB: Well, because I didn't do it very well. Not that it was hard. I mean, I always loved the challenge of learning. I regretted it that I didn't discipline myself for more ballet training in that I couldn't do double pirouettes with ease. I'd get tense before I'd have to do it. I would say that was my weakest point, the ballet training.

VC: It's incredible, because when people think of you, they think of you in *Choros.*

JRB: But I was very good in it. I'm not saying I was bad. I am talking about how I felt about myself, how I felt about it. I never worked on pointe. I was a very strong dancer, very, very strong. And I had enough ballet training that *Choros* was just right. I just had enough to make *Choros,* to feel comfortable in it. But to this day, occasionally, I have dreams about *Choros.* It's like I hear the music, and I can't find my costume, and I can't find my way, and there are new people in the company, or I may see Lucille [Ellis]. It's a frustration. And I did *Choros,* both parts, during different periods while I was in the company, and I never got over my nervousness before when I heard the music start. Never.

VC: I guess a legend has come up about how the Ailey company handled *Choros.*[1] Did you hear anything yourself?

JRB: Well, I went and worked with the girls. Delores Harper and I went and spent a whole day working with the girls once because I believe Clifford Fears taught them the ballet, but he concentrated on the boys, and the girls really didn't know what they were doing. And I think it got to the point where no one really taught them correctly the ballet.

VC: And Miss D wasn't around.

JRB: No.

VC: I got the word down the line that it was just too strenuous for them, and they complained about it. But you're saying that maybe they just didn't [learn it properly].

JRB: Well, I think that what was so unique about the Dunham Company was that we had to, at a moment's notice, go from one technique to another. And I think that a ballet dancer or a modern dancer is not accustomed to doing that. And *Choros* is very demanding. You have to go from ballet into—what do you call it?—samba, folk. A completely different attitude psychologically, and your body is working in total contrast rhythmically as well. So, *Choros* was much more demanding. And another thing, you had to look ta-da-ta-da [*hums*]. It all had to look easy, but it was very, very difficult.

VC: There is a delicateness about that piece, but you know underneath it's really strong.

JRB: But it was important for the audience not to feel that it was hard. It should have just, you know—when you get into the rhythmic samba part, that's where they [the Ailey dancers] had the trouble. They didn't know how to emote. At *that* time. Maybe now, because one of the girls that was doing it, that I worked with, was one of the younger up-and-coming dancers. She's one of his leading dancers now, so perhaps now she could.

VC: In a way, *Choros* came into the Dunham repertoire later on, in fact, but then if you consider that the company goes back to 1938, 1939—

JRB: Yes.

VC: It sounds to me like it's a maturer piece even for her.

JRB: Well, *Choros 1*, of course, was the only *Choros* that was performed for many years, until she did *2, 3,* and then *4*.

VC: Were you aware of the person you were to replace once you went from the school into the company?

JRB: Who? Gloria [Thornburg]? Oh, my goodness, I knew Gloria very well.

VC: Okay. How did that transition work?

JRB: Well, I was a scholarship student, and even before I started teaching, we had an experimental group at the school. We all had duties, like running the elevator, and we had our own costumes. So, when the company was in New York, Gloria used to be at the school a lot, and we became very friendly. We were quite good friends before I joined the company.

VC: Did you learn her roles from her?

JRB: No, I didn't.

VC: She got married and left the company and then—

JRB: I'm trying to remember. I do have a little blank spot about when I actually was learning. I think I learned a lot of the choreography, like *L'Ag'ya, Shango,* and so on. She [Dunham] would just throw you in it. But there was a period when Eloise Anderson was in the company. And Eloise and I went down to Philadelphia to audition for Dunham because Dunham had not seen me dance for about a year or so. Of course, I had become much stronger in the technique itself. This was just before she went to Europe in 1948. And so, Dunham took me in the company then, from that audition, and about a year, or a year and a half later, someone—I forget who it was—had left the company in Europe, and Eloise came [and joined] the company.

vc: How long were you actually with the company? It sounds like you were with them in the school since about 1944?

jrb: Well, since Caravan Hall, since 1944. I was with her for about seven years I think. And then after I left the company, the last time I performed with her was her last performance at the Greek Theater. I came in because she needed me to do some of the roles that someone who had replaced me couldn't do for one reason or another.

vc: That means you were with her for *Caribbean Rhapsody* in Europe?

jrb: No.

vc: 1948? That's what the whole show was called.

jrb: Oh, yes.

vc: That would be 1948, 1949.

jrb: Oh, yes, 1950, 1951, the whole South American tour, a Broadway run, Ciro's, El Rancho, Vegas, and Reno, Nevada.

vc: Until about 1954, 1955?

jrb: No, no, 1953. And I did *Mambo,* the film, actually.

vc: Let's go back, just for a second. How would you say that the Experimental Group within the Dunham complex, differed, if it did, from the touring company, from the professional company?

jrb: Well, as under-subsidized as the Dunham Company was, the Experimental Group was pitiful. We had no money. We had to make our own costumes. We weren't getting paid, but it was a tremendous education and I think to a great degree it prepared me for the company. That's why a theater orchestra or a second company is so important for a main company to be able to draw upon. And I think that the Experimental Group really should have been more [able to] serve that purpose.

vc: I have never thought of it as—you know how they have Ailey I and an Ailey II—I never thought of it as Dunham II. Because of the nature of some of the things that they did, that's why I phrased that question as I did. It sounded to me like [the Experimental Group] was more educational, that they would do lectures.

JRB: That's all that we could do. That's all we were asked to do.

VC: Freebies!

JRB: But it was a tremendous training for being able to perform the technique.

VC: That puts it into perspective. For some reason, I never have asked anybody that question, because so many other people I've talked to came straight into the company. Like Archie [Savage], like Lucille [Ellis]. You really worked your way up.

JRB: Well, there was no school in their day, in the beginning, you see, so they had their own reality.

VC: Okay, let's take you on tour. First stop is London. Can you recall the high?

JRB: Vividly.

VC: All right. You tell me what you want to tell me.

JRB: What do you want to know?

VC: Obviously, I've gone through all the numbers with her [Dunham], every single one of them as though we were going to reconstruct [them], but then I also tell her she can throw in some of the juice, you know personal memories, how the audience reacted et cetera. I am trying to get it from several angles. I have a couple of questions that I want to ask you about the tour but I am sort of interested in, say, opening night in London, the kinds of things you remember vividly.

JRB: I thought you meant the whole period. The actual opening night I don't recall vividly. I recall being on the top floor, sharing a dressing room with Eartha [Kitt], with Kitty, who was my roommate. We eventually got an apartment in London. And I will just never forget the whole period because it was my first time with the company.

We had to wear white panties—they had little ruffles on them—with certain costumes, and black panties with others. And since we were four flights up, very often, Kitty and I would have to do our quick changes. We'd have to bring our clothes down and do it in the wings. And very often we'd forget the black panties. I remember getting to the stage manager and saying, "Please"—after he'd called "places in five minutes" on the intercom—"please, Kitty, will you bring down my black panties?"

Also, when you joined the Dunham Company, you had a duty. Everyone had a duty to do. Have you ever been told about that? Well, mine was ironing the white ruffles of the skirts. Jon Lei and I had to do that three times a week, and this was before the nylon seersucker came out a few years later when Mr. Pratt replaced those skirts with a fabric that did not have to be ironed. But for a few years, I had to iron, and I swore that if I ever got married, I would scrub floors, I would do anything, but I would never, ever iron again! And I haven't, and I never will. [*Laughter.*] But I graduated to the hats with Dolores. That wasn't until I was a principal dancer. I ironed for a long time.

VC: So your memory of that whole tour was constant excitement, I would imagine.

JRB: Yes and no, because it was a very interesting time in that it was shortly after the war and there was still rationing in England. A lot of very interesting things took place because we went back—When was it? 1951? 1950? No, in 1949, the following year, or was it two years later? I don't remember because we went to the Cambridge Theatre. We opened at the Prince of Wales.

But what I started to say was, [being] in a country that had just had such a devastating experience in the war, we too had to have ration books. And so we could have one egg a week. I smoked in those days, and so, cigarettes—now *that* I remember vividly, you know, holding on to butts or finding butts and dancing barefoot in very little heat in England. We'd keep brandy in the wings. Really. Gordon Simpson always had his little nip there for us, so I started to have a taste here and there just to keep warm. So that whole period, even touring the provinces, we lived in what they called digs, and the sheets were wet and it was just damp. We were very gaseous all the time. It was very difficult.

On the other hand, it was quite an experience. And also I was Richie's [Richardena Jackson] understudy, which later on became a very important thing for me because when Richie got married, I took her roles. And I was very serious about dancing. My mother has kept letters, the letters that I wrote to her, and I am always saying my legs are getting stronger, and I was very serious. I even started a book—I don't know where it is—where I sketched the costumes. Because dance notation was a complete failure, and I tried to say what the choreography was. It was like a big ledger. I don't know where that book is today. And it was just all breaking me into many, many, many things. And of course, your first question was, what did I get out of the experience? And I said it was multi-fold because I started working within the company in different periods, in different ways. I mean at one point then, I became her [Dunham's] understudy and I actually did do her role twice, once in Argentina and once in Jamaica.

vc: I was going to ask you that. You seem to have been perhaps one of the few folk around at the time who could have done Dunham's roles, and I guess it always comes up when she's reconstructing. Especially now, who would do her roles? Were you ever approached—I'm going to skip now to recent times—to actually do some of Ms. Dunham's roles if you were to dance?

jrb: No.

vc: Did you dance in the gala at Carnegie Hall?

jrb: No.

vc: Okay, you've told me about some of the low points, especially in the one—

jrb: But it was also a big excitement like you said. I found everything exciting. Oh, the work was so exciting!

vc: How would you say that the reception and the performance in London differed from performing in Paris?

jrb: Well, the difference between the English and the French.

vc: How would you characterize that?

jrb: I'll put it this way. They're both colonial powers, and I think in those days—as well as probably today—they found black people exotic and fantastic, as long as they weren't too cerebral, I suppose. That's where *Southland* comes in and her problems with it. However, I think that the English express their racism—they express themselves emotionally in a different way. So of course, the French were more outgoing. But when we went back to England—of course this was sometime later, this was after Frances [Taylor] joined the company—we moved five times, there was such discrimination in housing. Now in Paris, it was the other way. No matter where we went there was champagne, and we were just the last word. To a point. Well, I think it's well known that Parisians don't invite you to their homes. Like I said, I feel as long as you were exotic and in the theater—and you know, it was at that sort of level, I do believe. And of course now that I am older and wiser, I am sure of it. Then we went to Algiers, and the first thing that we saw was a Frenchman with a stick. You know, a policeman. I think the success of the Dunham Company in Europe was—I don't think it could have been more incredible. Harry's success now seems to be so fantastic, but the company's was the same.

I don't know if anyone has mentioned this to you—it's just an aside—but when we went to London, performing in London were the Berry Brothers, the Nicholas Brothers, June Richmond—she's dead now—Duke Ellington's band with Ray Nance, who is also dead. That was 1948. George Kirby. He was on the ship with us when we went over.

vc: No one has mentioned that, that there was so much competition.

jrb: Competition, yet camaraderie. We're all friends to this day. We all got to know each other because we all ended up living in a place called Airways Mansion.

vc: Oh, what was that?

jrb: Little flats. Except Dolores, and Richie, and Lucille and Van [Vanoye Aikens], and Lenwood [Morris]. I think they rented a house some-where. We underlings [were there].

vc: I guess I said "competition" because you just wonder how much of an audience you can pull in.

jrb: Oh, in those days, it was just the beginning of black entertainers coming to Europe, and it was just an explosion. The Peters Sisters had been there, and of course Josephine Baker—we know that. But it was really the beginning of seeing other forms of black entertainment. And I think it was the first in terms of dance—it wasn't eating fire and drums. It was such a high caliber. This was just something that the European audiences liked.

vc: How would you characterize the audience response the second time the company came through to those same places in Europe?

jrb: Very favorable as well. I don't remember a let-down or a getting used to the excitement of the company. As always, reviews are better in some cities than in others.

vc: And South America? That period is probably the least well docu-mented. I am not really sure why, because she [Dunham] kept every-thing, absolutely everything.

jrb: Well, in a way, that was one of the most productive periods from *her* point of view. I can't imagine that it would be the least documented.

vc: It is, compared to England.

jrb: Because that's where *Southland* was choreographed, number one. She did a lot of research herself in Brazil—I was with her—in terms of the Candomblé. There are so many things during that period that were so important. I can't believe that [it's not well documented]. Unless she is the only one that—I am thinking in terms of the other people that were in that tour. Have you spoken with anyone that was in that tour?

vc: I don't mean from the point of view of the company. I mean in the press.

jrb: Oh, yes. I see. In terms of the press. Oh, I think I could understand that very well. Brazil was quite well publicized as I remember. But don't forget in South America there is no middle class. You have peasants, which is most of the country, and the wealthy, which came to the theater. And I think that's your answer.

vc: Do you remember the piece that she did called *Tango?*

jrb: I danced in it.

vc: That one is interesting to me because it's one that she did fairly late, and I think that if you were there until 1953, then you must have danced in it before she changed it into a fairly political piece. When you danced *Tango,* was it dedicated to—

jrb: No. To whom?

vc:—to a woman pianist who had died between the time that you danced it and the time that Dunham went back in 1954. It's one that people remember. I didn't bring the photograph along, but Ms. Dunham is standing there like this, in this really tight black dress. And she has a look on her face that you don't usually see, which is a look of anger. And I asked her, "Miss D, how come you're in so few of these photographs?" And she told me this whole thing, how they had been there before, and when they came back, this woman, this friend of theirs, had "disappeared." Well you know what that meant. She then took *Tango* and turned it into a political piece, which it had not been before. And she hated the way she looked because she doesn't like to see herself angry. But it was one of the few times you saw that particular look on her, on the stage. It's not like she destroyed the copies, but she just somehow didn't have many prints of them. That's going to be a little bit after your time, but I always want to ask people about *Tango,* how they saw it, especially someone who'd remember over the period when it first started and then when she went back.

jrb: I don't think there is anyone who went through both periods because I was the one that danced it, you see, before the other period. I don't know who did it after me. I can't imagine anyone doing it after me. [*Laughing*]. I'm not sure. I really don't know.

vc: Now when you danced it, was it a dance of seduction?

jrb: No, it was definitely a dance—as far as I was concerned—of tremendous intensity. I mean, when I danced it. The fascination that I have to this day is to hear the tango rhythmically. It was that extreme tension that doesn't require—it's an inner tension, the tango. You have to be so intense because your feet and legs are working and because there's a certain posture you have to maintain.

That's another thing that was so wonderful because we went to all these places, and we went and danced all these dances. This was another one of her great gifts, I think. For instance, when we were in Colombia, I remember that we went out one night to this place where they were doing a *cumbia*. And she'd say, "Get up and dance," and little did we know that she was already transposing that in theatrical terms, you see. So, by the time we got up on the stage to do it, we had felt it because we had been a part of it in real life. So, she knew what she was doing in that sense.

vc: You know, I have a feeling that most people who talk about Dunham do *not* see the South America period as a period that was that rich and that creative.

jrb: Good Lord, and *Southland* is—

vc: We are going to get to that. Let's see if we can make a list of the roles that you played over the long period that you were with the Dunham Company. *Choros.*

jrb: Then I replaced Richie as the Zombie in the second act of *L'Ag'ya*. I danced that role. *Choros, Son, L'Ag'ya.* I *loved* doing that part, the zombie scene.

vc: I think *L'Ag'ya* is my favorite.

jrb: Yeah, it's wonderful. Let's see. *Adeus Terras.* I have neck problems to this day I think because of that. You know I had to whip my hair on that table. Anyway, let's see what else. *Tango,* of course. It's one of my favorites. I felt that was me.

vc: Were you partnered?

jrb: Yes, with Lenwood.

vc: You mentioned that the company had to move several times for reasons of racism in London.

jrb: Well, not the company, but you see, it was Jackie [Walcott], Frances [Taylor], and myself. There were three of us, because Kitty and I no longer roomed together. This was not the first time. This was the second time in London when we were at the Cambridge Theatre.

vc: Doesn't it seem a little ironic that you, not being black, would have to move?

jrb: Yes, I know. We tried everything. We tried my going first and securing it. We tried every combination and finally gave up and went to Airways Mansion. We had a cute little place.

vc: Were there situations, racial situations, the company got into that were very difficult for you?

JRB: No, it just underscored my commitment politically. Especially in Nevada.

VC: That's one I've never heard. I never thought to ask. [*Laughter.*]

JRB: Really? Well, first of all in El Rancho, Vegas, which since has burned down—I am trying to think, this was 1950. Let's see, we were just coming from the South American tour, so it was 1951. And at that time, blacks could not eat on the Strip, let alone sleep, or go into the casinos, and we had to eat in the kitchen. In terms of living quarters, there was literally the other side of the tracks. And there were two places to stay: Mrs. Lawrence's Guesthouse and Mrs. Shaw's Motel. And Mrs. Lawrence didn't want us to sit on her spreads, you know. So, it was just terrible. Lenwood and Ural [Wilson] were living in a trailer where you could see the heat shimmering. I mean, it was just horrible.

There was one nightclub—naturally called the Cotton Club—where we would hang out all night and just get drunk and sleep all day, so that we wouldn't have to face the day. As a matter of fact, that's when the first atomic explosion happened. I remember it so well. However the second time back there—I am trying to think what year that was. It couldn't have been the same time—because we were there, I think twice—but Frances was my roommate, Frances Taylor. Our baggage was in this big, air-conditioned room in the hotel; the trunks and the costumes were living in luxury, and we were living in these inhuman, really terrible circumstances.

Then when we went up to Reno; there was only one house to live in and the only place we could eat was the bus station because of the interstate traveling. And we'd sit up there all night in the bus station. We played slot machines, got drunk, ate. So, it just reinforced, you know, my—I've always been a political person, it just took different forms. I had political parents and I've always been community-oriented, even as a younger person.

VC: All right. I am still in those questions I ask everybody. What would you consider your favorite Dunham piece, or role? It doesn't have to be something you've been in, but something that's your favorite.

JRB: It's *impossible,* because her creativity was so diverse. It's like, I love hot colors, I love earth tones, I love pastels. How can you have a favorite? I love classical music, I love folk, I love salsa. You can't have a favorite. I maybe would have a group of favorites, and for different reasons. I love *L'Ag'ya* because I love anything that has drama or a story. So, that's one reason I love that. I love *Nañigo* because of the energy and the excitement of the piece. Hmm. It's very difficult to say. I think one of my favorites would be *Rites*—and I think that John Pratt plays no small part, he has a tremendous part, in much of the work. And I think *Rites* is one example of that. When I feel myself working and when I see it, I see John Pratt as well as Katherine Dunham. I think too few people think about that. That was a part of her and that was a part of the visual theater. And I don't think he ever really got his credit.

VC: He hasn't, because I talked to him a number of times and—

JRB: I think that he is a genius as well.

VC: Absolutely. I said to him, "Mr. P, has anybody done any kind of an extended article or anything on you?" And he told me only once did he remember getting good notices from one guy in London. I'm not even sure that I have found that piece he was talking about. So I sat with him and said, "Let's look at *mises en scène*," and I asked him about changing curtains and so on. I just think he is absolutely wonderful.

JRB: He is a genius.

VC: He is outrageous, that guy.

JRB: He could take a rag and mount it, and his understanding—He understood the cultures as well, which is very unusual for a white Canadian.

VC: Yours was such a visual, visual company.

JRB: Oh, good Lord. And the *Veracruzana* suite? Oh my goodness. That's the first time I ever sang in my life, by the way. I replaced Kitty singing those songs. I'll never forget when she left the company. Having lived with her—and I speak Spanish well enough—I knew the songs, so I went to Miss D and I said, "I can sing those songs." She said, "Oh, please." I said, "Try me." And I did, and I sang [her songs] for the rest of the time in the company.

VC: I am interested that you said that you had a constellation of favorites.

JRB: It's impossible [to choose one favorite]. In fact, I would do it the other way. I could perhaps think of some that I like not so much.

VC: What's your least favorite?

JRB: One would be *Bolero*.

VC: Why?

JRB: I think it's a bit trite, both musically and [dramatically]. I think the beat and so on isn't as interesting and sophisticated.

VC: That's an old piece.

JRB: It's what someone—I can imagine, especially in that time in history—would expect a black company to be doing. I can't explain it.

[*Hums song.*] We loved the costumes because it was one of the few we felt pretty in. Sexy.

VC: Maybe that's why she left it in there, so you guys could feel real good.

JRB: But do you understand what I'm saying?

VC: I do. I do.

JRB: Not that I didn't like it, but it was one I would say would have a lower evaluation. Let's see what else. There are very few because they are all so different. I know that there were some that I hated to do. Like *Cakewalk.*

VC: Why?

JRB: Because the hats were so heavy. It felt awkward.

VC: Nearly everyone who has answered that question has not had a least favorite at all. It's always been the one that was most strenuous to perform that was the least favorite.

JRB: Really? That could be the greatest to me. You see, *Choros* was one of my most exciting moments, but it was the most difficult.

VC: I like what you said about *Bolero* because what we've been doing is looking at how long a piece stayed in the repertoire, and it had been on the program since 1937.

JRB: In my time, we didn't do it that often, just on certain tours. She had things that she just did in nightclubs and didn't do in the theater. What was the one where we went around in a wheel? *Rhumba Trio? Rhumba Trio.* That was great in the nightclub, but it wasn't right for the theater. Let me try to go through the program. I think all the second-act ballets, which either told a story or, like *Rites* that were in three parts, were I think absolutely extraordinary. And that's *Veracruzana, L'Ag'ya,* and *Rites,* and then *Southland.*

VC: We are going to get to *Southland.*

JRB: That's something else. *Shango* is just fantastic. It was the perfect closing in the first act. I think it reflected her studying years and her genius for adapting authenticity in theatrical vocabulary. And it epitomized that.

VC: That's so well put. It's sad. It has been just recently reconstructed, but it just doesn't have the power. It really has to do with the type of training that people have.

JRB: Also we had the experience in Brazil and in Haiti. And having that, that assimilates into you. When you have had the experience, when you drank the *kashasa,* you got up, and you partook of the ritual. And having had that experience, even though you know you are on the stage, something happens that is not the same as someone saying, you do eight of these and six of these. It's something else and there'll never be a company like we were, for largely that reason.

VC: You were such an anthropological band of beings. I don't think any group is going to ever come close. You have to have an incredible amount of courage to do what you all did—and I am not talking about the social barriers. I am talking about really taking part in that life, the same way you would take part in going to the dance halls here. You go to them in Cuba, and you go to them wherever you are, and a lot of dancers do not want to do that these days.

JRB: Yes, of course. We did not only do it because—I think this is something very key. I think no one really realizes it. Dunham perhaps had us go to a *cumbia* because she was going to mount it, and she knew how important it was to have an experience. But we just happened to be a group of livers. We smoked, we drank, we had love affairs. We did not take care of ourselves. We were not disciplined in terms of our health and so forth. We also brought that on stage. We weren't sterile, because we lived life, and that projected itself from each and everyone of the company, I do believe.

VC: I think it was Tommy [Gomez] who said that. You used the word *emote,* but he said there was the sense that you had to project. Miss Dunham has said that too.

JRB: Absolutely. And I don't care how many *tours jetés* or *tours en l'air* or pirouettes [one can do] if it doesn't say something.

VC: And it's not good enough just to smile.

JRB: No, no.

VC: Were you in *Mambo?* Or were you there with her when she did it?

JRB: No I wasn't with her. But really, it was a bizarre coincidence because I had left the company, and I decided I was going back to Italy. I had a one-way ticket. I went to Paris, where our trunks were. I got our trunks and I went to Italy, coincidentally just when she [Dunham] came to Rome to do *Mambo.* And what made it more of a coincidence was in the beginning Silvana Mangano was supposed to dance. Her character was supposed to dance *La Valse.* And I was the only one who knew the role, so I was hired to do that film—to be Silvana Mangano in long-shot. But they never did it in the film.

VC: They took it out?

JRB: They decided not to use it, so what happened was that I became a member of the company. Have you seen that film?

vc: I have been waiting to see that film.

jrb: It's a terrible film, just terrible. By the way, James Dean—when he was alive and I was at the commissary out at Universal—came over and said my scene was the best thing in it. The making of that movie could make a movie. The intrigue that was going on. We [the dancers] were just in scenes, they did a ballet, which I didn't think was very good. There was a Carnival scene that was fun, and we were all through the picture. Van, Lenwood. I am trying to think—There was a nucleus of the Dunham Company that was in it.

vc: So what would you consider your most memorable performance with the company?

jrb: *Southland.* There is no question about it.

vc: Why is it the most memorable?

jrb: For many reasons. First of all, it was choreographed in 1951. But you see, there came a point when I left the company. I began to think that movement wasn't enough, so I became interested in acting. I always wanted to make noises or sounds because the frustration of the movement wasn't enough. I eventually did study acting, and I was going into acting, until I met my husband, so of course we had a family, and it all kind of stopped. Which I don't regret. It was by choice. However, it had a tremendous effect on me because it was there all the time, the desire to act, and I think the only way I could do it [*Southland*] was make it an acting problem.

When we first started rehearsing in Argentina we were all very tired because we were doing two shows a day and then rehearsing. And I will never forget when she was staging the moment when I had to absolutely scream in repulsion. You know the story, I think. And scream "Nigger!" "Wait," I said, "I can't do it." She said, "But you *have* to do it." "But I can't." I insisted. "Try," she said.

The whole company was sitting around like this [watching]. Now Frances Taylor and Jackie were roommates, and Delores and I were roommates. But the four of us always tried to get adjoining rooms, and we called each other "Sadie." And then we became The Sadies. We are tighter today than ever. Our children have grown up together. We go away every year together.

vc: That's outrageous. I had no idea.

jrb: So the four of us were living in a little suite in Argentina. And I was really exhausted because I also worked with the composer, the man that wrote the music, and I had to do it over and over, while he was composing and creating as well. So Delores stopped waiting for me, you know, to eat and stuff like that.

One night—Lenwood was at a different hotel—I was in bed, and Frances and Jackie were up, and as I drifted off, I could just hear them yackety yack. Dolores came in, and I awakened, and I heard Dolores start talking about me. She was saying, "You noticed the way she says it more than . . ."

By that time, it was about two o'clock in the morning. I put my clothes on and went to Lenwood's hotel. I was crying. I said, "Dolores, my Sadie, who I live with, [she's] closer to me than my own sister. [I can't believe] that she would turn on me." I said, "I can't handle it. It's too much for me." We sat up all night, and he said "You've got to do it. You know how important it is. It's because you are so good." The only way, the key for me to do it so well, was to use my feelings about the character I was playing, to use that hate for that person and transpose it to Jon Lei. That was the only way to get it out.

So it became a very definite acting problem for me, and I solved it that way. And I guess I was so good at it that I had problems. And then it wasn't just Delores, but Claudia McNeil. I paid an emotional price during that period. I felt so tired also. It was so avant-garde to do then, that drama, at that time, and the subject matter alone at that time was just so fantastic. I was just so supportive of her politically.

I don't know if you know what happened. At that time we were being wined and dined by the American embassy, and we were in Buenos Aires, Argentina, for three months, and then we did one performance of this in Santiago, Chile. And the American embassy asked Dunham not to do it, so she said she was going to do it anyway. Then when we went back to Argentina, our friends weren't inviting us anymore. The word probably got out and all that. But she was very smart when we did it in Paris. I think John Pratt went to Paris ahead and said we were doing it. He didn't ask permission or anything like that. I don't remember exactly. So there were no problems. I have all the clippings and stuff from the press. I have a book, pictures of myself.

vc: I would love at some point to see that. For some reason *Southland* is not as well-documented as it should be.

jrb: You see, that's another thing. She wanted to reconstruct it, and I told her I felt that because the world has changed, the third act, it would have to be updated. It's politically obsolete. And she didn't do that. It's all valid if you update the ending. It's a shame because in its time it was so ahead of its time. Not only the subject matter, but as a form of dance drama—because I was on that stage alone for twenty-five minutes doing mime, telling a lie, you know, of the rape and so on.

VC: Twenty-five minutes?

JRB: It had to have been twenty minutes, fifteen minutes, something like that. And the night before in rehearsal, Lenwood kicked my ankle by accident, and I did the whole thing with a sprained ankle. I had to have Novocain before every performance, and she would wait in the wings with ice before every performance, and a shot of brandy.

VC: You and that brandy. [*Laughter.*]

JRB: Well, I can't drink brandy anymore, but it did come in handy.

NOTES

1. *Choros* was mounted for the Alvin Ailey American Dance Theater in 1987 as part of "The Magic of Katherine Dunham," a full-evening program of Dunham's dances saluting her lifetime achievement *[Eds.]*.

Foreword to Katherine Dunham's
Dances of Haiti

Claude Lévi-Strauss

The French translation of *Dances of Haiti* by Katherine Dunham is indeed timely; it enhances measurably the existing public image of this artist. Katherine Dunham appears herein not only as a dancer and choreographer but also as a solidly trained specialist holding advanced degrees from the University of Chicago and Northwestern University[1]—major institutions that have long made their authority felt in the fields of observation, analysis, and ethnographic theory. This short study, presented now to the French reader, provides an exemplary work of clarity and substance.

Further, Haiti and Haitian subjects are the order of the day. Within a few short years we have had revealed to us, first, the literature of Haiti through the writings of the late Jacques Roumain, the Thoby-Marcelin brothers, and many others, then a surge of extraordinary primitive painting, which burst forth suddenly with an intense and lyric vitality from the brushes of men, often illiterate, to whom the very concept of painting— and certainly its accessories—has been a complete novelty. Undoubtedly this was to be expected (since it has long held the attention of excellent specialists); but perhaps with more acuity these artistic works have shown how a culture, doubly transplanted (a culture transported from Africa onto American soil, imbued in its new dwelling place with a religion and philosophy originating in Europe, especially in France) has proven capable

SOURCE: Claude Lévi-Strauss, foreword to Katherine Dunham, *Les danses d'Haïti* (Paris: Fasquelle Éditeurs, 1950), translated by Jeanelle Stovall in Katherine Dunham, *Dances of Haiti* (Los Angeles: University of California, Center for Afro-American Studies, 1983). Copyright 1983 by the Regents of the University of California and Katherine Dunham. Reprinted by permission of Katherine Dunham.

of retaining its cohesive force while gaining freedom through the existence and vitality of its beliefs and rites.

In the large periodic table of human societies, Haiti could therefore not miss appearing as a social molecule whose small dimensions retained remarkable proprieties, a molecule formed, it would seem, of atoms capable of releasing exceptional quantities of energy. This fact alone should justify the impassioned attention devoted increasingly by sociologists and ethnographers to the Haitian society.

An unquestionable originality marks Katherine Dunham's book among all these works. Her penetration into the life and local customs of the country was doubly facilitated by her common origin with the inhabitants and by her theoretical and practical knowledge of aspects of dance. To the *dignitaires* of the Vodun who were to become her informants, she was both a colleague, capable of comprehending and assimilating the subtleties of a complex ritual, and a stray soul who had to be brought back into the fold of the traditional cult; for the flocks of slaves lost on the large continent to the north had forgotten how to practice and had lost the spiritual benefits. These two reasons placed the researcher in a favored position.

In addition to these somewhat personal advantages, her book has the great merit of reintegrating the social act of dance, which serves as her central theme, within a total complex. Katherine Dunham proposed not only to study a ritual but also to define the role of dance in the life of a society. Her study is based, therefore, on a triple system of references: the opposite and complementary aspects of the sacred and the secular; the interrelated physiological and psychological aspects of dance from the individual's point of view; and the dual psychosociological nature of a dance form that, even in its most individualistic manifestations (I refer here to the phenomena of possession), validates "conventional behavior," and follows "established patterns." In the face of behavioral manifestations that could be viewed as an arbitrary release of instinct, a derangement of the mind, or an outbreak of the unconscious, the author reasonably refuses to envisage anything other than purely "symbolic and representative" workings, whose main (if not exclusive) role is that of "confirming the realities of cult affirmation." This approach contributes importantly to the study of relationships between sociology and psychopathology. Phenomena exist in our own society that could happen only through deception or under the guise of apparent mental derangement; and yet these same phenomena, placed within another sociological context, could be factors of collective cohesion and spiritual enrichment. This fact provokes serious thought about certain restrictions placed on our civilization during its development which are perhaps the price unconsciously paid for deriving other advantages.

The mass confusion of the twentieth century, expressed partially by this growing vogue of ethnographic research, is that we no longer can discern very well these advantages or their value. We have some vague aspirations, certainly not to an exchange of situations granting us the fate of other groups (because we know the high price they pay in the form of exploitation, physical poverty, and malnutrition), but at least to a new "deal" that would allow us to reshuffle and alter the positions of the card game; it is not even certain that this is possible. But precisely because the Haitian culture is a syncretism, it provides a privileged field of study for observing those phenomena of collaboration among different traditions; herein lie the only hope for a better and freer life for these peoples long humiliated and the one possibility for the others to discover a vaster and more complete humanity. In short, such a collaboration could give rise to a new humanism. Mankind would not be limited, as in the Renaissance period, to a mere fraternization of the most exceptional minds in solely intellectual pursuit but would be united in the common enjoyment of the material resources still denied to some and of spiritual wealth still possible for others to rediscover with the guidance of their brothers.

NOTES

1. Although Katherine Dunham is famously associated with both the University of Chicago and Northwestern University, she does not hold an advanced degree from either institution [Eds.].

Katherine Dunham

An Appreciation

ALFRED MÉTRAUX

The Katherine Dunham I present to you is not too well known to the public. It is Katherine Dunham the ethnographer and the scientist. Well before I associated her name with marvelous dancing, I had read about her in a letter by the Department of Anthropology of the University of Chicago. It was about a young student whose talent and ambition made it possible to foresee some original work in a field in which I was particularly interested: mainly the study of Vodun cults in the West Indies. Not too long after that, I met this new recruit of our branch of science. The first time I saw her she was bent over her notes in a class of Mexican archaeology. The memory of our first conversation is deeply engraved in my mind. However "graduate Katherine Dunham's" ambitions were not such that one could predict the brilliant artistic career that made her famous. She was interested in the dance, and we had a taste of her talent at the sound of a phonograph, but her dream was about trips to far away places, studies, rites, initiations and secret ceremonies. She was also hoping to obtain the means for going there to undertake an analysis of West Indian dances, a project that did materialize thanks to the help of an American foundation.

SOURCE: Alfred Métraux, "Katherine Dunham: An Appreciation," from the program for performances of *Bamboche!* at the 54th Street Theatre, New York, in the week of 22 October 1962. Copyright 1962 by the Alfred Métraux Estate and Katherine Dunham. Reprinted by permission of Katherine Dunham.

NOTE: *Bamboche!*, a dance revue in three acts and thirteen scenes, was created and directed by Katherine Dunham. It opened 22 October 1962 at the 54th Street Theatre and closed 28 October 1962 after eight performances.

Katherine Dunham attended a school that was even stricter than all departments of anthropology: namely that of the Haitian Vodun sanctuaries. How often have I heard people talk about "Miss Katherine," the strange woman from the United States, who was dancing on the peristyle of the temple as if she had been brought up in Vodun. She had nothing to envy from the *hounci* (the gods' servants). I met her masters. One of them was Ti-cousin, whose famous sanctuary I visited, near Léogâne. Vodun, in its Haitian, Cuban, or Brazilian form, is like the cults of Dahomey and Nigeria, from where it stems, a "danced religion." The gods are honored by dances. It is by dancing that the worshipers communicate with them, and when the god descends on his horse, during the mystic dance, they say that he "dances in the head." Katherine Dunham, by virtue of her racial origin, her scientific background, and her talent as a dancer, combined exceptionally well all the conditions required to penetrate into the heart of this fairly unknown religion. Her talents as an ethnographer can be appreciated in several of her works. In the one dedicated to Jamaica, she writes about the descendants of the brown Negroes that she studied right in the mountains where she went looking for them.

But it's in her book, translated into French under the title of *Les danses d'Haïti* (Haitian Dances), that the originality of her contribution can be seen the most clearly. It is not a common thing to see an ethnographer talk with knowledge of facts about as subtle a phenomenon as the muscular and psychological mechanism that creates favorable ground for mystical ecstasy. Katherine Dunham, who danced barefoot, in the midst of the *hounci* for all the gods in the Vodun pantheon, felt upon herself the breath of the *loas* (spirits), and was able, in her capacity of ethnographer, and dance specialist, to describe to us the gradual abandon of the dancer, climaxing in a "state of complete surrender in which body and soul are ready to receive the god."

Would it be indiscreet to reveal at this point that Katherine Dunham went through all the stages of initiation in a Vodun sanctuary and that she actually penetrated all the mysteries of the *kanzo* rites? To see the way she handles the *ason* (the sacred rattle) I am brought to believe that her science in the ritual and her talents took her all the way to the top of the Vodun hierarchy. In any case, it is from her experience as an ethnographer, acquired right on the spot, that Katherine Dunham borrowed the most beautiful themes for her dances. She has tried to release in a nutshell the moments in which the rituals reach their highest point. Rhythms of drums, songs and dances, bring us an echo of the ceremonies that, from Cuba to the Amazon, convene the African gods on American soil. These invocations, transposed on the stage, are so powerful at times that what starts as the actors' mimic changes into an authentic trance, How many in the audience did suspect that last year the snake-god Damballa had descended upon a Parisian scene?

A malevolent legend surrounds Vodun. Those who fervently practice the cults and those who learned to love them are grateful to Katherine Dunham for having brought to the white world the profound beauty and humanity of a religion in which the American Negroes have found new reasons to hope and to live.

Notes on Dances for *Aïda*

KATHERINE DUNHAM

ACT I, SCENE 2: SCENE ANALYSIS. The priestesses' scene in *Aïda* is for me essentially a rite of Women's Mysteries; a perhaps rare occasion to demonstrate before the uninitiated the sacredness of the anointed, some small part of their traditional, inviolable importance, not only in single events such as releasing of the sacred sword and veil for the conquest of war, but in the total life, death, and survival process of their race. The main objective must not then be one of dance, in the conventional sense, but should aim to capture in design and emotional projection the importance of the ritual moment in terms of the entire opera. The meaning of the final scene, the entombment of the lovers who have offended the sacredness of

SOURCE: "Dances by Dunham," program for performance of Giuseppe Verdi's *Aïda* at the Metropolitan Opera House, New York City, 14 December 1963. Copyright 1963 by Katherine Dunham. Reprinted by permission.

NOTE: In her first choreographic assignment for the Metropolitan Opera, Katherine Dunham has brought an unusual perspective and point of view to the dances for the new production of Verdi's Aïda. This is to regard the music not merely as an interpolation in a nineteenth-century Italian opera, but as the opportunity to recreate a vista of life as it might have been in the period of the pharoahs.

For the Triumphal Scene, Miss Dunham's conception includes (a) Bedouin girls "swathed voluminously in shades of pale and indigo blue, antecedents perhaps of the Blue Women of Gulimin in southern Morocco"; (b) a "band of four high-leaping Somalis from south of Ethiopia," a composite type recreated "in the absence of clear records of pre-historic black Africa"; (c) a band of Nubian warriors who perform the "striking, punching, kicking, and springing movements of traditional Karate"; (d) women "brought in as slaves, hostages, or concubines" from across the Red Sea, from the areas now known as the Middle East; (e) the townswomen, who enter "for a grand climax of revelry."

the pharaoh, gains in intensity and purity when directly related to this previous scene of invocation. The aura of immersion in the mystic and ritual contact with the god Ptah through the intermediary of the chosen, the purified, and the initiated should cling to the very decor and heighten the deeper significance of the final scene of the opera, moving it from one of tragedy and possible pathos to one of transcendence and union in the Universal Whole—"Life of the Universe, myth of eternal love" as chanted by Ramfis and the priests.

The brief music conventionally allotted to the priestesses for dancing seems to me the least significant moment of the scene. What does allow for true interpretation are the passages sung by Ramfis, priests, and priestesses. These are far more appropriate for the ritualized primitive ecstasy called for by both story and lyrics—the words translated as "guardian," "avenger," "spirit of fertility," all of these unhampered by the conventional harmonies of modern instruments lend to an authenticity, no matter how little archaeological substantiation we may find. The acolytes, their principal of slightly higher protocol, the eunuch figure masked in the head of Ra, should serve as catalysts throughout the entire scene, contributing whether in choreographic pattern or in motion, to the devotional element with which the scene should be permeated.

The selection of performers able to emanate a virginal quality but at the same time almost awesome, at times fearful dedication to their mission is essential.

ACT 1, SCENE 2: CHOREOGRAPHY. Behind a scrim, slowly rising pools of light disclose the sacred altar at the base of a gigantic figure of the pharaoh, and before it the gold-tinted, dog-headed figure of the eunuch serving Ra [i.e., Anubis, guide to the afterlife]. On the first musical phrase the sacred bark is placed on the altar by slaves. Passing through the pools of light, almost as somnambulists, two priestesses purify the temple with incense vaporizing from brass bowls. One turns slowly, rising and sinking as though intent on reaching every level of the atmosphere: another edges forward on her knees, breathing some spiritual essence from the incense held at arms length before her. The two change positions halfway across the stage, arrive at the pedestals of burning incense already in place, then, almost overcome, salute each other ritualistically, incline toward the Anubis figure who divides with a distaff the veil covering the altar, and in a backward sinking movement place the bowls between their knees from where the Ra figure takes them to be offered before the altar. The two priestesses

prostrate themselves before the altar; they should, by their dramatic projection, have established the quality of a woman's secret ritual, should
convey the impression of having undergone a period of ritual preparation
before entering the inner temple. One feels that they are drugged, partly
by the incense, partly by the chant, partly by some powerful emanation
from the lotus flowers which they wear.

With the arrival of the two priestesses at the altar, the lines of priests
moving into position from the ramparts above the altar and two descending staircases should be in view. Two other priestesses are seen at the
upstage corners of the ramparts. They descend by the stage right staircase
as another two priestesses enter from stage left. They are led by the high
priestess and they also should project the feeling of entering into the temple from an inner sanctuary after a long and arduous confinement. They
should carry themselves as true instruments of Ptah, as those select, to
whom the destiny of Egypt has been entrusted. The high priestess wears
draped over her shoulders the veil which she will, after passing it over the
body of a young virgin who becomes possessed, venerate before the Ra
figure, offering it to Ramfis, who places it on the shoulders of Radames.[1]

This passing of the veil does not take place in immediate sequence but
is spaced though the scene to arrive just before the climax as Ptah indicates
acceptance of the devotions.

The dance proper of the priestesses is one of designs reminiscent of temple bas-reliefs, augmented by series of extensions, "spread out thy hand
over the soil of Egypt"—union with each other and with the god figures,
symbolic floor patterns, prostrations. During the duet between Ramfis
and Radames there are patterns and postures of attentive expectance, but
no movement; there is action again on the choral chants. A final ecstasy is
climaxed by the orgiastic possession of the youngest of the priestesses
coinciding with the burst of fire from the altar. The response of Ptah is evi-
denced in the body of the virgin as well as the flames from the sacred boat.

In résumé, we should have experienced with the priestesses their semi-
stupor upon entering, the interpersonal contact in their salutations, the
zealous veneration of the god personified in the altar and the figure of the
pharaoh—the heavily sensuous atmosphere punctuated by the possession
of the virgin which should signify a sign of recognition from the god, and
the orgiastic climaxes of movements directed toward the male figure which
point up the sexual, the fertility theme characteristic of the sect of Ptah.

The closing scene should, in contrast to the tense, comatose expectancy
of the opening, be one of complete purification, of catharsis, of conviction

of victory and re-affirmation of a transcendent nature, of the unity of the votaries with the gods.

Note: In the last scene of the opera, two priestesses often return to fortify Amneris in the death scene. It would be my recommendation that some god figure or figures more closely connected with the traditional Egyptian rites of the dead be portrayed; the transformation into Ptah, into a Lotus, the human head springing from a Lotus, into animal forms.[2]

There are also in the same references highly decorative plates of funeral processions signifying the peaceful and dignified passage of the deceased into his future abode which would, it seems to me, highly authenticate this scene and relieve it of any suggestion of sentimentality. These plates might appear behind Amneris as decor, or the figures and offerings themselves be represented as set pieces and supporting elements.

I must apologize for offering this suggestion at such a late date, but the reference material has been buried in archives not accessible until now.

NOTES

1. While Ramfis is high priest, it is probable that he may have at no time entered into the sanctuary of the virgin priestesses. He could very well regard their high priestess with the respect of equal protocol as well as a certain awe in recognition of the power of the female in the hierarchy of Egyptian gods.

2. E. A. Wallis Budge, *The Egyptian Book of the Dead* (London: Kegan Paul, Trench & Turner, 1928), 264–73.

The Caribbean Islands
Now and Then

KATHERINE DUNHAM

TRINIDAD. There was still a mynah bird whistling throaty rich tones in the central patio where I first stayed in Port of Spain twenty years ago. The hotel itself had become seedy—or had I been blinded by the wonder of it all during those student years? The plants in possession of the borders of the patio were not as flamboyant; a bar disfigured one end and wicker chairs and tea tables were replaced by chrome-legged cocktail units. My friend, Mrs. Audrey Jeffries, was ill, and so we could not meet and talk over old times: the trip to Congo Village to see the *bamboula;* the *calinda* danced by the old folk in white starched embroidered petticoats and gold collars; the Shango, a secret religious ritual, from which I was evicted when the sound of my camera, which I was operating through a crack in the "temple" door, superseded the squawking of the sacrificial white cock.

The calypso nights must still be there, especially during Carnival, but I was looking for the Lion and the Lord Beginner and would take no less, remembering sleepless nights when restless bands roved the streets challenging each other to verbal bouts, filling the still, hot air with biting political or social comment done to that rhythm only approximated for me in the current West African High Life. Or if the breeze were fresher and cooler, they would pass jest after jest back and forth in verse form like shuttlecock players on a hot tin roof: music, girl friends, lovemaking, amatory successes and failures, abnormal appetites, pathetic little personal secrets all bandied about in song to the beat of drums, scrape of coconut

SOURCE: Katherine Dunham, "The Caribbean: Islands Now and Then," *Show Magazine* (November 1963). Copyright 1963 by *Show Magazine*, Inc. Reprinted by permission.

grater, shuffle of feet and gasp of seed-filled rattles. Rich voices out of black satin throats.

Port of Spain has seemingly worked hard at earning itself a clean bill of health in the Caribbean. There are no more leprosy-marked vendors on corners surrounded, it seemed inevitably, by trays of things to eat. No more covert Chinatown with a hint of the sinister in the mah-jongg games glimpsed in smoky back rooms, the click of counting-boards tattooing against the wall and hum of an Indian dance drama, and a squalor unbelievable in the Western Hemisphere. A great deal of amalgamation has taken place, and the three dominant racial groups—East Indian, African, and Mongolian—no longer stand out as distinct, often opposing if not warring, components. From the airport on up into the hills, the miscegenation is seen in skin color, hair texture, in that indefinable handsomeness that results from the blending of major stocks, with, of course, the Caucasian still offering its contribution to the melting pot.

There was bigotry in Trinidad then; there seems to be less now, though it is hard to know on such a short visit. I would suspect that there are still havens of the white-skinned, even though discreetly cloaked under the classification of "private" clubs. The mark of the British is there, stronger, I feel, than the once rival Jamaica. It is a mark which may mean the reluctance to lose hold, to patronize, but which carries with it opportunities for good living, for order, for efficiency. I felt a new Trinidad which I appreciated; but all of these new things only make the memory of the old sharper.

JAMAICA. Kingston, like Port of Spain, has changed in its physical aspects; more concrete, more automobiles, more asphalt, and practically none of those old convertible Packards and Cadillacs manned by courteous and grizzled coachman types left. The Myrtle Bank Hotel had held its own, adding a few shops and a boardwalk to the sea and no doubt air conditioning; and this in spite of luxury spas too numerous to mention, like the millionaire's haven, Frenchman's Cove, and my preferred hostel, the Blue Mountain Inn.

In spite of the industrious feeling of Kingston, the streets hold a strange peasant quality so attractive to tourists. The vendors work unmercifully but wittily at a single sale; their wares are colorful and plentiful, and a kind of energy, associated in some intangible way with a new-found independence, livens the marketplaces, street corners, and country crossroads.

The bearded men of the Rastafari cult are an innovation, but in the past there were on every country road the white-robed Pocomania followers

and the Shepherds with their Moody-and-Sankey-hymn–chanting flocks.[1]
Jamaica has assimilated more from America than from Trinidad; it seems
less British and more on its own economically uncertain feet. Here I feel
more a pride in race and new freedoms than in land; for the bend, the
pull, the yen is toward London: to expatriate and take one's chances, no
matter what hair-raising episodes are reported from friends and relatives
who have gone ahead, or by the grapevine.

But the beauty of the vegetation I had forgotten, or had been aware
of only in that isolated wild area inhabited by the Maroon people in the
craggy Blue Mountains. This time I passed by the South Camp Road
Hotel, having declined from dingy colonial elegance to dull Rotarianism,
and looking like a Charles Addams or William Faulkner creation behind
its grove of shedding royal palms. On and up to the center of Kingston
and an old English inn perched on a ravine over a water torrent. The
dining room might have been in the West End, the bar in Bombay. But
the waiter with breakfast and the maid changing linen and the road curv-
ing a precipice and the great boulders in the riverbed and the giant trees
at a crossroads and shrubbery on the mountain facing us were suddenly
all Jamaica.

The trip to Montego Bay was a marvel of lushness. Perhaps it was the
company of expatriated Haitians excited to have news of relatives and
friends, or relief from the ever watching eye of the Big Brother Society of
the Black Republic. But every mountain curve embraced a cottonwood
larger than a country store, gnarled, prehistoric in impact, hirsute with
moss, wise, full of mystery, a shelter for the legendary duppies and rolling
calf.[2] Bananas grew in orderly plantations, then ran wild and uncared for;
ferns made bridges over fens, hibiscus drooped into our open windows
and bamboo filled the pockets of slow-running streams. The breadfruit,
the mango, the chocho, and the akee held their own, with coffee plants
and sugar cane scattered between. Somewhere along the road we bought
barbecued wild pork spattered with hot sauce from a porteress known to
our host. I thought of our hunts among the Maroons in the cockpits, and
the community barbecues afterward. I thought further back to Thirty-
fifth and State Streets in Chicago and of the open pit where a wizened
cousin several times removed of this same porteress speared ribs for us—
thrill seekers of the Thirties from the University of Chicago.

Days later, on the way back to Kingston, I examined people more than
shrubbery. They were neither happy nor friendly. The Maroons, who had
seemed so inhospitable on my first field trip, seemed welcoming princes

in comparison with the surly acknowledgments and reluctant greetings I received. An unnecessary insolence, camouflage for fear and, above all, uncertainty of the ever-pressing future.

At the meetings in Kingston I said a passing "hello" to my old acquaintance Dr. Miguel Bustamente and was cordially received by my longstanding friend Prime Minister Norman Washington Manley. I played with the idea of heading a National Dance Theater, then left the island, bathed in visions of green mysterious luxuriance, but taking away impressions of a crystal nonchalance, a disillusionment not common in the Caribbean.

HAITI. Haiti is enigmatic. Nothing is as it was, nor should it be. And still in other ways too much is as it was. My love affair with this island of witchery is classic. And still one tires of the effort to understand and the struggle for equilibrium. Offhand, I would miss, most of all, the men's starched white suits, emblem of respectability and semi-slave labor, worn by the unpaid 'ti moune; I would miss the girls' natural braided hair, virgin from pressing irons, and ladies discreet enough to wear all black and veils when visiting government officials to ask for favors for husbands or brothers at a price never admitted later even to themselves. There are more automobiles now, and more roads, and more holes in the roads. And in the capital itself, one jumps over the same open drains and stumbles into the same ditch down the same collectors' item curbstones as in my student years.

It seems a vicious circle with improvement only on the outer edges. And still, complain as we do—we who live there—we go on living there (if we are allowed to) or return (same conditions).

The most primitive, the most exotic, the most basic of the Caribbean in life fundamentals, Haiti gives most trouble and causes most grief, inside and out. Like a mistress too beautiful and necessary to let go, those who have known the dark island love her for what they have known and hate her for senseless infidelity; for nonfulfillment.

Here are the deep and withdrawn faces of Africa itself, not of those acculturated with new and fresh grievances. Women on donkeys seem hard, sullen, until they smile; unlike the hill people of Jamaica, they will smile if handled gently. Among the old there are still kind faces in the presence of more poverty than one should have to bear for so long, with such affluence just next door, and the babies open like chocolate flowers at the slightest attention.

This is the Haiti that I know, that, along with the deeper, hidden mysterious interior, keeps me here in spite of reason and sense.

Although my good friend Dumarsais Estimé, former president of Haiti, razed the slums in the south of the capital to construct a park ground for the Caribbean bicentennial, the slums in the center and to the north of the city range like active pox sores. With a smattering of other languages, odd pieces of European clothing, and occasional radios and juke boxes, there are strange resemblances to Chicago or Harlem or Saint Louis slums a few years back.

The guide-chauffeurs (as distinguished from ordinary cab or private cab drivers) help things not at all with tourists; they are a surly lot, tougher than the teamsters' union. On the whole, they are avaricious and sadistic, refusing most of the time to give an inch on rates, which are the highest in the Caribbean. The rare exceptions are chiefly of the old school, clean, neat, starched, and gallant when acting in capacity of guide rather than chauffeur, or the clean, sport-shirted, and well-traveled younger group.

Now I see women in the famed National Guard. During my field study days, women had no suffrage. Mrs. Price-Mars, wife of the delegate from Haiti to the United Nations and mother of Luis Mars, the ambassador from Haiti to the United States, spent much of her time campaigning for the rights of her sex. Now, in their brown uniforms with starched collars, women ride beside the military elite and occupy lesser posts in the military hierarchy. Women are also in business now, serving as salesgirls in stores where once, except for the Syrian matriarchs at the cash registers, they entered only when chaperoned.

Deforestation to make charcoal for the many iron cooking pots has made the once green hills as scraggly as the back of a mangy lion. Along with others, I seethed over the fall of the majestic pines (in the pine forests there is constant replanting) and of the great *figié* and cottonwoods to make way for insignificant roads or re-routable telephone cables.

One could go on and on caviling, but there is always the fact that Haiti is the most dramatic, the most exotic (whatever that means by now), the least diluted by Western ways, the most fundamental in terms of ethnic culture and life principles (here I speak of the vast peasant population) of all the Caribbean islands. Perhaps, too, we complain because we are concerned. Even the tourists who used to fume at the constant attacks from beggars and confidence men will return someday, seeking what they themselves do not know. But I know even after visiting green Jamaica and the sybaritic beaches of Nassau and Paradise Island, the gods of Haiti have not yet retreated in the face of the white man and his magic.

Notes

1. Dwight Lyman Moody (1837–1899) and Ira David Sankey (1840–1908) were revivalist evangelicals who wrote numerous Gospel hymns. Moody wrote the words and Sankey wrote the tunes *[Eds.]*.

2. Duppies are ghosts. The rolling calf is the animal form assumed by especially dangerous duppies *[Eds.]*.

Caribbean Tourist Tips

Katherine Dunham

On a map, the islands of the Caribbean lie between North and South America like puzzle pieces floating on a blue background, with the Leewards and the Windwards a young girl's pink necklace. The candor of chroniclers from Moreau de Saint-Méry to Seabrook,[1] the romance trailing behind a ship heavy with tourists, the markets and native costumes and language, the seaport capitals each with something different to say—these are the attributes which insure the position of the Caribbean as a most seductive mistress south of the border. Certainly Central America is unparalleled in richness of lore, remarkable flora and fauna, and impressive colonial remains. Yet the trek to the Caribbean continues.

Of twenty-odd voyages to or from the Caribbean since my student anthropologist research years, few have been by ship, yet these were most memorable. And each time I indulge in the luxury of time-saving by jet from Miami or Puerto Rico or New York or Madrid, I long for proximity with the white-fringed cobalt and emerald sea beneath.

When I set foot for the first time on an ocean-going vessel, a Royal Netherlands ship—and wept as we drew away from the unfamiliar shoreline of Manhattan—I dressed for dinner as I had somehow imagined one always did at sea, and blushed with embarrassment to find myself the only one of a half-dozen passengers with any such idea.

I fell in love with the entire Dutch people on that one trip. I have ever found again the sumptuousness of meals, the kindliness of service, the gentleness of covering the inevitable *faux pas* of the first ocean voyage,

SOURCE: Katherine Dunham, "Caribbean Tourist Tips," *Travel Magazine* (February 1964). Copyright 1964 by *Travel Magazine,* Inc. Reprinted by permission.

the eagerness to point out the beauties of sea as we sailed and land as we neared port. Through the years admiration for the Dutch courtesy has been reaffirmed many times, not the least on their own territory, and again at my own *habitation* near Port-au-Prince in Haiti when the wife of an official of the now unfortunately inactive Royal Netherlands Line approached me at a garden party to thank me for a reference to this trip of twenty years before made at a lecture earlier that day.

My second sea voyage was on the deck of one of the Compagnie Générale Transatlantique fleet. Twice the size of the little Netherlands ship, she was brimming over with adventurers bound for the Amazon, petty officials returning from the provinces to the Guineas, wives visiting convict husbands, and ladies of leisure resting, if prudent, for the strenuous receptions at their various destinations. Here a mattress on the deck was my berth, the universe of the unbelievable Caribbean sky my ceiling.

Though grateful now for what was a memorable impression, my deck trip was by no means by choice. Indiscretions in Haiti and Jamaica, time overstayed among the Maroon people of Jamaica, a delay of remittance from the foundation sponsoring my trip—all of these had depleted my allowance which, with the mismanagement of the inexperienced and over-enthusiastic, had no likelihood of lasting the year for which it was destined.

In my eagerness to fit into what I was led by my friends to expect in Martinique, I committed the first error in sound field-research technique—to listen with no cross-reference. And so I arrived to install myself at the modest Hôtel de Paris in Fort-de-France, a serious student anthropologist requesting of the management the new-type mosquito netting through which the deadly fer-de-lance could not bite its way, and singing ribald songs in Marseillaise dialect to the chambermaids to impress them with my knowledge of nursery rhyme patois! These were not my only errors, but so many times then and now I have offered thanks to others for experienced words of counsel.

As callous, as rough-shod as American tourists have always been by reputation when confronted with the unfamiliar on foreign ground, I have never felt it willful that the customs of others are so often considered without true value. One of our problems is to learn how to leap gracefully over the barriers of language. When confronted with the unintelligible—as most American educational institutions seem content with the written rather than the oral use of a foreign tongue—my compatriots, from shop clerks to ambassadors, resort to a kind of child's talkee-talkee. Or they simply refuse to learn the local language or dialect because of the embarrassment of hearing themselves speak a foreign tongue. And what pleasures, what securities, what new experiences and heightened status can be achieved, what floodgates opened at the first bright contact of words understood! The job of learning a few basic words or colloquialisms of greetings and farewells, market needs, directions, affirmations and negations, simple directions, price inquiries, and ordinary foods is not as formidable as some would believe. For my part, whether in Japan or Morocco, Haiti or Pernambuco, I come prepared, or seek out the nearest book shop to find the simplest, smallest tourist phonetic dictionary and phrase book. Most natives are delighted and flattered at this mark of esteem and interest, and redouble their efforts to offer information, matching, as it were, their wits with the enigmatical printed pages.

I have never ceased regretting my stubbornness about learning cult songs in the idiom my first years in the Caribbean. Drumming came easily to me through earlier exposure and coaching by the Africanologist Melville Herskovits. Even so, it is extremely unwise to touch musical instruments at any native dance or ceremony unless invited, or, if you have complete familiarity with a community, you request permission. Only when instruments are exposed in the marketplaces for tourist consumption can you feel completely safe in handling them. Otherwise you run the risk of incurring the wrath of not only the proprietor but the gods, for handling most used instruments or instruments which are personal property or are in private homes. Additionally, some edifices have, as in Africa, either been formally baptized and named or have by assimilation, a sort of osmosis, acquired special properties which may be diminished if handled by the profane.

Frequently that necessary item, a tourist guide, hoping for extra remuneration, will assume authority to encourage some curious or exhibitionist tourist to try his hand at a personal drum. I have seen the helpless reluctance with which a proprietor will hand over his instrument. But the guides are notoriously insensitive, particularly when exhibiting superior knowledge or class protocol, and the peasant or stall owner or musician or even high priest of Shango depends today on these intermediaries for his living for the entire year made during the brief tourist seasons. There is no payment equal to his relief or gratitude when an enlightened traveler courteously thanks the guide but refuses to touch the object, indicating that surely he would not compete with such a "maestro."

These cases are particular ones, but still ritual ones. It is good to be acquainted with a few of the rhythms of each area, to recognize them when played, to compare them, and, should the occasion arise, even demonstrate one after assurance that no taboo has been infringed upon.

Although I had long since matriculated from scholar to performer before mastering a repertoire of songs to match drum rhythms and dances in the non-English-speaking languages of the Caribbean, from my first night in Jamaica and its counterpart in Trinidad, I was grateful for a Middle West strict-Methodist childhood. On the outskirts of the bands of white-robed Shepherds and their bass-drum orchestras, I joined in syncopated renditions of Moody and Sankey hymns to the delight of spectators and gratification of followers. If you have the entire year to prepare for a vacation which may even accidentally sidetrack into field investigation, or just primary pursuit of native rhythms and rituals, instead of hovering around the remnants often set out for the unknowing, then surely a study of the vast library of music of all of these islands is warranted. And I have yet to see the tourist who could resist successively the Vodun of Haiti, Pocomania of Jamaica, limbo of the Bahamas, Shango of Trinidad, beguine of Santo Domingo, and so on down the line of sacred rituals and secular amusements.

The field techniques which contribute to fullest participation are many and diverse. As it is not possible within the scope of one sitting to enlarge upon all of them, I list a few taboos, distilled from many active years on both sides of the fence, which may make life easier for a vacationer. At least, they are worthy of consideration by a traveler capable of sensitivities, well meaning, sincere in his interest, and free of condescension in his attitudes.

1. Never make derisive or derogatory remarks in any language. Somewhere, someone will understand English, French, Dutch, German, Spanish, Portuguese, Arabic, even Russian. And most West Indian domestics, chauffeurs, guides, or hotel servants are by polite custom or insatiable curiosity in constant attendance whether in sight or not.
2. Be friendly with the opposite sex but never lose sight of the fact that most tropical peoples externalize their pleasures and emotions, and most Latin men are by habit flirtatious. But there is no society more conservative than the elite, even bourgeois, of these charming islands. Frequently gossip is the most rapid and certainly most entertaining means of spreading news, and though you may be only a few hours in port, they should be hours free of complication.
3. Unless specifically qualified, avoid discussion of political attitudes or problems. The Caribbean is in a state of changing social and political

structure, and visitors are not invited to participate in the process. In most cases this does not restrict genuine interest without evaluation. In others, it means not even too much interest. Your tourist bureau or embassy can be of help in advice on this side of things.

4. Like public behavior, clothes should follow your own national costume, but with all modesty that allows for comfort. Legs well covered are the rule for bush visits, feet well covered whether in town or out, and under no circumstances ladies in slacks, unless yachting.

5. It is fun to dance to the local ballroom dances. It is better to start learning at home or on shipboard. But no matter how well you dance, it is never wise to try and out-dance the natives. The rum on every island is the drink—not only is it a subtle courtesy but it is custom. It is also best health- and behavior-wise. Something about the tropics makes a number of north-country drinks harder to support, and nothing is more ridiculous than the man who cannot gauge his alcohol, or more shocking than the woman who becomes an exhibit.

6. When photographing, as you surely will want to do, whether from mountain top into valley, following a carnival procession, or picking out physical types, it is always best to be on sure ground. The professional will either be discreet or will have such an air of authority that he stands a good chance of being accepted without question or protest. But some situations may be embarrassing, even dangerous, or at least annoying. Try and refuse demands for money or tips. A kind of friendly good will, and a promise of a later print, may save a riot for hand-outs. If on uncertain ground—babies are usually a risky subject, the machine pointed at them may constitute a sort of evil-eye—a friend or guide is advised. Today, most public monuments, parks, market places, crossroads, and beaches may be photographed without question. The clever photographer sets his camera as best he may with the brilliant, tricky Caribbean lighting, then waits for an unsuspecting subject to pass while he ostentatiously fixes his attention on the background. On filming special communities, ceremonies, and dances, a Polaroid camera which gives immediate prints for distribution may prove invaluable.

Viewed in retrospect, my years of applying field techniques have paid themselves off many times the world over. Any set of rules at first glance seems to infringe upon the freedom you look forward to when leaving suburbia or a college lecture room and booking passage by air or sea to far places. But those who have traveled extensively either for business or pleasure soon learn that like all assignments in life there are certain keys which facilitate mobility, which augment pleasure, stimulate interest, and gratify curiosity and wanderlust.

The list of suggestions, cautions, advice, even rules governing getting the utmost from excursions into strange territories, grows as you increase in sensitivity and interest. A cruise to the Caribbean is no longer only the exquisite beauty of matchless night skies with stars within reach, an ocean like black velvet at night and bottomless sapphire in the day, a moon that you can read by and a sun that bursts like a rocket into early morning, puts you to sleep at midday, and precipitates a flame ball into the sea at cocktail time. A cruise is also a time of unspoken obligation to know more, to return to suburbia better informed, even while enjoying all of those intoxicating beauties on ship and others on shore. These few notes may serve as guidance for seasons to come—from one who has often hidden in the hills at the first "all ashore" siren!

Notes

1. Médéric-Louis-Élie Moreau de Saint-Méry (1750–1819), a native of Martinique, was a lawyer, historian, and publisher who played an active part in the early days of the French Revolution. Having incurred the enmity of Robespierre, he fled to North America, where he opened a bookshop and printery in Philadelphia. His *Déscription topographique, physique, civile, politique et historique de la partie française de l'Isle Saint-Domingue* was published in 1797–1798. William Buehler Seabrook (1886–1945) was a travel writer whose book on Haiti, *The Magic Island,* was published in 1929 *[Eds.].*

Getting the Show on the Road

An Excerpt

RUTH BECKFORD

In 1963, [Katherine Dunham's] brother-in-law Davis Pratt, a professor in the Design Department of Southern Illinois University, Carbondale, convinced the Fine Arts Department that her archives should be established there and that she should be an artist in residence. Although the University of Texas was also interested, Illinois was her home and seemed a more fitting location to house her history. So, from 1964 to 1966, whenever time permitted, she was artist in residence at SIU.

In 1965 Dunham resumed a relationship with Senegal, [in West] Africa, originally begun in 1962 while she was gathering dancers and material for the show *Bamboche!* In Senegal she found that the effect of her company on European whites was documented in reviews, but that its effect on black students was not. On the occasion of her first audience with Senegalese president Léopold Senghor she was told that, when her company first opened in Europe, it had caused a cultural revolution that paralleled their political and economic revolutions. Different peoples' chiefs-of-state in sub-Saharan Africa had been encouraged and inspired by her formula and format, adding course material from their own countries.

Dunham's presence in Africa thus opened a new vista for blacks. Afterward, when her company performed in Paris, she saw to it that the American embassy gave free tickets to African students, much to the chagrin of managements since shows were always sold out. Fortunately, the students saw her performances and, on occasions when she would return to Africa

SOURCE: Ruth Beckford, *Katherine Dunham: A Biography,* with a foreword by Arthur Mitchell (New York: Marcel Dekker, 1979), 60–62. Copyright 1979 by Ruth Beckford. Reprinted by permission.

for new material, she was received with open arms. The African students recognized her knowledge as well as the cultural, sociological, artistic, and political significance of her work. They felt she belonged to them.

In 1965 Dunham rallied her company together for another appearance in this country at the Apollo Theater, a famous black vaudeville house in Harlem. Dunham instinctively felt that this would be her company's last appearance. They appeared by accident when the act that was originally scheduled canceled out due to the summer race riots. When they arrived, Dunham sensed that to gather the dancers, rehearse, inspire, protect, baby, and discipline them was too hard. She knew it was no longer her career and that she was no longer receiving the personal satisfaction that made the hardships of being star, producer, and touring with a company worthwhile.

So, in the following year she returned to Africa between such projects as appearing at the Apollo, starting a new school, undertaking a Paris tour, choreographing an Italian show that starred Marcello Mastroianni, and establishing her archives at SIU in Carbondale. She felt that it was logical to align herself with the Festival of Black Arts in Dakar, Senegal, where Senghor had requested that she return as unofficial U.S. ambassador. In 1966 she made three trips as a U.S. specialist.

There were tragic moments on this assignment. She knew that she was acting for the United States and, consequently, resisted the temptation to expose to Africa what she felt were America's true racial attitudes. Instead, she continued to work and kept strong feelings of responsibility toward her country. Still, she possessed an unwillingness to give in to all of its dictates, in recognizing that she belonged to and was surrounded by the black struggle. Not until she returned to the United States after being appointed to a position of technical and cultural advisor in Africa by President Senghor and had taken her present-day assignment in East Saint Louis did she realize that her battle against racial injustice had only begun. She thought that the events of discrimination she had experienced on the road were incidental, like living her book, *A Touch of Innocence*. She was equally certain that the results of the labors of her friends during university days would have contributed toward settling the racial question. In Senegal in 1966 she realized that she had aided in spearheading Africa's cultural revolution. Furthermore, she felt that she belonged to the African intellectual complex and wanted to understand and develop with the African country.

After the festival was over, she remained in Senegal to train its national ballet. She was not happy with the company's objectives; whereas they wanted to work with "new" creative forms, she felt good theater demanded that they recreate from their own authentic cultural heritage. Even if today, in retrospect, she feels their African objectives were right, at that time she was far more interested in being a guide and in building a way for the Senegalese people to find security in living while training and developing their own indigenous resources.

Plan for an Academy of
West African Cultural Arts

KATHERINE DUNHAM

The Île de Gorée in the harbor of Dakar, Senegal, is ideally situated for a West African cultural arts center. This is not only because of its geographic position but because of Senegal's traditional cultural leadership in French-speaking Africa. The interest of the president of the republic in visual and performing arts has been known in these French-speaking countries and in Europe for many years and has now become known in many other countries of the world through translations of Léopold Senghor's writings and his intellectual leadership.

That a national academy of arts and letters, of fine arts, should be under proposal in Senegal at the same time as the National Academy of Arts and Humanities has been passed as a law and the Kennedy Center of Performing Arts is in formation in the United States seems strongly indicative of the common thinking of the two countries, and of two chiefs of state who simultaneously felt the importance of mass cultural education in their countries.

The National Academy at Dakar operates now under the Commissaire des Arts, Maurice Sonhar Senghor, brother of His Excellency Léopold Senghor, President of the Republic. In a small group of rehabilitated army shelters, music, painting, weaving, pottery, fundamentals of drama, and ballet for children are taught. The needs for expansion in cultural arts cannot be satisfied here, nor is the teaching staff adequate for the plans of

SOURCE: Katherine Dunham, "Plan for Gorée as Residence Academy for West African Cultural Arts," unpublished paper, written in 1965, in the Katherine Mary Dunham Papers, Special Collections, Morris Library, Southern Illinois University, Carbondale. Copyright 1965 by Katherine Dunham. Reprinted by permission. Minor changes of editorial style have been made.

development. This is, however, a remarkably serious beginning and is expected to continue in the capital as a school of fine arts.

On my last visit to Senegal, in April 1965, my interest was to examine the possibilities of a dance academy of international proportions. On many points regarding the interpretation of dance the president of the republic and I have agreed for some time: Dance is a social act, and a social expression. It is likely that vocal sound and the conscious rhythmic motion that makes dance were born at one and the same time, long before man spoke. The clan, tribal, family life, and anxieties, fears, determinations, and emotions, tender and cruel, have been danced since known man. Also his history, mores, ethics, religion, and philosophy; and it was a thing of participation, and fulfillment of a life need.[1] This meaning of dance has not been buried in the Westernization of most African peoples, of most other countries changing their forms of social structure and government, which we term "emerging."

The most complete studies of dance encompass not only the complex surrounding dance—that is, music, instruments of accompaniment, artifacts, and social organization—but enter easily into the fields of design, psychology, the humanities, and the social sciences. It has been on this basis that the former and present Dunham schools have operated and from this complex has come my own career and more than twenty-five years of world touring of the Dunham Company.

Before my departure for Africa this April, and in keeping with the work which I have been doing as artist in residence and professor at Southern Illinois University, I requested and received permission from the president of the university, Delyte Morris, to include the university in the plan for an academy at Senegal should this be worked out to the satisfaction of all concerned.

It now seems time for universities the world over to supplement government action in expanding cultural and educational horizons, and Southern Illinois University is well on its way to a firm position in this respect. Exchange programs are presently under way in Nepal and Mali, and Peace Corps training for Nepal and Senegal is a part of the university's International Services. Working with the State Department and host countries, great progress has been made in deepening understandings and exchanging cultural patterns that eventually result in the dissolution of social and racial prejudices. The following statement further supports the validity of our wish for the academy at Gorée. The arts, visual and performing, are, because of their freedom from language barriers among the most effective agents of contact, communication and persuasion. Now that the State Department has begun to concern itself with not only the exportation but the importation of fine arts from the exterior, a further step would seem to me to be the assumption of a definite position on the part of the agencies of the American government and private foundations, it being assumed that the two are working a common end, in guidance, selection, training, and education of artists in countries which need and wish this aid.[2]

In the interim since the above recommendation was presented to the Ford Foundation, universities the world over have been making rapid strides toward assuming greater responsibility in government and international affairs. Since heretofore it has not been the policy of the United States to include its educational institutions in foreign policy, the progress in international relationships made by Southern Illinois University are indeed to be commended. The university director's enthusiasm for the plan at Gorée follows the general thinking toward an enlarged cultural attitude.

The idea of a dance academy in the conventional interpretation has always seemed too limiting to me. Therefore, in continuing discussions with the president of Senegal and his associates, and later in Washington with G. Mennon Williams, head of African programs at the U.S. Department of State, and Miss Erin Hubbert, liaison for West African programs, and, finally, with members of the university staff, the idea developed from a dance academy into an academy of West African cultural arts. Mrs. Shelley, liaison officer of UNESCO, stressed the importance of archives.

In certain areas of Africa, advancement in technology is measured in terms of estrangement from all aspects of ancestral, social, religious, and cultural arts programs. This has resulted often in the destruction of monumental and irreplaceable works of art, the suppression of music, song, and dance forms that revolve around ritual and ceremony. One of the important functions of the academy could be to serve as an agent of research and record of these forms that may, without this foundation's support, dissolve into the rapidly changing world history that could easily leave mankind with no record of his past.

LOCATION. Gorée, a small island lying approximately twenty minutes by motor launch from the Senegal mainland, was at one time a trading post for slaves gathered from the West Coast and interior of Africa. The main structure of the building and the cubicles in which the slaves lay, chained spoon-fashioned, waiting embarkation for the West Indies, the Middle Passage, and the small door through which they passed single file down a rocky beach to the slave ships, are still intact at Gorée. The existence of these remains as well as those of other colonial structures creates an atmosphere ideal for students seriously interested in design, art, and aesthetics, and the partial isolation of the island ensures a serious concentration of study in the performing arts.

The fact that buildings practically ready for occupation exist is fortuitous; the former recreation center and barracks of the French Army occupies approximately a half kilometer of beach line on the north side of the island. These barracks are complete with sleeping rooms, sanitation, mess halls, two villas, and an exercise area evidently used by the military and as a children's playground. This barracks has recently been turned over intact to the Senegalese government, and was requested of the president by me for use as the academy. Should this not be feasible during the period of the festival (hotel space may be at a premium during this time), I do not find this serious, as a number of months will be required to finalize the academy as visualized.

PHASE ONE. During my State Department assignment in Senegal (six months beginning on or about 15 November 1955) training and choreographing for the National Ballet and recruiting and auditioning new material from the interior will be a major part of my activity. Any remaining time will be spent in attempting to pass judgment on future teaching material, and to evaluate students and potential teachers. I shall make every effort to investigate what folk material should be classified for permanent archives and for documentary as well as theater use. The existing mess halls and officers' entertainment halls can serve during the first months of operation as studios for dance with the following renovations and requisitions.

Since the period of Phase One would coincide with the six months prior to the festival, Southern Illinois University participation in these early stages seems timely. Reconstruction of the slave quarters to a degree sufficient for safe inspection and frescoing the walls with appropriate scenes for tourist interest is one project which I have suggested to the Design Department of the university. A festival or permanent booklet on the slave area as well as other colonial ruins might also result from this period of residence.[3]

NOTES

1. Katherine Dunham, "Lecture Notes on the Dance in Modern Society," Faculty Club, Southern Illinois University, 4 June 1965.

2. Katherine Dunham, "Recommendation for a Program of Cultural Expansion in Three Areas," submitted to the Ford Foundation, 6 January 1964.

3. Further information on La Maison des Esclaves on the Île de Gorée is now available in French and English on a Web site mounted by UNESCO: http://webworld. unesco.org/goree. *[Eds.]*.

Address Delivered at the Dakar Festival of Negro Arts

KATHERINE DUNHAM

Monsieur le Président, distinguished members of the Colloquium, honored guests, and visitors.

With the passage of time, one of my increasingly developed characteristics has become a respect for, as well as dependency upon, the intuitive; not in the sense of the mystic, but based upon a good long period of experience and exposure to the ways of other nations and other peoples. So without thinking twice I have known that the world would be grateful for the event that is the reason for our being here today.[1] Now that the nervous tension of pre-festival has passed, those of us who have so hoped for and worked toward its success can realize that if nothing else were to happen during the festival, we have had our compensation in the beauty of the city and its people, the combined sophistication and primitiveness of the spectacle of Gorée staged by Juan Mazel to the poetry of an old friend, Jean Brierre; the treasures of the dynamic museum, this gathering together in the colloquium of specialists, friends, and intellectuals from all over the world; the brilliant opening at the Daniel Sorano Theater by the Nigerian players in a remarkable production of Wole Soyinka; and the elegance of the audience of the inauguration itself—these things alone would make this occasion a history-making event.

To some of us who have dreamed of such an event since the earliest days of *Présence Africaine,* to have made of this festival a *fait accompli* is

SOURCE: Katherine Dunham, address delivered at the first World Black and African Festival of Arts and Culture, Dakar, Senegal, 3 April 1966, unpublished paper in the Katherine Mary Dunham Papers, Special Collections, Morris Library, Southern Illinois University, Carbondale. Copyright 1966 by Katherine Dunham. Reprinted by permission. Minor corrections and changes of editorial style have been made.

nothing short of miraculous. This in a country, or I should say, in a world, where man has begun to drift away from magic and believes no more in miracles.

I have thought much over a statement made by the president of the republic, Léopold Sédar Senghor, that the failure of the festival would represent the failure of negritude in general and of Senegal in particular. To me, could anything as inconceivable have occurred, this would have indicated neither the failure of negritude nor of the Senegalese people, but of the conscience of the entire world.

Now when I have seen in these few days so many friends who in effect have contributed directly or indirectly to my thinking, even to my life of action, I realize that no man with an honest mission walks alone.

Today there is no one comparable to Dr. Price-Mars,[2] and there was no one comparable to him when in June 1936 in Pétionville, Haiti, he received my credentials from the universities of Chicago and Northwestern, from Herskovits, Redfield, Franz Boas, Malinowski, and Warner, and took me, a lone student social anthropologist, to my first Vodun ceremony. It was a ceremony venerating the ancestors who had come over from a land known to the Haitians as "Nan Guinée." Then began the intensive work under Dr. Price-Mars, and because it was work with a man who loved not only his country and his people but all humanity, I feel that the gateways to my own ancestors were opened by Legba and that from then on my path, though difficult, was clear.

Haiti was the most complex of all of the areas of my studies but in many ways, with its complex of vestigial cults brought over by, among others, Aradas, Yorubas, Ibos, Congos, Mandingoes (Koromantees went to the British islands, Angolas to Brazil, and so on), it furnished the basis for a study that was accepted by the University of Chicago as a master's thesis. Some of the results are in this small book,[3] a concentrated analysis of the dances of Haiti which has served many an academician of ritual, music, and dance as a guide book for social organization, artifacts, musical accompaniment, classification, and the interrelation between form and function.

My first Haitian experience also served me for the construction of a large part of the material which went into the primitive and folk aspects of the Dunham performing company, which still serves our schools in New York, Stockholm, and Paris as a basis for training technique, and which will undoubtedly serve other world tours of the same company at some future date. But I say to those of you who need guidelines that none of this could have been done—neither the development of the intellectual stimulus nor the professional success, which has taken us into more than fifty different countries of the world—had not the approach been that of the humanist preceding the scientist. Great art comes from love and is a constant dedication in love. If this is coupled with clear vision, durability, insight into the necessary techniques and the materials with which to work, I see no barriers in front of either institution or individual.

I see Louis Achille here and am carried back to Martinique where his father took over from Price-Mars and acquainted me with that tiny island and what was left of song, ritual, and dance; out of this experience, of months of living in a tiny fishing village, grew a ballet, *L'Ag'ya,* which Arnold Haskell, the British critic, has called "the *Giselle* of the Caribbean"! And Gbeho, a musicologist from Ghana,[4] reminded me the other day that his entire company of dancers and musicians sat through matinee and evening shows in London, staying between shows to exchange drum rhythms with our Haitian and Cuban and Brazilian drummers.

Before approaching the very brief formal paper that I have prepared for the Colloquium, I would like to pass on some thoughts which have come to me and which seem applicable after our many hours of *Commissions.*

At one time a dear friend of mine, Bernard Berenson, asked me if I had a definition for beauty. Until now I have not found it, but somehow I felt a close tie between aesthetics and nature in the sense of living close to nature. I feel that those of us who have inherited industrial and now atomic societies tend to see only the externals, but that those who think in terms of symbology find some hidden meaning which transforms, to them, the very appearance of the object. I like a quote which I found recently in Christmas Humphreys's *Buddhism* (London: Cassell, 1962): "The Buddhist artist's aim is to teach by the symbolic value of his artifact the way to spiritual experience of which his art was the outward and visible sign." I have brought in this quotation from Eastern thinking because of a conviction that there is a strong relationship between African and Eastern thinking, in that, for both, identity is a basic principle. From Arthur Waley's *Zen Buddhism and Its Relation to Art* (London: Lozac, 1922), applied to the field of artistic activity, this is a definition of the highest form of conception, the purest kind of inspiration: the knower becomes the object of his knowledge, the artist the thing he envisions or conceives, and if he possesses the proper means of exteriorization he will transmit in symbols or shapes or signs something that contains a spark of that eternal stream of life or consciousness which abides when forms decay.

The other day, in a Colloquium discussion the question as to whether the advisability of separating dance and music into sacred and secular as I have done in *Dances of Haiti* was hanging in a state of immobile suspension. One or more participants remained with the feeling that African art expressions are all sacred. I feel that some compromise can be met without too much difficulty, but in support of the importance of the sacred, let me read loosely some deductions from my readings in Buddhist art. "The spirit of worship released and gave expression to the highest emotions in which the roots of all great art are found. When to this deep devotion . . . was added the intuitive awareness that life in all its forms is one indivisible Life, and all its expressions but fleeting carriers of that Life, the way is clear for that release of spiritual energy which flowered in the greatest period of Indian art." In all art, there is an insincerity if the stream of spiritual experience is not followed. There must be an intensity of devotion, and a strong inspiration to sustain the richness which Africa possesses. Whether this should be a respect for the traditional, a new set of ideologies, or both remains to be seen.

In experiencing Wole Soyinka's *Kongi's Harvest*[5] at the Daniel Sorano Theater I could not help but remark how well and how carefully the demands for a successful performing arts presentation are followed out: that the perceiver must enter in, be one with, be a part of, not bound by the limits of the stage. In this way series of mysteries of personal interpretations become intelligible. We spoke so often in our committee of the language barrier imposed by the theater of acting, but if we think that:

There must be originality. Influence is inevitable but nothing that is copied is true art.
Art must have the quality of spontaneity, no matter how highly trained, and from this an exhilaration diffuses which the observer feels.
A spiritual, aesthetic, and utilitarian life of the nation must progress as a whole. I think of Japan, where every movement is one of symbology, where great emotional economy is practiced, and where a 450-pound sumo fighter is able to perform a tea ceremony.

I would say that Mr. Soyinka possesses to the highest degree another quality of theater, which is the knowledge of economy. Where to stop so that the beholder participates, supplying maximum to minimum with an absence of visible skill. If the basic requirement of the performing arts are fulfilled, our concerns about language barriers are indeed minimized.

Now I come to a question that has puzzled me for some time: what should the spiritual strength of Africa be? I talk not of the potential but of the guideline for the future, for the young who are children today, so that we who, because of our very natures, would wish to participate will know our direction. If we think of all of Africa or of Africa in its total, because that is what we are here for, then we think of negritude, of culture, of ancestry. The conflict in achieving oneness is small beside the reward. This has been done in other parts of the world and can and will be done in Africa; for a further enlightenment on this concept of unity, I would suggest that *The New States of Africa* (1961) by John Joseph Vianney become a first in your bibliography.

During our very interesting committee sessions it occurred to me that there was among certain of the participants a kind of mistrust, a *méfiance* at the likelihood of a reversal to the traditional, or I should say more specifically, to a nostalgia of the traditional that might serve to inhibit "modernization," and I have put *modernization* in quotes. My "methodology," and again I put this word in quotes, my procedures in these many years of the same or closely related struggle has been the combination of ideology with education in the traditional and contemporary forms. As a matter of fact, ideology can be a non-aggressive finding of self through total historic examination, no matter what religion or tribe or language.

The school, which operated, again unsubsidized, in New York from 1943 until 1957, and which has been reopened on a smaller scale in New York during the past three years, offered [a broad] curriculum. . . . Unfortunately, after the first three and a half years, I found it financially impossible to remain in full residence at the school and although we had been touring from 1939 in the United States and Canada, I found that to support a company of the magnitude of ours it would be necessary to tour outside the country. For many years the troupe was classified among the first three or four touring companies in the world. In 1947 we spent a summer in Mexico, which you will find elaborated upon in Miss Eartha Kitt's autobiography. In the summer of 1938, we were to have spent three weeks in London at the Prince of Wales Theatre. We stayed for three months and then moved into Paris, which has unashamedly and in so many instances admitted our influence on world art. I say these things not so much for myself as for you, so that you will realize that nothing is insurmountable, particularly with the will to evolve, which I know is a fundamental quality of the African people.

My friend the psychiatrist Harry Stack Sullivan used to call this the "diffused optimism" of the Negro race. As much as I would like to count upon the recognition of the potential of Africa by the rest of the world, and in this I mean a recognition that is concrete and will pave the material way, which would save so much wear and tear, and so much real deprivation on the part of the dedicated artist or leader, as much as I would like to offer encouragement in this direction, I must say and I believe that I am simply repeating the words of the first speaker of this Colloquium, Monsieur André Malraux—this is something the motivation of which must be done by you and you alone. Of course this is not an inclusive you, and then whatever else follows could be considered manna from heaven.

NOTES

1. A series of meetings of African and African diasporic writers, begun in Rome in 1956, led to the organization of the first World Black and African Festival of Arts and Culture in 1966. Better known as the World Festival of Negro Arts, it was held in Dakar, Senegal, in April 1966 *[Eds.]*.

2. Jean Price-Mars (1876–1969) was a Haitian physician, public official, diplomat, ethnologist, and historian of his country's sociological and intellectual development. Besides various governmental posts, Dr. Price-Mars was a founder of the Society of Haitian History and Geography, the first director of the Haitian-American Institute, and president of the University of Haiti *[Eds.]*.

3. Dunham's thesis, "Dances of Haiti: Their Social Organization, Classification, Form, and Function," was submitted to the Department of Anthropology at the University of Chicago in partial fulfillment of the requirements for a master of arts degree in 1937. It was first published in Spanish (*Las danzas de Haiti*, 1947), then in French (*Les danses d'Haïti*, 1950), and finally in English (*Dances of Haiti*,1983) *[Eds.]*.

4. Philip Comi Gbeho (1904–1976), composer of the national anthem of Ghana.

5. *Kongi's Harvest* was first produced in Lagos, Nigeria, in 1965. Soyinka revived it for the Dakar festival in 1966 *[Eds.]*.

Dunham Jailed
Following Protest

Katherine Dunham, Negro dancer and artist in residence at Southern Illinois University, was charged with disorderly conduct last night when she objected to the booking of one of her students as a suspect in recent racial disorders here.

The police said Miss Dunham had been asked to leave the booking office at police headquarters when she became irate but that she had refused to do so. An officer picked her up and carried her to a second-floor cell, where she spent three and a half hours before she was released on bond.

Miss Dunham, who is fifty-seven years old, teaches at the university's Alton campus, near East Saint Louis.

Mrs. Clarice Braddix of East Saint Louis, mother of Darryl Braddix, the student Miss Dunham defended, said her son apparently had been implicated by another youth in window smashing in a Negro section of the city the night before.

Miss Dunham and Miss Jeanelle Stovall, who was identified by the dancer as a vacationing employee of the United Nations, had gone downtown with Mr. Braddix. The police approached them on the street and the two women accompanied the youth to headquarters. Mr. Braddix, a twenty-one-year old freshman, was charged in a warrant with criminal damage of property and held in lieu of $10,000 bail.

Miss Dunham said tonight: "When I asked what the charges against Darryl were, I was told to mind my own business. One cop started pushing me around and two other pig cops started twisting my arms. I asked if I were under arrest and they said: 'You sure are.'"

SOURCE: Associated Press, East Saint Louis, Illinois, 29 July 1967, "Katherine Dunham Is Jailed 3½ Hours Following Protest," *New York Times,* 30 July 1967. Copyright 1967 by Associated Press. Reprinted by permission.

Katherine Dunham

GWEN MAZER

It is early morning in Haiti, with a brilliant blue sky and sunlight gleaming on the gently waving palm fronds. Katherine Dunham, hair fluffed into a moderate Afro, arms and neck strewn with gold amulets and chains, is sitting on her dining terrace sipping rich Haitian coffee. Her amber brown skin glows with a honeyed sheen, her eyes slightly veiled with the pain of seeing and knowing too much. She is wearing a crisp, white, loose-fitting dress that seems even whiter against the green profusion of the surrounding garden.

Katherine Dunham found the keys to success and fame when she unleashed the movements and rhythms she discovered as an anthropology student studying the origins of dance in the Caribbean. Here it is forty years later.

We are preparing to drive to Ibo Beach, a resort of comfortable beach houses on a small island forty-five minutes from Port-au-Prince. Katherine wants to spend a few days near the ocean basking in the sun and sea wind. It is a good atmosphere, she says, in which to sort her thoughts.

After a pleasant drive we arrive, accompanied by her administrative assistant and right hand at Southern Illinois University, Jeanelle Stovall, and Rosie Rubenstein, who runs Residence Katherine Dunham in Haiti. After being shown to our cottages and comfortably settled, Dunham curls up on a chaise lounge. Her eyes facing out to sea, she begins to talk.

"When I was a child, I used to play a game with my brother Albert about how I would go to the moon, to Africa, have all sorts of adventures.

SOURCE: Gwen Mazer, "Katherine Dunham," *Essence* (December 1976). Copyright 1976 by *Essence* Communications Partners. Reprinted by permission. Minor corrections of names and dates have been made.

"My greatest struggle was the decision between anthropology and dance. My parents were mystified as to why my brother and I had gone off into these strange academic pursuits. My brother was a philosopher. My father wanted him to enter his dry cleaning business. They eventually accepted the theatrical part of my life because of the favorable publicity. But the idea of anthropology was more than they could understand. They wanted me to be a schoolteacher, but it seemed such an uninteresting profession compared to the world I saw open to explore—to know other people's ways of being and thinking.

"After being trained in anthropology, I knew I was not meant to be confined. There were other places to be. Having escaped the Midwest, I was not going to be held by the color bars of the United States. I was so intensely interested in what I was doing that to do without things or go hungry seemed fairly normal. One does live by other than bread. The inner life must be fed. What comes to you, comes a great deal by what you believe in.

"I performed with my first so-called company at the 1933 World's Fair in Chicago," she goes on, "then at a small theater where my former teacher, Ludmilla Speranzeva, had arranged for us to appear. Erich Fromm saw me perform there, and he and Charles Johnson urged the Rosenwalds to consider me for the fellowship. They used to come around to our Cube Theater, this stable where Ruth and Bill Attway and I worked. I think the only way a person inclined toward intellectual and artistic freedom could survive in those days was within a group of people considered bohemians. Arna Bontemps, Langston Hughes, Charles White, Charles Sebre, we were a people's liberation group. I very naturally gravitated toward that group with the help of my brother. Without that atmosphere I don't know how many of us would have continued.

"In 1934 I was a guest star of the Chicago Opera. After that I formed several companies and finally my own, the Dunham Dance Company."

Traveling rarely with any endowment, her company, dancers, drummers, musicians, costumes, and sets visited fifty-seven countries around the world. From South America to the Far East she left a trail of headlines, triumphs, and hard work behind her, presenting all aspects of black culture on stage and fighting segregation in hotels, restaurants, and theaters. Her arrival in London in 1948 was heralded in the press as comparable to the arrival of Diaghilev's Ballets Russes in Paris in 1909. At the same time Ms. Dunham was invited to address the Royal Anthropological Society, of which she was made a member. In the American South an enthusiastic but segregated audience clamored for a speech. She announced that she would never play at the theater again until the audience was integrated. In São Paulo, Brazil, she instituted a suit against a hotel for discrimination that caused the president to pass a national law forbidding discrimination in public places. She received his personal apologies.

When the company performed in Paris for the first time, there were no blacks in the opening-night audience. She immediately made sure tickets were set aside and that the African students at the Sorbonne were made welcome. Among them were Léopold Senghor, now president of Senegal, Sékou Toure of Guinea, and many of the ministers of Nigeria and Dahomey.

"I had to dance. I danced to something so much vaster than the audience. I felt part of a universal setting. It justified all the hardships. Mood, movement, choreographic patterns, posture were all so natural to me. What I did on stage was considered daring. I thought of myself as rather conservative. Being on stage was, for me, making love. It was an expression of my love of humanity and things of beauty. This is what took Europe by storm. Initially I was embarrassed by discussions about sexuality and my legs. I didn't realize that sexuality was a dominating factor in my life or that it was different for anyone else.

"I loved going to the theater. I'd always go a couple of hours before performance to absorb the atmosphere. I liked seeing the show hung, the platforms set up. The floor would become my living room, and I would lie on the stage to prepare for the audience. I didn't understand why the company didn't spend as much time in the theater as possible. So I was always disciplining to keep it at its peak.

"The company thought I loved authority. I hated it. But as producer, director, and star performer, I would finally have to insist on complete order. Intermission was my time to compliment and correct. Everyone in the company would gather. I became so sensitive to the whole management of the stage, lights, music. Every part of me would see right and wrong.

"For me the greatest part of performing was the intensity of meeting the challenge of different situations, different locations and people. Mistakenly or not, I felt also that I had to carry on part of my intellectual life while performing. At the time the real satisfaction in my life was performing, but it gave me great pleasure to know that I had this other capacity in hand.

"When I founded the Dunham School, the curriculum was often criticized. Why the teaching of the humanities, philosophy, languages, aesthetics, as well as the Dunham Technique? I believe these things are necessary for the complete person, and so to be the complete dancer I could not simply teach dancing."

Sounds of the sea lull us and she begins to talk of rhythms, relationships, and love. "It is so necessary to find and understand your individual rhythm. That's why I believe it is important to maintain close contact with nature. It helps to restore our inner balance, which can be both a healing and selective force. I believe the best relationships are built on mutual rhythms. We are more alike in this than on the basis of race. My own nature is basically turned inward—self-examining—so it is very easy for my rhythm to be disturbed.

"I don't pretend to understand love. One of my faults has been my inability to love single-mindedly. Many years of conversation and friendship with psychoanalyst and writer Erich Fromm have helped me develop a greater knowledge of myself. I do know that you can become too involved and spoil the very thing you think you want. I don't want love invading my privacy and being worn out by too much familiarity. It's part of my fight for absolute freedom. I think that love is the tender care and concern that is left after the thrill of pursuit and the rapture of capture is over. We must learn to remain objective and detached enough. What counts, if you really love someone, is to be able to stand on your own love and not worry about whether they love you back.

"One of the great loves of my life was Bernard Berenson, the art historian. He was eighty-three years old when we met. He was the catalyst for one of the most important turning points in my growth and character. David Aster and Serge Tolstoy, the grandson of the writer Leo Tolstoy, had written to Berenson about me. He invited me to lunch at his Villa i Tati, just outside of Florence, and I was late. When I arrived he was pacing the terrace looking very irritated. No one ever kept him waiting, and I thought I would die of embarrassment. But our rhythms meshed, and we became immediately close.

"He took the time to bring me closer to myself. He helped me to a greater confidence in myself as an anthropologist and performer in the theater. A deep relationship evolved over ten years. At one point I seriously considered giving up my career, going to I Tati and burying myself in his library.

"I felt an intense desire to be near him. Once he said that had we met sooner, something could have come of it. He was famous for his courtships of beautiful and elegant women of the world. It was difficult for me to put myself in the category of these women, but if I take his view of it,

I believe he felt that I filled certain of his needs. If this were not the case, I probably would not have seen so much of him. I certainly depended on him to strengthen my confidence in myself.

"He was always kind and thoughtful of my wishes. There was a great feeling of sexuality in his courtship with me. I certainly would have relinquished a sexual life to be with him. Though sex is one of the accepted patterns of relating, there are other ways. To deny sex in an intellectual relationship would be unfortunate. Yet if I had to choose, for the most part, I would choose the intellectual. If one can have both, it's really ideal.

"When we met, Berenson was rather frail and could no longer travel. He asked me to be his eyes, to write him my impressions as I traveled. I wrote pages, on the Peróns, Argentina, life in Japan. I would wait breathlessly to hear his opinions of my observations and writing. It was through him that I gained the confidence to write my first book, *A Touch of Innocence* (New York: Harcourt, Brace, 1959). He said to me that two things were like making love—the theater and writing.

"Nothing is accidental—the people you meet, fall in love with—it all rests on inner rhythms. We just have to be receptive and ready to follow where it takes us.

"I came to Haiti in 1936 as an anthropology student from the University of Chicago under a Rosenwald fellowship to study the dances of the Caribbean and to learn about their form and function. After traveling through Trinidad, Martinique, and Jamaica, I finally settled in Haiti. I lived at the Excelsior Hotel, a sort of Bemelman's dream, gingerbread style, with Victorian cupolas and curlicued terraces, run by two very proper Haitian ladies, the Rouzier sisters.

"I'm sure I was both a mystery and a trial to many Haitians, who certainly were not used to foreign young ladies taken to driving into the hills at all hours of the night following the sound of drums to observe or participate in the dances and ceremonies. I soon realized that the dances and the rituals of the Vodun were one. Fortunately there was a strong recognition among the priesthood of the blood relationship of all people whose ancestors came from Africa. So I photographed, recorded, filled notebooks with observations, learned the dances, and was initiated into the Rada-Dahomey cult.

"In Haiti, Brazil, Cuba, and other parts of the Caribbean the Vodun god structure has maintained itself as a vital and practiced belief. In the dances the gods who possess you through the rhythms and vibrations become your gods. This has left me with many gods to serve," she says smiling in her enigmatic way.

"Once the Haitians understood my interest in learning, they were pleased to teach me about the Vodun without proselytizing. One of the things the cult religions brought to me is the firm belief in having guidance and protection by the ancestors and the gods. In these ancient and deep beliefs of African lore there is a spiritual key for survival today and the development of man. We really need more black anthropology students, there is so much research," sighs Dunham.

"Here at Residence Katherine Dunham we have ceremonies regularly. Our head priest, two *mambos* (high priestesses), and our drummers have been attached to the place from the beginning.

"I'm so attached to this country. I have a lot of faith in Haiti in spite of its great problems. I've been to many of the islands of the Caribbean. Some of them are very neat and clean as opposed to the helter-skelter mid-town Port-au-Prince. Yet the island itself is so beautiful. Its mountains, beaches, its people really do possess a magic. This has really been home since the 1940s. I believe that if black Americans were to come here, they would find a great deal of the spirit and the feeling that they expect to find in Africa."

Days later, back in Port-au-Prince, I sit with Katherine on the terrace enjoying the late afternoon sun, talking, and sipping coconut water, her conversation rising and flowing in crystal-quick thoughts interspersed with her constant shadows of introspection. From the main terrace the view of the surrounding jungle is one of nearly biblical splendor—coconut and royal palms, mangoes, breadfruit, papayas, banana, orange, and lemon trees, tropical oak, and mahogany. Flowers growing in wild profusion, varieties of hibiscus, poinsettia bushes, jasmine, gardenia, ferns, and orchids hang in baskets from the trees.

"I bought the property of Habitation Leclerc over thirty years ago," she continues. "It was originally the home of Pauline Bonaparte Leclerc, Napoleon's sister. I was fascinated by its history and beauty, and I wanted to see this large rain forest protected. I'd always hoped that the forest of Leclerc could be like the Hope Gardens in Jamaica. There has always been a sense of mystery in the forest of Leclerc, something very special. You know this area from Bimini on down through Haiti is thought by many scholars to have been the seat of Atlantis."

Several years ago the larger part of the Dunham property was turned over to foreign investors who created the now-famous luxury resort Habitation Leclerc. A smaller part of the property houses Residence Katherine

Dunham, a large main structure, color-washed a soft Mexican pink, supported by nine massive arches of stone facing a large, clear, fresh-water pool. A separate wing houses Dunham's private quarters. Residence Katherine Dunham functions with a twofold purpose: It is a quiet, elegant inn to a selected list of guests as well as a place for holiday seminars and studies of the various philosophies. "Eventually I want to establish a school here of the arts and sciences for serious students of anthropology, the humanities, the occult, tropical medicine, and dance," Dunham says.

Over twenty-five people consider themselves part of her Haitian residence, and Katherine Dunham has assumed responsibility for them. Helping with their financial problems, schooling the children, attending to medical problems, administering to the births and deaths are part of her everyday routine. Years ago, moved by the poor health and inadequate nutritional facilities in Haiti, she opened a medical clinic on the property, treating hundreds of patients monthly. Her cause was supported by various doctors in the United States who sent her medical supplies.

Currently Katherine Dunham is a professor at Southern Illinois University in Edwardsville and director of the Performing Arts Training Center and Dynamic Museum, a branch of the university located in East Saint Louis. "In 1967 I accepted a professorship at the university, planning to stay a single semester. Once there, I was so moved by the terrible situation of East Saint Louis, the hopelessness, apathy, and utter despair that had been intensified by the riots, that I remained. As an anthropologist and a humanist I felt that I could give something, make individuals aware of themselves, their environment, and create a desire to be alive. When I come to Haiti now, it is to rest and breathe fresh air."

In Haiti Ms. Dunham leads a very secluded life, rarely venturing into the nightlife. She is not one of the expatriate Americans who gather in the evening at Oloffson's Hotel. "I suppose that it is still expected of me to be glamorous. Take Josephine Baker, she went to her death living in the image of herself. I don't want to do that. At the same time I feel that I let some people down when I don't dress up, go out, and do the things I did when I was living my career in the theater. People wouldn't have to question me, ask me if I'm Katherine Dunham, if I'd kept my image. But now other things interest me. Writing my books, *Island Possessed* (New York: Doubleday, 1969) and now *Kasamance* (New York: Odarkai, 1974), has given me the desire to spend more time writing. I have also been compiling the ten years of correspondence between Bernard Berenson and myself, which I plan to publish as 'Love Letters from I Tati.'"

Katherine Dunham has written numerous short stories, including a mystery, and many magazine articles as well. The list of committees, organizations and boards on which she serves are too numerous to mention. In Paris she was decorated with the Palme Académique for her distinguished contribution to the cultural life of France. The Haitian government named her to the Légion d'Honneur et Mérite and made her an honorary citizen of the country.

"If people could only understand they belong to a much vaster society than they live in, this would give them courage to live life with less fear of death. A bit of the whole is in everybody. You take your participation in the total."

Perhaps it is so that in the hills of Haiti, Katherine Dunham, thinker, dreamer, woman of the mysteries, dancing to ancient thoughts and rhythms, has found the secret of life—dancing the *yonvalou,* the prayer dance of her god Damballa, the god of motion and life.

Her Careers Are Manifold

VANDY BREWER

Katherine Dunham came gingerly down the staircase, holding onto the banister with one hand and the arm of her assistant with the other.

Reaching the bottom, she smiled and extended her hand in greeting.

"I had knee surgery in Haiti, and I haven't been able to make it up and down stairs easily," she explained.

Dressed in a knitted robe of many colors, the internationally known dancer-choreographer, educator, anthropologist, and authority on black culture sipped a cup of Haitian coffee as she sat on the tufted leather love-seat in the parlor of her home at 532 North Tenth Street, East Saint Louis.

Large sea shells covered a heavy round table in the middle of the room. Books filled the built-in shelves. African carvings were placed around the room. An easel with a half-finished painting on it was set up next to an aquarium. All of the room reflected the multiple interests of the woman herself.

Of the painting, she said, "Oh, that . . . well, I have painted for some time and have had several shows, but I've gotten away from it lately and can't seem to get interested in it again."

Many of the carvings—which she gathered during her travels around the world—will be on display today at the Dunham Museum, 1005 Pennsylvania Avenue, East Saint Louis. The museum will open at 3:00 P.M. and will feature Miss Dunham's collection as well as donated collections of Haitian, South American, and African artifacts.

SOURCE: Vandy Brewer, "Katherine Dunham, Her Careers Are Manifold," *East Saint Louis (Illinois) Metro East Journal*, 18 December 1977. Copyright 1977 by *Metro East Journal* Company. Reprinted by permission.

"I have been collecting these things for almost a lifetime," she said. "Some of my collection began in Paris in 1947–1948 among the Africans who were there."

Although she now prefers to be known as an educator, civic leader, and author, she admits she only in recent times has been able to think of herself other than in terms of her onstage image.

Yet she does not miss dancing at all.

She and her Katherine Dunham Company—thirty-five to fifty dancers and musicians—had toured "almost without stopping" from 1937 to 1960. They had performed in nightclubs and on Broadway, in motion pictures and on television, and in theaters around the world. And when she retired in 1965, she was "really exhausted."

"It was getting too difficult to meet union demands and train people as I wanted to train them," she said.

"What has been hard has been a personal adjustment to a lack of the audience, and I missed the company terribly at first. When I went to Japan and wrote a book of the first eighteen years of my life, I wept for the first two weeks."

Nevertheless, she said, she is satisfied with her decision.

"I have had the most brilliant career anybody could want to have. I don't know that I had more to give."

"I cannot get people to just say 'The Training Company of the Performing Arts Training Center' . . . I am not interested in gaining competition with my past."

Besides, she said, the dancers at the training center are carving out their own reputation in dance.

Although no dance company now bears her name, people persist in calling the dancers at the SIU East Saint Louis Center's Performing Arts Training Center the "Katherine Dunham dancers."

Miss Dunham is a professor at SIU-Edwardsville and director of the Performing Arts Training Center. She said the center is important to young dancers because it gives them the training they want and encourages them to pursue academic subjects as well.

She said dancers need general studies, but it is hard to convince them of that. She was an anthropologist before she decided to become a professional dancer and she believes in educating the total person.

The well-rounded person, she believes, should study the humanities and should have some knowledge of philosophy and other aesthetics. At

SIU–East Saint Louis, dancers are encouraged to "work as hard as they can" at dancing, but are cautioned to "not let that be their total existence."

She has never given up her interest in anthropology, and recently returned to a methodical study of cults which she began in 1935. At that time, major cults were headed by the likes of Aimee Semple McPherson and Father Divine. She finds interesting parallels between the 1930s and recent years when interest in mysticism and cultism again is flourishing. Even in Haiti, where she has a home, there are "more and more gods I never heard of. New ones are cropping up all the time."

In her own home she maintains an altar "to honor the Cuban saints who are my protectors" and says she is "deeply involved in the cults that have their origin in African animism in Cuba and Brazil and Haiti. These are my main points of interest."

Her study of the cultural origins of black people in America has been a lifelong passion, one she fostered long before black awareness was in vogue. She recalls that her early days as a dancer were difficult because the black community at that time "was not in the least bit interested in having presented a (dance) technique that was based on blackness."

Her museum is continuing to promote interest in black culture heritage. The museum had been in the Beulah residence in East Saint Louis, and was closed in 1974.

"In the time in between there has been a gradual, continual education to an interest in other cultures. It's sometimes very subtle, but it's going on all the time, even with Alex Haley's *Roots*,"[1] she said, with a smile.

NOTES

1. *Roots,* Alex Haley's account of his African American family's history, was published in 1976, after twelve years of research and creative reconstruction. One year after publication, a television miniseries, *Roots: The Saga of an American Family,* was watched by an estimated 130 million viewers. For his work on the script, Haley received the Pulitzer Prize and the Spingarn Medal in 1977. The book has been translated into thirty-seven languages and has sold millions of copies around the world *[Eds.].*

The Dance with Death

MARTHA SHERRILL

The Katherine Dunham Watch has begun: she is prepared to starve herself to death, she says. America has lost its conscience, she says. America
has forgotten what it stands for. America, where her mother settled from
French Canada to marry her father, a black man. America, where she
danced and held Broadway and Hollywood audiences enraptured and
kept them that way for decades. America, where she retired from the
stage in 1963 to settle in here in East Saint Louis, this desolate backwater
of urban neglect, to teach poor black kids about performing arts and self-
esteem and dance and African culture.

America. It's an embarrassment what is happening. Send these, the
homeless, tempest-tossed, to me . . .

"They are treated badly, maybe because they are very, very poor," she
says of the Haitian refugees our country has been sending back. "Once
it was the richest country in the Caribbean. But poor now, and black
black."

This is about blacks, she says. America takes in all sorts of refugees, she
says, gives money to so many miserable places. But here are thousands
of blacks and their children—from the poorest country in the Western
Hemisphere—who stepped into flimsy boats, left their troubled island,
crossed the sea with trash bags of belongings, were intercepted by the U.S.
government, held at a naval base in Cuba for weeks, and now are being
slowly sent back to Haiti in Coast Guard ships three times a week, armed

SOURCE: Martha Sherrill, "The Dance with Death: Katherine Dunham and Her
Fast for the Troubled Masses from Haiti," *Washington Post,* 16 March 1992. Copyright
1992 by the *Washington Post* Company. Reprinted by permission. Ms. Dunham's fast
lasted for forty-seven days.

with souvenirs of their trip to America: Huggies diapers, a ready-to-eat meal in a cardboard box, and, oddly, a selection of books on art and music.

In protest, Katherine Dunham is ready to die.

She could be living in Paris or London, of course, this beautiful legend, this dark priestess of the dance world, but she's here in dumpsville and keeping to her bed with her Advil and Ocean Spray cranberry juice and Evian water and tea from Tibet that's supposed to bring her tranquility. Pulse is good. Vital signs are fine. Her blood pressure has dropped a bit, the doctor says. But the spirit of Katherine Dunham remains strong—despite forty-four days of fasting in support of the Haitian refugees, two weeks in the hospital for dehydration. And despite her age, which is eighty-two.

Certain discussions now take place, in a downstairs drawing room where the white muslin curtains are closed: Is she too weak to talk, and if not, for how long can she talk, and how long should she rest beforehand? She's feeling well but tired. Her eyes are on the blink. Friends and family answer phone calls and the doorbell and wear sneakers in the way of all tiptoeing families with a loved one upstairs resting in bed with the TV going but the volume very low.

Statues of Buddha share rooms with the baby Jesus, with Chinese temple dogs, with icons of the Virgin Mary, with brass crabs and strange beads from the Vodun ceremonies Dunham has been attending since 1935, when she made her first trip to Haiti to study ritual dances for an anthropology paper.

"Whatever you do," warns her daughter Marie-Christine Dunham-Pratt, "don't ask her to quit her fast. She says she won't see anyone who does that."

In this sort of atmosphere—of big-heartedness and warmth and walking softly—the folded letter from national security adviser Brent Scowcroft reads a little cold. Time and place can do that to a letter. It's distant, as far away as typed words on white paper with THE WHITE HOUSE embossed at the top can seem.

Dear Ms. Dunham:
Thank you for your recent letter to the president concerning the plight of the Haitian boat people. I want to assure you that the president shares your concerns on this most difficult problem. . . .

Her fast began February 1, when the boat people started being forcibly returned to Port-au-Prince. On February 3, she telegraphed President Bush—who had awarded her the National Medal of the Arts at the White House two years ago:

I find the most recent decisions regarding Haitian refugees shocking.
Please believe me, Mr. President, those returned will receive no welcome.
Having lived in Haiti sporadically for fifty years, I find it too valuable to
ignore. . . . My anxiety has reached the depths of despair and grows daily.

The Bush administration contends that most of the boat people—now
nearly sixteen thousand—are "economic" refugees, not "political" refugees—coming here to flee poverty, not persecution for supporting the government of President Jean-Bertrand Aristide, which ended by military coup
last September. Once returned to Haiti, they have been fingerprinted and
photographed by Haitian authorities. Some claim they have been tortured
and beaten. The State Department, through its spokesman Margaret Tut-
wiler, first insisted that there was no evidence in the past eleven years of
any repatriated Haitians being persecuted. More recently it announced it
would be investigating these allegations of violence and repression, but in
the meanwhile, the boat people would continue to be returned.

In her upstairs bedroom, *The Paper Chase* is playing on TV and John
Houseman is making a speech, although the volume is turned very low.
Katherine Dunham is propped up on five huge white pillows—the Mat-
terhorn, it looks like. Her face is doughy but smooth. Her eyes are black
and deep-set and alive. She's wearing a purple shirt. She's covered by a
quilt she brought back from one of her many trips to Haiti—she's an honorary citizen there. Gold bracelets keep falling together on her arms as she
moves. Her gray hair has been recently corn-rowed and woven with tiny
yellow and pink silk threads.

Is she feeling well?

"I'm feeling well."

Her voice is low and assured and cultured, the sort of voice that be-
friended Prince Aly Khan and millionaire Doris Duke, charmed art historian Bernard Berenson and choreographer George Balanchine in its youth,
and later gently thanked the clapping crowds at Carnegie Hall and the
Kennedy Center and on Broadway for so many standing ovations and
gala tributes and eighteen honorary Ph.D.'s—in dance, in anthropology,
in social work, in law.

"I will fast until there's a positive change for the Haitians," she says.
"Haiti must be brought into a vision of the entire world. It's treated like a
stepchild now, from what I've seen myself for years. It's as though Haitians
were subhumans. In the very least, they should be given temporary protected status here."

It may seem old-fashioned or naive—this hunger strike, this fast, this passive militancy and humanitarianism. In Washington, it may seem silly to care about anything so much. Politics. It's only politics and paperwork and delays. Who can do anything these days to change the world?

"I need President Bush to answer my telegram himself," she says. "I don't care if it's a phone call or a letter—as long as it's an answer."

Vigils are held every night, outside the short cyclone fence around her simple brick house. Sometimes just a handful of people stand holding candles. Sometimes more. Yesterday, there was a rally of five hundred people. The NAACP is behind her. The American Jewish Committee. The American Bar Association. The AFL-CIO. A leader from the American Indian Movement is expected to show support soon. A rally was held two weeks ago in New York—at the Statue of Liberty—organized by movie director Jonathan Demme and producer Edward Saxon; they worked most recently together on *The Silence of the Lambs.*

Katherine Dunham, though, lying in her bed upstairs, surrounded by the warm, spicy smell of the YSL Opium lotion on the night table, by the millions of shells and rocks brought back from the islands, by heating pads and blankets and teapots, has remained calmly at center stage of this protest. It is impossible to upstage her: Jerry Brown hopes to turn up before tomorrow's primary. Paul Tsongas's sister, Thalia Tsongas Schlesinger, addressed the rally yesterday and walked in a protest march.

"Clinton's not in any big hurry to show up here," says Mark Silverman, Dunham's press coordinator, "since he's got the state sewed up."

Louis Farrakhan came by for forty-five minutes last week. Dick Gregory arrived February 12 and stayed—plan a fast, he'll be there—and has been thrown in jail three times by local police for chaining himself to the doors of the federal courthouse, among other things, and has already developed a conspiracy theory about the repatriation of the Haitians. It's all a CIA plot, Gregory believes, to cover up huge shipments of military hardware to Cuba because an invasion is imminent.

"It's bigger than some refugees," he told the *Riverfront Times.*

Marie-Christine Dunham-Pratt has flown in from Rome to be with her mother, to help answer phones and all that. "She's not talking today," Dunham-Pratt says to one caller, in a sort of continental English accent. Dunham-Pratt has the unadorned face and clothing of so many daughters of glamorous women, and seems as unused to attention as her mother is used to it. An orphaned child from Martinique, at five she was adopted by Dunham and her late husband, John Pratt. At six, she was sent to boarding schools in Switzerland and France. Now forty-four, she has lived in Rome for the better part of two decades, but sees her mother at least twice a year, at her house in Haiti and at her famous dance workshops—the Dunham Technique Seminars—held in the States.

"It was very nice, actually growing up as her daughter," says Dunham-Pratt. "Especially during the years when she was a big star. It was always a big event when she came to visit me in school. In Europe, she was almost a bigger star than she was in America—in France especially. They'd never seen anything quite like her before."

Before Katherine Dunham, black dance had never been seen on concert stages. She distilled ceremonial rituals from the West Indies and Africa, making a new eclectic ethnic style of her own. It was called Afro-Caribbean and Afro-Cuban and Afro-American. As a college student, she had worked her way through a master's program in anthropology at the University of Chicago, by dancing. The week before final examinations, she was offered a part in her first Broadway show—*Cabin in the Sky*. She went to the dean of the anthropology department and asked them what to do.

"When are you dancing again?" he asked her.

So, in a little theater on the South Side of Chicago, she looked out in the audience, and there he was—the dean—watching her dance. The next day, she met him at school. "I think," he said, "you should go on with your theater life."

She stretched. She danced to drums. She crossed her lean arms above her dark, wide-set brows and moved with grace and animal sense. People used all those words to describe her: sinuous and sultry, an enchantress, an artist, a pioneer. In the 1940s, she became a huge star of cabarets and Broadway and Hollywood, choreographing *Cabin in the Sky* with Balanchine for the stage, then making the movie version,[1] then choreographing and making more movies: *Star Spangled Rhythm* and *Stormy Weather* and *Casbah* and *Mambo*. Impresario Sol Hurok had her legs insured by Lloyd's of London. She performed with sets and costumes designed by Pratt—her college sweetheart, a white man, and her husband of forty-nine years—and there were headdresses and plunging necklines, pompom fringes and tiny beads, glittering bangles on her arms.

"We spoke on the phone when she was on her second day of fasting," says Dunham-Pratt. "That's how I found out. I didn't know quite what to think at the beginning. I did ask her to stop. I don't anymore. She needs to go through with this, to go all the way. There are so few people in life who care so much about something."

Upstairs, *The Paper Chase* continues on TV and Katherine Dunham shifts her bare legs around under the sheets. She talks about staying in John Houseman's house in Hollywood once. The only time she thinks about food now, she says, is when a commercial comes on with a picture of a grilled lobster or something. She rolls an Advil between two fingers, then plays with a string of beads with a big blue Egyptian scarab.

"I'm beginning to discover—to know more about myself," she says. "I think that everybody has a cosmic consciousness. We know—anyone who is at ease with themselves knows—that we are here for a purpose. I don't question it. . . . So many times, people tell you what you can't do. I don't think about those things. I think mostly about what I can do and what needs to be done."

There are all sorts of electrical cords coming together into a knot under her bed. A couple of them are winding up inside it—to heating pads and the like—but it's as though Dunham's hooked up to some outlet too, the ultimate direct current, a peaceful but high-voltage plug-in to the Big Upstairs, to all things important and immaterial.

"I've had so much of what I've wanted in life," she says, "that I have no reason to commit suicide. I cannot hasten or shorten my own death. When it happens, it happens. I don't feel that I have a death wish. But surely, I can't tell you when I'll stop this fast. It will be when I hear something positive."

Her daughter is asked about this, later. "Yes," says Dunham-Pratt. "She told me she was willing to die. She'll continue the fast until she gets some satisfaction. She wants to hear from Bush directly. It's between her and Bush now, in a way."

And if she doesn't hear—and she dies—will this be worth it?

"Yes, definitely," says Dunham-Pratt, looking first to the floor, then at a white muslin curtain. "When someone sacrifices for a cause, it's always worth it. If it wasn't, it would be tragic."

NOTES

1. George Balanchine and Dunham collaborated on the choreography for numbers danced by her and her company in the Broadway staging of *Cabin in the Sky* (1940). Dunham appeared in the leading role of Georgia Brown, the Temptress. In the film version of *Cabin in the Sky* (1943) Lena Horne appears as Georgia Brown. Dunham was not involved in production of the movie *[Eds.]*.

PART III

Stories and Poems

Come Back to Arizona

KATHERINE DUNHAM

Florie Jackson, Elizabeth Mayfield, Peggy Riley, and Florie's two cousins, Tom and Edward Stanton, were out in the garden discussing whether they should use the bottom or the top floor of the barn for their circus.

"I think the top would be best, because people couldn't look in without paying," announced Florie.

"Well, we would close the door, anyway," said Tom, "but somebody might fall through the window if we went upstairs."

"I think . . ." began Peggy, but she was interrupted by Mrs. Jackson, who came into the garden.

"Oh, Florie! Guess what!" she exclaimed. "I just got a letter from your Uncle Jim in Arizona, and he wants you to come and spend the summer with him."

"Oh!" beamed Florie, "won't that be too delightful!"

"But," said her mother, "that is not all. You can take your four friends with you."

"Oh! Oh! Oh! Won't we have lots and lots of fun though!" they all cried at once. Then they forgot all about the circus and got their heads together to talk about Arizona, while Mrs. Jackson went to see the children's mothers. When she came back the look on her face betrayed her before she got a chance to speak. Peggy got up and started to dance around, the rest following. They danced until they were breathless and then dropped on the cool green grass to rest.

SOURCE: Katherine M. Dunham, "Come Back to Arizona," *The Brownies' Book,* vol. 2 (August 1921). A periodical edited by W. E .B. Du Bois and published by Du Bois & Dill, New York. Reprinted by permission of Katherine Dunham. Ms. Dunham was twelve years old when the story was published.

"Now," laughed Mrs. Jackson, "since you are through I will tell you when you are going. You'll leave a week from today." Then she ran away with her hands over her ears to escape the expected noise.

"Just think," said Elizabeth a little later, "we leave the day after school closes."

"And it's a ranch," joined in Florie. "We will have ponies and everything." As she spoke of ponies she glanced to where the boys had been sitting, but they weren't there. "Where did Tom and Edward go?" she asked.

"Here we are," called Tom, and she saw them standing over by the garden gate.

"Won't Annabelle and her friends be jealous when they hear that we are going to Arizona, though?" said Elizabeth. "But how could we tell her?"

"Oh" I know," cried Peggy, . . . and they started a whispered conversation which did not last long, however, for Tom and Edward soon came back.

That night it took a long time for the Sandman to close five little pairs of eyes. In fact, he had to come around twice before he was sure their owners were asleep.

Sunday, Elizabeth and Peggy came over to Florie's house to talk about clothes, while her cousins went outside to talk about cowboys.

"Oh! won't it be grand to see us flying around on fiery steeds and capturing bandits," exclaimed Edward. And indeed he did not know how near he came to telling the truth.

The next day it happened that they were studying the western states in school, and when they came to Arizona, Florie raised her hand.

"What is it, Florie?" asked Miss Anderson.

"Miss Anderson," began Florie, "Saturday mother got a letter from my Uncle Jim in Arizona, and he wants me to take some of my friends and go out there to spend the summer on his ranch."

"Oh! Won't that be fine!" said Miss Anderson. "When you come back you can tell us all about Arizona."

That recess and at noon there was no limit to questions from the schoolchildren. Everyone crowded around, excepting Annabelle and her friends. As Florie was in the middle of one of her conversations about what they intended to do out West, Annabelle passed by and said to one of her companions, "Huh, what do we care about Arizona? I am going to get a new wristwatch anyway, so there!"

The rest of the week passed haltingly but happily for the children. It seemed as though Saturday would never come. The time came, however, when father drove five excited little children to the station. They did not have to wait long before the train arrived, and after many good-byes, kisses and hugs, the children climbed aboard.

I will not go into details about their journey to Arizona, but I will say that it was delightful and that they saw many interesting sights.

When they arrived at the small station Uncle Jim and a few cowboys were there waiting.

"Hullo," said he as he lifted Florie up and planted a kiss on her cheek. "Ain't this Florie? You was just a little mite last time I saw you."

"Yes," she answered. "This must be Uncle Jim." She introduced her friends to him. All the while the cowboys had been fidgeting from one foot to the other, and when they saw Uncle Jim helping the children into the wagon (borrowed especially for the occasion), one of them said, "Well, Jim, ain't you goin' to interduce us?"

"Oh, yes, excuse me, children. Florie, meet Larry," he began. Then he introduced them in turn.

They soon came to a large ranch-house, surrounded by acre after acre of land. Behind it were several corrals. When Tom caught sight of it he jumped up and down crying, "Now for the bandit round-up, Edward."

Uncle Jim laughed a hearty big laugh, then a serious look came into his face.

"SD are havin' some trouble," he said. "Them greasers over to the Samson ranch are kinda kickin' up lately."

I will skip over the first few days while the children are getting acquainted with the ranch. It was the next week when Uncle Jim suggested that they go on a picnic. "You can go over to Mountain Cliff," he said, "or any place around here, so as you don't go no further than a mile." The cook packed them a nice big lunch and their uncle let them use some none-too-fast ponies.

"They better watch out for them bandits," said Lanky Joe (so called for his long legs).

"Oh, we'll be all right," assured Edward. "Tom and I have our guns, anyway," and so saying he pulled out a toy cap-pistol.

"They can go out by Dobson's cave, can't they?" asked Larry, a tall cowboy, as he shifted a lump of tobacco to the other side of his mouth.

So after being carefully directed where the cave was, the children started, Tom carrying the lunch-basket.

"Won't it be nice," said Elizabeth. "I'm glad Larry thought of it."

"I guess it will be cool, too," said Peggy, as she glanced reflectively at the prickly cactus that dotted the dry ground as far as the eye could reach. "Seems like you can't get out of the heat."

When they got there it proved to be a big roomy cave, very cool indeed. The girls spread an old table-cloth, which the cook had packed for the purpose, on the floor, and set it with the most delicious food. Tom and Edward went in back of the cave to get some water from a rippling little spring which was shaded by an old, almost leafless tree. When they came back, they both wore a very excited look on their faces.

"Guess what?" began Tom.

"No, I want to tell," complained Edward. "You're always first."

"Oh, go ahead then," said Tom disgustedly. "I wish I didn't have a brother."

Edward took no offense, but began, "You know the back of the cave reaches way out to the spring. When we went out there we heard some-one talking. At first we thought it was you but the voices didn't sound like it and we couldn't hear you anyway. The first one we heard said, "Now listen, Bill, tonight at about eleven o'clock they will turn in. Then we can get away with some of those new horses they got. They ain't been branded yet." The other one just said "All right."

"What shall we do?" asked Florie. The rest were silent, then Elizabeth said, "I think we should stay right here while Edward runs as fast as he can to get help." They all agreed to this and as Edward was about to start he said, remembering their slow journey to the cave, "suppose I could run faster than any one of those ponies."

Then he started off. They were within a mile of the ranch, so it did not take Edward very long to get there, though he had to stop several times to rest.

Wasn't everyone surprised to see a small boy running with all his might to Uncle Jim.

"What's the matter?" asked the man anxiously. "Has anything gone wrong?"

Edward just sat and panted. At last he said, "There are some bandits in the cave. Run quick!" Two cowboys mounted their horses, without having to be told, and started off.

The children were beginning to get frightened.

The two men crept cautiously back into the cave. Evidently the bandits were getting ready to leave, for one of them said, "Now remember, tonight at twelve o'clock." Then they started out but didn't get very far, for one of the cowboys spoke up in a gruff voice saying, "Hands up!" The bandits lost no time in doing so, for they didn't know just how many men were there and they thought too much of their skins to offer any rebellion.

They were then marched to the ranch and you may believe that there was much surprise. The children were highly rewarded by the sheriff and when they were leaving (two months later) the cowboys crowded around the station shouting, "Come back to Arizona! Come back to Ariz—on—a!"

Afternoon into Night

KATHERINE DUNHAM

Umberto Rodriguez Morales slowly took off his elegant rented matador vest, his tight-fitting breeches, his soiled white stockings, and his low-heeled pumps and handed them to his admiring peon. He moved mechanically, trying to hold together the pieces that were bursting inside him, trying to shut out the picture of what had happened. Polero was not the first man he had seen killed in the bullring, nor were his the first entrails that Umberto had seen quivering on the angry horns of the victorious bull. But Polero had died not by accident or a slip or a weak thrust or a faulty turn but simply because at the crucial moment of the killing, when it was one or the other, Polero had given in.

From five feet away Umberto had seen it all. Automatically he had stepped forward and thrust his *espada* into the death spot in the neck of the bull, just behind the massive skull. Then he had stood still, while the peons rushed a stretcher for what was left of Polero and the horses of the *picadors* dragged the dead bull in the opposite direction. The crowd, shocked, strained from the wooden seats to watch the removal of the tragedy. It was the last fight of the day. A woman broke through the guards and ran across the ring screaming after the stretcher bearers. Boys climbed walls to see more. An American woman fainted. Confused, frightened, hushed, the crowd filtered out of the arena, a lover cheated of an unnatural satisfaction.

Umberto slid into his cheap wide-shouldered zoot suit, excused his peon,

SOURCE: Katherine Dunham, "Afternoon into Night," *Band Wagon* 13 (June 1952): reprinted in *Best Short Stories by Negro Writers,* edited by Langston Hughes (Boston: Little, Brown, 1967). Reprinted by permission of Katherine Dunham.

and by short cuts and rear exits managed to leave the arena, unmolested by the crowds that were waiting to acclaim him the hero of the day.

Bright sun, take back your rays. How can heat and light be cold, too? When he talked to the mightiest of bulls they drank in the insults of his words and were angrier still. When he talked to women an infinite tenderness quivered between them as though he knew too well the secret fabric making up women. Polero was pure Indian, remote, sulky, sometimes cruel. Bright sun too warm to be without.

Umberto found himself in the park beside the Palación. He sat on a bench and closed his eyes. Now he saw Polero as he knew him best. Polero ready for the kill. Umberto wondered if others who had known him felt as he did.

Always just before the kill Polero would look at his friend and pupil Umberto. In the arrested moment before the kill he would look at Umberto. A glance so hidden beneath long lashes, so much a part of his casual arrogance that Umberto could never be sure that it was for him. Sometimes he felt afraid, too, of what he might see there. At that moment, knowing that he should feel some recognition beyond anything he had ever known, Umberto's bloodstream would stand still. With another self he strained to reach out to something that he had never known. Another self made up of Mexican peasant bleakness and an arrow-like tautness that could, at a touch, shoot a clean straight line into the heavens. The killing would happen then, and swelling waves of applause would bring him back to the ring. He would follow the procession beside his hero, picking up the flowers, slippers and scarves that showered from the boxes.

This way he had stood that afternoon, a bronze statue. The late sun glinting from the shining embroidery of his bolero, superb in peacock blue satin and silver, gathering from behind, and above, and all sides, electricity from the suspended onlookers. Polero was magnificent, standing between them and their miserable fears of impotency and destruction, uniting them with the beast in death.

A connecting link between these people and their fears, protecting them from the fury and destruction of the beast. A symbol of the triumph of the reason and skill of man against the unreason of fear. Someone had to make death fine and glorious.

A street urchin came to him with a hollowed-out bamboo full of orchids and gardenias from Xochimilco. The smell was heavy and sweet. He got up from the park bench and moved on. He quickened his step to pass Tonio's bar. It was here that all of the bullfighters gathered on Sunday night after the *corrida*. There were always women waiting for them. There was one especially for Polero. The woman who had run screaming across the arena. Now he knew that he had heard her voice for the first time that afternoon. A deadened section of his brain relayed her scream, and it shot out like a radio in full blast. Over and over again as she ran across the trampled earth. "No! No! Holy Virgin, he cannot! He cannot! He cannot!" Umberto could see her now, blinded by the low rays of the sun, stumbling over the trampled earth, ankle-deep in the blood-soaked sawdust; in that light, her red shoes turned shining black.

They would all ask him why Polero had died. They would all turn to him with questions that he could not answer. That woman, and other women, would cling to him and weep, because they knew that he too loved Polero. They would turn their grief on him, a thing now mixed with a great fear that settled in his stomach and his groin. Polero was looking at him, Umberto, as he died. Looking at him and smiling, and they must all have seen it.

He was about to turn into the Estrellita, but a woman at a charcoal stove recognized him and started to speak. She thought better of it when she saw his face. He hurried on, hat pulled down, head bent low, trying to hunch his shoulders and walk casually, instead of with the proud chest and swaying hips of the bullfighter. Even so they all knew him, and turned to stare as he passed. To get out of the street he slipped into a bar and went far back into a corner and ordered a drink. He turned his back to the tired band of mariachi players. "Noche de ronda," they sang, "noche de tristeza. . . ." Infinite sadness of the Mexican peon. Aztec and Mayan sadness of centuries . . . In the fly-specked mirror behind the bar he saw the dregs of the night life of Mexico City. *Indios,* Spanish, *mestizas, mulatos* crowding into the mirror and in the midst of them Polero's eyes and mouth, talking to him.

Polero spoke always with the silent things; the turn of his head, his hands, the tempo of his breathing. When they were children, boys of nine and fourteen in the same village, it was always Umberto who talked. If he could release now that stream of child talk, perhaps his pain would go. Talk into the mirror to Polero.

Umberto ordered another drink. His blood was rushing faster now, and he felt hot and breathless and expectant. He looked in the mirror again, to see if Polero were still there. Instead the red eyes, distended nostrils, and slobbering mouth of the bull were before him. He closed his eyes and heard the sound of its breathing. He had heard it so many times before, but this seemed closer, more terrifying, as though all of doom would sweep down on him if he opened his eyes. He stood waiting, feeling his own blood and his own entrails spilling on the floor of the bar. When he opened his eyes he saw that a man was behind him looking into his eyes in the mirror. A man whose head hung low and from whose lips a line of saliva drooled out to a glass held in midair. It was this man's breathing, this man's sound. He might have been the bull. Instinctively the muscles of the fingers of Umberto's right hand twitched. He stepped quickly to one side, stomach muscles tense, thighs pressed together. The red eyes continued to look into the mirror. Umberto flung fifty centavos on the counter and hurried out past the mariachi players. He threaded his way through *touristas* and natives, in real flight now, as though to save not only his body but his soul.

He treaded narrow streets, finding the back ways. There was no place to go. Before, he was moving blindly, to push out thinking from his mind. Now he was fleeing from a thing—an essence which he felt would mean real destruction if ever it caught up with him.

No place, in flight, to escape this thing that had become real.

He began to run, and as he ran he felt the man behind him. He turned sharply into an alleyway and waited for footsteps. The only sounds were night sounds of the quieting street, and the tight rush of his own breathing. He knew that somehow everything was drawing together into one picture. Pieces falling in place that he couldn't put into words. It was well past midnight. He stopped at a street stove and bought an oily *tostado* from one of the scrawny vendors. He had eaten nothing since early morning. As he reached to his pocket to pay her, he heard the thick drop of a coin in her tin cup and the woman thanked the man behind him. He felt his forehead suddenly cold and his throat contracted so that he could hardly swallow. He stayed there and ate the *tostado,* forcing it down his dry throat, trying to control the sound of his breathing and wondering where to turn for escape.

Mexico City is wide awake until dawn. The Salón México was just a few squares away, and Umberto sought refuge there. The man did not follow him, and upstairs, in the corner by the band, he felt a moment of real safety and relief. He had often been here to dance himself. Now he enjoyed watching the small Indians in white trousers and bright blankets jitterbug with girls in cheap satin and lace Sunday dresses. Umberto began to relax. He felt sleepy, drugged, carried away by the flashing bright colors on the dancers, and by the heat. Then one of the jitterbug dancers started across the floor to greet him. The whole room seemed to stop in suspended motion and turn toward him, and all of their faces were alive with the same question. . . . In panic again, he turned and ran down the stairway and into the street.

Outside there was no moon, and the only light came from the street signs and here and there a kerosene lamp behind shutters. He stepped out of the Salón México, and as he turned from the door he felt a hand on his shoulder. He became suddenly rigid and then sprang around with the force of a whip. It was not his voice but he heard himself say: "What do you want?" The sound scarcely left his lips and his throat hurt even to make room for the words. The ugly soft face of the man pressed closer to him. Breath passed heavily over loose lips; in the neon light reflected from the sign above, they were wet. The man spoke, panting. Out of the head of the bull his voice soft and high, straining with tortured desire. He spoke in the familiar *tú* instead of *usted*. Disjointed words, things men say to women. Umberto stood transfixed, his entire body swept with mingled fear and revolt. The man stopped talking. Three drunken cattlemen stumbled by, and Umberto turned mechanically to continue his flight. The man held him by the arm. "Oh, no," he said, and the high sweet voice came again as a surprise. "Don't go." He moved closer to Umberto and one hand fell on the smooth hard muscles of the bullfighter's right arm. "I know what happened. I saw it all. I have watched every time he fought for years, watched you both. I know why he did it, and you know too." They were walking now, and Umberto was trying to shut out what he was hearing. But if the words didn't come from the man outside, they continued just the same, his own self supplying them in a steady stream feeding into his consciousness; so that it became as though he were finally telling himself all of these things which he had always known.

They walked and turned into a stairway. It was dark and hot and the eagerness of the man filled the narrow hallway to bursting. On the third step Umberto stopped and closed his eyes and leaned his head against the wall. He heard the bellow of death agony of the bull and when he opened his eyes he saw the burning eyes of Polero, Polero's mouth smiling. This creature was really the bull, and if he did not kill it he would be killed by it. Polero had been killed by it. All of the fear that had been drawing closer around Umberto in his flight from the arena came together now in this black stairway. He did not want to die, he did not want to be killed by this bull.

He was moving upward again. It was still intensely black but with a hand on each wall beside him, he continued to climb slowly, guided by the breathing of the man in front of him; then by a thick wet hand on his. He moved first like someone who was very ill, then like a very young boy. As he continued to climb in the darkness, he felt the man closer and closer to him. That afternoon in the torn arena blood gushed from the mouth of the bull, but not before Polero died, smiling, looking. Umberto's grief broke, silent and clean as an arrow released from its bow. Just as surely as that, he knew that he would never fight again.

Baio

KATHERINE DUNHAM

Sueño debajo del palmar
Con el amor que ha de llegar
En este tibio atardecer
Pienso en la fiebre que tendré
Soñoliento corazón
Late al ritmo del ballón

Mi corazón hoy es feliz
Estando tu aquí junto a mi
Mi corazón hoy es feliz
Pues te quiero con frenesí
Ay, que lindo es el amor
Ay, que bueno es el amor

Hoy yo me siento tan feliz
Que me da ganas de bailar
Al compás de este balancear
Escucho el rumor del mar
Balancéame mi amor
Que me quiero emborrachar

Source: Katherine Dunham, "Baio," lyrics to music by Bernardo Noriega, dated Rome, 18 January 1954; in the Katherine Mary Dunham Papers, Special Collections, Morris Library, Southern Illinois University, Carbondale. Copyright by Katherine Dunham. Used by permission.

A balancearte mi amor
Siento una gran sensación
Y brillará más el sol
Pues el también es feliz
Al mirame junto a ti
Al mirarme tan feliz

Oye a lo lejos el cantar
De la gran brisa tropical
Verdes rumores del palmar
Que nos invitan a bailar
Al compás de este ballón
Vamos pronto a bailar

Béguine

KATHERINE DUNHAM

Aille lavé linge ou Miranda
Aille trempé yo an d'leau savon a
Sanmedi dansé palais schoelche
Dimanche couri, dipeche ou
    an l'eglise

Lindi bon marin fok ou levé
Pou lavé linge sale ou Miranda
Le dos ou coumencé fait ou mal
Fok pas plain Miranda
An ni songé doudou ou
Lavé linge moin a
Si ou lavé i bien
Boute canne moin a ce pou ou
Lè ou vini caille moin au soué

Toutt' ti fi connait' lavé linge yo
Mais piece pas peu lavé yo con ou
Toutt' ti fi connait' dansé beguine
    Pas con Miranda
        Pas palé

SOURCE: Katherine Dunham, "Béguine," lyrics to music by Bernardo Noriega, dated Buenos Aires, 28 October 1954, translated by Lucie Guannel; in the Katherine Mary Dunham Papers, Special Collections, Morris Library, Southern Illinois University, Carbondale. Copyright by Katherine Dunham. Used by permission.

The Babies of Biafra

Katherine Dunham

The babies are crying,
Black Mother,
And the earth groans
Beneath the weight
Of her own distended bosoms.

The babies cry,
Black Mother.
From small dry throats
Past parched tongues
And withered lips
The little ones
Gather strength enough
To gasp out their agony.
The planes fly low but cannot fly
Above the tortured city bearing food
For fear of treachery.

The hunger rages on.
The Old
Have long since withered.
The proud Biafra Chiefs
Lie spattered on the pavement,

SOURCE: Katherine Dunham, "The Babies of Biafra," in *A Galaxy of Black Writing,* edited by R. Baird Shuman (Durham, N.C.: Moore Publishing Co., 1970). Copyright 1970 by Katherine Dunham. Reprinted by permission.

Dropped
From overstuffed entrails
Of the greedy vulture.

Fear of poison here
Fear of guns there

The hungry know no fear
But gape obscenely
At the living, walking
Eating.
Gape into the brazen sky
Too weak
To curse the enemy
Or pray to Ibo gods
Or Christ.

They are alone among themselves.
Earth and bush
Have swallowed kin
With strength enough
To travel,
And earth and bush
Await the last fine blood
Of tribe and clan.

The babies are crying,
Black Mother.
Surely now we are forsaken.
Surely now we mourn.

Brother against brother
Our tears come slowly
When they come at all,
And red as blood.

My tribal marks turn in
And yours turn out.
Four wives are mine
By Moslem law
While you have one.
Allah versus Jesus.

Bible, Koran,
Hunger stalks us all
And babies fall
From weakened arms
To lie unburied,
No more recognizable
As Man.

Surely now we are forsaken.
Surely now we weep.
Our tears come slowly
When they come at all,
And red as blood.

The babies cry,
Black Mother
What shall we do?

Charité

KATHERINE DUNHAM

One morning at the Kenscoff crossroads a young woman named Charité stopped and allowed a friendly young man washing his feet in the stream running beside the road to help her remove her loaded basket. Charité greeted friends among the other porteresses, and knew that they were all wondering if this was the moment for the birth of Charité's first child, because she was very round in front, her distended bellybutton showing through her scant shift. Those who knew her best were worried, because the child was overdue, and Charité had not been at all well, in spite of long massages and incantations from the old crone at Furcy who looked after Charité these days, and in spite of potions and infusions of herbs and teas brewed from leaves and roots and tree bark and toad's hide and other secret and special things by the *bocor,* or bush priest or medicine man, who had taken Charité on as his special obligation.

Charité was loved by everyone who knew her, and admired by those who didn't. To begin with, she never indulged in idle gossip. Whenever she told news, it was of very simple and very good things. Her nature was as gentle as her manner, and her manner was charming as she herself was. She was even more, she was beautiful.

There is in Haiti a blood mixture producing a physical type known as *marabout.* This is considered one of the most perfect mixtures, of classic African beauty, and many a lover sighs out confessions of his love for a *marabout* in poetry or song. To begin with, the *marabout* is for some

SOURCE: Katherine Dunham, "Charité," section 1 of "Elifait," an unpublished work, written circa 1972, in the Katherine Mary Dunham Papers, Special Collections, Morris Library, Southern Illinois University, Carbondale. Copyright 1972 by Katherine Dunham. Used by permission.

reason rare. They are velvet-smooth of complexion, with the skin color of a desert night sky. Fine, relatively small features and this unusual skin, together with coal black hair neither straight nor kinky has made many Haitians believe that Fulani and other Moorish African tribes were imported as slaves, and also that early in captivity on the island there may have been some mixture with the few remaining Arawak Indians who nearly all died while enslaved by the colonists before the Africans were imported to work in the sugar and cotton and coffee fields. Whatever the ancestral strain, this beauty was epitomized in Charité. Her eyes were large and soft and black, with very white whites and fringed by long, silky upper and lower lashes.

Charité dropped her eyes as she squatted beside the others at the crossroads and told her anxiety to her dearest friend. Her fine skin dripping wet, and milk from her full breasts stained the sweat-soaked front of her dress. "M' pas conné," she murmured to her friend, "I don't know. I don't know why I am afraid. Other women have babies and everything is all right. But the doctor at the clinic at Pétionville told me to expect him a month ago. I'm afraid, Marie-Celeste. What will happen to the poor thing if I die, and what will happen to me if he dies!" Everyone knew that since Charité's husband had been killed by a boulder tumbling down onto the main road from a rock cliff above Furcy she had lived only for the child, which she never referred to excepting as "he." Marie-Celeste, the same age as Charité but mother of seven girls, tried to comfort her friend. At fourteen she had borne her first child, and one each year after that, excepting for skipping a year, and the next were twins. At twenty-one Marie-Celeste felt far older than Charité, who had waited five years for her first baby, and now seemed obsessed with the idea that her dead husband was lonely back in Africa, Guinée, and would want the company of either his wife or his son as soon as possible.

The other porteresses shook their heads and clucked in sympathy. They helped Charité to her feet and adjusted her full tray. They then turned to each other for help, the last one stopping an old man trotting behind a donkey overburdened with firewood to lift her tray to her head. "I will pay you on my way back, old man!" she sang merrily, and the old man chuckled and beat his stubborn donkey with a piece of firewood trying to keep up with the porteresses to hear them gossip and exchange jokes and pleasant conversation. But the line of porteresses was ahead of him, and the donkey was stubborn and tired. Those who did not stop to bargain with the cooks of the resort hotels now dotting the countryside, or of the villas of the rich, would arrive at Pétionville well before he did. And those who had many opportunities to sell out their wares along the road as they approached the small town seldom did so. Because then they would be forced to calculate in *gourdes* and *centimes* rather than bartering their wares for oil and kerosene and matches and rice and dried beans and salt fish and pepper and salt and tiny red hot peppers. Also they would be deprived of one of the things they looked forward to most on market day—the chance to join in the bustle and gaiety of the market, and to pick up bits of news as some of us do from papers and magazines and the radio and television.

The Market Place
at Pétionville

KATHERINE DUNHAM

The marketplace at Pétionville is not far from the town square with its clipped green grass, bubbling fountains, and pavilion where now and then the army band gives concerts on Sunday afternoons. In the evening young students stroll up and down the square hand in hand, or sit on the stone benches and recite their next day's studies in philosophy or science or literature. The marketplace has a cement floor, a tin roof supported by cement posts at intervals, and is open on all sides during the day and at night when the porteresses from far places cook their evening meal over charcoal fires, smoke pipes or an occasional cigarette, chatter, sing, meet lovers, and finally sleep before the dawn return to wherever home is. On the periphery of two sides of the market small donkeys are fastened to the posts. For the most part they are scrawny, sore-spotted, and weary. Under-fed dogs lounge among the donkeys and piled beside them are burlap bundles, cooking pots, sacks of charcoal, and odd objects belonging to their owners. Inside the market it is cool and dark, and it takes a little while to become accustomed to this interior after the blinding sun and heat of the town. Each vendor has a steady commerce with his or her own favorite porteress, and of course the living space adjoining the stall is reserved for them.

When Charité and her companions reached the market it was in full early morning progress. There were a few travelers in corners who must

SOURCE: Katherine Dunham, "The Market Place at Pétionville," section 2 of "Eli-fait," an unpublished work, written c. 1972, in the Katherine Mary Dunham Papers, Special Collections, Morris Library, Southern Illinois University, Carbondale. Copyright 1972 by Katherine Dunham. Used by permission.

have been very tired or had drunk *clairin,* raw white rum, the night before instead of *kola,* the bottled Haitian fruit-flavored drink. They were folding their covers and stretching and yawning before going outside to the public pump for their morning toilets. One by one kerosene lamps were all extinguished, as were charcoal fires smoldering from the night before. Some children were still asleep, but most of them were already crawling under the stalls playing hide and seek. Babies were wrapped in rags and tucked away on bundles of straw in corners, and grown-ups were squatting, their heads covered with shawls until the morning sun heated the tin roof, sorting out piles of fresh and dried fruits and vegetables.

Charité loved most of all the neat trays of all sorts of beans and rice and peas. It was among these she stumbled on the morning of her descent from Furcy so that the owner of the stall had to catch her tray of vegetables and Marie-Celeste, just behind, held her to keep her from falling. Then of course someone had to catch Marie-Celeste's tray to keep it from toppling over. An egg fell from its nest at the apex of the mound of vegetables, and many old people shook their heads as they watched the yellow and gelatinous inside slip from the stall where it had broken to slide and drip to the cement floor of the market. This was not a good omen at all so near a birth. And to make matters worse, a black bird swooped suddenly into the market enclosure, cawing derisively. In spite of every effort to keep it away or chase it out with brooms and straw hats and handkerchiefs, it careened wildly through the market place, its mean yellow beak wide open, lurched down over the ring that had formed around Charité to protect her, skinned over the neat trays of beans and rice and peas upsetting them, then, after beating its wings wildly against the tin roof and the cement posts, took off toward the mountain path of Furcy.

This was the worst sign of all, and Charité knew it. She crawled under the stall clinging tightly to Marie-Celeste's hand, biting her lips to keep from crying out in pain. A midwife began kneading her stomach, and in a few minutes a tiny bundle wrapped in rags was handed out from under the stall. Women went to fetch warm water and a half of a dried gourd served as a basin to bathe the new-born child. Charité lived long enough to hear its first wail, then, smiling, spoke her dead husband's name. An old, old, woman came forward and took the little bundle in her arms as men covered Charité's lifeless body. It was the unspoken custom of the market that any ill befalling one was shared by all. So they planned a night ceremony of dancing and drumming and singing to the *mystères,* the spirits governing the dead, and gathered *centimes* and *gourdes* and portions from their produce to pay the undertaker so that Charité might have a proper funeral.

The body was removed from the market, and housewives outside the immediate circle surrounding the young women went about the business of haggling over pennies without ever even knowing what had happened. Marie-Celeste sat under the stall of the bean seller and wept. She bargained extra hard that day with the contents of Charité's basket and her own. In spite of seven hungry mouths at home, the returns would go to mark a grave beside that of Charité's husband in the tiny cemetery of the hamlet of Furcy. The old woman who had taken the baby turned out to be the great-great-great grandmother of the tiny bundle that was to be known as Eliphet, after the prophet in the Old Testament, or "Elle li fait!" meaning that she has done it, or "Eh! Li fait!," it is done or made. In our story the boy is called Elifait. The old woman left the market, mumbling to herself, leaning on a cane with one hand, sheltering the boy child in the crook of her other arm. She refused all help and went her way down into the city of Port-au-Prince.

At the moment of Elifait's birth some recall thunder over Kenscoff and Furcy, though there were no rain clouds. Others said the loud blast was a cannon salute from a military boat from Santo Domingo visiting Port-au-Prince.

The Census Takers

KATHERINE DUNHAM

By the end of the week The Plan was put into action. Who in the Royal Palace would have imagined that every village and hamlet and compound and even isolated huts in field and forest including many villages far and beyond the highways would be visited by a Royal Queen! Of course by now news had traveled far and wide that *something* of importance was taking place in the kingdom, but as many as there were tale-tellers just so many were the versions. Some said that Ouagadesh was a thousand miles underground in the desert. Some said the King Dougo-Wawa Sotoko Toure-Kafiakingi kept ferocious animals in cages and entertained his guests by having them loosed while slaves fought them for the amusement of the guests. All agreed on one point, no one had ever seen the Royal Queen Wives of Ouagadesh, each of whom was the daughter of some powerful kingdom. Another point of accord was that the King was exactly as wide as he was tall, and he was not at all a short man. It was said that when he led his army to battle he was so impressive carried on a litter strapped onto the backs of sixteen coal-black Arabian stallions, each keeping such perfect step until to the enemy the enormous armored figure seemed to be floating toward them so that they stood transfixed and forgot what the fighting was all about and reasonable treaties were signed by both sides. Everyone also agreed and all legends verified the fact that though he might not be handsome, and even if he did weigh more than seven hundred

SOURCE: Katherine Dunham, "The Census Takers (of Marriageable Maidens)," part 3 of *Kasamance: A Fantasy*, illustrated by Bennie Arrington after original drawings by John Pratt (New York: Odarkai Books, 1974). Copyright 1974 by Katherine Dunham. Reprinted by permission.

pounds, Dougo-Wawa Sotoko was just, reasonable, and of a very good nature unless unreasonably aroused.

The King of Kasamance was quite in favor of The Plan. So a day was set and each Royal Queen set forth on a visit to one or more villages to talk with the mothers and marriageable daughters of the kingdom. They were to pose as Census Takers of Marriageable Maidens and not to tell just yet the importance of the Great Occasion, which would be some time after the *hivernage*[1] to allow the jungle roads and ditches and potholes to dry, and to allow for the King of Guagadesh to arrive at the Capital of Kasamance. At this very minute the *juju-ists,* who were, of course, the first to be aware of the details of The Plan, were examining goats' entrails and the *fetichists* were reading cowries and snakes' and lizards' entrails, and Ialu Boku was going his own way to find out a more exact date for the arrival of the King of Ouagadesh.

The Plan was that each Royal Wife would arrive without warming at the compound or village or hut at early morning when the girls of marriageable age were just waking up. In this way she would see them before they began grooming for the day and find out just which ones had qualities befitting such an important responsibility. But no one would know who the stranger was because she would be dressed very simply, be traveling on foot (a royal bodyguard was always somewhere hidden in the bush near by, and a covered palanquin of reeds was handy for any move that was too far a distance for the Royal Wives—who were not at all accustomed to more exercise than to move at a leisurely pace from one place to another within the palace walls, chiefly in the women's compound—to go on foot). If an overnight trip was necessary, the pause would be planned to take place at the village of some Chieftain or Councilman's family where strict secrecy of the traveler's identity would be exacted from the host.

The First Wife had planned well. Since there had been no census in ten years, a scribe accompanied each wife and upon a secret code between the two wrote only the names of the eligible young maidens with marks of Fair, Passing, and Excellent (later this would, for the First Selection, be only Passing and Excellent). The King, the explanation went at each case and compound, wanted to complete his archives; so all were more than willing to comply and saw nothing strange in a woman Census Taker since Marriageable Maidens were the subject.

In this way early one morning Abila, one hundred and twelfth wife in order of protocol in the court of Kasamance, and a very plain and unassuming person, especially in her faded *pagne* and turban, and with her breasts covered as befitting a woman of her years, entered the village of Ojumbulo, where her first stop was at the *case* of Tojo Ifumbe, owner of many rice fields and father of six daughters, all of marriageable age. Abila stayed hidden at the edge of the forest for a while, watching their morning preparations. The village of Ojumbulo was just about like any other Kasamance village or compound, and the *cases* or single houses of Tojo Ifumbe the rice tiller were just about like all others. One for the father and one or more favorite wives, depending on if they could get along together, one for nursing and expecting mothers, cared for by an older wife, one for boy children, and one for girl children. If a man were not so affluent there might be some doubling up, but things always worked out somehow and of course there were warehouses and perhaps cattle pens and sometimes a guest house and sometimes on the edge of a field or forest there were houses for the very very old or very very sick who were fed and cared for but just waiting to die. The young girls who would go to the rice fields on the day we are speaking of emerged from the shadow of the marriageable maidens' *case,* six of them, not fully awake, all stretching and yawning and winding their colorful *pagnes* around their slender thighs and legs. Some grumbled and shivered before the sun hit them through the silk cotton tree that sheltered the *case,* but with the first rays of sun they laughed and told each other their dreams and teased each other and ran to look at the new babies and to salute their mothers and their fathers and brothers who were by now awake and tumbling out of the boys' house.

While this was going on an old woman poured water for the marriageable maidens from a large pottery jug into *calbasses,* bowls or gourds cut in half, and two young wives pounded *petit mil* in a mortar and tossed the wooden pounding stick in the air, singing while they pounded. The six young girls of courting age brushed their teeth, chattering like birds while the old women kept replenishing the *calbasse* of water which the girls poured over each other. When they had dried and wrapped fresh *pagnes* around their hips, they bound their short braids in head cloths and formed a circle around a *marmite,* or earthen pot, of porridge brought to them by the First Wife into which they dipped with their fingers to eat. Then they washed their hands and faces and teeth again, picked up their head baskets and started down the path toward the rice paddies. Each checked carefully to see that she was wearing her own special *juju,* or charm, against the bite of poisonous snakes, for without these they would not be protected from the hateful serpents who lived in the paddy fields but who fled at the sight or sound or order of these special charms.

It was at this moment that Abila stepped from her hiding place with her scribe-secretary behind her. She introduced herself to the head wife, had the scribe read her credentials, complimented the first wife on her well-run household, and asked to see the daughters of marriageable age. All of Tojo Ifumbe's daughters were handsome, but one in particular had attracted Abila's attention from the very beginning. With proper training, here, if ever, was the wife for the King of Ouagadesh. Her name was Kine-Kan. She was taller than any of her brothers, some of whom were of age and now stood aside wondering when it had begun to matter to count women in a royal census. But besides standing out from the others because of her slender height, Kine-Kan had skin like black starlight, teeth whiter than cowrie shells, and dimples in her velvet cheeks. She also had a very long neck (which the one hundred and twelfth Royal Wife could already see ringed with gold and turquoise necklaces stretching from the lovely valleys of each shoulder blade to the tip of her proud little chin). Kine-Kan's arms were long and as fluid as the Gambia River when she made the slightest movement, and her uncovered bosoms were like round soft fruit just about to become ripe. No fault could be found with her slim waistline or long straight limbs. Perhaps—that is, if one could get that far for looking at other things—some might consider her pointed-in feet as a slight defect. But then the grace of the slender feet themselves with long supple toes quite made up for that. Her long gentle hands seemed to caress everything they touched, each finger tipped by a shining pink nail, for Kine-Kan was very proud of her fingernails and polished them with pink *jonga* dust every spare moment.

Of course Abila took information on all of the other daughters, but her mind was made up. She thanked the entire family graciously and said that now a plan was on foot at the palace to inscribe girl babies as well as men children in the royal archives. The young grown-up brothers hurried off to tell their clan brothers of such foolishness, and the entire household, excepting Tojo Ifumbe, who was shoveling rice into sacks at the warehouse, thanked the gracious Census Taker and the scribe-secretary and offered them breakfast, which they politely refused.

Notes

1. In West Africa, the *hiverage* is the winter season of rain and heavy winds. For definitions of other special terms, see the glossary at the back of this book [Eds.].

PART IV

Dunham Technique

Interview with
Katherine Dunham

VÈVÈ A. CLARK

VÈVÈ A. CLARK (hereafter VC): What was your technique like in the early Forties? We know what we learned from Miss Beckford[1] and we can learn only so much from photographs of the period.

KATHERINE DUNHAM (hereafter KD): I was greatly influenced by the Kamerny Theater,[2] Ludmilla Speranzeva, Kreutzberg [Harald Kreutzberg], La Argentina, and East Indian manner. I was influenced by almost everything that came through Chicago during the period. I think I was starry-eyed. Chicago attracted people who came, appeared at the Auditorium Theatre, gave a few classes, and a number of them here and there remained. It must have been a little richer at that time than New York. I would try to study with these visitors. My main teacher was Ludmilla Speranzeva who had come to the United States with the Chauve-Souris,[3] and stayed. She had been trained at the Kamerny Theater, and taught there. She was raised in the tsarist court until the revolution. Her father was chief telegrapher for the tsar.

VC: Was the Kamerny Theater connected to the tradition of the Maryinsky that led to the Ballets Russes then identified with Cecchetti?

KD: Yes, to a degree, but I would say that it was a branch that emphasized theater perhaps as much as dance. It worked on the theory that dance had been too long treated as a precious, elite art form in Russia. I was so very much influenced by the arms and feet of this particular ballet

SOURCE: *Film Culture Magazine* (1978); reprinted in VèVè A. Clark, Millicent Hodson, Catrina Neiman, and Francine Bailey Price, *The Legend of Maya Deren: A Documentary Biography and Collected Works,* edited by Hollis Melton (New York: Anthology Film Archives, 1984). Copyright 1978 by *Film Culture Magazine.* Reprinted by permission.

dancer, Olga Preobrajenska from whom I had one lesson in Paris. At that time, Dunham Technique included the low shoulder, broad back line, and the hand coming off without splayed fingers [*she demonstrates*]; and then the straight back line so that you didn't have this arch here [*imitating exaggerated arch in lower back*], which for years the Bolshoi had. All these things came from Speranzeva as far as ballet technique went. Adolph Bolm. I did some work with him. My ballet background was very classical and very pure from these people who had broken away from the old Russian tradition.

But surely, in searching for what my own body could do, and in searching for (maybe I didn't even know it) what might develop out of black people, people like La Argentina and Kreutzberg and Mary Wigman gave me a great deal of hope.[4] For some time while teaching classical ballet, I began to become discouraged about the physical structure of the American Negro body attempting to dance classical. I'm not yet sure that there isn't something to it. On the other hand, it may have to do with the thing I was telling you about the success of the *coumbite,* something that has to do with rhythm. I think that fundamentally people are more to be differentiated on the basis of their rhythmic cycles than on the basis of their race or color, or this or that. One of the survival mechanisms in black people has been a rhythmic pattern that relates more to universal rhythmic patterns than among some other people.

vc: Science may be just now catching up with you with the study of biorhythms.

kd: Mmm, hmm. Very well, because I *firmly* believe in it. I think that there are black people who have it and there are those who don't.

vc: Reading through the clippings from the period of the early Forties, I've always been interested in the fact that almost every critic would point out that when you came on stage, you did everything "without seeming to put out any energy." I wish you would comment on that.

kd: I think I'm getting back to that concept of *dynamic energy.* What you are you don't have to talk about. It shows. With a feeling of confidence in your movement, truth in it is just about all you need. Where the question of taste comes in I don't know. I have seen people do utterly ridiculous things—[Maya Deren] is one with that shoulder shaking. She believed in it, deeply, but it was embarrassing. I've seen people do that in dance. From my point of view, I've never approached the theater without humility as an essential quality. I owe the people because they would come to see me. I used to tell the company, if there are only ten people in the audience, you owe them more than if there are thousands because they had come. It used to all be quite effortless. Part of the style of my work—like Graham's from her back—came from my knees. Having always had arthritis, I have probably developed more of that dynamic energy. I didn't try to outdo anyone in terms of leaps. I put myself in a position where there was no competition, and that gave me a great security. I'm finding myself even now thinking up programs and courses that are not following but leading, where there is a minimum of competition.

NOTES

1. Ruth Beckford, former member of the Dunham Company and instructor of Dunham Technique, wrote the authorized Dunham biography. It was published in New York by Marcel Dekker in 1979 [Eds.].

2. The Kamerny Theater was a small, intimate theater founded in Moscow in 1914 by the Russian director Aleksandr Tairov to support experimental synthetic theater that incorporated all theatrical arts–ballet, opera, music, mime, and drama–as an alternative to the naturalistic presentations of Konstantin Stanislavsky's realism at the Moscow Art Theater [Eds.].

3. Nikita Balieff's Théâtre de la Chauve-Souris à Moscou (Bat Theater of Moscow) was a Franco-Russian vaudeville troupe that toured Europe and the United States during the 1920s. The program, consisting of playlets, sketches, songs, and dances, changed frequently [Eds.].

4. La Argentina (Antonia Mercé, 1888–1936) was a famous Spanish classic dancer. From 1928 to 1936 she made six transcontinental tours of North America. Harald Kreutzberg (1902–1968) was a German dancer who studied with Rudolf von Laban and Mary Wigman. He danced in the United States in the 1930s and late 1940s. Mary Wigman (1886–1973), German dancer, studied with Dalcroze and Rudolf von Laban. In 1914, she became von Laban's assistant. She made her first appearance in the United States in 1930 [Eds.].

Katherine Dunham
School of Arts and Research

Brochure, 1946–1947

Katherine Dunham School of Arts and Research
including
Dunham School of Dance and Theater
Department of Cultural Studies
Institute for Caribbean Research

220 West 43rd Street
New York City
New York

The Katherine Dunham School of Arts and Research offers individual classes and courses in all of the dance and theater studies and cultural courses for the professional and lay student.

The Dunham School of Dance and Theater is making a unique departure in the field of professional schools of dance and theater in offering special two-, three-, and five-year courses leading to professional, elementary, and master graduate certificates in the fields of dance, drama, and cultural studies. For the first time it is possible for the serious student to receive the professional training which is absolutely essential to a professional career upon the stage, as a teacher or as a research investigator, and at the same time to acquire a knowledge in the academic courses found

SOURCE: Brochure for the Katherine Dunham School of Arts and Research, New York, N.Y., 1946–1947. Copyright 1946 by Katherine Dunham. Reprinted by permission. The typography of the original brochure has been altered to suit the format of the present book.

only in upper-level educational institutions, taught by the finest faculty in the United States.

KATHERINE DUNHAM　　　DORATHI BOCK PIERRE
President　　　*Administrative Director*

STAFF

JOHN PRATT, *Consulting Director.* DIONE LEWIS, *Katherine Dunham Enterprises.* VERNE VAN BEYNUM, *Registrar.* SYVILLA FORT, *Supervisor, Dance Department.* EDGAR PECK, *Office Assistant to Mrs. Pierre.* RAMONA GOMEZ, *Secretary.* RAI KEELING, *Secretary to Miss Dunham.*

FACULTY

Dance Division

HENRI AUGUSTIN (Percussion). Born in Haiti. Associated with Miss Dunham for years as advisor in Haitian folk rhythms and folklore.

LENA BELLOC (Dance Notation). B.S., San Francisco State Teacher's College. Von Laban system of dance notation. Librarian, Modern Ballet Theater, San Francisco.

TODD BOLENDER (Ballet). Choreographer, Ballet Russe de Monte Carlo. Formerly with American Ballet, Philadelphia Ballet, Ballet Caravan. Associate founder-choreographer, American Concert Ballet.

MARIE BRYANT (Tap and Boogie). Featured in Duke Ellington's *Jump for Joy* and *Are You with It?* Featured in motion pictures *Jammin' the Blues* and *Ziegfeld Follies.* Dance instructor for Martha Raye, Arlene Judge, and others.

SYVILLA FORT (Dunham Technique, Ballet). Graduate, University of Washington and Cornish School of Theater Arts. Featured dancer with Katherine Dunham Company for five years. Instructor, experimental dance, at Martha Washington School for Girls.

TOMMY GOMEZ (Dunham Technique). Featured dancer with Katherine Dunham Company for six years. Now appearing in *Show Boat.*

IRENE HAWTHORNE (Ballet, Classic Spanish Technique). B.A. University of California. Featured ballerina, Metropolitan Opera Ballet. First dancer, *Sing Out, Sweet Land.* Solo artist, San Francisco Symphony Orchestra.

José Limón (Modern Dance). Soloist, Humphrey-Weidman Dance Group. Leading dancer and choreographer for numerous Broadway shows. Solo appearances with Philadelphia and New York Symphony Orchestras. Fellow, Bennington College, U.S. Army, 1943–1945.

Dorathi Bock Pierre (History of Dance). University of Oregon. Editor, author, dance critic, and lecturer on dance and drama. Former critic-contributor, *American Dancer* and *Dance* magazines. Editor-publisher, *Educational Dance* magazine.

Angiola Sartorio (Choreutics, Eukinetics). Studied music in England and dance in Germany with Rudolf von Laban and in France with Mme Egouou. Appeared with Royal Opera, Rome, and Civic Ballet, Florence, Italy. Soloist-teacher with Kurt Jooss and Ballets Jooss.

Archie Savage (Dunham Technique). Former featured dancer with Katherine Dunham Company.

Lavinia Williams (Dunham Technique, Russian). University of California. Appearances in Broadway shows, Ballet Theatre. Studied and danced in France, Italy, and Germany. Member, Katherine Dunham Company.

Drama Division

Herbert Berghof (Acting). Graduate, Vienna State Academy of Dramatic Art. Played over 120 important roles in leading theaters of Europe. Appeared in five Theater Guild plays. Directed Broadway shows and is active in radio.

Kurt Cerf (Acting). Municipal Theater, Leipzig. Directed Children's Theater there. Instructor, New Theater School. Speech instructor, Warner Brothers. Flight instructor and transport pilot, U.S. Army, 1942–1946.

Katinka Loeser DeVries (Words and Their Meaning). Graduate, University of Chicago. Instructor, Latin School for Girls, Chicago. Associate editor, *Poetry* magazine.

Alice Hermes (Voice and Speech). M.A., Columbia University. Teacher of English, New York high schools. Instructor of speech, Dramatic Workshop, American Negro Theater.

Ela Kula (Make-up). Graduate, Pratt Institute and Chicago School of Design.

Dione Lewis (Production, Subjective and Objective Techniques). American Academy of Dramatic Art, Yale University.

Producer-director, Litchfield Playhouse. Assistant to Paul Czinner for *The Two Mrs. Carrolls.*

JOHN PRATT (Visual Design). Ph.D., University of Chicago. Advisor and designer for Katherine Dunham Productions. Designer, Labor Stage, New York; Chicago Repertory Group; Ruth Page, Agnes de Mille, Grace and Kurt Graf; motion pictures; etc.

MARIAN RICH (Voice and Speech). Graduate, Radcliffe College. Harvard Dramatic Club. Instructor, Westchester Playhouse, Neighborhood Playhouse, Paper Mill Playhouse, New School, etc.

ALFRED SAXE (Acting). Broadway director and actor. Motion picture director and teacher. Founder-director, Hollywood Actor's Laboratory Theater.

KARL VOLLMOELLER (History of Drama, Playwrighting). Playwright-producer-director with Max Reinhardt for 39 years. Wrote and produced *The Miracle, Turandot, The Blue Angel,* and many others, Specialist and authority in Greek drama and history of drama.

KATE WARRINER (Voice and Speech). Graduate, Saint Timothy's School, Maryland, New York School of Theater. Theater study in Bath, England, and with Max Reinhardt in Salzburg, Austria. Speech coach for Margaret Webster, Maurice Evans, and American Repertory Theater.

Cultural Studies Division

BEN FREDERIC CARRUTHERS (Spanish). B.S. in education, University of Wisconsin; M.A., University of Illinois; Ph.D. University of Havana, Cuba. Former associate social scientist, Office of Coordinator of Inter-American Affairs.

CAMILLA DELEON (Music Appreciation, Music Reading). City College, Columbia University graduate; postgraduate and teacher's diploma, Juilliard Music School.

JEANNE GENET (French). Born in France and privately tutored. Lectures and translations, art, commercial and literary subjects.

ALTA GUSAR (Introductory Psychology, General Anthropology). B.A., Barnard College, Ph.D. candidate, Columbia University. Field and research study, New York University, Hunter College, and Northwestern University.

BASIL MATTHEWS (Philosophy of Religion, Scientific Methods and Logic). Graduate, Saint Mary's College, Trinidad, B.W.I. Entered Order of Saint Benedict, Trinidad. Benedictine College, University

of Louvain, Belgium. University College, Cambridge, England.
Ph.D., Fordham University. Fellow, Rockefeller Foundation. Founder-
director, Institute of Social Research, Trinidad.
MARGARET SKINNER (Deportment). Honors graduate, Cambridge
University, England. M.S., Trinity College, Dublin, Ireland.

CERTIFICATE APPLICANT REQUIREMENTS

Twenty-five hours a week

The Dance Division requires ten hours per week in major and five hours
in minor each week. Ten hours elective within prescribed studies. The
Drama Division and Department of Cultural Studies require twenty-five
hours each week within prescribed studies.

CERTIFICATES OFFERED

Dance and Drama Divisions

Two-year course leading to Professional Certificate
Three-year course leading to Research Assistant Certificate
Five-year course leading to Master Teaching Certificate

Department of Cultural Studies

Two-year course leading to Field Report Certificate
Three-year course leading to Research Assistant Certificate
Five-year course leading to Institute Associate Certificate

REQUIRED COURSES FOR CERTIFICATE APPLICANTS

Dance Division

FIRST YEAR. Fifteen hours dance. Ten hours elective: Percussion, Music
Appreciation, History of Dance, Visual Design, Choreutics, General
Anthropology, Language.
SECOND YEAR. Fifteen hours dance. Ten hours elective: Form and Space
and Form and Function, Eukinetics, Dance Notation, History of
Dance, Design, Anthropology.

Drama Division

FIRST YEAR. Twenty-five hours elective: Acting, Voice and Speech, Words
and Their Meaning, Production, History of Drama, Body Movement
for Actors, Visual Design, Philosophy, Language.

SECOND YEAR. Acting, Voice and Speech, Production, Design, Make-up, Bódy Movement for Actors, Playwriting, Language, General Anthropology.

Department of Cultural Studies

FIRST YEAR. Twenty-five hours elective: Language, Philosophy, General Anthropology, Scientific Methods and Logic, Words and Their Meaning, Aesthetics, Voice and Speech, Introductory Psychology, Body Movement or a dance technique, Percussion and Use of Native Instruments.

SECOND YEAR. Aesthetics, Psychology, Specific Anthropology, Philosophy of Religion, Projective Group Testing, Language, Music Appreciation, Caribbean Folk Lore, Caribbean Social Dances, Body Movement or a dance technique.

1946–1947 SCHEDULE

Fall Term: Monday, September 30, 1946, to Saturday, December 21, 1946
Two-Week Christmas Vacation
Winter Term: Monday, January 6, 1947, to Saturday, March 29, 1947
Spring Term: Monday, March 31, 1947, to Saturday, June 21, 1947
Special Eight-Week Summer Course: July 7, 1947, to August 30, 1947

SCHEDULE OF CLASSES

Classes for adults are taught on weekdays, Monday through Friday, from 8:00 a.m. to 6:00 p.m. The brochure lists all courses offered, with names of instructors and hours of instruction. Children's dance classes are taught on Wednesday and Saturday. Once a month, children are instructed in deportment at a Sunday tea party.

TUITION

CERTIFICATE APPLICANT RATES: Three hundred and fifty dollars per term. Special rate for veterans taking full course of studies, or Certificate Applicants. Applicants for individual courses must register by the term.

RATES (Adult Classes)   Total hours

Per Term	1 class a week	(1 hour)	$30.00	12
	2 classes a week	(2 hours)	52.50	24

3 classes a week	(3 hours)	69.00	36
4 classes a week	(4 hours)	84.00	48
5 classes a week	(5 hours)	97.50	60

—Special rates for 6 or more classes weekly—

Private lessons: 1 hour $10.00   ½ hour $6.00

Quarterly or term rates for 15 classes weekly or over include ½ hour private lesson weekly.

RATES (Children's Classes)   Total hours

Per Term	1 class a week	(1 hour)	$14.00	12
	2 classes a week	(2 hours)	24.00	24
	3 classes a week	(3 hours)	36.00	36
	4 classes a week	(4 hours)	48.00	48
	Drama Classes		20.00	

RATES (Theater Courses)

Per Term	Elementary Acting (twice weekly required)	$78.00
	Voice and Speech	42.00
	Playwriting	45.00

ALL TUITION FEES PAYABLE IN ADVANCE

Make checks payable to

DUNHAM SCHOOL OF DANCE AND THEATER

—Special discount on all rates to dance and theater professionals—

—Scholarships available to worthy students—

The Dunham Schools

KATHERINE DUNHAM

A Dunham school was first established in Chicago in 1934. It did not exist with continuity, however, until 1944, when it was re-opened in New York in Caravan Hall, Isadora Duncan's old studio, as a school of dance and theater. It moved in 1945 to 220 West 43rd Street. From studies in dance, speech, drama, and allied theater techniques, the school expanded in 1952 into the Katherine Dunham School of Cultural Arts.

The expansion of the school was due to the addition of lectures and courses in the social sciences and humanities and to a recognition, on my part, of a need for a rounded education, particularly in the social sciences, to fill requirements for dance technique investigation and its development for theater or educational use. The school functioned thus until 1957 with no subsidies and a minimum of donations. The program proved too extended for private enterprise, and my personal earnings could no longer underwrite its costs on such a scale; particularly since much of my work was in countries where payment was in non-transferable foreign currency.

From 1957 until November 1962, the training in Dunham Technique and allied techniques of dancing was confined to the performing company with limited apprentices and master classes wherever stationed (Mexico, Australia, New Zealand, and Near and Far East, Europe, etc.). A brief attempt at a school in Port-au-Prince, Haiti, proved impractical under existing economic and political conditions in that country.

SOURCE: Katherine Dunham, "The Dunham Schools," an unpublished paper, dated 1964, in the Katherine Mary Dunham Papers, Special Collections, Morris Library, Southern Illinois University, Carbondale. Copyright 1964 by Katherine Dunham. Reprinted by permission.

In November 1962, a series of classes was organized at the Ballet Russe School, and in January, the cost of rental being too high for the hours available, the Dunham School moved to a small studio in the Chelsea Hotel (New York City). This proved to be impractical because of the nature of our requirements—space, freedom to use assorted percussion instruments, irregular hours, unhampered circulation of peoples of varied racial, national, and cultural backgrounds.

We have now found what could be considered an ideal permanent location and have been at 440 West 42nd Street since 1963. The present school will not attempt a staff proportioned as that of West 43rd Street. Exposure to allied education will be through guidance to other sources, with occasional lectures and films on related subjects. We have access to a small theater in the same building and will encourage frequent student performances as well as appearances of professionals prepared at least partially.

One of our objectives will be to stimulate the interest of and prepare a working program for young people of deprived backgrounds who are not conditioned to training for the performing arts, and who have no opportunities to pursue these studies. Other objectives will be to continue the analysis and cataloguing of primitive techniques of dance and the complexes surrounding them; to explore further the workings of the Dunham Company and the dance technique which has served as a model for a large part of dance development, in many countries of the world for more than twenty-five years. Important, also, will be the re-education of the professional dancer of today who is, in my opinion, fast losing in all performance prerequisites excepting perfection of superficial techniques.

An important aspect of our school has always been the existence of a performing company growing out of or attached to it. This serves as a model to the student as well as an incentive for those who otherwise might be inclined to doubt a career in the performing arts, particularly in the social structure existing in America. It is therefore important in planning the physical structure of the school that the needs, as a base for the company, be taken into consideration and that a part of the basic training curriculum be the extensive repertoire of the company.

One can foresee the collection under one roof of all archives and materials of both school and company over the years since my first research in the Caribbean as a fellow of the Rosenwald Fund and Guggenheim Foundation in 1935–1936. Our immediate concern, however, is the establishment of facilities for basic training and research as outlined above.

Dunham Technique Seminars

JOYCE ASCHENBRENNER

In the annual Dunham Technique Seminar, the atmosphere vibrates with the force of percussion and the *élan vital* of energetic dancers. The two-week seminar, held since 1984 in the Saint Louis–metro-east (Illinois) region, is an intensive learning experience. It is also a celebration of Katherine Dunham's long, eventful, and influential career.

Those attending the seminar have included through the years—many of them every year—former members of the Dunham Company, as master instructors. Drummers from Senegal, Ghana, Argentina, Barbados, Brazil, Cuba, Haiti, New York, and the Saint Louis–East Saint Louis area provide complex, diverse rhythms for the dancers. Dunham Technique students of various skill levels, as well as other dancers and non-dancers, come to learn from the masters. The origins of those traveling to the seminar reflect the international tours and influence of the original Dunham Company: Australia, Peru, Paris, Spain, Germany, California, Connecticut, New York, Chicago, Denver, Trinidad, Haiti, Jamaica, Rome, Senegal, Japan, Israel, and Brazil are some of the locations in and outside the United States. They arrive in Saint Louis to retrain, re-energize, and restore the unique qualities of Dunham Technique that they have lost or that have been diluted by practicing other dance styles during the year. Many are dance instructors, and quite a few have dance schools and groups of their own.

SOURCE: Joyce Aschenbrenner, *Katherine Dunham: Dancing a Life* (Urbana: University of Illinois Press, 2002), 203–8, 210, 212–13. Copyright 2002 by the Board of Trustees of the University of Illinois. Reprinted by permission. The notation system has been changed because of abridgment of the original text.

Several generations of Dunham Technique students mingle and learn from one another. All participants learn about "Miss D's" philosophy and the history of the Dunham Company and the Dunham Technique. The master instructors discover the differences that have developed in other regions where the technique is taught. The rapport and camaraderie that develop are crucial to the transmission of Dunham traditions.

Dunham has dreamed of holding the seminars at her residence in Port-au-Prince; however, the political situation there has persuaded her to continue housing it in various schools in the metropolitan Saint Louis area, most recently, at East Saint Louis Community College. Although it is very demanding and difficult for her, the seminar is too important and valuable an experience to all participants to be abandoned. In 1998, when she was eighty-nine, she said she could not be concerned about how old she is, that these last years she is just "scrabbling" to get the things done she needs to. In the summer of 2001, at ninety-two, she seemed even more driven, extending the master class beyond the allotted time and exhausting many of the dancers, who had already had classes in Cuban, African, "jazz" dance, or Dunham Technique. Her desire to communicate what she has learned, to get things right, comes through clearly in these sessions, and the students respond with great respect and a concern to carry on her mission.

In the master class, Dunham—dressed in an African robe or other distinctive garb—presides with absolute authority and dignity. In recent years sitting in a wheelchair, she directs with incisive comments, expressive hand gestures, and her total body; she works closely with the drummers, in a fashion reminiscent of the Vodun priest. As Lucille Ellis explained, "They carry the power of the drum that she needs."[1] When the dancers are slow to pick up the beat or get into formation, she threatens that the drummers will get bored or tired waiting for them and will quit.

The drummers greet her with a spirited salute when she arrives for the master class. The mutual respect between master instructors and the drummers forms the solid foundation of all seminar classes and reflects the honor and regard all drummers accord "Madame," who recognizes and appreciates their power. She learned intricate and subtle rhythms and movements from such drummers as Papa Augustin and the Cubans La Rosa Estrada and Julio Mendez. On tour in Brazil, Puerto Rico, and Cuba, and in Haiti, she visited the drummers' families.

When the Cubans entered her life, Dunham asserted, they greatly influenced her. "They have a way of externalizing their religions; the music, drums, and dance form a religion that is with them all the time," Dunham explained.[2] She was introduced to Estrada and Mendez by the Cuban anthropologist Fernando Ortiz.[3] The Cuban *rhumba* and the *nañigo* became staples of the Dunham Company repertoire. Marta Vega, the director of the Caribbean Cultural Center in New York, has pointed out that Katherine Dunham was the first to take the *bata,* or Cuban double-headed drum, to New York.[4]

Dunham brought an appreciation of the origins of Latin rhythms in African religions to audiences in the Latino community in New York, as well as elsewhere. Her staging of the dances, displaying the cultural context, influenced Cubans and other Latinos to make their own artistic presentations. Recordings of Latin rhythms by Tito Puente and Chano Pozo acquainted North Americans with the vitality of the Cuban beat.[5] Pozo, who was a drummer in the Dunham Company, played with Dizzy Gillespie's band, introducing Latin rhythms into jazz. Other Cuban drummers in the company included Francisco Aguabella and Albert Laguerre, and Gilberto Valdés, "a brilliant young composer and conductor," wrote music based on Afro-Cuban themes for the company.[6]

When she visited Senegal and trained the royal dance troupe, Dunham worked closely with Senegalese drummers and musicians, bringing them to the United States to perform and teach in her program. Drummers paid homage to Dunham in a 1988 tribute performance in Chicago. Mor Thiam, the Senegalese master drummer, started the program with a crash of his *jimbe* from the back of the auditorium, then he led a parade of thirteen or more drummers down the aisle to the front where she sat, and they serenaded her for several minutes. It was a spirited introduction, and it raised the excitement level of both audience and performers to a high pitch.[7]

Marta Vega maintains that it is Dunham's relationship with the drummers that gives her technique a solid grounding in the spiritual life of those in the African diaspora. Knowledgeable drummers help control the spirits that can otherwise disrupt performances, while ensuring the authenticity of rhythmic movement. In 1979, Dunham wrote, "I would, when developing exercises which later became Dunham Technique, work closely with what drummers were available. As a school we taught Haitian, Cuban, and Brazilian drumming, with smatterings of what I had recorded or could remember from first-hand experience."[8]

The master instructors sit at her side or nearby in the master class. In recent years, there has been a serious erosion of staff. In 1993, Talley Beatty received a Scripp's Award and took time out for personal renewal.[9] Ricardo Avalos traveled from Los Angeles to take his place. Avalos, an Argentinian, was originally hired as a drummer, but he also danced with the Dunham Company and taught at the Performing Arts Training Center (PATC) in East Saint Louis. He had not returned to the area for many years. Beatty came back to attend the seminar in 1994, but he died the following year. His death was keenly felt by participants, especially Dunham.

Through the years, other instructors have died or dropped out because of ill health, and others have taken their places. When Lucille Ellis, who had had a serious stroke, missed the 1995 seminar, her classes were taught by Dana McBroom-Manno, a former Dunham Company dancer. Joe Sircus, a Cuban drummer, was memorialized in the 1996 seminar, and Lucille Ellis, Tommy Gomez, and Ronnie Marshall all died in 1998–1999. Walter Nicks, a former dance director at the Dunham School in New York, stepped in to teach Dunham Technique classes, while Sara Marshall, Ronnie Marshall's wife, picked up Ghanaian dances that he had taught.

Dunham was absent from the 1995 seminar because she was in Haiti, where she had been honored in a ceremony at the Presidential Palace. Hurricane Andrew and then ill health delayed her return. This was the first seminar she had missed, and the dancers, some of whom had come primarily to see her, were disappointed. In the spirit of the Dunham Company, others substituted in master classes, and the seminar presenters VèVè Clark and Marta Vega provided dynamic learning experiences about the sources and social and cultural contexts of Dunham Technique. . . .

Dunham rules the demonstrators for the master class—Theodore ("Theo") Jamison, tall and solidly built; Keith Williams; and, on occasion, Doris Bennett-Glasper—with an iron hand. They are accomplished dancers who were among the original students in PATC. Jamsion and Bennett-Glasper, along with Ruby Streate and Darryl Braddix, have been instructors at the Children's Workshop, which represents the only current dance group—except for Cleo Robinson's Denver company—that has permission to perform Dunham choreography and copy her costumes.

In the master class, Dunham educates the dancers about subjects ranging from politics and culture to love and sex, relating them to dance. She instructed the students to achieve the sinuous movements of the *yonvalou* by envisioning what it was like to be a snake, with no legs and having to project itself forward through a series of wavelike motions. She described this type of imitation through mental imaging as characteristically African. In the same class, Dunham noted that Congolese movement stresses the middle part of the body as the focus of power, medical treatment, and sexuality. She alluded to the fierceness and independence of the Congolese in Haiti and the tall, very dark, handsome men. She is aware that some people criticize her for spending too much time talking, so that the dancers are not warmed up when they perform the movements. Nevertheless, she feels that they need to know these things and that she will never get all of her views and ideas written down.

She also imparts detailed information about the dance movements, how they were developed, as well as the philosophy behind her technique. When she first returned from Haiti, she incorporated into her pieces movements taken from dances she had learned in the Caribbean. She described the first movement she used from her field research, based on the *combite* procession in which the toes grip the earth and then release in a zigzag pattern across the ground, leaving furrows. She used such isolation of body parts in choreography before she incorporated them into a technique. She pointed out the difference between a dance movement and technique: as a system of prototypes providing the basis for choreography. Dunham Technique consists of paradigms utilizing different muscle groups, displayed in progressions across the floor. It is fundamentally a synthesis of African and balletic movement, with the systematic isolation of body parts characteristic of African and East Indian dance. She worked with Uday Shankar and Vera Mirova in developing isolation technique, although the basic movements and choreographic patterns were African.[10] A flexible back and relaxed knees are central to the technique; these are characteristic of the *yonvalou,* so important in Dunham's life.

The East Indian influence continues to be felt in the master classes. She emphasizes the seven *chakras,* points on the body where energies are focused, and the need to be aware of them at all times. She admonished the class, "Don't be afraid of the *chakra* [groin], that's where most of your energy comes from. Get acquainted with it."[11] The externalization of sexual energy in African and Latin movements that has energized audiences and brought about critical reaction to performances was also therapy to the girl and woman who had fought against a strict Methodist upbringing and a domineering father.

Dunham is a severe taskmaster. She characterized her role in the class as one of providing criticism, and she takes her charge seriously. A reviewer wrote in 1957, "Hard on herself, she is hard on others, but despite long hours, stormy scenes, and low pay . . . the company stays with her."[12] In 1993, while students were working strenuously in ninety-five-degree temperatures and high humidity, with no air conditioning, their energy sometimes flagged. Resolutely, the eighty-four-year-old woman, weakened by a spell of pneumonia, insisted, "Never say 'I'm hot.' Never say 'I'm tired.' Just go on."[13] These were the words of a star performer who went on stage while suffering from knee pain and many bouts of illness. Marjorie Scott commented, "[She missed] one performance in Quito, Ecuador, [when] she went on a trip somewhere and the boat got stranded and she didn't get back. That was the only time in all the time I was with her that she missed a performance . . . you'd see her going on [stage] sick or sorry."[14] . . .

Katherine Dunham has stated her criteria for teaching Dunham Technique: First, one must have a sense of compassion; second absolute honesty is critical; finally, one must study as much as possible and be a perennial student, constantly learning.[15] "I don't believe you can teach choreography," Dunham lectured in a class, "Your teacher gives you materials, and you put it into your own ideas."[16] . . .

At present, Dunham Technique is being taught by former company members and their students, by others who studied at the Dunham School, and by former PATC company members. Lavinia Williams and Pearl Reynolds taught Dunham Technique in the Alvin Ailey company. Their places were later taken by Joan Peters, who had held a children's scholarship at the Dunham School in New York. When Syvilla Fort, who directed the Dance Division of the school while Dunham was on tour, left to form her own school, she took Peters and others in the children's group with her.

According to one scholar, Richard Long, Fort became "for many years one of the leading teachers in New York City."[17] He referred to Dunham, along with Pearl Primus, as "canonical" in producing dance teachers and mentioned a considerable number of dancers associated with Dunham who have international reputations as teachers. Among others, he cited Carmencita Romero, who has taught in Cuba, Italy, Japan, Spain, and Germany; Lavinia Williams, who taught in Haiti, the Bahamas, Guyana, Jamaica, Germany, and New York; Vanoye Aikens, a faculty member for many years at the Royal Swedish School of Dance; Walter Nicks, who taught in New York, Scandinavia, and France and in the 1970s had his own company in the United States; and Syvilla Fort, Claude Marchant, Tommy Gomez, Archie Savage, Ruth Beckford, Glory Van Scott, and Pearl Reynolds, all of whom have taught primarily in the United States. Lucille Ellis, Clifford Fears, Lenwood Morris, Ural Wilson, and many of those who have attended the seminar also taught in universities and community centers.

NOTES

1. Lucille Ellis, interview by author, 13 August 1991, Dunham Technique Seminar. Center of Contemporary Arts.

2. "Conversations with Katherine Dunham," 12 August 1994. Videotape in Katherine Dunham Museum, East Saint Louis, Illinois.

3. Ortiz not only did research on African-Cuban history and culture but also was a lawyer and political activist who served in various public offices.

4. In a presentation at the Katherine Dunham Technique Seminar, August 1995, Parks College, Cahokia, Illinois. The Caribbean Cultural Center in New York collaborated with the New York City Department of Cultural Affairs in mounting two exhibitions, *The Worldview of Katherine Dunham* and *Katherine Dunham in Cuba, 1947: Documentary Photographs by Carmen Schiavone,* on the occasion of her eighty-fifth birthday.

5. Tito Puente and Max Roach, among others, honored Dunham at the 1994 celebration sponsored by the Caribbean Cultural Center.

6. "Program for *Bal Nègre*" (1946), in *Kaiso! Katherine Dunham: An Anthology of Writings,* edited by VèVè A. Clark and Margaret B. Wilkerson (Berkeley: Institute for the Study of Social Change, 1978), 98–100.

7. Tommy Gomez described this in an afternoon seminar on 14 August 1990, Dunham Technique Seminar, Center of Contemporary Arts.

8. Katherine Dunham, "Open Letter to Black Theaters," *Black Scholar* 8 (July–August 1979): 5.

9. This was the Samuel H. Scripps American Dance Festival Award. Dunham received it in 1986.

10. Numerous mentions in personal conversations and "Conversations with Katherine Dunham," Dunham Technique Seminar, 1975–2000.

11. Katherine Dunham, master class, 8 August 1994, Dunham Technique Seminar, Central City Visual and Performing Arts High School.

12. David Wisely, "Dance Show Is Done on a Necklace," *Auckland Star,* 10 April 1957, 7.

13. Katherine Dunham, master class, 11 August 1993, Soldan High School.

14. Marjorie Scott, interview by author, 10 June 1993, East Saint Louis, Illinois.

15. "Conversations with Katherine Dunham," 10 August 1992, University City High School.

16. Katherine Dunham, master class, 13 August 1993, Soldan High School.

17. Richard A. Long, *The Black Tradition in American Dance* (New York: Rizzoli, 1989), 158.

Dunham Technique

Barre Work and Center Progressions

ALBIRDA ROSE

BARRE WORK

Sequence 1: Placement

The student faces the barre, feet parallel and as wide apart as his/her shoulders, arms are down to the side, focusing straight ahead. The arms are placed at the insertion of the hip joints, palms flat, fingers facing in.

Sequence 2: Dunham Presentation

This is the Dunham presentation of the arms. On the count that is set, the student begins to raise the arms forward, in four counts. Halfway up, the arms stop, palms are flat, elbows and shoulders are balanced equally. In this halfway position, hold for four counts. The arms continue rising above the head (hands slightly in front of face) and are held in this position for four counts.

While holding the position above, the student checks for correct body alignment:

- The head is centered
- The shoulders are well balanced over the chest area
- The chest is lined up over the waistline
- Waistline is directly over hips through to the thighs
- Thighs are directly over the knee

Albirda Rose, *Dunham Technique, A Way of Life* (Dubuque: Kendall/Hunt Publishing Company, 1990.), 32–33; 38–41; 69–70; 80–81; 93–97. Copyright 1990 by Albirda Rose. Reprinted by permission. Minor editorial changes have been made. The original text includes diagrams of movement exercises and detailed variations of each sequence.

- The knees are directly over the toes
- Feet are in parallel (approximately eight inches apart)

Sequence 7: Body Rolls

Through the development of strength and abdominal muscle control from the previous exercise [flat back], the student should have a visual working knowledge of the pelvic area.

At this point the student begins to understand the use of the pelvic area. The large gluteus maximus muscles are used in this position where the pelvis inserts into the thigh muscles and the front area of the pelvic girdle. In the flat back position, the student will contract and release the pelvic area from both the front and back (this may take some work). The instructor should have the students place their fingers into the soft tissue area in order for them to feel where the start of the movement should begin.

The fingers should be placed so that they can feel the contraction and release of the muscles. This could be a very difficult aspect of the technique, but once perfected the rest will flow accordingly. The instructor must make the students aware of where the pelvic girdle and where the pelvic contraction exist. The instructor should note that this entire sequence is done in the flat back position and that the "release" does not indicate hyperextension of the pelvis or lower back, but that the back returns to the flat back position.

- In the pelvic area, contract and release should be repeated approximately four times working each specific area
- Using the gluteus, contract and release and repeat four times
- Move into the lower back area, contract and release four times (The student is still in the flat back position.)
- Move up into the middle back area, contract and release four times
- Upper back area, contract and release, repeat four times
- Head area
- Then all of these body parts are put together in continuous motion to complete the full body roll.

At the completion of the body rolls in flat back, the students should hold for four counts, again focusing and finding their balance, being in total alignment; then the right hand comes off the barre, sweeps down along the right side of the hip, elbow comes up, palm reaching down with slightly cupped hand; then repeat with the left hand.

Depending on the level of the student, this could be done with both arms together or with one arm at two different counts. Beginners should do one arm off at two different counts so that they can feel where their balance point is, then the other arm comes off in the second count. More advanced students can take off both arms in one count and hold the position, knowing where they are in space without losing balance. At the completion of the sets, the flat back position is held.

Then the arms and hands are brought in toward the body, palms facing toward the body, and the back is still flat. Starting at the pelvis, the pelvic contraction starts a body roll placing each vertebrae on top of each other, slowly; from the pelvis, gluteus, lower back, middle back, upper back, shoulders, neck and head until standing position is reached with proper alignment.

As this is being done, the arms are in a continuous flow of motion. They come up, in four counts, above the head. Again the shoulders are down, focus is straight ahead, chin is up and you frame the face as a perfect picture and the entire position is held.

If this is a level-one class (beginners), this exercise should be done with flat feet; if level-two or -three students, they can begin, as they contract, to start the pelvis movements and roll up on four or eight counts. Again, the student should be aware of their own center, knowing that their pelvis is in alignment, tailbone is long, neck is long, chin is slightly lifted while looking straight ahead, shoulders down and relaxed. Hold, then slowly come down completing the movement in four or eight counts. Arms come back down to the beginning position.

PROGRESSIONS

To start progressions, the students should line up at one end of the room, three to four people across. When one group has completed a phrase the next group should start four to eight counts behind the first group depending on the exercise. The suggested rhythm for beginning progressions is Ibo.

Sequence 1: Dunham Walk

The Dunham Walk is done within the understanding of body alignment and placement. The basic walk using the feet is executed with a feeling of a continuous flowing energy through space. The movement begins with the foot stepping away from the body, the right foot using the toe, ball, arch, and heel. The knee is in plié until the entire foot makes contact with the floor. The weight is shifted to left foot and repeated. This is a gliding movement across the floor that is always in plié. The upper torso is held high, and the chin is lifted as the student begins to glide in plié with the feeling of the rhythm coming from within as they move. As they glide and move across the floor, a presence and/or energy level equal to that of being in a processional giving homage must be maintained. The movement should cover space and the student should be in command of that space. The walk is done in a parallel position to the rhythm Ibo.

The arms are in Dunham presentation second position. The arms are parallel to the floor, palms are flat facing the floor, fingers closed, elbows lifted. The walk starts off gently to the rhythm, stepping to every beat. The object is to hold the hands and arms lifted so that the energy is held consistently as the glide through space is maintained through the entire body. The movement can be started with the left or the right foot. It can be moving backward or forward with any variation that the instructor suggests.

Sequence 4: Traveling Isolations

Note: This movement can be done to the rhythm that the instructor chooses. If already working with Ibo, you may want to continue in that rhythm.

Traveling isolations should move from the head, though the shoulders, chest, and hips. The basic concept is to give the students an understanding of how to move and isolate a certain part of the body in conjunction with locomotion movement and to move that part of the body across the floor. The beginning isolations should be done standing in one place working each body part. Now we begin to put those body parts on top of a rhythm moving through space.

Begin in plié, stepping with a flat foot. In plié the student gets the feeling of being in contact with the earth as opposed to flying in space and losing control. The rhythm base is found through the pelvic and abdominal areas, knees bent, using the floor.

PROGRESSIONS IN CULTURAL CONTEXT

Beckford states that progressions is "the term used for a movement pattern done across the floor." Not only are progressions simple movement patterns done across the floor, but they are the students' opportunity to increase their ability to perfect the movement that they have done at the barre or isolation from stationary floor center. The student combines these movement combinations in the sequences in which the teacher directs him/her and begins to move across the floor from one designated starting point to another. The student then must put it all together; rhythm, style, and quality of movements. The centering, focusing, alignment, and attention must all come to a point of intersecting for total execution of the movement phrase.

Progressions in Cultural Context are built around the same basic principle of simple progressions, moving from one point in the room to another. The difference is that now specific rhythm forms are used, rhythms that reflect a cultural heritage of a specific group. The main cultural influence that Miss Dunham uses is that of Haiti, but it is not the only rhythm style that appears. These rhythms usually have specific dance steps that accompany them, and these steps usually reflect the basic concept of that dance or why that dance is performed.

This aspect of the technique is a direct influence of Miss Dunham's work as an anthropologist and her belief in synchronization. Her research done in Haiti gives the basic information and concepts for Progressions in Cultural Context. Damballa, Yanvalou, Zépaules and others are specific rhythms or deities that are represented in the Vodun ceremonies or the basic celebration of everyday life in Haiti, Martinique, Jamaica, Cuba, or other West Indian cultures. The other area of representation is jazz dance. Miss Dunham recognized the rhythm and movement style connection between jazz dance of African American culture in the United States and that of the islands of the West Indies.

There were no dance techniques that would give Miss Dunham and her dancers the unique style, strength, and rhythm needed to perform her choreography with the authenticity and the quality that were needed. Progression in Cultural Context is the fusion of what she needed to train her dancers. This type of technique helps give the audience an accurate visual perception of the dances. The early technique work at the barre, center floor, isolation, and basic progression are the foundations for the development of movement in cultural context, or movement that has been created specifically for performance by the choreographer.

Miss Dunham's descriptions of several of these rhythms or dances were first listed in her book *Dances of Haiti,* or have been documented in descriptions of specific choreographies that were done for stage.

Damballa

Damballa is the serpent god in the Vodun religion. The movement that represents this particular deity is a slow undulating movement of the torso. The movement breakdown has been described throughout the foundation of the techniques from the barre work to center floor as body rolls. If the student has already perfected this movement concept, then the execution of Damballa and its variation will be simple.

The upper torso is moving in continuous fluid motions that move throughout the entire spine.

> Yonvalou, the dance of humility and assurance. This dance to the serpent Damballa, the Haitian Vodun god, begins at the base of the spine by contracting or tucking under the hips in an upward tilt. Like a ripple in a pool of water, the movement starts to follow up the spine to the neck and finishes at the neck and head only to start again in the hips in an unbroken circuit (Beckford 52).[1]

This movement does not stop, so one is not aware of where the movement begins or ends. The position of the legs, knees and feet can use several variations as the upper body is moving through the motion. The knees always bend within the rhythmic pattern of the movement. The feet move in a step-together-step from side to side, forward and backward, in circles, slow or fast. The movement can also add level changes from high to low, and variations on tempo, fast, slow or very slow.

Yanvalou

Yanvalou is the religious dance that honors Damballa. Yanvalou has a specific rhythm that is usually in $\frac{3}{4}$ or $\frac{6}{8}$ time. The movement concept is the same as Damballa, undulating movements of the torso. This undulating free-flowing movement can manifest itself in any part of the body: arms, hands, hips as well as the torso. The student should be able to do the movement so that an observer would not be able to see where the movement starts or ends; it should always be continuous. The tempo of the movement is usually set by the drummers. The variations on this dance are many. The movement can travel in any direction, use all levels possible and any body parts. Even within a traditional ceremony itself, the level of improvisation is unlimited.

Zépaules

Zépaules is a dance of the Vodun done for the deities Legba and others. Lcgba is the god that is the gatekeeper. This particular dance is a perfect example of why Miss Dunham developed isolation. . . . Zépaules is a movement that uses rapid shoulder isolation. Thus, keeping the other parts of the body still, the main emphasis is on the shoulders moving in unison, pushing downward. The shoulder movement is of a percussive quality that pushes downward, then up with the feeling of the energy going through the back of the body.

The movement of the feet accompanying the body is the same rapid tempo as the shoulders. The movement is usually small steps taken in a forward direction, with knees bent slightly. The feet leave the floor in a flat position lifting off and returning the same.

Mahi (my-ee)

The Mahi can really be called the dance of the feet. (Williams 9).[2] Mahi is a fast rhythmic tempo, with very percussive movements. The knees are bent with the upper torso being carried in a stately manner with movement variation from isolation to smooth undulation movement as body rolls. The feet are the main focus of this dance. With flat feet, one foot is picked up (one at a time) moving forward, then to the back in an arc motion. The other leg never leaves the plié position at the knee. The same foot is then placed down in the back of the support foot, almost in a straight line behind it. This is all done in a constant motion, moving in a forward direction, with the movement alternating from one side to the other. This particular movement combines polyrhythm, with the upper torso at a different tempo and quality of movement. This is also one of the most difficult movements to perfect or teach. One should give her/himself the opportunity to have hands-on experience of this particular exercise.

NOTES

1. Rose is referring to Ruth Beckford's *Katherine Dunham: A Biography* (New York: Marcel Dekker, 1979) *[Eds.]*.

2. See Lavinia Williams Yarborough's *Haiti-Dance* (Germany: Bronners Druckere, 1958). Williams was a principal dancer with the Dunham Company who eventually settled in Haiti and became a prime exponent of Dunham Technique *[Eds.]*.

How She Began Her Beguine

Dunham's Dance Literacy

MILLICENT HODSON

Katherine Dunham is a bona fide dancer and scholar, both at once. The combination is rare in the dance world, which has yet to acknowledge Dunham for the new level of literacy she has brought to the art. The myth of unthinking dancers is still too pervasive to allow full recognition of a woman like Dunham, her 1969 *Dance Magazine* Award and other honors notwithstanding. But her time is coming because the world is catching up with her, not just the dance world but people in medicine, psychotherapy, community organizing, sociology, and in a sense, even the sharks making millions on the jogging and disco fads. Dunham realized that it was rhythm we had lost in our lives, sometime around the Industrial Revolution when automation, alienation of the worker from work, the replacement of extended families and choral dancing by nuclear families and coupling for the waltz, when all these things began. A progressive woman, a visionary and an activist, she did not propose a single-minded return-to-nature program, although she disappeared for a period in the Caribbean islands "to see firsthand the primitive dance in its everyday relationship to the people."[1] It was her goal to take the knowledge of "primitive" rhythms and use it to change the quality of modern urban life. By way of doing so, she would preserve the culture of her ancestors; she would give new life to their spirits. In the course of doing so—making these rhythms at home in the moment—she would alter the history of American dance.

SOURCE: Millicent Hodson, "How She Began Her Beguine: Dunham's Dance Literacy" in *Kaiso! Katherine Dunham: An Anthology of Writings,* edited by VèVè A. Clark and Margaret B. Wilkerson (Berkeley: Institute for the Study of Social Change, 1978), 197–200. Copyright 1978 by the University of California, Berkeley. Reprinted by permission.

Dance is a way of knowing. In the myriad of Dunham's gifts to the world, she brings us closer to this truth. Working in words or working in movements, she begins and ends with the body as the instrument of knowing. In Dunham's vision the body embraces mind and psyche. What is seen and measurable, what is called science, this exists on a continuum with active wondering about the invisible, what is called religion or magic. This continuum has a concrete life in the central nervous system, winding snakelike up the back from the sacrum bone to the complex lobes of the brain. Rhythm is the coordinating function of the central nervous system, making instantaneously real in our limbs what is being signaled in the mind and psyche (elsewhere known as soul). Dunham identified schizophrenia, alienation, apartheid, the separation of music and dance— each of these phenomena on a different order of reality she identified as the breaking of rhythm.[2] When the rhythm is broken, whether in an individual or in a whole society, malaise is the result, disintegration, the diffusion of energy. If rhythm is the proof of unity, of the evolution of form, then dance is the way of knowing. In an early essay Dunham defined dance as "the profound urge to rhythmic motion and organized pattern."[3] She saw it as the key to our "potentialities for personal and social integration."[4] She understood the search for rhythm through dance in a holistic context that anticipates the contemporary need to discover other states of body consciousness, either through ancient methods of exercise and meditation or new methods of therapy. Again, the world is catching up with this dancer and scholar who has for several decades included martial arts and metaphysics in the training of her performers. She begins and ends with the body as the instrument of knowing:

> the desire for unity directs itself toward an idea of the divine, toward nature, toward the unifying of the various personalities making up each individual self, toward a search for a concept of good, or simply toward an unseen light. When some degree of unity is arrived at, some degree of relief from malaise is the reward.[5]

Katherine Dunham began her career in the mid-1930s, coming out of the Great Depression and the University of Chicago when it was a mecca of social thought, coming out of classical ballet and as much Spanish and Russian dance as she could find in Chicago, coming out of a racially mixed family that was socially derived from theater people on the one hand and conservative Protestants on the other. Coming out of all this,

Dunham is her own best storyteller. In the excerpts which follow she tells us, among other things, how she began her beguine. The anecdote stands as a metaphor for her rare synthesis of scholarship and the practice of dance. A few days before her virgin voyage as anthropologist, Katherine Dunham learned the beguine from Bronislaw Malinowski. As wildly fantastic as it sounds, it is true. Malinowski, who exists in the popular imagination as a lonely social scientist writing up reports on the Trobriand Islanders, taught Miss Dunham how to do the beguine—Katherine Dunham, who would shortly exist in the popular imagination as the exponent of Caribbean rhythms. Dunham raised the ghost of the beguine and other African-derived dances which had found their way, cooled off and cleaned up, into the Chicago ballrooms of the 1930s. After the now legendary voyage researching these dances in the islands, Dunham began her writing career with a short article for *Esquire* in 1939 about the beguine in Martinique. The article, published under the *nom de plume* Kaye Dunn, is entitled "La Boule Blanche."[6] It is a kind of equation of how Dunham writes about dance. She begins with the body, recording the actual movements and the context of sound that accompanies them. Then she analyzes the dancer in terms of social class and individual style, and she analyzes the dance according to its function at that nightclub, on that island, in that branch of the African bloodline. Finally, because of the vivid detail that carries you through the analysis, she makes you feel the ambiance, as though you were there, which makes you want desperately to dance the beguine yourself. So she ends as she begins with the body as the instrument of knowing.

In the excerpts which follow, we learn, from Dunham's point of view, the state of the art of dance when she began ("The so-called modern schools . . ."), the history of her career ("Lecture-Demonstration"), and the way she would herself document the work she has done ("Dunham Technique: Prospectus" and chapter summaries for a book). She is astute in her reckoning of the state of the art; unburdened by categories (ballet, modern, ethnic, etc.), she speaks of all the strains of dance as "so-called modern" and shows what strength each has given the art as a whole. In brief, Dunham explains that Isadora Duncan let dance out of the cage of the old ballet and that Sergei Diaghilev (in exile with the Russians in Paris) gave structure to the new energy Isadora unleashed. It is a fact that Diaghilev's first choreographer, Mikhail Fokine, did his signature work *Les Sylphides* under the influence of Isadora dancing in Moscow in 1905 to music of Chopin. *Les Sylphides* was originally called *Chopiniana,* and it

broke with the ballet of the time by freeing the arms and torso into continuously flowing, Duncanesque movement. Dunham, perhaps recognizing
a kindred soul, gives Duncan her due as Diaghilev and his choreographers
never did. In her state-of-the-art essay, Dunham concludes that Mary
Wigman in Europe and Martha Graham in America were the climax to
that first phase of the revolution in dance. Dunham does not stop to point
out that both of these dancers established movement vocabularies based
on the bodily freedom—especially of the arms and torso—which Isadora
prescribed. Nor does Dunham discuss how both Wigman and Graham
developed Diaghilev's ideas of *mise en scène*—the extension of a coherent
visual design from the choreography through the decor, the collaboration
of painters and sculptors with choreographers to achieve this coherent
design, and the exploration of historical material as the source for contemporary forms in the theater. Dunham carried these advances in movement
vocabulary and *mise en scène* into the second phase of the dance revolution.
She recognized the weak links and how her particular background and
goals could strengthen them. The Dunham Technique makes available to
the "modern schools" of dance the liberation of knees and pelvis that is
fundamental to African dance. Dunham created exercises based on the
principles of traditional dances derived from Africa. Her choreography,
evolving from the same principles, established for the modern dancer a
new vocabulary of movement for the lower body. Dunham's contribution
in terms of *mise en scène* is equally significant. Working with John Pratt
and others, she set a new level of design for dance theater, extending the
lines of dance movement through the cut and color of costumes, using the
tropical context of her dances to awaken the kinesthetic sense of the audience. But it is in the adaptation of historical material to the modern stage
that Dunham's genius fully flowered.

   In the excerpt on the "so-called modern schools,"[7] Dunham identifies
her own role; for "primitive" dance, "it is the work of a student of ethnology as well as a student of the dance to observe and record that which
can be transferred to the field of art and which will serve as a stimulus."
Dunham brought to Broadway, Hollywood, and even the Metropolitan
Opera the idea of authenticity in its use of historical materials. The issue
to contend with was exoticism, a basic trait of Western theater that reflects, step by step, the progress of imperialism. Whoever was currently
being colonized was turned into the romantic "other" in the theater of
Europe and America, from the court spectacles of the Renaissance to the
films of D. W. Griffith. The tradition continues in subtler forms into the

present. Early on it became a convention to play out this xenophobic ritual with as much opulence as possible, as though, unconsciously, to pay back the plunder. By the 1890s, performers could hardly move for the amount of scenery, bulk of costumes, and expanse of fantasies from the burgeoning empires. From this rubble of cardboard and kings the dance revolution broke out. Duncan and Diaghilev, later Wigman and Graham and others—all of them slashed away at the ideology, the movement vocabulary, and the *mise en scène* of the old theater. All of them sought purer models for theatrical form, especially in the Greek and Eastern theater. Katherine Dunham, reaching through her own historical past, found the model in Africa—as it had survived through her ancestors in the Americas. Unlike her predecessors in dance, she was trained to organize scientifically what she found in her research. Even Diaghilev, scholarly though he was in tracing things out for his ballets, was unsystematic and left no record of his search for others to continue. Dunham, on the other hand, was taught the standard techniques of research and in using them for her work in the Caribbean she set a new level of literacy in dance. As she confides in the "Lecture-Demonstration" excerpt, remembering her stay in Haiti:

> For a long time I was merely a happy participant in every dance that I could manage to get to for miles around. Then my academic training got the better of me and I began to get seriously into the question of the choreographic form, psychological and sociological significance, organization and function of what I was seeing and participating in.[8]

She goes on to detail her criteria for differentiating the dances, and later explains, as her focus turns from research to choreography, her principles of adapting ritual or festival material to the stage:

> What would be the connection between the carnival dances, whose function is sexual stimulus and release, and almost any similar situation in a Broadway musical, for example, the temptation scene on the River Nile in *Cabin in the Sky?* It would be the similarity in function, and through this similarity in function the transference of certain elements of form would be legitimate.[9]

Perhaps it required a black American, perhaps even a woman, to be so conscious about plunder and so conscientious about the evolution of form.

Dunham's commitment to historical integrity connects in an arc to her ideas about rhythm and the integration of the self in society. For a dance to be real to history is comparable to an individual being real to himself or herself, to his or her origins. How Dunham must have startled the Metropolitan Opera by the authenticity of her 1963 production, in which the Ethiopian princess was a black performer and the Egyptian army was composed of Somalians, Nubians, and other groups which archeology identifies as the population of black Africa at the time of ancient Egypt. Dunham insisted on authenticity not only in characterization but also in plot. She saw the priestess scene as a secret rite of women's mysteries, changing the scene from an exotic showpiece to the crux of the transformation ritual she saw the whole opera to be. In her notes for the Triumphal March in the opera, Dunham reflects on the issue of exoticism which she had countered in her work for almost three decades:

The Triumphal March of *Aïda* has always been a production challenge. Until the last decade, however, authenticity counted for less than random extravaganza. Today with television, motion picture spectaculars and distant lands readily accessible to the general public, the production staffs of operas of exotic themes are obliged to restudy scores and original notes and research in ethnic and archeological backgrounds in order to satisfy a more demanding audience and give a new authority to material tending heretofore to underestimate too often the value of reality.[10]

By developing tools to make the past a source of new creative energy Dunham carried the dance revolution into its second phase. The Dunham Technique not only teaches rhythmic movement but also embodies an ideology for use of rhythm in contemporary life. Dunham's dances and books not only elaborate authentic material but provide a model for research, enabling us with her to continuously create the world in which we dance.

NOTES

1. Dorathi Bock Pierre, "A Talk with Katherine Dunham," *Educational Dance* (August–September 1941): 7.

2. These perceptions run throughout Dunham's work. She deals with them specifically in "Notes on the Dance," in *Seven Arts,* ed. Fernando Puma (New York: Doubleday, 1954), and in an address entitled "The Historical Necessity of Music."

3. Dunham, "Notes on the Dance," 69.

4. Ibid., 70.

5. Ibid., 71.

6. Katherine Dunham, writing as Kaye Dunn, "La Boule Blanche," *Esquire* (September 1939): 92ff.

7. Katherine Dunham, untitled, undated statement beginning "In the so-called modern schools." [Reprinted herein as "Need for Study of Dances of Primitive Peoples."]

8. Katherine Dunham, "Lecture-Demonstration of the Anthropological Approach to the Dance and the Practical Application of This Approach to the Theater," UCLA, 1942, p. 7. [Reprinted herein as "The Anthropological Approach to the Dance."]

9. Ibid., 9–10.

10. Katherine Dunham, production notes for *Aïda,* act 2, scene 2, p. 1, for the Metropolitan Opera Company, New York, 1963. [Reprinted herein as "Notes on Dances for *Aïda.*"]

Form and Function in Primitive Dance

KATHERINE DUNHAM

Laymen who attend dance concerts, dance teachers, and even performers are usually unconcerned with the function of dance. Instead, they are concerned, largely, with its aesthetic principles, its technique, the ideology of modern forms, and the form of the choreography. As an anthropologist, however, I became increasingly interested in the functions of dance, both religious and secular, in primitive and folk societies. Accordingly, when the opportunity to make a study of primitive dance presented itself, I emphasized the importance of observing the interrelation of form and function as it expressed itself in such a context. The result of these observations was incorporated in a study of the dances of Haiti, prepared for a master's degree in anthropology at the University of Chicago.

For a number of reasons, Haiti presented a particularly fertile field for the study of primitive dance. On the one hand, it had not been greatly industrialized and in isolated sections of the island original African forms and rituals were preserved almost intact. Furthermore, the French had never been as merciless in their cultural domination of colonies as had the British, and thus again the preservation of authentic and original forms was more characteristic of Haiti than of other islands of the West Indies. In other words, the authentic context within which the interrelation of the

SOURCE: Katherine Dunham, "Form and Function in Primitive Dance," *Educational Dance* 4.10 (October 1941): 2–4. Copyright 1941 by Katherine Dunham. Reprinted by permission.

NOTE: This article also appears, virtually verbatim, as chapter 7, "Interrelation of Form and Function," of *Dances of Haiti* (Los Angeles: University of California, Center for Afro-American Studies, 1983), 59–62. The original text has been corrected to conform to the later version.

forms and functions of the dances would most spontaneously manifest themselves was available to me. The following is a portion of the study that deals with these considerations. (See Figure 1.)

To discuss the interrelation of form and function of the dance involves a great deal of speculation. At times this relationship is asymmetric—the form determines the function without the reverse being noticeably true. Other actions between the two are symmetric, as in the case of the *banda* funeral dance.[1] Here the *grouillé* form[2] causes externalization of grief, but at the same time the function determines the form. With the large *danse collé,*[3] the closeness and compactness of the mass engenders social cohesion, while at the same time the gregarious, recreational impulses and the desire to externalize and share experiences draw people together in mass form. For the most part, however, the form of the dances has a determining effect on the function, in lesser or greater degree. The *caribinien,* or *contredanse,* is a native adaptation of the European square dance. In this, men and women face each other on four sides of a square, and partners alternate frequently. The floor pattern is involved, and the formality of the dance is stressed. The principle of choreography as an agent of sexual attraction operates to a far lesser degree here than in the case of the *Congo paillette.*[4] The pattern of the *Congo paillette* directs one man to one woman, and the movements are directly symbolic of pursuit and capture, without the formal embellishment of the changes of partner and elaborate choreographic pattern as in the *contredanse.*

The form so far discussed refers to choreography or floor pattern. There is an even more basic interrelation between form of body emphasis and function. In my discussion of the function of the sacred dance, I point out that the dance is an essential in motivation and direction of religious ecstasy and thus is a continuance of cult worship. This is achieved by expression of the ethos of the cult, in the same way that observations as to the ethos and character of a people may be deduced from a general knowledge of the form of their dance.

Priests of Pétro[5] have in some regions (namely, environs of Léogâne) submerged the purely religious functions of the cult and emphasized the working of magic, often "black," or of a destructive nature. In general, the Pétro cult is known for its violence and as a cult of blood. Though I have attended only one real Pétro ceremony (these are rare and more inaccessible than some of the other "services"), from a knowledge of the dance Pétro, I would be inclined to add it as further substantiating evidence as to the violent character of the cult.

FIGURE I. Functions of the Dances of Haiti

SECULAR DANCES

Seasonal Dances (large crowd)

Play, recreation
Externalization of inhibitions
Externalization of energy
Social cohesion
Greater social integration
Sexual stimulus and release

Occasional, Social Dances (small gathering)

Sexual selection
Sexual attraction
Development of artistic values through exhibition of skill
Development of the artist
Social cohesion
Gratification of exhibitionist tendencies through
 audience-performer relationship

SACRED DANCES

Cult Dances

Ritual
Preparation for reception of *loa*
Secret ritual functions to induce or break hypnosis
Establishment of cult solidarity by motivation and
 direction of religious ecstasy through dance

"Loa" Dances

Representation or symbol of *loa*
Establishment of contact between individual and deity

Funeral Dances

Externalization of grief
Escape from secret ritual function

The dance *Pétro-magi* may be called one of opposition. In order to shift rapidly on half-bent knees, and to use feet and heels with force, it is necessary that the muscles of the back be rigid. It would seem that this produces an excitement quite apart from the hypnotic effect of dances of other cults and the sexual stimulus of other dances. The atmosphere of a true Pétro ceremony is hostile and negative. The possessions are apt to resemble frenzy rather than ecstasy. At the baptismal ceremony witnessed on *veille de Noël* (Christmas Eve) in the plains near Croix-des-Bouquets, the ignition of flares of gunpowder at a given time caused such pandemonium that the impulse of an outsider was to seek shelter until the various Pétro *loas* (deities) had vented their emotions and departed.

There are fewer possessions by gods at a Pétro ceremony; the form of the dance apparently leads to uncontrolled motor activity or hysteria rather than to ecstasy or hypnotism. Undoubtedly, somewhere in the secret rituals of this cult there are beliefs requiring force and an attitude of opposition to natural forces. Perhaps one of these is black magic. At any rate, the ethos of the cult is publicly expressed through this dance, and the solidarity of the cult is assured by the producing of similar effects in all of the worshipers. This seems to be a symmetric relationship between form and function, some of the ritual or social functions apparently determining this particular form.

To illustrate again the effect of dance form on cult solidarity, we may examine the dances of the Rada-Dahomey cult, chief of them being the *yonvalou*. One of my Haitian friends aptly termed the *yonvalou* the "prayer" of the Vodun. The dancing of the *yonvalou* produces a state of ecstasy remarkably near that which the medieval Christian saints are supposed to have experienced through prayer and meditation. It would seem that the fundamental purpose of prayer is release from emotional conflict by an establishment of contact with some superior being, or a complete externalization and loss of one's ego in that of the essence or being with whom the communion is desired. The movement of the *yonvalou* is fluid, involving spine, base of the head, chest, solar plexus, and pelvic girdle. The effect is complete relaxation. There has been no tenseness or rigidity of muscles: instead, a constant circular flow acts as a mental narcotic and neural catharsis. The dance is decidedly soothing rather than exciting, and one is left in a state of complete receptivity. It is in this state that contact with the *loas* most often occurs.

Contrary to the Pétro cult, the Rada-Dahomey cult is known to be beneficent in nature. It has connected with it no bad *loa*, no *loa* whose demands would cause difficulty or would willfully do harm. Nor does the cult practice magic. The *houngan* or *mambo* (priests of the cult) may indulge in divining, or in a little prescribing of amulets for an improvement of health or luck, but this is not directly associated with cult duties. In some instances, of course, divining is necessary ceremonially, and a worker of black magic would not be countenanced. Here we have the ethos expressed in the positive, flowing quality of the dance, as well as further substantiation of hypotheses as to psychophysiological effects of body emphasis. In this prayer dance I cannot say whether the condition of ecstasy is achieved more readily by the completion of a circuit within the body (circular flow through spine, chest, and solar plexus) or whether, in a state of acceptance, mind and body are left freer to receive the suggestion of possible contact with these *loa*. Perhaps both are equally true.

Another dance of religious ecstasy is the *zépaules,* which stresses shoulder action. But here the ecstasy is of a slightly different quality than in the *yonvalou*. It seems that the regular forward-backward jerking of the shoulders and the rapid contracting and expanding of the chest ensure quick, regular breathing. This forced rapid breathing brings about self-hypnosis and auto-intoxication, states bordering on ecstasy. The action of the *zépaules* is less fluid than that of the *yonvalou,* and the effect is more of excitement bordering on hysteria than ecstasy.

The form of dances of sexual stimulation, sexual release, and sexual symbolism operates directly on these functions by emphasis on parts of the body associated with the sex act. In the *danses des hanches,* such as the *Congo paillette,* the symbolism serves as a stimulus as much as the body emphasis. The effect of this symbolism was noticed after having danced the dance as an amusement without being conscious of the symbolism, and later dancing it with an understanding of the fecundation principle behind it. True, the agitation of the haunches is exciting, but it does not act as a sexual stimulus to the same degree as the *grouillé* and *ventre* (stomach) dances. The hip-twisting and stomach dances, on the other hand, seem to serve as a direct stimulus that, if participated in at length and under the impetus of the crowd, reaches a climax and then releases this tension. It would seem that the centering of movement and attention on the particular muscles involved serves to stimulate the particular sections of the nervous system involved, and that this stimulus reacts again upon the form of the dance, causing it to become more vigorous and extreme. Undoubtedly, association of ideas plays a major part in these reactions, but any further discussion of the interrelation of this particular phase of form and function will have to be left to the psychologist.

NOTES

1. The *banda* is a dance that takes place in the presence of the corpse before the interment. It has a sexual character, in keeping with the African philosophy that closely associates procreation with death, perhaps as a compensatory effort. The body emphasis here is on the forward-thrust hips, and the *grouillé* movement is sustained throughout *[Eds.]*.

2. The *danses grouillés* form one of the larger categories in which Haitian dances may be divided according to form. They are the hip-twisting dances common to Mardi Gras and Rara festivals, as well as some of the sacred dances and many of the social dances. The form consists of a grinding movement of the forward-thrust hips and is directly associated with sexual activities *[Eds.]*.

3. *Collé* is an inclusive term applied to dances performed *en masse,* where the density of the crowd is such that the dancers have the sensation and appearance of being glued together *[Eds.]*.

4. The *Congo paillette* is one of the *danses des hanches* group, as far as form is concerned. In these, practically the only movement is in the rapid agitation of the extended haunches, accomplished by a rapid shuffling motion of the feet *[Eds.]*.

5. Pétro is a branch of Vodun. As compared to the Dahomey rites, whose deities are, in general, benevolent, Pétro deities, or *lwa* are often perceived as violent and sometimes malevolent *[Eds.]*.

The Anthropological Approach
to the Dance

KATHERINE DUNHAM

During the early part of my college career it seems to me that I must have annoyed my professors to no end by being late to classes, failing to get papers in on time, and skipping class now and then in order to keep up with my less academic interest—the technical training in the dance. During the later part of my college career, which for economic and other reasons, was separated from the earlier period by some several years, I am afraid that I annoyed my professors even more by trying to find some twist in whatever subject I happened to be struggling through that would connect it with my outside activity, namely, the dance.

In trying to bring about this extraordinary marriage of two seemingly unrelated interests, I would find myself, in archaeology, interested in Mound Builder cultures of the Mississippi Valley almost entirely because of the implications of their ceremonial artifacts. Ethnology excited me very much because in every unfamiliar people or custom I saw a great possibility of establishing an exotic mood in the theater. In physical anthropology I measured some two hundred or so little schoolchildren, trying to find out what the posterior projection of the calcaneus had to do with elevation—their ability to leap and spring. In linguistics, I must confess I found no way to combine my two interests. Social anthropology offered

SOURCE: Katherine Dunham, "A Lecture-Demonstration of the Anthropological Approach to the Dance and the Practical Application of This Approach to the Theater," delivered at the University of California at Los Angeles, October 1942; unpublished paper in the Katherine Mary Dunham Papers, Special Collections, Morris Library, Southern Illinois University, Carbondale. Copyright 1942 by Katherine Dunham. Reprinted by permission.

the best possible solution for joining my wish to be an anthropologist, and the great physical urge to be a dancer.

I must say that through this rather hectic experimental period, I found only the greatest sympathy in the attitude of my professors toward what I was trying to do. Now and then I was forced to become a little bit suspicious at some one of them assuring me, after some concert or other, that I really should concentrate primarily on the dance. But on the whole it was through such general interpretations as these of Redfield, Radcliffe-Brown, Malinowski, Herskovits, and others, that I was able to arrive at a sane translation of classroom and field material in terms of the theater.

During one of my more serious periods at the University of Chicago, it occurred to me that the dance, as a specific and extremely important social trait, had received relatively small consideration from anthropologists. It occurred to me, also, that someone who could actively participate in this activity would be able to arrive much more clearly at the function of the dance in a specific community than the field worker who depended primarily on observation.

Dr. Redfield stressed the essential unity of activity—the cohesiveness of all elements in a simple society; this would mean that the dance would be related to other traits in that society. Dr. Herskovits gave me a more than adequate background for my West Indian research, both through African material and through his own West Indian material. Radcliffe-Brown lectured in terms of function, so that I was always reminded to look for the purpose and the use of whatever I saw, as well as the form. As for Dr. Malinowski, I shall always be grateful to him for giving me my first lesson in the beguine just a few days before I left for my field trip.

In spite of all of this very academic-sounding background, it was really on the basis of a ballet which I directed for the Chicago Civic Opera that I received my fellowship from the Julius Rosenwald Fund. After six months' training with Dr. Herskovits at Northwestern University, I felt sufficiently prepared to set out from island to island in the West Indies and look for the elements of the dance in the simple society which I hoped later to develop into an analysis of primitive dancing.

The West Indies, I felt, was a very important field, because there one finds forms completely primitive as well as those in a process of acculturation. African forms still survive vigorously, chiefly in the ceremonial life; now and then even a Carib Indian form persists.

Before narrowing down to a specific region, I wish I could give you an adequate definition of dance. The closest one that I can figure out is to think of the dance as "rhythmic motion singly or in a group," for any one of the following several purposes:

1. *Play.* The Bushman of South Africa will often dance around a center pole for several hours of the day in one direction and then for several hours of the day in another direction, for no apparent reason other than that it amuses them.
2. *Release and building of emotional and physical tension.* The sacred dances fall primarily in this category: for example, funeral dances release the emotion of grief, and there are many religious dances whose chief function is to build the participants to the point of ecstasy. War dances serve to increase physical and emotional tension.
3. *Establishment of social cohesion or solidarity.* The Carnival dances popular all over the West Indies serve as a good example of this.
4. *Exhibition of skill.* This exhibition may be either in solo or group form and may be either a demonstration of amateur spontaneity or of professional virtuosity.

The history of each island of the West Indies, whether it be Dutch, French, English, Spanish, or otherwise, is practically the history of every one of the other islands. Carib Indians were indigenous to the islands. With the coming of Europeans the native population died out practically to a man, and great numbers of West Coast Africans were imported to work the cane and coffee fields and banana plantations. African slaves became a matter of course. Often the slaves en route to North America were dropped for a while in the islands of the West Indies to become acclimatized. Certain of the foreign peoples preferred certain tribes; the Koramantee were favorites of the English and Dutch; the Congo, Ibo, Mandingos, and Rada and slaves from the highly developed kingdom of Dahomey seemed to find themselves primarily in the French islands.

The island of Haiti, French before it became a republic, offered material for a thesis which somewhat appalls me as I look at it now, in the scope of its approach. The title of it is "The Dances of Haiti: A Study of Their Material Aspect, Organization, Form, and Function."

As you know, Haiti is the larger part of an island in the Greater Antilles, the smaller part being the Spanish-speaking republic of Santo Domingo. Like most of the West Indian islands, Haiti has one main port town, several lesser towns, and a great many small, entirely native villages. The economy is agrarian, with 5 percent of the population, known as elite or "mulatto," living on the labor of the other 95 percent in the export of coffee, bananas, and rum. The North, the region of Christophe and the Citadel,[1] is the stronghold of the "black" population; the South, where the capital, Port-au-Prince, is located, is the stronghold of the mulatto "elite." Port-au-Prince is in the center of a magnificent bay, and above it are mountains, and between it and the North are the dry, dusty plains of the Cul-de-Sac, and more mountains. My work in Haiti centered chiefly in these plains, in the mountains above Port-au-Prince, and in the mountains of the North. Introduction into each community was usually made by someone of the Port-au-Prince elite, or by some scholar, or perhaps by a peasant from another community. Some six months in Jamaica, Martinique, and Trinidad had more or less familiarized me with field technique, and Martinique had accustomed me to the sound of the French Creole language. In each community I would rent a native hut and take up residence more or less on the same basis as the natives themselves, and patiently await an occasion to dance, or to find out what to expect in the way of dances.

Fellow field workers always take a great interest in the way another field worker gets what he or she wants out of a community. I found that for every island a different approach had to be used. Haiti was the least difficult of the several which I visited. After taking up residence and allowing enough to be known about myself to put the community at ease, I would frankly ask about the dances of that region, when one was expected, and what were the occasions to dance. Then I would busy myself with the other life of the community—going out in boats with the fishermen, to market with the women, and sitting around the charcoal fires at night listening to gossip and improving my Creole. Pretty soon someone would hear of a dance in a nearby community and would remember that I had been asking about dances. I might be invited, or I might learn by accident and invite myself, sometimes I would hear drums several miles away and would enlist the aid of someone from my compound or group of native huts to help me locate them. Perhaps we would find them, perhaps not. If we did not, more than likely it was because a secret cult dance was in progress, and no one would give us accurate directions. In general, after a few days in a community, everyone for miles around would know all about me and what I was there for, and unless a dance was of a particularly sacred nature, there would be no trouble at all in being invited to it, or in just walking in on it. As time went on, occasions would come up which would allow me to plan a dance myself, as for instance at Descay-ettes, in the mountains above Port-au-Prince, when the priest Julien warned me of some difficulties that I was in, and I persuaded him to perform a three-day ceremony to appease the gods for a while. [Anecdote: embar-rassing experience of not becoming possessed.]

For a long time I was merely a happy participant in every dance that I could manage to get to for miles around. Then my academic training got the better of me, and I began to get seriously into the question of the choreographic form, psychological and sociological significance, organiza-tion and function of what I was seeing and participating in.

Gradually, out of a maze of strange names, instruments, songs, and patterns, I managed to arrive at a somewhat comprehensive classification of the dances of the area of Haiti, on the basis of the following criteria of differentiation:

1. Their sociological significance in the community.
2. Their material aspects (drums, clothing, symbols, etc.).
3. Their form, both in choreographic development and in body emphasis.
4. Their function, sociological and psychological.
5. Their organization, from the loose-knit Carnival band to the highly organized Vodun ceremony.

Before describing the classification resulting from these criteria of dif-ferentiation, I would like to elaborate on two of the criteria, organization and form. A section from the paper which I mentioned earlier will illus-trate organization. [See "Form and Function in Primitive Dance" for a summary of this thesis.] So much for organization.

Since form is the most important external feature of any dance, I can best illustrate its possible variations by calling on members of the company to demonstrate. [Extemporaneous.] In Haiti, the natives have descriptive terms which I found very useful in differentiating one type of dance from another.

grouillé [twisting, grinding of the hips]
collé [glued]—any dance done close together, usually in crowds. Imagine the
    effect of a great mass of people dancing a *danse grouillé* as at Carnival.
do-ba [low bending of the back]
zépaules [*des épaules,* of the shoulders]
du ventre [of the belly, stomach]

des hanches [of the hips, haunches]
de pie [*des pieds,* of the feet]
(Also interesting to see what drummers will do).

As to function, the material is far too lengthy and detailed to bring into such a general discussion. However, I would like to read through for you a chart which is the result of this section of the research. [See Figure 1 in "Form and Function in Primitive Dance."] A discussion of the interrelation of form and function, with which I concluded my analysis of the dances of Haiti, went over, I am afraid, into the realm of theory; but since the idea of a possible interrelation is extremely important, I will read some paragraphs from this concluding section. [See dissertation: "Inter-relation of Form and Function."]

As in the primitive community, certain specific movement patterns could be related to certain functions, so in the modern theater there would be a correlation between a dance movement and the function of that dance within the theater framework. And certainly a broad and general knowledge of cultural patterns can be advantageously brought to bear upon the problems of relating form and function in the modern theater. Or so has been my theory and so my practice in my own theater experience. What would be the connection between the Carnival dances, whose function is sexual stimulus and release, and almost any similar situation in a Broadway musical, for example, the temptation scene on the River Nile in *Cabin in the Sky?* It would be the similarity in function, and through this similarity in function the transference of certain elements of form would be legitimate.

I feel that I have burdened you enough with material from this paper. You are probably wondering what connection such academic-sounding material may have with the dance in the theater. I would like to show you how such materials have inspired the creation of and given background to a number recently completed.

[Members of the Dunham Company perform.]

NOTES

1. Henri Christophe (1767–1820) was a freed black slave who served as a general under Toussaint Louverture during the Haitian Revolution (1791–1804). Vying with others for political power and military control, he eventually became provisional chief of northern Haiti. In 1811 he declared himself King Henri I and began a reign modeled on the absolute monarchies of Europe. The pomp and splendor of his reign are still evident in the ruins of Citadelle La Ferrière, a formidable mountaintop fortress near Cap Haïtien *[Eds.].*

Notes on the Dance

Katherine Dunham

The challenge to master space and gravity seems to be a characteristic inherent in the more complex of animal species. Often this challenge takes a symmetrical expression involving form and time. The leaping, bounding, and running of the young of the four-legged, the complex patterns of bird choreography, the seasonal mass theater of elephant herds are all evidences of this profound urge to rhythmic motion and organized pattern. As though in a continuous effort to arrive at an organic unity with nature, dance, loosely defined as "rhythmic motion," has persisted through the various phases of man's physical, psychological, and socio-organizational changes from prehistory until now.

To define is often to limit unconditionally, and the attempts to define deep-rooted and fundamental inner springs, senses, atavistic patterns should be in correct thinking superfluous. "Rhythmic motion," however, is too sparse a definition for dance unless automatically is included a body of experiences of sounds, feelings, and intentions. In a search for definition, I once arrived at the following:

> Dance is a rhythmic motion for one or more of a number of reasons: social cohesion, psychological or physiological catharsis, exhibitionism, autohypnosis, pleasure, ecstasy, sexual selection, play recreation, development of artistic values, stimulus to action, aggressive or non-aggressive, extension and affirmation of social patterns, and others.

SOURCE: Katherine Dunham, "Notes on the Dance, with Special Reference to the Island of Haiti," in *Seven Arts,* edited by Fernando Puma (New York: Doubleday, 1954), 69–76. Copyright 1954 by Katherine Dunham. Reprinted by permission.

I realize that this formula enters more into the terms of description than definition, which often occurs when by a certain continuous extension of correlated characteristics the only answers seem to be over-complexity or over-simplicity. Verbalization is apt to end in sterility, and the aesthetic experience such as makes up a large part of any art creation eludes explicitness with a tantalizing facility. (Even now I see, however, that I, like numerous other creative artists, have fallen into this pitfall and try to explain with many words an experience which is firmly rooted in man's essential being and may well be a key to his potentialities for personal and social integration.)

The universality of dance has long been recognized by historians, philosophers, graphic and plastic artists, and of late has become a subject of interest to anthropologists, psychologists, and physiologists; there has begun to emerge in recent years a strong popular concern for this expression not only from a theatrical or entertainment point of view, but *in terms of* its examination as a cultural trait, comparative analysis of its different forms and its significance, sociological, biological, and psychological. But as the cultural importance of the dance is brought to prominence by such media as the folklore theater, exploitation by camera, and the ever-growing library of descriptive travel lore, there arises in modern society a dispute which has finalized itself in placing dance in that ambiguous position between science and art, between exposition and entertainment. This dichotomy seems to me to be a useless one, as the paths of art and scientific discovery too often cross, even merge, to allow for dispute. In primitive societies dance is an accepted functional element of both personal and community life, and for this reason the conflict of classification does not arise. The ecstasies, repressions, challenges, sorrows, and pleasures of peoples still living in a folkloric or primitive state find expression and are channeled, controlled, or released as the case may be by ritualized dance. And it is from a careful observation of the dance as a community expression that many useful hypotheses of culture type or pattern, psychology, and philosophy may be arrived at.

Man's desire seems to move in two directions, one toward the deep atavistic backward pull of some darker millennium past, the other toward greater integration and a more unified existence. Depending on the character of the individual and the type of culture in which he finds himself, depending on elements still unknown to psychologist and physiologist, the desire for unity directs itself toward an idea of the divine, toward nature, toward the unifying of the various personalities making up each individual self, toward a search for a concept of good, or simply toward an unseen light. When some degree of unity is arrived at, some degree of relief from malaise is the reward.

Since there is every evidence of the ascendancy of malaise in our own industrialized societies, it becomes increasingly timely and of interest to observe in societies still enjoying a primitive or folk state to what degree dance serves as a unifying element, to what degree rhythmic motion reaches into the depths of community and individual life and effects equilibrium, maintains balance, channels emotion. This interest need not confine itself to societies classified as primitive or folk; modern society also exposes itself to comment through its demonstrations of rhythmic motor activity. We have somehow in our process of absorbing the refinements of civilization arrived at the conclusion that we are no longer to be measured by the same set of equations as govern peoples still living in a folk or primitive state. This is obviously a fallacy, and many of the intense crises of modern living when viewed from the vantage point of evolution or acculturation become less ominous and more amenable to solution. Dance in modern society is almost totally confined to social ballroom situations, or various forms of theater and entertainment. The tastes of a nonparticipating public, that is, the spectator, are important in analysis, however, and certainly if we observe mass tastes in social dancing in a cross-section of the most highly industrialized metropolitan centers we find a pattern fairly generally followed during the past century of rapidly changing mores, ethics, economics, and credos.

The rhythm of the average metropolitan center is not one to induce integration—quite the contrary. Or perhaps as yet we human beings are still too cradled in the movement of the earth womb to adapt to the ever-increasing heterodoxy imposed upon us by our mode of life. Our pace is uneven, our bearing has lost the composure of its stature, and our spirit has no oneness with the air that we breathe. We are dominated by a cross-current of rhythms and motions emanating from countless man-created machines and institutions, from fears, anxieties, and loss of faith. The rhythms of the human body itself—the beating of the heart, the motion of breathing, the delicate system of waves emanating from the brain centers, the flow of the bloodstream, and the unconscious urging of the muscles are in constant competition with the cacophony and disharmony which are the fruits of our industrial age. In the dance hall the giddy jazz of the 1920s catapulted into the frenetic delirium of the Lindy Hop and its subsequent developments. A decade later, having seemingly reached a vertiginous height, a search into the past brought to the fore again the 1920s—the Charleston, Dixieland, energetic country folk dancing. A curious combination of jazz and bolero came out of Cuba toward the end of the 1940 decade in the form of the "mambo" and has swept a tornado through the Caribbean, the Americas, and Europe. Since the great waltz era, which had its inception immediately preceding the industrial revolution, the social dancing of modern man, which after all is the sole vestige remaining to him of dance as a cultural trait apart from the theater, has exhibited the increased neurasthenia, the growing lack of integrative tendency, and the fundamental disharmony in which we find ourselves today.

There is every biological evidence that an essential sense of order exists in all living organisms, a movement not haphazard or without form, a pattern of life more carefully choreographed than any of the ballets of the masters. The search for visual evidence of this order has and still fortunately does preoccupy philosophers, scientists, and creative artists. The obvious, almost prerequisite point of departure in this quest would be an examination of those societies still living in a state relatively free from the extended complex of industrialism.

Although I have chosen to make the island of Haiti the illustration of many and varied theses expounding the unity between man and his gods, man and the elements of nature, and man and a set of fundamental governing rhythms, I would not be able to make the statement with any honesty that the peoples of the island of Haiti are free from neurasthenia. For some of them African gods have turned into schizophrenic superstition; for others the strain of reconciliation between these gods and Catholicism creates deep conflict; for many others the anxieties of the caste-color system are psychologically insupportable. But one can hardly set foot on the island without being aware at once that some cohesive agent is strongly at work.

The Republic of Haiti occupies about one third of the area of the island known at one time as Saint-Domingue, earlier named Hispaniola by its discoverer, Christopher Columbus. The remaining portion of the island, less attractive in many geographical aspects, is made up of the Dominican Republic, Spanish in provenance. While Haiti is French in the contacts and customs of its upper classes, the influence of the brief North American occupation and the subsequent influx of tourists is fast being absorbed into its culture pattern. The great body of illiterate peasantry speaks French Creole, works the cane, coffee, and sisal fields in a concerted rhythm known as the *combite* to concerted singing under a professional concertmaster, fishes in the deep sea, and derives a special dance movement of the god Agwe from the motion of the waves. At night when the Haitian peasant huddles around a small charcoal fire to recite stories and bits of gossip, statement, interrogation, and expostulation become a gentle interweaving into a rhythmic pattern. Added to this, nine evenings out of ten, guitar, maracas, and bongo, Cuban importations, will be stimulating a *bamboche,* or social get-together, in one of the many neighborhoods such as Carrefour, or a juke box will be playing endless "mambos" in the endless cafés along the ocean front on the road to Léogâne. In the hills above Port-au-Prince the drums of Rada-Dahomey, beaten primarily with sharp sticks on a five-foot tree trunk headed with a pegged ox hide, pierce the chill mountain air and penetrate into the low coastline to send a thrill of excitement across the Champs-de-Mars where mulatto lovers hold hands on stone benches. Legba, Ogun, Damballa, Aïda Ouedo—invocations to these and a score of other gods can be heard from the steps of the sugar-icing presidential palace, and a group of porteresses swinging down from Pétionville may with no warning whatsoever break into a ballet of shoulder movement and shuffling feet. Out of the bowels of the earth in the south the Congo drums answer with the disturbing sex groan which characterizes the percussive accompaniment to this hierarchy of deities. From Croix-des-Bouquets the sharp infuriated anger beat of the more violent Pétro cult catapults into the plains of the Cul-de-Sac in defiance of the gentler, more benevolent deities of its neighbors. If it is night, it is the drums; if it is day, it is the sound of the sharp hooves of scrawny, mean little donkeys on pavement, rock, or dust, the banter of their mistresses, and the endless padding of bare feet streaming down from the hills to market and back up into the hills again, always in rhythm and always, even seen from far, in choreographic pattern. Immediately one is aware that these essential rhythm patterns penetrate every phase of island life.

Industrialism has not yet descended upon Haiti with full force. The several modern factories remain almost entirely unabsorbed into the basic culture of the island and seem insignificant beside those patterns handed down for centuries and surviving the shock of displacement, impact with foreign cultures, revolution, occupation by American Marines, and tourist invasion. Undoubtedly, the phenomenal success of the ragged bands of revolting slaves against the armies of Napoleon has done much to shape the character of the modern Haitian, peasant or elite. Certainly this success gave every reason for a reinforcement of the belief in the African gods and their Haitian complements and the violent extermination of all

material vestiges of the former colonial state left free play for the development of a society purely folk and highly individual in character.

One feels a cohesive element when setting foot on the island, and this
cohesive element is rhythm. In spite of whatever political or social quarrel
may be in vogue at the time, the Haitian of any given class whatsoever
responds to the pulse beat of the Vodun drum. His social status may inhibit
a direct reaction, but to deny the response would be like a true Spaniard
denying a blood surge at the sight of the promenade into the bull ring or
a temperature change at the cry of a flamenco singer. The folk, the uninhibited, will respond by direct motor reflex even if the relationship to
the origin of the sound or sight be an indirect one.

There is another, a more intangible, quality to elemental rhythm than
those sounds and motions associated with conscious action and one becomes aware of this at all sorts of odd moments, in observing the reactions
in movement and sound of a crowd around a cockfight; the unconscious
falling into sculptural groupings at road crossings or in market places; the
cries of street vendors, and the half dance of burdened longshoremen
loading a coffee cargo. For the elite, the only physical participation may
be at Carnival time or at parties or night clubs. For the large body of the
population, the peasant, the worker in the field, the small shopkeeper on
a dusty road, it is always a dancing through of one's emotions, experiences,
joys, sufferings. A dancing out of oneself that makes life bearable, because
the life of the Haitian peasant is not an easy one.

The emotional life of any community is clearly legible in its art forms,
and because the dance seeks continuously to capture moments of life in
a fusion of time, space, and motion, the dance is at a given moment the
most accurate chronicler of culture pattern. The constant interplay of conscious and unconscious finds a perfect instrument in the physical form, the
human body which embraces all at once. Alone or in concert man dances
his various selves and his emotions and his dance become a communication as clear as though it were written or spoken in a universal language.

The possibilities for research in the field of rhythm and motion in relationship to the measure and control of individual personality traits are
almost unlimited; some note has been taken in relationship to community
traits and culture pattern, but to date both of these special studies remain
more in the field of scattered and cursory documentation than in analysis.

Need for Study of Dances of Primitive Peoples

KATHERINE DUNHAM

The so-called modern schools of the dance, which had their birth in the interpretive dance of Isadora Duncan and the revolutionary productions of Sergei Diaghilev, and which have reached their climax in such schools as those of Martha Graham and Mary Wigman, have drawn upon the classic Greek, the primitive, and the Oriental to furnish a technique which would relieve choreography of the geometric patterns of the formal ballet. To create, rather than to imitate, is now the major problem of the dancer, and to create in such a pure and tangible manner that the result will offer beauty and inspiration to lovers of art.

From my own observation, I would say that the dance of the primitive has been scarcely touched, and this, perhaps, because unlike the classic Greek and the Oriental, it is the work of a student of ethnology, as well as a student of the dance, to observe and record that which can be transferred to the field of art and which will serve as a stimulus for creation. Additional work in ethnology, particularly research work among the Indians and Negroes of America, island peoples, and primitive Africa, would contribute to science a comparative analysis of the dance which has, I believe, not received adequate attention from scientists. In art, it is likely that a study of the dances of various groups of primitives would lead to the discovery of those principles of technique which are fundamental and universal in character, and to their incorporation into a basic dance form which has not yet been developed by the modernists.

SOURCE: Katherine Dunham, untitled statement, undated, in the Katherine Mary Dunham Papers, Special Collections, Morris Library, Southern Illinois University, Carbondale. Copyright by Katherine Dunham. Reprinted by permission.

Although my primary interest in the dance is creative, I realize the necessity of highly specialized training. For this reason I would study at the schools mentioned above, so that I would be capable, in every sense of the word, to train a group of dancers with which to interpret the materials collected in research and to produce ballets which I am confident such research would inspire.

The dance as an art form is an increasingly strong social force, and undoubtedly contributions to the development of new, vital material and technique would be of great social significance.

Dunham Technique

Prospectus

KATHERINE DUNHAM

There are two ways to approach the technique known as Dunham. One would be in a first, separate work such as planned some years ago—a *Primer of Primitive Rhythms,* analyzing, with drawings and photographs, the origin of the source material on which I have drawn in anthropological research. This would be approaching the matter purely chronologically, and comparatively; that is, classifying what could serve among varied primitive peoples as classic. This study would not, however, develop into the area which has produced the final stages of our technique as seen in theater presentations and classrooms.

A more general book strongly recommended at this time could be known simply as *Dunham Technique* and would embrace an introductory amount of analysis of original primitive movements, illustrating in what ways these movements have developed into the technique of our school and theater; had they been directly borrowed, had they gone through a process of change, and to what degree and why. This would be a book of theory, interrupted rhythmically by illustrative analysis and photographs.

Disturbed in my early years of social anthropology at the lack of emphasis on the complex of the dance in primitive society, I proposed that my scholarship from the Rosenwald and Rockefeller foundations be directed toward an effort at repairing this lack. Also involved was an element of rebellion against the often condescending attitudes toward not only Negro performing arts but those of all deprived, minority, "exotic" folk.

SOURCE: Katherine Dunham, "Dunham Technique: Prospectus," an unpublished paper, dated February 1963, in the Katherine Mary Dunham Papers, Special Collections, Morris Library, Southern Illinois University, Carbondale. Copyright 1963 by Katherine Dunham. Reprinted by permission.

Oriental dancing at its commonest level became "kootch," African dancing, "shake" or "grind," American Indian dancing, hopping about bent
double, West Indian and South American, a melange of sensual shoulder-
shaking and pelvic undulating. Pacific regions were vaguely mixed up in
fantasies of knee-slapping orgies of wildly swaying grass skirts. There is, of
course, some truth in all of this, but surely these expressions of thousands
of years' combined culture could be better oriented. To observe, record,
classify, and teach became an aim of mine, and in so doing to establish
a rigorous discipline and form much as must have been intrinsic in the
evolving of classical ballet from primitive northern ritual to country fair
celebrations to court entertainment to Covent Garden.

Theory, the basis for selecting the area examined and particular movements from these areas, a further delving into my favorite study, the interrelation of form and function should occupy one half a volume the
text of which should be about thirty thousand words. The other half
would be the description and process of development of large groupings
of movements or methods of technique; from whence strength and balance, function of trained breathing, process of transferring training from
muscle consciousness to utility exercise to variations on movements to
choreography—this well illustrated with photographs.

Those photographs which I could supply would be chiefly mood ones,
or ones of general pattern. The step-by-step development of a selection of
basic movements would be left to a dance photographer. I suggest Carmen
Schiavone, who has done some of this for me and who now seems willing to cooperate further. In the last pages of the Richard Buckle book
are some photographs by Schiavone.[1] Also available is a large quantity of
photographs from the dance training classes around which much of the
film *Mambo* (1955), starring Sylvana Mangano, was based.

It is difficult at this stage of planning to set an exact limit to photographs. I would suggest thirty, of which I could supply one half almost
exclusively in the general pattern and atmosphere category (backstage
and in rehearsal in most countries of the world). An arrangement with
Schiavone would of course be the responsibility of the publishers.

For a cover I suggest a plate similar to the stroboscopic photograph of
L'Ag'ya by Gjon Mili and see no reason why the solid cover of the book
should not carry the same photograph, following from front completely
around the book as has been the format of some of our souvenir programs.

From fan mail and inquiries the world over, especially since the closing
of our New York school a few years ago, I would say that the publication

of such a book is consummately timely. I feel a personal need for it in order to clarify a technique much diffused but little understood.

CHAPTER I

In order to do this book I have been forced to read a great deal about myself, which I might have continued to glance over perfunctorily or avoid the rest of my life, as is my tendency with reviews, critical and complimentary alike. Somehow I have felt that the freshness of ideas both of oneself and one's work, the bloom of constant discovery, the necessary anguish of self-doubt which comes of itself from the inner being of the artist without help from the critic might be thrown out of balance, however so slightly by moving too closely into the orbit of what others think of one or one's creations.

The analysis of my own technique or even the description of it has been one of the most difficult problems of a long and rewarding career. Articulate about most incidents of my life or work to a degree which has permitted me to lecture, perform, and write without inhibition, when confronted with the inevitable demand to describe what I do or what our theater is about or just what Dunham Technique consists of I become painfully mute, unreasonably reluctant. It is, I have finally decided, because this part of my life is still too close, too much a part of fiber and being to be put into perspective and set apart for analysis.

At one time or another, either as self-defense or because it is truly one of my basic concepts, or both, I made the statement that "to describe is often to limit."[2] Finally, however, I feel the growing separation of a complete delivery, the beginnings of a certain objectivity which allows me to put on paper some of those principles of a technique, an approach to theater called "anthropological."[3] This metamorphosis has come about in me not only by a natural process of time and gestation but because a return to America for a few months, instead of days or weeks, for the first time in many years has awakened me rudely to the great changes that have taken place in the entertainment world since I knew it, to the poverty of ideas which has started a whole era of what is described accurately, though uncomfortably, as "brain picking" as opposed to mere plagiarism or mild copying or inevitable similarities through exposure and influence.

George Balanchine continues his cool, erudite destiny; Martha Graham emerges too rarely from an island accessible only to the initiated; Hanya Holm is there but seldom seen; Agnes DeMille writes; Jack Cole seems to have tired of turning out originals for carbon copies; Jerome Robbins has entered the uppermost echelon of Broadway and now belongs to producers and directors. The others are there, but in each one, with the exception of the Bolshoi Ballet or some imported folk dance theater, there is the shameless imitation if not of actual pattern, of idea.

Originality has an unmistakable quality of its own. When a thing comes from somewhere other than oneself and one's own experience, conscious or subliminal, when there is no true creative stimulus, only a drive to produce by any means and for gain, rather than gratification, when there is no defiance of the norm, no honest daring propelled by a soul exigency, no innocence and no spontaneity, then there is no art. It is not difficult for the creative artist or artisan, and finally for any observer whose senses have not been dulled by a surfeit of mediocrity to sense the true, the original. And it becomes the obligation of the artist not only to continue to produce the original but to remain on such a steady course that even though change does and must take place within himself his original concepts remain firm, fixed and recognizable, and in all great art, time-resistant.

My old friend Bernard Berenson says that

in art, as in all matters of the spirit, ten years are the utmost rarely reached limits of a generation. The new generation follows hard on the heels of the old. Its instincts for change and self-assertion, far from being the same, are naturally opposed, and the newcomers, looking coolly at the achievements of their immediate precursors, end with a feeling of vague but extreme dissatisfaction.[4]

If this be true, I would say that dance in America is rapidly falling from the pinnacle of the classification of "art." The loss of adventuresomeness so marked in choreographers of more than a decade ago may be the result of insecurity brought about by the dwindling market, a market swallowed up methodically by the great glass furnace of television. A style has been set which requires a minimum of creativity, with the premium rather on cleverness as far as direction goes; and sadly, because of the nature of this particular expression, the instrument itself changes standards. The student who at once must make classic sacrifices to find the means to study, to train, to rehearse, who traveled across the country or continents to spend time with his mentor, and whose very being, apart and aside from his technique and convictions of execution and performance vibrated with belief in and respect for his *alma mater* now passes from one class to another with his small rehearsal bag, flitting like moths but getting no closer than the plate-glass window illuminated obliquely by a neon sign.

This I call the "audition age." Bright and sunny, svelte of figure, neat and polished, passing the lower grades of a wide number of techniques, the young ones give an impressive soulless audition. In thinking back two decades, vitamins have made them taller, nutrition stronger, ambition ruthless, and array of unions unyielding. But too often even the technique slips backward upon contract signing. Rehearsals that were once a joy of creative inter-exchange have become clock watching by the union representative, nervous measuring out of material by the choreographer, with too often mechanization as the result. The time to inculcate, infuse, instill, develop, impart, educate is no longer there. Like sheep at a given moment they leave with no backward glance, none of the eagerness to know and understand and belong to the whole idea so necessary in the performing arts. This may be another explanation for the static quality of the dance today, for its poverty of new things and the diminished creativity of the choreographers.

Sol Hurok, the only true impresario left in this country, perhaps on the grand scale in the world today, continues to impart or have a hand in imparting the colossus of the Bolshoi Ballet, and Sadler's Wells, the large-scale national dance groups and folk festivals. But these seem remote as inspiration not only to the single performer removed to a dream world outside his wildest hopes of participation, but set no aim competitively or inspirationally for the choreographer or producer simply by the impracticality of attempting anything in such large measure there today. (Unless, of course, subsidized by private or government funds, a condition much rarer than one would think.)

The identification with the single performer, La Argentina, Argentinita, Harald Kreutzberg, Mary Wigman, Martha Graham; the not-out-of-reach small touring companies of Devi-dia, Humphrey-Weidman, José Limón, even more recently the ballet companies graven in dance history but scarcely touring in the country—Jerome Robbins, Ballet Theatre, Agnes DeMille—this is fast fading from the horizon of the dance student today. Instead he sees a future of more and more infrequent Broadway musicals (best-seller casts hardly exceed four in all), practically no dance spectacular television shows, the Hollywood musical scene shifted to foreign countries for such gigantic productions as might use dance extras, slow freezing out of dancers on television except for a few stock in-trade programs, the dance concert practically unknown except for a few die-hard series, and night clubs, like Broadway shows, with few exceptions veering from full productions to single performers and small acts.

All of this means that what there is of conviction, what remains of dance as an art should be put before the public in every possible form: film, articles, books, lectures, photographs, for preservation.

CHAPTER 2

I have held auditions in just about all of the sixty or so countries visited by me and fifty-odd in which we have performed. There was a time when these auditions were either an education, a discovery of the new, or a joy in rediscovery of the known; a good showing of the technique of Bill Robinson, or Jack Cole or Uday Shankar or our own school. Naturally, since most auditions are held with an eye toward passing a board of examiners, those held by us were either by local folk groups wanting an opinion or evaluation from one whose specialty had been an analysis of their own or similar cultures, or by aspirants to our company who had been exposed to our technique through film, performance attendance, contact with former company members or the Dunham School instructors. . . . Quite naturally these latter sought to please by presenting what they had been taught as our technique or conceived it to be.

In 1934 I did my first formal dance training, outside "terpsichorean" free-style movements in school extracurricular sessions, with Mark Turbyfill, onetime ballet master of the Chicago Opera. This was in classical ballet, and Mark had been a respected disciple of Adolph Bolm. Adolph Bolm gave a special session or two, as did Argentina, Kreutzberg, Ruth Page; visitors to our classes were the nephew of Anna Pavlova (important only for name-dropping), Léonide Massine, stars and choreographers of the first Ballet Russe to tour America, Escudero, the Oriental expert Vera Mirova, others who escape me. I was moving from Mark Turbyfill to Quill Monroe, once dancing partner of Argentina, to the *maestra* who would lead me through her Chauve-Souris variety show experience, her Kamerny Theater dramatic polish, her Karsavina and Preobrajenskaya classical ballet technique, her Russian gypsy affiliations, and her own nonconformist attitudes into a style and decision of my own. I took roots between Mark Turbyfill and Ludmilla Speranzeva (known as Paetz when it was unpopular to be "Speranzeva") and practiced castanets with Quill Monroe and finger positions with Mirova until Robert Redfield opened the flood-gates of social anthropology.

Notes

1. Richard Buckle, *Katherine Dunham, Her Dancers, Singers, Musicians,* illustrated by Roger Wood and other photographers (London: Ballet Publications, 1949) *[Eds.]*.

2. Lecture, Auckland, New Zealand *[Eds.]*.

3. "Anthropological Approach to Theater," lecture, Yale University, 1939.

4. Hanna Kiel, ed., *The Bernard Berenson Treasury* (New York: Simon & Schuster, 1962).

The World in Dance and Ritual

World Dance Film Project

K ATHERINE D UNHAM

There is great possibility that dance is the oldest form of human expression. This would be in its strictest sense, of course, as rhythmic motion. In the absence of a written language the research student in dance is faced with many problems but is nevertheless on safer ground than the research student in music. Figurines, statues, bas-reliefs, cave drawings such as those found in Spain and those of South African Bushmen, and other areas of prehistoric remains depict man dancing alone or in groups. His dance may be freeform, imitative, symbolic, representative; it may be to tell and preserve the history of his tribe, to relate incidents seen or heard of, or to venerate or appease the gods. It would seem that of all things man must do by the structure of his physical and spiritual self, he must at some time or another, unless hopelessly inhibited by convention, move rhythmically in extended and repeated patterns, in choreography.

The changing nations of the world, those moving at atomic speed from primitive to folk to urban settings, cling to the last moment to the expressions of the culture into which they have been born, but sooner or later these mores become diffused or absorbed into the new or superimposed setting and, changing form, are pushed backward, to emerge rarely and only under special circumstances, or are lost forever. And with the loss of any part of the complex of cultural traits in any society a link from past to present, perhaps present to future, is lost.

SOURCE: Katherine Dunham, "The World in Dance and Ritual: World Dance Film Project," unpublished paper, dated January 1964, in the Katherine Mary Dunham Papers, Special Collections, Morris Library, Southern Illinois University, Carbondale. Copyright 1964 by Katherine Dunham. Reprinted by permission.

The only satisfactory record of dance has been film. And the adequacy of dance film to date must be questioned. Surely we have seen portions of the dance life of peoples of the world for many years, but in my estimation the film is yet to be made which penetrates into the totality of the complex structure surrounding the dance, either visually or dynamically. It is such a film that I would propose making, and such a film can be made only by a combined professional in the field of the performing arts, and in methods of anthropological research.

The documentary aspect of such a film is of great value, but it is only one aspect. Museums and other institutes, set up for the preservation of and investigation into the customs of other peoples would profit greatly. But dance securely structured into motion, sound segmented, and brought by the camera and the controlling artists and technicians into our own concepts of motion, kinesthetics, aesthetics, would be the ultimate film to be produced. How would a group of monkeys in their grotesque cavortings on the bas-relief walls of the Angkor Wat blend visually and dynamically into a dance situation? What sensations would be evoked if the feet, legs, the ruffles and underskirts of a ballerina on pointe were in meaningful motion against a deserted rocky shore or an 11th Avenue dock; or if a series of leaps led to the heights of a skyscraper in construction, or an oil pump in a Texas desert dissolved into a Mayan or Aztec ritual? These are extreme examples and might not even be used. But out of a world of ideas, rituals, meaningful objects, colors, people, and animals would come the inner essence and outer force of motion so that even inanimate objects and graphic and plastic art would join in the impact of the projection of the body, sections of the body, groups, masses in motion.

Focal Rites

New Dance Dominions

ROY THOMAS

For more than four decades Katherine Dunham has been a pioneer of choreo-cinema; hence, the serious student of dance-on-film would do well to consult the Dunham canon for what it reveals about the dancer as anthropologist, choreographer, performer, teacher, and filmmaker. Only three aspects of Dunham's achievements in film will be considered here: (1) the documentation of dance and dance environments, (2) the transmutation of primitive dance data, and (3) the uses of dance films in classroom instruction. An examination of these three facets of Dunham's work will not only reveal the range of her work in film but also the ways in which she employed film to enhance dance, without diminishing either art form. Moreover, the infrastructure of Dunham's system is to be located in such an examination—techniques that gave rise to her balletic innovations, art film style, and curriculum design. An exhaustive treatment of Dunham's film achievements would include comparative studies by other anthropologists who have filmed dance, analyses of advantages and limitations of film documentation of dance, longitudinal studies of Dunham's choreography for the stage and commercial film, and a close reading of her written technical commentaries on the earliest film footage.

It is no great surprise that in 1936 when Dunham was preparing to go to Haiti, there was, among anthropologists, so little enthusiasm for the use of the motion picture camera as the primary recording instrument in the field. A few anthropologists—one of Dunham's teachers among them—

SOURCE: Roy Thomas, "Focal Rites: New Dance Dominions" in *Kaiso! Katherine Dunham: An Anthology of Writings,* edited by VèVè A. Clark and Margaret B. Wilkerson (Berkeley: Institute for the Study of Social Change, 1978), 112–16. Copyright 1978 by the University of California, Berkeley. Reprinted by permission.

had made strong pleas for anthropological films because of their value for future research.[1] There were attempts in 1937 to establish anthropological film archives in London and Berlin, but these early projects failed. Such reluctance prevailed despite the fact that there was no notational system in existence to record with fidelity the dances of other cultures. Armed with her 16 mm Kodak Special II camera, Katherine Dunham was in the vanguard of those anthropologists who believed that the motion picture camera provided not only the best but the "only possible method of re-cording the often extempore movements of individual dancers and their interrelationships."[2] So, for the twenty-year period 1936–1956 she was actually behind the camera more than she was in front of it or beside it. It is quite clear that Dunham sensed—maybe for the first time—that dance is more than human bodies moving in space and time. From behind the camera she was also learning lifestyles, recording pulse beats, charting parabolas of ecstasy and sorrow with all the high seriousness and oblivion of a griot whose images will sway the future.

We see her on the tiny island of Martinique in 1936 filming fisherfolk, funerals, some workers on a sugarcane plantation, other workers at a sug-arcane mill. She establishes definitively the time and place with footage of beaches, mountains, landscapes, and seascapes. She films the *l'ag'ya* at Le Vauclin and a *béguine* at Fort-de-France. That same year she went to Haiti, where she filmed the Mardi Gras in Port-au-Prince, scenes of pos-session by Damballa, a Vodun center at Descayettes, and a cockfight. The historic *kalenda* [*calinda*][3] and *banda* funeral dance were filmed in Trini-dad as well as the majestic shay-shay at the public dance hall in Kingston, Jamaica.

Other films made in 1936 show Dunham engaged in both ritual and routine activities with the home folks.[4] Dunham dancing like the Haitian women, with the Haitian women; visiting the iron market at Port-au-Prince; walking and observing along the roads to Cap Haïtien and Saint Marc. When a fire breaks out at Peter's Bakery, she is there; when President Trujillo arrives at Port-au-Prince, she is on the scene. Rivers and streams run through these films. And monuments—La Citadelle, Dessaline's Statue—bring together past and present. On this her first field trip, Dunham shot ten thousand feet of black-and-white film, approximately eight thousand feet of this shot outdoors. A close look at these films is in order.

In reviewing the footage today I am impressed with Dunham's eye for broad dance movements as well as for individual phrasing and nuance. Long shots of recurring theme statements and transitions of a line of male dancers precede close-ups of foot, arm, and hand movements. And even though the drums are inaudible, the beat is clearly depicted as heads, torsos, and shoulders counterpoint the rhythms of the feet and legs. Frames explode with percussive movement, whirls, leaps. The pans show indispensable complements of people, architecture, and place; the close-ups underline the direction, size, and level of movement. Throughout these films Dunham communicated to us a sense of time and space uniquely Haitian, Jamaican, Trinidadian. There is nothing in these films which suggests garnish; there are no leers or sneers. Nor is the camera planted so as to merely photograph a dance corps or copy drummers caught up in the passion of their message. The camera is in the dances; the camera person dances. Here is the kind of involvement generally frowned upon by academicians;[5] a point to which I shall return later in this discussion.

Important because it comments on and extends Dunham's visual record of Haiti is the footage shot by Fred Alsop during the 1936 trip. Here one sees Dunham as participant in various cultural activities moving among informants without artifice or superfluous compliance. Her facial language, gestures, apparel are the best evidence of her method. She would ask for instructions about a particular drum, an explanation of a game being played by boys, the name of an instrument. We see Dunham in the same space as her auditors, utilizing not only her visual sense but her tactile, olfactory, and gustatory senses as well in getting to know the people who created and danced the movements which were becoming her own.

In 1950–1951 Dunham went to Brazil, Sicily, Barcelona, and Colombia to do more filming. She shot religious rituals, bullfights, and dances such as the *macumba, frevo,* and *samba.* Six years later she visited New Zealand, where she filmed men dancing the *haka*[6] and women performing both the long poi and the short poi. This footage from Latin America, Europe, and New Zealand is no less informative or impressive than the film shot in the Caribbean.

At the outset I stated that one must look to Dunham's earliest fieldwork, if he would discover the genesis of her choreographic vocabulary and system. I proceeded to identify specific subject matter, places, and what I perceived to be her goals at the time. Further, I have mentioned briefly films in which she appears, since I believe these constitute a valuable commentary on Dunham's own filming. We need at this point to review Dunham's choreography after her return to the United States.[7] Did she make wise choices of subject matter in the field? Was her camera technique adequate for comprehensive data collection? Were the time, funds, and energy expended commensurate with the results obtained? In order to answer these inquiries, we should examine the films of dance concerts performed by the Dunham company and commercial films made at Hollywood studios.

Over the years, Katherine Dunham has succeeded in preserving many of her famous choreographies on film. The film of the Dunham Company's show for 1943–1944, for instance, is a representative one in that it contains scenes from a variety of Dunham dances as well as a complete ballet. Included are dance sequences from *Tropics: Rara Tonga, Batucada,* and *Bolero.* The ballet *L'Ag'ya* appears in this footage along with *Barrelhouse, Flaming Youth, Cakewalk,* and *Havana 1910.* In the film of Dunham's 1947 show are *Nañigo, Haitian Roadsides, Shango,* and again *L'Ag'ya.* In 1956 the Dunham Company made a film for television entitled *Historia de un Tambor,* which included *Rites de Passage #2, Artibonite, Cumbia,* and *Cakewalk.* Of the fifteen dances listed, eleven are based on Caribbean and Latin American themes; four are derived from the dance forms of blacks in North America. This ratio is sustained throughout the films of the Dunham Company: Seventy-three percent of the dances are derived from Dunham's fieldwork in the Caribbean, Brazil, Mexico, New Zealand, and Europe.

Dunham sought to recreate the setting and ethos of the original dances as authentically as possible. What we see in the films of the company is not a duplication of the *l'ag'ya* which Dunham witnessed in Martinique. All of the original material is translated and transmuted. The *l'ag'ya* is an acrobatic dance which Dunham filmed in the little town of Le Vauclin in Martinique. The original is a film of ritual wrestling in which stalwart young men move toward and away from each other, now circling, now feinting with a lateral move. Hand and forearm, head and shoulders move in complex rhythmic orchestration. Posture is prominent in this dance: the crouch, backbend, bow are all executed with a fluidity and energy that are breathtaking. The ballet *L'Ag'ya* in the Dunham Company repertoire consisted of three sections divided into eight different dance sequences: "Market Scene," "Pas de Deux," "Zombie Scene," "Mazouk," "Beguine," "Charm Dance," "L'Ag'ya Fight," and "Death Scene." This ballet is a story of romantic love depicting the pursuit, conflict, and resolution characteristic of this genre in dance theater. The ritual competition of the original is translated into dramatic tensions by Dunham's new creation. The various dances are based on forms that come from Martinique, Haiti, Brazil, Trinidad, and Jamaica.

If one views *Rites of Passage,* he will see formal aspects of the *banda* funeral dance which Dunham filmed in Trinidad. The *batucada,* a dance of fisherwomen in Brazil, becomes a dance of flirtation in the company repertoire. Looking at the original film footage, at Dunham's written material on these dances, and at her fresh creations, I am convinced that she not only gained a profound understanding of the content, form, function, and technique of these dances in their native environments, but she also understood the necessity of working out an aesthetic unique to these materials and correspondent with her own genius and worldview.

In 1941 the Dunham company was invited by Warner Bros. Studio to make a twenty-minute film entitled *Carnival of Rhythm.* The film contains four dances, all of which are grounded in Dunham's field studies: *Ciudad Maravillosa, Los Indios, Batucada,* and *Adeus Terras.* This short film is the single Hollywood production in which a professional film editor and choreographer determined jointly what the final film would look like. In 1942 Dunham jitterbugged with Eddie "Rochester" Anderson in *Star Spangled Rhythm* and did the choreography for the hula dancers in *Pardon My Sarong.* Dunham and her company danced in *Stormy Weather* in 1943. In 1948 she played Odette and danced with her company in *Casbah.* She did the choreography for *Green Mansions* in 1959. Except for *Carnival of Rhythm* and *Casbah,* Dunham's participation in Hollywood films was brief, but it is not unimportant from a historical point of view.

Since Edison's 1896 film *The Dancing Nig,* white filmmakers had been filming black dance. Throughout the silent-film era most of these films were intended to provoke laughter. After the advent of sound pictures in 1927, an occasional black adviser would be called in to assist Vidor (*Hallelujah*) and Stone (*Hearts in Dixie*), but these advisers received neither film credit nor steady employment.

When Dunham was invited to Hollywood in 1941, she went as choreographer, performer, and camera person. Her discrete experiences with the Hollywood studios were less than satisfying: she was particularly displeased with the stilted and unimaginative camera shots of her company in most of the films. Nor was she unaware that the dances in most of the feature-length films were additive, not an integral part of the story.[8] However, the cumulative effect of Dunham's participation, 1941–1959, has been positive.

The principal significance of Dunham's choreography and performance in commercial film is that it helped to prepare the way for an increasing use of black dance, dancers, and choreographers in Hollywood films made in the Fifties through to the present day. Current opportunities for black choreographers in Hollywood studios are directly related to the dance images reflective of the liberating and recreative powers of African-based dance and music. Taken together, *Carnival of Rhythm* and the sequences from *Stormy Weather* and *Mambo* (1955) form the triptych of Dunham Technique in commercial films.[9] Needless to say, the Hollywood films are not as rewarding for the student of dance as are those documentary films of Dunham choreography discussed earlier, but because of the far-flung distribution network of commercial films, this triptych has been seen by millions of viewers on both sides of the Atlantic Ocean. Fortunately one can advance from these to in-depth and extensive study of Dunham in the company films.

When it comes to dance instruction there are no students more fortunate than those who study with Katherine Dunham or any one of the graduates of Dunham's school. Such students have access to Dunham's own written works, the many films and videotapes, and to those disciples who have studied and performed with Dunham at one time or another. My attention here will be focused particularly on film as an instrument of instruction.

In studying Dunham's film footage of the 1930s, a student receives information about dances in particular cultures. The student also is able to learn techniques for making films in the field. These films are authoritative in showing what to look for, how to look, proper uses of the camera, and so on. These films constitute the Dunham dance lexicon, an invaluable "text" for all students of dance.

Juxtaposed with the above footage should be the films of the company performing. Careful analysis here will provide students with a sure sense of technique in the art of creating dances.

A group of films and videotapes has been made expressly for teaching Dunham Technique. This third example of Dunham film footage contains very concentrated dance sequences which depict the technique from different angles, distances, and at different speeds. These have been filmed at different times and places—in Oakland, California; New York City; Atlanta; Chicago; East Saint Louis, Illinois, by Dunham's assistants. What these films tell us is that Dunham Technique is part of a system that has been undergoing subtle changes over the last four decades. I shall comment on the nature of these modifications later.

In a given academic quarter Dunham will be using all three categories of film mentioned above, sometimes individually, other times in pairs, or the three back-to-back. The films are preceded by carefully planned lectures and followed by discussion and analysis. Film segments are rerun enabling students to read movement in detail. The films do not replace actual work at the barre nor do they displace demonstrations on the floor. Rather they are complementary in that they show the student in images that are concise, clear, and eloquent the uses of his body in space.

Earlier I stated that the Dunham system is undergoing constant change. Films depicting the technique of that system must be modified accordingly. When Dunham originally choreographed *Nañigo, Choros #1, Rites of Passage,* and *Homage to Scott Joplin,* the company consisted of particular dancers, each with his or her own strengths, graces, idiosyncrasies. Dunham's own worldview was different from what it is today. When today's young dancers perform the dances mentioned above, they touch the dances with the fire of their own imagination. The dances are not the same. Films tell us so. Dunham realizes as much in that she can descry new directions, construct new combinations, and hear different accompaniments than at the beginning. She can criticize her own dance history on film.

In light of the discussion about Dunham Technique I should like to make clear the distinction in the system before making my final observations.

Repeated viewings of films by and about Dunham have indicated to me that what is referred to as Dunham Technique is only one aspect of what is really the Dunham system, an entity with a distinctive philosophy, aesthetic, and critical method. This system, as depicted in the films, is based on a monism which postulates a single unity for all life, one changeless and timeless truth manifest in different ways. This unity undergirds all temporal societies, orders, and kingdoms. In order to understand fully any part of society, one must look at it in the context of the whole. A single charm, song, prayer, dance, vocation transmits as much information about its environment as about itself.

The aesthetic for such a view naturally finds completeness and beauty in the correspondence of parts with the whole, that whole with other wholes so that ultimately there is universal harmony. Isolated dance movements, individual parts of the body, single spaces are completed and fulfilled in relationships. Mental health is related to physical health similarly.

Dunham Technique must be understood in the light of the philosophy and aesthetic of the larger system from which it derives. Many students have learned Dunham Technique without this understanding. The films show the technique explicitly and the system implicitly. The technique is codified, demonstrated, and transmitted daily; the system, on the other hand, is not immediately perceived, not directly demonstrable.

Basic Dunham Technique involves vigorous work at the barre, isolations, movement, and control of energy flow. The technique perfects the body; the system clarifies the mind. Such a system decrees change, demands rigorous self-interrogation.

Dunham is unafraid to call the creating self into question. For the creative artist to settle down is to forfeit the creative impulses. Over and above style information, idiom, an individual teaches, finally, what she is. Dunham teaches a respect for truth, an open-mindedness, and a penchant for self-criticism that is essential for those who would master the technique and learn the system.

Finally, viewing Dunham as ethnographer, performer and instructor, one comes to understand the ritual of observation that invariably attends the filming of all human behavior. I described Dunham and her camera as *entering* into the dance which she was filming. According to Ruth Beckford's biographical account, Dunham believes that "the best dance films will be made when the cinematographer is also a dancer."[10]

Unlike biologists, architects, engineers, doctors, and others who employ film in research, the students of human behavior—anthropologists, psychologists, psychiatrists—generally involve more of themselves in the act of filming. This involvement, I contend, enhances rather than diminishes the value and use of the film because the filmmaker responds affectively to those projections emanating from the people being filmed. This affective response precludes that objectification of human beings which sometimes stifles personal interaction.[11] The highest desideratum for the student of human behavior is to bring the thinking and feeling dimensions of his personality into the most dynamic interplay possible with the new culture.

The kind of observation called ritual is not without its guidelines; it has demands that are as compelling as those informing rituals. Suggested here is a way of seeing with a heightened sense of expectancy, even epiphany. The Ritual Observer looks with the inner as well as the exterior eye. Like all such ceremony there must be preparation, anticipation, and concentration in order to maximize receptivity. Such looking almost always leads to the discovery of new worlds, new truths about the human condition and physical universe. It is at this point that I locate Dunham with her camera transporting us to the interiors of dance in the human experience. Our vision is so affected that we can never again move or perceive in the old time-space relationship. Indeed, we foresee with her new dominions for the world of dance and enter into a universe just the other side of the ordinary.

Notes

1. See the detailed account in Anthony R. Michaelis, *Research Films in Biology, Anthropology, Psychology, and Medicine* (New York: Academic Press, 1955), 193–96.

2. Ibid., 189.

3. This West African–derived form, known also as *mousondi,* has stimulated the widest controversy of any dance form since the early eighteenth century. Harold Courlander, *The Drum and the Hoe: Life and Lore of the Haitian People* (Berkeley: University of California Press, 1960); Lynn Fauley Emery, *Black Dance in the United States from 1619 to 1970,* with a foreword by Katherine Dunham (Palo Alto, Calif.: National Press Books, 1972).

4. Fred Alsop, who met Miss Dunham in Haiti, shot approximately five thousand feet of film in which Dunham appears in person, 1936–1937.

5. Michaelis, *Research Films,* 167. Also in John Collier Jr., *Visual Anthropology: Photography as a Research Method* (New York: Holt, Rinehart & Winston, 1967), 196.

6. See Suzanne Youngerman, "Maori Dancing since the Eighteenth Century," in *Dance in Africa, Asia and the Pacific: Selected Readings,* edited by Judy Van Zile (New York: MSS Information Corp., 1976), 127–47.

7. Dunham returned to the United States after eighteen months in the field but has continued to make intermittent trips to the Caribbean and other parts of the world in subsequent years.

8. Most of the Hollywood films containing black music and dance were not musicals, as that genre is defined. They were anti-musical.

9. In these three, one is able to see a total of forty-five minutes of Dunham Technique.

10. Ruth Beckford, *Katherine Dunham: A Biography* (New York: Marcel Dekker, 1979).

11. A considerable amount of the gawking aspect noticeable in early anthropological films is the work of a mythical, detached, and objective camera operator.

Dance as a Cultural Art and
Its Role in Development

Katherine Dunham

In Africa, as in the rest of the Third World, we hear often the word *development* and understand it to mean movement in the direction of industrialization, toward science and technology, toward the nuclear age, toward better jobs and housing for all people. This is a leap we feel is vital for our survival. And while that may be true, we need concomitantly to reflect carefully on the implications of what we are aspiring toward, in what way such knowledge, once achieved, will be harnessed for the benefit of our people rather than their potential destruction. In our haste to reach the level of the industrialized world, we have not even questioned whether that "level" is above or below our present state; we only know, at all cost, that it must be attained. The impact of the mass media, of the "Early Bird" Satellite, of transistor radios, of Hollywood movies, have all subtly caused us to belittle or be ashamed of what we presently have, and to cast it aside without first having really looked and examined it to see if it may be of use and of value in our quest for this new civilization. We have been subtly taught to think that our art forms, our culture, our way of being, are archaic and without value; that they are uncivilized and unworthy, that our creative thinking and expressions are savage, pagan, and thus we strive to escape all which labels us as belonging to "backward societies." We are tempted to feel that if we allow ourselves to reflect on our true tradition, on our heritage, that we will tend to stagnate and never catch up.

SOURCE: Katherine Dunham, "Dance as a Cultural Art and Its Role in Development," address delivered by Jeanelle Stovall on the occasion of Léopold Sédar Senghor's Seventieth Birthday Celebration, Dakar, Senegal, in 1976; unpublished paper in the Katherine Mary Dunham Papers, Special Collections, Morris Library, Southern Illinois University, Carbondale. Copyright 1976 by Katherine Dunham. Reprinted by permission.

We feel if every priority, as set apart by the dominant society, is not placed on economic and political growth, that we will be continuously viewed by the rest of the world as ignorant and incapable. In our rush to adopt blindly all the superficial trappings of development that we hear of and see in other countries—the fashion clothing, beautiful homes, fine cars, skyscrapers, computers, synthetic furniture; and so on, we disregard what we already have, which, if properly implemented, can accelerate the acquisition of these material goods, and simultaneously assist us to more wisely and humanely utilize them—better than they have been in the past in our so-called civilized and developed world.

It seems ironic, when individuals in industrialized countries are seeking a missing element, that something which became lost or was the price to be paid for achieving their present state, that Africa and the rest of the Third World are anxiously looking toward these countries as readymade models to be imported with all the solutions, rather than taking the time, without fear, to take stock of the present and past wealth, already existent in Africa; to know and understand all aspects of it and then adapt that which is positive and useful along with the advanced techniques of the industrialized societies and evolve a better solution for development. The developed countries themselves, at this stage, need help. Why must Africa follow their leadership without contributing a possible solution which could be of benefit to the entire world?

Acquisition of techniques and larger incomes mean nothing if they are still misused or misunderstood. If we continue to have complexes about our own past, how can we expect others to respect it; how can we do more than join the rest of the confused world, rather than helping to salvage it for a better tomorrow?

This does not mean that one should stop seeking the knowledge and techniques of the industrialized world, simply that one must also seek and study what already exists; that which is our cultural heritage, and improve upon it as well, and see through it the potential for a stronger state rather than regarding it as an impediment; rather than feeling that the heritage is subsidiary, is insignificant in relation to all else, and that concentration must be brought to bear on scientific advancements only. . . .

Man seeks harmony with his universe. When he is in discord with it, his psyche is affected and thus his ability to survive. The arts provide this harmony and this is perhaps why those nations having attained the highest levels of scientific and technological developments find an emptiness which they deny but seek to fill by looking to other areas for spiritual enhancement.

Those of us presently in the state of utilizing art forms as an integral part of our traditional background, who have not separated out the arts from our daily living, find more equilibrium and unity within our existence. Writer and analyst Dr. Erich Fromm has stated that "all art is humanistic." So when we think in terms of our aspirations to "development," as it exists in the rest of the world, we must bear in mind that we have an obligation to that world to provide a more balanced development, a development in which the arts continue to go hand in glove with our economic, political, social growth; for they are the expression of all these and must be retained as the central motivating force of our lives. We must utilize them to the hilt in order to ensure that our society will be a more humane one, and that we will be able to cope if we utilize the various techniques to remain in accord with, rather than to exert control over, our universe. We will find that the more aware we all are of our heritage, the more forceful it will become. Being born into or living through the traditions of our heritage does not make us automatically aware, but making the effort to carefully sift and determine those things in our heritage of humanizing value, and spread that knowledge to us all does lead to awakening. Our dancers, our painters, our sculptors are as important as our scientists, doctors, and engineers. They must, not only by reflex but through deliberate in-depth training and education in all aspects of our culture, help to intensify and accelerate the acquisition of the other more technical forms of development.

When we express our cultural heritage to the rest of the world, it must be not with arrogance but with authority: the authority which comes through the deep rather than superficial or habitual understanding of what we are. Every artist is a potential emissary—an ambassador from his country and thus a powerful international force. How important it is for us to realize that our negotiations must take place with the rest of the world, not only on the level of trade and aid, of technical assistance and foreign exchange, but also on the level of world understanding through true cultural exchange. This means that every effort must be ensured to make certain that our cultural interpretation of what we are is so true, that it cannot lead to misinterpretation but rather to acceptance and respect, which then in turn facilitates the other exchanges we desire to undertake.

The necessary communication among disparate groups in this or any part of the world cannot occur spontaneously. Awareness must precede the understanding which results in communication and leads to cooperation and exchange.

Our objectives therefore must be to seek methods for bringing about the essential awareness through a universal perspective. Only when individuals and nations are able clearly to be aware of theirs and other cultures, see their true values and grasp the universality of these, will the facilities emerge for communication and exchange.

Our commitment to development must then not merely be for the sake of proving to the rest of the world that we can achieve the same imitation, but that commitment must be a strong one to ourselves so that we can more positively utilize its force for the well-being of mankind in general and our people in particular.

I define the culture of a people as the sum total of its thinking. The cultural arts of a people therefore would be the expression through art of the sum total of this thinking. My prior comments on development and our cultural heritage were inspired by the recollection that during the very interesting committee sessions held in 1966 during the colloquium of the first World Festival of Negro Arts, it occurred to me that there was among certain of the participants, a kind of mistrust, a *méfiance* at the likelihood of a reversal to the traditional or more specifically to a nostalgia of the traditional which might serve to inhibit "modernization." However, after a decade, and many events which have developed, I feel certain one would now agree that as a process rather than a theory, art is the use of techniques already known or learned for the express purpose of transcending the barriers which prevent the perfect unity of form and function, and that the emotional life of any country or community is clearly legible in its art forms. This makes it imperative that we do not cast aside or underestimate the most important element in our development process.

Being most experienced in dance as an art form and being convinced of its necessity to man, I make more reference to the dance as an example, but the validity holds true for all art forms; further, dance, of all art forms, best illustrates why we must not ignore it. It is a natural impulse—as much a part of us as eating or sleeping, an integral expression of all societies no matter at what technological level. . . .

Alone or in concert man dances his "selves" and his feelings, his knowledge and his intuitions, and his dance becomes a communication as clear as though it were written or spoken in a universal language. Because dance seeks continuously to capture moments of life in a fusion of time, space, and motion, the dance is at a given moment the most accurate chronicler of culture pattern.

Man's desire seems to move in two directions; one toward the deep atavistic backward pull of some darker millennium past, the other toward greater integration and a more unified existence. Unified with what? With an idea of the divine, with nature, with the various personalities making up each individual self; with a concept of good, a drive toward an unknown light, depending on elements still unknown to psychologist and physiologist.

These desires of man may be found expressed in any of the art forms of his community, but in none are they more clearly or fundamentally expressed than in dance. Because here the continuous interplay of conscious and unconscious find a perfect instrument in the physical form, the human body, which embraces all factors of interplay at once.

In spite of this age of nuclear warfare, T.V., Cinemascope, VistaVision, visits to the moon and Mars, and other witnesses to man's increasing mastery of natural forces, there still remain a few very simple and refreshing truths: Among these is the fact that all living organisms seem to have an irrepressible urge for voluntary action. When this voluntary motion is executed, not for any of the simplest utilitarian purposes such as walking, running, or climbing to reach a certain point, and when it follows a rhythmic pattern singly or in groups, it becomes the manifestation known as "dance." . . .

In African societies the dance has reached relative stages of development determined by the pattern of the society, its beliefs and needs, but all of these stages are at a high level in comparison to the Western world.

Modern society exposes itself to comment through its demonstrations of rhythmic motor activity. The industrialized world has somehow, in the process of absorbing the refinements of civilization, arrived at the conclusion that they are no longer to be measured by the same set of equations as govern peoples still living in a less industrialized state. Many of us of the Third World fall prey to these same beliefs and run away from our own riches to align with this obvious fallacy. However, many of the intense crises of modern living, when viewed from the vantage point of evolution or acculturation, become less ominous and more amenable to solution.

In the United States, the dance has become minimized, in that it is confined in its more developed forms to the professional stage and to those who have mastered the techniques through years of training—in other words, a highly specialized group. This is, it seems to me, an unfortunate circumstance, and surely a great deal is lost individually and socially by this removal of a natural and needed expression to the professional. . . .

Socially, dance is important because of the strong integrative influence it exerts in general, and because of its adaptability to the expression of the social and emotional trend of a society. To the individual, when a true cultural instrument, it means expression through movement, the coordination of mental and physical activities, the concrete achievement of an act by means of the various disciplines of the diverse techniques.

When some degree of unity is arrived at, some degree of relief from malaise is the reward. Since there is every evidence of the ascending of malaise in the individualized and technically governed societies, it becomes increasingly timely and of interest for those countries to be able to observe in African societies how and to what degree dance serves as a unifying element, between man and his universe, to what degree rhythmic motion reaches into the depths of community and individual life and affects equilibrium, maintains balance, channels emotion.

It seems perfectly natural to me to investigate and continue those pursuits of my anthropological days and then carry the findings as a creative artist to the stage. In Third World societies, dance is an accepted functional element of both personal and community life and for this reason conflict of classification does not arise. The ecstasies, repressions, challenges, sorrows, and pleasures of people in many Third World countries find expression and are channeled, controlled, or released, as the case may be, by ritualized dance.

Man has become so specialized in the industrialized world that he has separated himself almost totally from his arts except insofar as they occasionally fulfill some far-fetched need during his moments of leisure. He has become so compartmentalized that he finds difficulty in relating one area of living to another. Education should prepare man for life application; the psychologist sees little or no relation between his field of expertise and the dance. In the industrialized world, one is taught to execute one's specialty and is unable to relate that to all else.

More and more, however, one discusses, in conferences and meetings, the arts and their effect on the quality of life; one recognizes a void but still finds it indefinable.

In Africa, all life is integrated in art expression—the arts form an integral and functional part of living. Dance, music, art all have their significance in fulfilling one's life. Man still responds to natural impulses without pushing them aside and thus is a more total being.

Those who interpret these art forms of Africa to the rest of the world must know the art form—not only in the externals, but in its fundamental meaning to the society, its social organization, its historical importance and its form related to its function. Without this knowledge of the history, the ethos and mores, we are apt to present only entertainment, airport art, or at most a superficial view of a trait of the culture, of a people deserving far more attention, and thus give rise to minimization.

Therefore the "return to the sources," the tendency to revert to the traditional, should not mean a turning of one's back on "modernization," and thus something to be feared, but rather the coming into full awareness of one's cultural heritage in order to better reinforce and intensify one's development, through pride and knowledge of one's heritage.

The pride of a people cannot be thrust upon them, but it is vital for development; if it is not there, it must come of itself; it cannot exist in certain situations without guidance and without aid. Any true pride that I have seen in people comes from knowledge and accurate evaluations, whether of self, race, or country. A continent as rich as Africa in the life means of the Western world today, with a heritage of art forms still unused, a profound knowledge of the rhythms by which every human organism lives, an unabused vitality, and a beauty conforming with nature rather than the fictionalized concepts—such a continent has an obligation to carefully examine the processes of tradition through education and expressions which will best forward the concept of development.

Too often when these arts are presented to foreign cultures they are not prepared for the industrialized world. This is not to mean they lack value, but simply because what has been performed through inheritance will be known and appreciated within the framework of its own inheritance, but runs the risk of misinterpretation outside its own culture; however, if each element of a performing company or each artist—even each politician, economist, or scientist—has been subjected to intense training in his own and related techniques, if his learning has been historic, socioeconomic, religious, aesthetic, organizational, and traditional, then the risk of misinterpretation is practically minimal.

There seems necessary, then, among the high priorities for development, in order best to present and protect the cultural arts of modern Africa, the need for an education within Africa, for respect and understanding of historical facts and prehistory findings. This must come from the collecting, classifying, and cataloguing of all available material in film, literature, photographic and recorded form, and all related materials.

The respect for historical values does not mean nationalistic or racialist attitudes or even retrogression. It is simply a look backward to better go forward. It is the simple knowledge of fact, which in all people, if presented truthfully, engenders of itself a desire to progress and to enjoy the freedom which comes of respect of self and of kind and the security of belonging to something of value. The best mode of expression of this is through the cultural arts. (I need not comment on the injury done to the American black youth in the omission from school textbooks of those facts of history, which would have elevated his being and spirit rather than categorically depriving it. I need not comment on the impact made on the African mind who first learned that his ancestors were the Gauls or that the geography of England was clearer to him than that of Africa itself).

As a prerequisite to development, therefore, we should ask, "What should the spiritual strength of Africa be?" I speak not of the potential but of the guideline for the future, for the young who are children today, so that we, who, because of our very natures, would wish to participate, will know our direction. If we think of all of Africa or of Africa in its total, because that is what we are here for, then we think of negritude, of culture, of ancestry. The conflict in achieving oneness is small beside the reward.

As Benedetto Croce has said, "The task of art today is to reestablish life among the fragmentary, specialization characteristics of industrial and technological society."

The gauntlet is therefore thrown to us. Shall we pick it up and show, through a continuous and close interrelationship between our cultural arts and our search for new techniques, that we shall provide the answer to the perfect form of development? Or shall we continue to take our cultural heritage, our arts for granted, and continue as have other nations on the same road to unbalanced development? It is now up to us.

I hasten to add, however, that the evidence is there, that we have indeed begun to consider the importance of our cultural heritage in development. From every indication seen in African dance which has been exported to the rest of the world, since the first World Festival of Negro Arts in Dakar, one can note a growing awareness. There have been great changes in style and technique of presentation which have not altered the cultural force but rather enhanced the theatrical impact.

One can conclude therefore, that the potential solution, now existent in Africa, through the humanization of industrial development, by means of the cultural arts, can and will be achieved by Africa, for the betterment of all mankind.

PART V

Preserving the Legacy

Performing Arts Training Center as a Focal Point for a New and Unique College or School

KATHERINE DUNHAM

PERFORMING AND RELATED ARTS

It may be said that art is as old as man. The research of anthropologists has proven that historically, prehistorically, man played music, danced, designed, painted, and produced sculptures, however crude. Philosophers, since man has been literate, define and redefine art and examine its relationship to the individual and society. Man is a social being, and the arts, verbal and nonverbal, provoke sensations of sound, color, meter, or movement, and these provoke social feelings. In the fragmentary, specialized, industrial, and technological societies of today, art becomes more important than ever to answer man's need to participate, to experience total involvement, to restore psychic balance, to compensate for the spiritual inadequacies of the present. In one way or another, the philosophers of the human experience all agree that art brings the generative idea, the revelation, the vision awaited by man to set him free and at the same time provide a mechanism for that most important of all drives, creative participation.

In our capsule of arts training here in East Saint Louis, we have seen art serve as one of the methods of arousing awareness, of stimulating life to be thinking, observant, comparative, not automatic; of surpassing alienation, and of serving as a rational alternative to violence and genocide.

SOURCE: Katherine Dunham, "Performing Arts Training Center as a Focal Point for a New and Unique College or School," unpublished paper, dated 1970, in the Katherine Mary Dunham Papers, Special Collections, Morris Library, Southern Illinois University, Carbondale. Copyright 1970 by Katherine Dunham. Reprinted by permission.

An anomaly is taking place in the national spectrum of the arts that could create confusion unless one takes into consideration the drastic change in attitudes toward the arts during these last years of our present century. . . . The National Committee for Cultural Resources[1] points out the following:

1. Strong and rising interest in the arts in all communities
    (a) larger audiences
    (b) more community activities and programs
    (c) increased financial support from individuals and corporations
    (d) wide geographic spread of the arts
    (e) comparison of gross national product of the arts with other industries
    (f) percentage of college arts center costs paid for by tuition
    (g) demonstrate improved quality of life because of the arts
2. Substantiating research on the impact of the arts
    (a) geographic spread of the arts
    (b) economic contribution of the arts as evidenced by real estate tax employees, tourism, auxiliary revenues generated, etc.
    (c) verification of multiplier
    (d) comparison of the contribution to the gross national product by the arts and other industries
    (e) educational contribution of the arts
    (f) social contribution of the arts
    (g) rehabilitation, and social service value of the arts, e.g. day care, senior citizen, prisoner and addict rehabilitation
    (h) improved quality of life due to the arts
3. Political strength of the arts
    [As the impact of the arts is a field to be researched for exact statistics, but which even now indicates, by voting in the Senate and the House, the interest and consideration already given the arts.]
    (a) evidence of rising political strength in fifty states and the federal government
    (b) case histories of six most rapidly developing state aid programs
    (c) examples of votes by body (Senate and House), party (Republican and Democrat), political leaning (liberal and conservative), locality (rural and urban)

On the other hand, along with increased audience and participation in the arts, there is what the Committee for Cultural Resources terms a "national crisis in the arts," all phases of which have been researched and have available documentation: (a) demonstration of cost inflation, (b) increasing need for non-local aid from state arts councils and the National Endowment for the Arts, (c) increased need resulting from increased services to the communities, (d) failure of city and local aid to keep up with inflation, and (e) reduction of programs and art activity. In view of the above findings, answers must be found. Private sectors can no longer be counted on in quantities to meet the need: (a) ticket prices are now maximized, (b) ticket prices and admissions cover only one half of the gross costs for performing arts, one third for visual arts, and one fourth for community arts, (c) increased financial support. from individuals, corporations, and local sectors unable to keep up with double-digit inflation, (d) foundation support being reduced by declining value of assets.

The answer, then, seems to be that, until massive government aid is established, we must turn to institutions of learning, whether state or privately supported.

The Performing Arts Training Center (PATC) of Southern Illinois University, East Saint Louis, Illinois, is a multidisciplinary approach to arts training. It is based on the administrator's belief that the artist must be educated as a person, a living, developing humanist, aware, as all artists are, of the happenings of the times, but aware with the equipment that will serve him in his technique and as an instrument for social balance and, if necessary, and this is a constant in all societies, of social change. For this reason all schools which have carried my name, and all schools in many countries of the world—Italy, Sweden, Germany, France, South America, Australia—which teach the method and philosophy that have made this particular formula an international success follow the format of performing arts, applied skills, and humanities. The Performing Arts Training Center follows this format, and to the thinking of its administrators and directors, successfully. Our evaluations are pragmatic and at times personal, but nevertheless worthwhile.

In view of the crisis in the arts so well presented by the Committee for Cultural Resources, where then should arts turn for a maximum of understanding, development, and funding? I repeat, to the institutions of higher learning. From a recent résumé of the Performing Arts Training Center I quote:

MISSION AND SCOPE OF PATC. The Performing Arts Training Center is a unique effort to motivate and stimulate the unchallenged young people of the East Saint Louis area through the arts. This effort has proven to be an innovative approach to integral, interdisciplinary education and cultural awakening. To achieve these objectives, the approach of the Performing Arts Training Center is multifaceted:

1. THE PERFORMING ARTS TRAINING PROGRAM of both credit and noncredit classes in the fields of performing arts, applied skills, and humanities.
2. THE PERFORMING COMPANY, a semi-professional group, composed of staff and students embodying the achievement of the training in dance particularly.
3. THE KUTANA PLAYERS, originally with Southern Illinois University at Carbondale, forming the nucleus of a developing dramatic capacity within the overall training program.
4. THE DYNAMIC MUSEUM, reversing the priorities of ordinary museums, placing educational use before matters of acquisition or preservation of treasures; this is an objective which, for lack of funds and expertise, has not yet been fully achieved.
5. COMMUNITY SERVICES PROGRAM, involving both students and staff of the center in a variety of services to the community.

The mission of PATC lies, then, in three primary areas: academic, community services, and performing companies. Through a continuously developing program, we aim to train 100 academic students per academic year and to orient toward community teaching at least 350 of the 800–1,000 participants who matriculate per quarter in the community services program. We further aim to encourage, where possible, community students to undertake academic pursuits. The performing companies comprise students being trained in academic and community classes.

As PATC endeavors to fulfill its educational mission, major emphasis will be placed upon the further development of upper undergraduate and graduate curricula. However, in meeting the needs of contemporary society, not only must the center strive toward a high-quality academic program which is more widely and easily available, but it must also be prepared to continue to service the entire community to its fullest capacity.

PATC aims to seed the locality with residents of the area who, having benefited from the program themselves, will then become participants in the educational process for their locality, as student-instructors in community service projects. Through such programs, the center hopes to exert an influence for growth and adaptation upon the leaders and educators of the area.

OBJECTIVE. The overall objective is to employ a creative and flexible educational methodology in pursuit of the fullest possible humanization and socialization of the individual and the community, through a program which emphasizes the performing and cultural arts as its principal implement.

METHOD. Adaptation is the key method in all efforts of the Performing Arts Training Center. It is made to utilize most effectively the special talents and competencies of the staff. With regard to the academic program, the course schedule is so arranged as to embrace the concept of integral education. A wide range of subjects is offered, from the simplest physical education course, through the arts and crafts, the martial and performing arts, to the more academic subjects of dance anthropology, philosophy, history, and literature, The aim here is to provide a context in which the growing student may taste the range of educational possibilities, stimulating his curiosity and in some cases preparing him to move on into more conventional institutions of higher learning, while at the same time tapping the specialized competencies of the staff. Every effort is made to stimulate the student with challenges he is ready to carry; to avoid crushing him with burdens he is not ready to bear. Such a program calls for great sensitivity, dedication, and competence on the part of the staff member.

ROLE OF THE UNIVERSITY IN COMMUNITY SERVICES. It is the opinion of the PATC administrators that in order to confront the myriad problems of modern society, it is indeed timely for institutions to adopt nontraditional approaches for stimulating and rechanneling the energies and leisure time of mankind into socially and individually productive patterns. The concept of a university as a focal point of an endogenous elite has proven inoperable for the simple reason that the greatest part of the population of this country does not, for one reason or another, enjoy this privilege. It is therefore up to an institution of learning to facilitate the egress of its learning and learned body into those areas of the population where the elements from the university and the elements of the people will operate in a situation of exchange. Thus, any research the university may foster in a community should only be for the purpose of problem solving or providing some way for the community to benefit from this research. The same should be true of teaching in the community or exposing the community to advanced knowledge. The substructure of the university depends upon its relationship with a wider body, and this wider body is the community outlying the university. In this way, recruitment is less a goal, and matriculation follows a normal pattern of choice. There is no longer the barrier of suspicion or reticence between the community and the university. The university automatically becomes a field of action when extended into the community and recognizing that this contact facilitates a capacity to progress and to contribute, the community of its own accord then becomes a part of the quintessential structure of the university.

CONCLUSION

The Performing Arts Training Center of Southern Illinois University in East Saint Louis has all of the elements to justify its transition into a school or college. The resistance to do so to date stems, in our belief, from stultified, conservative-traditional attitudes toward higher education, especially as related to malnutritioned communities. The ivory towers of the *apartheid* colleges and universities, restricting staff and matriculates to the edicts of guidelines and textbooks are beginning to crumble. In their place have arisen new horizons of thinking, of universities without walls, of new and innovative methods and programs to fill the needs of those students who are now aware of the wonder of living and developing and serving.

Our proposition is that PATC follow the requirements of the first two college years, taking into consideration general studies. The performing arts would be both required and offered as electives. The two upper-level years would begin a concentration on one or more of the performing arts, depending on choice and aptitude, but always with counseling by a knowledgeable staff member. By the time of graduation the student should have been exposed to the principal opportunities offered in his chosen field—teaching, a professional or business career, or research. The certificate of graduation would be from PATC, rather than from the traditional institution, clearly noting the field of concentration, the major and minor.

NOTES

1. Operating from the Lincoln Center for Performing Arts, New York, New York.

Cultural Fusion and
Spiritual Unity

EUGENE REDMOND

Armed with the aggregate experiences of more than three decades of living, dancing, and studying in fifty-seven countries, Katherine Dunham returned home in the 1960s to meet one of the biggest challenges of her career. The initial step in this challenge was an invitation from Southern Illinois University (SIU) at Carbondale to spend eleven weeks there as artist in residence (and to do the choreography for and staging of the opera *Faust*). The invitation, coming in 1964, was a high priority item for Miss Dunham, who has substantial roots in Illinois—beginning with her birth in Chicago and her childhood in Glen Ellyn and continuing up through her study of anthropology and dance at the University of Chicago. As a returning member of what we sometimes call the "expatriate" group of Afro-American artists and intellectuals, she was seriously rethinking ways of employing the arts in the service of struggle and community education at home. She was no stranger to the historical causes behind this new thrust, since for most of her life she had been in the breach of social agitation and change. But the political and cultural climates of the contemporary period had forced her to reopen questions about the arts as rituals of therapy and human development.

After the successful run of *Faust*, Miss Dunham relocated to the northern campus of SIU in East Saint Louis; there she found an excellent laboratory and limitless raw resources to implement her ideas and formulas for community educational theater. First as a visiting artist in the Fine Arts Division, then as cultural affairs consultant to the Edwardsville campus,

SOURCE: Eugene Redmond, "Cultural Fusion and Spiritual Unity: Katherine Dunham's Approach to Developing Educational Community Theater," unpublished paper dated 11 June 1976. Copyright 1976 by Eugene Redmond. Used by permission.

and finally as director of the Performing Arts Training Center (PATC) and the Dynamic Museum in East Saint Louis, Miss Dunham and her staff worked tirelessly to establish contact with funding agencies, related academic departments and administrators of SIU, and the black communities of the area.

SIU's Experiment in Higher Education (EHE), jointly funded by the state of Illinois and the Office of Economic Opportunity in the federal Department of Health, Education, and Welfare (OEO-HEW) and emerging at the same time as PATC, played a very important role in Miss Dunham's larger plan. Both EHE and PATC were structured around an aim of recruiting inner-city youngsters who were either turned off by or would not have been accepted into traditional higher education programs. EHE and PATC faculties redesigned curricula, developed and wrote new texts, participated in team-teaching projects, and created strong instructor-counselor relationships with students. The superb teaching faculty of EHE has included such giants as Oliver Jackson (painter and philosopher), Joyce Ladner (sociologist), Donald Henderson (theoretician), and Henry Dumas (writer). Miss Dunham, who taught in both EHE and PATC, also assembled a brilliant group of teachers and consultants, many of them former students or members of her troupe: Christian de Rougement (who now supervises a Dunham School in Paris), Ural Wilson, Jeanelle Stovall, Mor Thiam of Senegal, René Calvin of Haiti, Lenwood Morris, Mademoiselle Susanne Diop of the Senegalese Supreme Court, Glen Standifer, Oscar Brown Jr., Tommy Gomez, Charles White, Julius Hemphill, Clifford Fears, Archie Savage, and Camille Yarbrough. Some of the PATC faculty were available on a short in-residence basis (Mlle Diop, Brown, White), while others were permanent.

Additionally PATC has produced outstanding actors, dancers, percussionists, and a traveling company from among the native youngsters of East Saint Louis. A former student, Jackie Thompson, has just opened the Thompson School of Dunham Technique and Allied Art in Springfield, Illinois. A sampling of other outstanding young talent developed by PATC includes Darryl Braddix (dancer), Ronald Tibbs (actor with the American Conservatory Theater in San Francisco), Marsha Robinson (dancer, MFA candidate at the University of California, San Diego), Anne Walker (dancer, singer, and cultural programs director for the city of East Saint Louis), Arthur Moore (brilliant percussionist), Pam Kay (dancer), Warrington Hudlin (Yale University alumnus, martial arts expert, and writer), Sherman Fowler (poet and cinematographer), John Brooks (actor and television commentator), and Cathy Allen (director of Spirits of the Dance Troupe). This inexhaustive list points up two things: (1) at the vital human level of beans-and-bread PATC offers serious black youngsters several exciting and marketable alternatives to traditional and obsolete educational programs; and (2) the word *dance* is too narrow to capture or suggest what Katherine Dunham has on her mind.

In comprehending Miss Dunham, then, one has to think not just of dance, not just of drums, not just of primitive rhythms, but of a totem-woman of African spirituality and cultural wealth. Taken as an author (of poetry, fiction, fantasy, and articles), seen as the choreographer of several movies and ballets, appreciated as a re-shaper of a neo-African ethos through rigorous use of anthropology and folk materials, viewed as a philosopher and mystic and seer, loved as the mothering influence on Afro-American dance and the arts—examined in all these spheres, the Dunham World must then be given the breadth of space and place that we accord a W. E. B. Du Bois or a Paul Robeson. So when she took up residence at 532 North Tenth Street in East Saint Louis, amidst crumbling buildings, night-piercing sirens, and on the turf of the Imperial War Lords (a youth gang), she brought at least the above listing. But more, she brought the Dynamic Museum—her own artifacts, memorabilia, and the human remnants of her various companies—which showcased her decades of work and travel primarily to show the dignity of "dark-skinned people."

Much giving was required of Miss Dunham and East Saint Louisians before PATC could become more than an idea. Acceptance of the concept was predicated on the willingness of local politicians, church groups, educators, and especially youth. Convincing inflexible school administrators and teachers that the performing arts were sound educational investments was only one of the countless hurdles and obstacles that confronted Miss Dunham. However, by the time the teaching-performing faculty and students had been acclaimed in Kansas City, Atlanta, Bridgeport, Chicago, Detroit, Washington, D.C., Los Angeles, and Saint Louis, PATC had become a permanent resident in its adopted home. It is now an East Saint Louis institution that reverberates throughout black communities in the Midwest. Its presence also brought renewed attention to native daughters and sons—artists like Miles Davis, Oliver Nelson, Leon Thomas, Julius Hemphill (and the Saint Louis–based Black Artists Group), Eugene Redmond, Grace Bumbry, Bobby McClure, Ike and Tina Turner, and Barbara Ann Teer, many of whom, though known, had not before been celebrated as "products" of the area.

Correlative to identifying and giving recognition to local artists is the maintenance of a shrine of local heroes, martyrs to the struggle, and folk characters. Nowhere is this concept actualized more profoundly than in *Ode to Taylor Jones,* a Dunham-produced ballet-tribute to Taylor Jones III, an East Saint Louis black activist killed in an automobile accident in 1967. *Ode,* partially written by Eugene Redmond, who shared the lead role in the production, had successful tours of the midwestern, southern, and eastern United States during 1968–1970. The strength and success of *Ode to Taylor Jones,* with its rich use of archival theatrical materials from black and other cultures, rested in concepts and ideas Miss Dunham had been nurturing and refining for more than forty years. In 1966 at the first World Festival of Negro Arts, she gave a talk on "The Performing Arts of Africa." One key to understanding the Dunham concept of cultural homogeneity, as it is presented in the *Ode,* is found in this poignant passage:

> After many efforts to arrive at some conclusive decisions when thinking of dance, I have decided upon this, that dance is not a technique but a social act and that dance should return to where it first came from, which is the heart and soul of man, and man's social living. I create movements in form in response to what I feel or know. This feeling knowingness and responsiveness are evident without my knowing it.[1]

She noted that "dance is rhythmic motion of a conscious organism for the purpose of releasing one's needs."[2] Reference was also made to "non-man directed or cosmic choreography."[3] Deeply interested for many years in psychology, religion, the subliminal and mythical implications of ritual, and racial intellect/intuition as it emerges from and returns to its verbal and gestural archives, Miss Dunham continued to translate this complex and complicated network of mysteries and powers into meaningful components of a community-based theater. The *Ode to Taylor Jones* represented yet another successful employment of her synthesis. And a glance at any program or outline for a presentation will show how her use of indigenous structures and messages become integral to her larger philosophy of the residential arts.

Body-sermons, drum-lectures, song-sagas, gesture-thoughts, and love-prayers are all vibrant elements in the Dunham cosmos. The ontology of a people, she believes, is seen in what they do and especially the way they dance—in the expanded sense of that word. Moreover, that ontology can be enhanced by selectively borrowing from other cultures. Thus the *Ode to Taylor Jones*, ostensibly neo-African in structure and attitude, used a Scottish precision march to suggest an honor guard for the fallen young warrior. Characters move along rungs of a ladder to achieve various dramatic effects while some of the background music is also transplanted. Underlying and interweaving all this tension are African-Carribean–Afro-American folk and street forms which illustrate both the urgency and the authenticity of the tribute.

On 15 October 1969, PATC participated in a Black Arts Festival at Rockhurst College in Kansas City, Missouri. Some indication of the devastating breadth and energy of the Dunham concept can be seen in the program: *Brazilian Quadrilles, Choros #1 and #4;* African songs and drums; African dance number, *Chaka*; poetry by Eugene Redmond of Southern Illinois University; *Libertad,* original choreography by Katherine Dunham; *The Lesson,* with explanatory recitation by Eugene Redmond; finale, *Ode to Taylor Jones* by Theater Company. On another occasion a Dunham production of *Dream Deferred* was presented with Haitian folk dances and drumming. In yet another community setting a new work, *Psychedelia,* which examined some of Miss Dunham's ideas about the counter-culture, was staged along with guest appearances by Oscar Brown Jr. and Jean Pace. A 1970 program featured an African suite of songs and drums (*Fati-Fati-Goloman*), a South American suite (*Carnival; Damballa; Papa Loi, Mama Loi; Los Indios*), *Drums of Casamance* (including the Senegalese drummer Mor Thiam), *Bolero, A Moorish Dance from Afrique du Nord*), African Jazz Orchestra (featuring African and Afro-American artists), Poems of Militancy, Afro-Jazz (Hemphill and Thiam), and *Cakewalk* (including the strut, cakewalk couples, and a baton twirler).

In practically every production there is conscious, built-in, attention to all the needs and dreams of black people. But the Dunham approach to complete theater never understates Afro-Americans. For while the East Saint Louis project has required much shifting and re-ordering she nevertheless refuses to compromise those principles and expectations on which she has built several life times of important work. Indeed even Miss Dunham's presence in East Saint Louis may seem somewhat anachronous when one looks over her past experiences and travels and when one knows that she has homes in Haiti (where she became a Vodun initiate) and in Dakar, Senegal (where she has served as "technical cultural advisor to both the president and the minister of cultural affairs"). But being a different kind of black scholar-artist, Miss Dunham, a complex and formidable woman, had little difficulty seeing the ties between the dancing children of Port-au-Prince, Dakar, or East Saint Louis. As a scholar-artist of processes that are practically applied (without a resultant loss of cosmic and spiritual strength), she implements ideas from the book of the world.

I have said elsewhere that six months of daily contact with "Miss D" is at least worth a B.A. from Fisk, Oxford, or U.C., Berkeley. Anecdotes alone could fill the space taken by this article. But one will suffice. One evening several community organizers and consultants to Miss Dunham were summoned by her and told that we would be flying to New York City to discuss contemporary issues with Erich Fromm. Some of the people thought it was a joke. But a few hours later we were engaged in tireless exchange (for several days) with an important thinker who challenged us with alternative ways of viewing our missions and ourselves. So, in addition to our cherished audiences with "Miss D" we never knew whom or what we might meet or see! This area alone deserves a book!

Under Miss Dunham's Godwomaning aegis, a cultural-educational institution of inestimable importance has been developed in East Saint Louis. Just as she suggested in 1966 that dance be allowed to return to its original purpose, so she returned to her own sources and purposes. This allowed her to reach the peak of syncretization toward which she had been evolving; but she also exemplified a solid prototype for the black scholar-artist-activist. For nearly half a century she has worked at reconstructing the links and bones of black life. Carefully retracing the paths of her forebears she has been able to develop new weapons for fighting the hydra-headed monster known as racism, alias prejudice, alias oppression. At the same time she has not compromised her creative spirit with transient causes, sociological imperatives, or petty emotional blindnesses.

To think or write about Katherine Dunham is no easy task. And one would hope at least to suggest the spontaneous brilliance and professional dexterity of her life and work. Even so there can be no "conclusion" of a discussion of "Miss D." Right now these lines are splitting and seeking entrance into my thoughts of Miss Dunham:

> *18 hands*, holding blood-blessed branches,
> Make hollow drums deep and long,
> Like the unwritten diaries of Katherine Dunham
> Whose sacred legs still straddle continents.[4]

Notes

1. Katherine Dunham, "The Performing Arts of Africa," in proceedings, *Premier festival mondial des arts nègres: Colloque / First World Festival of Negro Arts: Colloquium* (Dakar: Éditions Présence Africaine, 1968), 478–79.

2. Ibid., 479.

3. Ibid.

4. From "The 18 Hands of Jerome Harris" by Eugene Redmond. Copyright 1967 by Eugene Redmond.

Institute for
Intercultural Communication

JEANELLE STOVALL

As pressures of daily living and survival itself increase, individuals and nations have come to realize that the fabric of mankind consists of a network of channels of communication which permits men to know themselves and to appreciate others. Such channels, utilizing the arts and humanities as media, have been constant subjects for research and planning in the career of Katherine Dunham, both as artist and as social scientist. Her appearances in more than fifty-seven countries of the world, with a full company of performing artists, have reinforced her conviction that the arts and humanities help immeasurably in the process of removing barriers between diverse cultures, and in neutralizing alienation of the individual from his own society. Over the past ten years, spent in the urban community of East Saint Louis, the universality of this belief has become increasingly clear; longstanding urban problems cry out for solutions; the public policies intended to solve them are often alien and inappropriate to the lifestyles and subcultural values of city residents.

Based upon these realizations and convictions, therefore, Miss Dunham has established an institute, the Institute for Intercultural Communication, in order to create, document, research, and present means of facilitating and extending communication among peoples of diverse cultures and of varying degrees of social and economic condition, through the media of the arts, the social sciences, and the humanities.

SOURCE: Jeanelle Stovall, "Institute for Intercultural Communication," unpublished paper, undated, in the Katherine Mary Dunham Papers, Special Collections, Morris Library, Southern Illinois University, Carbondale. Copyright by Jeanelle Stovall. Used by permission.

Goals

The program of the institute is directed toward humanization and social-ization of the individual and of the community as a whole. On the one hand, it aspires to combine artistic potentials of the individual, the local community, and the framework of world culture as a whole to achieve its goals; on the other, it seeks more effective means for understanding and the development of more productive governance, via seminars, policy papers stemming from the cultural heritage of world representation, and a program of policy forums.

The Institute for Intercultural Communication will pursue an intensive research program, seeking new ways to lower the walls of alienation and suspicion between individuals, groups, and cultures of every kind and in every place. Its principal goals are humanization and socialization.

- Humanization is a condition in which man is concerned about his fellow men; to the end that man may find alternatives to frustration, hatred, and violence, which are indeed the major social illnesses of today.
- Socialization, in its full dimension, connotes the process of helping men to liberate themselves from every form of alienation with respect to themselves and others; it is concerned with promoting recognition of true individual worth and discrimination of values, encouraging a sense of pride in personal talents, resources, potentialities, and achieve-ments. It further connotes the end achievement of fullest participa-tion in the social life which is its goal. Inherent in this is a sense of respect for the talents, interests, and culture of other men, toward the end of facilitating universal personal fulfillment which is simultane-ously a service to, and an enrichment of, ones own culture.

Objectives

The overall objective of the institute is that of guiding and encouraging people toward a fuller awareness of themselves and their potential cultural contributions to society, while enabling them to develop a greater under-standing of the cultural dynamics of others. Specific objectives are the following:

- To carry forward the work begun by Katherine Dunham in the cul-tural and performing arts and the humanities.

- To develop stronger communications links between cultural and subcultural groups within the nation and the world at large.
- To offer education and training directed toward solving problems arising from cultural deprivation, especially acute in urban communities.
- To establish an effective medium for the exchange of ideas.
- To establish a dynamic museum exhibiting major works of the arts and crafts, representing the diversities and commonalities of geographically separated societies.
- To integrate cultural considerations with urban governance and public policy.

METHOD

The Institute for Intercultural Communication proposes to carry out research of various cultures of the world, bringing members of these cultures or subcultures into contact to the extent possible with academic and community groups of the area. It will sponsor workshops, public policy forums, and seminars, with the assistance of scholars from various disciplines from this and other parts of the world. These scholars will undertake to clarify the political, economic, social, historical, and cultural conditions of this or another country, to demonstrate how one person's insights can shape public policy. Through travels and national and international meetings, institute members would encourage and foster greater interest in the study of urban problems, among other problems, from a cultural perspective.

- With the establishment of the Dynamic Museum, the Institute for Intercultural Communications would provide a tangible resource for influencing individuals able to appreciate outstanding contributions from various countries of the world.
- The Institute for Intercultural Communication will develop research and documentation of communications media, cross-cultural and intercultural, and it will disseminate data locally and to other areas of the country and the world. Through a combination of the arts, humanities, and other disciplines, relationships will be established between the heretofore alienated; attempts will be made to render more comprehensible and effective the media of communication, and to engender a feeling of awareness, security, and understanding among those whose experiences have been limited to economically and socially depressed communities, usually as members of an antisocial subculture.

• The Institute for Intercultural Communication will work closely with other educational institutions in the conduct of workshops, public forums, and seminars for other communities and countries; it will engage fellows and consultants, to the extent possible, for the development of new methods of communication. These new methods, as well as other items of importance, will be communicated by an ongoing publication program of the institute. Further, it will provide scholarships or stipends when and where possible, to encourage individuals to pursue studies in cultural aspects of arts training and governance.

THE KATHERINE DUNHAM ARCHIVES AND DYNAMIC MUSEUM

To those cognizant of the extensive and diverse dimensions of Katherine Dunham's life, as theatrical performer, writer, dance anthropologist, humanitarian, and educator, there is great concern regarding the accumulated wealth of material produced by and about her, not yet adequately collected, organized, and utilized. The documentation, exploitation, and exhibition of these works constitute an essential objective of the institute's program. Film, slides, audio and visual tapes, plus intensified work on the archival collection of Miss Dunham and her professional company would therefore round out the work of the institute.

GOVERNANCE

The Institute for Intercultural Communication will be housed in East Saint Louis, Illinois. It will be governed by an international board of directors with Katherine Dunham serving as the president and chief executive officer. The participating staff will be composed of a community of scholars and professionals from the arts, the humanities, and the social sciences.

Katherine Dunham Museum

JEANELLE STOVALL

A Dunham Museum exhibit was first developed in October of 1967 in Alton, Illinois. This development was the direct result of Miss Dunham's decision to come to Southern Illinois University as an artist in residence. Miss Dunham moved to the university's East Saint Louis center to attempt to create a living museum as well as a performing arts training center. An important part of Miss Dunham's life has been her interest in folk art, the objects and actions that are a creative extension of man's effort to express and preserve the nature of the society and time in which man lives. The Dunham Museum exhibit focused on the folk art from a number of countries from across the world. Included in the collection was a significant assortment of West African wood carvings and Caribbean artifacts.

Since the first displays in Alton, considerable changes have taken place in the circumstances surrounding the collection. In the first place, the collection has been expanded and in its new setting in East Saint Louis, the displays promise to approach even more fully the ideal exhibit setting. Any museum attempts to fulfill three functions in relation to its objects: acquisition, preservation, and education. As previously mentioned, the collection has been expanded and at the same time the quality of pieces in the collection has been maintained. The curators hope that the museum will become a focal point of educational experiences for its visitors. The Dunham Museum collection consists of furniture, paintings, musical instruments, costumes, decorations, photographs, sketches, a broad range of

SOURCE: Jeanelle Stovall, "Katherine Dunham Museum," unpublished paper, dated 1977, in the Katherine Mary Dunham Papers, Special Collections, Morris Library, Southern Illinois University, Carbondale. Copyright 1977 by Jeanelle Stovall. Used by permission.

ethnic art objects, and a cross-section of personal belongings documenting the life of the museum founder, Katherine Dunham. Objects will be available at all times for wearing, touching, making sound with, and generally exploring. These types of living displays will enable museum patrons to place themselves in the cultural atmosphere created by the actual displays.

Also included at the Dunham Museum will be an extensive collection of books that will constitute a resource library for scholars and interested laymen. The library will concentrate in four areas: African culture, the American black, dance, and the general humanities.

LOCATION

An East Saint Louis location for the Dunham Museum was selected because the people in this area have long been denied a visual experience as forceful, vigorous, and available as this facility is. The museum will be a source of pride to the community because of the nature of its contents, the superior quality of the objects, displays, and programs that will be available and the easy accessibility the facility will offer area residents. The museum's displays have been in one location or another in East Saint Louis since 1969. After many years of involuntary moving about the community, the Dunham Museum is now located in the former YWCA building on Pennsylvania Avenue at Tenth Street. With the help of the East Saint Louis Chamber of Commerce and a number of civic-minded corporations, the Dunham Museum has raised sufficient funds to purchase and renovate this building.

KATHERINE DUNHAM BACKGROUND

Katherine Dunham has been the driving force behind the creation of this living museum of the Third World and primitive cultures. As a student of anthropology and of dance, Miss Dunham lived among the "lost" tribes of West Africa in the Caribbean islands. Early in her dual career, she learned the cultural rhythms and dances of the Maroon tribe of Jamaica, which had never been known by "civilized societies." Upon her return to the United States, her dances began to exhibit the passionate movement she had seen while watching the Maroon tribe portray the ceremonies attached with growing up, selecting a mate, and proving one's courage. The honesty, passion, humor and courage she had witnessed years earlier became incorporated in her dance performances. Her work became expressive interpretations of highly developed cultural and primitive structures. Miss Dunham's dancing has been refined and improved over the many years she spent traversing the world. During these travels she brought back art objects of all types. In the Dunham Museum visitors will be walking through exhibits of elegantly sculptured masterpieces, totems, bronzed figures, colorful tribal dresses, and an assortment of tribal drums. As an Illinois native, originally from Chicago, Miss Dunham is excited by the opportunity to bring folk art to people in her native state.

MAJOR POINTS ABOUT THE DUNHAM MUSEUM

The principal goals of the Katherine Dunham Museum are the following:

- To serve as a living museum for the people of the bi-state area (Illinois and Missouri).
- To operate a resource center, both in display and research materials, for the local community.
- To promote community unity in East Saint Louis and improve the cultural atmosphere of the area.
- To maintain a place where people can assemble to learn about and discuss folk art from various countries of the world.
- To promote sufficient interest among members of the community to support this type of undertaking financially and at the same time raise funding for later expansion and growth.
- To aid in the improvement and rehabilitation of the East Saint Louis area by making a commitment to local neighborhoods and businesses that the Dunham Museum will stay in the area and do what it is able to help others settle and develop East Saint Louis.
- To serve as a collection point for those interested in donating or exhibiting other artifacts in the area.
- To save those relics and materials that are priceless to the many, many people interested in their background and history as well as those concerned with the overall development of man.

The museum needs whatever human resources are available, be it donated time, help in organizing events and activities or some other event that will prove to be beneficial to the steady growth of the museum.

The museum needs interested members who believe in the concept of the museum and in its continued existence.

The museum needs the financial support of those interested in redeveloping the East Saint Louis area as well as in providing a meaningful facility for the development of cultural and artistic activities.

The museum will be a successful and lasting endeavor with tremendous community support that looks to expand that support as much as possible.

Honoring Katherine Dunham, 26 May 1976

St. Clair Drake

This is the year of America's bicentennial celebration, of the Declaration of Independence of the United States. Twenty-eight years from now, in the year 2004, another New World nation will celebrate its bicentennial, a black nation, the sovereign state of Haiti.

The Haitian slaves rose in rebellion in 1791, freed themselves, and then fought a thirteen-year war for independence that resulted in the emergence of the second independent state in the Western Hemisphere. The name of Toussaint Louverture became a household word among Afro-Americans as the founder of a black nation, a brave warrior, and an astute statesman. Haiti remained the only black nation, other than Ethiopia, until Liberia declared its sovereignty in 1847, and these three remained the only black sovereign states until the 1950s. From the beginning of her professional career, our distinguished honoree has functioned as a good-will ambassador from the Afro-Americans of the United States to Haiti. As an interpreter of Haitian culture to us she has no peer—and to all the world, I might add. Her role was recognized when she was made a *grand officier* of the Haitian Legion of Honor and Merit.

During the 172 years of Haiti's existence, that country had to fight continuously for its survival as an independent nation. In 1914 the United States Marines landed in Haiti and stayed there for over twenty years. In organizing their resistance to invasion and domination, two important

SOURCE: St. Clair Drake, address given at the opening reception of the Kaiso exhibit, Women's Center, University of California, Berkeley, 26 May 1976, in *Kaiso! Katherine Dunham: An Anthology of Writings,* edited by VèVè A. Clark and Margaret B. Wilkerson (Berkeley: Institute for the Study of Social Change, 1978), xi–xv. Copyright 1978 by the University of California, Berkeley. Reprinted by permission.

things happened. Among the illiterate but proud peasant masses, the guerilla fighting forces took up arms. Within the ranks of the intellectuals, a few individuals began to give voice to the aspirations of the ordinary people by making known to the world the folklore, the music, the dance, and the religious concepts of the poverty-stricken but resilient and courageous ordinary people. Their poetry, novels, and essays had a quality similar to that of black intellectuals in other parts of the world who were fighting against racism and for human dignity. What the Haitian men of letters were doing fused with the literary work of West Indian and African intellectuals who were developing the concept of *négritude,* and with the work of the Afro-Americans who were creating the Harlem Renaissance. I begin with these remarks about pan-African history because I want to recount an incident involving Katherine Dunham that I had the privilege of observing.

One of the leaders of the *négritude* movement had been a poet from Senegal, Léopold Senghor. He was associated with a group of Africans and West Indians in Paris who established the Society for African Culture (SAC) after World War II, an organization that began to publish the magazine *Présence africaine.* A number of Americans then proceeded to organize the American Society for African Culture (AMSAC), affiliated with the Paris-based SAC. After Senghor had become president of the Republic of Senegal, SAC accepted his invitation to hold the first World Festival of Negro Arts in that country in 1966. AMSAC sent a large contingent, and I went as an official American representative to the festival colloquium, along with the poet Langston Hughes and several artists. When SAC was organized, it was decided to give the office of the president to Haiti's outstanding scholar, Dr. Jean Price-Mars, who had been the spiritual leader of the Haitian literary movement during the American occupation. Now, in 1966, he was invited as the most honored guest at the first Festival of Negro Arts. When President Senghor held his official reception at the Executive Pavilion, an event of high symbolic significance took place. I saw Dr. Price-Mars, a man in his nineties, move forward to be greeted by Senghor leaning on the strong, younger arms of Katherine Dunham—the aged Haitian scholar, doyen, elder statesman, the father of the *négritude* movement, so to speak, being escorted by the Afro-American woman of distinction to meet the president of an African state who was also a leading poet of *négritude.* I watched entranced.

I was to see a lot of Katherine Dunham before I left Dakar. I watched her functioning in varied roles, but the episode involving Price-Mars is etched indelibly on my memory. What could have been more appropriate than to have Price-Mars presented by an Afro-American artist who had exhibited profound respect and understanding where Haiti was involved? When the conference was over, President Senghor asked Katherine Dunham to remain in Senegal for a year as cultural adviser to the government.

Before Katherine Dunham came to participate in the Dakar conference and festival, she had already given us two books upon which a solid literary reputation rested: an autobiography appropriately and felicitously named *A Touch of Innocence* and the book on her pilgrimage to the cockpit country of the Maroons of Jamaica, *Journey to Accompong*. I enjoyed the first as an intensely human document and the second as an important contribution to the field of humanistic anthropology as well as to what we now call Black Studies. We had known her as a short-story writer before these books appeared as well as for a highly professional piece in the prestigious journal *Acta antropológica* on "Las danzas de Haití."

Three years after the festival we all rushed to read *Island Possessed* and marveled at her ability to produce this profound book about Haiti while carrying on her professional career in the performing arts on a vast international stage. The production of this work indicated a discipline of her total personality that paralleled the kinesic discipline that made her such a superb dancer. But we should have expected that after reading *A Touch of Innocence*. The long-overdue biographies are beginning to appear that will render assessment by admirers and critics. We are very happy that she "got her licks in first" with an autobiography. We hope that before the very long life we predict for her ends she will also do her memoirs.

I want to mention four anecdotal items that reveal why my generation of anthropologists has made a legendary figure of Katherine Dunham. Let others appraise her as an artist and writer. I prefer to muse over some concrete episodes in her life that have significance for me and for some of my friends in anthropological circles.

I entered the anthropology department of the University of Chicago in 1937 to work on an advanced degree. There were very, very few black students at that university in those days. Somebody told me that a wonderful person was probably going to be in some of my classes sometimes, a young woman who had established a Negro School of the Dance in Chicago soon after the Depression began and who made a smash hit in 1931 by presenting *Negro Rhapsody* at the Chicago Beaux Arts Ball. I don't think our paths ever crossed in a class, but students in the anthropology department talked about Katherine Dunham continuously. The first thing that put her "ace-high" in our books was an article that she and a Japanese graduate student published on the predecessors of the Black Muslim group in one of the academic journals. We considered it a great tribute to our two fellow students that they were permitted to become participant-observers in this religious group, which divided all mankind into Europeans and Asiatics and whose members wore red fezzes, called themselves "beys," studied and mastered the Koran, and walked the streets of Chicago and Detroit with great pride and self-confidence. It was predicted that she would be a very eminent anthropologist someday.

The second episode that kept tongues wagging around the anthropology department was the matter of her Rosenwald grant. Most black graduate students in those days—and I was in that group myself—depended upon the Rosenwald Fund for financial aid at crucial moments. When the fund published a book called *Investment in People,*[1] the name of nearly every Afro-American scholar, artist, and writer was in it. Katherine Dunham applied for a grant to go to Haiti to study the dance there. We assumed she was gathering data for a Ph.D. dissertation. She handed in a thesis for her master's degree a couple of years after going to the Caribbean, a work entitled "The Dances of Haiti: A Study of Their Material Aspect, Organization, Form, and Function." It was certainly of Ph.D. quality, but she had done a very sensible thing. Instead of wasting her talent preparing for incredibly boring Ph.D. exams in physical anthropology, archaeology, and linguistics as well as in the fields more relevant to her interests—ethnology and social anthropology—she decided to do what she did best, and what she had always yearned to do. She formed a dance troupe, did the choreography herself, and went on to win accolades from the New York press for *Tropics* and *Le Jazz "Hot."* The reviewer for the *Herald Tribune* said "Katherine Dunham is laying the groundwork for a great Negro dance," and another critic observed that "not the least of Katherine Dunham's gifts is beauty." Meanwhile she was publishing magazine articles and acting in the movies. As we drudged away at the university, condemned by lack of artistic talent and beauty to become academics, we did not look at her with envy but with admiration, not only for her professional skill but also for being able to parlay a year of successful fieldwork in anthropology on a Rosenwald grant into the launching of a stage career. Later, she received a coveted Guggenheim award.

Our admiration, and perhaps even awe, was increased when we read early in 1941 that she was going to lecture to the Anthropology Club of Yale University graduate school on "the practical application of primitive materials to the theater, demonstrating her discourse with the aid of ten performers." One of "our own" had created a new field in anthropology, and Yale had recognized it. This was not the last time we were to exult a bit over things like this. We came to expect them of Katherine Dunham, like the time when she lectured before the Royal Anthropological Society of Great Britain. We insisted upon claiming her as a fellow anthropologist because that brought honor to us, and we are glad that she still plays an active part in organizations like the Inter-American Institute for Ethnomusicology and Folklore and that she is president of a Foundation for the Development and Preservation of Cultural Arts.

Finally, our rapport and identification with her was increased immeasurably when, upon one occasion, an attempt was made to Jim Crow her at a hotel in Rio de Janeiro. That incident became an international *cause célèbre*. We were indignant. The government of Brazil expressed its shame and claimed to have taken corrective action through anti-discrimination legislation. What happened to her there as a black woman of high achievement was a reminder to all of us that it could happen to us too, that racism was not yet dead even for those who seemed to "have it made." It forced us to rededicate ourselves to the fight for black liberation. *Our* Katherine Dunham had been mistreated and insulted. We were determined that race prejudice must be rooted out *everywhere*. Her present association with the Institute of the Black World is a measure of *her* commitment to struggle.

I wish to thank the organizers of this reception for according me the privilege of participating in this event to honor Katherine Dunham. I was always in Africa, the West Indies, or somewhere else where her dance troupe were not. I missed *Caribbean Rhapsody* during a decade of its performances all over the world, and I have missed *Bamboche!* in more recent years. And, of course, I was not at the Benibashi in Tokyo when she and her dancers performed there in 1957 or at the bull ring in Lima, Peru. I've had to remain content with watching her on television or at the movies instead of seeing her and the dancers in the flesh.

But I have followed her career with fascinated interest, reading every account of her triumphs that I have seen in the press, reading her books as they appeared for both edification and enjoyment, and admiring the harmonious blending of academic anthropological interest with expert skill in choreography and artistic performance. When she decided to share her skill and wisdom and insight by taking on the role of a university faculty member, I was happy to see her finally honor our profession by her choice. She has established schools of dance, theater, and cultural arts in

New York, Haiti, Paris, and in Italian cities. Now, she has chosen to give her talents to a performing arts training center in East Saint Louis, Illinois. The Afro-American community considers this a profound act of dedication and identification with the milieu from whence she came. But, for those of us who have known her, this comes as no surprise.

Notes

1. Edwin R. Embree and Julia Waxman, *Investment in People: The Story of the Julius Rosenwald Fund* (New York: Harper Bros., 1949).

Dunham 101

An Interview with Glory Van Scott

VÈVÈ A. CLARK

Glory Van Scott began to study at the Dunham School soon after she arrived in New York in the early 1950s. She made her Broadway debut as a featured performer in *House of Flowers* in 1954 and later appeared in many other musical shows and dance ensembles, including those of Talley Beatty and Walter Nicks. She joined the Dunham Company in 1959 and remained with it until its dissolution at the end of its third European tour in 1960. While pursuing her performing career, she earned a doctorate in philosophy of education and theater arts. She continues to be active as a theatrical producer and director in New York. The following is an abridgment of an interview conducted on 12 September 1999, in Saint Louis, Missouri.

VÈVÈ A. CLARK: [hereafter VC] A couple of things I want to ask you have to do with Dunham Technique. How would you describe what Dunham Technique does for the body if you were talking to someone who knows nothing about it?

GLORY VAN SCOTT: [hereafter GVS] Well, first off, I always say that Dunham Technique makes very strong bodies. Dunham's dancers are among the strongest of all dancers. There are a lot of things that Dunham dancers can do technically that other dancers cannot do. They don't have the stamina. You build that stamina dancing Dunham Technique. The men are very strong and virile and marvelous and developed beautifully. And I think that's part of it. I think it is a technique that is of the earth; when you do it, you put your foot on the earth and you lift it or whatever; if you're going toward the sky, you are taking the whole body. It's a very alive technique, very difficult, but a very natural and a very beautiful technique.

Often we would walk down the street, and you could tell one dancer from another just by the way they walked. "Oh, that's a Dunham dancer, that's a Graham dancer, that's a ballet dancer."

The Dunham dancers also have a flow about themselves. There's a— I think, in a sense—a mystique about them and the way they carry themselves. For example, if you were taking classes from Lenwood Morris, who's a ballet dancer, Dunham dancer, and a ballet master of the Dunham Company, if he's teaching someone and he sees there's a little rip in tights, he'll tell you "No, no, no. You sew that up. We don't look at skin through any tights. There are no holes here." Dunham dancers are always dressed a certain way. I'll know them anywhere. One of the oldest ones is Carmencita Romero, and she looks a certain way, and you say, "Well, that's Dunham."

There's a whole thing about them, and you get that from the horse's mouth. Miss Dunham is like that, and you see that when you're in the company, and you know you're expected to act a certain way, to look a certain way. You're a Dunham dancer.

VC: Tell me what you learned from Dunham Technique at the barre.

GVS: You get your center, you get your access, you get the strength from that barre. By the time you come from those exercises at the barre, and you go to the center of the floor, you can do them without holding onto the barre or anything else. That's what happens. You get very strong from the barre. Those barre exercises are fantastic.

VC: That's a very nice way to put it. I'll remember that. So at the advanced level that you and the other dancers achieved, if you do it long enough, it really stretches [the muscles]. I came to the Dunham Technique after having been a highly trained runner, but that was almost nine years later, and Dunham Technique stretched me in places where, boy, I thought I was already stretched.

I do want to ask you a couple of questions about your own relationship with Miss D because each person I've talked to has an anecdote. When you talked about Lucille [Ellis], you said "mom"—

GVS: Well, Lucille was like a mom to me, like a second mother to me, and I was her brat. She referred to me as that, and I teased her in the company. She used to tease me, and everybody always knew we had that wonderful relationship. With Miss Dunham it was different. With Miss

Dunham I refer to myself as her little monster, which means that if something needs to be done that might very well be unpleasant for somebody to do, in order to straighten out some business or anything that's wrong, I'm the one to go and do that. And it doesn't bother me to do it if it needs to be done.

As I said, she has always referred to Beryl Reynolds, Barbara McVey, and me as Hope, Faith, and Charity, but she's never told us who's Hope, who's Faith, or who's Charity. And even if I ask her today, she'll start giggling and won't tell me which one she's referred to as Hope, Faith, and Charity. But no, I have the utmost respect and regard for her. She's a genius, which we know. One of the nicest things was when I wrote a musical on Sojourner Truth, and I played her. It was at the Kennedy Center and theaters all over, and Lewis Johnson had choreographed it. Clyde Barnes, when he was reviewing it, said that Miss Dunham was my guru and that I was in the overachiever class of Katherine Dunham. That was a great honor.

vc: Surely, it is.

You know, each person in the company had a unique position. Do you want to tell me what your unique position might have been? Beyond the monster stuff, I mean, and the baby.

gvs: I think, with me, it's as an emotional chronicler of the company.

vc: What do you mean by that?

gvs: It means that I retain memories and scenes and visions of walking down the streets and what we encountered. What I saw. The people. I used to get up very, very early and go out to market and watch the people and record these things. I was very much aware that I was in a different kind of situation—different countries, different flavors, different everything. And I took note of all of this and recorded it in my mind and wrote scenes down. For me, it was more than just the performing. It was also the chronicling of scenes that I saw and felt. Sometimes I just dip down into myself and feel connectives.

For example, I had something happen once. We were coming from Lebanon on a ship, and we had to stop. The ship was in port, and we were getting ready to leave, and so vendors would come on board to sell things. I saw this beautiful little locket of Nefertiti. It was gold and turquoise, and I wanted to buy it. So I said to the vendor, "How much is that?" And he said to me, "You give me kiss. You give me kiss." And I pulled up, and I looked at him, and I said, "Would you ask Nefertiti for a kiss?" He looked at me; he looked down on the ground; and he handed it to me. Like that. Turned and left with his bag, off the ship. Gave it to me. No charge. Nothing. Didn't look at me when he left. I cannot tell you why I say things like that, but they just come out.

VC: When you say "a chronicler," does that mean that then you go back and talk to Miss Dunham, and you tell her "This is what I've seen and written about," and it winds up in her choreography? The only reason I ask you this is that [she has said that] a lot of her choreography [comes from observations]. *Woman with the Cigar,* she said, when I talked to her, comes from a woman she saw coming off the—

GVS: Well, no, I don't necessarily go to her and tell her. It's chronicled in terms of my life in that company and at some point when I write, I'm sure it will come. Miss Dunham has always said that I have to write about some of the Dunham experience, and I've told her that I will. I promised her, at some point I will. But there are things [I remember]. There are beautiful images and things.

VC: So these are images that you think will come up in your writing?

GVS: Yes, there's no question of it. It's extraordinary. The travel, the people, the language, the culture. The beauty of it all. And it didn't matter if it was an area that was poor or an area that was very rich. Your memories are rich. I have to thank Miss Dunham for having her company so that I could partake of it in that way, because if you go on a private trip you wouldn't go to that many myriad places, nor would you be in places that long, nor would you exchange the kind of things that you exchange with your fellow company members. You wouldn't travel with such a big group.

That's because you're really going from country to country and studying. There was one time when we were doing one-night stands all through Italy, and you came out and got on the company bus, they took you somewhere, and you went in and you came out, and you went into the theater, and you performed, and you came out and said, "So, are we sleeping on the bus on the way to somewhere else, or are we going to bed tonight?" To the point where you were just punchy.

Then I remember once picking up the phone and saying, "Excuse me, I don't mean to sound stupid, but where is this? Where are we? Oh, now we're in Switzerland." Because we were moving so fast. It was extraordinary. I couldn't do that now, but at that time we were young and vigorous, and everything was new.

Another time, I had a date with three Greek guys. They came in packs to take you out, and we had a wonderful time. And they had photos taken with me, with them grinning just for the enjoyment of exchanging culture. Just enjoyment.

VC: There's something truly serious that we need to address, and I'm not sure you were in the company then, but what do you make of, maybe reflecting back now, of all this brouhaha over *Southland?*

GVS: I wasn't in the company. That was ages and ages before I was ever in town.

VC: When did you come into the company?

GVS: 1959. I was in the last company.

VC: Yes, I know. What is your memory of the last—

GVS: The only thing I can think about in terms of *Southland* is that earlier Miss Dunham had said to me that *Southland* came about because of my cousin, Emmett Till, who was killed by racists in Mississippi; but then subsequently she said that it may have been something that happened some years before. But I know that she is very moved by the death of my cousin, which of course affected us in many ways.

What do I make of *Southland?* I think that, again, as someone has said, the dancers were probably happy to get away from the difficulties that they had in America, and once they were touring and traveling in different countries they didn't even have to address any of that. They were stars abroad; they were accepted beautifully; they had a wonderful time; and then they had to come back into our own culture where people were discriminating. They were not ready to do that. I guess when she was considering the ballet they probably thought, "We don't want to do that, because we've lived it, and we don't want to go back to it." I can understand that. At the same time, I do understand why she would do it, because I also would have done it.

VC: I can't remember the date of the Emmett Till murder.

GVS: It was in 1955. And he was fourteen years old.[1]

VC: When I was interviewing Miss Dunham, she said exactly the same thing. It wasn't until Emmett Till's death [that she made the connection] as far as the ballet [was concerned]. But the ballet was created in 1951, and I knew something was wrong, so of course I went to the Communist newspapers and that's how I found out the names of the persons [involved]. They obviously show up [in newspaper accounts], but I think it's important for us to set our own record straight.

Now, in 1955, do you remember anything about how the family reacted to that personal tragedy?

GVS: Well, I still can't talk about it, meaning that at some point I will write about it, but it is one of the those things where your mind just freezes and doesn't take in the enormity of it. Because it's almost like, "This cannot be happening to me, cannot be happening to my family, cannot be happening." That's the first thing: disbelief. And then one has to get on and deal with that. And it has made me stronger; it hasn't made me weak. One has to do what one has to do in this world, and one has to take whatever blows come, but it doesn't mean that you take them lying down. You pick the battles, and you the pick the way in which you fight the injustices. My parents were very political, and I picked the battles that I have fought. I just know that I'm combative, and I know that I'm an activist, so it was different for me. I don't come from a family who sits back and takes things. They are active about things if there's any kind of injustice.

VC: Is that a way to explain why, maybe, Miss Dunham relies on you to be the "bad cop"?

GVS: It could be. Because I'm not afraid of confrontation if there's an issue, if there's a problem. I don't care who you are. I can confront it and make you confront it and deal with it, and say, "I love you, but I don't like this situation, and this has to change, and this has to be the situation." I don't have problems with that.

VC: How much did she know about your background? Correct me if I'm wrong, but, given what we have on the audio tapes, what you've just been telling me, it seems to me that the two of you do share [a similar background].

GVS: She knows I'm a kid who came out of Chicago.

VC: Okay. And the penchant for activism?

GVS: Yes. She knows about that.

VC: Do you want to talk about that?

GVS: Yes, she knows that, and she knows that I'm not a person who just sits back. Even in the company I was like that. If I thought something was not right, I'd say it. My upbringing has been really that of a humanist, and very progressive. My parents used to say, "You can say what you want to say to us if you say it respectfully. You have that right to say it." So, I was never brought up where kids were silent. We'd sit in the dining room and discuss things, and whatever was wrong we'd talk about. Nothing was swept under the rug or anything.

VC: Let's move to what motivated you to take on and produce "The Magic of Katherine Dunham"?

GVS: Not "The Magic of." It would be the Katherine Dunham Gala.

VC: That was in seventy—

GVS: 1979. The Katherine Dunham Gala. What motivated me [was a meeting with Miss Dunham]. I was by then a principal dancer with Agnes DeMille's company, and she and Miss Dunham were friends. Agnes DeMille wanted to have *Floyd's Guitar Blues* for her company, and she wanted me to dance it. So I had come down to East Saint Louis to learn it from Miss Dunham, which I did. After I had learned it, Miss Dunham and I were sitting and talking. We have "Dunham 101," which I do when I sit with her and have one-on-one talks. In the course of talking, after she'd seen me do the dance, she was saying, "Oh, I'd love to see the Dunham dancers again." I looked right at her and said, "Oh, you will." She said, "I will?" I said, "Yes, I'll produce a gala, and we'll have the dancers, and you'll see them again."

Now, I didn't have one nickel to start producing any so-called gala and get those dancers. But I looked at her and I said, "We will." I went back to New York and got an application from the National Endowment for the Arts, filled it out, and where it says "organization," I wrote in there with big bold letters "I am the organization." They laughed about that. "I am the organization," which I was. They knew my track record for things, I wasn't an unknown person or anything. And so they said to me, "Okay. We will give you the money to get it videotaped" and da-da-da. And if I would only wait until then, perhaps the next time I could get a gala. I said, "Hmm. No way, José." I got my matching funds, and I got the gala. I got it videotaped. I got it photographed. Everything.

They said, "My God. First time out of the barn with that, and it was a huge success." People were hanging from the rafters. And it was really done. I wanted three different generations of Dunham dancers, the PATC ones,[2] my generation, and then the rest of their generation interacting. It was marvelous. It was a marvelous, marvelous occasion, and I'm very happy that I did it. I'm ever so happy about that.

VC: Yes, I was there. I was telling Sara [Johnson] this morning how I slipped out of Yale in the midst of a job interview so I could get down to New York.

I wonder if you can tell us the range of reviews that you got? I know it's hard to summarize, but, from one end into the next, what do you remember about it?

GVS: Well for one, they were very happy to see the works again, and then refer to older dancers and when Miss Dunham did it. I did her role in *Cakewalk* this time where she used to do it and things of this sort, but it was the nostalgia of it. It was so wonderful to see these works again and these different generations. Just a wonderful thing. It was what we called in the 1960s a happening. And everybody was happy.

vc: Do you remember any of the negative criticisms that you received?

gvs: No. No.

vc: Because I do remember people [criticizing the production], and I was thinking, "Why would anyone say anything so stupid?" People, if we get into the nostalgia mode, said that those pieces were originally seen with a full orchestra.

gvs: That is not what you even address. If you did that, then you would not have any touring. They're not touring around with an orchestra. Martha Graham is not touring around with an orchestra. No company can afford that, so what you do, and the way in which I handle things like that, is you go right past it or you look at them and say, "Are you willing to put up the money for us to have a full orchestra?" And they look at you, and you say, "If you're not, then you must consider that we do the next best thing, which is we have recorded music, and that's what all the companies do." Maybe on an opening night you have a full orchestra, but the cost is prohibitive.

What you learn to do with those kind of things, because those are not legitimate criticisms, is [know] that if the person really realized where you are at this stage in the world, they would know why the companies cannot carry this. And, yes, there are different people dancing these roles. Well, if they're not, you have to resurrect some people who are in their graves. And that is where you have to be careful. You want things to be done. They can't be done always by the people who originally did them. The world moves on; things move on. If it has to be only the people who originally did it, then that means you will not have any progress. And I am one who'll say "Yes, maybe they don't do it this way, but that's the next best thing." But you have a choice. You can't resurrect those people. Then do the works die because those people are not going to get to it, or do you put other people there and do the best that they can do so that the works stay alive? You've got a choice, and you make the decision.

vc: I think that the one issue that people didn't deal with at the time is that these are ballets for the most part of the 1940s, and some of them—I'm not going to say a majority, but some of them—under the financing of Sol Hurok were performed at a time when you could have a full orchestra.

GVS: Everything. You had everything then. You had all the money to do everything.

VC: But people don't think historically. And I think that you just put this whole thing in perspective.

So, here's the last question I have. We've been here now for two days talking about conceptualizing the legacy of Katherine Dunham. Again, if you had to explain to someone who never met the woman, knows nothing about her, the youth who don't care, because they're into MTV or whatever, how would you explain what the legacy of this woman in fact is?

GVS: I'd probably say, "Do you know what a comet is?" And they'd say, "Yes." "So, would you like to touch a comet? I have a comet right there before you." "Yes." " Then I'll introduce you to Miss Dunham and her world."

NOTES

1. In August 1955, Emmett Till, an African American boy from Chicago, was brutally murdered while he was visiting relatives in the Mississippi Delta. Unaccustomed to the strict segregation of the races in the South, he had whistled at a white female store clerk as she walked across a parking lot. Two days later, her relatives kidnapped him in the middle of the night. He was never seen alive again. The two men accused of his murder were quickly acquitted by an all-white jury. They later publicly admitted that they were guilty. Widely covered in the press, the case attracted international attention as an outrageous miscarriage of justice and was a signal event in precipitating the civil rights movement in the United States. In May 2004 the U.S. Department of Justice announced that it was opening a criminal investigation into the case in light of new evidence that implicated other participants in the grisly crime *[Eds.]*.

2. Dancers from the Performing Arts Training Center, Southern Illinois University, East Saint Louis *[Eds.]*.

The Kennedy Center Honors

CARLA HALL AND JOE BROWN

On the stage of the Opera House, Hollywood greats told tales of other Hollywood greats overcoming adversity, and in the audience Kennedy Center honorees wiped back tears as the tributes grew sumptuous and moving. It was all for five Americans with distinguished careers in the performing arts—all awarded Kennedy Center Honors last night in this sixth annual ceremony: Frank Sinatra, 67; Jimmy Stewart, 75; Elia Kazan, 73; Virgil Thomson, 87; and Katherine Dunham, 71. Seated in the Presidential Box along with Ronald and Nancy Reagan, they applauded each other and took the kudos they received with grace.

It was a night of tears and applause and funny stories and tributes in which people thanked others for changing their lives. And it was a night when President Reagan stepped away for a while from the anguish in Lebanon—though the military activity there cast a long shadow from which no one completely escaped. It was a night of the older meeting the younger: Mikhail Baryshnikov dancing to Sinatra's crooning; the New York City Breakers, young kids dancing fast and soulfully, bounding off the stage, careening down the aisles, slapping hands with Gene Kelly as they passed him during their salute to Dunham. And Agnes DeMille, who was a 1980 honoree, proclaimed that when choreographer Katherine Dunham first came to New York, "No one, no one, who saw her then could possibly forget her."

Between moving tributes to the honorees, the incorrigible Art Buchwald

SOURCE: Carla Hall and Joe Brown, Abridged version of "The Kennedy Center Honors," *Washington Post*, 5 December 1983, p. B1. Copyright 1983 by the *Washington Post* Company. Reprinted by permission.

took to the stage, booming in his nasal voice: "Mr. President, it's now exactly 8:14 P.M. Do you know where Prince Andrew is? And don't you wish you were with him?" The audience broke into guffaws.

"First of all," Buchwald continued, "I would like to thank the Secretary of Defense for permitting the press to be here. The original Pentagon plan was to allow the press to watch the show from the island of Barbados."

Buchwald lamented, "This is not an easy time for political humorists—because the government is now funnier than we are." Buchwald urged the president to take care with his Latin American policy. "If the Kennedy Center goes Communist," Buchwald warned, "the Hollywood Bowl will go next."

Carol Burnett and retired brigadier general Chuck Yeager, the test pilot who broke the sound barrier, accompanied by the Cadet Chorale from the U.S. Air Force Academy, serenaded Stewart with "Auld Lang Syne," part of the closing scene in the Frank Capra movie *It's a Wonderful Life,* in which Stewart starred.

Burnett began by saying, "I have not kept it a secret over the years that I have been in love with James Stewart my whole life." Of her first meeting with Stewart, when she was a star-struck kid visiting the sound stage of *The FBI Story,* she said: "I stepped into a bucket of whitewash, and I didn't turn around—I dragged it all the way across the sound stage thinking, 'Maybe he'll think I did this on purpose.'" Burnett then sang "Easy to Love" with the one-hundred-voice Air Force Academy Cadet Chorale, the only song Stewart ever sang in a movie (to Eleanor Powell). Stewart, from the Presidential Box, blew Burnett a kiss and saluted Yeager while the 2,100 in the audience looked on.

A bearded Burt Lancaster remembered Stewart as "a lean gangly, idealistic young man, grown into what has been called the most complete cinema personality on the screen . . . as an actor he is respected for what he has done, and as a man he is respected for what he is." As Stewart rose to the audience's applause, Nancy Reagan leaned over and kissed him, and his old friend, the president, shook his hand.

Warren Beatty spoke of working with director Kazan. "Elia Kazan gave me my start in the movies, so I'm going to try and use a little restraint here and not embarrass him," said Beatty, adding, "I think he's the greatest American director who ever lived, so I was lucky to observe this man in my first picture." Beatty addressed President Reagan, asking him to use his influence with Kazan to get Beatty the part of Kazan in a movie of his life.

"I think actually you could be a big help in that," Beatty said. "Do you think you could take him aside and at least mention to him that I look Greek? Who knows, Mr. President—in five years you might want me to take him aside and mention you. Let me put it this way—it would be the nicest thing I ever did for a Republican," Beatty said as a clever, filmed biography of Kazan loomed behind on a huge screen.

Next up for Kazan was Anthony Quinn, who won his first Oscar in Kazan's *Viva Zapata!* Quinn and the cast of his current Broadway show, *Zorba!* performed two numbers from the show.

"I say this unabashedly. You gave me freedom . . . but then you gave all your actors that freedom, and that was your genius," Quinn said and then growled out the song "I Am Free" from *Zorba!*

Each artist was honored with a filmed biography, which had as a running thread the theme of how each artist overcame major stumbling blocks on the way to success: Kazan spent seven years searching for a producer for his film *On the Waterfront;* Frank Sinatra lost his voice at the peak of his popularity; Dunham took her shows to places where blacks couldn't even sit in the audience; and Virgil Thomson spent six years writing *Four Saints in Three Acts,* which no opera house in New York would touch.

John Houseman, speaking of Thomson, said he was "awed by his wisdom, his clarity of vision and his profound sense . . . that made him the nearest thing to a guru in my life."

Houseman brought on the cast of the current New York production of *The Mother of Us All,* Thomson's second opera, with text by Gertrude Stein. "It's about the winning of political rights for women," Houseman said, "a subject that was apparently not completely resolved by that production."

Gene Kelly, a 1982 honoree, told the audience of his first meeting with Sinatra in New York. "I decided to check out this new kid on the block. My first impression was 'He just looks awful!' He was a skinny runt, and then he opened his mouth and it was awesome."

Perry Como came on with a large children's chorus and sang "Young at Heart" in tribute to Sinatra with new lyrics: "Though you once were the rage on the Paramount stage . . . Though you're past middle age—Frank, you'll always be among the very young at heart."

"Once each year, we gather here to give Art Buchwald an opportunity to make fun of the Kennedy Center deficit," said Kennedy Center chairman Roger L. Stevens, "and to give all of you a chance to do something about it." (Stevens also said the center would make about $500,000 from the evening. The show was produced by George Stevens Jr. and Nick Vanoff, and was taped to air on CBS December 27.)

Stevens then introduced a big surprise—American Ballet Theatre artistic director Baryshnikov, who performed Twyla Tharp's new ballet, *Sinatra Suite,* in black tie to five Sinatra standards. Before he left the stage, Ol' Blue Eyes and Misha saluted each other across the hall.

Before his dance, Baryshnikov read a telegram from one Sinatra fan who couldn't make it last night. It read: "All the best from the kid on the block. Jimmy Cagney."

Agnes DeMille walked slowly onstage in a full sky-blue gown, and seemed moved as the audience rose to its feet for her. Dunham blew DeMille a kiss toward the stage.

She said Dunham gave a gift to all artists. "She told us what art really is—communication—a direct speech of the heart. Oh, Katie, bonnie Katie, we love you."

Master of ceremonies Walter Cronkite ended the tribute in typical Uncle Walter style, addressing the five honorees. "For you, the show will always go on—for that's the way it is. You know, that's the way it's been for most of a century. You've graced our stages, you've graced our lives, you graced our history. And now it's time for you to take another bow and for us to show our gratitude." The audience rose for the last time as the honorees held hands and raised them high.

The glittering crowd loved it all.

Dance's Dynamic Duo

Alvin Ailey in Collaboration with Katherine Dunham

Alan M. Kriegsman

"The Magic of Katherine Dunham"—the evening-long program Tuesday and Wednesday nights that will launch a week of performances by the Alvin Ailey American Dance Theater at the Kennedy Center Opera House—is a testimonial from one charismatic dance personage to another. It's a tribute by Ailey, one of the greatest pioneers of black American dance, to Dunham, an equally great pioneer of an earlier era and a lifelong inspiration to Ailey. Just about everyone even remotely interested in dance has heard of Dunham, now 75, who was the recipient of the $25,000 Samuel H. Scripps Award two years ago, joined the list of Kennedy Center honorees in 1983 and has been profiled by public television's prestigious *Dance in America* series.

The outward facts of her career as a dancer, anthropologist, choreographer, and teacher are also known to many—her anthropological studies at the University of Chicago and her extensive field trips to the West Indies and Africa; her forging of a new dance technique distilled from her ethnic researches; her founding, in the late 1930s, of one of the earliest black dance troupes, later to be known as the Katherine Dunham Dancers; the period of her reign as a radiantly glamorous star of Broadway, Hollywood, and the cabaret circuit, dating from her 1940 stage appearance in *Cabin in the Sky,* which she choreographed with George Balanchine; the opening of her immensely influential New York school in 1945, and the worldwide tours of her revues, designed by her late husband John Pratt; and since the

SOURCE: Alan M. Kriegsman, "Dance's Dynamic Duo: Alvin Ailey in Collaboration with Katherine Dunham," *Washington Post,* 8 May 1988, p. G1. Copyright 1988 by the Washington Post Company. Reprinted by permission.

mid-1960s, her continuing work with youngsters in East Saint Louis, as the founder of the Performing Arts Training Center at Southern Illinois University.

Despite all this, only a relative smattering of older fans has actually seen the dances and dance theater pieces created by Dunham. It was precisely to remedy this lack that Ailey set out to mount his company's homage. Dunham herself supervised virtually all of the lengthy rehearsals and enlisted the help of Vanoye Aikens—her dance partner for two decades—as well as former Dunham dancers Lucille Ellis, Tommy Gomez, and Pearl Reynolds in reconstructing the works. Every effort was made to match the original productions. Pratt's original sets and costumes have been used or precisely copied.

The resulting program has three acts. The first is an Afro-Caribbean suite of seven dances; the second is *L'Ag'ya,* a folkloric dance dramatization involving romance, witchcraft, and vengeance, set in eighteenth-century Martinique; and the third and last highlights the dance traditions of black America—the self-explicating titles are *Field Hands, Plantation Dances, Spirituals, Flaming Youth, Barrelhouse,* and *Cakewalk.* The Dunham program proved an immensely challenging undertaking for Ailey and his troupe. Originally budgeted at $300,000, it wound up costing closer to half a million.

"It turned out to be a big splashy production," said Ailey in his New York office a couple of weeks ago. "Bigger than we realized, bigger than we could pay for." The premiere at New York's City Center last December was preceded by six weeks of rehearsal and required a thirty-piece orchestra plus five drummers and five singers (the music is too expensive for touring, so tape will be used at Kennedy Center).

"But it really was a fabulous coming together of elements," Ailey said. "We'd rehearse five hours a day and we had a merry old time, and then Katherine would give us these lectures. Let me tell you, we know about every rock and leaf in the Caribbean by now."

According to Ailey, Dunham couldn't herself remember all the moves and positions, but "she remembered what it was not." "'It was not that,' she'd say, watching the dancers. 'Try something else.' When no one, neither she nor her colleagues, could remember a passage, she'd fill in, and she changed a few things the others remembered.

"She was wonderful with the dancers, who were quite a bit in awe of her. The first day of rehearsal she told them: 'I know you've probably heard the stories that I'm a mystic and a clairvoyant and a Voodoo priestess and all

that. It's all true. I'll just say that I promise not to use any of my powers—
unless I have to.'"

Ailey says the dancers of his company had less trouble mastering
Dunham's technical demands than her overtly theatrical approach to the
material. "They found it difficult to project as performers, difficult to let
go, to 'sell' the dance a little bit more than they're used to. I think it had
to do with the 'cool' of today's younger dancers. They're just not accustomed to giving out feelings that much."

Dunham also was an absolute stickler for detail, Ailey notes. "She has
such an acute mind, and it never stopped working, you know. At one point
she wanted to fire the entire orchestra. 'I'm tough,' she said. She heard a
couple of trombones out of tune and she was ready to call up the orchestra manager to get in a whole new crew. And after every day of rehearsal
she gave us pages of notes, packets of them, filled with criticisms of the
dancing, the rhythms, the lighting, even the speed of the curtains."

Ailey first saw Dunham and her troupe perform in 1945, when they
brought her *Tropical Revue* to the Biltmore Theatre in Los Angeles. He
was fourteen at the time. "I'd taken some tap by then, but I wasn't really
dancing yet. But I was completely bowled over by Miss Dunham and her
dancers, and I think the seeds were planted right then and there for my
desire years afterward to bring these dances back. I know I do not want to
see these dances die—that would be criminal."

In the later 1940s, Dunham returned for appearances at a chic Los
Angeles nightclub, and this time Ailey got to know some members of the
Dunham company, but not yet Dunham. "I met Lucille Ellis, and she let
me in to the show every night, but there was no coming near Madame
herself. It wasn't until many years later that I came to know her as a person and friend."

Still, those performances were dearly treasured by the teenage Ailey.
"There she was, gorgeous and glittering in gold bangles, doing black culture, and playing Ciro's, where we, as blacks, couldn't even enter in those
days."

After "The Magic of Katherine Dunham," the Ailey programs at the
Opera House—the first in Washington since 1985—will feature four additional Washington premieres as well as seven works from the repertory.

Two of the pieces new to us are by choreographer Ulysses Dove—
Bad Blood, to a score by Laurie Anderson, and *Vespers,* a dance for six
women with percussion music by Mikel Rouse. The other two premieres
are by Ailey: *Survivors,* a collaboration with the company's associate artistic

director Mary Barnett to a Max Roach score, about the plight of South Africa's Nelson and Winnie Mandela; and *Caverna Magica,* a thirty-five-minute ensemble work created for the Royal Danish Ballet to music by Andreas Vollenweider.

Also to be seen are Ailey's *For Bird with Love* and *Revelations,* Judith Jamison's *Divining,* Talley Beatty's *The Stack-Up,* Billy Wilson's *Concerto in F,* Elisa Monte's *Treading,* and Jennifer Muller's *Speeds.*

Ailey Does Dunham

ALAN M. KRIEGSMAN

"The Magic of Katherine Dunham," the program that launched a week of performances by the Alvin Ailey American Dance Theater at the Kennedy Center Opera House Tuesday night, was just that—magic. A spectacular salute to Dunham, the much-honored, 75-year-old native Chicagoan who created her own choreographic universe inspired by her anthropological studies and research, the evening had a degree of theatrical panache seldom seen on the dance stage apart from full-length ballet classics

The production—choreographed, staged, and directed by Dunham, with wonderfully striking sets and costumes based on original designs by her husband, artist John Pratt (who died in 1986 at age 74)—recreates dances and dance-theater pieces dating from 1937 through 1950, arranged into three acts. Each of the acts has its own theme. The first includes a demonstration of Dunham technique, introductory to a suite of Afro-Caribbean dances. The second is a complete dance drama, *L'Ag'ya,* in three scenes, set in an eighteenth-century fishing village in Martinique. The third, *Americana Suite,* ranges across the spectrum of black American dance forms from the era of slavery to the jazz age. In addition to *L'Ag'ya,* the other two acts contain pieces, *Shango* in the first and *Flaming Youth—Chicago 1920,* that are integral mini dramas complete with specific decor and thoroughly individualized characters.

The Ailey dancers must have worked like demons to realize this ambitious project under Dunham's supervision, the more so to have achieved so brilliant a result. If they inevitably stamped the material here and there with

SOURCE: Alan M. Kriegsman, "Ailey Does Dunham," *Washington Post,* May 12, 1988, p. D4. Copyright 1988 by the *Washington Post* Company. Reprinted by permission.

signs of their own generation, they nevertheless seemed entirely at home with these historic dances and performed them with a kind of relish and intensity that could only have arisen from deep commitment. The program as a whole is a testimonial to the amazing reach of Dunham's imagination, as well as her mastery of stagecraft. Not every one of the individual dances could be counted a masterwork, which was in any case far from the original intention—many of these pieces originated as elements in traveling revues, and their entertainment value is never in doubt. But the effect of the evening is decidedly cumulative, the sum much greater than the parts.

Central to the program is the idea of cultural assimilation and transformation. The first couple of numbers, illustrating Dunham technique, show how she distilled dance forms of the Caribbean, Latin America, and Africa into a codified system of stage dancing—she actually made a new dance language, embracing rhythms, shapes, and degrees of bodily freedom until then unknown to American dance. The rest of the program displays this language in action in the widest diversity of contexts, further transformed by additional ingredients from Dunham's background.

Dunham's own earliest dance studies were in classical ballet, and Ailey relates how in rehearsing the program, she kept asking, in certain sequences, for "Preobrajenska arms" (Olga Preobrajenska, 1870–1962, was an illustrious Russian dancer and pedagogue, long resident in Paris). It was startling to see, in the middle of passages otherwise dominated by swiveling hips, rolling shoulders, and undulant torsos, a flash of *pirouettes, brisés,* and *sissonnes,* seamlessly blended into the phrasing. It was also fascinating to note how such African-derived motifs as rippling backs or rotating pelvises migrated not only to various parts of the Latin world but also from American plantations to Chicago cabarets, all in different dance guises reflective of their respective locales and musical scaffoldings.

The Afro-Caribbean section took in such dances as *Afrique,* a village scene dressed in stunning fabrics, in which a local queen (this must have been a Dunham role) with a coronet, gold necklaces, and a bare midriff is borne upon a pallet by four tribesmen; *Choros,* a Brazilian quadrille to a lilting Latin beat; *Nañigo,* a vigorous, athletic dance for men based on a once-secret African ritual; and *Los Indios,* an amusing rustic vignette about two South American native women and their encounter with a flirtatious young flute player. In *Shango,* the Yoruba ceremony that climaxed the first act, a youth (Dereque Whiturs) possessed by the snake god—and slithering contortedly on his belly—is released from the spell by priestly incantations and exits in jubilation astride a huge log toted by six men.

The evening's single most stirring work was the elaborately staged *L'Ag'ya* (1938), much graced by the performances of April Berry and Andre Tyson as young Martinique lovers and Gary DeLoatch as Julot, the jealous suitor of the triangle. In the wonderfully eerie second scene, amid the greenish nocturnal mists of the jungle, Julot fearfully encounters the living dead and their sovereign, Roi Zombie (a fiendishly cackling Dudley Williams), from whom he secures a magic love totem. In the final scene, Julot bewitches Berry with the charm into a writhingly seductive dance, but is then defeated by Tyson in the Capoiera-like combat of l'ag'ya (a Martinique martial art). In the end, Julot treacherously stabs his rival in the back, and Berry is left lamenting over his body like a stricken bird.

The big production number of the *Americana Suite* was *Flaming Youth,* a rousing, atmospheric evocation of the social dances of the 1920s, such as the Charleston, the Black Bottom, and the Mooch, featuring Desiree Sewer as the vampish Kansas City Woman and Christopher Huggins as Snakehips Tucker. The suite also sampled folk and social dances from the plantation days to minstrelsy, ending with a jaunty *Cakewalk.*

The program would actually benefit from some judicious editing; running three hours in its present form, it gets to be rather overwhelming. There are very few numbers one would readily lose, but one or two might go without serious damage to the overall concept, and a few others could probably be shortened. In any case, this precious gift of restoration does honor to Dunham, Ailey, his superbly versatile dancers, and American dance generally.

The Jamaican Connexion

REX NETTLEFORD

"The course of dance in America has been plotted by three mighty matri-archs—[Isadora] Duncan, [Ruth] St. Denis, and [Katherine] Dunham."
So spake Walter Terry of *Dance Magazine* when Katherine Dunham, cho-reographer, dancer, and social anthropologist received the Albert Schweitzer Music Award in 1977. The unpardonable omission of the great Martha Graham aside, Mr. Terry's proclamation had a ring of retributive justice about it seeing that Ms. Dunham's work was in her time often dismissed by the racist, Eurocentric and snooty observers in her native USA and rel-egated to the periphery of art. Not unlike the resonant dismissal later on of much of Jamaican dance theatre by yet another visiting "critic" as "rustic simplicities and back-a-yard ballets."

Well, I saw what to the uninformed might well have been such "rustic simplicities and back-a-yard ballets" at the City Center in New York in early December, 1987. It was a three-act evening-long tribute to Ms. Dunham—a kind of retrospective of her repertoire of dances created somewhere between 1938 and 1958. The evening could have been one hour shorter but those who know the value of this icon, we were richer for the experi-ence. *Rites de Passage* might have made greater impact than *L'Ag'ya*. A great artist after all deserves to be remembered by his/her best works. Yet there were more than glimpses of that greatness. She had brought back old warriors like Lucille Ellis, Pearl Reynolds, and Tommy Gomez of blessed memory as well as Vanoye Aikens to remount the works on the bodies of

SOURCE: Rex Nettleford, "Katherine Dunham: The Jamaican Connexion (or *Journey from Accompong*)," *Kingston (Jamaica) Sunday Gleaner*, 3 January 1988. Copyright 1988 by the *Gleaner* Company, Ltd. . Reprinted by permission.

the young Alvin Ailey dancers. This is as it should be. For "Black Dance" has long determined the mainstream of American dance-art without receiving proper acknowledgment. There still exist overt and covert reservations about "things ethnic" (read non-white) being able to claim centre place in the ethos.

The New York tribute to Dunham was of more than passing interest to us in Jamaica at the time since the work of the previous thirty years in Jamaican dance and dance-theatre had sought to root form and feeling as well as classic expressions in the realities of Jamaican and Caribbean life and existence. It continues so to do. Ms. Dunham herself drew heavily on the Caribbean region as source of energy and for her quite monumental work which was being celebrated by a younger generation. The Gala performance (at $450 US per seat) must have been a joyous affair. The Jamerican entertainer and actor Harry Belafonte presided over the glitter and substance of African American artistry. His wife, the former Julie Robinson, had been a memorable member of the great Dunham company which toured and conquered Europe in the fifties.

They also conquered Kingston in 1950. And that was when I first saw them. I journeyed from Montego Bay, three hours' drive away, as a schoolboy and was taken by the hand into the Carib Theatre by a famous woman of Jamaican letters and theatre, the late Una Marson, who procured the tickets for us both. It was an unforgettable experience.

Ms. Dunham was in the hospital recuperating from an unscheduled appendicitis operation, but the show went on; and I recalled many of the dances which I was to see thirty-seven years later on a New York stage. The future Graham and Ailey dancer Clive Thompson (who was younger than I), and now back with us in Jamaica as choreographer with the NDTC was also in the audience at the Carib, as I later discovered, and he has often stated how impressed he was with the sheer excitement that the dancers brought to the work on the Carib Theatre stage. They pushed him to the Ivy Baxter studio and beyond.

For my part, I returned to Montego Bay convinced that what I was doing at the time with the Worm Chambers Vaudeville Group at the Strand and Roxy "Theatres" as well as with fellow students at Cornwall College and with yard youths in the backyard where I lived was dead right—that the likes of us had something to say for ourselves in our music and our dance. I had no idea then, that Ms. Dunham had in fact done field study in Jamaica among the Maroons in Accompong and had written a book (her report) entitled *Journey to Accompong*. I was to learn later that Haiti, Brazil, Jamaica, Trinidad—the Caribbean Basin—provided her with much of her inspiration for a definitive dance idiom which was to start several black Americans on their professional international careers in dance, the theatre, and entertainment. Claudia McNeil stayed behind for a couple of years in Jamaica and sang her way into the hearts of Jamaicans over Radio ZQI. She was to blossom into a stage and film actress.

When I later met and worked with Ivy Baxter, Beryl McBurnie, and Lavinia Williams (one of Ms. Dunham's earliest dancers), things all fell into place. The rustic simplicities and back-a-yard experiences of the Caribbean were indeed the richest sources for a mode of artistic expression with its own validity and cultural integrity. That that expression must be on the basis not of self-indulgent "art for art's sake" assumptions but of deep and serious study of text and context is something yet to be appreciated even by many of our own people. So just as Ms. Dunham was dismissed by traditionalists as a social anthropologist parading as an artist, others after her have been threatened with the imposition of the label of minstrel rather than as self-respecting creators with the capacity to think for themselves, to organize rationally (never mind that Balanchine insisted that he was merely an assembler of steps), or to possess a vision that takes one beyond the ephemeral nightly performance. Ms. Dunham, according to legend, was heard to pray that she would never hear the word jungle again. For that is where her detractors placed her in much the same way as Jamaican dance-theatre without arabesques and European classical music is relegated to rustic simplicity and the back-a-yard.

But the integrity of Ms. Dunham's work has outlived the detractors and vindicated her supporters, some of whom might well have loved her *Tropical Revue* merely for its "exoticism," but many of whom focused on the originality and profundity of her contribution to American and African diasporic culture through the performing arts. She had earned her Bachelor of Philosophy in Social Anthropology from the University of Chicago in 193[6] and was to discover that much of her people's (any people's) grasp of their own being, or the way they think and come to know about existence, or their world view, comes through in the ritual of dance and song, or rhythm, of play, of storytelling. She knew the instant impact of a theatre production over a written thesis but more than that, the power of the synthesis of field and stage, of life and art. She was highly successful; giving to the United States yet another showpiece of achievement by a society that was vibrant, energetic, capable of openness despite the scourge of Jim Crowism, and full of hope. Ms. Dunham was more than social anthropologist, more than dancer, more than choreographer. She was an effective apostle of Black dignity and New World hope, a child, like Zora Neale Hurston, of the twenty-first century—textured, insightful, delight-fully complex.

She rightly became an icon to many from the Plantation American world who aspired to excellence. She became a survivor and oftentimes found warmer welcome in distant lands other than her own country. "Whatever her rating in America may be, the daughter of slaves has come as a conqueror to Europe," wrote Richard Buckle of London in 1951. London and Paris did fall at the feet of the charismatic "Miss D" and her "magnificent dancers and musicians." She still resides in Haiti—strife-torn but ancestrally reinvigorating. And she once thought of relocating her company in Jamaica, in 1960 when I first met her face to face at a rehearsal of the LTM pantomime Carib Gold, which I was then choreographing and co-directing. But America (the U.S.A.) is growing up and she has been celebrated in East Saint Louis where her memorabilia and papers are preserved waiting for further safekeeping as part of the heritage of all of the Americas and where seminars promoting her technique and dance philos-ophy have been conducted. I hope this colloquium will lead positively to the direction of resources towards the endurance of the Dunham legacy. The Alvin Ailey Dance Theater tribute followed naturally on the growing maturity of a society that had at last acknowledged the worth of Porgy and Bess, which was finally regarded as "good enough" to play at the Metropol-itan Opera House after fifty years of snubbing. We in Jamaica aim to avoid continuing on a similar and perilous route and wake up to our own possi-bilities—thanks to Ms. Dunham. The paradox is that Ms. Dunham herself, like Belafonte, who has done well on his parents' country's folksongs, knew from early on the tremendous richness of the cultural soil of the Carib-bean. "In 1930," writes a Dunham biographer, "a chance attendance at an ethnological lecture fired her imagination with an idea which has been the guiding impulse of her career: that in the dances of the Caribbean Negroes she might find the cultural heritage of which their American cousins had been deprived although it was theirs by right of their African blood. Could she forge a link with the past and revive among her people . . . a sense of their traditions and history?" She did, while some Jamaican creators here were saying that there is little in Jamaican material out of which to shape a classic dance idiom. Beryl McBurnie of Trinidad thought otherwise and Berto Pasuko the Jamaican dancer sought refuge in Britain and Europe, where he was a forerunner of Ms. Dunham with his Ballets Nègres.

Her *Shango* remains as fresh today as it was in 1950 when I first saw it. And *Rites de Passage*, which drew on Africa for its kinetic and movement quality, must surely rank as one of the finest dance works anywhere. Her return in this retrospective is important for millions of people concerned more with their cultural sovereignty than with being merely titillated.

The task is nowhere yet finished. Even Anna Kisselgoff, the eminently intelligent critic of the *New York Times,* in reviewing the gala performance betrayed the enduring tensions that threaten the metropolitan "mainstream" arbiter of creative work that is forced into a predetermined narrow orbit. She was admittedly deferential. But the difficulty of attributing to Ms. Dunham's lifelong work a logic and consistency of its own came through. Many from the background of Africa-in-the-Americas would never agree that *Choros,* the Brazilian quadrille described by Ms. Kisselgoff as a "polished gem," was the "program's masterpiece." The question inevitably is: by what and whose criteria? Nor should anyone with any knowledge of or respect for the texture and diversity of Caribbean- and African-Americans' traditional life and history, find "astounding . . . the variety that the choreography extracted from her specialized interests," as Ms. Kisselgoff astoundingly did. Corresponding "specialized interests" of other dance pioneers have thrown up no less variety as George Balanchine and Martha Graham themselves demonstrated. But in fairness to the critic there was praise for "Ms. Dunham's shrewd mix of show business, art, and anthropology," which I would like to think acknowledges the fact that there are alternative and valid options to the aesthetics of cerebrated modern dance.

Jamaica joins in tribute to this high priestess and matriarch who shares with the Caribbean's own Beryl McBurnie, who flourished as la Belle Rosette in New York when Dunham was still exploring a vision which happily is not yet lost to a younger generation. That generation, to which the new breed of Ailey dancers belong, as do all young dancers in the Americas at end of century, needs to understand that determining their own destiny, which they insist on, means the responsibility of creating their own art out of their ancestral and existential realities. Dunham is a welcome challenge, then, lest they forget!

She deserves to be celebrated, her work merits the test of endurance. We at the University of the West Indies, through its Cultural Studies program, feel an obligation to target her work and her vision as a topic for research, analysis, and wider dissemination in a continuing struggle to bring sanity and good sense to the new millennium.

The Yoruba Orisha Tradition
Comes to New York City

MARTA MORENO VEGA

The work of Katherine Dunham, Zora Neale Hurston, and Pearl Primus—
building on the research of Melville Herskovits and W. E. B. Du Bois—
introduced an intellectual perspective of the African Diaspora into the
arts. These artists worked studiously to incorporate an international racial
and cultural legacy into an African-based aesthetic which could serve as a
unifying link for Africans in the Diaspora. Dunham, for example, insisted
that the members of her dance company understand the cultural traditions of creative expression in their respective countries, and her school
at 43rd Street and Broadway nurtured developing and accomplished artists who embraced the African Diaspora in their creative expression. "Our
school," writes Dunham in an unpublished autobiography,

> became the popular meeting place of Caribbean, Central and South Amer-
> ican diplomats, painters, musicians, poets, and the like. At our monthly
> "Bottle Blanches" we usually presented new and *untried* Cuban orchestras
> such as Pérez Prado, Tito Puente, Mongo Santamaría, and Bobby Capó.
> Cuban Julio Iglesias toured with us for a couple of seasons. Celia Cruz came
> to these affairs both as a guest and entertainer. Among our regular partici-
> pants and followers were Helen Hayes and her daughter, Lena Horne,
> Xavier Cugat, and many others.

Dunham's work with the Maroons of Jamaica and with traditional African communities in Haiti, along with research in Cuba, Martinique, and

SOURCE: Marta Moreno Vega, "The Yoruba Orisha Tradition Comes to New York
City," *African American Review* 29.2 (1995) 201–6. Copyright 1995 by Marta Moreno
Vega. Reprinted by permission.

Senegal—among other locations—filled the productions she staged for international audiences with images, symbols, music, dance, instruments, and ritual practice of the African Diaspora. But Cuba held a special attraction for her.

On Dunham's first trip there, in 1938, she met the families of the drummers Julio Mendez and La Rosa Estrada and performed rituals that they had been unable to accomplish in New York City. And to maintain an African Diaspora focus in her dance company, she incorporated the expertise of researchers like Fernando Ortiz and Lydia Cabrera; the writing of Afro-Cuban poet Nicolás Guillén; and the music of the composer Ernesto Lecuona in her productions. "Cuban music and ritual," she writes, "were inextricably interwoven into my life—both personal and professional."[1]

When Dunham could not find drummers for her company in 1952, she returned to Cuba and recruited Julito Collazo and Francisco Aguabella, renowned percussionists in the Latino, jazz, and popular music communities who had been trained in the Orisha tradition.[2] Julito Collazo would become one of the pioneer members of a small group of Yoruba traditional practitioners who were instrumental in establishing Orisha worship in New York City. He settled in New York in 1955 when Dunham's touring company ran out of funds, and, along with Francisco Aguabella, he performed the songs, dances, and music of Afro-Cuban traditions and spread these traditions to international audiences.

In 1955, there were approximately twenty-five people in New York City who were believers in the Orisha tradition (Collazo interview). The founding member of the Orisha tradition in New York City was Babalawo Pancho Mora (Yoruba name, Ifa Morote). who arrived in New York in 1946 and, soon after, established the "first *ile,* or house of the *orishas"* there (Murphy 50). Mora had been initiated as a high priest of Ifa in Cuba on January 27, 1944, by Babalawo Quintin Lecon, a renowned Cuban Ifa priest, and was the first *babalawo* in New York to practice Ifa divination (Murphy 49–50).

Mora's belief in this ancient tradition and his desire to maintain his belief system motivated him to found the first Orisha community in the city. From his pioneering work, the tradition has grown to include thousands of initiates from all walks of life and ethnic groups. He has initiated several thousand godchildren from varied professions and international backgrounds, and has traveled extensively to Latin America and nationally to perform rituals and spread the practice of Santería (Mora interview).

On December 4, 1955, Francisco Aguabella and Julito Collazo attended their first Santería ritual in New York, a celebration to Chango (Santa Barbara) by *santero* Willie, also known as El Bolitero (The Numbers Runner), an Afro–Puerto Rican initiated in Cuba by Pancho Mora's sister.[3] Aguabella and Collazo found out about the ceremony, which took place at 111th Street and Saint Nicolas Avenue in Harlem, at the world-famous Palladium night club, where many Latin musicians gathered and played.[4]

After observing for a time the ceremony at the home of Willie El Bolitero, Collazo and Aguabella joined in the singing. They attracted much attention, since few people at the time knew the Yoruba chants to the *orishas*. As the son of the renowned *santera* Ebelia Collazo del barrio San Miguel in Cuba, Julito Collazo had grown up in the Orisha religion and learned the intricacies of this African-based tradition (Collazo interview).[5] At the age of fifteen, he was accepted into a neighborhood *batá* drum group and began his professional career. Simultaneously, Julito became more involved with other Afro-Cuban religions and increased his knowledge of the philosophies and rituals of each sect. Under the guidance of the renowned traditional *batá* drummer Pablo Roche of Cuba[6] and of master traditional drummers Raúl Diaz, Trinidad Torregrosa, Nicholas Angarica, and Miguel Somodeville, Julito Collazo became *omo* Añya, initiated in the secret knowledge of the *orisha* Añya, owner of the drum.

The Yoruba community between 1955 and 1959 included important figures in the entertainment field who helped promote the songs and music of the Santería tradition. The presence of Cuban musicians like Frank "Machito" Grillo and Mario Bauzá, founder of the Afro-Cubans Orchestra, influenced Afro-American jazz as well as Latin music. Bauzá's introduction of master Afro-Cuban drummer Chano Pozo to Dizzy Gillespie, and the incorporation of Chano Pozo—an initiate of Afro-Cuban religions—into Dizzy's orchestra, opened new musical horizons in African-American jazz.

The continued collaboration among Chano Pozo, Mario Bauza, and Dizzy Gillespie further served to popularize traditional Afro-Cuban music. Gillespie continued throughout his career to incorporate the music of Santería, the rhythms of Abakua rituals *(nañigos),* Kongo music, and others, because of his close association with these Cuban musicians. Together they developed "Cubop," the integration of two African-based musical styles:

Chano taught us all multirhythm, we learned from the master. . . . He'd teach us some of those Cuban chants and things like that. . . . You have different ones, the Nanigo, the Arrara, the Santo (music to the Yoruba

Orisha) and several others, and they each have their own rhythm. . . .
They're all of African derivation. (Gillespie 319)

The percussionists Carlos "Patato" Valdéz, Cándido Vicenty, and Mongo
Santamaría were also very influential, and the affinity of the Puerto Rican
musicians culturally and musically with Afro-Cuban music and musicians
established a strong bridge of exchange. Tito Puente, the internationally
known Puerto Rican musician, left the Afro-Cubans Orchestra during
this period to establish the Tito Puente Orchestra. The circle of musicians
that were part of his group included Puerto Ricans Willie Bobo and Ray
Barretto and Cuban Vincentico Valdéz. Although few of the Cuban musicians were initiated (Collazo interview), they were surrounded by Santería
practice in Cuba, and so they brought the philosophy, belief system, and
rituals with them to New York City. The passing on of these traditions
to Puerto Ricans during the early days of Santería practice in New York
City was critical to its growth. In fact, the first initiates in New York City
were Puerto Ricans. The similarity of languages, histories, geographic
location in the Caribbean, and racial and cultural expressions provided the
basis for easy communication and exchange.

The center of Orisha activity was located on the Upper West Side,
where most of the Afro-Cuban and Afro–Puerto Rican community resided. The Rendezvous Bar at Lenox Avenue between 113th and 114th
Streets, where stowaways from Cuba "hung out," and the beauty parlor of
Illuminada at 110th Street and Madison Avenue were popular meeting
places among Orisha believers. The concentration of Latinos in these areas
enhanced the familiarity between the two cultural groups and nurtured
the growth of the Orisha belief system.[7]

In 1956, the Afro-Cuban percussionist Mongo Santamaría organized
the first public performance of Orisha music and dance at the Palladium
night club, in tribute to the Yoruba *orisha* Chango. Julito Collazo performed songs and dances for the *orisha* Chango and made a broad audience aware of this ancient African belief system.[8]

The music of Santería continued to receive popular exposure when Tito
Puente asked Julito Collazo to participate in recordings of his orchestra.
These recordings introduced Yoruba chants for the first time in contem-
porary commercial recordings in New York City. *Latin Percussions,* one of
Tito Puente's classic albums is considered the first commercial recording
of Santería music (Collazo interview).

Another traditional leader who advanced Yoruba tradition in New York

City was Cuban-born Mercedes Nobles (Yoruba name, Oban Yoko), who traveled to New York in 1952. Yoko's mother was eight years old when her Afro-American grandparents moved to Cuba during World War I. In 1958, Yoko returned to Cuba and was initiated into the Yoruba tradition on March 9 as a priestess of Chango. Julito Collazo played for her first *cumpleaños de Santo,* her Orisha birthday celebration, on March 9, 1959 (Collazo interview).

During the late 1950s, as the Orisha community expanded in New York City, believers would return to Cuba to perform initiations. In 1961, Oban Yoko, with the consent of her *orisha,* performed the first initiation of Orisha ("mounting of the *orisha,*" or *hacer Santo*) on the head of Julia Franco, at 610 West 136th Street in Manhattan. Yoko went on to establish a *casa de Santo* ('House of Orisha') in New York City. When I interviewed her in 1981, she had initiated thirty-two people into the Orisha tradition, and as the first *santera* to initiate a recognized Orisha godchild in New York City, she established precedents for performing initiation ceremonies there. The reaction to this pioneering move was much criticized (Collazo, Scull).[9] However, Oban Yoko's pioneering spirit gave Orisha a permanent home in New York, and the presence of *babalowos* Pancho Mora and Bebo sanctioned this first step in initiating devotees in New York City. Not only did Yoko's courageous and pioneering action validate New York City initiations, but local initiation allowed people who could not afford to travel to Cuba to become recognized members of the Orisha community.

The influx of Cubans escaping the Cuban Revolution of 1959 further accelerated the belief in the Orisha tradition in New York City, as Joseph Murphy points out:

> Since the Cuban revolution of 1959, the United States has seen a reinfu-
> sion of Africanity into its melting pot. Thousands of *santeros* have come as
> exiles, bringing the orishas to America again. This has meant a second, if
> less brutal, transplantation and a second acculturation of Yoruba religion.
> This time an entirely new set of ethno-historical factors has come into play
> as *santeros* acquire North American culture and Americans feel the impact
> of Santería (115).

The growing community of Latinos, the establishment of *botánicas,* where ritual products could be sold, and the creation of Latino neighborhoods served to facilitate the practice of the religion, and as a consequence the presence of Orisha became increasingly public in the Latino community. The handful of practitioners in New York City in the early 1950s were joined by several thousand others by 1964, the year Pancho Mora held a public drum ceremony that attracted three thousand people, including Latin music stars Julio Collazo and Machito (Murphy 50). During the 1960s, Mongo Santamaría also held public celebrations to the *orisha* Chango in Latino *teatros*.

During this period, recreations of Cuban *batá* and conga drums were used. The first *batá de fundamento* was brought to New York City from Cuba in 1979.[10] These drums were ritually prepared, given voice *(darle voz a tambor)* by Papo Angarica in Cuba, a *babalawo, omo* Añya, musician, son of a famous *santero, oriyate,* and historian. Sacred drums receive the same ritual birth as people: just as initiates are born from believers—thus maintaining and extending ritual family ties through the community—the drum is born from another sacred drum, thus establishing historical and traditional linkages.

Since there were no sacred drums in the United States before Omelio Scull acquired his, it was not possible to "give birth" to sacred drums developed in New York City. Now various sets of sacred *batá* drums exist outside Cuba. One set belongs to Orlando "Puntilla" Rios, *omo* Chango, *omo* Añya, who came to the United States during the Mariel Boatlift in 1981. He is one of the most influential ritual drummers and performers of the Afro-Cuban Yoruba tradition in New York City. Once he established himself in the Orisha community, he had a set of sacred *batá* drums consecrated. Another set belongs to Puerto Rican percussionist and *omo* Añya, Louis Bauzo, who, as a traditional musician and leader of a traditional dance company, has helped promulgate the Orisha tradition.

The first African Americans to be initiated into the Yoruba belief system were Oba Sergiman and Christopher Oliana in 1959. Already versed and initiated into the Haitian system of Vodun, they sought to expand their spiritual knowledge and cultural centeredness. Pursuing Black Power strategies to empower the African American community, Oba Sergiman opened the first African American temple in West Harlem devoted to the *loas* (divinities of Dahomey) of West Africa and Haiti and the *orishas* of Cuba (originally of Yorubaland, West Africa).[11] He notes that his pride in the reclamation of Africa as part of the African American experience came with much struggle.

African Americans and Cuban Americans had to confront cultural barriers and racist attitudes before the *orishas* could encompass both communities. The participation of the African American community in Yoruba traditions increased Orisha exposure, but publicity made the Cuban traditional community uneasy, since many of its members were illegal aliens trying to maintain a low profile. The images of Catholic saints in Cuban / Puerto Rican Yoruba practice created another point of conflict between Latinos and African Americans, who wished to remove all images of western European oppression from the tradition. These issues motivated African Americans to look increasingly toward Nigeria for their development in the Orisha traditional belief system.

African Americans actively sought to incorporate the *orishas* of Cuba and *loas* of Haiti into the Black Power Revolution as a means of confronting the division between the African American and Latino communities. The inclusive vision of *santeras* Asunta Serrano, Mercedes Nobels, and Juana Manrique, along with *babalawo* Pancho Mora, helped embrace African American initiates. In the Harlem community, African Americans discovered the gods of Africa at their back doors. The Cuban and Puerto Rican communities had brought and preserved the *orishas* and made them available to the African American community. The work of anthropologists and artists like Zora Neale Hurston, Katherine Dunham, Pearl Primus, Percival Borde, W. E. B. Du Bois, and others had provided culturally grounded principles which guided the thinking, work, and practice of cultural activities of the late sixties and seventies. And Black Arts activists, in turn, incorporated the symbols, languages, images, rhythms, songs, and dress that connected our Diaspora experiences to *our root cultures.* The work of Puerto Rican visual artist Jorge Soto incorporated the symbols of *orisha* Chango, the thunder-god. The work of African American artists Amiri Baraka, Larry Neal, and Barbara Ann Teer reflected the understanding of Yoruba philosophy and practice. The works of cultural nationalists connected political struggle to cultural expansion, providing creative expressions directly connected to our historical legacies and continuity.

Works Cited

Collazo, Julito. Telephone interview. February 1995.

Dunham, Katherine. Autobiography. In progress.

Gillespie, Dizzy, with Al Fraser. *To Be, or Not . . . to Bop: Memoirs.* Garden City: Doubleday, 1979.

Mora, Pancho. Personal interview. New York, May 1981.

Murphy, Joseph M. *Santería: An African Religion in America.* Boston: Beacon Press, 1988.

Scull, Omelio. Personal interview. Puerto Rico, March 1994.

Sergiman, Oba. "History of the Orisha Tradition in New York City." Caribbean Cultural Center, New York, February 1994.

Thompson, Robert Farris. *Face of the Gods: Art and Altars of Africa and the African Americas.* New York: Museum for African Art, 1993.

Voko, Oban. Personal interview. New York, May 1981.

NOTES

1. Dunham adds, "I am definitely Yemanja. She is my guide and my mother, unless I happen to be involved in Buddhist research. Fortunately, there is not conflict between Yemanja sent out to sea in her gift-laden barque on the shores of Corcavado in Brazil, or a river whose name I do not know in Ibadan, Nigeria, or a leaky Haitian boat sent out to sea, hardly seaworthy, with a timeworn Yemanja lying on the prow on her sequin-covered bedspread, or on my balcony at Leclerc in Haiti, or right here on my small altar in East Saint Louis, Illinois. Frankly, I feel as much Cuban as anything else." (Dunham autobiography)

2. All of the leading performers who have been instrumental in the promulgation of Orisha tradition were part of the cultural aesthetic movement nurtured by Katherine Dunham. Before they became major performing artists in the Latino community, Mongo Santamaría, Tito Puente, Celia Cruz, Pérez Prado, Julito Collazo, and Francisco Aguabella all exchanged information and ideas in the nurturing environment Dunham established. The interrelationship of the cultural experiences of the African American and African Latino communities dates to the mid-Thirties, and the music of Tito Puente, Celia Cruz with La Sonora Matancera, and Celina would educate New York audiences in the songs and celebratory messages and practices of the Orisha tradition of Cuba.

3. In Cuba, December 4 is the feast date of Chango, and of Santa Barbara, the Catholic saint, who is used as a camouflage for the African *orisha* Shango.

4. Conga drums were played at the ceremony in 1955 by the Afro-Cuban musician Arsenio Rodríguez, who came to New York City around 1949, and his brother Kid, who was initiated with the *orisha* Ogun in Cuba, before coming to New York City (Collazo interview). During this period, the sacred *batá* drums used in Yoruba ceremonies had not been introduced to New York City. The *toques* (drum ceremonies) were played with conga drums solely. Collazo's account differs from Robert Farris Thompson's statement "Julito Collazo and Francisco Aguabella brought *batá* to the United States in 1955" (170). Actually they brought their skill in playing the *batá* drums and their knowledge of *toques*. Omelio Scull introduced the first set of Cuban *fundamento* drums to New York City. The first set of sacred *batá* drums arrived in New York City in 1979 (Scull interview). When Collazo first started playing *toques,* he played solo with conga drums and sang simple Yoruba chants, so that people could follow the call and response in ceremonies that provide the energy to call the *orishas* to earth to manifest themselves.

5. Collazo's mother had been initiated in Cuba by an African named Dominga Latuan.

6. Pablo Roche was a major informant for anthropologist Fernando Ortiz in his research documenting African traditions in Cuba.

7. In the early Sixties, the courts became aware of the practice of Orisha. A *santero* accused of manslaughter killed a chicken in court before the judge who was to decide his sentence, and the judge became so irate that he had the *santero* deported to Cuba. In Cuba, the *santero* was freed, since the laws of the United States did not apply to Cuba. The man is still living there (Collazo interview).

8. Robert Farris Thompson says that the first time he saw Julito Collazo perform for the *orishas* was at the Palladium night club during the Chango presentation. They were formally introduced by the orchestra leader of the Afro-Cubans, Frank "Machito" Grillo, child of the *orisha* Chango.

9. Omelio Scull also participated in this first initiation *lavando Elegun and Obatala* ("washing the *orishas* Elegua and Obatala"). This *is* part of the Orisha ritual of initiation and rebirth into the Yoruba belief system.

10. According to Omelio Scull, Olu Anya de Oba De'e (a Yoruba name indicating ownership and name of the sacred batá drum set), a master traditional drummer, brought the drum to New York City.

11. In a presentation to the Caribbean Cultural Center in New York City, Oba Sergiman recognized the need to connect the Black activist movement to a culturally grounded philosophy and lifestyle. He identified a division within the Black Power Movement between political activists and cultural activists. Sergiman's cultural activism led him to develop the first temple in West Harlem and later to establish Oyotungi Village, a Yoruba community in South Carolina.

Katherine Dunham, a Pioneer of Postmodern Anthropology

HALIFU OSUMARE

Katherine Dunham has always been a highly self-motivated applied anthropologist who works in dance and theater, both professionally and for community development. She, in fact, was one of the few African American anthropologists of the 1930s.[1] Moreover, Dunham's research-to-performance choreographic method and her published ethnographies reveal striking resonance with contemporary postmodern anthropology theory. The anthropologist Victor Turner observed that "in the modern consciousness, cognition, idea, and rationality were paramount. In the postmodern turn [since the 1970s] cognition is not dethroned but rather takes its place on an equal footing with volition and affect."[2] Indeed, Dunham has been on a quest not only cognitively to discern the relationship of Caribbean dances and rituals to their social structures but also to exert her personal will on academia through the synthesis of anthropology and dance as equal disciplines. She accomplished her dual purpose through exercising her powerful affectivity, turning her gaze to the anthropological method of fieldwork and thereby opening our awareness to the multiple dimensions of engaging the participation side of participant-observation. Summarily, Dunham created performance ethnographies on the world's greatest stages, privileged the voices of her informants in her publications, created visions of cross-cultural communication, and engaged in self-examination within the fieldwork process that far exceeded any of her contemporaries. Her resulting products and flamboyant processes reveal a postmodern anthropologist ahead of her times.

SOURCE: Halifu Osumare, "Katherine Dunham, a Pioneer of Postmodern Anthropology," unpublished essay. Copyright 2000 by Halifu Osumare. Used by permission.

In Chicago, Dunham was located in the crucible of anthropology's evolution at the same time that she was in a locus of the developing modernist
dance aesthetic. Working on her master's degree at the University of Chicago with the seminal architects of anthropology theory—such as A. R.
Radcliffe-Brown, Bronislaw Malinowski, and Robert Redfield, as well as the
great Africanist and Caribbeanist Melville Herskovits at Northwestern—
seems to have been almost predestined for Dunham. The post-Boasian
1930s provided an open-ended theoretical landscape for her anthropology
professors to explore their newfound discipline. They were, therefore,
receptive to myriad forms of human behavior, including expressive culture
like dance, ritual, and performance. As Dunham has revealed, "Social
anthropology offered the best possible solution for joining my wish to be
an anthropologist, and the great physical urge to be a dancer."[3]

Dunham conducted her field research in Haiti, Jamaica, Martinique,
and Trinidad, beginning in June 1935 during a sixteen-month field trip.
Her research yielded two ethnographies, *Journey to Accompong,* with an
introduction by anthropologist Ralph Linton, in 1946, about the Maroon
society of the Jamaican Blue Mountains, and *Island Possessed* in 1969, the
story of her intense relationship with Haiti that includes her initiation
into the Vodun religion. Her eventual master's thesis, "The Dances of
Haiti" [submitted to the Department of Anthropology at the University of Chicago in 1937 or 1938] was a major ethnological treatise in the
structural-functionalist school, based on her work with Malinowski and
Radcliffe-Brown. It was published in Spanish and English in 1947; in
French, with a foreword by Claude Lévi-Strauss in 1950; and belatedly in
English in 1983 by UCLA's Center for Afro-American Studies.

While pursuing her graduate course work, Chicago also provided seminal dance teachers and performance doyens, offering Dunham an all-
important gestation period for creative development away from the jaded
gaze of the New York dance scene. When Dunham was not allowed as
a young black dancer to take regular studio classes, segregated America
ironically provided her the benefits of private lessons with Russian ballet
dancer Ludmilla Speranzeva, a former member of Nikita Balieff's Chauve-
Souris company. Dunham's growing dance technique and her charismatic
persona won her featured stage opportunities with modern dance pioneers
Ruth Page and Mark Turbyfill at the Chicago Opera Company in productions such as the 1934 *La Guiablesse.*[4] Her own first dance company, Ballet
Nègre (later reconstituted as the Negro Dance Group) was formed during
these pre-Caribbean times. Dunham's crucial training period in Chicago

in both anthropology and dance, preceding her Caribbean fieldwork and her famous internationally touring dance company, furnished her just the right dose of academic and artistic encouragement that nurtured the anthropological and artistic iconoclast that Dunham was to become.

DUNHAM, ANTHROPOLOGY'S DEVELOPMENT, AND POSTMODERNISM

The present mood within the social sciences and the humanities is one of reassessment. Within academia, jargon such as "multiculturalism," "diversity," and "Afrocentrism" on the cultural side and "subjectivity" and "reflexivity" on the theoretical side is frequently employed in both scholarly analysis and academic policy. These terms have become buzzwords for complex agendas of rethinking our portrayal of the past and our construction of an inclusive and/or Other-centered present that privileges subjective methods over illusive "objectivity." Anthropologists Marcus and Fischer have analyzed the theoretical aspects of the paradigm shift: "It is not just the ideas themselves that are coming under attack, but the paradigmatic style in which they have been presented."[5] The contemporary postmodern movement is a theoretical era that becomes a challenging affront to previous sacrosanct modernist paradigms of conceptual representations of reality. Dunham realized both the cultural and theoretical deficiencies in the academy long before it became professionally trendy:

> Disturbed in my early years of social anthropology at the lack of emphasis on the complex of the dance in primitive society, I proposed that my scholarship from the Rosenwald and Rockefeller Institutes be directed toward an effort at repairing this lack. Also involved was an element of rebellion against the cliché often condescending attitudes toward not only Negro performing arts but those of all deprived, minority, "exotic" folk.[6]

Her keen sensitivity, probing intellect, and outsider status as a black artist-academic during America's segregation era all converged to locate her clearly in a prescient stance in relation to the theoretical and methodological changes that were yet to come.

Historically in anthropology, Franz Boas had ushered in the modern era of the discipline as the father of American cultural anthropology. He challenged the grand theories of social evolutionism fostered by Herbert Spencer, as well as cultural difussionism promulgated by Grafton Smith and Friedrich Ratzel, whose theories had in tandem created the "often condescending attitudes toward . . . 'exotic' folk." Boas set the discipline of anthropology on the road to a more "scientific" framework by developing the concept of cultural particularism, by which each culture could be viewed within its own context. Boas's students, Benedict, Mead, Kroeber, and others went on to add other conceptual frames, such as individual personality and the spurious concept of "national personality" to the equation; while theorists like Edward Sapir introduced linguistic and other psychological considerations.

Yet all of these modernist approaches, from the level of theory, presupposed a universal ordering of specific units of social organization that could be viewed in the same systematic manner by every researcher, rendering similar data. The prevailing model was that a single theoretical framework, as imposed by the anthropologist, yielded insights that were objectively measurable, revealing the "truth" about a culture. These modernist paradigms utilized the participant-observer method, but only to a point. The anthropologist, it was thought, must keep a somewhat objective stance in order to write authoritatively about the observable facts. The major presuppositions were/are (1) objectivity on the part of the researcher, (2) utilization of the same conceptual models in all cultures, (3) measurable objective truths will always emerge.

The postmodern theoretical era, since the seventies, has predictably revised these assumptions. About so-called objectivity, Stanford anthropologist Renato Rosaldo contends that

> the myth of detachment gives ethnographers an appearance of innocence, which distances them from complicity with imperialist domination. Prejudice and distortion, however, putatively derive from vices of subjectivity, passionate concern, prior knowledge, and ethical engagement. . . . [I] contest the equation of analytical distance and scientific objectivity by arguing that social analysts should explore their subjects from a number of positions, rather than being locked into any particular one.[7]

From her first field study in the Caribbean, Dunham enlisted multiple approaches to anthropological methods, long before perceptions such as Rosaldo's became commonplace.

Her earliest ethnography provides ample proof of her presaging today's accepted anthropological perspectives. We know from *Journey to Accompong* that she utilized a functionalist theoretical frame by recording the various

social institutions in relationship to each other. Kinship, ownership patterns, religion, work group organizations, clothing and material culture,
age, gender (unusual for her time), and social interaction were the sequen-
tial subject matters of her chapters. Yet, she had come there "to study
and take part in the dances." Being a trained dancer of African descent,
she easily learned the dances of the Jamaican Maroons, and immediately
participated in their acculturated European set dances that were accompanied by fiddles and hand clapping. However, Dunham was not satisfied
with these discovered dance gems. She had come to observe "the Koromantee war dance most of all," the ancient dance of the long forgotten
Asante ancestors of the Gold Coast (today's Ghana). Through patience
and some conniving to remove the repressive Colonel (chief of the settlement), she finally achieved her goal toward the end of her short six-week
stay in Jamaica:

> I plead with Ba' Weeyums for a Koromantee war dance, and find that it is
> no other than the wild dance which I saw only a suggestion of at Ol' Mis'
> Cross's gravedigging. In this I join, along with Simon Rowe and others
> who have only watched so far. The few young people who are here, how-
> ever, do not join in these traditional dances. They are ashamed, and I am
> sure that I shock them greatly; on the other hand, I feel that they watch us
> rather wistfully, wishing that they had the courage to give themselves for
> a moment to their traditions.[8]

Through her intense engagement of the participatory insider role with
the dancing Maroons, she gained historical insights that were embedded
within the dancing act itself:

> The war dances are danced by men and women. . . . The songs are in lusty
> Koromantee, and from somewhere a woman procured a rattle and is shak-
> ing it in accompaniment to Ba' Weeyums [the drummer]. Some of the men
> wave sticks in the air, and the women tear off their handkerchiefs and wave
> them on high as they dance. . . . A few of these turns, and we separate in a
> melee of leaping, shouting warriors; a moment later we are "bush fightin',"
> crouching down and advancing in line to attack an imaginary enemy with
> many feints, swerves, and much pantomime. At one stage of the dance Miss
> Mary and I are face to face, she no longer is a duppy, but a Maroon woman
> of old days, working the men up to a pitch where they will descend into
> the cockpit and exterminate one of His Majesty's red-coated platoons.[9]

Dunham's willingness to engage the Maroon dances on the culture's own terms, treating dance as another social system, allowed her a unique view into the role of the nearly forgotten Koromantee dance as a part of the Maroons' hard-won battle for independence from the British. She thus was one of the first to demonstrate the continuity of West African war dances that served enslaved Africans with similar purposes in the colonial New World. It is significant that this discovery was cognized in the act of dancing, a total immersion in enactment with the people. It has only been from today's contemporary scholarship that we realize the importance of Dunham's early transatlantic performance connections. As Africanist anthropologist Margaret Drewal revealed in the nineties about African-based performance, "[it] is a primary site for the production of knowledge, where philosophy is enacted, and where multiple and often simultaneous discourses are employed."[10]

During Dunham's sixteen-month research trip, Haiti was, by far, the island where she furthered this intense participatory approach, penetrating to the deep structure of Haitian thought exemplified in Vodun. Although the cultural-relativist, participant-observation technique had been the theorized anthropological method since Boas, her professors were clearly taken aback at the fervor in which she employed participatory fieldwork techniques. During the period when Dunham was undertaking the second level of initiation into Vodun, the *canzo* ceremony, a 1936 letter from Herskovits reflects the limits of anthropology's participant-observation method and Dunham's courage to transcend those attempted imposed boundaries:

> Once again, I am disturbed at the amount you are trying to do, this time principally because of your health. I hope you haven't contracted malaria, but whatever it is, you owe it to yourself not to try to do quite as much as you are. *I am a little disturbed also at the prospect of your going through* canzo *ceremony, and I am wondering if it would not be possible for you to attend merely as a witness.* Of course, as you know, the trial by fire is an integral part of this initiation, but I wouldn't like to see you suffer burns as a result of going through it. However, you know best in such matters. *I am not surprised that the natives are amazed at the way you pick up the dances, and that it induces them to believe that you probably have inherited* loa [a spiritual force] *that makes this possible.*[11] [my italics]

Dunham thus breaks academic tradition. She literally dances into uncharted territory in the 1930s when merely "being there" with pad and pen was deemed enough participation. Her immersion method, along with her thorough and meticulous survey of each society's social systems in relation to its dances, yielded not only Geertzian "thick description" but also a probing of the motives of the fieldworker herself in relation to her entire agenda in the field.[12] She expressed an anthropological postmodern sensibility long before it was even cognized, let alone articulated.

Dunham's emic-participatory approach was further demonstrated in her intuitive understanding that the oral literature and linguistic syntax of a people may contain perspectives on cultural values and worldview. She discovered in the language of her culture bearers a process of creolization that was the hallmark of New World experience. She not only recorded Maroon folk tales and songs, which was the normative Boasian method, but in *Journey to Accompong* she also wrote entire chapters using their English patois. Her chapter "Ninth Day" records the "Why 'm waitin' boy" story completely in vernacular. This privileging of the native voice enables the reader to adopt an insider's view of how the English language was adapted over the centuries into the Jamaican Maroons' own linguistic nuances. The story itself turned out to be a particular tale that recorded an underlying rebellious trait of the Maroons that helped propel them to revolt against British slavery, establishing their current settlements as a separate nation in the Jamaican Blue Mountains under a treaty with England. Together with written records by nineteenth-century historian Robert Renny, whose account is included in Dunham's ethnography, a more complete picture of Jamaican Maroons is systematically revealed.

Extensive use of oral history as a part of ethnography has only been legitimized in the last twenty years. In 1980 Rosaldo, in an essay in *Social Analysis,* puts the etic/emic approach into proper perspective:

> Doing oral history involves telling stories about stories people tell about themselves. Method in this discipline should therefore attend to "our stories" [written archival records], "their stories" [folk tales, songs, and in this case also dances] and the connections between them.[13]

Much of postmodernism's deconstruction is derived from literary criticism. Postmodern ethnography, in style and content, re-maps the Other from the periphery to the center of Western revisionist thought. Postmodernist James Clifford "treats ethnography itself as a performance emplotted by powerful stories. These stories simultaneously describe real cultural events, and make additional, moral, ideological, and even cosmological statements."[14] Postmodernism, then, as a "new" academic perspective, gives the researcher the permission to bring folk elements, his or her personal reflections, cross-cultural musings, and even political and moral analysis to the description of field observations.

Dunham's *Island Possessed*, published during the civil rights era, is a melange of literary devices employed to describe her many years of research in the trouble-filled, yet intoxicating island of Haiti. She tells fascinatingly interwoven stories of her friendship with several Haitian presidents and repercussions of the American occupation of Haiti that ended only right before her field research as well as giving graphic details of her initiation in the much maligned Vodun religion. "One seldom finds within the covers of one short book a harmonious combination of biography, anthropology, dance, and folklore," reflects one of the reviews of the book at that time.[15] Later, in response to a *critical* review of Dunham's ethnographic eclecticism, anthropologist Joyce Aschenbrenner reflected on Dunham's analyses of Haitian politics and politicians in *Island Possessed:*

> The inclusion of political and international figures, as well as insightful historical material, in my view, places the ethnographic descriptions in the context of a broad social and political analysis; this is more in tune with contemporary thought than descriptions treating societies as if they were self-contained.[16]

Dunham's courage to tackle the thorny politics of Haiti, as well as her own personal centrality to it vis-à-vis her relationships with key Haitian presidents, partially positioned her discourse in political-economy anthropological discourse, today known as the political economy school championed by Eric Wolfe, Talal Asad, and others.

Yet Dunham never expressed a conflict between her more "objective" structural-functionalist representation with her insider "impressionist" accounts, or her many digressions, for that matter, into what is now called the self-reflexive "confessional" genre of ethnography. Aschenbrenner, who along with Caribbeanist VèVè Clark, has done some of the most extensive critical analyses of Dunham as an anthropologist, contends that Dunham was, in fact, more in conformity with anthropology's true disciplinary mission:

> In reality, the academic profession as well as others in which anthropologists find themselves, with rigid compartmentalization and emphasis on "received"

knowledge, is in inherent opposition to the importance of fieldwork and
the holistic approach of anthropology. The more one becomes involved
with another culture, the less attractive and compelling academic aims and
imperatives are. . . . It was the conflict between these ideals and those of academia that led her to develop her own way of doing anthropology, applying her insights from the field to the arts.[17]

Dunham was never able to separate herself from her subjects or her subject in either research method or textual strategy. She was clearly on a mission that included her complete immersion in the customs, belief systems,
and lives of her chosen culture bearers. This is, in essence, the reflexive,
interactive approach, of many of today's anthropologists. But Katherine
Dunham used these approaches and methods in the 1930s, fifty years
before they began to be engaged by reputable anthropologists pushing
the envelope of the discipline. By any measure—theoretical perspective,
fieldwork methods, use of textual strategies with oral history, and today's
self-reflexive literary criticism approach—Katherine Dunham was a pioneer
of what we today call postmodern anthropology. She was never a conform-
ist to any single theory, school, or specific method. Dunham was and is an
inner-directed iconoclast, who respected her anthropological mentors, but
in the end had to do it her way.

Dunham's Adapted Theories and Applied Anthropology

Katherine Dunham developed her own theoretical paradigms that directly
resulted from her marriage of anthropology and dance. Her theory of intercultural communication, which corresponds to cross-cultural comparative
perspectives in anthropology today, is how she perceived her choreographic
works that were performed on the worlds' theatrical stages. Cultural fusion
was accomplished within the physicality of the Dunham dance technique
by merging Caribbean folk movement with modern dance and ballet. She
investigated intercultural communication also through her journalistic reflections about how her fusion dance form, as the foundation of her ballets,
might affect audience members who knew little to nothing about the cultures from which her performed ethnographies were drawn.[18] Dunham's
returning of her anthropological considerations to her native United States
and other cultures during her international tours, through her interaction with theater audiences, was, in effect, applying theory to the reality
of cultures interacting in the real world. Her staged ethnographies were

essentially what today's postmodernists call the "repatriation of anthropology as cultural critique."[19]

Dance theater became a prime laboratory for Dunham, where Afro-Caribbean cultures could "migrate" through the performance of her choreography and through the personhoods of her individual dancers in the act of performing the Dunham *oeuvre*. In this sense, Afro-Caribbean culture migrates and interacts with the consciousness of audiences from other cultures all over the world. Through her Caribbean research, Dunham accessed what Clark calls a "repository of memory" contained in the historical legacy represented by New World creole dances. Her research-to-performance method allows this "repository of memory" to act upon other cultures, thereby creating a "dance literacy," as well as intercultural communication.[20]

Dunham's cross-cultural approach through choreography rested on the functionalist anthropological theory of form and function, where manifestations of a particular cultural trait were directly connected to their functioning within the theorized integrated cultural pattern and social structure of a people. As Albirda Rose has pointed out, Dunham's adaptation of form and function was to demonstrate "how dance relates to particular cultural patterns and belief systems."[21] Both theories, of intercultural communication and of form and function, merge in her third theoretical frame, socialization through the arts. Here, Dunham directly applies what she personally learned in the dance and music-based cultures of the Caribbean: dance, music, festival, and ritual become socializing tools for effective functioning in the society. Since 1967, she has been implementing this concept through various nonprofit artistic and educational institutions within the poverty-ridden community of East Saint Louis, Illinois. Today, at age ninety-one, she continues her efforts there, particularly for youth, through the Katherine Dunham Centers of Arts and Humanities.

No matter what angle from which we view Katherine Dunham, this doyenne of dance provides a facile parallel with contemporary postmodern anthropology. Yet, this parallelism is solely for the sake of analyzing her immense contributions to scholarship and the arts. Dunham need not know today's anthropological paradigms and attendant jargon, for she implicitly reflects and transcends them. Since the 1980s, for example, with the addition of the dancer's envisioning of the Eastern-inspired *chakra* energy points along the spinal column to her barre technique, she continues to search for deeper human connections and intercultural communication. Katherine Dunham, as a visionary artist, may still be way ahead of her time.

NOTES

1. Perhaps Zora Neale Hurston, as a student of Franz Boas, was the only other. It is also significant that the two most prominent black anthropologists of that early era were women.

2. Victor Turner, *The Anthropology of Performance* (New York: PAJ Publications, 1980), 80.

3. Katherine Dunham, "Lecture-Demonstration of the Anthropological Approach to Dance," in *Kaiso!*, edited by VèVè A. Clark and Margaret B. Wilkerson (Berkeley: Institute for the Study of Social Change, 1978), 200. [Reprinted herein as "The Anthropological Approach to Dance."]

4. Ruth Page's ballet *La Guiablesse* (The Devil Woman), based on a Martinican legend, was set to a commissioned score by black composer William Grant Still. First performed for the Chicago World's Fair in 1933, it was restaged for the Chicago Opera Company in 1934.

5. George E. Marcus and Michael M. J. Fischer, *Anthropology as Cultural Critique: An Experimental Moment in the Human Sciences* (Chicago: University of Chicago Press, 1986), 7.

6. Katherine Dunham, "Dunham Technique: Prospectus," in *Kaiso!*, eds. Clark and Wilkerson, 205. [Reprinted herein.]

7. Renato Rosaldo, *Culture and Truth: The Remaking of Social Analysis* (Boston: Beacon Press, 1989), 168–69.

8. Katherine Dunham, *Journey to Accompong* (New York: Henry Holt, 1946), 134–35.

9. Ibid., 135–36.

10. Margaret Drewal, "The State of Research on Performance in Africa, " *African Studies Review* 34.3 (1991): 8.

11. VèVè A. Clark discovered this correspondence between Herskovits and Dunham in the Herskovits archives at the Africana Library of Northwestern University. Clark first presented her discovery in her paper "Performing the Memory of Difference in Afro-Caribbean Dance: Katherine Dunham's Choreography, 1938–1987," at the Katherine Dunham Symposium, Stanford University, May 12, 1989. The fields of dance and anthropology owe a great debt to her for her interest and research in this matter.

12. "Being there" is a term coined by Clifford Geertz in *Works and Lives: The Anthropologist as Author* (Stanford University Press, 1988), and the term "thick description" is a famous ethnographic term used in his development of symbolic anthropology in *The Interpretation of Cultures* (New York: Basic Books, 1973).

13. Renato Rosaldo, "Doing Oral History," *Social Analysis: Journal of Cultural and Social Practice* 4 (September 1980): 89.

14. James Clifford, "On Ethnographic Allegory," in *Writing Culture*, edited by James Clifford and George Marcus (Berkeley and Los Angeles: University of California Press, 1986), 98.

15. Joseph Schraibman, review of *Island Possessed* by Katherine Dunham, *Books*, November 16, 1969.

16. Joyce Aschenbrenner, "Anthropology as Lifeway: Katherine Dunham," in *Kaiso!*, ed. Clark and Wilkerson, 186.

17. Ibid..

18. See, for example, "La Boule Blanche," *Esquire* (September 1939): 84–85, 126, and "L'ag'ya of Martinique," *Esquire* (November 1939): 92–93, 158. [Both reprinted herein.]

19. Marcus and Fischer, *Anthropology as Cultural Critique,* 117

20. VèVè A. Clark, "Katherine Dunham: Method Dancing or Memory of Difference," in *African-American Genius in Modern Dance* (Durham, N.C.: American Dance Festival, 1992), 5–8.

21. Albirda Rose, *Dunham Technique: "A Way of Life"* (Dubuque, Iowa: Kendall/ Hunt, 1990), 20.

Katherine Dunham

One-Woman Revolution

WENDY PERRON

All roads lead to Katherine Dunham. Well, not all. But sometimes it seems to be so. Jazz dance, "fusion," and the search for our cultural heritage all have their antecedents in Dunham's work as a dancer, choreographer, and anthropologist. She was the first American dancer to present indigenous forms on a concert stage, the first to sustain a black dance company, the first black person to choreograph for the Metropolitan Opera. She created and performed in works for stage, clubs, and Hollywood films; she started a school and a technique that continue to flourish; she fought unstintingly for racial justice. She could have had her own TV show called *Dance Roots.*

Dunham, ninety-one, is in Manhattan, where she is working on an autobiography, "Minefields," while undergoing physical therapy for her surgically replaced knees. Surrounded by former dancers, friends, and a bright-eyed two-and-a-half-year-old goddaughter, she regales them with stories, songs, and warm-hearted joking.

The young Katherine Dunham studied ballet with Mark Turbyfill of the Chicago Opera and the Russian dancer Ludmilla Speranzeva. When she was only twenty-one, with Turbyfill's help, she formed the short-lived Ballet Nègre. Soon after, she started the Katherine Dunham Dance Company, which was based in Chicago during the early years. Carmencita Romero, who danced with Dunham from 1933 to 1941, said the company performed a mix of cultures even then. "We did Russian folk dances with full skirts,

Spanish dances influenced by La Argentinita and Carmen Amaya and plantation dances like *Br'er Rabbit an' de Tah Baby.*"

In 1935 Dunham, under the aegis of a Rosenwald fellowship, traveled to the Caribbean to research African-based dances. She returned in 1936, having passed rigorous initiation rites to become a *mambo*—a Vodun priestess. She soon choreographed pieces that reflect Haitian movements, for instance, the *yanvalou,* in which the spine undulates like the snake god Damballa. But more than that, she absorbed the idea of dance as religious ritual. She has said, "In Vodun we sacrifice to the gods, but the top sacrifice is dance." *Shango* (1945), which depicts such a sacrifice, hypnotized audiences during the Alvin Ailey American Dance Theater's celebration of Dunham in 1987.

Dunham also focused on American dance forms. "I was running around getting all these exotic things from the Caribbean and Africa when the real development lay in Harlem and black Americans," she says. "So I developed those things in jazz." Her revue *Le Jazz Hot* (1940) included vernacular forms like the Shimmy, Black Bottom, Shorty George, and the cakewalk. That same year, Dunham collaborated with George Balanchine in choreographing the Broadway musical *Cabin in the Sky.* She recalls, "He took an Arab song and taught it to me for a belly dance." About their collaboration, she confesses, "He was a help, but I was pretty adamant about what I wanted to do. We had a wonderful time together."

In 1943, the international impresario Sol Hurok presented Dunham's company in *Tropical Revue* at the Martin Beck Theater on Broadway, adding Dixieland jazz musicians to boost its commercial appeal. The show became a hit, enjoying a six-week run, unusual for such a revue. Dunham was a glamorous performer, and it is rumored that Hurok had insured her legs for a million dollars. In an interview with biographer Ruth Beckford, Dunham demurred, saying the amount was a mere quarter million.

Dunham opened a school in New York in 1945. Dana McBroom-Manno, who was a student there and later danced with Dunham, describes the Dunham Technique as modern with an African base.

> You use the floor as earth, the pelvis as center, holding torso and legs together. You work for fluidity, moving like a goddess, undulations like water, like the ocean. High leaps for the men. You elongate the muscles, creating a hidden strength. We use both parallel and turned out, so it's easy to go from Dunham into any other technique. The isolations of the hips, ribs, shoulders that you see in all jazz classes were brought to us from the

Caribbean by Miss Dunham. Also, she [talked about] Indian *chakra* points [in yoga, points of physical or spiritual energy in the body].

Romero, who has taught dance history at the Alvin Ailey American Dance Center, emphasizes the spiritual. "In Africa, all dance is based on animals, plants, the elements of the universe. The Dunham Technique gives you a feeling of release and exhilaration by letting the body go."

The Dunham School, in the Times Square area, thrived for ten years. Its thirty teachers offered classes in ballet, modern (José Limón was one of the modern teachers), "primitive," acting, martial arts, and more. Among its students were James Dean, Arthur Mitchell, Butterfly McQueen, and Doris Duke. Donald Saddler, recently reminiscing, said Marlon Brando would come and play drums. Sometimes jazz bassist and composer Charles Mingus would come with a group of his musicians and play for classes.

Out of the school came a student group, directed by the legendary Syvilla Fort, that included Julie Robinson [now Julie Robinson Belafonte], Walter Nicks, and Peter Gennaro. This group performed at schools and benefits. Belafonte—who met her husband, Harry, through one of these performances—recalls: "We were taught the rhythms of the movements with drums and with song in other languages: for instance, Portuguese and Haitian patois. In class anyone could break into song at any time."

The Dunham Company was an incubator for many well-known performers, including Eartha Kitt, Talley Beatty, Janet Collins, and Vanoye Aikens. In the 1940s and 1950s, its heaviest touring years, the company visited an astounding fifty-seven countries. Audience response was heady. Glory Van Scott, who danced with the company in 1959 and 1960, says, "Everywhere we went, audiences went crazy. In Paris, we'd do our show, and then we'd go dancing half the night at the Samba Club. The audience loved us so much, they would follow us there. It was unreal."

But the company encountered racism at home, and Dunham responded with defiance. In 1944, while touring in segregated Louisville, Kentucky, she found a "For Blacks Only" sign on a bus and pinned it to her dress on stage. Afterward, she declared to the audience that she wouldn't come back to a place that forbade blacks to sit next to whites.

In Dunham's *Southland* (1951), an impassioned response to the lynchings of Southern blacks, Julie Robinson played a white woman whose false accusation of rape leads to a black man's murder. "It was very, very difficult for me," Belafonte recalls. "I had to transpose my hatred of the character . . . it was an acting problem. I had to overcome it in myself."

Audience reaction was strong. Says Belafonte, "Everyone in the audience cried when we did it."

The company premiered *Southland* in Santiago, Chile, despite warnings from the State Department, which wanted U.S. cultural exports to project only positive images. Possibly as a result, Dunham did not win support from the department, which funded tours by Martha Graham, José Limón, and Paul Taylor. (In the days before the National Endowment for the Arts, this was the only program that sponsored international dance touring.) But another possible reason is that the State Department's dance panel called her work "torrid."

Dunham has lived her credo that "all artists are humanists." Her home in Haiti, Habitation Leclerc, served as a medical clinic—as well as a tourist attraction, with its nightly drumming and dancing—for many years. Having given injections of vitamin B and penicillin to ailing dancers, she administered first aid for parasites and joint diseases. Once a week, local doctors helped her to diagnose and treat patients in exchange for the medications that she could get them from New York.

Dunham moved to East Saint Louis, Illinois, during the racial troubles of the 1960s. Despite death threats and bomb scares, she helped a gang of black youths by giving them classes in martial arts, drumming, and dance. During the period, the police were picking up young black men as a matter of course. On one occasion, Dunham railed against this racial profiling, getting herself thrown in jail.

While in her eighties, she made national headlines by going on a hunger strike to protest the U.S. government's policy of returning Haitian refugees to face starvation and repression in their native land. She was supported in this effort by comedian Dick Gregory, filmmaker Jonathan Demme, and the Reverend Jesse Jackson, along with hundreds of other Americans. It was only at the coaxing of Jean-Bertrand Aristide, the deposed and later reinstated president of Haiti, that she ended her fast after forty-seven days.

Asked about her courageous stand, Dunham says simply, "You can't learn or acquire these things; I think they're just put in you from the beginning."

She is very happy about the Dunham Institute, to be held in August [see following, "Instituting Dunham," by K. C. Patrick]. She feels it is an extension of her destiny to teach—"My guiding voices tell me I should teach, and that's what I've been doing my entire life." The Dunham Technique is being taught all over the country. McBroom-Manno, who has taught Dunham Technique at Adelphi University, the Alvin Ailey American Dance Center, and now at the Ninety-second Street Y Dance Center in New York, says, "I teach Dunham Technique as a way of life. Nutrition, African-based religions, and social conscience are all part of it." Walter Nicks and Romero, who has taught dance history at the Ailey center, keep Dunham Technique alive in Europe, while McBroom-Manno passes it along in the United States.

"Everybody is an anthropologist," Dunham says. "My objective is to see that different cultures get to know each other." McBroom-Manno relates how, as a scholarship student getting free lunch at the school, she was required to learn the traditional Japanese tea ceremony. "We would be squirming and carrying on, but she wanted us to learn the serenity and silence of that tradition." In preparing for *Aïda* (1963), McBroom-Manno and the rest of the cast, dancers from both Dunham's group and the Metropolitan Opera ballet company, studied karate at the Dunham School to perfect a processional before the African king.

Her influence is global. She helped to train the Senegalese National Ballet, and her performances inspired the start of many national groups, such as Ballet Folklórico de México. Her numerous awards include the Dance Magazine Award in 1968, the Kennedy Center Honors, the American Dance Festival Scripps Award, the Albert Schweitzer Award, and just, this spring, the Duke Ellington Award.

She is still concerned about Haiti. During a May 25 interview, she was gratified to hear that very day that Haiti had help free elections without incident.

But her thoughts linger on the art of dance. "Dance has been the stepchild of the arts for a long time. I think now it's time for it to take its place among the other arts."

It is also time for Katherine Dunham to be honored as one of the great innovators in the field of dance and one of the great humanitarian artists in history.

Instituting Dunham

K. C. PATRICK

For seventeen summers, Katherine Dunham has conducted an institute in Saint Louis, Missouri (across from East Saint Louis, Illinois, where she has a home), to teach Dunham Technique to eager dancers. This year, though, when Jannas Zalesky learned that Dunham would be in New York for an extended stay, she conceived the idea of sponsoring a Dunham Institute at City Center August 12–18. Zalesky is head of City Center's Outreach Education Department, which arranges training and resources for dance educators and artist teaching in New York's enormous school system. Directed by Judith Dakin, City Center is not only an award-winning performance venue and home to major professional dance companies but also a major player in linking schoolchildren to the arts, providing arts training to their teachers, and engaging professional artists to share their expertise in schools. City Center also works closely with agencies such as Career Transitions for Dancers.

The Dunham Institute is perhaps the grandest program the Outreach Education Department has attempted. It is intended not only to encourage celebrating Dunham and her contributions to dance and society during the 2000–2001 schoolyear but also to use her holistic approach to dance as a model for dance education in public schools as well as in the dance community at large.

As a social scientist, Dunham explored such questions as what motivates a people to dance or express themselves in movement; her dance technique evolved to embrace the cultural context of each society that produced it.

SOURCE: K. C. Patrick, "Instituting Dunham," *Dance Magazine* (August 2000): 45. Copyright 2000 by *Dance Magazine,* Inc. Reprinted by permission.

Her dancers learned more than movement techniques; they were encouraged to explore and understand humanity's similarities, rather than its differences.

"Her technique and philosophy are universal," says Dr. Glory Van Scott, a scholar and former Dunham dancer. "Teachers used to get hold of her global vision. More than dance, she's life. She demanded that you do something with your life. When you take a page from her life and attach it to your own, then you do more than you thought you could."

All sessions at the Dunham Institute are to be presented by nationally recognized experts on the dances of the African diaspora, including several former Dunham Company dancers. The teaching roster includes Scott, VèVè Clark, Walter Nicks, Julian Jean, Brenda Dixon Gottschild, Joe Nash, Gil Noble, E. Gaynell Sherrod, Jeanelle Stovall, Mor Thiam, and Jawole Willa Jo Zollar. Surprise guests and drop-ins are likely to visit the sessions. Dunham Institutes are always a reunion of sorts.

Classes in Dunham Technique and Haitian dance and Afro-Caribbean music and instrumentation require daily participation. Panel presentations and seminars that look at Dunham's work in a larger social, political, and historical context are scheduled throughout the week. As is her custom, Dunham will conduct an evening conversation. A performance finale will showcase new dance works that have been created in the spirit of her life work.

Materials developed for and out of the institute will be made available on the New York City Board of Education Project ARTS Web site: www.nycenet.edu/projectarts/.

"With our historic and ongoing connections to the dance community, City Center is both delighted and honored to take a leadership role in celebrating Ms. Dunham's career and work with this momentous project," Zalesky said.

APPENDIXES
GLOSSARY
CONTRIBUTORS

Appendix 1

Stage Choreography by Katherine Dunham, 1937–1972

This partial list of Dunham's stage choreography, alphabetically arranged, was prepared by Katherine Dunham (to her best recollection), Jeanelle Stovall, and VèVè A. Clark. All dances for which no place or date is indicated were choreographed in rehearsal and were not performed. This list also does not include the dates of productions originating at the Performing Arts Training Center in East Saint Louis, Illinois.

Dance Performances

Acaraje, from *Hommage à Dorival Caymmi,* Arcachon, France, August 1952

Adeus Terras, Rome 1949

Afrique, Rome 1949

Afrique du Nord, Cave Supper Club, Vancouver, 1953

L'Ag'ya, Federal Theatre, Chicago, 27 January 1938. In five scenes: Ouverture, Market Scene, Pas de Deux, Zombie Scene, Festival Scene.

A las Montañas, Abraham Lincoln Center, Chicago, 1938. Solo concert only (first public staging). Played in October 1937 as part of *Péruvienne* with *À la Cenote.*

Amazon

Anabacoa, Club Antilles in the Hotel Chalfonte–Haddon Hall, Atlantic City, New Jersey, 1963

SOURCE: Ruth Beckford, *Katherine Dunham: A Biography* (New York and Basel: Marcel Dekker, 1979), 131–35. Copyright 1979 by Ruth Beckford. Reprinted by permission. Minor corrections have been made.

Angelique (or *Angelico* from *Haitian Suite*), Ciro's, Hollywood, 1948

Argentine Country Dances

Babalu, Curran Theatre, San Francisco, December 1941

Baby San

Bahiana, University of Cincinnati, 1939

Bajao

Bal Nègre, Belasco Theatre, New York, and tour, 1946

Bamboche!, 54th Street Theatre, New York, 1962

Banana Boat, Empire Theatre, Manila, 1957

Banda

Barrelhouse, 1938

Batucada, Teatro Esperanza Iris, Mexico City, 1947

Bertha the Sewing Machine Girl (from *Pins and Needles 1940*), Windsor
    Theatre, New York, 1939

Big Ballet, from the film *Mambo,* 1954

Biguine-Biguine, 1937; sometimes entitled *Béguine* or *Béquine-Béguine*

Black Panther

Blues Trio, Ciro's, Hollywood, 1948

Bolero, Teatro Esperanza Iris, Mexico City, 1947

Boogie Woogie Pray

Br'er Rabbit an' de Tah Baby, Goodman Theatre, Chicago, 1938

Cakewalk (from *Br'er Rabbit an' de Tah Baby*), Goodman Theatre, Chicago,
    November 1938

Callate, Royal Alexandra Theatre, Toronto, January 1944

Caribbean Rhapsody, Prince of Wales Theatre, London, and tour, 1948

Carnaval, Broadway Theatre, New York, November 22, 1955

Carib Song, Adelphi Theatre, New York, October 1945

Caymmi (Hommage à Dorival Caymmi), Arcachon, France, August 1952

C'est Lui, Martinique Club, New York, 1947

Choros, first performed at Royal Alexandra Theatre, Toronto, January 1944,
    nos. 1–5

Ciudad Maravillosa, 1939

La Comparsa (from *Motivos*), Temple Theatre, Portland, Oregon, January
    1946

Concert Rhumba, 1939

Congo Femme (from *Haitian Suite*), Curran Theatre, San Francisco, Decem-
    ber 1941

Cuban Danzon, Brooklyn Academy of Music, New York

Cumbancha, 1939

Cumbia, Cave Supper Club, Vancouver, 1953

Diablitos

Diamond Thief, New York, 1962

Dora, Cave Supper Club, Vancouver, 1953

Dos Hermanos

Doudou

Drum Ritual

Drum Session

Field Hands (from *Plantation Dances*), Windsor Theatre, New York, May 1940

Flaming Youth, 1927, New Britain, Connecticut, February 1944

Floor Exercises, Dunham Experimental Group, Montclair Y.W.C.A., Montclair, New Jersey, 7 November 1947

Florida Swamp Shimmy, 1937

Floyd's Guitar Blues, Ciro's, Hollywood, 1955

Frevo, Paris, 1951

Haitian Roadside, Temple Theatre, Portland, Oregon, January 1946

Haitian Suite (includes *Congo Paillette, Yonvalou,* and *Zépaules*) Abraham Lincoln Center, Chicago, January 1937

Harry (I'm Just Wild about Harry), Ciro's, Hollywood, 1955

Havana 1910/1919 (from *Promenade* in *Tropical Revue*), Opera House, San Francisco, March 1944

Honey in the Honeycomb, Cave Supper Club, Vancouver, 1953

Honky Tonky Train (from *Le Jazz "Hot"*), Curran Theatre, San Francisco, December 1941

Hounci Canzo

Incantation, Cave Supper Club, Vancouver, 1953

Los Indios, Santiago de Chile, December 1950

Island Songs, Goodman Theatre, Chicago, 1938

Jazz Finale, Ciro's, Hollywood, 1955

Le Jazz "Hot" (includes *Boogie Woogie Prayer, Honky Tonky Train,* and *Barrelhouse*), Goodman Theatre, Chicago, 1938

Jazz in Five Movements, Théâtre National, Paris, March 1949

Lazarus

Lotus Eaters, 1937

Macumba, Ciro's, Hollywood, 1948

Madame Christoff (Sarabande to Madame Christophe, Queen of Haiti), Goodman Theatre, Chicago, October 1937

Maracas

Mexican Rumba, Goodman Theatre, Chicago, November 1938

Missouri Waltz, c.1948

Mozart

Nañigo (from *Motivos*), Temple Theatre, Portland, Oregon (?), January 1946

New Jazz

New Love, New Wine, Ciro's, Hollywood, 1955

Nibo (from *Island Songs*), Goodman Theatre, Chicago, 1938

Nostalgia, Temple Theatre, Portland, Oregon (?), January 1946

Octoroon Ball, Mexico, 1947

Ode to Taylor Jones, 1968

Para Que Tu Veas, Royal Alexandra Theatre, Toronto, January 1944

Péruvienne, Goodman Theatre, Chicago, 1938

Plantation Dances, Windsor Theatre, New York, May 1940

Planting Rice, Manila, 1957

Preludios, Santiago de Chile

Processional

Quirino (from *Street Scene*), Prince of Wales Theatre, London, fall 1948

Ragtime (from *Nostalgia*), 1946. Performed as a separate piece at Ciro's, Hollywood, 1948.

Ramona, vocal group, Ciro's, Hollywood, 1952

Rara Tonga, originally the opening section of *Primitive Rhythms,* first performed at the Goodman Theatre, Chicago, October 1937. Performed as a solo at the Forrest Theatre, New York, November 1943.

Rhumba Jive, Curran Theatre, San Francisco, 1941

Rhumba Rhapsody

Rhumba Trio, Instituto Nacional de Bellas Artes, Mexico City, 1947

Rhumba Variations

Rites de Passage, Curran Theatre, San Francisco, December 1941. Scenes include (1) Puberty, (2) Fertility, (3) Death, (4) Women's Mysteries.

Samba, Brazilian Suite, 1954

Saudade da Brazil, Goodman Theatre, Chicago, March 1938

Schulhoff Tango, Abraham Lincoln Center, Chicago, January 1937

Shango (from *Carib Song*), October 1945

Sister Kate, Manila, 1957

Son (from *Primitive Rhythms*), October 1938

Southland, Teatro Municipal, Santiago de Chile, January 1951

Spanish Earth Suite, Goodman Theatre, Chicago, 1938

Spirituals, Théâtre des Champs-Elysées, Paris, 1951

Street Scene, Prince of Wales Theatre, London, 1948
Strutters Ball (from *Plantation Dances*), Forrest Theatre, New York, November 1943
Tango (from *Jazz in Five Movements*)
Ti' Cocomacaque, Sankei Hall, Tokyo, 1957
Tropics, Abraham Lincoln Center, Chicago, 1937
Tropical Revue, Forrest Theatre, New York, November 1943
La Valse, Palacio de Bellas Artes, Mexico City, 1947
Valse Creole
Veracruzana. Ciro's, Hollywood, 1948
Washerwoman, Paris, August 1952
Wine Door
Woman with the Cigar, 1938
Xaxado (from *Carnaval*), Broadway Theatre, New York, 22 November 1955
Yemaya, Ciro's, Hollywood, 1955

Musical Plays

Cabin in the Sky (in collaboration with George Balanchine), Martin Beck Theatre, New York, and national tour, 1940–1941
Ciao, Rudi (artistic collaborator), Rome, 1965
Les Deux Anges Venus, Théâtre de Paris, 1965
Tropical Pinafore, Chicago, 1939
Windy City, Great Northern Theatre, Chicago, 13 May 1947

Operas

Aïda, Metropolitan Opera House, New York, 1963
Faust, Southern Illinois University, Carbondale, 1965
Treemonisha, Morehouse College, Atlanta, 27 January 1972; Wolftrap Farm Park for the Performing Arts, Vienna, Virginia, 1972

Appendix 2

Film Choreography by
Katherine Dunham 1939–1964

This list of Dunham's film choreography, chronologically arranged, was originally researched and documented by Giovannella Zannoni for publication in Ruth Beckford's 1979 biography of Miss Dunham. For this new edition of *Kaiso!* it has been researched and amended by Claude Conyers.

1939. CARNIVAL OF RHYTHM. Released 1941. Country: U.S.A. Language: English / Spanish / Portuguese. Color (Technicolor). Runtime: 18 minutes. A Warner Bros. production. Directed by Jean Negulesco. Written by Stanley Martin. Short film entirely dedicated to Katherine Dunham and Company, including Archie Savage and Talley Beatty. Choreography by Katherine Dunham. Costume design by John Pratt. Includes *Ciudad Maravillosa* and early versions of *Los Indios, Batucada*, and *Adeus Terras,* all Brazilian dances set to Brazilian music.

1942. STAR SPANGLED RHYTHM. Country: U.S.A. Language: English. Black and white. Runtime: 99 minutes. A Paramount Pictures production. Directed by George Marshall. Principal players are Betty Hutton, Eddie Bracken, Victor Moore, and numerous Hollywood stars appearing as themselves. Featured dancers are Vera Zorina and Katherine Dunham. Dunham appears as the dance partner of Eddie "Rochester" Anderson in "Sharp as a Tack," a production number with music by Harold Arlen and lyrics by Johnny Mercer. The song is sung solo by a zoot-suited Rochester; the dance is a strutting jive duet choreographed by Danny Dare and Katherine Dunham (uncredited).

SOURCE: Based on Giovannella Zannoni, "Film Choreography by Dunham," in Ruth Beckford, *Katherine Dunham: A Biography* (New York: Marcel Dekker, 1979), 136–39.

1942. PARDON MY SARONG. Country: U.S.A. Language: English. Black and white. Runtime: 84 minutes. A Universal Pictures production. Directed by Eric C. Kenton. Principal players are Bud Abbott, Lou Costello, Virginia Bruce, and Robert Paige. Featured performers are Nan Wynn, Marie McDonald, The Four Ink Spots, and Tip, Tap, and Toe. Dances designed and staged by Katherine Dunham. No personal appearance by either Katherine Dunham or her company.

1943. STORMY WEATHER. Country: U.S.A. Language: English. Black and white. Runtime: 78 minutes. A Twentieth Century–Fox production. Directed by Andrew L. Stone. Principal players are Bill Robinson and Lena Horne. In this show-business story of a song-and-dance man (Robinson) and his romance with a beautiful singer (Horne), Ada Brown, Fats Waller, Cab Calloway, and the Nicholas Brothers appear as themselves. Dooley Wilson appears in a supporting role, and Janet Collins (uncredited) is featured in one production number. Katherine Dunham and Her Dancers appear during the break in Lena Horne's performance of the title song, "Stormy Weather," an urban version of the blues. In 2001, *Stormy Weather* was added to the National Film Registry by the National Film Preservation Board.

1948. CASBAH. Country: U.S.A. Language: English. Black and white. Runtime: 94 minutes. A Universal Pictures production. Directed by John Berry. Principal players are Yvonne De Carlo, Tony Martin, Peter Lorre, and Tommy Gomez. Katherine Dunham (uncredited) appears as Odette; Eartha Kitt appears as herself. Katherine Dunham and Company appear in two scenes, the Ramadan Festival and the Casbah Nightclub; choreography by Katherine Dunham.

1949. BOTTA E RISPOSTA. Country: Italy. Language: Italian. Black and white. Runtime: 93 minutes; cut to 80 minutes for U.S. distribution. Produced by Dino de Laurentiis for Teatri della Farnesina, Rome. Directed by Mario Soldati. Principal players are Nino Taranto, Isa Barzizza, and Suzy Delair. Louis Armstrong, Fernandel, Katherine Dunham and Company, and Isa Miranda are featured. Includes the following numbers from the Dunham repertory: *Batucada* and *Jazz in Five Movements* (segment). The title of the film, *Botta e risposta,* is an Italian idiom meaning "sharp reply to the point," "repartee," "witty retort." The international English title is *I'm in the Revue.*

1954. MAMBO. Released 1955. Country: Italy and U.S.A. Language: English. Black and white. Runtime: 110 minutes. Produced by Carlo Ponti and Dino de Laurentiis for Teatri della Farnesina, Rome, and Paramount

Pictures, Hollywood. Directed by Robert Rossen. Original music by Dave Gilbert, Angelo Francesco Lavagnino, Bernardo Noriega, and Nino Rota. Principal players are Silvana Mangano, Michael Rennie, Vittorio Gassman, and Shelley Winters. Katherine Dunham appears as a dance teacher. Includes exclusive and rare footage of the Dunham Company in classroom demonstrations of Dunham Technique. Five numbers were choreographed by Katherine Dunham expressly for this film: *Coboclo do Mato* (sung and danced by Katherine Dunham), *Baiao* (never performed on stage), *Sube Espuma* (danced by Katherine Dunham; later performed on stage in a different version), *New Love, New Wine,* and *Mambo* (performed on stage in a different version under the title *Mambo Finale*).

1954. DIE GROßE STARPARADE. (*The Great Star Parade;* also known as *Gloria-Starparade* and *Liebessender*). Country: West Germany. Language: German. Black and white. Runtime: 98 minutes. Produced by Artur Brauner and Léon Canel for CCC Film Kunst, GmbH, Berlin. Directed by Paul Martin. Original music by Michael Jary. Principal players are Adrian Hoven, Renate Holm, Gunther Philipp, and Michael Jary. Featured dancers are Katherine Dunham and Company, Heinz Holl, Harald Horn, and Liane Müller. Costume design for the Dunham company by John Pratt. Includes the following numbers from the Dunham repertory: *Choros* (no.1 and no. 4), *Shango,* and *Tropics.*

1955. MÚSICA EN LA NOCHE (*Music in the Night*). Released 1958. Country: Mexico. Language: Spanish. Color. Runtime: 85 minutes. Produced by Alianza Cinematográfica Mexicana, Mexico City. Directed by Tito Davidson. Featured dancers are Carmen Amaya and Company and Katherine Dunham and Company. Includes the following numbers from the Dunham repertory: *Dora* and *Cakewalk.*

1958. GREEN MANSIONS. Released 1959. Country: U.S.A. Language: English. Color. Runtime: 104 minutes. Produced by Metro-Goldwyn-Mayer. Directed by Mel Ferrer. Based on the novel by William Henry Hudson. Principal players are Audrey Hepburn and Anthony Perkins. Original music by Bronislau Kaper and Heitor Villa-Lobos. Choreography by Katherine Dunham. No personal appearance by either Katherine Dunham or her company.

1960. KARAIBISHE RHYTHMEN (*Caribbean Rhythms*). Country: Austria. Language: German. Black and white. Produced for television by WDR Fernsehen, Köln, West Germany. Directed by Gunther Hassert. A television special devoted to Katherine Dunham and Her Company.

Includes the following numbers from the Dunham repertory: *Afrique, Rhumba Trio, Choros* (nos. 1 and 4), *Cumbia, Samba, Floyd's Guitar Blues, Strutters' Ball,* and *Cakewalk.*

1964. THE BIBLE / LA BIBBIA (also known as *The Bible . . . In the Beginning*). Country: U.S.A. and Italy. Language: English. Color (DeLuxe). Runtime: 174 minutes. Produced by Dino de Laurentiis for Twentieth Century–Fox and Seven Arts. Directed by John Huston. Written by Vittorio Bonicelli, Christopher Fry, Jonathan Griffin, Ivo Perilli, Mario Soldati (uncredited), and Orson Welles (uncredited). John Huston appears as Noah and supplies the voices of God, The Serpent, and the narrator; George C. Scott and Ava Gardner appear as Abraham and Sarah; Peter O'Toole portrays the Three Angels. Katherine Dunham conceived, staged, and choreographed the dance sequences for two scenes: the Festival and the destruction of Sodom and Gomorrah. No personal appearance by Katherine Dunham or her company.

Appendix 3

Selected Bibliography of Writings by Katherine Dunham

Items are arranged in chronological order within each category. Compiled by Sara E. Johnson.

BOOKS

Katherine Dunham's Journey to Accompong. With an introduction by Ralph Linton and illustrations by Proctor Fyffe ("Ted") Cook. New York: Henry Holt, 1946. Reprint, Westport, Conn.: Negro Universities Press, 1971.

Las danzas de Haití (in Spanish and English). Translated by Javier Romero. *Acta antropológica* (Mexico) 2.4 (1947). Published in French as *Les danses d'Haïti,* with a foreword by Claude Lévi-Strauss. Paris: Fasquelle Éditeurs, 1950. Revised and published in English as *Dances of Haiti,* with photographs by Patricia Cummings. Los Angeles: Center for Afro-American Studies, University of California, 1983.

A Touch of Innocence: Memoirs of Childhood. New York: Harcourt, Brace, 1959. Reprint, University of Chicago Press, 1994.

Island Possessed. New York: Doubleday, 1969. Reprint, University of Chicago Press, 1994.

Kasamance: A Fantasy. Illustrated by Bennie Arrington after original drawings by John Pratt. New York: Odarkai Books, 1974.

"Minefields." An autobiography in progress. As yet unpublished.

ARTICLES AND ESSAYS

"La Boule Blanche" (under the pseudonym Kaye Dunn). *Esquire* 12.3 (September 1939): 92–93, 158.

"L'ag'ya of Martinique" (under the pseudonym Kaye Dunn). *Esquire* 12.5 (November 1939): 84–85, 126.

"The American Negro Dance and Its West Indian Affiliations." In *The Negro Caravan,* edited by Sterling A. Brown, Arthur P. Davis, and Ulysses Lee, 990–1000. New York: Dryden Press, 1941.

"Thesis Turned Broadway." *California Arts and Architecture* (August 1941): 19.

"Form and Function in Primitive Dance." *Educational Dance* 4.10 (October 1941): 2–4.

"Goombay." *Mademoiselle* (November 1945).

"Notes on the Dance, with Special Reference to the Island of Haiti." In *Seven Arts,* edited by Fernando Puma, 69–76. New York: Doubleday, 1954.

"The Caribbean: Islands Now and Then." *Show* (November 1963).

"Caribbean Tourist Tips: Avoid Friction by Preparing for Your Caribbean Vacation." *Travel* (February 1964).

"Open Letter to Black Theaters." *Black Scholar* 8 (July–August 1979): 5.

Stories and Poems

"Come Back to Arizona." *The Brownies' Book* 2 (August 1921). A periodical edited by W. E. B. Du Bois and published by Du Bois & Dill, New York.

"Afternoon into Night." *Bandwagon* 13 (June 1952). Reprinted in *Best Short Stories by Negro Writers,* edited by Langston Hughes. Boston: Little, Brown, 1967.

"Baio." Lyrics to music by Bernardo Noriega, dated Rome, 18 January 1954.

"Audrey." *Phylon* 15 (June 1954): 147–53.

"Béguine." Lyrics to music by Bernardo Noriega, dated Buenos Aires, 20 October 1954.

"The Crime of Pablo Martínez." *Ellery Queen's Magazine* (1964).

"The Babies of Biafra." In *A Galaxy of Black Writing,* edited by R. Baird Shuman. Durham, N.C.: Moore Publishing Co., 1970.

"Elifait," 1972. An unpublished manuscript in the Katherine Mary Dunham Papers, Special Collections, Morris Library, Southern Illinois University, Carbondale.

Speeches and Lectures

"Lecture Demonstration on the Anthropological Approach to Dance and the Practical Application of This Approach to the Theater." Delivered at the University of California, Los Angeles, October 1942.

"Comment to a Louisville Audience." Made in Memorial Auditorium, Louisville, Kentucky, 19 October 1944.

"The State of Cults among the Deprived." Address delivered to the Royal Anthropological Society, London, 1948.

"O estado dos cultos entre os povos deserdados." Paper given at the conference of the Teatro Experimental do Negro, Rio de Janeiro, June 1950. Published in *Quilombo* (Junho–Julho 1950): 5–7, 10.

"This Historic Necessity for Music." Address delivered 11 November 1963. Published in *Musical America* (December 1963): 157–58.

"Lecture Notes on the Dance in Modern Society." Delivered at the Faculty Club, Southern Illinois State University, 4 June 1965.

Address delivered at the first World Black and African Festival of Arts and Culture (also known as the first World Festival of Negro Arts), Dakar, Senegal, 3 April 1966.

"Reflections on Survival." Commencement address delivered to the graduating class of MacMurray College, Jacksonville, Illinois, 21 May 1972.

"Dance as a Cultural Art and Its Role in Development." Address delivered by Jeanelle Stovall on the occasion of Léopold Sédar Senghor's seventieth birthday. Dakar, Senegal, in 1976.

Miscellaneous Writings

Unless otherwise noted, the unpublished papers below are housed in the Katherine Mary Dunham Papers, Special Collections, Morris Library, Southern Illinois University, Carbondale.

"Statement on need for study of dances of primitive peoples." Undated.

"The Dance in the National Youth Administration." 1941–42.

"Preface." In *Isles of Rhythm* by Earl Leaf. New York: A. S. Barnes, 1948.

"Dunham Technique: Prospectus." February 1963.

"Dances by Dunham." Program for performance of Giuseppi Verdi's *Aïda* at the MetropolitanOpera House, December 14, 1963.

"The World in Dance and Ritual: World Dance Film Project." January 1964.

"The Dunham Schools." 1964.

"Plan for Gorée as Residence Academy for West African Cultural Arts."
1965.

"Performing Arts Training Center as a Focal Point for a New and Unique
College or School." 1970.

"Foreword." In *Black Dance in the United States from 1619 to 1970*, edited
by Lynne Fauley Emery. Palo Alto: National Press Books, 1972.

Appendix 4

Selected Bibliography of Writings about Katherine Dunham

The following bibliography includes a selection of textual sources. There is a wealth of information, including audio interviews, videos, and electronic sources that are also available. Items are arranged alphabetically, by author or by title, in each category. Compiled by Sara E. Johnson.

BIOGRAPHIES

Aschenbrenner, Joyce. *Katherine Dunham: Dancing a Life.* Urbana: University of Illinois Press, 2002.

Beckford, Ruth. *Katherine Dunham: A Biography.* New York: Marcel Dekker, 1979.

Biemiller, Ruth. *Dance: The Story of Katherine Dunham.* Garden City, N.Y.: Doubleday, 1969.

Dominy, Jeannine. *Katherine Dunham.* Senior consulting editor, Nathan Irvin Huggins. With an introductory essay by Coretta Scott King. New York: Chelsea House, 1992.

Donloe, Darlene. *Katherine Dunham.* Los Angeles: Melrose Square, 1993.

Greene, Carol. *Katherine Dunham, Black Dancer.* Chicago: Children's Press, 1992.

Harnan, Terry. *African Rhythm–American Dance: A Biography of Katherine Dunham.* New York: Knopf, 1974.

Haskins, James. *Katherine Dunham.* New York: Coward, McCann & Geoghegan, Inc., 1982.

O'Connor, Barbara. *Katherine Dunham: Pioneer of Black Dance.* Minneapolis: Carolrhoda Books, 2000.

Related Works

Aschenbrenner, Joyce. *Katherine Dunham: Reflections on the Social and Political Contexts of Afro-American Dance.* With notations of the Dunham Method and Technique by Lavinia Williams Yarborough. CORD 1980 Dance Research Annual, 12. New York: Congress on Research in Dance, Inc., 1981.

Buckle, Richard. *Katherine Dunham, Her Dancers, Singers, Musicians.* Illustrated by Roger Wood and other photographers. London: Ballet Publications, 1949.

Caribbean Cultural Center. *The Worldview of Katherine Dunham.* Edited by Gayle Louison and Mora J. Byrd. Catalog for two photodocumentary exhibitions celebrating the life and work of Katherine Dunham. New York: Franklin H. Williams Caribbean Cultural Center African Diaspora Institute, 1994.

Clark, Vèvè A., and Margaret B. Wilkerson, eds. *Kaiso! Katherine Dunham: An Anthology of Writings.* Berkeley: University of California, Institute for the Study of Cultural Change, CCEW Women's Center, 1978.

Hughes, Langston, and Milton Meltzer. *Black Magic: A Pictorial History of the Negro in American Entertainment.* Englewood Cliffs, N.J.: Prentice-Hall, 1967.

Kitt, Eartha. *Thursday's Child.* New York: Duell, Sloan & Pearce, 1956.

Lloyd, Margaret. *The Borzoi Book of Modern Dance.* New York: Knopf, 1949. Reprint, New York: Dance Horizons, 1969.

Long, Richard A. *The Black Tradition in American Dance.* Photographs selected and annotated by Joe Nash. New York: Rizzoli, 1989.

Rose, Albirda. *Dunham Technique: A Way of Life.* Dubuque: Kendall/Hunt, 1990.

Woody, Regina L. *Student Dancer.* Boston: Houghton Mifflin, 1951.

Articles, Reviews, and Press Notices, 1938–1965

"Andre Drew School of the Dance." *Ebony* (June 1956): 27–30.

"Anthropologist." *New Yorker* (22 February 1941): 14.

"Anthropology, Hot," *Time* 35.12 (18 March 1940): 32.

B, Sig. "Success for the Dunham Ballet." *Dagens Nyheder* (Copenhagen), 15 June 1959.

Baignères, Claude. "Ballets Folkloriques; Katherine Dunham à Paris." *Musica Disques* (January 1960): 14–16.

"Balanchine Stages a Play." *Dance Magazine* (November 1940): 10–11.

"Ballet Beauty to Seek Dance Fame in U.S." *Jet* (1 July 1953): 34–35.

"Ballet on Bare Toes." *Ekstrabladet* (Copenhagen), 15 June 1959.

Beiswanger, George. "Broadway Steps Out." *Theatre Arts* (January 1941): 32–39.

Beyer, W. H. "State of the Theatre." *School and Society* (3 June 1950): 342.

Bland, Alexander. "Katherine Dunham & Co." *Ballet* 12.3 (March 1952): 4–17.

"Bring 'Em Back Dancing: Hunting Talent in Western Africa." *Life* (16 November 1962): 99–100.

Buckle, Richard. "The Adventures of a Ballet Critic." *Ballet* 11.8 (September 1951): 28–30.

"Bull-ring Performance in Lima." *Dance News* 18.4 (April 1951): 4.

Butcher, Fanny. Review of *Touch of Innocence*. *Chicago Tribune*, 25 October 1959.

Cain, Harold. "Two on the Aisle." *Portland (Oregon) Evening Express*, 11 February 1960.

"Career Sketch." *Dance and Dancers* (January 1952): 5.

"A Caribbean Rhapsody." *Dancing Times* (July 1948): 526.

Christout, Marie-Françoise. "Katherine Dunham." *Dance and Dancers* (January 1960): 29.

Chujoy, Anatole. "Katherine Dunham and Company at Broadway Theatre, New York." *Dance Magazine* (January 1956): 9.

Cluzel, Magdeleine. *Glimpses of the Theatre and Dance*. Trans. Lily and Baird Hastings. New York: Kain Publishers, 1953.

Comons, Grace. "The Hard Way." *Hartford Courant*, 21 November 1959.

"Composer Here for Showing of 'La Guiablesse'." *Chicago Defender*, 8 December 1934.

Cosman, Milein. "Pages du journal d'un français à Londres." *Ballet* 6.2 (November 1948): 36–39.

"Crowd at Negro Dance Recital: Folk Dances of Many Lands Featured in Dance Recital," *New York Age*, 13 March 1937, 9.

Davis, Luther, and John Cleveland. "Partly Primitive: Katherine Dunham, the Marian Anderson of the Dance." *Collier's* (11 January 1941): 22–23+.

Denby, Edwin. "Miss Dunham in Review." *New York Herald Tribune*, 26 September 1943.

"DK a Success—All the Same." *Aktuelt* (Copenhagen), 15 June 1959.

Drutman, Irving. "Anthropology Plus Jazz." *Negro Digest* 2 (December 1943): 47–48.

"Dunham Dance Graduates." *Ebony* (June 1953): 48–53.

"Dunham Dancers on Stage." *New York Post,* 19 October 1940.

"Dunham Dances." *Christian Science Monitor,* 29 April 1950.

"Dunham Dances." *Life* (8 November 1943): 69–72.

"Dunham Denounces Kentucky Jimcro," *People's Voice* (11 November 1944): 28.

"Dunham Returns to Broadway." *Musical America* (December 1955): 25.

"Dunham's Return." *Newsweek* (1 May 1950), 74.

"Dunham's Revue to Broadway." *Dance Magazine* (October 1962): 3.

Eaton, Quaintance. "Dunham Dance Group Returns after Two Years in Europe." *Musical America* (May 1950): 7+.

"Eleven New Dancers for Met Ballet." *Dance Magazine* (October 1963): 3.

Elias, Albert J. "Conversation with Katherine Dunham." *Dance Magazine* (February 1956): 16–19.

Farjeon, Annabel. "Lives of Dancers." *Dance Magazine* (March 1961): 21–22.

Guthman, Louise, et al. "Reviews of the Month." *Dance Observer* (January 1956): 10–12.

Haines, Aubrey B. "Katherine Dunham: Anthropologist-Dancer, Part 1." *Dance Digest* (December 1956): 445–48.

———. "Katherine Dunham: Anthropologist-Dancer, Part 2." *Dance Digest* (January 1957): 14–17.

Harrison, John. "Katherine Dunham: Review of Jamaica Performance." *Ballet* 11.6 (July 1951): 52.

Haskell, Arnold L. "Balletomane's Log Book: The Value of a Dancer." *Dancing Times* (October 1954): 16.

Herring, Doris. "Katherine Dunham and Company in *Bamboche.*" *Dance Magazine* (December 1962): 30+.

———. "Reviews: Katherine Dunham and Company, November 22–December 17, 1955, The Broadway Theatre." *Dance Magazine* (January 1956): 11+.

Herzog, Emily. "K. Dunham, Anthropologist." *Who* (May 1941): 42–44.

Hubner, Alma. "Primitive Rhythms in Paris." *Dance and Dancers* (May 1950): 19.

Hughes, Allen. "Revue by Katherine Dunham." *New York Times,* 23 October 1962.

Hughes, Langston. Review of *Touch of Innocence. New York Herald Tribune,* 25 October 1959.

"An Interim of Dancing: Negro Dance Recital Enthralls Audience," *New York Amsterdam News,* 13 March 1937: 9.

Jackson, Frank. "Katherine Dunham Again." *Ballet Today* (February 1952): 14.

Janeway, Elizabeth. "A Way of Looking at the World." *New York Times,* 8 November 1959.

"K. Dunham's 'La Boule Blanche.'" *New York Amsterdam News,* 10 July 1948: 7.

"Katherine Dunham." *Crisis* (June 1950): 344.

"Katherine Dunham." *Paris théâtre* (October 1954): 45.

"Katherine Dunham: Ambassador with Hips." *Our World* (September 1950): 42–44.

"Katherine Dunham and Dancers in Ti' Cocomacaque." *Theatre Arts* 26:8 (August 1942): 524.

"Katherine Dunham Appears in Revue: Program of Primitive and Comic Choreography." *Musical America* (October 1943): 15.

"Katherine Dunham, Four Dances." *Theatre Arts* (April 1945): 251.

"Katherine Dunham Leaves Havana Engagement to Choreograph a Film in Italy." *Dance Magazine* (November 1953): 3.

"Katherine Dunham Spices Up Dance Revue." *Ebony* (August 1955): 25–27.

"Katherine Dunham, Teacher." *Dance Magazine* (June 1945): 28.

"Katherine Dunham's New Show." *Sepia* (November 1962): 71–74.

Lowe, Ramona. "Being a Close-up on Miss Dunham," *New York Amsterdam News,* 18 September 1943, 8B.

L'Rue, June. "Want to Learn to Dance?" *Pittsburgh Courier,* 20 December 1952.

Martin, John. "The Dance—A Negro Art: Katherine Dunham's Notable Contribtution." *New York Times,* 25 February 1940.

———. "Dance Recital Given by Negro Artists," *New York Times,* 30 April 1931: 27.

———. "Dunham." *New York Times,* 14 May 1950.

———. "Elysian Jazz." *New York Times,* 10 November 1940.

———. "Katherine Dunham Gives Dance Revue." *New York Times,* 20 September 1943.

———. "Katherine Dunham Returns." *New York Times,* 23 November 1955.

———. "Negro Dance Art Shown in Recital." *New York Times,* 19 February 1940.

———. "Tropical Revue." *New York Times,* 3 October 1943.

"Master of Arts." *American* (May 1945): 135.

Matthias, Blanche C. "Katherine Dunham" *Opportunity* (April 1941): 112.

Mendes, Murilo. "Uma negra e sua equipe." *Quilombo* (June–July 1950).

Mishnun, V. "Dunham Tropical Revue." *Nation* (9 October 1943): 416.

"Miss Dunham Trains Dancers for New Film." *Ebony* (October 1958): 121–22+.

"Movies in the Making: *Green Mansions.*" *Dance Magazine* (February 1959): 22–23.

Nascimento, Abdias do. "Katherine Dunham e Nós." *Quilombo* (Junho–Julho 1950).

Newnham, John K. "Why Call It Mambo?" *Dancing Times* (May 1955): 499–501.

Orme, Frederic L. "The Negro in the Dance as Katherine Dunham Sees Him." *American Dancer* (March 1938): 10, 46.

"People Are Talking About. . . ." *Vogue* (November 1953): 84–85.

Pierre, Dorathi Bock. "Katherine Dunham." *Dance Magazine* (May 1947): 11.

———. "A Talk with Katherine Dunham." *Educational Dance* (August–September 1941): 7–8.

Pittman, John. "Dunham Dance Group Returns for Another San Francisco Triumph," *People's World,* 3 January 1942.

Pollack, Robert. "All-Negro Folk Ballet Steals Federal Show." *Chicago Daily News,* 28 January 1938.

Porter, A. "Anthropological Katie." *Collier's* (24 February 1945): 68–69.

Porter, Dorothy B. Review of *Katherine Dunham's Journey to Accompong. Journal of Negro Education* (1947): 201–2.

Provines, June. "She's Got Haitian Rhythm." *Chicago Tribune,* 26 February 1938.

Rice, Vernon. "Katherine Dunham." *New York Post,* 1 April 1940.

Sabin, Robert. "La Danse aux U.S.A." *Formes et Couleurs* 6 (1947).

Schallert, Edwin. "Katherine Dunham Revue Sensational." *Los Angeles Times,* 9 April 1945.

Schorrs, Daniel. "Dances of Dunham Surprise to Dutch: 'Caribbean Rhapsody' Leaves Festival Audience Rapt but Hesitant with Applause." *New York Times,* 14 July 1949.

"Shore Excursion, Katherine Dunham in Tropics." *Theatre Arts* 24 (1940): 319.

Smith, Cecil. "Federal Dance Project Gives First Program." *Chicago Tribune,* 28 January 1938.

Terry, Walter. "Dash of Ethnic Spice." *New York Herald Tribune,* 18 October 1962.

————. "Miss Dunham Back with Best Work." *New York Herald Tribune,* 14 October 1962.

————. "The Negro Dances." *New York Herald Tribune,* 28 April 1940.

"The Sitter Out: A Caribbean Rhapsody." *Dancing Times* (July 1948): 526.

Todd, Arthur. "America." *Dance and Dancers* (January 1956): 37–38.

————. "The Art of the American Negro is One of Our Foremost National Treasures." *New York Times,* 2 July 1961.

"Torridity to Anthropology." *Newsweek* (27 January 1941): 62.

Watt, D. "Musical Events." *New Yorker* (29 April 1950): 83.

Woods, Keith. "Around the World: New Zealand." *Ballet Today* (February 1958): 10.

Wyatt, E. V. R. "Tropical Revue." *Catholic World* (February 1945): 454.

————. "Theater." *Catholic World* (January 1956): 310.

ARTICLES, REVIEWS, AND PRESS NOTICES, 1966–1990

Agostini, Alfio. "'The Magic of Katherine Dunham' e di Alvin Ailey." *Balletto Oggi* 51 (1988): 34–35.

Allen, Zita D. "MemorabAileya." *Dance Magazine* (August 1974): 22–27.

Anderson, Jack. Review of "The Magic of Katherine Dunham." *Dancing Times* (February 1988): 435–36.

Barnes, Clive. "At the Ailey: Fun, Love, and Sin." *New York Times,* 3 December 1972.

Barzel, Ann. Report from Chicago. *Dance Magazine* (May 1981): 14.

Barzel, Ann, Mark Turbyfill, and Ruth Page. "The Untold Story of the Dunham-Turbyfill Alliance: The Lost Ten Years." *Dance Magazine* (December 1983): 91–98.

Berger, Renato. "Katherine Dunham: An Ingenious Dancer and Choreographer Devoted to Traditional, Modern and Avant-Garde Dance." *Ballet International* 13.6–7 (June/July 1990): 30–35.

Bowen, Tullia. "Making Television Dance." *Ballet News* 1.11 (May 1980): 26–29.

Bourguignon, Erika. Review of *Island Possessed. American Anthropologist* 72 (December 1970): 1132–33.

Bowers, Theresa. "Katherine Dunham Gala." *Dance Magazine* (May 1979): 48–49.

Clark, VèVè A. "Katherine Dunham's *Tropical Revue." Black American Literature Forum* 16.4 (Winter 1982): 147–152. Reprinted in *Caribe: Special Dance Issue* Vol. 7.1/7.2 (1983) and in *Caribbean Dance From Abakuá to*

Zouk, edited by Susanna Sloat, 305–19. Gainesville: University Press of Florida, 2002.

"*Dance Magazine* Gives Awards: Carla Fracci, Erik Bruhn, Katherine Dunham." *Dance Magazine* (May 1969): 11.

"The Dazzling Color of Alvin Ailey's Dunham Tribute." *Ebony* 43.7 (May 1988): 86–89.

DjeDje, Jacqueline C. Review of *Katherine Dunham: Reflections on the Social and Political Contexts of Afro-American Dance* by Joyce Aschenbrenner with Lavinia Williams. *Ethnomusicology* 26.3 (September 1982): 473–74.

"Dunham, Bruhn, Fracci Receive 1969 Dance Magazine Awards." *Dance Magazine* (July 1969): 44–46.

"Dunham in D.C." *Dance Magazine* (December 1983): 4.

"Dunham Will Receive Scripps Dance Award." *New York Times,* 1 May 1986.

Eismann, Marianne. "Dunham." *University of Chicago Magazine* 77.4 (Summer 1985): 14–19.

Guatterini, Marinella. "Katherine Dunham, tra la magìa nera e il varietà." *Balletto Oggi* 49 (November 1987): 25–26.

Guy, Edna. "Negro Dance Pioneers." *Dance Herald* 1.3 (1976): 5–6.

Hall, Carla, and Joe Brown. "The Glitterati Sparkle for an Evening of Gala Tributes." *Washington Post,* 5 December 1983.

Hardy, Camille. "Echoes of the Drum: Katherine Dunham on Ritual Dance in the Personal Theater." *Ballet News* (November 1983): 26, 28–29.

———. Review of Alvin Ailey American Dance Theater. *Dance Magazine* (April 1988): 37–39.

Harris, Dale. "New Life for Old Dances." *Wall Street Journal,* 8 January 1988.

Janowitz, Katherine. "Katherine Dunham: Divine Drumbeats." *Arabesque* (July–August 1980): 10.

Johnson, Helen Armstead. "The Wrong Step: Beckford on Dunham." *Dance Chronicle* 3.4 (1979–1980): 476–82.

Kastor, Elizabeth. "Kennedy Center Makes Its Picks: Sinatra, Stewart, Dunham, Kazan, Thomson Honored." *Washington Post,* 29 July 1983.

"Katherine Dunham." *Dance Research Journal* 14:1/2 (1981/1982): 68.

"Katherine Dunham Is Jailed Three Hours Following Protest." *New York Times,* 30 July 1967.

"Katherine Dunham Museum Opens." *Dance Herald* 4.2 (1979): 1.

"Katherine Dunham Pioneers: Celebration of Women Dancers." *New York Amsterdam News,* 24 January 1981.

Kisselgoff, Anna. "Katherine Dunham Gala Is Occasion for Nostalgia." *New York Times,* 17 January 1979.

Kokich, Kim Alexandra. Review of "The Magic of Katherine Dunham." *Ballet Review* 16.1 (1988): 8–11.

Macdonald, Annette. "Katherine Dunham and Her Contributions to American Modern Dance." *Dance Research Journal* 21.2 (Fall 1989): 41–43.

McDonagh, Don. "Katherine Dunham." In *The Complete Guide to Modern Dance,* 167. Garden City: Doubleday, 1976.

———. "Three Revivals Close Exuberant Season by Ailey Dancers." *New York Times,* 4 June 1974.

Nettleford, Rex M. "Dance Study Supplement, Part 8. *Dancing Times* (May 1990): 1–8.

———. "Katherine Dunham: The Jamaican Connexion (or Journey to Accompong) *Sunday Gleaner* (Kingston, Jamaica), 3 January 1988.

Philp, Richard. "Miss D's Day: Ailey Launches a Katherine Dunham Renaissance." *Dance Magazine* (December 1987): 50–55.

Ploski, Harry A. "The Black Entertainer in the Performing Arts." In *The Negro Almanac,* edited by Harry A. Ploski and James Williams, 1115–68. Detroit: Gale Research, 1989.

Reid, Georgia. Review of *Katherine Dunham: A Biography* by Ruth Beckford. *Dance Research Journal* 14.1–2 (1981–1982): 68–69.

Resnikova, Eva. "Tropical Fever in Midtown." Review of Alvin Ailey American Dance Theater, "The Magic of Katherine Dunham," City Center, New York. *New Criterion* (February 1988): 59–62.

Rosen, Lillie F. "A Katherine Dunham Gala, Carnegie Hall, N. Y. C., January 15, 1979." *Dance News* (May 1979): 12.

Rudnicki, Marianne Danks. "Detroit Celebrates Katherine Dunham." *Dance Magazine* (August 1984): 88.

Sandler, Ken. "A Celebration of Women in Dance, Thelma Hill Performing Arts Center, Brooklyn, March 15, 1981." *Ballet News* (April 1981): 8.

Segal, Lewis. "Dunham Honored as Pioneer in Bad Old Days Awards." *Los Angeles Times,* 3 December 1990.

Smith, Bill. "Katherine Dunham Was Born to Dancing and Social Activism." *Saint Louis Globe Democrat,* 11–12 September 1982.

Sommer, Sally "Under Her Spell: Alvin Ailey Brings Back Katherine Dunham's Vamps and Voodoo." *Connoisseur* 217 (December 1987): 138–43.

Terry, Walter. "Dunham's Legacy." *Saturday Review,* 26 May 1979, 56–57.

Tobias, Tobi. "Some Like It Hot." *New York,* (4 January 1988): 40–41.

Williamson, Liz. "That Eclectic, Elusive Dance Called Jazz." *Dance Magazine* (February 1978): 63–75.

Wright, Arthur. "The Dunham Technique—What It Is." *Attitude* 2.1 (June 1983): 5–6.

Zimmer, Diane. Review of *Katherine Dunham: A Biography* by Ruth Beckford. *Dance Book Forum* 1 (1981): 20–21.

ARTICLES, REVIEWS, AND PRESS NOTICES, 1991–2003

"40th Annual Capezio Dance Awards." *Dance Teacher Now* 13.5 (May/June 1991): 41–42.

Akinyemi, Omonike. "National News: Dunham Speaks from the Heart." *Dance Magazine* (January 1993): 22+.

Anawalt, Sasha. "Her Body on the Line: Katherine Dunham Uses Dance to Examine Racism." *Los Angeles Times,* 24 June 2001.

Anderson, Jack. "Awards Given for Dance and Performance Art." *New York Times,* 25 September 2001.

"Apropos the Empress at 90." *Drumvoices Revue* 8.1–2 (Fall/Winter/Spring,1998/99): 10–20.

Asante, Kariamu Welsh. "Moving in Concert: Katherine Dunham and Pearl Primus, Artists and Activists." *Sage* 8.2 (1994): 2–3.

"At 70, Dance Festival Still Has Spring in Its Steps." *Christian Science Monitor,* 12 July 2002.

Barad, Elizabeth. "Haiti Dances to a Different Drummer." *Dance Magazine* (August 1994): 38–41.

Ben-Itzak, Paul. "National News: Dunham Legacy Stands at Risk." *Dance Magazine* (January 1995): 40, 42.

Bloch, Alice. "Katherine Dunham Fasts for Haiti." *Dance Magazine* (May 1992): 14–15.

Burt, Ramsay. "Dance, 'Race,' and Sexuality: Katherine Dunham's *Rites de Passage* and Martha Graham's *Night Journey* in Boston." In *Embodying Liberation: The Black Body in American Dance,* edited by Dorothea Fischer-Hornung and Alison D. Goeller, 79–89. Hamburg: LIT, 2001.

———. "Primitivism, Modernism and Ritual in the Work of Mary Wigman, Katherine Dunham, and Martha Graham." In his *Alien Bodies: Representations of Modernity, "Race," and Nation in Early Modern Dance,* 160–89. London: Routledge, 1998.

"Caribbean Center Salute to Katherine Dunham." *New York Times,* 8 October 1994.

Cash, Debra. "Jacob's Pillow: 70th Anniversary Season." *Ballet Review* 30.3 (Fall 2002): 11–13.

"Choreographer Ends Her Fast Protesting against Deportation." *New York Times,* 20 March 1992.

Clark, VèVè A. "Dunham, Katherine." In *International Encyclopedia of Dance,* edited by Selma Jeanne Cohen et al. Vol. 2, 458–460. New York and Oxford: Oxford University Press, 1998.

———. "Performing the Memory of Difference in Afro-Caribbean Dance: Katherine Dunham's Choreography, 1938–1987." In *History and Memory in African-American Culture,* edited by Genevieve Fabre and Robert O'Meally, 188–204. New York and Oxford: Oxford University Press 1994.

Daly, Ann. "From Living Treasures, Coins of Artistic Wisdom." *New York Times,* 26 August 2001.

"Dance Legend Katherine Dunham Celebrates 90th Birthday" *Jet* (19 July 1999): 16, 18.

Dayan, Joan. "Haiti's Unquiet Past: Katherine Dunham, Modern Dancer, and Her Enchanted Island." In *Women at Sea: Travel Writing and the Margins of Caribbean Discourse,* edited by Lizabeth Paravisini-Gebert and Ivette Romero-Cesareo, 281–91. New York: Palgrave, 2001.

DeFrantz, Thomas. "Payback Time: Dollars from Diva to Diva." *Village Voice,* 24 January 2001, 67.

Dulan-Wilson, Gloria. Interview. "Women of Courage: Katherine Dunham, High Priestess of Protest." *Crisis* (October 1992): 26.

"Dunham $1 Million Birthday Gift." *Jet* (17 July 2000): 36.

"Dunham Hospitalized as a Result of Protest." *Dance/USA Journal* 9.3 (Winter 1992): 7.

Dunning, Jennifer. "A Dance Icon Sees a Lovely Now in the Mirror." *New York Times,* 14 Aug. 2000.

———. "A Legendary Teacher Continues Her Magic." *New York Times,* 13 June 2000.

———. "The Simple Secret of Teaching Dance." *New York Times,* 15 September 1991.

Durbin, Paula. "The First Lady of Caribbean Cadences." *Américas* 48.1 (January–February 1996): 36–41.

Eichenbaum, Rose. "A Conference for Blacks in Dance: Legends of African-American Dance—Chuck Davis, Cleo Parker Robinson, Katherine

Dunham, and Others—Converge in Denver." *Dance Teacher* 21:5 (May–June 1999): 67–71.

Eigner, Janet B. "Compassion's Voices: St. Louis' Aida Connection." *DCA News* (Winter 1998): 1+.

Eley, Susie. "The Power of One." *Dance Teacher* 22.9 (November 2000): 49–52, 54.

Fischer-Hornung, Dorothea. "The Body Possessed: Katherine Dunham Dance Technique in *Mambo.*" In *Embodying Liberation: The Black Body in American Dance,* edited by Dorothea Fischer-Hornung and Alison D. Goeller, 91–112. Hamburg: LIT, 2001.

———. "An Island Occupied: The U. S. Marine Occupation of Haiti in Zora Neale Hurston's *Tell My Horse* and Katherine Dunham's *Island Possessed.*" In *Holding Their Own: Perspectives on the Multi-Ethnic Literatures of the United States,* edited by Dorothea Fischer-Hornung and Heike Raphael-Hernández, 153–68. Tübingen: Stauffenburg, 2000.

Gleik, Elizabeth, Nina Burleigh, and Mary Harrison. "Hunger Strike: Dance Legend Katherine Dunham Ends Her Fast for the People of Haiti." *People* (30 March 1992): 42–43,

Goldman, Phyllis. Review of Cleo Parker Robinson Dance Ensemble. *Back Stage* (26 September 2003): 45.

Gonzalez, David. "In Katherine Dunham's Eden, Invaders from Hell." *New York Times,* 6 August. 2002.

Grey, William Daniel. "The Capezio Dance Award." *Dance Pages* 8.4 (1991): 18–20.

Hall, Corey. "Katherine Dunham's Legacy, Tradition, and Strength Honored at Benefit Dinner." *Hyde Park Citizen,* 30 January 1997.

Hill, Constance Valis. "Katherine Dunham's *Southland*: Protest in the Face of Repression." *Dance Research Journal* 26.2 (Fall 1994): 1–10. Reprinted in *Dancing Many Drums: Excavations in African American Dance*, edited by Thomas F. DeFrantz, 289–316. Madison: University of Wisconsin Press, 2002.

Johnson, Robert. "Capezio Offers 1991 Dance Awards. *Dance Magazine* (May 1991): 16.

Kensey, Barbara L. "Katherine Dunham: Choreographing a Way of Life." *High Performance* 18.1–2 (1995): 78–79.

Kisselgoff, Anna. "Katherine Dunham's Timeless Legacy, Visible in Youth and Age." *New York Times,* 16 September 2003.

Kraut, Anthea. "Between Primitivism and Diaspora: The Dance Performances of Josephine Baker, Zora Neale Hurston, and Katherine Dunham." *Theatre Journal* 55:3 (October 2003): 433–50.

Manning, Susan. "Modern Dance, Negro Dance, and Katherine Dunham." *Textual Practice* 15.3 (2001): 1–19.

Mazo, Joseph H. "The Real Thing." *Dance Magazine* (March 1994): 66.

McDonagh, Don. "Jazz Dance: The Blues." *Dance Magazine* (January 1998): 88.

"Missouri Group Gets Dance Collection: Missouri Historical Society to Receive Katherine Dunham's Collection of Costumes, Instruments, Papers and Films." *New York Times,* 8 January 1992.

Moore, Nancy G. "Forever Touched by Your Legacy: 90th Birthday Tribute to Katherine Dunham." *Dance Magazine* (September 1999): 102–4.

———. "Preserving the Legacy of Katherine Dunham." *Dance Magazine* (November 1999): 40, 44.

Moore, William. "Beautiful and Brainy." *New York Amsterdam News,* 28 March 1992.

———. "Dance Artist, Scholar Katherine Dunham Continues Hunger Strike." *Attitude: The Dancer's Magazine* 8.3 (1992): 5.

———. "Katherine Dunham Ends Hunger Strike." *Attitude: The Dancer's Magazine* 8.3 (1992): 6.

———. "Katherine Dunham Is Very Much Alive and Well, Thank You." *Attitude: The Dancer's Magazine* 7.3 (1991): 5.

———. "President Aristide's Visit Ends Dunham's Hunger Strike." *New York Amsterdam News,* 28 March 1992.

———. "Teaches Her Own Technique Every Summer." *Attitude: The Dancer's Magazine* 7.4 (1991): 28.

———. Will President Bush Respond Too Late to Katherine Dunham's Hunger Strike?" *New York Amsterdam News,* 21 March 1992.

Moreno Vega, Marta. "The Yoruba Orisha Tradition Comes to New York City." *African American Review* 29.2 (1995): 201–6.

Nash, Joe. "Pioneers in Negro Concert Dance." *Michigan Citizen,* 22 December 2002.

Oberdorfer, Kathryn. "Spotlight on Katherine Dunham." *Dance Teacher Now* (February 1994): 28+.

Obituary: "Thomas Gomez, 77, Stage, Film Dancer." *Back Stage* (11 December 1998): 42.

Parks, Gary. "Reviews of the Century: Great Moments from the Pages of *Dance Magazine.*" *Dance Magazine* (March 1999): 7.

Patrick, K. C. "Circle of Dance 1996: A Glance Backward." *Dance Teacher Now* (December 1996): 105+.

———. "Instituting Dunham." *Dance Magazine* (August 2000): 45.

———. "Starting Here: Legacy." *Dance Magazine* (August 2002): 10.

Perpener, John O. III. "African American Dance and Sociological Positivism during the 1930s." *Studies in Dance History* 5.1 (Spring 1994): 23–30. Volume title: *Of, By, and For the People: Dancing on the Left in the 1930s,* edited by Lynn Garafola, 1994. Distributed by University of Wisconsin Press.

Perron, Wendy. "One Woman Revolution: Katherine Dunham." *Dance Magazine* (August 2000): 42–45, 74.

———. "The Teach-Learn Connection: Hunter College Shares the Legacy." *Dance Magazine* (August 2002): 46.

Ramsey, Kate. "Melville Herskovits, Katherine Dunham, and the Politics of African Dance Anthropology." In *Dancing Bodies, Living Histories: New Writings about Dance and Culture,* edited by Lisa Doolittle and Anne Flynn, 196–216. Banff: Banff Centre Press, 2000.

Regitz, Hartmut. "Never Stop Dancing." *Ballettanz* (April 2002): 15.

Samuels, Shayna. "Grant Money Goes to Perpetuate Katherine Dunham's Work." *Dance Magazine* (May 2001): 38.

Schulman, Jennie. "Dance Legend Dunham to Receive Tribute." *Back Stage* (12 September 2003): 11.

Sherrill, Martha. "The Dance with Death." *Washington Post,* 16 March 1992.

Solomons, Gus Jr. Report from New York. *Ballet Review* 28.4 (Winter 2000): 8.

Thom, Rose Anne. "Moving Image: From Africa to Avant-Garde." *Dance Magazine* (June 2001): 70–71.

"A Tribute to Katherine Dunham." *Talking Drums! The Journal of Black Dance* 5.1 (January 1995): 23.

Turner, Renee. "Dance Divas!" *Heart & Soul* (February 1999): 72–76.

Vaccarino, Elisa. "Vodu, le danze di Haiti." *Balletto Oggi* (August 1991): 46.

Dissertations

Banks, Kimberly Jaye. "Representations of Vernacular Culture: Women as Culture Bearers in the Works of Claude McKay, Langston Hughes, Zora Neale Hurston, and Katherine Dunham." Rutgers, State University of New Jersey, 2002.

Burroughs, John Hamby. "Haitian Ceremonial Dance on the Concert Stage: The Contextual Transference and Transformation of Yanvalou (Vodou)." New York University, 1995.

Compton, Tamara L. "Mary Hunter Wolf: Director, Producer, Educator. Building Communities through Theatre." University of Nebraska, 1992.

Foulkes, Julia Lawrence. "Dancing America: Modern Dance and Cultural Nationalism, 1925–1950." University of Massachusetts, Amherst, 1997.

Gwynn, Eleanor W. Faucette. "A Key Determinant of Dance Style : The Structural Use of the Dance Instrument as Illustrated by the Choreography of Katherine Dunham's *Rites de Passage.*" University of Wisconsin, Madison, 1978.

Hazel, Risa Marie. "Voodoo and the Failure to Know in Some Contemporary American Narratives." University of Minnesota, 2001.

Moreno Vega, Marta. "Yoruba Philosophy: Multiple Levels of Transformation and Understanding (African Americans)." Temple University, 1995.

Nester, Deborah Craig. "'Gwine By': Colonial Women's Travel Literature and the West Indian Marketplace." University of Miami, 2001.

Perpener, John O. III. "The Seminal Years of Black Concert Dance (Afro-American, Modern Dance)." New York University, 1992.

Sherrod, Elgie Gaynell. "The Dance Griots: An Examination of the Dance Pedagogy of Katherine Dunham and Black Pioneering Dancers in Chicago and New York." Temple University, 1998.

Spoor, Suzanne Jaqueline. "Searching for a Black Republic: The Textual Invention of Haiti by United States Black Artists in the 1930s." University of Maryland, College Park, 1999.

Glossary

ag'ya, l'ag'ya, or *ladja*—The fighting dance of Martinique; a martial art.

Ayida Wèdo or Aïda Ouedo—The *lwa* of fertility, rainbows, and snakes; wife of Danbala.

bamboche—A peasant-style social dance in Haiti, a "get-together to have a good time."

bamboula—An older form of tambourine or drum used in the West Indies; a dance to the accompaniment of this instrument.

barre—A horizontal handrail used as support by dancers during classroom exercises. Also, the series of exercises performed while holding this handrail.

béguine or *beguine*—The national popular dance of Martinique and its accompanying music.

bèkè—Creole term used for white planters and their descendants in Martinique and Guadeloupe.

belair or *bèlè*—An African-derived social dance in Martinique.

bocor (French) *bòkò*— Vodun priest who practices divining and/or magic in addition to working with the *lwa* and the dead.

caille or *lakay*—A hut or small house; cabin.

Calinda or *calenda*—A dance of African origin, known from the seventeenth-century colonization of the Antilles; one type associated with stick fighting/dancing and satirical song; another type of dance for couples characterized by lascivious pelvic movements.

cambois, quimbois—A charm or potion made by a practitioner of Quimbois, an African-derived religion in the French Caribbean.

canaris—Earthen vessels for storing or transporting water.

Candomblé—An African-based religious system in Brazil.

Carnival—The festival season preceding Lent.

case—In West Africa, a round house with a thatched roof made of rushes or palm leaves.

chandelle—Spiny plant, candelabra-shaped, of the cactus family.

Chauve-Souris—Nikita Balieff's Théâtre de la Chauve-Souris à Moscou, a Franco-Russian vaudeville troupe that performed in the United States throughout the 1920s; Dunham's ballet teacher, Ludmilla Speranzeva, was a member of the troupe during the 1925 season.

Combite, coumbite—An organized community work-group effort of friends and neighbors, often engaged in building, harvesting, road repair, and so forth. Song and dance accompany work movements.

couleuvre—Nonvenomous serpent; in Haiti the cult representation of Damballa.

cowries—Small, brightly colored, glossy sea shells, used for divination; formerly used in Africa and South Asia as money.

Creole—A person born in the Americas, often of mixed racial and cultural ancestry; adjective used to describe something/someone native to the Americas; a language of the Caribbean. French-based Creoles are spoken by approximately 8.5 million people in the Caribbean (Haiti, Guadeloupe, Martinique, Dominica, St. Lucia, French Guyana), South America (Venezuela), North America (Louisiana), and the Indian Ocean (Réunion, Seychelles, Mauritius). Haitian Creole specifically is the most widely spoken Creole in the world. As a general rule, the lexicon is French, and the syntax is based on variety of African languages.

Dahomey, Rada-Dahomey—One of the two spirit pantheons in the Vodun religion of Haiti; often associated with the "cool" spirits.

Danbala, Damballa—One of the most important of the Vodun divinities; the supreme Rada serpent *lwa,* associated with water, wisdom, and fecundity. An egg is his sacrificial food.

danse collé—A large group dance in which dancers are closely packed (i.e., "glued").

danse de pie, danse des pieds—A dance of the feet.

danse des épaules, zepaule (Creole)—A dance of the shoulders.

danse des hanches—A dance of the hips, haunches.

danse du ventre—A dance of the belly, stomach.

fetishist—A priest who makes magic charms.

feuilles—Leaves or medical herbs gathered for medicine or magic.

gris-gris—Fetish, talisman, magical charm; bird used in making charm.

hivernage—In West Africa, the winter season of rain and heavy winds.

hounci, hounsi, or *ounsi*—An apprentice or servitor to the Vodun who assists in the rituals of the temple.

Houngfor, hounfort or *ounfò*—The Vodun temple; structure dedicated to the Haitian *lwa* for permanent housing and ceremonial offerings; repository of artifacts associated with the mystic spirit of the gods.

houngan, oungan—A Vodun religious leader who facilitates the communities contact with the *lwa.*

juba—A popular plantation folk dance, a modified form of the *majumba.*

juju—A fetish or magic charm. Also, the magic of such a charm.

Kanzo—A stage of initiation in Vodun.

Koromantee or Kromanti—Name used by the Maroons of Jamaica to describe themselves, their songs, their dance rituals, and their language.

Léogâne—A town in southwestern Haiti.

lwa, or loa—The spirit or deity who, originally from Africa, may take residence in the head or occupy the entire body in ceremonies.

Majhumbwe—A section of the *bélair.*

Mazouk—The creole mazurka of Martinique.

Mento—A genre of Jamaican music.

mambo—A high priestess of Vodun.

maroon—Fixtures throughout the Americas, maroon communities were semi-autonomous groupings of runaway slaves and their descendants. In Jamaica, these communities achieved formal recognition of their independence by the British colonial authorities in the Treaty of 1738, which ended the First Maroon War.

négritude—An ideological and literary movement begun in the 1930s and characterized by an affirmation of African cultural values; usually associated with the Martinican poet Aimé Cesaire, the Senegalese poet Léopold Sédar Senghor, and the French Guyanese poet Léon Gontran Damas.

orishas or *orichas*—Guardian spirits, aspects of a supreme being, Olodumare, manifested as forces of nature; central to the Yoruba-derived belief systems known as Regla de Ocha, Lucumi, or Santería (Cuba, Puerto Rico, United States), Candomblé (Brazil), and Shango Baptist (Trinidad).

pagne—A length of cloth wound around the body into a long skirt for women or, occasionally, a short one for men.

petit mil—Millet, an edible grain or cereal.

Pétro or petwo—One of the two spirit pantheons of Vodun; associated
    with Congolese origins and "hot" spirits.

prix-de-cloche—"Prize of the bell," an advanced degree of Vodun initiates.

prix-des-yeux—"Prize of the eyes," or "price of the eyes"; clairvoyance.
    The highest degree of Vodun initiates.

Rara—Haitian festivals and parade celebrations that take place every
    weekend during Lent, characterized by group singing, dancing,
    masquerade bands, and playing of homemade musical instruments.

Santería—A Yoruba-derived religious system of Cuba, Puerto Rico, and
    the United States. Also known as Lucumi or Lukumi and as Regla de
    Ocha.

'ti moune—a system whereby children engaged as house servants, or
    restavecs, in Haiti.

Vodun—The dominant religious system practiced in Haiti, taken from
    the word for spirit or god.; the hierarchy of gods governing the belief
    system; given various various spellings in French (Vaudou, Vaudun,
    Vodou), Spanish (Vudú), and English (Voodoo). In April 2003,
    Vodou was recognized as an official religion of Haiti.

yonvalou—A Haitian dance done during Vodun rituals; a solo dance of
    fluid movements leading to an ecstatic state in which contact with the
    lwa may occur.

Contributors

JOYCE ASCHENBRENNER is Professor Emerita of anthropology at Southern Illinois University at Edwardsville. Among her publications are *Katherine Dunham: Reflections on the Social and Political Contexts of Afro-American Dance* (1981) and *Katherine Dunham: Dancing a Life* (2002). She is currently the acting curator and education coordinator of the Katherine Dunham Museum in East Saint Louis, Illinois.

EDWARD BARRY was a staff writer for the *Chicago Daily Tribune.*

SUE BARRY wrote for *People's World,* a Communist Party newspaper produced on the West Coast.

ANN BARZEL is a noted journalist, historian, critic, photographer, and filmmaker who has devoted her long life to the art of dance, particularly to dance in Chicago and the Midwest. Trained as a dancer, she became a critic for the *Chicago Times* in 1946 and later for the *Chicago American,* where she wrote dance reviews for twenty-seven years. The Ann Barzel Dance Research Collection, an extensive archive including theater programs, dance magazines, books, records, photographs, and films, is accessible in the Ann Barzel Reading Room of Chicago's Newberry Library.

RUTH BECKFORD joined the Katherine Dunham Dance Company in 1943 and toured the West Coast and Canada. She has taught Dunham Technique at the University of California at Berkeley, Mills College, and Oregon State College, among other schools. In 1954 she taught at the Dunham School in New York, and from 1954 to 1961 she was director, dancer, and choreographer for her own company, the Ruth Beckford

African Haitian Dance Company. She is the author of *Katherine Dunham: A Biography* (1979).

VANDY BREWER was a staff writer for the *Metro-East Journal* in East Saint Louis.

VÈVÈ A. CLARK is an associate professor of African American Studies at the University of California, Berkeley. She was Ms. Dunham's archivist from 1977 to 1983 and has published several articles on various Dunham ballets. She has written widely on Haitian performance and political theatre, and is currently preparing a manuscript on Ms. Dunham's career, entitled *Performing the Memory of Difference.*

CLAUDE CONYERS has had a dual career in publishing and dance. He retired from his position as vice president and editorial director of the scholarly and professional reference department at Oxford University Press, U.S.A., in 1999. Trained as a ballet dancer from childhood, he danced professionally in South Africa and Canada during a four-year hiatus in his publishing career. He is a member of the board of directors of the George Balanchine Foundation and the editorial board of the Society of Dance History Scholars. He currently works as a freelance writer, editor, consultant, and project manager.

ST. CLAIR DRAKE was a pioneer in the field of sociology, best known for his *Black Metropolis: A Study of Negro Life in a Northern City* (co-authored with Horace Cayton in 1945) and *Black Folk Here and There* (1987).

CARLA HALL and JOE BROWN are staff writers for the *Washington Post.*

CONSTANCE VALIS HILL is a jazz dancer, choreographer, and scholar of performance studies. Having taught at the Ailey School in New York, the Conservatoire d'Arts Dramatique in Paris, and New York University's Tisch School of the Arts, she is currently a Visiting Five-College Associate Professor of Dance at Hampshire College in Amherst, Massachusetts. She has contributed articles and reviews to numerous journals, magazines, and newspapers and is the author of *Brotherhood in Rhythm: The Jazz Tap Dancing of the Nicholas Brothers* (2000).

MILLICENT HODSON, choreographer and dance historian, began her professional career as a graduate student at the University of California at Berkeley, where she staged programs of performing arts in museum settings as a way of maximizing the visual space with choreographic work. She and her husband, Kenneth Archer, are best known as dance reconstructionists. Together they have completed more than ten reconstructions of historic dance works by Vaslav Nijinsky, Jean Börlin, and George Balanchine, the most famous of which is Nijinsky's *Le Sacre de Printemps*.

ZORA NEALE HURSTON was the most prolific African American woman writer in America from the early 1930s until her death. During that thirty-year period, she published seven books and many short stories, magazine articles, and plays, from which she gained a reputation as an outstanding folklorist as well as an accomplished storyteller, essayist, novelist, and playwright. Among her books is *Tell My Horse* (1937), which contains a chapter on the Maroon settlement at Accompong in Jamaica but deals mainly with the Vodun religious system of Haiti. Her autobiography is *Dust Tracks on a Road* (1942).

SARA E. JOHNSON is an assistant professor of comparative literature at the University of California, San Diego. She has performed extensive academic fieldwork in Haiti, Cuba, the Dominican Republic, Senegal, and Martinique and has published several articles examining Caribbean literary, musical, and religious traditions. She is currently completing a book on the cultural legacy of the Haitian Revolution in the Americas.

EARTHA KITT, a legendary star of stage and screen, began her entertainment career in the 1940s as a dancer with the Katherine Dunham Company, playing on Broadway in *Bal Nègre* (1946) and touring Mexico and America. Following a European tour, she remained in Paris, where she achieved celebrity as a nightclub singer. Her further appearances on Broadway have ranged from *New Faces of 1952* to a revival of *Nine* in 2003. She has also appeared in numerous movies and television shows and has toured internationally as a cabaret singer. Her autobiography, which includes accounts of her experiences with the Dunham Company, is *Thursday's Child* (1956).

ALAN M. KRIEGSMAN served as performing arts critic (music, dance, theater, film, television) for the *Washington Post* from 1966 until 1996, when he retired and was named critic emeritus. In 1976 he won a Pulitzer Prize for his dance writing, and he remains the sole recipient of that honor for dance criticism. His writings on the performing arts have also appeared in the *Saturday Review, Cultural Affairs, Horizon, Musical Quarterly*, and other periodicals. He has taught courses on the arts at numerous colleges and universities, including Columbia, Barnard, Juilliard, Harvard, and Temple. Archives of his research are compiled in the Alan M. and Sali Ann Kriegsman Collection at the Library of Congress.

CLAUDE LÉVI-STRAUSS was the leading figure in post–World War II French ethnology. After fieldwork experiences in Amazonia (1935–1939) and wartime expatriation from France at the New School for Social Research in New York (1942–1945), he joined the Musée de l'Homme in Paris and later the École Pratique des Hautes Études. In 1959 he received the first chair of social anthropology at the Collège de France and in 1973 was voted a member of the Académie Française. Most of his works have been translated into English, among them *Structural Anthropology*, 2 vols. (1963, 1976), *The Savage Mind* (1966), *The Raw and the Cooked* (1969), *Structuralism and Ecology* (1972), and *The Naked Man* (1981).

SUSAN MANNING is an associate professor of English, theater, and performance studies at Northwestern University. Her teaching cuts across diverse genres of twentieth-century theatrical performance, while her research concerns the cultural politics of modern dance. Her first book, *Ecstasy and the Demon*, winner of the 1994 de la Torre Bueno Prize, examines the shift from modernist bodies to fascist bodies in the choreography of Mary Wigman. Her second book, *Modern Dance, Negro Dance: Race in Motion*, explores changing relations between modern dancers and African American choreographers in New York City from 1930 to 1960. Currently she is the convener of the Chicago Seminar on Dance and Performance and the president of the Society of Dance History Scholars.

JOHN MARTIN was the first full-time dance critic on a major American newspaper. In 1927 he was asked to write dance reviews for the *New York Times* by the paper's music critic, who wanted him to help out for six months. Martin held in the job for thirty-five years, retiring only in 1962. During those years, he was more than a reviewer; he was an advocate and crusader for dance, particularly the new "modern dance" of such young choreographers as Martha Graham and Doris Humphrey. He was also appreciative of the work of Katherine Dunham, which he helped to popularize through his column in the *Times*.

GWEN MAZER created and edited the popular monthly "Lifestyle" column for *Harper's Bazaar*.

ALFRED MÉTRAUX is considered one of the most important European ethnologists of the twentieth century. Under the auspices of the United

Nations Educational, Scientific, and Cultural Organization (UNESCO), he studied indigenous cultures throughout South America, in Haiti, and on Easter Island. His major works available in English include *Voodoo in Haiti* (1959) and *Haiti: Black Peasants and Voodoo* (1960).

ABDIAS DO NASCIMENTO is a painter, poet, playwright, essayist, theater director, publisher, university professor, and political figure. Among other accomplishments, he was the publisher of *Quilombo,* a Brazilian periodical, and founder of the Teatro Experimental do Negro in Rio de Janiero. Considered one of the foremost scholars of Afro-Brazilian culture, he is Professor Emeritus of the State University of New York at Buffalo and author, coauthor, or editor of numerous books, including *Africans in Brazil: A Pan-African Perspective* (1992) and *Orixás: Os deuses vivos da Africa* (*Orishas: The Living Gods of Africa in Brazil*; 1995).

REX NETTLEFORD, a native of Jamaica, is a dancer, choreographer, author, and educator and a leading figure of intellectual life in the Caribbean. As founder, artistic director, principal choreographer, and former lead dancer of the National Dance Theatre Company of Jamaica and as professor and chancellor of the University of the West Indies, he has had a profound impact on the arts and education throughout the Caribbean basin. He is also editor of *Caribbean Quarterly,* the region's oldest journal, and the author of numerous books, including *Dance Jamaica: Cultural Definition and Artistic Discovery* (1985).

FREDERICK L. ORME wrote for *American Dancer* in the 1930s.

HALIFU OSUMARE has been involved with dance and the performing arts for over thirty years as a dancer, choreographer, teacher, administrator, and scholar. She is currently assistant professor of American studies at the University of California, Davis. She was a soloist with the Rod Rodgers Dance Company in the early 1970s and is a certified instructor of the Katherine Dunham Technique. She organized Ms. Dunham's residencies at Stanford University and the University of Hawaii.

RUTH PAGE was a ballet dancer, choreographer, company director, and writer. In the mid-1920s she settled in Chicago and soon began her long association with opera ballet, first with the Ravinia Opera and then with the Chicago Opera, for which she served as ballet director. In that capacity she gave Katherine Dunham her first important performing experience, in the title role of Page's ballet *La Guiablesse* (The devil woman), mounted for the Chicago Opera in 1934. In later years she choreographed numerous ballets and toured widely with her own ballet companies.

K. C. PATRICK is a staff writer for *Dance Magazine.*

WENDY PERRON is a dancer, choreographer, and journalist based in New York City. She danced with the companies of Sara Rudner, Kenneth King, and Trisha Brown during the 1970s and was director of her own company from 1983 to 1994. She has served as the chair of the dance division at Bennington College, as associate director of the Jacob's Pillow Dance Festival, and as teacher of dance technique, composition, improvisation, criticism, and history at Princeton, Rutgers, and New York University. She writes widely on dance and performance and is a well-respected journalist. In 2004 she was appointed editor in chief of *Dance Magazine* and *Young Dancer.*

DORATHI BOCK PIERRE was a writer, editor, modern dancer, dance historian, dance critic, educator, actress, publicist, administrator, and philanthropist. From 1938 until 1942 she was editor and publisher of *Educational Dance,* a periodical, and in subsequent years she was the administrative director of the Katherine Dunham School of Arts and Research in New York City. She was the editor of her father's autobiography, *Memoirs of an American Artist, Sculptor Richard W. Bock* (1989), and a benefactor of the Bock Museum on the campus of Greenville College in Greenville, Illinois.

EUGENE REDMOND is the author of six volumes of poetry and the editor of *Drumvoices Revue.* A longtime collaborator of Ms. Dunham's in the East Saint Louis community, he teaches in the English department at Southern Illinois University at Edwardsville.

ALBIRDA ROSE began her dance training with Ruth Beckford, a former member of the Dunham Company, at the age of eight. The author of *Dunham Technique: A Way of Life* (1990), she is currently a member of the Certification Board for Dunham Technique. She has collaborated with colleagues concerning the certification process since the project's inception in 1993 at the Dunham Technique Seminar in East Saint Louis. She is a professor in the School of Music and Dance at San Francisco State University.

MARTHA SHERRILL has been a staff writer at the *Washington Post* since 1989 and has also written for magazines such as *Esquire* and *Vanity Fair.*

JEANELLE STOVALL worked with Ms. Dunham for over thirty years. She was the director of the Katherine Dunham Museum in East Saint Louis and played an active role in the Performing Arts Training Center, the Katherine Dunham Centers for Arts and Humanities, and the Dunham Academy.

ROY THOMAS taught for many years in the African American studies department at the University of California, Berkeley. Highly recognized for his work on Langston Hughes, he also organized the first international festival of Black film in Berkeley in 1973. He and Ruth Beckford brought Ms. Dunham to UC Berkeley as a visiting scholar in 1976.

MARK TURBYFILL was a Chicago-based poet, painter, dancer, and journalist. In the 1920s and 1930s, he was a principal dancer with the nation's first ballet company, Allied Artists, and he partnered ballerina Ruth Page in her early experimental works. He was the first ballet teacher of Katherine Dunham and, notably, tried to help her found a Negro ballet company in the 1930s. He is today best known for his dance criticism in Chicago newspapers of the early 1930s. His poems appear in *The Words beneath Us: Balletic Poems* (1951) and *A Marriage with Space* (1974); his letters are held by the Morris Library of Southern Illinois University at Carbondale; and his paintings are housed at the Smart Gallery on the University of Chicago campus.

MARTA MORENO VEGA, founder of the Franklin H. Williams Caribbean Cultural Center in New York City, also served as the chair of the Katherine Dunham Legacy Committee. She is the author of *Altar of My Soul: The Living Traditions of Santería* and coproducer of the documentary *When the Spirits Dances Mambo.*

PETER WADDINGTON wrote for *Opera and Concert.*

GIOVANNELLA ZANNONI is a filmmaker and served as Ms. Dunham's film archivist during the 1960s and 1970s.

Index

Abercrombie, Gertrude, 102
Academy of West African Cultural Arts,
    plan for, 407–11
acculturation, 228
Achille, Louis, 414
activism, 4, 9–10; agitprop, dance as,
    331–37; avoidance of radical affilia-
    tions, 104; civil rights movement
    and KD, 230, 263, 337; cultural
    grounding for, 611n11; dance as social
    protest, 257–58; fast, protest against
    US policy on Haitian refugees, 430–
    35, 627; funding of projects linked to,
    627; fund-raising for American
    Friends of Spanish Democracy, 4,
    189, 337; KD arrested after protest,
    418, 627; Louisville speech, 255;
    paradigm shift in American concert
    dance and, 256–66; Scott on, 583;
    Southland as protest, 345–63; Spanish
    Civil War, 104–5, 337
Adeus Terras, 374, 535
Africa: African dance, 217; African
    Diaspora and traditions, 3, 4, 7, 10,
    217–25, 258–61, 320–40, 603–11;
    Afro-American, KD on term, 241;
    Afrocentrism, 614; development and
    dance in, 540–47; development and
    loss of cultural heritage, 409; Egypt
    as setting for "In My Old Virginia
    Home on the River Nile," 239–41,

246; pan-African cultural organiza-
    tions, 573; religious traditions of, 3,
    220; World Black and African
    Festival of Arts and Culture, Dakar,
    405, 412–17, 543, 547. *See also* Senegal
African American temple, West Harlem,
    608
Afrique, 281, 596
Afro-American, KD on term, 241
Afrocentrism, 614
"Afternoon into Night," 444–49
agitprop, 331–37
Aguabella, Francisco, 483, 604–5
Ag'ya, L'. See L'Ag'ya
ag'ya, l'. See l'ag'ya
Aïda (ballet, Page), 500
Aïda (opera), 10, 628; notes on dances,
    388–91
Aïda Ouedo, 64, 518
Aikens, Vanoye, 9, 115, 117, *157, 158, 169,*
    333, 486, 598, 626; interview with,
    274–87; in *L'Ag'ya, 161;* singing career
    of, 279–81
Ailey, Alvin, 591–97, 599
Albert Schweitzer Award, 628
Alemán, Miguel, 303
Alfonso, Don, 126
Allan, Lewis (Abel Meeropol), 347,
    360n10, 361n30
Allen, Cathy, 559
Alsop, Fred, 66, *151,* 533, 539

David Gere, University of California, Los Angeles
Sandra Noll Hammond, Santa Rosa, California
Constance Valis Hill, Hampshire College
Marion Kant, University of Pennsylvania
Lizbeth Langston, University of California, Riverside
Madeleine Nichols, Dance Division, New York Public Library for the Performing Arts
Cecilia Olsson, Stockholm University
Jean Van Delinder, Oklahoma State University
Judy Van Zile, University of Hawaii at Manoa